DINING
WITH
DELPHINA

D1531424

WHITEFIELD BOOKS
waitsfield vermont

For information address:
Whitefield Books, Inc.
Waitsfield, VT 05673

Library of Congress Catalog Card Number: 91-66096
ISBN: 0-9630835-0-3

Printed in U.S.A.
First Edition

To Dr. Steve

FOREWORD

It is my fervent desire that good cooks learn to organize their menus in order that they may enhance the enjoyment of the dining experience. To that end, I have devoted many happy hours of cooking, dining and entertaining. Herewith is the harvest of those hours. I hope that this book will bring you as much pleasure as it has given me...creating it for you.

Sincerely,

DELPHINA

TABLE OF CONTENTS

DINING
WITH
DELPHINA

PRESENTATION

The dining room creates an atmosphere that has much to do with the enjoyment of food. However, a beautiful room, while desirable, is not a necessity; more important is a room that evokes serenity. Agreeable colors, comfortable chairs and lovely plants will enhance the ambiance as will a background of soft pleasant music. But do keep in mind the fact that the more elegant the room the greater the expectations for the food presented will be.

Dinner by candle light is the ultimate relaxation. Candle light sets the mood, and the world beyond ceases to exist. Odd numbers of people around the dinner table produce interesting conversations. Have you noticed that too? The conversation is less likely to break up into pairs. Also, for the sake of conviviality, if there are more than eight people present at dinner, two smaller tables are preferable to one larger one.

Even though blooming plants in the dining room are charming, I'm reluctant to place fresh flowers on the dinner table. Fresh flowers on the table only upstage the food which should, after all, be a work of art and receive full attention. The food is the flower. Nor should anything be placed on the table, with the exception of candles, that does not pertain directly to the food.

However flower patterns on tablecloths, placemats, napkins and china can be very effective. The use or non use of tablecloths, placemats, or a bare table are some of the tools with which we have to work to set the scene. The pattern, color and style of the napery should be in keeping with the tableware and the food being presented. A dining table covered with a skirt that reaches the floor is romantic. Placemats give the greatest range of texture, from straw to lace. If you are leaving your beautiful table bare of cloth or placemats, then be sure to use huge linen dinner napkins in the European fashion. I am fortunate to have my grandmother's on which she embroidered her initials. At the start of dinner see that the napkins are discreetly folded and resting on the service plate at each place setting.

Choosing a basic pattern for tableware, and then supplementing it with pieces of a solid, harmonizing color is a good idea both aesthetically and financially. It gives flexibility. Searching out varied and interesting antiques in shops and at yard sales, to use as accent pieces, can be an endless source of amusement.

Any kind of tableware made of wood, especially if it's maple, Oriental china both Chinese and Japanese, Mexican pottery, enameled tinware, both patterned and plain, French white ovenware, fine English china, new or old glassware from oven proof baking dishes to cut crystal, modern plastic dinnerware in flamboyant colors, silver serving pieces and

Indian brass serving trays are favorites. Selections of flatware and drinking glasses are infinite and of course must harmonize with the tableware as well as the budget.

What is important is that the tableware compliment in style, color and texture, the food being presented, whether it be a salad on a glass plate, chile in an earthenware bowl or artichokes on a silver platter. The tableware completes the total picture that contributes to the ultimate enjoyment of the food. Also visualize what the food will look like once it has been served from the main dish, if that be the case, onto the individual dinner plate, especially certain baked casserole dishes. Often the food would make a far more attractive presentation if it were baked in individual baking dishes. A couple of sets of individual size baking dishes can make your repertory appear to have greatly expanded. And of course any dinner plate which can go into the oven is a real treasure. A great luxury is having certain plates or dishes that are reserved for certain foods or certain occasions. Such as the particular color, design or texture of a plate that flatters a certain food. It would make the occasion more special. It's a luxury of storage space really.

Service plates, though not a necessity, add a touch of elegance to any table. They are slightly larger than the dinner plate and are already at each place setting before the diners come to the table. The first course soup cups, bowls or plates are set upon the service plates and they are removed along with the first course when it is cleared away. In the same frame of reference, the plates of each course must remain at each place setting until the last person has finished the course. Do not be too anxious to clear the table. It makes guests feel that they have either eaten too fast or too slow. Providing finger bowls of warm water after a course of corn on the cob or any food which is eaten with the fingers is thoughtful and practical. It's good to have some little bowls that can be used for that purpose. And finally, while we are on the subject of food presentation, let's not over look the drama of simplicity.

MENU DESIGN

A successful dinner must first be viewed in its entirety, as if it were a great painting. Like all art forms menu design gains freedom through discipline. Menu patterns are helpful outlines. They are useful in bringing balance and harmony to any meal. They create order and avoid repetition and waste. A menu insures that the character of each course will dramatize and add to the pleasure and enjoyment of the following courses. The very liquid quality of that wonderful first course, soup, is the perfect prelude to the diverse character of the entrée course. Then the slightly tart dressing of a crisp salad refreshes and prepares the palate for the appreciation of the sweetness of a fruit or rich dessert. And the final course of hot coffee or tea is meant to encourage digestion. Time and reason, not to mention appetite dictate that there can be only one principal dish in a dinner upon which attention is lavished. It is the chef d'oeuvre. It is the focal point of the menu, the feature by which the selection of the other dishes and courses in the dinner are guided. Requirements for the construction of a successful dinner are subtle and varied. All the components of a meal are interrelated and must fit together harmoniously in order to achieve a pleasing, satisfying picture.

Menus appear simply as suggestions in the paragraph at the beginning of all the principal recipes. Though they are merely suggestions, they have been carefully developed. These menus fall into five major patterns that comprise from three to five courses. Coffee and tea served at the end of dinner are regarded as an important course.

As an additional guide to menu planning you will find that the recipes and consequently the menus have been casually arranged into groups representative of the four seasons. The menu patterns are as follows.

MENU I

soup
entrée and accompaniment vegetable plus optional pilaf
salad, bread and butter plus optional cheese
fruit, nuts, or cookies
tea and coffee

MENU II

principal soup
salad, bread and butter plus optional cheese
fruit, nuts, or cookies
tea and coffee

MENU III

soup
principal salad, bread and butter plus optional cheese
fruit, nuts, or cookies
tea and coffee

MENU IV

soup
salad, bread and butter plus optional cheese
principal dessert
tea and coffee

MENU V

bouillon soup
blue plate special
fruit or ice cream

SOUPS

Serving soup is a social grace. Ladling a delicious soup from a beautiful, brimming tureen, into warm soup plates, one at a time, and passing them to each of the diners at the table could be called the soup ceremony. It is the prelude to gracious dining and almost no civilized dinner should begin without it. However, soup can also assume another role and a hearty soup can become the principal dish of the main course.

Every household should be equipped with several soup tureens. Does that sound extravagant? It need not be for a number of receptacles can be used as tureens. Consider an attractive enameled soup kettle filled with a thick bean soup. It can be brought right from the stove to the table. The kettle becomes the tureen. Or a lovely glass bowl becomes the tureen for the chilled summer soup. Tureens for first course soups can be smaller than those for the larger principal soups. However, it is nice to have at least one big beautiful soup tureen which is the pride of the household. Always be sure that the tureen is warm before putting the soup into it. To warm a soup tureen fill it with hot tap water and allow it to stand five minutes. Drain it, dry it, then transfer the hot soup to the warm tureen. Incidentally, soup tureens make wonderful wedding gifts.

Equally as important as the tureen are the cups, bowls, or soup plates into which the soup is ladled. They must be in harmony with the character of the soup such as china for the lighter soups, earthenware for the heartier soups and glass for cold soups. The lighter first course soups are best ladled into small bowls or consommé cups, those with a handle on either side. They usually have about a one and a half cup capacity. The round, small size soup spoon known as a consommé spoon is really necessary to use when eating soup out of a cup or a small bowl. They are harder to find than they one were and you might have to scout around for them. Most of the principal soups fit well into old fashion soup plates and are eaten with larger soup spoons. Like the tureen, soup cups, bowls and plates must of course be warmed before hot soup is ladled into them.

While we are on the subject of soup, I must tell you that I never serve crackers or bread with any soup, with two exceptions. People are prone to crumble crackers into their soup which distorts its flavor. Moreover, bread with the soup course ruins appetites for the rest of the dinner. The two exceptions are split pea soup with which croutons have become somewhat traditional and gazpacho which is both a principal soup and a salad all in one.

first course soups

The principal soups also appear in the first course, but the term "first course soup" is used to designate the less substantial soups which are a prelude to the dinner that follows. All of the criteria which apply to the selection of an accompaniment vegetable can be utilized in the selection of a first course soup, seasonal availability, taste, type, texture, color and tradition with the exception of cooking method.

First course soups vary in consistency from simple broth based soups whose variety can be multiplied by any number of small additions which change their character, to the slightly thicker soups such as sorrel soup whose consistency falls just short of having enough body to place it among the principal soups. The gradations in consistency and texture of first course soups are what make them perfect for pairing with either lighter or more substantial entrées, salads and desserts. For instance, broth based stracciatella is a good foil for substantial lasagna. While sopa de tortilla pairs perfectly with a dinner that has a simple entrée of corn on the cob.

Chilled first course soups are an introduction to summer meals. They are a dream come true for the cook cum host or hostess for they require no last minute attention.

One thing is certain when serving the first course soup—no matter how good it is. Allow each diner to have just one serving, appetites must remain keen.

consommé jardinière

herb broth

saffron consommé royale

egg drop soup

borscht (elegant rather than earthy)

tomato essence

new york state cheddar soup

watercress soup

sopa de cacahuete

noodle soup

cold avocado soup

cold curried buttermilk soup

jellied consommé madrilène

mushroom bisque

sorrel soup

avgolemono

cucumber soup

stracciatella

vichyssoise

home style tomato soup

purée of fava bean soup

sopa de tortilla

matzoh balls in garlic broth

potato dumplings in paprika broth

french onion soup

consommé jardinière

an assortment of vegetables - (1 heaping çup sliced)
6 cups clarified stock broth - (see clarified stock broth)
1 Tablespoon unsalted butter
1 teaspoon sherry
1 teaspoon honey
1/2 teaspoon salt
1/2 teaspoon celery salt
pinch freshly cracked black pepper

Trim, cut into small pieces if necessary and thinly slice any vegetables that you happen to have on hand. (To illustrate: small mushrooms, with stems intact, sliced lengthwise, slender carrots sliced crosswise, string beans sliced diagonally, upper parts of celery ribs sliced crosswise, white turnips cut into little wedges, etc.)
Bring the remaining ingredients to boil in a large saucepan over high heat. Add the sliced vegetables all at once and cook them, covered, for 5 minutes from the moment they are in the broth, regardless of when the broth returns to boil, adjusting the heat to keep the broth slowly boiling or until the vegetables are just tender. Ladle the consommé jardinière into warm soup cups and serve immediately.

about 6 cups

herb broth

3 Tablespoons large pearl tapioca
6 cups clarified stock broth - (see clarified stock broth)
1 cup water
1 Tablespoon butter
1/2 teaspoon honey
1/4 teaspoon salt
dash freshly cracked black pepper
1/4 teaspoon dried marjoram
1/4 teaspoon dried thyme
1/4 teaspoon dried chervil

In a bowl, soak the tapioca in the combined broth and water, 24 hours, covered and refrigerated.

About 1 hour before serving time, transfer the mixture to a large saucepan and bring it to boil over medium high heat, stirring constantly. Reduce the heat to low and simmer the broth, covered, stirring frequently, about 55 minutes or until the tapioca pearls are clear. Add the remaining ingredients, crushing the herbs well as you do so, and simmer the broth 5 minutes longer. Ladle the herb broth into warm soup cups, and serve immediately.

about 6 cups

saffron consommé royale

royale custard - (recipe follows)
parsley leaves - (2 teaspoons chopped)
6 cups clarified stock broth - (see clarified stock broth)
1 Tablespoon unsalted butter
1 teaspoon honey
3/4 teaspoon salt
1/2 teaspoon celery salt
pinch white pepper
1/4 teaspoon crushed saffron threads

Prepare the royale custard in advance as directed.

Chop the parsley fine and reserve it.

Bring the remaining ingredients to boil in a large saucepan over high heat. Reduce the heat to low and simmer the broth, covered, 10 minutes.

Place 5 or 6 custard cubes or cut outs per serving in the bottom of warm soup cups, and carefully ladle the broth into the cups. Sprinkle a pinch of the chopped parsley over each serving, and serve the saffron consommé royale immediately.

6 cups

Note: Especially lovely in white soup cups.

royale custard

1 egg - at room temperature
1 egg yolk - at room temperature
1/2 cup clarified stock broth - (see clarified stock broth)
dash salt

A round 5 1/2 inch in diameter baking dish or pan will produce the desired 1/2 inch thick custard made with the quantity of ingredients listed above. First, cut out a piece of wax paper to fit the inside of the bottom of the dish. Butter the dish, lay the wax paper in it, then butter the wax paper. Set the dish aside.

In a bowl, using a wire whisk, beat the egg and yolk until they are light. Slowly beat in the broth, add the salt and pour the mixture into the prepared dish. Place a trivet (or two chopsticks) in a large baking pan and set the dish on it. Pour enough hot water into the large pan to reach 3/4 of the way up the sides of the dish. Put the waterbath arrangement in a preheated 325 degree oven and bake the custard 25 minutes.

Lift the dish out of the waterbath and allow the custard to cool to room temperature. Then cover the dish and refrigerate it at least 1 hour or up to 24 hours for convenience. Now, turn the custard out onto a flat surface and carefully peel off the wax paper. Cut the custard into 1/2 inch cubes or tiny fancy shaped cut outs.

In either case carefully slice off the thin skin which formed on the top of the custard while it was baking and place the little custards on a plate. They can be prepared in advance and refrigerated 2 or 3 hours, but bring them to room temperature before serving.

egg drop soup

1 egg - at room temperature - (see cooked eggs note)
6 cups clarified stock broth - (see clarified stock broth)
1 Tablespoon soy sauce
1/2 teaspoon peanut oil
1/2 teaspoon salt
1/2 teaspoon celery salt
3/4 teaspoon sugar
dash white pepper

Gently stirring it, strain the egg through a fine strainer into a tea cup.

Bring the remaining ingredients to boil in a large saucepan, covered, over high heat. Uncover, and remove the pan from the heat. The moment the broth stops bubbling, stir it swiftly in one direction until it spins by itself. Immediately pour the strained egg, from a teaspoon in a very thin stream, into the spinning broth. Ladle the egg drop soup into warm soup cups, and serve immediately.

6 cups

Note: The effect is total if the soup is served in small Oriental, lotus shaped bowls with china spoons.

borscht
(elegant rather than earthy)

1 pound beets - 2 large
6 cups clarified stock broth - (see clarified stock broth)
1/2 cup water
2 Tablespoons distilled white vinegar
1 teaspoon honey
1 teaspoon brown sugar
1 teaspoon salt
small pinch white pepper
1 cup sour cream - at room temperature

Scrub, cook and peel just 1 of the beets as directed. (See boiled beets.) Then cut it into thin julienne matchsticks and reserve them.

Meanwhile trim, peel and coarsely grate the other beet. The yield should be about 1 1/2 cups. Bring the broth and water to boil in a large saucepan over high heat. Add the grated beet and when the broth returns to boil, reduce the heat to medium low and simmer the broth, covered with lid ajar, 15 minutes. Strain the broth through a large strainer set over a bowl and allow the beets to drain 5 minutes. Discard the grated beets.

Return the broth to the saucepan over medium heat. Add the vinegar, honey, sugar, salt and pepper and heat the broth covered, until it just comes to simmer. Add the julienne beets and heat 3 minutes longer. Ladle the broth into warm soup cups, and serve the borscht immediately along with a bowl of the sour cream. Let each diner stir whatever size dollop of sour cream into his borscht he pleases.

6 cups

Note: This beautiful ruby color broth can be served either hot or cold.

tomato essence

6 pounds tomatoes - about 12 medium - (12 cups chopped)
1 teaspoon plus optional salt - divided
1 bay leaf
5 black peppercorns
1 Tablespoon olive oil
1/2 teaspoon plus optional honey - divided
1/4 teaspoon celery salt
dash cayenne
1/4 teaspoon dried thyme
1/4 teaspoon dried basil

Select fully ripened garden tomatoes. Cut out the stem buttons and coarsely chop the tomatoes.

Place them, sprinkled with the 1 teaspoon of salt, along with the bay leaf and peppercorns in a large heavy saucepan over medium low heat. Allow the tomatoes to gently stew in their own juices, covered, 1 hour, stirring occasionally.

Set a colander lined with two layers of wet wrung out cheese cloth, over a bowl. Pour the stewed tomatoes into it, tie the corners of the cheese cloth together and hang the bag up over the bowl to drain for 1 hour. Do not press the bag. The yield should be 6 cups of tomato liquid.

In a large saucepan over medium heat, bring the tomato liquid, oil, the 1/2 teaspoon of honey, the celery salt and cayenne to simmer. Add the thyme and basil, crushing them and simmer 5 minutes. Taste the soup to determine whether more salt or honey is necessary. Ladle the tomato essence into warm soup cups, and serve immediately.

6 cups

Note: The most exquisite of all soups.

new york state cheddar soup

1 1/2 cups pale ale
4 1/2 cups stock broth - (see stock broth) - divided
3/4 cup flour
1/2 teaspoon salt
1/2 teaspoon turmeric
1/8 cayenne
2 Tablespoons butter
1 teaspoon honey
1 pound New York State extra sharp Cheddar cheese - (4 cups grated)
1 Tablespoon English mustard powder
2 Tablespoons water

Pour the ale out into a bowl and allow enough time for it to become flat.

Pour 1/2 cup of broth into the blender or processor. Add the flour, salt, turmeric and cayenne. Add 1 1/2 cups more broth and blend or process the mixture for 1 minute. Transfer the mixture to a large saucepan set over medium high heat. Rinse out the container of the machine with the remaining stock broth and add it to the saucepan. Add the flat ale, butter and honey, stirring constantly until the mixture comes to boil. (If the mixture becomes lumpy, pass it through a fine strainer and return it to the saucepan.) Reduce the heat to low, place a heat diffuser under the pan, and very gently, simmer the mixture, covered, 55 minutes, stirring frequently. Remove the pan from the heat, allow the mixture to cool to room temperature, then refrigerate it 24 hours. At serving time, bring the mixture to simmer again, on a heat diffuser over medium heat, stirring.

Meanwhile, coarsely grate the cheese and reserve it.

In a small cup make a paste out of the mustard powder and water, then stir it into the soup mixture and simmer 5 minutes longer. Remove the pan from the heat and add the cheese, 1/2 cup at a time, stirring until the cheese has melted. Ladle the New York State Cheddar soup into warm soup cups, and serve immediately.

about 6 cups

watercress soup

celery - 1 large rib - (1/2 cup chopped)
watercress - 2 bunches - (8 loosely packed cups leaves and tips)
1 teaspoon celery salt
5 Tablespoons unsalted butter - divided
1/2 teaspoon salt
5 cups stock broth - (see stock broth) - divided
4 Tablespoons flour
1/4 teaspoon white pepper
1 cup heavy cream - at room temperature
1 teaspoon honey
1 teaspoon English mustard powder
2 teaspoons water
4 egg yolks - at room temperature - (see cooked eggs note)

Trim, scrape the strings from, and chop the celery.

Strip the leaves and only the tiny branch tips from the stems of the watercress.

Sauté the celery, sprinkled with the celery salt, in 1 tablespoon of butter in a large saucepan over medium heat, for 3 minutes. Add the watercress, sprinkle with the salt and cook 5 minutes, stirring. Add 1 cup of the broth, increase the heat to high, when the broth comes to boil, reduce the heat to low, and simmer the watercress, covered, 15 minutes. Remove the pan from the heat, allow it to cool a bit then purée the vegetables, along with their cooking broth, in the blender or processor or pass them through a food mill set over a bowl.

Melt 3 tablespoons of the butter in a large saucepan over low heat. Using a rubber spatula, blend in the flour and pepper until they absorb the butter. Slowly, stir in the remaining broth, the cream and honey. Then stir in the puréed watercress. Place a heat diffuser under the pan and gently simmer the soup, covered, 55 minutes.

(The soup can be prepared up to 24 hours in advance up to this point cooled to room temperature, refrigerated then reheated before continuing with the recipe.)

In a cup, make a paste out of the mustard powder and water then stir it into the soup.

Gently stirring them, strain the yolks through a fine strainer into a small bowl. Very slowly, stir 1 cup of the hot soup into the yolks then slowly stir the yolk mixture into the soup, simmer the soup 1 minute and remove the pan from the heat. Now, stir in the remaining 1 tablespoon of butter and ladle the watercress soup into warm soup cups, and serve immediately.

Note: The flour stabilizes the yolks, and they will not curdle when simmered. They will just thicken the soup nicely.

sopa de cacahuete

celery - 1 large rib - (1/2 cup diced)
1/2 teaspoon celery salt
4 Tablespoons butter
4 Tablespoons flour
4 cups stock broth - divided
1/2 cup chunky style peanut butter - (see note)
1 cup heavy cream - at room temperature
1 Tablespoon soy sauce
1 teaspoon light molasses
1 teaspoon honey
1 drop liquid smoke
3/4 teaspoon salt

Trim, scrape the strings from, and dice the celery very small.
Sauté the celery, sprinkled with the celery salt, in the butter in a large saucepan over medium heat, 3 minutes. Reduce the heat to low, and using a rubber spatula, blend in the flour until it absorbs the butter. Slowly stir in 1 cup of the broth, then add the peanut butter and stir until it has melted. The mixture will be very thick. Slowly stir in the rest of the broth and the cream. Add the remaining ingredients, place a heat diffuser under the saucepan and very gently cook the soup, covered, 1 hour. Ladle the sopa de cacahuete into warm soup cups, and serve immediately.

5 1/2 cups

Note: Be sure to use old fashioned natural peanut butter, with no additives, just peanuts and salt.

noodle soup

about 2 ounces rutabaga - (1/3 cup chopped)
celery - 1 small rib - (1/3 cup chopped)
about 2 ounces green bell pepper - 1/2 medium small - (1/3 cup chopped)
about 1 ounce mushrooms - 2 medium large - (1/3 cup chopped)
about 3 ounces tomato - 1 small - (1/3 cup chopped)
1 teaspoon salt
1 teaspoon celery salt
1/4 teaspoon freshly cracked black pepper
1 1/2 Tablespoons olive oil
1 1/2 Tablespoons butter
6 cups water
1 bay leaf
1 teaspoon honey
2 Tablespoons soy sauce
1/2 teaspoon curry powder
about 4 ounces fine dried egg noodles - (2 cups)
1/4 teaspoon dried thyme
1/4 teaspoon dried marjoram

Peel, and chop the rutabaga small.

Trim, scrape the strings from and chop the celery small.

Core the bell pepper, trim away any white membrane and chop the pepper small.

Wipe the mushrooms with a damp cloth, trim the butt ends of the stems and chop them small.

Peel and seed the tomato as directed. (See peeled tomatoes and see seeded tomatoes.) Chop it small.

Sauté the chopped vegetables, sprinkled with the salt, celery salt, and black pepper in the oil and butter in a large saucepan over medium heat, stirring, for 5 minutes. Add the water, bay leaf, honey, soy sauce and curry powder. Raise the heat to high until the water comes to boil then reduce it to low and simmer the vegetables, covered, 5 minutes. Raise the heat to high again. When the soup boils, add the noodles, thyme and marjoram, crushing the herbs. Cook the noodles, covered with lid ajar, for 5 minutes from the moment they are in the soup, regardless of when the soup returns to boil. Stir them occasionally with a wooden spoon and adjust the heat to keep the soup gently simmering until the noodles are just tender but firm. Remember, the noodles will go right on cooking in the hot soup even after it is served. Ladle the noodle soup into warm soup cups, and serve immediately.

about 7 cups

cold avocado soup

1 Tablespoon dried cilantro
1 Tablespoon boiling water
4 cups yogurt
about 3 pounds 4 ounces knobby skinned avocados - about 5 or 6 small
2 cups cold water - divided
6 Tablespoons fresh lime juice
3 Tablespoons honey
2 1/2 teaspoons salt
1 teaspoon celery salt
1/2 teaspoon ground cumin
1/4 teaspoon white pepper
1/8 teaspoon cayenne

Crush the cilantro into a cup, pour the boiling water over it and allow it to steep while you prepare the soup.

In a large mixing bowl, using a wire whisk beat the yogurt until it is perfectly smooth.

Cut the avocados in half and reserve the pits. Scoop the flesh out of the shells and liquefy it with 1 1/2 cups of the cold water and all the remaining ingredients in the blender in 2 batches or in the processor. Stir the liquefied avocado into the yogurt. Rinse out the container of the machine with the remaining 1/2 cup of water and add it to the yogurt mixture. Stir in the cilantro and its soaking water. Then add the reserved pits. They will keep the avocado soup from discoloring. Refrigerate the soup, covered, 2 hours. Remove the pits and ladle the soup into cold, individual size glass bowls, and serve the avocado soup very cold.

6 cups

cold curried buttermilk soup

2 cups puréed stock vegetables - (see puréed stock vegetables)
1 cup water
2 Tablespoons corn oil
2 Tablespoons honey

2 Tablespoons curry powder
1 1/2 teaspoons salt
1 1/2 teaspoons ground coriander
1 teaspoon ground turmeric
1/2 teaspoon ground cumin
1/4 teaspoon cayenne
4 cups buttermilk - cold

Liquefy the vegetable purée with the water in the blender or processor.

In a large saucepan, over medium low heat, combine the liquefied purée with all the remaining ingredients except the buttermilk. Heat the mixture, covered, stirring occasionally, about 30 minutes to allow the flavors time to develop and blend.

Turn the mixture into a large mixing bowl and let it cool to room temperature. Then stir in the buttermilk and refrigerate the soup, covered, 2 hours.

Ladle the soup into cold individual size glass bowls, and serve the buttermilk soup very cold.

about 7 cups

Note: Liquefying the purée gives the soup a smooth texture.

jellied consommé madrilène

3 pounds ripe tomatoes - 6 medium - (6 cups chopped)
1/2 teaspoon plus optional salt
1 bay leaf
1/2 cup plus optional cold water
3 cups clarified stock broth - cold - (see clarified stock broth)
1 Tablespoon agar-agar granules - (see note)
1 teaspoon plus optional honey
dash cayenne
1 teaspoon fresh lemon juice
lemon wedges

Remove the stem buttons and coarsely chop the tomatoes. Place them, sprinkled with the 1/2 teaspoon of salt, in a heavy saucepan, with the bay leaf, over medium low heat. Allow the tomatoes to gently stew in their own juices, covered, about 1 hour, stirring occasionally.

Set a colander, lined with 4 layers of wet, wrung out cheese cloth, over a bowl. Pour the tomatoes into it, remove and reserve the bay leaf. Tie the corners of the cheese cloth together and hang the bag up over the bowl to drain for 1 hour. Do not press the bag. If the yield is more than 3 cups of tomato liquid do not use the excess it would unbalance the recipe. (Drink it.) If the yield is not enough, add water.

In a large saucepan combine the tomato liquid, the 1/2 cup of water, the stock broth, the agar-agar, the 1 teaspoon of honey, the cayenne and the reserved bay leaf and bring the mixture to boil over high heat, while stirring constantly. Reduce the heat to medium high and cook 10 minutes, still stirring constantly. Now pour the mixture into a bowl, stir in the lemon juice and taste it. This is the time to add a little more salt and/or honey if necessary. Allow the consommé to cool to room temperature and set, then refrigerate it for at least 2 hours.

At serving time, using a large spoon, spoon the consommé into cold individual size glass bowls and serve the jellied consommé Madrilène along with a dish of the lemon wedges for those who would like a sprinkling of lemon juice over their consommé.

6 cups

Note: Agar-agar is a gelatin derived from sea weed and is available at natural food stores.

mushroom bisque

2 large celery ribs - (2/3 cup minced)
1 pound mushrooms - medium - (5 cups sliced)
1/2 teaspoon celery salt
6 Tablespoons unsalted butter - divided
1 teaspoon salt
6 Tablespoons flour
1/4 teaspoon white pepper
5 cups milk - at room temperature

1 teaspoon honey
2 Tablespoons soy sauce
1 Tablespoon sherry

Trim, scrape the strings from, and chop the celery fine.

Wipe the mushrooms with a damp cloth trim the butt ends of the stems and very thinly slice the mushrooms, lengthwise, stems and all.

Sauté the celery, sprinkled with the celery salt, in 2 tablespoons of the butter, in a large frying pan (see utensils) over medium heat, stirring, for about 8 minutes or until it starts to shrink but before it starts to brown. Add the mushrooms, sprinkle with the salt and sauté about 10 minutes longer, while gradually turning up the heat until all mushroom liquid has evaporated and the mushrooms start to brown. Remove the pan from the heat.

Melt 4 tablespoons of the butter in a large saucepan over low heat. Using a rubber spatula, blend in the flour and pepper until they absorb the butter, then slowly stir in the milk and honey until the mixture is smooth. Add the sautéed celery and mushrooms.

Pour the soy sauce and sherry into the empty frying pan, set it over low heat, and using a rubber spatula, scrape the pan down well to deglaze it. Pour the pan juices into the soup.

Place a heat diffuser under the saucepan, and very gently, cook the mushroom bisque, covered, 1 hour and serve.

6 cups

sorrel soup

celery - 1 large rib - (1/2 cup chopped)
1 pound 2 ounces baking potatoes - 2 large - (2 1/4 cups chopped)
iceberg lettuce - about 1/2 large head - (4 packed cups shredded)
2 ounces untrimmed spinach - (1 packed cup trimmed)
1 ounce untrimmed sorrel - (1/2 packed cup trimmed)
1/2 teaspoon celery salt
8 Tablespoons butter
2 1/2 teaspoons salt - divided
6 cups water
2 teaspoons honey
1/4 teaspoon white pepper
chervil leaves - (1 rounded Tablespoon)
1 Tablespoon fresh lemon juice

Trim, scrape the strings from, and chop the celery.

Peel and dice the potatoes.

Core and shred the lettuce.

Wash and trim the spinach and sorrel together as directed. (See washed and trimmed spinach.)

Sauté the celery, sprinkled with the celery salt, in the butter in a large saucepan over medium heat, 3 minutes. Add the potatoes, sprinkle with 1 teaspoon of the salt and sauté 5 minutes longer. Add the lettuce, spinach and sorrel, sprinkle with 1 1/2 teaspoons of the salt and stir the greens in the butter for 1 minute. Add the water, honey and pepper. Increase the heat to high, when the water comes to boil, reduce the heat to low, and gently simmer the soup, covered, 55 minutes. Add the chervil, remove the pan from the heat and allow it to cool a bit. Then purée the soup, in batches, in the blender or processor or pass it through a food mill set over a bowl. Return the soup to the saucepan set over medium heat. When the soup simmers, add the lemon juice simmer 5 minutes ,and serve the sorrel soup immediately.

about 8 cups

Note: Only occasionally is sorrel available in the market. However, it is very easy of cultivation either in the garden or in a pot. It is perennial and is the first herb to pop up the minute the snow recedes; the deer love it. I've tried using wild sorrel in this soup at times but, interestingly, it doesn't seem quite as pungent as the cultivated, "French sorrel." The other indispensable herb in this soup is fresh chervil which you will also probably have to grow yourself. Chervil is a very worth while herb to grow, as it is delightful in salads and omelets as well as soups.

avgolemono

8 cups stock broth - (see stock broth)
1 small bay leaf
1/4 cup short grain white rice
1 Tablespoon virgin olive oil
1 Tablespoon butter
1 Tablespoon honey
1 1/2 teaspoon salt
1/2 teaspoon celery salt

1/4 teaspoon freshly cracked black pepper
1/2 teaspoon dried oregano
2 eggs - at room temperature - (see cooked eggs note)
2 Tablespoons fresh lemon juice

In a large saucepan over high heat, boil the broth, with the bay leaf, uncovered, 20 minutes or until it is reduced to 6 cups. Add the rice, oil, butter, honey, salt, celery salt, and pepper. Reduce the heat to low and simmer the broth, covered, about 20 minutes or until the rice is cooked. Add the oregano, crushing it and simmer 5 minutes longer.

Now, gently stirring them, strain the eggs through a fine strainer into a small bowl. Then, very slowly, stir the lemon juice into them. (If the lemon juice is added too quickly it can curdle the eggs.) Again, very slowly, stir 1 cup of the hot soup into the egg mixture. Still, very slowly pour the egg mixture into the soup while stirring the soup constantly. Leave the saucepan on the heat long enough for the soup to just barely start to simmer again, quickly remove the pan and serve the avgolemono immediately.

about 6 cups

Note: This method of adding the lemon juice and eggs is the "authentic" version. Frankly, I prefer to stir 2 tablespoons of cornstarch into the lemon juice and to use 4 eggs. It makes a more viscous soup and there is no concern about curdling because the cornstarch stabilizes the eggs.

cucumber soup

1 cup crème fraîche - (recipe follows)
1/2 teaspoon dill seeds
celery - 1 large rib - (1/2 cup chopped)
3 pounds 6 ounces cucumbers - 6 average, 7 to 8 inches long - (6 heaping
cups sliced and grated)
1/2 teaspoon celery salt
4 Tablespoons butter - divided
1 1/4 teaspoon salt
5 cups stock broth - (see stock broth) - divided
4 Tablespoons flour
1/4 teaspoon white pepper
1 1/2 teaspoon honey
dill leaves - (2 Tablespoons chopped)

The crème fraîche can be prepared well in advance as directed. Bring it to room temperature before serving time.

Toast the dill seeds in a dry pan over medium heat, stirring, for 3 minutes until they become golden and fragrant. Remove them from the pan immediately and crush them fine in a mortar or use a spice grinder. Reserve them.

Trim, scrape the strings from and chop the celery.

Peel the cucumbers and cut thin slices off of either end of all 6 of them until the slices measure 1 cup. (Check the slices for any bitterness.) Reserve the slices. Quarter the remainder of the cucumbers lengthwise, scrape out the seed and coarsely grate them.

Sauté the celery, sprinkled with the celery salt, in 1 tablespoon of the butter in a large saucepan over medium heat 3 minutes. Add the grated cucumber, sprinkle with the salt, and cook 5 minutes longer, stirring. Add 2 cups of the broth, increase the heat to high, when the broth comes to boil, reduce the heat to low and simmer the cucumbers, covered, 15 minutes or until they are soft. Remove the pan from the heat and allow it to cool a bit, then liquefy the vegetables, along with their cooking broth, in the blender or processor.

Melt 3 tablespoons of the butter in the large saucepan over low heat. Using a rubber spatula, blend in the flour and pepper until they absorb the butter. Slowly stir in the remaining broth, the honey, the liquefied cucumbers and the reserved, crushed dill seed. Place a heat diffuser under the pan and gently simmer the soup, covered, 45 minutes. Add the reserved cucumber slices and cook 10 minutes more.

(The soup can be prepared up to 24 hours in advance up to this point, cooled, refrigerated, then reheated before continuing with the recipe.)

Now, chop the dill leaves small, add them to the soup and cook 5 minutes longer.

In a bowl, using a wire whisk, slowly stir 1 cup of the hot soup into the crème fraîche. Then stir the crème fraîche mixture into the cucumber soup, and serve.

about 7 cups

Note: This soup can be enjoyed at any temperature.

crème fraîche

1 Tablespoon buttermilk - at room temperature
1 cup heavy cream - at room temperature

In a jar, stir the buttermilk into the cream. Cover the jar with wax paper, then screw the lid on tight and vigorously shake the jar for about 1 minute. Allow the jar to stand for from 12 to 24 hours until the cream thickens to about the consistency of sour cream. The crème fraîche will keep, refrigerated for as long as 4 weeks. (Write the date it was made on the lid.)

1 cup

Note: The trick here is to have a room temperature of 80 degrees. Crème fraîche is one of the bonuses of a hot summer day.

stracciatella

8 ounces untrimmed spinach - (4 packed cups trimmed)
2 eggs - at room temperature - (see cooked eggs note)
Parmesan cheese - (3 Tablespoons freshly grated)
Romano cheese - (1 Tablespoon freshly grated)
2 Tablespoons plus 2 drops olive oil - divided
6 cups stock broth - (see stock broth)
1 teaspoon honey
1 teaspoon salt
1/2 teaspoon celery salt
1/2 teaspoon freshly cracked black pepper

Wash and trim the spinach as directed. (See washed and trimmed spinach.) Leave the spinach in the colander.
Gently stirring them , strain the eggs through a fine strainer into a small bowl. Then stir the Parmesan, Romano and the 2 drops of oil into the strained eggs.
Bring the broth, honey, salt, celery salt, pepper and the 2 tablespoons of oil to boil in a large saucepan, covered, over high heat. Remove

the cover, toss in the spinach all at once, pushing it down with a wooden spoon, reduce the heat to low and cook the spinach for 5 minutes from the moment it is in the broth. Remove the pan from the heat, and using the wooden spoon, stir the broth swiftly in one direction until it spins by itself. Immediately pour the egg mixture, from a teaspoon, in a thin stream, into the spinning broth. Serve the stracciatella immediately while the spinach leaves are still bright green.

about 6 cups

vichyssoise

3 pounds leeks with tops - 4 medium bulbs, about 1 1/2 inches in diameter
- (2 1/2 cups sliced bulbs)
1 pound baking potatoes - 2 medium large - (3 heaping cups sliced)
chives - (1 Tablespoon snipped)
1 teaspoon salt
4 Tablespoons unsalted butter
4 cups stock broth - (see stock broth) - divided
4 Tablespoons flour
1/4 teaspoon white pepper
2 cups light cream - at room temperature

Cut the green tops from, trim and very thinly slice only the white part of the leeks crosswise. Rinse and drain them well.

Peel and thinly slice the potatoes crosswise.

Using a pair of scissors, snip the chives small.

In a large saucepan over low heat, sweat the leeks sprinkled with the salt, in the butter, covered, 15 minutes. Add 3 cups of the stock broth and the potatoes and increase the heat to high. When the broth comes to boil, reduce the heat to medium low and cook the vegetables, covered, about 15 minutes or until they are very soft.

Now, in a cup, slowly stir the remaining 1 cup of stock broth into the flour and pepper to make a smooth slurry, then stir the slurry into the mixture in the saucepan. Now, purée the mixture through a food mill set over a bowl. Alternatively, purée the mixture in the blender or processor.

Return the purée to the large saucepan set on a heat diffuser over low heat. Stir in the cream and very gently cook the soup, covered, 1 hour, stirring occasionally. You can either serve the soup hot or you can allow it to cool to room temperature, transfer it to a glass serving bowl, refrigerate it for 2 hours and serve it chilled. In either case, sprinkle the vichyssoise with the snipped chives before serving.

about 7 cups

Note: As I recall my mother never puréed the vegetables at all, but cooked the potatoes until they disintegrated. She would make a large quantity and we had it hot the first day and cold the second day.

home style tomato soup

4 Tablespoons butter
3 Tablespoons flour
3 cups plus 1 Tablespoon water - divided
1 can peeled tomatoes - 28 ounces - (3 1/2 cups)
1 bay leaf
1 teaspoon honey
3/4 teaspoon salt
1/2 teaspoon celery salt
1/4 teaspoon freshly cracked black pepper
1/4 teaspoon ground allspice
1 teaspoon fresh lemon juice
1 Tablespoon sweet Hungarian paprika
parsley leaves - (2 Tablespoons chopped)

Melt the butter in a large saucepan over low heat. Using a rubber spatula, blend in the flour until it absorbs the butter. Slowly stir in the 3 cups of water until the mixture is smooth. Drain the juice from the canned tomatoes into the pan. Then, add the tomatoes, cutting the stem button out of each tomato, and crushing it through your (clean) fingers into the pan. Add the bay leaf, honey, salt, celery salt, pepper, allspice and lemon juice. In a teacup make a paste out of the paprika and the 1 tablespoon of water then stir it into the soup. Raise the heat to medium, when the soup comes to simmer, reduce the heat to low and gently simmer the soup, covered, 55 minutes. Remove the pan from the heat and allow it to cool to room temperature. Then transfer the soup to a bowl and refrigerate it, covered, 24 hours.

At serving time chop the parsley small. Return the soup to the saucepan and bring it to simmer, covered, over medium heat. Add the parsley, simmer 5 minutes longer, and serve the home style tomato soup immediately.

about 6 1/2 cups

Note: The soup can also be served on the day that it is prepared. However, it is tastier the following day, after the flavors have been allowed to develop and marry.

purée of fava bean soup

1 cup plus 2 Tablespoons small or 1 1/4 cups large dried peeled fava beans
- 8 ounces - (see note)
6 cups water
1 bay leaf
1 pound eggplant - 1 medium
1 teaspoon plus salt
4 Tablespoons olive oil
4 Tablespoons butter
4 Tablespoons fresh lemon juice
1 Tablespoon plus 1 teaspoon honey
1 teaspoon celery salt
2 teaspoons ground cumin
2 teaspoons ground coriander
1/4 teaspoon cayenne
1 cup yogurt - at room temperature

Cull and rinse the beans. Bring the water to boil in a large saucepan over high heat then add the beans and the bay leaf. When the water returns to boil, reduce the heat to low and simmer the beans, covered with lid ajar just enough to allow the saucepan to breath, for from 1 1/2 to 2 1/2 hours, depending on their size, or until they disintegrate.
Meanwhile, trim, peel, and cut the eggplant crosswise into 1/2 inch thick slices. Spread the slices out on an oiled aluminum baking sheet or use aluminum foil. (Other metals discolor eggplant.) Lightly sprinkle the slices with salt ,and broil the eggplant in a preheated broiler, 6 inches from the

heat source for 5 minutes. Using a metal spatula, turn the slices over, lightly salt them again and broil them 5 minutes longer or until the slices are lightly charred on both sides.

Now removing the bay leaf and reserving it, allow both the cooked fava beans and broiled eggplant to cool slightly. Then purée them together with the bean cooking water, in batches, in the blender or processor. Return the purée to the saucepan, return the bay leaf to the purée, add the 1 teaspoon of salt and all the remaining ingredients except the yogurt and simmer the purée, covered, over low heat 30 minutes.

In a small serving bowl, using a wire whisk, beat the yogurt until it is perfectly smooth. Serve the purée of fava bean soup along with the bowl of yogurt and let each diner put a large dollop of yogurt in his own serving. The flavor peak of purée of fava bean soup is warm rather than hot.

about 8 cups

Note: Peeled fava beans are available at speciality and natural food stores.

sopa de tortilla

6 Tortillas
peanut oil
salt
4 ounces Monterey Jack cheese - (1 cup diced)
celery - 2 large ribs - (1 cup sliced)
6 ounces sweet Italian frying peppers - 3 medium - (1 cup sliced)
cilantro leaves - (2 Tablespoons chopped)
1 teaspoon salt
2 Tablespoons peanut oil
1 quart home canned tomatoes - (see home canned tomatoes)
4 cups water
1 teaspoon honey
1/2 teaspoon celery salt
1/8 teaspoon ground cumin
1/4 teaspoon cayenne
1/2 teaspoon oregano

Cut the tortillas in half then cut them across the short way into strips 1/4 inch wide. Heat about 1/2 inch of oil in an 8 inch frying pan over medium high heat. Before the oil smokes, fry 2 tortillas worth of strips at a time for about 2 minutes, turning, stirring and flattening them with a spatula. Be careful not to let them brown. When they are just crisp and golden, lift them from the oil with the spatula, drain them on paper towels and lightly sprinkle them with salt.

(The tortillas can be prepared up to 24 hours in advance. When they are cool, seal them in plastic bags.)

Dice the cheese into 3/8 inch cubes or smaller. Spread the tiny cubes out on a dinner plate to dry slightly for about 30 minutes. This will prevent them from sticking together when they are dropped into the soup.

Meanwhile, trim, scrape the strings from, and cut the celery into thin diagonal slices.

Cut the peppers, crossways, into thin slices, then trim the seeds and membrane out of the little rings.

Chop the cilantro small, and reserve it.

Sauté the celery and peppers, sprinkled with the 1 teaspoon of salt in the 2 tablespoons of oil in a large saucepan over medium heat, 5 minutes. Add the tomatoes, squeezing them through your (clean) fingers, with all their juices. Add the water, honey, celery salt, cumin and cayenne. Increase the heat to high. When the soup comes to boil, add the oregano, crushing it, reduce the heat to low and simmer the soup, covered, for just 10 minutes. Remove the pan from the heat. (At this point the soup can be transferred to a warm tureen.) Add the cilantro and allow the soup to stand, covered, 10 minutes. Add the tortilla strips and cheese, and serve the sopa de tortilla immediately.

about 8 cups

Note: This is a special and very delicious soup. It is always best made with home canned tomatoes and fresh cilantro. If you are not familiar with this herb now is the time to try it. Cilantro is the same herb as coriander whose seed we all know and love in Indian and Middle Eastern foods. But the flavor of the leaf is very different from that of the seed. The cilantro leaf has an off flavor that most gringos (North Americans) don't care for on first try. However, it combines well with tomatoes and once you've tasted it in sopa de tortilla you'll find it an indispensable herb in your kitchen. If you can't find it in the market, (our natural food store carries it) it's easy to grow.

matzoh balls in garlic broth

matzoh ball batter - (recipe follows)
6 cups clarified stock broth - (see clarified stock broth)
1/2 cup water
garlic - 1 head, about 12 cloves
1 Tablespoon plus 1 teaspoon butter
1/2 teaspoon salt
1/2 teaspoon celery salt
1/8 teaspoon white pepper
1/4 to 1/2 teaspoon sugar

Prepare the batter and refrigerate it as directed.

Bring the broth and water to boil in a large saucepan over high heat. Pull the garlic head apart to separate the cloves and add them to the broth. Reduce the heat to low and gently simmer the broth, covered, for 1 hour. Using a slotted spoon, remove the cloves, then add the butter, salt, celery salt, pepper and sugar to taste to the broth.

Before serving reduce the heat to very low so that the broth is just barely simmering. Using a teaspoon, shape the matzoh batter into little balls about 3/4 inch in diameter dropping them into the broth as they are made. When all the matzoh balls are in the pan, cover it, and gently poach them 15 minutes. Ladle the broth and matzoh balls into warm soup bowls, allowing up to 5 balls per serving, and serve the matzoh balls in garlic broth immediately.

6 cups

Note: You will be surprised at how mellow the broth is.

matzoh ball batter

1 Tablespoon butter
1 egg
2 Tablespoons water
1/4 teaspoon salt
1/8 teaspoon celery salt

pinch white pepper
1/4 cup matzoh meal

Melt the butter in a small pan over low heat. Remove it from the heat and allow it to cool a bit. In a small mixing bowl using a wire whisk, beat the egg, water, salt, celery salt, and pepper together. Stir in the matzoh meal, then the cooled butter. Refrigerate the batter, covered, for 1 hour.

batter for 20 or more matzoh balls

potato dumplings in paprika broth

potato dumplings - (recipe follows)
2 Tablespoons butter
2 Tablespoons tomato paste
6 cups clarified stock broth - (see clarified stock broth)
2 teaspoons honey
1 bay leaf
1 teaspoon salt
1/2 teaspoon celery salt
dash cayenne
2 teaspoons sweet Hungarian paprika
1 Tablespoons plus 1 teaspoon water

Prepare the batter for the potato dumplings and refrigerate it as directed.

About 20 minutes before serving time, melt the butter in a large saucepan over low heat. Stir in the tomato paste and the broth then add the honey, bay leaf, salt, celery salt, and cayenne. In a cup, make a paste out of the paprika and water then stir it into the broth. Raise the heat to high, when the broth comes to boil reduce it to low and simmer the broth, covered, about 15 minutes.

Meanwhile, make the dumplings as directed. Allowing up to 5 dumplings per serving, place the warm dumplings in warm soup bowls and ladle the hot broth over them. Serve the potato dumplings in paprika broth immediately.

6 cups

potato dumplings

parsley leaves - (2 Tablespoons minced)
8 ounces baking potato - 1 medium large
water
2 Tablespoons flour
1/4 teaspoon salt
1/2 teaspoon celery salt
pinch white pepper
1/4 teaspoon ground thyme
1 egg yolk

Mince the parsley and reserve it.

Scrub the potato under running water. In a saucepan over high heat, bring to boil enough water to cover the potato by 1 1/2 inches. Add the potato and cook it, covered with lid slightly ajar, for about 40 minutes from the moment it is in the water regardless of when the water returns to boil, adjusting the heat to keep the water slowly boiling, until the potato is just tender when pierced with a wooden skewer. Drain, peel, and cut the potato into eighths. Return it to the empty pan, set over low heat, and "dry it out," covered, for 2 or 3 minutes while constantly shaking the pan .

Pass the potato through a food mill set over a bowl. Stir the flour, salt, celery salt, pepper and thyme into the potato, blending the mixture well. Then stir in the egg yolk and minced parsley. Cover the bowl with a paper towel and lid and refrigerate it 2 hours.

About 30 minutes before serving time, shape the dumplings by scooping up a heaping teaspoon of the batter and rolling it between lightly floured hands to form a dumpling about 1 inch in diameter. Set the dumplings on a platter, as they are made.

This is the point at which to prepare the paprika broth.

About 20 minutes before serving time, in a large saucepan over medium heat, bring to simmer enough water in which to poach the dumplings. Then reduce the heat to very low. Carefully drop the dumplings, one by one, into the just barely simmering water. When all the dumplings are in the pan, cover it and gently poach them 15 minutes. Lift the dumplings out of the water with a slotted spoon and place them on paper towels to drain for a minute, rolling them around a bit to blot them.

20 or more potato dumplings

Note: The texture of the batter can vary. If it appears too soft, do not add more flour to it. Simply flour your hands more heavily when forming the dumplings.

french onion soup

1 pound tan skinned onions - 2 large - (4 cups sliced)
1/2 teaspoon salt
3 Tablespoons butter
6 cups stock broth - (see stock broth)
1 Tablespoon light molasses
1 teaspoon celery salt
1/4 teaspoon freshly cracked black pepper
1 teaspoon English mustard powder
2 teaspoons water
4 slices day old French bread - 3/4 inch thick
2 teaspoons butter - soft
Parmesan cheese - (1 Tablespoons freshly grated)
Romano cheese - (1 teaspoon freshly grated)
2 ounces Gruyère cheese - (1/2 cup grated)

Cut the onions in half, lengthwise, peel and cut them, crosswise, into 1/4 inch thick slices. Sauté the onions, sprinkled with the salt, in the 3 tablespoons of butter in a large heavy saucepan over medium heat 15 minutes, until they are golden but not brown. Add the broth, molasses, celery salt and pepper. In a cup make a paste out of the mustard powder and water then stir it into the soup. Cover the pan, raise the heat to medium high and when the soup comes to simmer, remove it from the heat, allow it to cool to room temperature, then refrigerate it 24 hours.

About 30 minutes before serving time, spread one side of each slice of bread with 1/2 teaspoon of the soft butter. Set the bread, buttered side up, on a baking sheet and lightly toast it in a preheated 250 degree oven, 20 minutes, then remove it from the baking sheet. Mix the Parmesan and Romano together and sprinkle 1 teaspoon of the mixture on the buttered side of each slice of bread. Coarsely grate the Gruyère and place 2 tablespoons of it on each slice.

Meanwhile, bring the soup to simmer again over medium heat, then ladle it into each of 4 warm, ovenproof soup bowls set on a baking sheet for convenience. Float 1 slice of bread in each bowl. Slip the baking sheet under a preheated broiler so that the top of the soup bowls are 6 inches from the heat source. Broil the soup 5 minutes, until the cheese is well melted. Carefully set the bowls on small plates set upon larger plates, and serve the French onion soup immediately.

4 servings

cream soups

The elegant cream soups are also first course soups. They are made of puréed vegetables and can be very practical since almost all of them if time allows, prefer to be made well in advance of serving, at least twenty four hours, and reheated. Their flavor develops and they thicken as they stand. In which case if there is an herb or seasoning to be added during the last 5 minutes of cooking delay adding it until the soup is reheated. Cream soups are not nearly so rich as they sound, most of them are principally made with milk.

cream of asparagus soup

cream of lima bean soup

cream of string bean soup

cream of broccoli soup

cream of brussels sprouts soup

cream of carrot soup

cream of cauliflower soup

cream of celeriac soup

cream of kohlrabi soup

cream of parsnip soup

cream of pea soup

cream of red bell pepper soup

cream of sweet potato soup

cream of pumpkin soup

cream of spinach soup

cream of stock vegetable purée soup

cream of tomato soup

cream of asparagus soup

celery - 1 large rib - (1/2 cup chopped)
2 pounds asparagus - (about 4 cups cut)
1 teaspoon celery salt
6 Tablespoons unsalted butter - divided
2 teaspoons salt
4 cups water - divided
6 Tablespoons flour
1/4 teaspoon white pepper
1 cup heavy cream - at room temperature
1 teaspoon honey
1/2 teaspoon dried tarragon

Trim, scrape the strings from, and chop the celery.

Rinse the asparagus in a basin of cold water. Snap off the butt end of each spear at the point where it breaks most easily. Do not bother to peel the spears but cut them into rather small pieces.

Sauté the celery, sprinkled with the celery salt, in 2 tablespoons of the butter in a large saucepan over medium heat, 3 minutes. Add the asparagus, sprinkle with the salt and cook 5 minutes more, while stirring well. Add 1 1/2 cups of the water and increase the heat to high. When the water comes to boil, reduce the heat to low and simmer, covered, about 30 minutes or until the asparagus is very soft. Now, pass the vegetables through a food mill set over a bowl, along with their cooking water, slowly pouring as much additional water over them as is needed to help ease the vegetables through the mill. Then, again using as much additional water as is needed, smoothly liquefy the purée in the blender or processor.

Melt 4 tablespoons of the butter in a large saucepan over low heat. Using a rubber spatula, blend in the flour and pepper until they absorb the butter. Slowly stir in the remaining water, the cream and honey. Then stir in the liquefied asparagus. Place a heat diffuser under the pan, and very gently cook the soup, covered, 55 minutes, stirring occasionally. Add the tarragon, crushing it fine and cook the cream of asparagus soup 5 minutes longer.

about 6 cups

Note: The asparagus needs to be both passed through a food mill, which removes any stringy fiber and then liquefied in the blender or processor which gives the soup a fine texture.

cream of lima bean soup

celery - 1 large rib - (1/2 cup chopped)
about 3 1/2 pounds unshelled lima beans - large - (4 cups shelled) - or about
20 ounces frozen
1/2 teaspoon celery salt
6 Tablespoons unsalted butter - divided
1 cup plus 1 teaspoon water - divided
1 drop liquid smoke
1 3/4 teaspoons salt
4 cups milk - at room temperature - divided
4 Tablespoons flour
1/4 teaspoon white pepper
1 teaspoon honey
1/2 teaspoon ground rosemary - (see ground rosemary)

Trim, scrape the strings from, and chop the celery.

Shell fresh lima beans or allow frozen limas to thaw and drain completely in a colander.

Sauté the celery, sprinkled with the celery salt, in 2 tablespoons of the butter in a large saucepan over medium heat, 3 minutes. Add the 1 cup of water, the liquid smoke and salt and increase the heat to high. When the water comes to boil, add the lima beans, when the water returns to boil, reduce the heat to low and simmer, covered, about 35 minutes or until the beans are very soft. Now, pass the vegetables through a food mill set over a bowl, along with their cooking water slowly pouring as much of the milk as is needed over the beans to help ease them through the mill. Sometimes some of the bean skins will not pass through the mill, just discard them.

Melt 4 tablespoons of the butter in a large saucepan over low heat. Using a rubber spatula, blend in the flour and pepper until they absorb the butter. Slowly stir in the remaining milk and the honey. Then stir in the lima bean purée. Place a heat diffuser under the pan, and very gently cook the soup, covered, 55 minutes, stirring occasionally. In a small cup make a paste out of the ground rosemary and the 1 teaspoon of water, then stir it into the soup. Cook the cream of lima bean soup 5 minutes longer.

about 7 cups

cream of string bean soup

1/2 teaspoon dill seeds
2 pounds Romano string beans - (7 cups cut)
1 1/4 teaspoon salt
8 Tablespoons butter - divided - (see note)
5 cups water - divided
4 Tablespoons flour
1/4 teaspoon white pepper
1/2 cup heavy cream - at room temperature
1 teaspoon fresh lemon juice

Toast the dill seeds in a dry pan over medium heat about 3 minutes, stirring until they become golden and fragrant. Remove them from the pan immediately and crush them fine in a mortar or spice grinder.

Trim the stems from the string beans and cut them into 1/2 inch pieces.

Cook the string beans, sprinkled with the salt, in 3 tablespoons of the butter in a large saucepan over medium heat 5 minutes while stirring well. Add 2 cups of the water and the crushed dill seeds and increase the heat to high. When the water comes to boil, reduce the heat to low and simmer the string beans, covered, 30 minutes or until they are very soft. Remove the pan from the heat and allow it to cool a bit. Then, using as much additional water as is needed, smoothly liquefy the string beans in the blender or processor along with their cooking water.

Melt 4 tablespoons of the butter in a large saucepan over low heat. Using a rubber spatula, blend in the flour and pepper until they absorb the butter. Slowly stir in the remaining water, the cream and lemon juice. Then stir in the liquefied string beans. Place a heat diffuser under the pan, and very gently cook the soup, covered, 1 hour, stirring occasionally.

The remaining 1 tablespoons of butter is stirred into the soup after it has been transferred to a warm soup tureen. Then serve the cream of string bean soup immediately.

about 6 cups

Note: Take note that the butter used in cream of string bean soup is regular salted butter, as opposed to the unsalted butter used in the other cream soups.

cream of broccoli soup

celery - 1 large rib - (1/2 cup chopped)
1 1/2 pound bunch broccoli - 3 average heads - (6 cups chopped)
1/2 teaspoon celery salt
6 Tablespoons unsalted butter - divided
1 1/2 teaspoons salt
1 1/2 cups plus 1 teaspoon water - divided
4 Tablespoons flour
1/4 teaspoon white pepper
4 cups milk - at room temperature
1 teaspoon honey
1/2 teaspoon English mustard powder

    Trim, scrape the strings from, and chop the celery.
    Cut the broccoli florets from the stalk. Trim and peel the stalk, first pulling the fibrous skin off with a knife and then using a vegetable peeler. Chop the broccoli florets and stalk small.
    Sauté the celery, sprinkled with the celery salt, in 2 tablespoons of the butter in a large saucepan over medium heat, 3 minutes. Add the broccoli, sprinkle with the salt and cook 5 minutes more, while stirring well. Add the 1 1/2 cups of water and increase the heat to high. When the water comes to boil, reduce the heat to low and simmer, covered, about 30 minutes or until the broccoli is very soft. Now, pass the vegetables through a food mill set over a bowl, along with their cooking water.
    Melt 4 tablespoons of the butter in a large saucepan over low heat. Using a rubber spatula, blend in the flour and pepper until they absorb the butter. Slowly stir in the milk and honey. Then stir in the broccoli purée. Place a heat diffuser under the pan, and very gently cook the soup, covered, 55 minutes, stirring occasionally. In a small cup make a paste out of the mustard powder and the 1 teaspoon of water then stir it into the soup. Cook the cream of broccoli soup 5 minutes longer.

about 7 cups

Note: This soup is best made with garden fresh broccoli.

cream of brussels sprouts soup

celery - 1 large rib - (1/2 cup chopped) .
1 1/2 pounds Brussels sprouts - (about 6 cups cut)
1/2 teaspoon celery salt
6 Tablespoons unsalted butter - divided
2 teaspoons salt
4 cups plus water
4 Tablespoons flour
1/4 teaspoon white pepper
2 cups light cream - at room temperature
1 teaspoon California white wine vinegar
1/2 teaspoon honey

Trim, scrape the strings from, and chop the celery.

Trim, and quarter the Brussels sprouts lengthwise.

Sauté the celery, sprinkled with the celery salt, in 2 tablespoons of the butter in a large saucepan over medium heat, 3 minutes. Add the Brussels sprouts, sprinkle with the salt, and cook 5 minutes more, while stirring well. Add the 4 cups of water and increase the heat to high. When the water comes to boil, reduce the heat to medium low and simmer, uncovered, (see note) about 30 minutes or until the Brussels sprouts are very soft. Drain the cooking water from the sprouts, measure it and add to it enough additional water for a total measurement of 4 cups and reserve it. Now, pass the vegetables through a food mill set over a bowl, slowly pouring as much of the reserved water as is needed over the sprouts to help ease them through the mill.

Melt 4 tablespoons of the butter in a large saucepan over low heat. Using a rubber spatula, blend in the flour and pepper until they absorb the butter. Slowly stir in the remaining reserved water, the cream, vinegar and honey. Then stir in the Brussels sprout purée. Place a heat diffuser under the pan, and very gently, cook the cream of Brussels sprout soup, covered now, 1 hour.

about 7 cups

Note: The flavor of Brussels sprouts will change if they are simmered, covered.

cream of carrot soup

celery - 1 large rib - (1/2 cup chopped)
about 3 1/3 pounds carrots - 7 large - (4 cups grated)
1/2 teaspoon celery salt
6 Tablespoons unsalted butter - divided
1 1/2 teaspoons salt
1 cup water
4 cups milk - at room temperature - divided
6 Tablespoons flour
1/4 teaspoon white pepper
1/2 ground turmeric
2 teaspoons honey
1/2 teaspoon dried marjoram

Trim, scrape the strings from and chop the celery.
Trim, peel and coarsely grate the carrots.
Sauté the celery, sprinkled with the celery salt in 2 tablespoons of the butter in a large saucepan over medium heat, 3 minutes. Add the carrots, sprinkle with the salt and cook 5 minutes, while stirring well. Add the water and increase the heat to high. When the water comes to boil, reduce the heat to low and simmer, covered, about 30 minutes or until the carrots are very soft. Remove the pan from the heat and allow it to cool a bit. Then, using as much of the milk as is needed, smoothly liquefy the vegetables, along with their cooking water, in the blender or processor.
Melt 4 tablespoons of the butter in a large sauce pan over low heat. Using a rubber spatula, blend in the flour, pepper and turmeric until they absorb the butter. Slowly stir in the remaining milk and the honey. Then stir in the liquefied carrots. Place a heat diffuser under the pan, and very gently cook the soup, covered, 55 minutes, stirring occasionally. Add the marjoram, crushing it fine and cook the cream of carrot soup 5 minutes longer.

about 6 cups

cream of cauliflower soup

1/4 teaspoon caraway seeds
celery - 1 large rib - (1/2 cup chopped)
1 pound 5 1/2 ounces cauliflower - 1 small head - (4 cups chopped)
1/2 teaspoon celery salt
6 Tablespoons unsalted butter - divided
1 1/2 teaspoons salt
1 cup water
4 Tablespoons flour
1/4 teaspoon white pepper
4 cups milk - at room temperature
1 teaspoon honey

Toast the caraway seeds in a dry pan over medium heat 2 or 3 minutes, stirring, until they become golden and fragrant. Remove them from the pan immediately and crush them fine in a mortar or spice grinder.

Trim, scrape the strings from, and chop the celery.

Break the cauliflower into florets and chop them small.

Sauté the celery, sprinkled with the celery salt, in 2 tablespoons of the butter in a large sauce the pan over medium heat, 3 minutes. Add the cauliflower, sprinkle with salt and cook 5 minutes, while stirring well. Add the water and crushed caraway seeds, and increase the heat to high. When the water comes to boil, reduce the heat to low and simmer, covered, about 30 minutes or until the cauliflower is very soft. Now, pass the vegetables through a food mill set over a bowl along with their cooking water.

Melt 4 tablespoons of the butter in a large saucepan over low heat. Using a rubber spatula, blend in the flour and pepper until they absorb the butter. Slowly stir in the milk and honey. Then stir in the cauliflower purée. Place a heat diffuser under the pan, and very gently cook the cream of cauliflower soup, covered, 1 hour, stirring occasionally.

about 6 cups

cream of celeriac soup

celery - 4 large ribs - (2 cups chopped)
1 pound celeriac - 1 large - (3/4 cups grated)
1 teaspoon celery salt
6 Tablespoons unsalted butter - divided
1 1/2 teaspoons salt
1 1/2 cups water
 4 cups milk - at room temperature - divided
4 Tablespoons flour
1/4 teaspoon white pepper
2 teaspoons honey
1 teaspoon fresh lemon juice

Trim, scrape the strings from, and chop the celery.
Wash, trim, peel and coarsely grate the celeriac.
Sauté the celery, sprinkled with the celery salt, in 2 tablespoons of the butter in a large saucepan over medium heat, 3 minutes. Add the celeriac, sprinkle with the salt and cook 5 minutes, while stirring well. Add the water and increase the heat to high. When the water comes to boil, reduce the heat to low and simmer, covered, about 30 minutes or until the vegetables are very soft. Now, pass the vegetables through a food mill set over a bowl, along with their cooking water. Then, using as much of the milk as is needed, smoothly liquefy the puree in the blender or processor.

Melt 4 tablespoons of the butter in a large saucepan over low heat. Using a rubber spatula, blend in the flour and pepper until they absorb the butter. Slowly, stir in the remaining milk, the honey and the lemon juice. Then stir in the liquefied vegetables. Place a heat diffuser under the pan, and very gently cook the cream of celeriac soup, covered, 1 hour, stirring occasionally.

about 6 cups

Note: The celeriac needs to be both passed through a food mill, which removes any coarse fiber, and then liquefied in the blender or processor which gives the soup a fine texture.

cream of kohlrabi soup

celery - 1 large rib - (1/2 cup chopped)
about 2 pounds kohlrabi, minus leaves - (about 3 pounds with leaves)- 6
                    bulbs, 2 to 2 1/2 inches in diameter - (4 cups grated)
1/2 teaspoon celery salt
6 Tablespoons unsalted butter - divided
1/2 teaspoon plus optional salt - divided
1 cup water
4 cups milk - at room temperature - divided
4 Tablespoons flour
1/4 teaspoon white pepper
1 teaspoon honey
2 Tablespoons soy sauce

Trim, scrape the strings from, and chop the celery.

Trim, peel and coarsely grate the kohlrabi.

Sauté the celery, sprinkled with the celery salt, in 2 tablespoons of the butter in a large saucepan over medium heat, 3 minutes. Add the kohlrabi, sprinkle with the 1/2 teaspoon of salt and cook 5 minutes, while stirring well. Add the water and increase the heat to high. When the water comes to boil, reduce the heat to low and simmer, covered, 30 minutes or until the kohlrabi is very soft. Now, pass the vegetables through a food mill set over a bowl, along with their cooking water. Then, using as much of the milk as is needed, smoothly liquefy the purée in the blender or processor.

Melt 4 tablespoons of the butter in a large saucepan over low heat. Using a rubber spatula, blend in the flour and pepper until they absorb the butter. Slowly, stir in the remaining milk, the honey and soy sauce. Then stir in the liquefied kohlrabi. Place a heat diffuser under the pan, and very gently cook the cream of kohlrabi soup, covered, 1 hour, stirring occasionally. Taste to determine whether a little more salt is required.

about 6 cups

Note: The kohlrabi needs to be both passed through the food mill, which removes any coarse fiber, and then liquefied in the blender or processor which gives the soup a fine texture.

cream of parsnip soup

celery - 1 large rib - (1/2 cup chopped)
1 pound parsnips - 5 or 6 medium - (3 cups grated)
1 teaspoon celery salt
6 Tablespoons unsalted butter - divided
1 teaspoon salt
1 cup plus 2 teaspoons water - divided
4 cups milk - at room temperature - divided
4 Tablespoons flour
1/4 teaspoon white pepper
1 teaspoon honey
1 teaspoon ground sage

Trim, scrape the strings from, and chop the celery.
Trim, peel and coarsely grate the parsnips.
Sauté the celery, sprinkled with the celery salt, in 2 tablespoons of the butter in a large saucepan over medium heat, 3 minutes. Add the parsnips, sprinkle with the salt and cook 5 minutes, while stirring well. Add the 1 cup of water and increase the heat to high. When the water comes to boil, reduce the heat to low and simmer, covered, 30 minutes or until the parsnips are very soft. Remove the pan from the heat and allow it to cool a bit. Then using as much of the milk as is needed, smoothly liquefy the vegetables, along with their cooking water in the blender or processor.
Melt 4 tablespoons of the butter in a large saucepan over low heat. Using a rubber spatula, blend in the flour and pepper until they absorb the butter. Slowly stir in the remaining milk and the honey. Then stir in the liquefied parsnips. Place a heat diffuser under the pan, and very gently cook the soup, covered, 55 minutes, stirring occasionally. In a small cup make a paste out of the ground sage and the 2 teaspoons of water then stir it into the soup. Cook the cream of parsnip soup 5 minutes longer.

about 7 cups

Note: The smooth texture of parsnips liquefied in the blender is essential to the success of this soup. Serve cream of parsnip soup as soon as it is ready for it does not reheat well. If you must reheat it, have it at room temperature and then very, very slowly reheat it over very low heat.

cream of pea soup

celery - 1 large rib - (1/2 cup chopped)
6 pounds unshelled peas - (6 cups shelled) - or about 30 ounces frozen
1/2 teaspoon celery salt
6 Tablespoons unsalted butter - divided
1 cup water
1 3/4 teaspoons salt
4 cups milk - at room temperature - divided
4 Tablespoons flour
1/4 teaspoon white pepper
1/2 teaspoon honey

Trim, scrape the strings from, and chop the celery.

Shell fresh peas or allow frozen peas to thaw and drain completely in a colander.

Sauté the celery, sprinkled with the celery salt, in 2 tablespoons of the butter in a large saucepan over medium heat, 3 minutes. Add the water and the salt and increase the heat to high. When the water comes to boil, add the peas, when the water returns to boil, reduce the heat to low and simmer, covered, about 30 minutes or until the peas are very soft. Now, pass the vegetables through a food mill set over a bowl, along with their cooking water, slowly pouring as much of the milk as is needed over the peas to help ease them through the mill. Sometimes, some of the pea skins will not pass through the mill, just discard them.

Melt 4 tablespoons of the butter in a large saucepan over low heat. Using a rubber spatula, blend in the flour and white pepper until they absorb the butter. Slowly stir in the remaining milk and the honey. Then stir in the pea purée. Place a heat diffuser under the pan, and very gently cook the cream of pea soup, covered, 1 hour, stirring occasionally.

7 cups

cream of red bell pepper soup

celery - 1 large rib - (1/2 cup chopped)
3 pounds red bell peppers - 6 to 8 medium to large

1/2 teaspoon celery salt
6 Tablespoons unsalted butter - divided
1 1/2 teaspoons salt
1 3/4 cups water - divided
6 Tablespoons flour
4 cups milk - at room temperature
1 teaspoon honey
 dash cayenne - just a dash
2 Tablespoons sweet Hungarian paprika

Trim, scrape the strings from, and chop the celery.

Prepare, roast and peel the peppers as directed. (See peeled red bell peppers.) Chop the flesh.

Sauté the celery, sprinkled with the celery salt, in 2 tablespoons of the butter in a large saucepan over medium heat, 3 minutes. Add the bell peppers, sprinkle with the salt and cook, 3 minutes while stirring well. Add 1 1/2 cups of the water and increase the heat to high. When the water comes to boil, reduce the heat to low, and simmer, covered, 15 minutes. Remove the pan from the heat and allow it to cool a bit. Then liquefy the vegetables in the blender or processor along with their cooking water until the mixture is smooth.

Melt 4 tablespoons of the butter in a large saucepan over low heat. Using a rubber spatula, blend in the flour until it absorbs the butter. Slowly stir in the milk, honey and cayenne. Then stir in the liquefied bell peppers. In a small cup make a paste out of the paprika and 1/4 cup of the water then stir it into the soup. Place a heat diffuser under the pan, and very gently cook the cream of red bell pepper soup 1 hour, covered, stirring occasionally.

about 6 cups

cream of sweet potato soup

celery - 1 large rib - (1/2 cup chopped)
about 1 pound 4 ounces sweet potatoes - 2 medium - (4 cups grated)
1/2 teaspoon celery salt
6 Tablespoons unsalted butter - divided
1 teaspoon salt
2 cups orange juice
3 cups milk - at room temperature - divided

4 Tablespoons flour
1/4 teaspoon white pepper
1 cup heavy cream - at room temperature
2 teaspoons honey
2 Tablespoons dry sherry
1 teaspoon ground ginger
1/4 teaspoon ground cloves
2 1/2 teaspoons water

Trim, scrape the strings from, and chop the celery.

Peel and coarsely grate the sweet potato.

Sauté the celery, sprinkled with the celery salt, in 2 tablespoons of the butter, in a large saucepan over medium heat, 3 minutes. Add the sweet potato, sprinkle with the salt and cook 5 minutes, while stirring well. Add the orange juice and increase the heat to high. When the juice comes to boil, reduce the heat to low and simmer, covered, about 30 minutes or until the potatoes are very soft. Remove the pan from the heat and allow it to cool a bit. Then, using as much of the milk as is needed, smoothly liquefy the vegetables, along with the orange juice, in the blender or processor.

Melt 4 tablespoons of the butter in a large saucepan over low heat. Using a rubber spatula, blend in the flour and pepper until they absorb the butter. Slowly stir in the remaining milk, the cream, honey and sherry. Then stir in the liquefied sweet potato. In a small cup make a paste out of the ginger, cloves and water then stir it into the soup. Place a heat diffuser under the pan, and very gently cook the cream of sweet potato soup, covered, 1 hour, stirring occasionally.

about 6 cups

Note: Slightly exotic!

cream of pumpkin soup

about 2 1/2 pounds buttercup squash - (2 cups baked mashed)
4 cups milk - at room temperature - divided
6 Tablespoons unsalted butter
4 Tablespoons flour
1/4 teaspoon white pepper
1 cup water

1 Tablespoon maple syrup - (the real thing)
1 1/2 teaspoons salt
nutmeg - (1/8 teaspoon freshly grated)

Prepare and bake the buttercup squash as directed. (See baked butternut squash.) Allow the squash to cool a bit. Scoop the flesh out of the skin, mash it, and measure out 2 cups of it. (Save any excess squash flesh for a bouillon soup. See bouillon soups.) Now, using about 2 cups of the milk, smoothly liquefy the squash in the blender or processor.

Melt the butter in a large saucepan over low heat. Using a rubber spatula, blend in the flour and pepper until they absorb the butter. Slowly stir in the remaining milk, the water, syrup, salt and nutmeg. Then stir in the liquefied squash. Place a heat diffuser under the pan, and very gently cook the cream of pumpkin soup, covered, 1 hour, stirring occasionally.

about 7 cups

Note: Buttercup is a dark green, somewhat turban shaped squash. It is preferable to pumpkin for use in "pumpkin" soup, as it always bakes dry, mealy and sweet, though butternut could be substituted. Both buttercup and butternut are generally smaller, more convenient to handle, and more commonly available than pumpkin. However, the traditional name—pumpkin soup—is retained.

One thing is certain don't try to substitute anything for real maple syrup in cream of pumpkin soup—it doesn't work! The sweetness of the squash may vary so add the maple syrup, judiciously, a little at a time.

cream of spinach soup

celery - 1 large rib - (1/2 cup chopped)
1 pound untrimmed spinach - (8 packed cups trimmed)
1/2 teaspoon celery salt
6 Tablespoons unsalted butter - divided
1/2 cup water
1 1/2 teaspoons salt
4 cups milk - at room temperature - divided
4 Tablespoons flour
1/4 teaspoon white pepper
1 teaspoon honey

2 Tablespoons fresh lemon juice
1 teaspoon English mustard powder

Trim, scrape the strings from and chop the celery.

Wash and trim the spinach as directed, allowing it to drain well in the colander. (See washed and trimmed spinach.)

Sauté the celery, sprinkled with the celery salt, in 2 tablespoons of the butter in a large sauce pan over medium heat, 3 minutes. Add the water and the salt and increase the heat to high. When the water boils, add the spinach, when the water returns to boil reduce the heat to low and simmer, covered, about 15 minutes or until the spinach is all very soft. Remove the pan from the heat and allow it to cool a bit. Then, using as much of the milk as is needed, smoothly liquify the vegetables, along with their cooking water, in the blender or processor.

Melt 4 tablespoons of the butter in a large saucepan over low heat. Using a rubber spatula, blend in the flour and pepper until they absorb the butter. Then slowly stir in the remaining milk, the liquified spinach and the honey. Place a heat diffuser under the pan, and very gently cook the soup, covered, 55 minutes, stirring occasionally. In a small cup, stir the lemon juice into the mustard powder until the mixture is smooth then stir the mixture into the soup. Cook the cream of spinach soup 5 minutes longer.

about 5 1/2 cups

cream of stock vegetable purée soup

6 Tablespoons unsalted butter
4 Tablespoons flour
1/4 teaspoon white pepper
4 cups milk - at room temperature
1 cup plus 1 Tablespoons plus 1 teaspoon water - divided
1 teaspoon honey
2 cups puréed stock vegetables - (see puréed stock vegetables)
1/2 teaspoon salt
1 teaspoon celery salt
rosemary - (1/2 teaspoon ground) - (see ground rosemary)
1/.2 teaspoon ground thyme
1/2 teaspoon ground (rubbed) sage
1/2 teaspoon ground ginger

Melt the butter in a large saucepan over low heat. Using a rubber spatula, blend in the flour and pepper until they absorb the butter. Slowly stir in the milk, the 1 cup of water and the honey. Then stir in the vegetable purée, salt and celery salt. Place a heat diffuser under the pan and very gently cook the soup, covered, 55 minutes, stirring occasionally. In a small cup, make a paste out of the ground rosemary, thyme, sage, ginger and the 1 tablespoon plus the 1 teaspoon of water then stir it into the soup. Cook the cream of stock vegetable purée soup 5 minutes longer.

about 7 cups

cream of tomato soup

2 cups tomato purée - 16 ounces - (best quality)
4 1/2 cups water
1 bay leaf
1 teaspoon salt
1/4 teaspoon celery salt
1/8 teaspoon cayenne
2 teaspoons honey
4 Tablespoons olive oil
6 Tablespoons flour
1/2 cup heavy cream - at room temperature
1/4 teaspoon dried basil
1/4 teaspoon dried thyme
1/4 teaspoon dried oregano

In a heavy saucepan over low heat, combine the first 7 ingredients, and very gently simmer the mixture, covered, 25 minutes.

Then, warm the oil in a large saucepan over low heat. Using a rubber spatula, blend in the flour until it absorbs the oil. Slowly stir in the cream, then the tomato purée. Place a heat diffuser under the pan, and very gently cook the soup, covered, 55 minutes. Add the basil, thyme and oregano, crushing them fine, and cook the cream of tomato soup 5 minutes longer.

about 7 cups

PRINCIPAL SOUPS

The principal soups are the substantial soups of the term, "soup supper." They require only a salad with some bread, perhaps cheese and then some fruit to comprise a full meal. Soup suppers tend to be informal meals, perfect for the family, but very popular with company as well. People seem to appreciate this simple form of food preparation. A bowl of steaming soup is a basic human need. Soup is nourishing, it is soothing, it is comforting, it is mother!

SECTION I

PASTA E FAGIOLI

MUSHROOM BARLEY SOUP

LENTIL AND ESCAROLE SOUP

MINESTRONE

 PASTA E FAGIOLI

Rosemary is the easiest of herbs to grow in the house. It's a handsome plant and is well worth growing for fresh rosemary is indispensable in this hearty soup. A small salad of sweet Italian frying peppers with some Fontina cheese and Italian bread will make a good salad course and poached pineapple slices will complete the supper.

2 1/2 cups dried cannellini - 1 pound - (see note)
1 bay leaf
5 cups reserved cooking liquid
celery - 2 large ribs (1 cup sliced)
Italian parsley leaves - (1/4 packed cup chopped)
1 teaspoon celery salt
6 Tablespoons olive oil
1 can peeled tomatoes - 28 ounces - (3 1/2 cups)
1 Tablespoons honey
1 1/2 teaspoons salt
1/2 teaspoon freshly cracked black pepper
3 ounces dried ditalini pasta
rosemary - 4 inch long sprig

Soak the beans and cook them, with the bay leaf, as directed. (See boiled dried shelled beans.) Drain the beans reserving 5 cups of their cooking liquid (add water if there is not enough liquid) and the bay leaf. Pass 2 1/2 cups of the cooked beans through a food mill into a bowl, using the 5 cups of cooking liquid to get them through. Add any skins that would not go through the mill to the bean slurry in the bowl. Reserve the slurry and the remainder of the cooked beans.

Trim, scrape the strings from, and very thinly slice the celery crosswise.

Chop the parsley small and reserve it.

Sauté the celery, sprinkled with the celery salt, in the oil, in the bottom of a large soup kettle over medium heat, for 3 minutes. Add the reserved bay leaf and bean slurry. Remove the stem buttons from the tomatoes and add them to the kettle along with all their juices, crushing the tomatoes through your (clean) fingers as you do so. Add the honey, salt and pepper and increase the heat to medium high. When the soup comes to simmer, reduce the heat to low and simmer the soup, very gently, covered, for 40 minutes, stirring it occasionally.

Increase the heat to medium, add the reserved beans, ditalini and rosemary and cook 15 minutes longer stirring more attentively now so that the pasta does not stick to the bottom of the kettle. (Pasta takes much longer to cook in thick soup than it does in water.) Now add the parsley and cook 5 minutes more or until the pasta is al denté. Serve the pasta e fagioli immediately.

about 12 cups

Note: Cannellini are white kidney beans. If they are unavailable substitute great northern beans.

 MUSHROOM BARLEY SOUP

A delicate blend of sweet herbs played against the tang of fresh black pepper is the bouquet of this soup. A small salad of egg, tomato and lettuce served with some whole wheat bread will make a substantial salad course. Serve poached cherries to finish.

celery - 2 large ribs - (1 cup sliced)
1 pound mushrooms - small - (6 cups sliced)
parsley leaves - (1/4 cup chopped)
1/2 teaspoon celery salt
3/4 teaspoon salt
2 Tablespoons butter
2 Tablespoons peanut oil
8 cups stock broth - (see stock broth)
1 cup water
2 Tablespoons soy sauce
1 teaspoon honey
1/4 scant teaspoon freshly cracked black pepper
1/2 cup barley - 3 1/2 ounces
1 teaspoon dried chervil
1/2 teaspoon dried marjoram
1/2 teaspoon dried basil

Trim, scrape the strings from, and thinly slice the celery crosswise.

Wipe the mushrooms with a damp cloth, trim the butt ends of the stems and thinly slice the mushrooms lengthwise.

Chop the parsley very small and reserve it.

Sauté the celery, sprinkled with the celery salt, in the butter and oil in the bottom of a soup kettle over medium heat for 3 minutes. Remove the celery with a slotted spoon and reserve it.

Add the mushrooms to the kettle, sprinkle with the salt and sauté them over medium high heat for about 8 minutes until all the moisture evaporates and the mushrooms start to brown. Add the stock broth, water, soy sauce, honey, and pepper to the kettle. Increase the heat to high, when the soup comes to boil, sprinkle in the barley, reduce the heat to low and simmer the soup, covered, 40 minutes, stirring occasionally. Add the reserved celery, simmer 5 minutes longer, add the chervil, marjoram and basil, crushing them and the reserved parsley, simmer 5 minutes more and serve the mushroom barley soup immediately.

about 10 cups

LENTIL AND ESCAROLE SOUP

Lentil and escarole soup can really be served any time of the year. Serve a salad of celeriac remoulade and some French bread following it. Enjoy mixed fruit over ice cream to complete the meal.

1/3 cup long grain brown rice
about 1 rounded cup lentils - 8 ounces
8 cups stock broth - (see stock broth)
4 cups water
2 bay leaves
2 teaspoons salt - divided
celery - 2 large ribs (1 cup diced)
3 ounces carrot - 1 large - (1/2 cup diced)
about 8 ounces escarole leaves - (3 packed cups cut)
about 3 ounces Romano cheese - (1/2 cup grated) - (see note)
6 Tablespoons olive oil
1 teaspoon celery salt
1/2 teaspoon freshly cracked black pepper
2 teaspoons honey

Steam the rice as directed. (See steamed long or short grain brown rice.) If the cooked rice measures more than 1 cup, do not use the excess, it would unbalance the recipe. (Save it for a bouillon soup. See bouillon soups.) Reserve the 1 cup of cooked rice.

Cull and rinse the lentils. Bring the stock broth and water with the bay leaves and 1/2 teaspoon of the salt to boil in a large soup kettle over high heat. Add the lentils. When the liquid returns to boil reduce the heat to low and simmer the lentils, covered with lid ajar only enough to allow the kettle to breath for about 30 minutes or until they are just tender.

Meanwhile, trim, scrape the strings from and dice the celery small. Trim, peel and dice the carrot small.

Rinse and drain the escarole discarding any tough or wilted leaves. Cut the escarole leaves crosswise into 1/4 inch wide slices.

Grate the Romano cheese fine and reserve it.

About 5 minutes before the lentils are done, sauté the celery and carrots, sprinkled with 1/2 teaspoon of the salt in the olive oil in a frying pan (see utensils) over medium heat for 5 minutes. Add the celery and carrots and all their cooking oil to the lentils.

Now, add the reserved rice, 1 teaspoon of the salt, the celery salt, pepper and honey to the kettle. Adjust the heat to keep the soup gently simmering and cook it 5 minutes. Then add the sliced escarole and cook the soup, uncovered now, 5 minutes longer.

Remove the kettle from the heat and stir in the 1/2 cup of reserved grated cheese. Serve the lentil and rescarole soup immediately while the escarole is still bright green.

about 12 cups

Note: The flavors in this soup are finely balanced. It does not need any more cheese. However, some people, through habit, feel that they must sprinkle more cheese on their serving. So keep a small bowl of extra grated cheese on hand but out of sight, in case someone asks.

 MINESTRONE

We could almost call this three day minestrone. The flavors need time to develop and mellow, but we don't want the vegetables to become overcooked. This method of cooking the soup briefly on three consecutive days works perfectly. Follow the wonderful minestrone soup with a tossed chicory salad, some Italian bread and then serve poached figs.

1/3 cup dried chick peas
2 bay leaves
reserved chick pea cooking liquid
water
3 1/2 ounces string beans - (3/4 cup cut)
celery - 1 1/2 large ribs - (3/4 cup diced)
4 ounces green bell pepper - 1 small - (3/4 cup diced)
4 ounces carrots - 2 medium - (3/4 cup diced)
4 1/2 ounces rutabaga - part of small - (3/4 cup diced)
4 1/2 ounces boiling potato - 1 medium small - (3/4 cup diced)
celery leaves - (1/2 cup chopped)
2 teaspoons salt
4 Tablespoons olive oil
1 can peeled tomatoes - 28 ounces - (3 1/2 cups)
1 Tablespoon honey
1 teaspoon celery salt
1/2 teaspoon freshly cracked black pepper
pinch cayenne
2 Tablespoons butter
1 teaspoon dried thyme
Parmesan cheese - (2 Tablespoons plus freshly grated)
Romano cheese - (2 Tablespoons plus freshly grated)

Soak the chick peas and cook them, as directed, with the bay leaves. (See boiled dried shelled beans.) Drain the chick peas reserving them, their cooking liquid and the bay leaves.

Trim the stems from and cut the string beans crosswise into 3/8 inch thick slices. The remaining fresh vegetables are cut into 3/8 inch dice. Trim, scrape the strings from and dice the celery. Core, trim away any white membrane from, and dice the bell pepper. Trim, peel, and dice the carrots, rutabaga and potato. Chop the celery leaves, reserving them.

Sauté all the prepared vegetables, except the celery leaves, sprinkled with the salt, in the oil, in the bottom of a large soup kettle, over medium heat, for 10 minutes, stirring them frequently. Remove the stem buttons from the tomatoes and add them to the kettle along with all their juices, crushing the tomatoes through your (clean) fingers as you do so. Now add enough water to the reserved cooking liquid to bring the total liquid measurement up to 8 cups and add it to the kettle. Add the reserved chick peas, bay leaves and celery leaves, the honey, celery salt, black pepper and cayenne.

Raise the heat to medium high. When the soup comes to simmer, reduce the heat to low and simmer the soup, covered, 5 minutes. Remove the kettle from the heat and allow it to cool to room temperature then refrigerate it 24 hours.

Next day allow the soup to come to room temperature. Then bring it to simmer over medium high heat. Reduce the heat to low and simmer the soup, covered, 5 minutes. Remove the kettle from the heat, allow it to cool to room temperature then refrigerate it 24 hours.

On the third day allow the soup to come to room temperature. Just before serving bring it to simmer over medium high heat. Reduce the heat to low, add the butter and the thyme, crushing it and simmer the soup, covered, 10 minutes. Add the 2 tablespoons each of Parmesan and Romano then serve the minestrone immediately along with a generous bowl of the cheeses mixed in proportions of 3 Parmesan to 1 Romano.

about 12 cups

SECTION II

TURNIP SOUP with cornmeal dumplings

GAZPACHO

BLACK BEAN SOUP

ZUCCHINI SOUP with pesto

OKRA GUMBO

TURNIP SOUP
with corn meal dumplings

I only make this soup when I have turnips in the garden. Turnips always reach the market minus their tops. However, turnip greens are often sold in bunches in early summer. So turnip soup is possible even if you don't have a garden. Don't miss it, the dumplings are addictive. Celery hearts vinaigrette would make a wonderful salad course served with some very simple crackers. And the dessert would have to be watermelon.

about 5 ounces white turnips - 1 medium large - 1 (1 cup diced)
celery - 2 large ribs - (1 cup diced)
8 ounces untrimmed turnip greens - (2 tightly packed cups trimmed,
                                                             chopped)
15 ounces unshelled lima beans - baby - (1 cup shelled) or about 5 ounces
                                                             frozen
corn - 2 ears - (1 cup kernels) or about 6 ounces frozen
corn meal dumpling batter - (recipe follows)
1 1/2 teaspoons salt
3 Tablespoons peanut oil
3 Tablespoons butter
8 cups stock broth - (see stock broth)
2 cups water
1 Tablespoons plus 1 teaspoon honey
1/4 teaspoon liquid smoke
1 1/2 teaspoons celery salt
1/4 teaspoon liquid hot red pepper
1/2 teaspoon dried thyme

Trim, peel and dice the turnips.
Trim, scrape the strings from and dice the celery.
Remove the stems from the turnip leaves. Wash the leaves well in cold water and drain them. Taking a handful at a time, chop them small.
Shell fresh lima beans or allow frozen limas to thaw and drain completely in a colander.
Husk the corn, carefully cut the kernels from the cob, separating them and crumbling them into a bowl. Or allow frozen corn to thaw and drain completely in a colander.
At this point, prepare the dumpling batter as directed and reserve it.
Sauté the turnips and celery, sprinkled with the salt, in the oil and butter in the bottom of a large soup kettle, over medium heat for 3 minutes. Add the stock broth, water, honey, liquid smoke and celery salt. Increase

the heat to high, when the liquid comes to boil, reduce the heat to low and simmer the soup, covered, 10 minutes. Add the greens and the fresh lima beans and simmer 5 minutes longer. Add the fresh corn or frozen corn and limas now if you are using them. Then carefully drop the dumpling batter, 1 rounded tablespoon at a time into the simmering soup. Adjust the heat to keep the soup gently simmering and cook, covered, 20 minutes longer. Add the liquid hot red pepper and the thyme, crushing it and cook 5 minutes more.

Serve the turnip soup immediately, allowing 2 corn meal dumplings per serving.

about 12 cups

corn meal dumpling batter

2 Tablespoons butter
2 teaspoons honey
1/4 cup all purpose flour
1 teaspoon baking powder
1/2 teaspoon salt
1 cup stoneground yellow corn meal
2 Tablespoons warm water
2 eggs - at room temperature

Melt the butter and honey together in a small saucepan over low heat. Remove the pan from the heat and allow the mixture to cool a bit.

Sift the flour, baking powder and salt together into a mixing bowl. Return any coarse corn meal which wouldn't go through the sieve to the mixing bowl.

In a small bowl, using a wire whisk, beat the water into the eggs until they are light then stir the butter mixture into them. Now stir the liquid ingredients into the dry ingredients. The batter will be very stiff.

batter for 12 dumplings

 GAZPACHO

Gazpacho is soup, entrée and salad all in one, three courses in a bowl. This recipe is ample for generous servings. Have some lovely crusty country bread with it and some Ricotta Salata cheese. Finish with chilled honeydew melon.

about 8 pounds tomatoes - 11 large
6 slices white bread
basil leaves - (1/4 packed cup)
2 Tablespoons sweet Hungarian paprika
1/2 cup olive oil
4 Tablespoons fresh lemon juice
4 Tablespoons cider vinegar
3 to 4 teaspoons salt
1 teaspoon celery salt
1/2 teaspoon cayenne
2 Tablespoons sugar
celery - 4 large ribs - (2 cups diced)
4 ounces red radishes, minus leaves - about 10 - (1 cup diced)
12 ounces red bell peppers - 2 medium - (2 cups diced)
about 1 pound cucumbers - 2 slender average - (2 cups diced)
parsley leaves - (4 Tablespoons minced)

Select fully ripe tomatoes. Remove the stem buttons and seed the tomatoes as directed, reserving the drained liquid from the seeds for the gazpacho. (See seeded tomatoes.) Coarsely chop the tomatoes. Tear the bread into small pieces. In the blender or processor, liquefy the tomatoes, bread, basil and paprika together with the reserved, drained liquid, in batches, until they are all liquefied. The yield should be about 16 cups. Pour the liquid into a large glass serving bowl and stir the oil, lemon juice, vinegar, salt to taste, celery salt, cayenne and sugar into it. At this point the soup should taste slightly sweet as the diced vegetables will balance the sweetness. Cover the bowl and refrigerate the soup 2 hours before serving.

Meanwhile, trim, scrape the strings from and cut the celery into 1/4 inch dice.

Trim and cut the radishes into 1/4 inch dice.

Core the bell peppers, trimming away any white membrane and cut them into 1/4 inch dice.

Peel and quarter the cucumbers lengthwise. Scrape out the seeds and cut them into 1/4 inch dice.

Mix all the diced vegetables together in a bowl and refrigerate them, covered, for 1 hour before serving.

Refrigerate individual soup bowls for 30 minutes before serving.

Mince the parsley leaves and just before serving stir them, along with the mixed diced vegetables into the soup and serve the very cold gazpacho immediately.

about 16 cups plus

Note: Gazpacho is best eaten right away. Do not allow the vegetables to stand in the soup for a period of time or they will entirely change its flavor.

 BLACK BEAN SOUP

After enjoying this black bean soup, serve avocados on the half shell accompanied by toasted flour tortillas with melted cheese on them. Oranges are the simple dessert.

2 1/4 cups dried black beans - 1 pound
2 bay leaves
2 eggs - at room temperature
celery - 2 large ribs with leaves - (1 heaping cup chopped)
1 pound red bell peppers - 2 large - (about 2 1/2 cups chopped)
1 1/2 pounds ripe tomatoes - 3 large - (3 cups chopped)
2 teaspoons celery salt
4 Tablespoons olive oil
1 Tablespoons honey
1 Tablespoons salt
1/2 teaspoon freshly cracked black pepper
4 Tablespoons butter
2 Tablespoons fresh lemon juice
1/2 cup Madeira
boiling water - optional
1 teaspoon dried oregano

Soak the beans and cook them with the bay leaves, as directed, until they are very tender. (See boiled, dried, shelled beans.)

Hard cook and peel the eggs as directed. (See cooked eggs. To save energy, rinse off the eggs and cook them in with the simmering beans.) Chop the eggs and reserve them.

Scrape the strings from the celery and coarsely chop it.

Core, trimming away any white membrane and coarsely chop the red peppers.

Remove the stem buttons from the tomatoes and coarsely chop them.

Sauté the celery and the bell peppers, sprinkled with the celery salt, in the oil in a frying pan (see utensils) over medium heat 10 minutes.

When the beans are soft, add the sautéed vegetables with all their cooking oil, the tomatoes, honey, salt and black pepper to them and continue to simmer them, 30 minutes longer. Then remove and reserve the bay leaves. Purée the beans and vegetables along with the reserved chopped eggs through a food mill set over a bowl then return the purée to the soup kettle.

Add the butter, lemon juice, Madeira and reserved bay leaves to the soup and simmer it, covered, over low heat 25 minutes. If the soup seems too thick at this point, add a little boiling water. Add the oregano, crushing it and simmer the black bean soup 5 minutes longer.

about 10 cups

ZUCCHINI SOUP
with pesto

This both beautiful and delicious soup is the answer to the question of what to do with all that over grown zucchini. Following the zucchini soup with pesto, serve a salad of sliced tomatoes, some Italian bread and a really good quality Parmesan, slicing it, as table cheese. Complete this summer supper with chilled green grapes.

1/2 cup pesto - (recipe follows)
celery - 2 large ribs - (1 cups chopped)
4 pounds zucchini squash - 8 medium - (12 cups coarsely grated)
1 pound potatoes - 2 medium large - (2 1/2 cups coarsely grated)
1 Tablespoons plus 1 teaspoon salt
4 Tablespoons olive oil
4 cups water
1 Tablespoons plus 1 teaspoon honey
1/4 teaspoon freshly cracked black pepper

Prepare the pesto first, as directed, and have it at room temperature.

Trim, scrape the strings from, and coarsely chop the celery.

Trim and coarsely grate the zucchini.

Peel and coarsely grate the potatoes.

Sauté the celery, sprinkled with 1 teaspoon of the salt, in the oil, in the bottom of a large soup kettle over medium heat for 3 minutes. Add the zucchini and potatoes, sprinkle with the remaining salt and sauté 5 minutes longer, stirring the mixture. Add the water, honey and pepper. Increase the heat to medium high, when the mixture comes to simmer reduce the heat to low and gently simmer the vegetables, covered, 30 minutes.

Purée the mixture through a food mill set over a bowl, then return it to the kettle. Heat the soup, covered, over medium heat until it comes to simmer. Then remove the kettle from the heat and allow the soup to stand, uncovered, 10 minutes.

Place the pesto in a small bowl and stir a ladleful of the soup into it. Then stir the mixture back into the kettle and serve the zucchini soup with pesto immediately.

about 12 cups

Note: This soup is served hot but not piping hot. Plan to consume it all at one meal for it cannot be reheated.

pesto

2 Tablespoons pine nuts
fresh basil leaves - (1/2 cup tightly packed)
4 Tablespoons olive oil
1/4 teaspoon salt
Parmesan cheese - (3 Tablespoons freshly grated)
Romano cheese - (1 Tablespoon freshly grated)
1 Tablespoon fresh lemon juice

Grind the nuts in the processor. Add the remaining ingredients and process until they have become a thick liquid. Alternatively, grind the nuts in the blender. Add all the remaining ingredients except the lemon juice and liquefy the mixture. Transfer the mixture to a bowl, rinse out the container of the blender with the lemon juice then stir it into the mixture in the bowl. Or for a really smooth pesto, pound the ingredients together using a marble mortar and pestle.

(The pesto can be prepared in advance and refrigerated, covered, in a nonplastic container. Bring it to room temperature before serving.)

about 1/2 cup

OKRA GUMBO

Delightful, substantial yet delicate, this soup must be made with home canned tomatoes. Follow it with iceberg wedges and whole wheat bread. Offer fresh blackberries for dessert.

celery - 2 large ribs - (1 cup sliced)
6 ounces green bell pepper - 1 medium - (1 cup sliced)
8 ounces okra - about 40 pods, 2 inches long - (2 cups sliced)
2 teaspoons salt
6 Tablespoons butter
1 quart home canned tomatoes - (see home canned tomatoes)
2 quarts water
1 Tablespoon honey
1 teaspoon celery salt
1/2 teaspoon freshly ground allspice
1/4 teaspoon freshly cracked black pepper
1/4 teaspoon cayenne
1 Tablespoon fresh lemon juice
1/3 cup short grain brown rice
Italian parsley leaves - (4 Tablespoons chopped)
1 teaspoon dried thyme leaves

Trim, scrape the strings from and thinly slice the celery crosswise.
Core, trimming away any white membrane and quarter the green bell pepper lengthwise. Thickly slice the quarters crosswise.
If necessary wipe the okra with a damp cloth. Trim the stems and cut the okra crosswise into 1/4 inch thick slices.
Sauté the prepared vegetables, sprinkled with the salt in the butter in the bottom of a large soup kettle over medium heat for 5 minutes. Add the tomatoes and all their juice to the kettle, squeezing the tomatoes

through your (clean) fingers as you do so. Add the water, honey, celery salt, allspice, black pepper and cayenne. Increase the heat to medium high and bring the soup, covered, just to boil. Then turn off the heat, add the lemon juice and allow the soup to cool to room temperature. Now refrigerate it overnight or 24 hours.

Meanwhile, cook the rice as directed. (See steamed long or short grain brown rice.) If the rice yields more than 1 cup do not use the excess as it would unbalance the recipe. (Save it for a bouillon soup. See bouillon soups.)

(The rice can be cooked in advance and allowed to cool.)

Allow the soup to come to room temperature. Just before serving time, chop the parsley small and reserve it. Add the thyme to the soup, crushing it and bring the soup to a simmer over medium high heat. As soon as the soup simmers, add the rice and reserved parsley, reduce the heat to low and simmer, covered 5 minutes longer. Then serve the okra gumbo immediately.

about 12 cups

Note: The flavor of okra gumbo develops while it is standing, rather than while it is cooking. Do not overcook it, and plan to finish it all in one sitting as it does not reheat well.

SECTION III

CUCURBITACEAE SOUP

CHOWDER HOUSE CHOWDER

CHICK PEA AND SWISS CHARD SOUP

OATMEAL SOUP

CORN CHOWDER

CUCURBITACEAE SOUP

Curcurbitaceae is the squash family used in this rich soup. It's a soup for a special day in autumn when the pumpkins are just starting to come in but summer squash is still available. Truly the pièce de résistance in a soup supper, follow it with a tossed spinach salad and some warm bread. Macintosh apples will round out the meal nicely.

15 pounds pumpkin - 1 medium large, with about 12 cup cavity
about 8 ounces zucchini squash - 1 medium, 7 to 8 inches long - (about
1 1/2 cups sliced)
about 8 ounces yellow straight or crook neck squash - 1 medium, 7 to 8
inches long - (about 1 1/2 cups sliced)
about 1 pound scalloped squash - 1 medium, 5 to 6 inches in diameter -
(about 3 cups sliced)
about 8 ounces cucumber - 1 slender average, 7 to 8 inches long - (about
1 cup sliced)
1 pound chunk any winter squash - (about 3 cups sliced)
8 ounces extra sharp New York State Cheddar cheese - (2 cups grated)
6 cups milk - at room temperature - divided
1 teaspoon honey
2 teaspoons salt
sage leaves - 20 large - (that's right!)
4 Tablespoons butter
4 Tablespoons flour
1/2 teaspoon white pepper

Select a pumpkin with an interesting stem to use as a lid handle. Carve a lid out of the pumpkin and scoop out all the seeds and membrane. Set the pumpkin aside.

Trim the zucchini and yellow squash. Cut them in half lengthwise and scoop out the seeds. Then slice them thin crosswise.

Trim the scalloped squash and cut it in half lengthwise. Scoop out the seeds if necessary. If the skin has hardened, remove it with a vegetable peeler. Slice the halves thin lengthwise.

Peel and slice the cucumber thin crosswise.

Remove any seeds from the winter squash and cut it into 2 inch squares. Cut the skin from the squash and cut the squares into slices that are a little thicker than the rest of the squash as it cooks more quickly.

Coarsely grate the cheese and reserve it.

Bring 4 cups of the milk to simmer in a large soup kettle set on a heat diffuser over medium heat. Add the honey, salt and all the sliced vegetables. Cover the kettle and watch for the milk to return to simmer which may take as long as 30 minutes. Then simmer the vegetables 15 minutes, adjusting the heat as necessary to keep the milk gently simmering. Add the sage leaves and simmer 15 minutes longer.

Meanwhile prepare a cheese sauce and time it so that it will be ready when the vegetables have finished simmering. Melt the butter in a medium size heavy saucepan over low heat. Using a rubber spatula blend in the flour and pepper, stirring constantly for 3 minutes. Slowly stir in the remaining 2 cups of milk while raising the heat to medium until the mixture simmers and thickens.

While the sauce is being made, warm the pumpkin shell slightly for about 15 minutes in a 200 degree oven so that it will not chill the soup.

Now, when the vegetables are ready, remove both the soup kettle and the saucepan from the heat. Stir the reserved cheese into the cream sauce, a handful at a time, until the mixture is smooth. Then gently stir the sauce into the soup. Remove the pumpkin from the oven and set it on a large round platter. Transfer the soup to the pumpkin shell, replace the lid and serve the cucurbitaceae soup immediately.

about 10 cups

CHOWDER HOUSE CHOWDER

Contains everything except the house. After this big chowder, serve some fresh coleslaw, a loaf of whole wheat bread and a wedge of Cheddar cheese. Present a plate of grapefruit sections for dessert.

1/3 cup dried navy beans
4 cups plus water - divided
2 bay leaves
about 5 ounces rutabaga - part of a small - (1 cup diced)
about 6 ounces carrots - 2 large - (1 cup diced)
about 5 ounces parsnip - 1 large - (1 cup diced)
celery - 2 large ribs - (1 cup diced)
6 ounces green bell pepper - 1 medium - (1 cup diced)
1 pound tomatoes - 2 medium - (2 cups diced) or use 2 cans peeled
tomatoes, 16 ounces each
parsley leaves - (2 Tablespoons chopped)

4 Tablespoons butter
8 Tablespoons flour
1/3 teaspoon white pepper
6 cups milk - at room temperature
2 teaspoons honey
1/2 scant teaspoon liquid smoke
2 teaspoons celery salt
1 teaspoon celery seeds
1 1/2 teaspoons ground turmeric
2 teaspoons salt - divided
4 Tablespoons peanut oil - divided
1 teaspoon ground rosemary - (see ground rosemary)
1 teaspoon ground sage
2 teaspoons dried summer savory
1/2 teaspoon liquid hot red pepper

Soak the beans, 12 hours or overnight in enough water to cover them by 2 inches. Drain and rinse them. Bring the 4 cups of water, with the bay leaves to boil in a large soup kettle over high heat. Add the beans and when the water returns to boil, reduce the heat to low and simmer the beans, covered with lid ajar only enough to allow the kettle to breathe, for about 1 hour or until they are just tender. Remove the kettle from the heat. Meanwhile, prepare the vegetables.

Trim, peel and cut the rutabaga, carrots and parsnips into 3/8 inch dice. Keep the vegetables separate.

Trim, scrape the strings from and cut the celery into 3/8 inch dice.

Core, trimming away any white membrane and cut the bell pepper into 3/8 inch dice.

Peel the tomatoes as directed. (See peeled tomatoes.) Remove the stem buttons, do not bother to seed them but coarsely chop the tomatoes. If you are using canned tomatoes, drain them. (Save the juice for a bouillon soup. See bouillon soups.) Remove any stem buttons and break up the tomatoes into pieces.

Chop the parsley and reserve it.

Melt the butter in a medium size saucepan over low heat. Using a rubber spatula blend in the flour and white pepper until the butter is absorbed. Slowly pour in the milk while stirring constantly and raising the heat to medium until the mixture simmers and thickens a bit. Then pour the mixture into the beans and add the honey, liquid smoke, celery salt and celery seeds. In a cup dissolve the turmeric in 1 tablespoon of water then add the mixture to the kettle and set the kettle, covered, on a heat diffuser over low heat.

Sauté the rutabaga, carrots and celery together, sprinkled with 1 teaspoon of the salt, in 2 tablespoons of the oil in a frying pan (see utensils) over medium heat for 5 minutes. Add the sautéed vegetables and all their cooking oil to the kettle and cook the chowder 15 minutes.

Now, sauté the parsnips and bell peppers together, sprinkled with, 1 teaspoon of the salt, in 2 tablespoons of the oil over medium heat for 3 minutes. Add the sautéed vegetables and their cooking oil to the kettle. Then add the tomatoes and cook the chowder 30 minutes longer or until the vegetables are tender.

In a cup dissolve the ground rosemary and sage in 4 teaspoons of water and add the mixture to the kettle along with the savory, crushing it. Add the liquid hot red pepper and cook the chowder 5 minutes more. Add the reserved parsley and serve the chowder house chowder immediately.

about 12 cups

CHICK PEA AND SWISS CHARD SOUP

Chick pea and Swiss chard is a substantial soup that tastes of summertime. For the salad course, serve baby artichokes vinaigrette accompanied by some crusty bread and an herb flavored Cream cheese. Then offer fresh peaches.

1 heaping cup dried chick peas - 8 ounces
2 1/2 quarts water
1 bay leaf
1 pound tomatoes - 2 large - (2 cups chopped)
5 1/2 ounces Swiss chard - (2 cups cut)
1/2 cup bulghar - 3 1/2 ounces
6 Tablespoons butter
1 Tablespoon plus 1 teaspoon honey
1 Tablespoon sweet Hungarian paprika
2 Tablespoons water
1 1/2 teaspoons salt
1 1/2 teaspoons celery salt
1/4 teaspoon freshly cracked black pepper
scant 1/4 teaspoon cayenne
rosemary - (1/4 teaspoon ground) - (see rosemary)
1/2 teaspoon dried thyme

Soak the chick peas, 12 hours or overnight in enough water to cover them by 2 inches. Drain and rinse them. Bring the 2 1/2 quarts of water, with the bay leaf to boil in a large soup kettle over high heat. Add the chick peas and when the water returns to boil, reduce the heat to low and simmer the chick peas, covered with lid ajar only enough to allow the kettle to breathe, for about 1 1/2 hours or until they are almost tender.

Meanwhile, peel and seed the tomatoes. (See peeled tomatoes and see seeded tomatoes.) Remove the stem button and coarsely chop the tomatoes.

Cut only the leaves of the Swiss chard in half lengthwise. Then cut both the leaves and the stems, crosswise, into 1/4 inch wide slices. Rinse the Swiss chard in a basin of cold water and drain it in a colander.

When the chick peas are ready, add the tomatoes, bulghar, butter and honey to them. In a cup, make a paste out of the paprika and the 2 tablespoons of water then add the mixture to the kettle. Add the salt, celery salt, black pepper and cayenne and continue to simmer the chick peas 25 minutes longer. Increase the heat to medium high and when the soup comes to a slow boil, add the Swiss chard, rosemary and the thyme, crushing it and cook the soup, uncovered, 5 minutes more. Serve the chickpea and Swiss chard immediately while the Swiss chard is still bright green.

about 12 cups

 OATMEAL SOUP

Oatmeal soup is a creamy, thick, comforting soup. Serve a salad of pressed cucumbers with oatmeal bread (naturally) and a mild Cheddar to go with it for the salad course. Poached apricots will make an easy dessert.

celery - 1 large rib - (1/2 cup diced)
3 ounces carrot - 1 large - (1/2 cup diced)
1 ounce parsnip - 1 piece - (1/4 cup diced)
about 4 1/2 ounces untrimmed kale - (1 1/2 tightly packed cups trimmed)
8 ounces unshelled peas - (1/2 cup shelled) - or 5 ounces frozen
8 cups stock broth - (see stock broth)
4 Tablespoons butter - divided

2 Tablespoons soy sauce
1 Tablespoon honey
1/2 teaspoon celery salt
1/4 teaspoon freshly cracked black pepper
1 1/2 cups oatmeal (not quick cooking)
1 cup light cream - at room temperature
1/2 teaspoon salt

Trim, scrape the strings from and dice the celery very small.

Trim, peel and dice the carrot and parsnip very small.

Cut away the stem and thick center rib from each leaf of kale. Rinse the trimmed kale in a basin or sink full of cold water then drain it in a large colander. Chop (not slice) the kale rather small.

Shell fresh peas or allow frozen peas to thaw and drain completely in a colander.

Bring the stock broth with 2 tablespoons of the butter, the soy sauce, honey, celery salt and pepper to boil in a large soup kettle over high heat. Sprinkle in the oatmeal, reduce the heat to low and cook the oatmeal, covered, for 5 minutes, stirring occasionally. Then add the cream.

Meanwhile, sauté the celery, carrots and parsnips, sprinkled with the salt in 2 tablespoons of the butter in a frying pan (see utensils) over medium heat for 5 minutes. Then add the diced vegetables and their cooking butter to the simmering soup along with the kale and the peas. Continue to simmer the soup, covered, 10 minutes longer, stirring occasionally. Serve the oatmeal soup immediately.

about 10 cups

CORN CHOWDER

I've been making this soup for years and I've tried any number of times to make my own cream style corn to use in it. But somehow it just never fills the bill the way almost any commercially prepared cream style corn does. Follow the corn chowder with a carrot and current salad and some homemade biscuits. Offer a bowl of crisp green apples to finish.

8 Tablespoons butter - divided
6 Tablespoons flour

3/8 teaspoon white pepper
3 cups water
6 cups milk - at room temperature
1 can cream style corn - 16 ounces - (2 cups)
1 can cream style corn - 8 ounces - (1 cup)
1 bay leaf
2 teaspoons salt - divided
1 teaspoon celery salt
corn - 6 ears - (3 cups kernels) or 15 ounces frozen
celery - 3 large ribs - (1 1/2 cups sliced)
9 ounces boiling potatoes - 3 small - (1 1/2 cups diced)
3/4 teaspoon ground thyme
2 teaspoons cold water

Melt 6 tablespoons of the butter in the bottom of a large soup kettle over low heat. Using a rubber spatula, blend in the flour and white pepper until they absorb the butter. Then slowly stir in the 3 cups of water until the mixture is smooth. Add the milk, cream style corn, bay leaf, 1 1/2 teaspoons of the salt and the celery salt and increase the heat to medium. When the soup comes to simmer, place a heat diffuser under the kettle, reduce the heat to low and gently simmer the soup, covered, for 30 minutes. Remove the kettle from the heat, allow it to cool to room temperature then refrigerate it 24 hours.

Allow the soup to come to room temperature. Then about 1 hour before serving time set the kettle on a heat diffuser over medium heat and slowly bring the soup to simmer.

Meanwhile, husk and trim the corn. Carefully cut the kernels from the cob, separating them and crumbling them into a bowl. Or allow frozen corn to thaw and drain completely in a colander. Reserve the corn kernels.

Trim, scrape the strings from and thinly slice the celery crosswise.

Peel and cut the potatoes into 3/8 inch dice.

Sauté the celery, sprinkled with 1/4 teaspoon of the salt, in 2 tablespoons of the butter in a large frying pan (see utensils) over medium heat for 2 minutes. Add the potatoes, sprinkle with 1/4 teaspoon of the salt and sauté 3 minutes longer. Transfer the celery and potatoes and the reserved corn kernels to the soup kettle and simmer the soup, covered, 20 minutes longer. In a cup, dissolve the ground thyme in the cold water then stir the mixture into the soup and cook 10 minutes longer or until the vegetables are just tender. Serve the corn chowder immediately.

about 12 cups

SECTION IV

KENNEBEC BEAN SOUP

SAMBHAR

CABBAGE SOUP

SPLIT PEA SOUP with croutons

 KENNEBEC BEAN SOUP

A bowl of this hearty soup will fortify you against any howling nor'easter. Serve a salad of tossed iceburg lettuce and some anadama bread with Coon cheese after the soup. Polished red apples will be dessert.

2 1/4 cups dried soldier beans - 1 pound
2 bay leaves
1 pound rutabaga - 1 small, about 3 inches in diameter - (3 cups cut)
celery - 2 large ribs - (1 cup cut)
sweet apple - 1 Macintosh or other
1 Tablespoons salt - divided
8 Tablespoons butter
2 1/2 cups water - divided
1/2 cup stoneground corn meal - about 5 ounces
1/2 cup cold water
1 Tablespoon honey
1/2 teaspoon liquid smoke
1/2 teaspoon celery salt
1/2 teaspoon freshly cracked black pepper
1/2 cup heavy cream - at room temperature
1 teaspoon dried summer savory

Soak the beans and cook them with the bay leaves, in a large soup kettle, as directed, allowing them to cook for at least 1 1/2 to 2 hours or until they are quite soft. (See boiled, dried, shelled beans.) Do not drain them.

Meanwhile, trim, peel and chop the rutabaga. Trim, scrape the strings from and chop the celery. Peel, core and chop the apple.

Sauté the rutabaga, celery and apple, sprinkled with 1 teaspoon of the salt in the butter, in a large frying pan (see utensils) over medium heat for 10 minutes. Reduce the heat to low, remove the pan from the heat, add 1 cup of the water, quickly cover the pan, return it to the heat and cook the mixture 20 minutes or until the vegetables are very soft. Remove the pan from the heat and let it cool a bit. Transfer the mixture with any of its remaining liquid to the blender or processor, add 1/4 cup of the water and liquefy it. Alternatively, use a food mill. Reserve the purée.

Bring 1 cup of the water with 1 teaspoon of the salt to boil in a medium size heavy saucepan over high heat. In a measuring cup stir the corn meal into the 1/2 cup of cold water then slowly stir the slurry into the boiling water. Reduce the heat to low and stir the mixture constantly for 5 minutes, smoothing out any lumps. Now, stir the reserved purée into the corn meal, rinsing out the blender, processor or food mill, with 1/4 cup of the water and adding it to the corn meal mixture. If the mixture must wait for the beans to be done, remove the pan from the heat and cover it.

When the beans are ready, using a wooden spoon, stir the corn meal mixture into them. Add 1 teaspoon of the salt, the honey, liquid smoke, celery salt, pepper and cream and cook the soup, covered, over medium low heat for 25 minutes, gently and frequently stirring it . Add the summer savory, crushing it and cook the Kennebec bean soup 5 minutes longer.

about 14 cups

SAMBHAR

Despite its list of ingredients, sambhar is quite easy to prepare. Tossed salad mix I with some pita bread and Ricotta Salata cheese will make a good salad course. Follow it with pomegranates.

3 heaping cups dried yellow split peas - 1 1/2 pounds
3 quarts water
6 1/2 ounces carrots - about 3 medium - (1 heaping cup sliced)
celery - 3 small ribs - (1 heaping cup sliced)
3 ounces mushrooms - medium small - (1 heaping cup sliced)
5 ounces Romano string beans - (1 heaping cup cut) - (see note)
about 6 ounces cauliflower - part of small head - (1 heaping cup florets)
1/2 teaspoon black mustard seeds
2 Tablespoons peanut oil
1/2 teaspoon ground cumin
1/2 teaspoon ground coriander
1/2 teaspoon ground turmeric
1/2 teaspoon ground fenugreek
1/4 teaspoon freshly cracked black pepper
1/4 teaspoon cayenne
1/4 teaspoon ground cinnamon
1/4 teaspoon ground cardamom
1/4 teaspoon ground cloves
6 Tablespoons butter
1 teaspoon salt
2 teaspoons celery salt

1 Tablespoon honey
1 Tablespoon fresh lemon juice

Cull and rinse the peas. Bring the water to boil in a very large, heavy soup kettle over high heat. Add the peas and when the water returns almost to boil, reduce the heat to low and simmer the peas, covered with lid ajar only enough to allow the kettle to breathe, for 2 hours, stirring occasionally until they are very soft. Purée the peas through a food mill set over a large bowl.

Meanwhile, prepare the vegetables. Trim, peel and cut the carrots crosswise into 1/4 inch thick slices. Trim, scrape the strings from and cut the celery crosswise into 3/8 inch thick slices. Wipe the mushrooms with a damp cloth. Trim the butt ends of the stems and cut the mushrooms lengthwise into 2, 3 or 4 slices depending on their size. Remove the stems from the string beans and cut them crosswise into 3/4 inch long pieces. Break the cauliflower up into very small, evenly sized florets, trimming the end of their stems to make them neat.

Warm the black mustard seeds in the oil in the bottom of the empty soup kettle, covered with lid ajar, over medium heat, 2 or 3 minutes until they have all popped. Reduce the heat to low and add the cumin, coriander, turmeric, fenugreek, black pepper, cayenne, cinnamon, cardamom and cloves. Allow the spices to warm and develop their flavors for about 1 minute, do not let them scorch.

Now, return the puréed peas to the kettle and add the butter, salt, celery salt and honey. Increase the heat to medium, when the soup comes to simmer, reduce the heat to low and very gently simmer the soup, covered, for 30 minutes, stirring occasionally. Now then, raise the heat to medium again, add the carrots and cook 2 minutes, add the celery, mushrooms and string beans and cook 2 minutes more. Add the cauliflower and cook 13 minutes longer or until all the vegetables are just tender. Then add the lemon juice and serve the sambhar.

about 12 cups

Note: If good quality Romano beans are not available, thawed, drained, frozen Romano beans can be substituted. In which case, they go into the soup 5 minutes after the cauliflower.

CABBAGE SOUP

Marinated mushrooms, served with dark rye bread and Cream cheese are served as the salad course after the aromatic cabbage soup. Poached plums complete this soup supper.

1/3 cup dried great northern beans
3 quarts water
2 bay leaves
2 1/2 teaspoons salt - divided
1 teaspoon celery salt
1/4 teaspoon freshly cracked black pepper
1/8 teaspoon liquid smoke
pinch cayenne
1/4 packed cup brown sugar (see note)
celery - 2 large ribs - (1 cup sliced)
about 1 1/2 ounces carrot - 1 medium small - (1/4 cup sliced)
1 pound cabbage - 1/2 small head - (4 cups shredded)
about 8 ounces boiling potato - 1 medium large - (1 1/2 heaping cups
sliced)
3 Tablespoons peanut oil - divided
3 Tablespoons butter - divided
1/4 cup rye flakes - (see note)
1/2 cup California white wine vinegar (see note)
1 1/2 teaspoons dried thyme

Soak the beans, overnight in enough water to cover them by 2 inches. Drain and rinse them. Bring the water, with the bay leaves, to boil in a large soup kettle over high heat. Add the beans and when the water returns to boil, reduce the heat to low and simmer the beans, covered with lid ajar only enough to allow the kettle to breathe, for 1 hour or until they are just tender. Add 1 teaspoon of the salt, the celery salt, pepper, liquid smoke, cayenne and brown sugar and remove the kettle from the heat.

Meanwhile, trim, scrape the strings from and thinly slice the celery crosswise. Trim, peel and thinly slice the carrot crosswise. Quarter, core, and cut the cabbage crosswise into 3/16 inch thick slices. Peel, quarter and thinly slice the potatoes.

Sauté the celery and carrots together, sprinkled with 1/2 teaspoon of the salt in 1 tablespoons of the oil and 1 tablespoon of the butter, in a medium size frying pan (see utensils) over medium heat for 3 minutes. Then add them to the soup kettle along with their cooking oil and butter. Sauté the cabbage then the potatoes, each separately, in like manner, using the same amount of salt, oil, and butter for each. Add them to the kettle, allow the soup to cool to room temperature then refrigerate it 24 hours.

Next day, allow the soup to come to room temperature then 35 minutes before serving bring it to boil, covered, over medium high heat. Sprinkle in the rye flakes, reduce the heat to medium low and simmer the soup about 10 minutes until the vegetables are just tender but firm, stirring occasionally with a wooden spoon. Add the vinegar and the thyme, crushing it and simmer 5 minutes longer. Serve the cabbage soup immediately.

about 12 cups

Note: Do not substitute any other type of vinegar. Even then white wine vinegars vary so you may want to proceed with caution when adding both the vinegar and the sugar.

Rye flakes are available at natural food stores. They are rolled ryeberries which look similar to oatmeal.

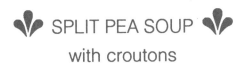

SPLIT PEA SOUP
with croutons

Time is the essential ingredient in split pea soup. It's the perfect soup to cook on a wood stove. Serve a red cabbage vinaigrette with toasted bread and Cheddar cheese for the salad course. Offer chilled yellow apples for dessert.

4 1/2 cups dried green split peas - 2 pounds
4 quarts water
2 bay leaves
6 Tablespoons peanut oil
6 Tablespoons butter
1 Tablespoon honey
2 teaspoons salt
2 teaspoons celery salt
1 teaspoon liquid smoke
1/2 teaspoon freshly cracked black pepper
croutons - (recipe follows)
1 1/2 teaspoons ground thyme
1 Tablespoon water

Cull and rinse the peas. Bring the 4 quarts of water to boil in a large, heavy soup kettle over high heat. Add the peas and when the water returns almost to boil, reduce the heat to low and simmer the peas, covered with lid ajar only enough to allow the kettle to breathe, for 2 1/2 hours, stirring them occasionally until they have almost all disintegrated. Then add the oil, butter, honey, salt, celery salt, liquid smoke and black pepper and continue to simmer the soup 30 minutes longer. Remove the kettle from the heat and allow it to cool to room temperature. Then refrigerate the soup 24 hours. Next day, allow it to come to room temperature before continuing with the recipe.

Meanwhile, the bread can be dried out to make the croutons. But do not toast the croutons in the frying pan until after the thyme has gone into the soup.

About 45 minutes before serving time, slowly reheat the soup on a heat diffuser over medium low heat, stirring occasionally until it comes to simmer. Now, in a cup dissolve the ground thyme in the 1 tablespoon of water then stir the mixture into the soup and simmer the soup about 10 minutes longer. Serve the split pea soup along with the basket of hot croutons.

about 13 cups

croutons

8 slices white bread
3 Tablespoons peanut oil
3 Tablespoons butter
1/4 teaspoon celery salt

Trim the crusts from the slices of bread and cut them into 3/8 inch cubes. Spread the bread cubes out on a 17 by 11 inch cookie sheet. If, at this point, they are left to stand, uncovered, 2 or 3 hours, it will reduce oven time. In any case dry the bread out in a preheated 200 degree oven for about 30 minutes. Remember, we are drying it not toasting it. When the bread is dry, immediately transfer it to an unsealed paper bag and reserve it.

At serving time heat the oil, butter and celery salt in a heavy 8 inch frying pan over medium heat. Add the dried bread cubes and toast them for about 3 minutes, while gently turning them with a spatula, until they begin to brown and have absorbed all the oil and butter. Transfer the croutons to a paper napkin lined basket and serve them while they are hot.

about 4 cups

bouillon soups

Did you ever cut off the top of a bunch of celery after it had been in the refrigerator for a couple of days because the leaves were all wilted? Or think how large the outer, tougher leaves of a head of cabbage were as you discarded them? Or think how expensive the asparagus was as you threw away those long butts? Bouillon soups are designed to save you from those anxieties, also to save vitamins, not to mention money.

There are so many soups that could be listed in this category that they are almost endless. Just to give you an idea of what bouillon soups are about and how easily they are made, here included are three recipes which quickly come to mind. They are celery, cabbage and asparagus bouillon. (Incidentally, use the celery leaves before they wilt.) But bouillon soups hardly need recipes. They are the product of a thrifty kitchen, they use peelings and scraps that might otherwise be thrown away. Save cooking water from dried beans, from vegetables, even the water used for steaming is flavorful. Add a couple of tablespoons of a grain, some noodles, a few lentils. For flavor and color there are soy sauce, tomato paste, curry powder, a little cream, some sherry—it's easy!

Then there is the all time great bouillon soup which really is not a bouillon soup, strictly speaking. If there is part of a dish leftover, just put it in the blender or processor with some milk and purée it. Reheat it with a little butter and serve it tomorrow night.

Bouillon soups are quick and easy and it would be wonderful to be able to list them in the formal menus but one is never quite sure of how they will turn out or even what will go into them. Sometimes they are excellent in which case do not hesitate to use them as the first course for a company dinner, if that is the way things work out. But for practical purposes bouillon soups are served as the first course in a blue plate special menu.

celery bouillon

cabbage bouillon

asparagus bouillon

celery bouillon

celery - leaves and upper branches - (2 cups chopped)
1/2 teaspoon black mustard seed
2 Tablespoons peanut oil
1 teaspoon celery salt
6 cups water
1 small bay leaf
1 teaspoon honey
1 1/4 teaspoons salt
1/2 teaspoon curry powder
pinch cayenne
2 Tablespoons millet

Rinse, drain and chop the celery leaves and branches small.

Warm the mustard seeds in the oil in a large saucepan, covered, with lid ajar, over medium heat, about 2 or 3 minutes, until they have all popped. Reduce the heat to low, add the celery, sprinkle it with the celery salt and sweat the celery, covered, 10 minutes. Add all the remaining ingredients except the millet and increase the heat to high. When the water comes to boil, sprinkle in the millet, reduce the heat to low and simmer the celery bouillon, covered, 35 minutes or until the millet is cooked.

6 cups

cabbage bouillon

cabbage - outer leaves and core - (2 cups shredded)
1/2 teaspoon caraway seeds
1 1/2 teaspoons salt
2 Tablespoons butter
6 cups water
1 small bay leaf
2 teaspoons honey
1/2 teaspoon celery salt
1/8 teaspoon black pepper
3 Tablespoons buckwheat groats

Shred the cabbage leaves and core fine.

Toast the caraway seeds in a dry pan over medium heat, stirring 2 or 3 minutes, until they become golden and fragrant. Remove them from the pan immediately and crush them fine in a mortar or spice grinder.

Sweat the cabbage, sprinkled with the salt, in the butter in a large saucepan, covered, over low heat, 10 minutes. Add the crushed caraway seeds and all the remaining ingredients, except the buckwheat, and increase the heat to high. When the water comes to boil, sprinkle in the buckwheat, reduce the heat to low, and simmer the cabbage bouillon, covered, 30 minutes.

6 cups

asparagus bouillon

asparagus - peelings and butt ends from 2 pounds
3/4 teaspoon salt
3 Tablespoons unsalted butter
6 cups water
1/2 teaspoon honey
1/8 teaspoon white pepper
2 Tablespoons white rice
1/4 teaspoon dried tarragon

Be sure that the asparagus whose peelings and ends are being used were well washed. Cut the butts crosswise into 1/4 inch thick slices, if possible.

Sweat the peelings and butts, sliced or not, sprinkled with the salt in the butter in a large saucepan, covered, over low heat, 15 minutes. Add the water and increase the heat to high, when the water comes to boil, reduce the heat to low and simmer the asparagus, covered, 30 minutes. Strain the bouillon through a colander, lined with wet wrung out cheese cloth, set over a bowl. Place a saucer, with a weight upon it, on the asparagus and allow it to drain 15 minutes, turning it over 2 or 3 times during that period and pressing on it. Discard the asparagus and return the bouillon to the saucepan set over high heat. Add the honey and pepper. When the bouillon comes to boil, sprinkle in the rice, reduce the heat to low and simmer the bouillon, covered, 15 minutes. Add the tarragon, crushing it, and simmer the asparagus bouillon 5 minutes longer or until the rice is just tender.

6 cups

ENTRÉES

In current usage the words entrée and main dish are synonymous. But here, we are going to separate their meaning in order to clarify menu design. Soups, salads, and desserts can become a main dish, set within limited categories, in three different types of menus. In this cookbook, the entrée is any main dish which is not a principal soup, salad, or dessert. Entrées can be more unlimited in their scope and diversity. They are the only main dishes which can be served with an accompaniment vegetable or a pilaf.

Consider first what the entrée will be and how the accompaniment vegetable will complement it for they set the pattern for the rest of the dinner. What is the season and the availability of the vegetables that will compose the entrée? They must be harmonious as well as prime. Whether they be the primaverae of spring or the harvest of autumn, we have the bounties of nature in infinite variety from which to choose.

The character and nature of the entrée can vary widely in style and form. What does it look like? Does it come wrapped in pastry? Is its shape indistinguishable in a casserole dish or very identifiable like a stuffed head of red cabbage? Is it heaped on a serving platter or presented on individual dinner plates. Is it a vegetable served simply in a delicious sauce or is it a fussy molded creation? Do you eat it with a spoon like a stew or with your hands like tacos? Is it a dish for a cold winter night or a hot summer day? Does it have ethnic origins, like a Spanish paella, a Hungarian goulash, or a Chinese stir fry?

Will the entrée be baked or broiled, what will the method of cooking be? How will timing work out and how much of the dish can be prepared in advance? These are all very important considerations.

It is the province of the cook, or chef if you prefer, to draw all these qualities together into a harmonious creation that both pleases our taste buds and our eyes and nourishes our bodies and our souls.

SECTION I

ENDIVES EN PAPILLOTES

BAKED HEAD OF CAULIFLOWER with curry sauce

ASPARAGUS QUICHE

PARSNIP PATTIES

TERRINE OF LÉGUMES AND VEGETABLES

RAVIOLI

YORKSHIRE POPOVER with gouda sauce

POMME DE TERRE ANNA

MOUSSAKA

DEEP FRIED GREEN BELL PEPPER RINGS

TIMBALES OF PEAS

STUFFED CUCUMBERS

CHINESE STIR FRY with chow mein

BROCCOLI STRATA

BAKED CARROTS with minted pea sauce

SPINACH ALFREDO

PAELLA

UMBELLIFERAE PURÉE

BLACK BEAN CHIMICHANGAS with longhorn sauce

STROGANOFF

ASPARAGUS HOLLANDAISE

CARROT SOUFFLÉ

FRIED RICE WITH SNOW PEAS

STOCK VEGETABLE CHARLOTTE

with tomato cream sauce

PARSNIPS À L' ORANGE

SPANAKOPITTA

CAULIFLOWER AND KASHA BAKED WITH CHEESE

PETIT POIS À LA DUCHESSE

SPRING FANTASY

BEAN SPROUTS FU-YUNG with sweet and sour sauce

❦ ENDIVES EN PAPILLOTES ❦

This sophisticated dish is deceptively easy to prepare. It involves four cooking steps, each of which is quite simple . Be sure that your endives are fresh and tightly furled with not the slightest tinge of green showing on the tips of the leaves. Serve a light noodle soup first, next accompany the endives en papillotes with braised carrots. Then have a salad of cauliflower vinaigrette with some French bread and—let' s have Brie. Offer fresh pears for dessert .

I cup wild rice - 8 ounces
8 Tablespoons butter - divided
2 teaspoons of salt - divided
6 ounces red bell pepper - 1 medium
parsley leaves - (4 Tablespoons chopped)
corn oil
I pound mushrooms - medium - (5 cups)
I/4 teaspoon freshly cracked black pepper
2 Tablespoons Madiera
I cup heavy cream
I pound 8 ounces endives - 8 plump
I/2 cup stock broth - (see stock broth)
I teaspoon sugar

Soak and steam the wild rice as directed. (See steamed wild rice.) In a warm bowl, toss the hot rice with 4 tablespoons of the butter, cut in pieces, and 1 teaspoon of the salt. Cover the bowl with a paper towel and lid or plate and keep it warm.

While the rice is soaking and steaming, prepare and peel the bell pepper as directed. (See peeled red bell peppers.) Cut 8 strips, 2 inches long and I/4 inch wide out of it and reserve them.

Chop the parsley small and reserve it.

At this point, cut 4 large hearts, about 15 inches long and 15 inches wide, out of parchment paper. Using a pastry brush paint the hearts with corn oil and set them aside.

Wipe the mushrooms with a damp cloth and trim the butt ends of the stems. Mince them fine. The food processor does it perfectly, but a little hand held mincer does a good job too. Sauté the minced mushrooms, sprinkled with 1/2 teaspoon of the salt and the black pepper in 2 table-spoons of the butter in a large frying pan (see utensils) over high heat, stirring, for about 5 minutes or until all the liquid has evaporated. Reduce the heat to medium. Remove the pan from the heat and stir in the Madiera, then the cream. Return the pan to the medium heat until the cream simmers. Then reduce the heat to low and gently simmer the sauce, uncovered, about 30 minutes, stirring occasionally, until it is reduced by about half. The sauce must be very thick. Remove the pan from the heat, cover it with a paper towel and lid and keep it warm.

Wipe the endives with a damp cloth and trim their butt ends if necessary. Melt 2 tablespoons of the butter in a large saucepan over medium heat. Add the endives, turning them in the butter. Add the stock broth, 1/2 teaspoon of the salt and the sugar. When the broth comes to simmer, reduce the heat to low and braise the endives, covered, 10 minutes. Pierce the endives at their butt ends with a wooden toothpick to determine when they are tender-firm. Handling them very gently, transfer them to a colander to drain. (Save any remaining braising liquid for a bouillon soup. See bouillon soups.)

Spread 1/4 of the wild rice out on half of each paper heart, leaving an uncovered 1 1/2 inch margin along the cut edge of the paper. Place 2 endives on each bed of rice. Generously spoon 1/4 of the mushroom sauce, in a band, across each pair of endives and sprinkle 1 tablespoon of the chopped parsley over each band of sauce. Then lay 2 of the reserved red pepper strips in an x over the parsley on each serving.

Fold the uncovered half of each paper heart over the filling. Seal the edges of the paper together, starting at the top of the heart, in little overlapping folds, pressing them closed and finally twisting the tail of the heart to completely seal the package. Brush the tops of the packages with more corn oil and place them on a large baking sheet. Bake them in a preheated 450 degree oven for 10 minutes until the paper is puffed and golden. Transfer the packages to each of 4 warm dinner plates. Serve the endives en papillotes allowing each diner to cut open his package with a knife.

4 servings

Note: Parchment paper is available at specialty stores and some super markets.

BAKED HEAD OF CAULIFLOWER
with curry sauce

Serve jellied consommé Madrilène as the first course for this simple yet elegant dinner. The cauliflower which is presented on a bed of peas and mushrooms is served with a very fine curry sauce . Next a carrot and currant salad is served with pita bread. Then follow with pomegranates.

4 pounds unshelled peas - (4 cups shelled) - or about 20 ounces frozen
about 6 ounces mushrooms - 16 medium
3 pounds cauliflower - I large head
3/4 teaspoon plus salt - divided
curry sauce - (recipe follows)
3 Tablespoons butter - divided

Shell fresh peas and reserve them.

Wipe the mushrooms with a damp cloth and carefully remove and discard the stems . (Save the stems for a bouillon soup. See bouillon soups.) Reserve the mushroom caps.

Trim away the leaves and surplus stem from the cauliflower head. Wipe the cauliflower with a damp cloth and lightly sprinkle it all over, with salt.

Wrap it tight in a double layer of aluminum foil, set it upside down on a baking sheet and bake it in a preheated 375 degree oven for 30 minutes. Turn the cauliflower right side up and bake it 50 to 55 minutes longer. That is I hour and 20 to 25 minutes total baking time . Pierce the cauliflower with a wooden skewer to determine when it is done. If the cauliflower has to wait for the other vegetables to be ready, remove it from the oven but don' t unwrap it .

About 30 minutes before the cauliflower is done, make the curry sauce and keep it warm as directed.

About 10 minutes before the cauliflower is done, steam the fresh peas as directed. (See steamed peas.) If you are using frozen peas, time them to be ready when the cauliflower is done . Blanch the still frozen peas in enough boiling water to cover them by I I/2 inches in a saucepan, uncovered, over high heat, I minute less than the recommended cooking time on the package, from the moment they are in the water, regardless of when the water returns to boil, stirring the peas with a wooden spoon. Don't over cook them. Drain them. In either case, toss the cooked peas with 2 tablespoons of the butter, cut in small pieces and I/2 teaspoon of the salt on a warm, round, 12 inch in diameter serving platter, spreading them out even.

At the same time as the peas are cooking and about 8 minutes before the cauliflower is done, sauté the mushroom caps, sprinkled with I/4 teaspoon of the salt in I tablespoon of the butter in a frying pan over medium high heat for 8 minutes. Arrange the mushrooms on the peas, around the edge of the platter, hollow side up and fill each cap with a few peas.

Unwrap the cauliflower and set it on the center of the bed of peas. Dribble 3 tablespoons of the curry sauce over the cauliflower and serve the baked head of cauliflower immediately along with a warm bowl of the curry sauce.

4 servings

Note: You'll want a serrated knife with which to cut the cauliflower.

curry sauce

I Tablespoon butter
I/4 teaspoon ground cardamom
I/4 teaspoon ground cinnamon
I/4 teaspoon ground cloves
I/4 teaspoon ground ginger
I/4 teaspoon cayenne
I/2 teaspoon ground coriander
I/2 teaspoon celery salt
I teaspoon ground cumin
I teaspoon ground fenugreek
I teaspoon turmeric
I teaspoon salt
I cup heavy cream - at room temperature
I I/2 cups milk - at room temperature
2 teaspoons honey
2 Tablespoon fresh lemon juice
5 egg yolks - at room temperature - (see cooked eggs note)

Melt the butter in a medium size saucepan (not a heavy one) over low heat. Add the next 11 ingredients and stir the spices for 1 minute. Stir in the cream, milk and honey while gradually raising the heat to medium. When the mixture comes to simmer allow it to simmer 3 minutes, then remove the pan from the heat and let it to cool a bit.

In a mixing bowl, using a wire whisk, slowly whisk the lemon juice into the egg yolks. Then slowly whisk in all of the cream mixture. Now, pass the sauce through a fine strainer back into the saucepan.

Return the pan to medium low heat and stir the sauce constantly using a rubber spatula, for 7 or 8 minutes, while lifting the pan frequently as for a hollandaise sauce, until the sauce thickens. Do not permit the sauce to simmer. Remove the pan from the heat, cover it with a paper towel and lid to keep it warm.

about 3 cups

ASPARAGUS QUICHE

Consommé jardinière begins this lovely springtime dinner. Accompany the marvelous, rich asparagus quiche with braised carrots then serve a tossed watercress salad and some French bread. Dessert will be poached pears.

prebaked 9 inch bottom diameter by 2 inch deep quiche shell - (recipe
follows)
2 pounds asparagus - (about 3 cups, cut)
celery - 2 large ribs - (1 cup diced)
8 ounces Swiss Ementhal cheese (Swiss cheese) - (2 cups grated)
2 cups light cream - at room temperature
1 cup heavy cream - at room temperature
2 teaspoons salt - divided
1 teaspoon celery salt
1/4 teaspoon white pepper
1/8 teaspoon freshly grated nutmeg
1 1/2 teaspoons English mustard powder
1 Tablespoon cold water
5 eggs - at room temperature
3 egg yolks - at room temperature
2 Tablespoons corn oil
3 Tablespoons unsalted butter
1 teaspoon dried tarragon

Prepare and bake the quiche shell in advance as directed.
Rinse the asparagus in a basin or sink full of cold water and drain

it. Snap off the butt end of each spear at the point where it breaks the easiest. (Save butt ends for a bouillon soup. See bouillon soups.) Select the 2 largest or best looking spears and lightly peel them below their heads, using a vegetable peeler. Trim off the bottom of 1 spear so that it is about 1/2 inch shorter than the other, then cut it into 2 equal parts, crosswise. Reserve the whole asparagus and the 2 pieces. Cut the heads off all the remaining asparagus, peel and cut the rest of the spears, crosswise, into 1/8 inch thick slices. There should be almost 3 cups of sliced asparagus, tips included. (Save all peelings for that bouillon soup.)

Trim, scrape the strings from and dice the celery small..

Coarsely grate the cheese and reserve it.

Bring the light and heavy cream to simmer, together in a saucepan over medium heat. Remove the pan from the heat and allow it to cool a bit. In a tea cup dissolve 1 teaspoon of the salt, the celery salt, pepper, nutmeg and mustard powder in the 1 tablespoon of cold water.

Using a wire whisk, beat the eggs and yolks together in a mixing bowl until they are just light. Slowly stir in the slightly cooled cream then the dissolved spices. Pour the custard mixture into the prebaked quiche shell (which is in its pan) and bake it, lightly covered with foil, in a preheated 325 degree oven for 30 minutes.

About 20 minutes after the pan goes into the oven sauté the sliced asparagus, plus the whole asparagus, the 2 pieces and the diced celery, sprinkled with 1 teaspoon of the salt, in the oil in a large frying pan (see utensils) over high heat for about 5 minutes, stirring constantly until any moisture evaporates. Remove the pan from the heat. Set the whole asparagus and the 2 pieces aside on paper towels and reserve them.

Now, remove the quiche from the oven and remove the foil. Using a wooden spoon, very carefully, gently and thoroughly fold the sautéed vegetables, the grated cheese, the butter, cut into bits, and the tarragon, crushing it, into the custard. Return the quiche to the oven and bake it, lightly covered with foil, 30 minutes longer. Remove the foil. Lay the reserved whole asparagus on the center of the quiche, place the 2 pieces on either side of it so that they form a cross. Continue to bake the quiche, uncovered now, 30 minutes more until it is puffed and golden brown. Remove the quiche from the oven, remove the rim from the pan and set the quiche on a cake rack and allow it to stand at room temperature for 25 minutes. Then set the asparagus quiche on an attractive platter to serve it.

6 to 8 servings

prebaked quiche shell

1 1/2 cups minus 1 1/2 Tablespoons all purpose flour
1 1/2 Tablespoons cornstarch
3/4 teaspoon salt
6 Tablespoons unsalted butter
2 Tablespoons margarine
3 to 3 1/2 Tablespoons plus 1 teaspoon cold water
1 egg yolk

Using all the above ingredients except the 1 teaspoon of water and the egg yolk, prepare, rest and roll out the pastry dough into a disc, 17 inches in diameter, using only the directions for plain pastry dough. (See plain pastry dough.) Fold the disc of dough in half and then again in half. Place the point of the folded dough in the center of a 9 inch bottom diameter by 2 inch deep, false bottom quiche pan. (See utensils.) Then unfold the dough, encouraging it to relax down into the pan. There should be 2 inches of dough hanging down all around the outside of the pan; trim the edges even. Dip your finger in some water and dampen the whole 2 inches of overhanging dough, all around, on the side that is facing you. Then fold the overhanging dough back into the shell, pressing it against the sides of the pan so that the dough pops up about 1/8 inch above the rim of the pan. Slip the pan into a plastic bag, seal it and allow the shell to rest, refrigerated, 30 minutes.

Now remove the pan from the plastic bag and fit aluminum foil down into the shell, using 2 sheets of foil if necessary, carefully folding the foil over the edges of the shell to cover the dough completely. Fill the foil covered shell with dried beans which you reserve solely for this purpose. It will require about 6 cups.

Bake the shell in a preheated 450 degree oven for 30 minutes. Remove the pan from the oven and, using a large spoon, remove the beans then carefully remove the foil. In a cup, using a fork, beat the yolk with the 1 teaspoon of water. Using a pastry brush, paint the entire inside of the shell with the beaten yolk. Return the pan to the oven and bake the shell 5 minutes longer. The quiche shell can be baked several hours in advance of being filled. In which case, remove the sides of the pan and carefully slide the shell off of the pan bottom onto a cake rack. When it is completely cool, seal it in plastic and leave it at room temperature. However return the shell to its quiche pan before it is filled and the asparagus quiche is baked.

prebaked quiche shell

PARSNIPS PATTIES

Golden delicate parsnip patties, lightly fried in lots of butter and served with roast tomatoes are a taste treat that everyone except gardeners and farmers has forgotten. New York State Cheddar soup will make an appropriate first course and a tossed spinach salad served with biscuits the salad course. Served poached peaches for dessert.

parsley leaves - (1/4 cup chopped)
2 pounds parsnips - about 10 medium - (6 cups sliced)
1/2 cup plus flour - divided
1 teaspoon salt
1/2 teaspoon celery salt
1/4 teaspoon black pepper
1 egg
6 Tablespoons butter
a few parsley springs

Chop the parsley leaves fine.

Trim, peel and slice the parsnips. Steam them over already simmering water 25 minutes or until they are very soft. Purée the parsnips through a food mill set over a bowl. Blend the 1/2 cup of flour, the salt, celery salt and pepper into them, then thoroughly beat in the egg. Stir in the chopped parsley and refrigerate the mixture, uncovered for at least 3 hours.

Just before frying, with well floured hands, shape the purée into 20 patties of about 2 tablespoons each, measuring 2 to 2 1/2 inches in diameter and 1/2 inch thick. Dredge them in flour and lay them out on waxpaper.

Fry the patties in the butter in a large frying pan, over medium heat, for 7 minutes on each side until they are golden brown. If the patties are fried in batches, divide the butter accordingly. Transfer the cooked patties to a warm serving platter. Cooked patties can be kept warm in a 200 degree oven until all the patties are fried. In which case use an oven proof platter. (I prefer to use my large rectangular electric skillet for this recipe. It accommodates all 20 patties at once.) Decorate the platter of parsnip patties with the sprigs of parsley and serve.

4 servings

Note: Parsnip patties have the added serving advantage of retaining their heat well.

This terrine of légumes and vegetables is a feast for the eyes as well as the palate. After a first course of saffron consommé royale serve the terrine accompanied by a barley pilaf. A salad of endive with bread and some Camembert cheese is the salad course. Strawberries over ice cream will round out this rather sumptuous dinner.

canned fava beans - (1/2 packed cup)
canned white kidney beans (Cannellini) - (1/2 packed cup)
canned chick peas - (1/2 packed cup)
canned black beans - (1/2 packed cup)
10 ounces untrimmed spinach - (5 packed cups trimmed)
1 teaspoon lemon juice
1/4 teaspoon sugar
8 Tablespoons butter - very cold - divided
1 1/2 teaspoons salt - divided
1/8 teaspoon freshly cracked black pepper - divided
4 eggs - at room temperature
8 ounces cauliflower - about 1/3 small head - (1 1/2 cups florets)
1/8 teaspoon white pepper
about 10 1/2 ounces carrots - 5 medium - (1 1/2 cups cut)
about 10 ounces mushrooms - small - (4 cups)

Drain, rinse and drain all the canned beans, keeping them separate. (Save extra beans for a bouillon soup. See bouillon soups.)
Prepare and blanch the spinach as directed. (See blanched spinach.) Immediately turn the drained spinach into a basin of cold water for 1 minute. Drain it into a colander, place a saucer with a moderate weight upon it on the spinach and allow it to drain about 30 minutes. Turn the spinach over 2 or 3 times, during that period, to get the moisture out of it, but don't squeeze it dry. Place the drained spinach, the fava beans, lemon juice, sugar, 2 tablespoons of the butter, cut in pieces, 1/4 teaspoon of the salt and a pinch of the black pepper in the processor. Process for 15 seconds, stop the machine, scrape down the bowl, process 5 seconds longer. Add 1 egg and process 5 seconds more. Transfer the purée to a small bowl and set it aside. (Alternatively, the legumes and vegetables could be passed through a food mill set over a bowl and their seasonings added. The butter would have to be melted before stirring it in and the egg beaten in with a wire whisk. The texture of the terrine would simply be a little coarser.) Rinse out and dry the processor bowl.

Break the cauliflower into small, even florets and steam them until just tender as directed. (See steamed cauliflower.) Immediately turn the steamed cauliflower into a basin of cold water for 3 minutes then drain it well. Reserve 2 small florets. Process the cauliflower, the kidney beans, 2 tablespoons of the butter, cut in pieces, 1/2 teaspoon of the salt, a pinch of the white pepper and 1 egg, the same as for the spinach. Set the purée aside.

Trim, peel and cut the carrots, crosswise, into 3/4 inch pieces and steam them as directed. (See steamed carrots.) Turn the steamed carrots into a basin of cold water for 3 minutes then drain them well. Reserve 1 small piece. Process the carrots, the chick peas, 2 tablespoons of the butter, cut in pieces, 1/2 teaspoon of the salt, a pinch of the white pepper and 1 egg, the same as for the cauliflower. Set the purée aside.

Wipe the mushrooms with a damp cloth and trim the butt ends of the stems. Slice all but 2 of the smallest mushrooms then cut the 2 in half, lengthwise. Sauté all the mushrooms, sprinkled with 1/4 teaspoon of the salt and a pinch of the black pepper in 2 tablespoons of the butter in a frying pan over medium high heat about 8 minutes, raising the heat as necessary to evaporate all the moisture. Remove the pan from the heat and allow the mushrooms to cool a bit. Reserve the 4 halves. Process the mushrooms, with all their cooking butter, the black beans and 1 egg, the same as for the carrots. Set the purée aside.

(The four purées can be prepared up to 24 hours in advance. Refrigerate them, tightly covered, then bring them to room temperature before continuing with the recipe. The pieces of cauliflower and carrot can be wrapped in plastic and the mushrooms in wax paper, refrigerated and brought to room temperature also.)

About 2 hours before serving time, cut out a piece of wax paper to fit into the bottom of an 8 3/4 by 4 1/2 by 2 1/2 inch deep, 4 cup baking dish. Butter the dish well, lay the piece of wax paper in the bottom of the dish and butter the paper well. Have the four purées on hand and stir each of them a few times while they are still in their bowls. Carefully spoon the spinach mixture into the prepared dish, smoothing it out even with a spatula and taking great care, around the edges, not to slop it against the sides of the dish. Tap the dish down firmly on the work surface once or twice to eliminate air bubbles. Now gently spoon the cauliflower mixture over the spinach, smoothing it out and tapping the dish as for the spinach. Repeat the procedure with the carrots, then the mushrooms. The ingredients should just reach the top of the dish. Set the dish on a trivet (or use 2 chop sticks) in a large baking pan. Pour enough hot water into the pan to reach 3/4 of the way up the sides of the dish and place the waterbath arrangement in a preheated 325 degree oven and bake the terrine 40 minutes. Lightly cover the terrine with buttered foil to keep it from browning and bake it 50 minutes longer.

Remove the foil and lift the baking dish out of the waterbath. Allow it to stand 10 minutes. The terrine will have puffed but it will settle. Run the point of a sharp knife around the inside edge of the dish. Cover the dish with a warm inverted serving platter. Holding the platter and the baking dish together, turn them over, tap the back of the dish with a wooden spoon then lift it off the terrine. Carefully peel off the piece of wax paper.

Working quickly, cut the reserved cauliflower florets in half, lengthwise. Lay them lengthwise, down the center of the top of the terrine, alternating them with the 4 reserved mushroom halves, all cut side down and touching. Cut the reserved piece of carrot crosswise into 4 slices then cut each slice in half. Lay a half slice of carrot on either side of the mushroom stems to make them look like leaves at the base of a flower, like tulips. To serve the beautiful terrine of légumes and vegetables, slice it crosswise.

6 servings

RAVIOLI

Be sure to allow enough time to make the ravioli. They take a good two hours to prepare, but the time can be cut in half if two people are working together. It's a fun project! Precede these very delicate ravioli with stracciatella. Then follow them with a salad of sweet Italian frying peppers and Italian bread for the next course. Finish with chilled honeydew melon.

48 homemade ravioli - (recipe follows)
ravioli sauce - (recipe follows)
4 quarts water
1 Tablespoon plus 1 teaspoon salt
2 Tablespoons butter - at room temperature
Parmesan cheese - (1 cup freshly grated)

Make the ravioli in advance as directed.
Prepare the sauce 1 hour before the ravioli are to be served or prepare it in advance and reheat it as directed.
Transfer the ravioli and the test pieces, (without the corn meal) to a colander. Bring the water, with the salt, to boil in a large kettle over high

heat. Slip the ravioli and the test pieces into the water all at once, stirring them with a wooden spoon. Cook them 3 or 4 minutes from the moment they are in the water regardless of when the water returns to boil, covered with lid ajar. Adjust the heat to keep the water slowly boiling and stir the ravioli occasionally. Fish out the test pieces with the spoon and taste them to determine when the ravioli are tender but firm. Drain them well in a colander and in the still warm kettle, toss them with the butter cut into small pieces.

Divide the ravioli equally among 4 warm dinner plates and ladle some of the warm sauce over each serving. Serve the ravioli immediately, passing around a bowl of the Parmesan cheese.

4 servings

Note: The serving size is 12 ravioli. However 8 ravioli per serving may suffice for some people, in which case there will still be ample sauce for 6 servings.

homemade ravioli

ravioli filling - cold - (recipe follows)
pasta dough - (see pasta dough)
1 egg yolk
1 Tablespoon water
2 Tablespoons corn meal

Prepare the filling well in advance of assembling the ravioli and refrigerate it as directed.

Roll out the dough as directed. (See machine rolled pasta dough.) Working with 1 sheet of dough at a time and with the aid of a ruler and a zig-zag cutting wheel, cut 6, 2 inch square pieces from the short end of the sheet. Cover the remainder of the sheet of dough with a dish towel, while you are assembling the ravioli, to prevent it from drying out.

Alternatively, roll out the dough as directed. (See hand rolled pasta dough.) Roll the dough out as thin as possible, encouraging it into a rectangular shape of at least 18 by 12 inches. Working with 1 sheet of dough at a time and with the aid of a ruler and a zig-zag cutting wheel, but 6, 2 inch square pieces from the short end of the sheet as above.

In either case, using a fork, beat the yolk and water together in a cup. Using a pastry brush, paint half the squares with the beaten yolk. Place 1 level teaspoon of the cold filling on the center of each of them then cover them with the remaining squares. Firmly press the edges of the ravioli together and trim the edges, as necessary with the zig-zag wheel. Toss the ravioli, as they are completed, onto a large jelly roll pan which has been scattered with the corn meal. Continue making the ravioli in like manner. If the dough has been properly rolled out, the yield will be 48 ravioli. Press any leftover scraps of dough together, two at a time, with beaten yolk, to use as test pieces when you are trying to determine if the ravioli are cooked.

Allow the ravioli to dry, uncovered, 15 minutes. Turn them over and allow them to dry 15 minutes longer. The ravioli are now ready to be cooked or, if you have made them early in the day, lightly cover them with a towel and refrigerate them 4 or 5 hours or until ready to serve.

48 ravioli

ravioli filling

parsley - (1/2 packed cup chopped)
1/2 cup bread crumbs - (see bread crumbs)
Romano cheese - (1/2 cup freshly grated)
1 cup Ricotta cheese
1/2 teaspoon freshly cracked black pepper

Chop the parsley fine and in a bowl combine it well with the remaining ingredients. Cover the mixture and refrigerate it for at least 2 hours.

filling for 48 ravioli

ravioli sauce

1/2 teaspoon fennel seeds
4 Tablespoons butter
1 1/2 cups tomato paste - 12 ounces
3 cups stock broth - (see stock broth)

2 Tablespoons light molasses
1 teaspoon celery salt
1/4 teaspoon freshly cracked black pepper
1/4 teaspoon ground rosemary - (see ground rosemary)
1/4 ground (rubbed) sage
1/4 teaspoon dried thyme

Toast the fennel seeds in a dry pan over medium heat about 3 minutes, stirring them constantly until they become fragrant and golden. Remove them from the pan immediately and crush them 1/2 teaspoon at a time in a mortar, or use a spice grinder.

Melt the butter in a medium size saucepan over medium heat. Add the tomato paste and stir in the broth and molasses. Add the crushed fennel seeds, celery salt and pepper. When the sauce simmers, reduce the heat to low and very gently simmer it, uncovered, 55 minutes, stirring occasionally. Add the rosemary, sage and the thyme, crushing it and simmer the sauce 5 minutes longer. Or, if you're planning to make the sauce in advance and reheat it, add the herbs only when the sauce is reheated.

about 4 cups

YORKSHIRE POPOVER
with gouda sauce

Yorkshire popover is a puffed and golden "tour de force" served with a delicious cheese sauce. Herb broth will make a light soup course. If bread is served with a tossed romaine salad, let it be something light and crisp. Poached pears will be dessert.

3 eggs
1 cup milk
1 cup all purpose flour
1 3/4 teaspoons salt - divided
about 13 ounces carrots - 4 large - (2 cups sliced)
1 pound unshelled peas - (1 cup shelled) - or about 5 ounces frozen
11 ounces cauliflower - about 1/2 small head - (2 cups florets)
celery - 4 large ribs - (2 cups cut)

about 6 ounces mushrooms - small - (2 cups whole)
4 Tablespoons corn oil
4 Tablespoons butter
1/4 teaspoon freshly cracked black pepper
Gouda sauce - (recipe follows)

In the processor, process the eggs, milk, flour and 1/4 teaspoon of the salt together 10 seconds. Alternatively, spin the ingredients in the blender until the mixture is smooth. Or in a bowl, beat the eggs until they are light. Stir in the milk and gradually sift in the flour and salt while stirring the batter. In any case, allow the batter to stand, covered, at room temperature for at least 1 hour or longer.

Have all the vegetables at room temperature, except the cauliflower which should be chilled.

Trim, peel and cut the carrots crosswise into 3/16 inch thick slices.

Shell fresh peas or allow frozen peas to thaw and drain completely in a colander.

Break the cauliflower up into small florets, cutting larger florets into halves or quarters. The cauliflower tends to cook more quickly than the other vegetables so keep it refrigerated until it is to go into the pan.

Trim, scrape the strings from and cut the celery crosswise into 1/2 inch thick slices.

Wipe the mushrooms with a damp cloth. Trim the butt ends of the stems and cut the mushrooms in half lengthwise.

Pour the oil into a 7 by 11 by 1 1/2 inch deep, 6 cup baking pan and add the carrots. Place the pan in the oven while it is being heated up to 425 degrees. This will give the carrots a little head start, since they take slightly longer to cook than the other vegetables. When the oven has heated to temperature, remove the pan and add the butter, cut in little pieces, to it. When the butter has melted, add all the remaining vegetables, a few at a time, mixing them up and turning them carefully with a large spatula to coat them well with the oil and butter and sprinkling them with 1 1/2 teaspoons of the salt and the pepper. Return the pan to the 425 degree oven and bake the vegetables 15 minutes.

Remove the pan from the oven. Stir up the batter, then carefully and evenly, pour it all over the vegetables. Again, return the pan to the oven and bake the popover 15 minutes at 425 degrees. Reduce the heat to 350 degrees and bake 30 minutes longer.

Meanwhile make the Gouda sauce and keep it warm as directed.

Serve the vegetable popover the minute it's done, bringing the pan right to the table, along with a bowl of the warm Gouda sauce. Cut the popover into squares and let the diners spoon the sauce over their own portions.

6 servings

Note: The pan and the vegetables in it must be good and hot in order for the batter to puff properly.

gouda sauce

12 ounces Gouda cheese - (3 cups grated) - (see note)
6 Tablespoons butter
6 Tablespoons flour
1/4 teaspoon white pepper
3 cups stock broth
3 egg yolks - at room temperature - (see cooked eggs note)

Coarsely grate the cheese and reserve it.

Melt the butter in a heavy saucepan over low heat. Using a rubber spatula, blend in the flour and pepper, stirring constantly for 5 minutes. Slowly stir in the broth while raising the heat to medium until the mixture simmers and thickens. Then reduce the heat to low again.

In a small bowl, using a wire whisk, beat the yolks until they are light, then very slowly stir about 1 cup of the hot broth mixture into them. Then slowly stir the yolk mixture back into the saucepan. Raise the heat to medium again, stirring until the sauce simmers. Simmer 1 minute and remove the pan from the heat. Now, 1/2 cup at a time, stir the reserved cheese into the sauce until it is melted and the sauce is smooth. Cover the pan with paper towel and lid to keep the Gouda sauce warm until serving.

about 4 1/2 cups

Note: Gouda is the Dutch cheese that looks like a flattened ball and is covered with red wax.

The flour stabilizes the yolks and they will not curdle when simmered. They'll just thicken the sauce nicely.

POMME DE TERRE ANNA

Steaming bowls of French onion soup is the first course. Next serve braised asparagus with this heavenly potato cake, then have a tossed salad of Boston lettuce. Follow with fresh strawberries.

8 Tablespoons butter - divided
3 pounds potatoes - small to medium size - (see note)
1 teaspoon salt - divided

Using some of the butter, butter an 8 inch cast iron frying pan well and refrigerate it. Butter a 9 inch square piece of aluminum foil and set it aside. Spread a piece of foil, with edges turned up, on the floor of the oven (under the heating element if it's electric) to catch any runover. Place a shelf at the lowest level in the oven and remove the other shelf for easier access.

Peel the potatoes, dropping them into a bowl of cold water to cover.

Remove the frying pan from the refrigerator and very heavily, butter it again.

Select 4 or 5 potatoes which will produce the most perfect round slices about 2 inches in diameter. Dry them well and slice them very, very thin. Lay the slices out on a paper towel and blot them. This is an important step.

Lay one potato slice in the center of the bottom of the frying pan. Lay more slices, in an overlapping pattern, slightly over and around it in a circle. Lay a second circle slightly over and around the first, but with the slices laid in the opposite direction. This should cover the bottom of the pan. Stand a third circle of overlapping slices around the sides of the pan, laying the slices in the opposite direction to the second circle and pressing them against the sides of the pan. Sprinkle the potatoes in the pan with 1/3 of the salt and dot them with 1/3 of the remaining butter, cut into bits.

Now, working quickly, dry, slice and blot the rest of the potatoes. They need not be as uniformly nor quite as thinly sliced as the potatoes already in the pan. Carefully lay half these slices in the pan then press down hard on them with your hands to compact them. Sprinkle them with half the remaining salt and dot them with half the remaining butter. Lay the rest of the slices in the pan, pressing down on them. They will be mounded up but will flatten as they cook. Sprinkle the rest of the salt over all and dot with the rest of the butter.

Set the pan on the stove over medium high heat for 5 minutes to give the potatoes a preliminary browning. Cover the potatoes with the piece of buttered foil and transfer the pan to the low shelf in the preheated 450 degree oven. Now set a heavy 10 inch cast iron frying pan on top of the foil to weigh the potatoes down and bake the potatoes 15 minutes. Then remove the 10 inch frying pan and carefully peel off the foil. Bake the potatoes 30 minutes longer. (If your oven heats unevenly, turn the pan once in the middle of the baking time to brown the potatoes evenly.)

Remove the pan from the oven and run a sharp knife down around the inside edges of the pan. The potatoes must be turned out onto a flat surface or their shape will be distorted. The bottom of a 9 inch springform pan is an ideal surface.

Cover the potatoes with the inverted bottom of the springform pan, firmly pressing it against the potatoes. Using pot holders, tilt the frying pan over a cup to catch about 2 tablespoons of excess butter which will run off. Now holding the frying pan and cover together, turn the two over onto the cover. Tap the back of the pan with a wooden spoon to help loosen the potatoes then lift it off of them. Violà! The pomme de terre Anna should be a golden brown work of art. Dribble the 2 tablespoons of runoff butter over the potatoes. Set the bottom of the springform pan on a serving dish and cut the pomme de terre Anna into wedges to serve it.

4 to 6 servings

Note: You always think all those potatoes will never fit into that little pan but they always do. Allow an hour to assemble this simple dish. If you use baking potatoes they will drop out of the pan like a dream. If you use boiling potatoes they are more likely to stick. However, the texture of boiling potatoes is more appropriate to the character of the dish. An "all purpose" potato is a good middle of the road choice. Maintain the pan you make pomme de terre Anna in, as you would an omelet pan, don't cook anything else in it!

 MOUSSAKA

Moussaka is a great make ahead party dish. You can be a guest at your own party. Start with cucumber soup, then have braised baby artichokes with the moussaka. Marinated mushrooms served with Feta cheese and some crusty bread will make the salad course. Purple grapes are the simple dessert.

moussaka filling - (recipe follows)
2 pounds eggplant - 2 medium, 1 pound each
salt
4 Tablespoons olive oil - divided
6 Tablespoons bread crumbs - divided - (see bread crumbs)
1 1/2 cups milk - at room temperature
1 1/2 Tablespoons butter
6 Tablespoons flour
3/8 teaspoon freshly grated nutmeg
1 egg - at room temperature
1 egg yolk - at room temperature

Partially prepare the filling until the moussaka is ready to be assembled, as directed.

Trim, peel and cut the eggplants in half, lengthwise. Lay the cut sides down and cut the halves lengthwise into slices 1/2 inch thick. Lay out the slices and lightly and evenly salt them. Allow them to stand 30 minutes, turn them over, salt them again and allow them to stand 30 minutes longer to drain away excess juices.

At this point finish preparing the filling as directed.

Now blot the eggplant on paper towels. Brown the slices for 1 minute on each side, using 1 tablespoon of the oil per each half eggplant, in a frying pan (see utensils) over high heat. Set the slices aside on paper towels.

Sprinkle 4 tablespoons of the bread crumbs in a buttered, 7 1/2 by 12 by 2 inch deep, 8 cup baking dish. Rotate the dish to evenly cover it with the crumbs. Using half of the eggplant slices, place a layer of the slices in the bottom of the dish. Do not allow them to overlap, but tightly fit them together, trimming the slices where necessary to do so and filling in any little spaces. Cover the eggplant with half of the completed filling, spreading it out even. Repeat the eggplant and filling layers once again.

To make the custard topping, slowly bring the milk to simmer in a small saucepan over medium heat. Remove the pan from the heat and allow the milk to cool a bit. Now, melt the butter in a medium size saucepan over low heat and using a wooden spoon, blend in the flour (which is no small task), then slowly stir in the cooled milk and add the nutmeg and a dash of salt. In a bowl, using a wire whisk, beat the egg and the yolk until they are light then stir them into the milk mixture. Alternatively, melt the butter in the warm milk. Combine the cooled milk mixture with the flour, nutmeg and salt in the container of the blender or processor and give it a spin. Add the egg and the yolk and give it one more little spin without allowing the egg to foam. (Easier.)

Now, carefully pour the custard topping over the last layer of the filling, covering it. Then evenly sprinkle 2 tablespoons of the bread crumbs over the custard. Bake the moussaka in a preheated 325 degree oven 1 hour. Remove it from the oven and allow it to cool to room temperature. Tightly cover the dish with foil and refrigerate it 48 hours. This step is essential for the flavors to develop and blend.

Before serving, remove the tight foil and bring the dish to room temperature. Reheat the dish, lightly covered with foil now, in a preheated 325 degree oven 30 minutes. Remove the dish from the oven and allow it to stand 30 minutes. The moussaka is served while it is just moderately warm, at which temperature it is at its fullest flavor.

8 servings

moussaka filling

2/3 cup dried chick peas - about 6 ounces
celery - 2 large ribs - (1 cup diced)
parsley leaves - (1/2 packed cup chopped)
1 cup shelled walnut halves - about 4 ounces
1 teaspoon celery salt
4 Tablespoons butter
3/4 cup tomato paste - 6 ounces
1 cup dry white wine
4 Tablespoons light molasses
1/4 teaspoon liquid smoke
1 teaspoon salt
1 1/2 teaspoons freshly ground allspice
3/4 teaspoon freshly cracked black pepper
3/8 teaspoon ground cinnamon
Parmesan cheese - (6 Tablespoons freshly grated)
Romano cheese - (2 Tablespoons freshly grated)
1/2 cup bread crumbs - (see bread crumbs)
1 1/2 teaspoons dried oregano
2 eggs

Soak and cook the chick peas as directed. (See boiled dried shelled beans.) Be sure they are well cooked. Drain them. If the cooked chick peas yield more than 2 cups, don't use the excess, it would unbalance the recipe. (Save it for a bouillon soup. See bouillon soups.) Spread the chick peas out on a platter and lightly crush them with a fork, crush not mash. Reserve them.

Trim, scrape the strings from and dice the celery.

Chop the parsley and reserve it.

Using a heavy knife, coarsely chop the walnuts and reserve them.

Sauté the celery, sprinkled with the celery salt, in the butter in a large frying pan (see utensils) over medium heat, 3 minutes. Add the tomato paste and slowly stir in the wine. Add the molasses, liquid smoke, salt, allspice, pepper, cinnamon and crushed chick peas. Reduce the heat to medium low and gently simmer the filling, uncovered, 30 minutes, stirring occasionally. Remove the pan from the heat and allow the filling to cool at least 30 minutes.

When the moussaka is ready to be assembled, stir the reserved parsley and walnuts, the Parmesan, Romano, bread crumbs and the oregano, crushing it into the filling. Lightly beat the eggs in a small bowl then thoroughly stir them into the filling.

 # DEEP FRIED GREEN BELL PEPPER RINGS

Breaded deep fried green bell pepper rings is a little known treatment of this popular vegetable. They fry up beautifully. Serve a cream of broccoli soup then accompany the pepper rings with individual bowls of stewed tomatoes set on dinner plates. Follow with a salad of potatoes in mayonnaise and finish with poached peaches.

2 pounds 4 ounces green bell peppers - 6 medium
1/2 cup flour
2 teaspoons plus salt - divided
2 teaspoon sugar
2 teaspoon paprika
1/2 teaspoon cayenne
1/4 cup sesame seeds
3/4 cup bread crumbs - (see bread crumbs)
2 eggs
2 Tablespoons plus water
4 cups peanut oil

Using a serrated bread knife, cut the peppers, crosswise, into slices 1/4 inch thick. Carefully cut the core and any white membrane out of the rings with the tip of a sharp knife. Use the end slices too, 1 pepper will yield about 8 rings.

Sift the flour, the 2 teaspoons of salt, the sugar, paprika and cayenne together into a shallow fruit or cereal dish.

Toast the sesame seeds in a dry frying pan over medium heat, stirring, for about 3 minutes until they become golden and fragrant. Remove them from the pan immediately. Combine the sesame seeds and bread crumbs and spin them around in the blender for about 1 minute until the bread crumbs are fairly fine. Place the crumb mixture in another shallow dish.

In a third shallow dish, using a fork, beat the eggs with the 2 tablespoons of water until they are light.

Dredge the pepper rings, one at a time, in the flour. The flour will not want to cling very well to the shiny skin of the peppers, but don't be concerned. Now, dip the rings in the beaten egg then dredge them in the bread crumbs. If the egg becomes thickened with flour, thin it with a little water. All the pepper rings can be prepared about one hour in advance of frying, and carefully stacked on a platter.

(Allowing about 15 minutes for the oil to heat to temperature, heat the oil in a deep saucepan, with a cooking thermometer clipped to the inside of it, over medium high heat to 365 degrees. Or use an electric deep fryer set at 365 degrees.) Fry the pepper rings, 3 at a time, for just one minute. They will be golden. Using a skimmer or slotted spoon, lift them from the oil and drain them on paper towels. Allowing 12 rings per serving, each serving will take 4 minutes to fry. Lightly salt the pepper rings and heap each serving in an individual size paper lined basket. Serve the deep fried green bell pepper rings immediately, they will not wait.

4 servings

 TIMBALES OF PEAS

Let's have consommé jardinière to start off this lovely dinner. Serve the accompaniment vegetable of fried potatoes already on the dinner plates with the timbales of peas. Watercress is the salad, served with French bread and fresh pears are dessert.

1 1/2 pounds unshelled peas - (1 1/2 cups shelled)
12 ounces Boston lettuce - usually 1 1/2 heads - (12 loosely packed cups torn)
6 Tablespoons unsalted butter
1 1/2 teaspoons honey
1 1/2 teaspoons salt
3/8 teaspoon white pepper
3 eggs - at room temperature
3 yolks - at room temperature
3/4 cup heavy cream - at room temperature

Shell the peas.

Wash the lettuce. Tear it into pieces as for a salad and spin it dry.

Melt the butter in a heavy saucepan over medium heat. Add the peas, lettuce, honey, salt and pepper and cook the vegetables, covered, 10 minutes, stirring them once or twice. At this point, remove 18 of the peas from the pan and set them aside, keeping them covered. Now, uncover the pan, increase the heat to high and cook the vegetables another 5 or 10 minutes, stirring them frequently until all the moisture has evaporated. Do not allow the vegetables to scorch. Pass the vegetables through a food mill set over a bowl. Then, using a wire whisk, thoroughly stir in the eggs and yolks one at a time. Stir in the cream.

Very thoroughly butter 6, 1/2 cup timbale molds. Evenly divide the vegetable mixture among them and firmly tap the molds down on the work surface once or twice to eliminate air bubbles. Set the molds on a trivet (cake rack) in a large baking pan and pour enough hot water into the pan to reach 3/4 of the way up the sides of the molds. Lightly cover the molds with one large piece of buttered foil. Place the waterbath arrangement in a preheated 325 degree oven and bake the timbales 1 hour and 15 minutes. A toothpick inserted in the center of each timbale should come out clean.

Remove the foil and lift the molds out of the waterbath. Allow them to stand 10 minutes then run the point of a small sharp knife around the inside edge of the molds. One at a time, cover each mold with a warm, inverted dinner plate. Holding the plate and the mold together, turn them over, tap the mold with a wooden spoon, then lift it off of the timbale. Decorate the top of each timbale with 3 of the reserved peas and serve the timbales of peas immediately.

6 servings

Note: I use beautiful little fluted molds from Germany, for this dish. If the molds are well buttered and the custard is allowed to stand the all important full 10 minutes, there will be no problem turning the timbales out of fancy molds.

 STUFFED CUCUMBERS

Stuffed cucumbers taste like summertime even when it isn't. Serve avgolemono soup first then braised baby artichokes with the cucumbers. Follow with a salad of fava beans vinaigrette. Poached plums will make a nice dessert.

1 pound ripe firm tomatoes - 4 small - (2 cups chopped)
celery - 2 large ribs - (1 cup chopped)
6 ounces green bell pepper - 1 medium - (1 cup chopped)
4 ounces radishes, minus leaves - about 10 - (1 cup chopped)
Italian parsley leaves - (1 cup chopped) - no substitute
2 pounds 4 ounces cucumbers - 4 average, 7 to 8 inches long
1 teaspoon celery salt
6 Tablespoons olive oil
2 teaspoons honey
1 teaspoon salt
1/2 teaspoon freshly cracked black pepper
1 1/2 teaspoons dried basil
3/4 cup bread crumbs - (see bread crumbs)
Parmesan cheese - (3/4 cup freshly grated)
2 eggs - at room temperature
2 Tablespoons fresh lemon juice

Peel and seed the tomatoes as directed. (See peeled tomatoes and see seeded tomatoes.) Remove the stem buttons and coarsely chop the tomatoes. Set them aside in a colander to drain.
Trim, scrape the strings from and dice the celery small.
Core, trim away any white membrane and dice the bell pepper small.
Trim and dice the radishes small.

Chop the parsley fine.

Peel the cucumbers, cut them in half lengthwise and scrape out the seeds with a small spoon. Pierce 4 or 5 holes through the cucumbers along the center of each cavity with a toothpick. Reserve the cucumbers.

In a large frying pan (see utensils), sauté the celery, bell pepper and radishes, sprinkled with the celery salt in the oil, over medium heat, 3 minutes. Raise the heat to high, add the tomatoes, honey, salt and black pepper and sauté 3 minutes longer while stirring the vegetables. Remove the pan from the heat, stir in the parsley and basil, crushing it and allow the mixture to cool a bit. Then stir in the bread crumbs and the cheese.

In a mixing bowl, using a wire whisk, beat the eggs until they are light while slowly adding the lemon juice, then stir the vegetable mixture into the eggs. Now generously stuff the cucumbers with the mixture. Place a cake rack over a baking pan and set the stuffed cucumbers on the rack so that they are cradled between the wires. Bake the cucumbers in a preheated 375 degree oven 20 minutes. Lightly cover them with foil and bake them 15 minutes longer. Transfer the stuffed cucumbers to a serving platter and allow them to stand 5 minutes before serving.

4 to 6 servings

CHINESE STIR FRY
with chow mein

Egg drop soup is the first course, of course! I'm saving my money to buy those covered metal dishes they use in Chinese restaurants to serve this stir fry in. White turnips vinaigrette accompanied by rice wafers are good choices for the salad course in an oriental dinner. Finish with a bowl of tangerines.

chow mein noodles - (recipe follows)
2 pounds bok choy (Chinese vegetable resembles Swiss chard) - 1 large
head - (8 packed cups cut)
2 cups long grain brown rice - 14 ounces
8 ounces tofu - (2 cups diced)
about 3 1/2 ounces shiitake mushrooms - large - (1 cup sliced)

6 ounces water chestnuts - about 12 - (3/4 cup sliced)
6 ounces snow peas - (2 cups)
4 ounces mung bean sprouts - (2 cups)
ginger root - (1 teaspoon freshly grated)
2 Tablespoons cornstarch
1 teaspoon sugar
1/4 cup cold water
6 Tablespoons soy sauce
6 Tablespoons dry sherry
2 teaspoons light molasses
6 Tablespoons peanut oil

Prepare the chow mein noodles in advance as directed.

Trim the bok choy where necessary and give the leaves a few lengthwise slashes. Starting at the base of the head, cut the bok choy, diagonally, into 1/4 inch thick slices. Rinse it in a basin of cold water, drain it well and spin it dry. Spread the bok choy out on paper towels, cover with more paper towels then roll the towels up and seal the bok choy in plastic bags. Allow it to stand 1 hour; the towels will absorb remaining moisture.

(The bok choy can be prepared up to 24 hours in advance, refrigerated, then emptied into a large bowl or colander and brought to room temperature before continuing with the recipe.)

Prepare the rice as directed. (See steamed long or short grain brown rice.) Keep the rice warm over hot water until serving.

Meanwhile, cut the tofu into 1/2 inch dice and blot it on paper towels.

Wipe the mushrooms with a damp cloth. Trim the butt ends of the stems as necessary and cut the remaining stems crosswise into slices 1/8 inch thick. Cut the caps lengthwise into slices 1/4 inch thick.

Trim, peel and cut the water chestnuts lengthwise into slices 1/8 inch thick.

Remove the stems and pull any strings from the snow peas. If any appear too large, cut them in half on a steep diagonal.

Pick off any remaining bean skins from the bean sprouts.

Peel and grate the ginger on a medium fine grater.

In a small saucepan, dissolve the cornstarch and sugar in the cold water, soy sauce and sherry, then stir in the molasses. Set the pan over medium heat and using a rubber spatula, stir the mixture constantly until it comes to simmer. Reduce the heat slightly and continue to simmer and stir for 2 minutes. Remove the pan from the heat and cover it with a paper towel and lid to keep the sauce warm. (The sauce will appear too thick and highly flavored before it is mixed with the vegetables.)

Set an 8 inch frying pan on or near the stove. Pour the oil into a wok and rotate the pan to coat it with the oil. Set the wok over high heat. Just before the oil starts to smoke, add the ginger and heat it 15 seconds. Add the tofu and mushrooms and stir fry them 6 minutes, using a wok spatula or long handled spoon, until the tofu starts to become a light golden color. Add the water chestnuts and stir fry 1 minute. Add the bok choy and stir fry 2 minutes. Add the snow peas and stir fry 4 minutes longer. Then add the bean sprouts and stir fry 1 minute more. Immediately remove the wok pan from the heat and set it on the eight inch frying pan. Wait 10 seconds while continuing to stir the vegetables. Now quickly pour the warm sauce over the vegetables, scraping out the saucepan with a rubber spatula, then, using two large spoons, toss the vegetables with the sauce for 1 minute. Equally divide the vegetables among warm dinner plates and serve the Chinese stir fry immediately along with bowls of the warm rice and a basket of the chow mein noodles. The diners serve themselves to the rice and the noodles.

4 to 6 servings

Note: Did you ever pour the uncooked cornstarch sauce into the hot wok only to have it congeal instantly and ruin your dish because the wok was so hot? Or have the vegetables overcook because the sauce took too long to thicken, in the wok over lowered heat? Those things can't happen if the sauce is made separately - especially for a large quantity of vegetables.

chow mein noodles

1 cup minus 1 Tablespoon unbleached all purpose flour
1 Tablespoon cornstarch
1/2 teaspoon plus salt - divided
4 Tablespoons plus 1 1/2 to 2 teaspoons cold water
about 2 cups peanut oil

Combine the flour, cornstarch, the 1/2 teaspoon of salt and the 4 tablespoons plus 1 1/2 teaspoons of water in the processor and process them 15 seconds. Stop the machine, scrape down the bowl and pinch the granular mixture together between your fingers. If it does not cling together to form dough, add 1/2 teaspoon more water. In any case, process 15 seconds longer, turn the still granular mixture out onto a very lightly floured work surface, gather the dough together and knead it 1 minute. The dough will weigh 8 ounces. Divide the dough into 4 pieces of equal weight and seal them in plastic. They do not need to rest.

Alternatively, sift the flour, cornstarch and the 1/2 teaspoon of salt together in a mixing bowl. Sprinkle them with the 4 tablespoons plus 1 1/2 teaspoons of water and stir the ingredients with a fork. Now, using your hand, knead the very crumbly mixture about 5 minutes or until a very rough dough begins to form. At this point, decide whether to add the 1/2 teaspoon more water. Turn the dough out onto a very lightly floured work surface and knead it, as best you can, for 3 minutes to form a cohesive mass even though the pasta machine will knead the dough later. Divide the dough etc., as directed above.

Roll out either the processor or hand made dough as directed. But use cornstarch rather than flour to dust it with. (See machine rolled pasta dough.) The dough may be very ragged during the first 1 or 2 passes through the rollers but it quickly smooths out and behaves. We want these noodles to be thick so stop after turning the number setting down about 2 times or when the sheets are about 6 inches square. The edges do not have to be neat and even.

(At this point, start heating the oil, it only needs to be 3/4 inch deep, in a deep saucepan over medium heat.)

Now, before cutting the noodles as directed, cut each of the little sheets into 3 rectangular pieces, each about 2 by 6 inches. Place a piece of wax paper under the machine and cut the rectangular pieces, the short way, through the 1/16 inch narrow cutting rollers, to make 2 inch long noodles. (See machine cut noodles.) Cut only one piece of dough at a time. The noodles do not need a drying period now.

Just before the oil starts to smoke slide each little batch of noodles, one batch at a time, into the hot oil and fry them just about 25 seconds, stirring them until they are light golden. Using a skimmer or slotted spoon transfer the noodles to paper towels and lightly salt them. Repeat with the remaining noodles.

(When the noodles have cooled to room temperature, they can be stored, in a cool place, in a tightly sealed plastic bag for up to 5 days.)

Bring the chow mein noodles to room temperature before serving.

about 8 ounces

Note: We want this dough to be nice and firm so resist adding the extra 1/2 teaspoons of water if you can. Don't let the dry roughness of the dough discourage you, especially if you are kneading the dough by hand. The processor is the preferred method here but it isn't absolutely necessary. However, it is necessary to use the pasta machine to roll out this very firm dough. Incidentally, chow mein are the Chinese words for fried noodles.

 BROCCOLI STRATA

Broccoli strata is really a savory bread pudding. Bread puddings are often, after being assembled, left to stand overnight in order to allow enough time for the bread to absorb the liquid. It would be a good idea to prepare all the vegetables, etc., the night before serving, assemble the dish in the morning and then leave it to stand all day in a cool place, before baking. The strata should come out of the oven just before the soup is served. While it cools, enjoy an herb broth and still have enough time to cook a colorful accompaniment vegetable of braised red bell peppers. Next offer tossed salad mix I, then serve poached peaches.

12 slices firm close textured white bread
celery - 2 large ribs - (1 cup diced)
1 1/2 pounds broccoli - 3 average heads - 1 bunch - (6 cups florets and cut)
1 can pitted black olives - 6 ounces - (1 heaping cup)
12 ounces Fontina cheese - (3 cups grated)
1/2 teaspoon celery salt
4 Tablespoons butter
1 1/2 teaspoons salt
1/2 teaspoon freshly cracked black pepper
2 Tablespoons hot water - in a cup
4 Tablespoons prepared grey mustard - (see note)
1 Tablespoon honey
2 cups stock broth - at room temperature - (see stock broth)
4 eggs - at room temperature

Trim the crusts from the slices of bread. On a cookie sheet, dry them out a bit in a preheated 250 degree oven for 10 minutes on each side. Remove them from the cookie sheet immediately and reserve them.

Trim, scrape the strings from and dice the celery.

Cut just the florets, with very short or hardly any stems, from the tops of the broccoli stalks. Break the florets into very small pieces. Trim and pull the fibrous skin from the stalks with a knife then peel them with a vegetable peeler. If the stalks are very thick, split them lengthwise. Cut the stalks crosswise into 1/4 inch thick pieces.

Drain, rinse and drain the olives. Break them into pieces.

Coarsely grate the cheese.

Sauté the celery, sprinkled with the celery salt, in the butter, in a large frying pan (see utensils) over medium heat 2 minutes. Add the broccoli sprinkle with the salt and pepper and sauté 3 minutes longer.

Reduce the heat to low. Remove the pan from the heat, add the hot water, cover the pan immediately, return it to the low heat and cook the vegetables 5 minutes. Raise the heat to high. Uncover the pan, add the olives and cook the mixture one minute longer, turning it with a wooden spatula, to evaporate any remaining moisture. Remove the pan from the heat.

In a bowl, blend the mustard into the honey until the mixture is smooth. Gradually stir in the stock broth.

In a large bowl, using a wire whisk, beat the eggs until they are light while slowly stirring in the stock broth mixture.

Pour enough of the egg and broth mixture into a buttered 8 by 8 by 2 inch deep, 8 cup baking dish to barely cover the bottom of the dish. Lay 4 slices of the bread in the dish. Don't be concerned if the slices do not fill the dish. They will swell. Sprinkle them with 1 cup of the grated cheese. Sprinkle 1/3 of the broccoli and olive mixture over the cheese. Repeat the bread, cheese and broccoli and olive layers twice more. Then carefully pour the egg and broth mixture over the dish so as not to disturb the broccoli and olives, letting it seep down into the dish. Now set the dish aside for at least one hour or longer in order to allow time for the bread to absorb the liquid.

Bake the strata in a preheated 325 degree oven 30 minutes. Lightly cover it with foil and bake it 45 minutes longer. Remove the dish from the oven and allow the broccoli strata to stand 30 minutes (yes 30) before serving.

4 very generous servings

Note: Be thoroughly familiar with the mustard you are using in this dish. Grey mustard works best, but too bland or too spicy will not do. The flavor and quality of the mustard are essential to the success of the broccoli strata.

BAKED CARROTS
with minted pea sauce

Have noodle soup first. Then serve cauliflower florets with this exquisite version of carrots and peas. After a tossed salad mix II and dinner rolls, offer fresh blueberries for dessert.

minted pea sauce - (recipe follows)
1 1/2 pounds carrots - 12 medium
1/2 teaspoon salt
1/4 cup water
mint sprigs - 4

Shell the peas for the sauce first but the sauce itself can be prepared and kept warm as directed after the carrots go into the oven.

Trim and peel the carrots. Lay them in a buttered baking dish just large enough to hold them in a single layer. Sprinkle the carrots with the salt, pour in the water and tightly cover the dish with foil. Bake the carrots in a preheated 375 degree oven 45 minutes or until they are tender when pierced with a wooden toothpick.

Using a metal spatula to transfer the carrots, equally divide them among 4 warm dinner plates. Ladle some of the warm sauce across the carrots and decorate each plate with a sprig of mint. Serve the baked carrots immediately along with a warm bowl of the remaining pea sauce.

4 servings.

minted pea sauce

4 pounds unshelled peas - (4 cups shelled) or about 20 ounces frozen
mint leaves - (4 Tablespoons chopped)
1 cup water - divided
1/2 teaspoon sugar
1/2 teaspoon salt
1/8 teaspoon white pepper
8 Tablespoons unsalted butter

Shell fresh peas or allow frozen to thaw and drain completely in a colander.

Coarsely chop the mint leaves.

Bring the peas, mint, 1/2 cup of the water with the sugar, salt and pepper to boil in a saucepan over medium high heat. Reduce the heat to medium low and simmer the peas, covered, 20 minutes or until they are very tender. Pass the peas and their cooking water through a food mill set over a bowl. Discard skins that don't go through. Then liquify the purée in the blender. Melt the butter in a saucepan over low heat and stir in the liquified peas. Rinse out the container of the blender with the remaining 1/2 cup of water and add it to the liquified peas. Heat the sauce until it is hot. Cover the pan with a trimmed piece of paper towel and lid and keep the sauce warm over very low heat until serving.

3 cups

Note: Mint leaves must be fresh, no substitutes.

SPINACH ALFREDO

A light consommé jardinière precedes this rich entrée. Spinach Alfredo looks best served on white dinner plates and is accompanied by broiled eggplant. Serve a salad of red bell peppers vinaigrette with Italian bread then some poached figs for dessert.

spinach noodles - (recipe follows)
2 pounds untrimmed spinach - (16 packed cups trimmed)
3 quarts water
2 Tablespoons reserved drained spinach liquid - optional
3 quarts water
1 Tablespoon plus optional salt
1/4 cup pinenuts
1 cup heavy cream - at room temperature - divided
2 egg yolks - at room temperature - (see cooked eggs note)
8 Tablespoons butter - at room temperature - divided.
Parmesan cheese - (3/4 cup freshly grated)
Romano cheese - (1/4 cup freshly grated)
1/4 teaspoon freshly cracked black pepper

Prepare the spinach noodles in advance as directed.
Prepare, (do not bother to tear into bite size pieces) blanch and drain the spinach as directed. (See blanched spinach.) Reserve 2 tablespoons of the drained spinach liquid. Now, taking the spinach a handful at a time, squeeze it to remove any excess remaining moisture and cut it into 1/4 inch thick 'slices'. Spread the 'slices' out on a dinner plate.

(The spinach can be prepared 24 hours in advance up to this point, covered with plastic, and refrigerated. Bring it to room temperature before continuing with the recipe.)

(Now, start heating the 3 quarts of water, with the one tablespoon of salt, in a large kettle set over high heat, for the noodles.)

Meanwhile, using a heavy knife, coarsely chop the pinenuts and toast them in a dry pan over medium heat, about 3 minutes, stirring, until they are golden. Remove them from the pan immediately and reserve them.

In a small bowl beat one tablespoon of the cream into the yolks and reserve them.

Bring the remaining cream with 4 tablespoons of the butter to simmer, in a medium size heavy saucepan, over medium heat. Sprinkle in the spinach, stirring with a fork and warm it, about 4 minutes, until the spinach is heated through. Reduce the heat to low then sprinkle in the Parmesan and Romano, stirring with a fork until the cheese has melted. Remove the pan from the heat and stir in the egg yolks. The mixture should be just loose enough so that it will combine easily with the noodles. If it looks too thick, add a little of the reserved drained liquid, one teaspoon at a time, go easy, do not add too much. Now stir in the pepper and taste the mixture. If you think it requires a little salt, add it. Cover the pan with a paper towel and lid and keep it warm, off direct heat.

By now, the water should be boiling. Drop the noodles all at once into the water. Give them a stir with a wooden spoon and cook the noodles, covered with lid ajar, for from 2 to 5 minutes, depending upon how thin or thick they are, from the moment they are in the water regardless of when the water returns to boil or until they are tender but firm, adjusting the heat to keep the water slowly boiling, stirring occasionally. Drain the noodles, and in the still warm kettle, toss them with 4 tablespoons of the butter, cut in pieces.

Divide the noodles equally among 4 warm dinner plates, pushing them to the edges of each plate to make a space in the center. Spoon the spinach mixture, equally divided, into the center of the noodles and sprinkle one tablespoon of the reserved pinenuts over the spinach on each serving. Serve the spinach Alfredo immediately.

4 servings.

spinach noodles

1 pound untrimmed spinach - (8 packed cups trimmed)
about 2 cups unbleached all purpose flour
1/2 teaspoon salt
2 eggs - at room temperature

Prepare and blanch the spinach as directed, however allow it to blanch 5 minutes. (See blanched spinach.) Immediately turn the drained spinach into a basin of cold water for one minute. Then turn it into a colander, place a saucer with a moderate weight upon it on the spinach and allow it to drain for 30 minutes, turning it over a couple of times during that period. The yield should be about 1/2 tightly packed cup of drained spinach. Taking a small handful of the spinach at a time, squeeze out all remaining moisture and mince the spinach fine.

Sift 2 cups of the flour and the salt together into a mixing bowl. In another bowl, using a wire whisk, beat the eggs until they are light, then using a fork, stir the minced spinach into them. Now, using the fork, stir the egg mixture into the flour. The dough will take longer to form than other pasta dough and will be sticky. Work the dough with a lightly floured hand. Two cups of flour always seems to be enough for hand rolled pasta, but if the pasta is going to be rolled out by machine, add a little more flour for a firmer dough. Gather up the dough and place it on a lightly floured surface. Wash, dry and lightly flour your hands. Knead the dough vigorously, folding it over itself and pressing it out repeatedly with the heel of your hand. If the dough is going to be rolled out by machine, knead it for 3 minutes to form a cohesive mass, even though the pasta machine will knead the dough later. If the dough is going to be rolled out by hand knead it for 10 minutes. Since spinach dough is a little more moist than other doughs, you may want to wash, dry and lightly flour your hands and the work surface once or twice more. The spinach pasta dough will weigh about 18 ounces.

For machine (see utensils) rolled pasta, divide the dough into 8 pieces of equal weight and seal them in plastic. They do not need to rest. Roll out the dough as directed, stopping before passing the sheets of dough through the narrowest setting of the machine. Make the machine rolled noodles, like hand rolled noodles, slightly thicker than other types of noodles. (See machine rolled pasta.) Allow the sheets of spinach pasta to dry 30 minutes on each side before cutting, because of their moistness. (See machine cut noodles.) Now, run the sheets of pasta through the 1/4 inch wide noodle cutting rollers of the pasta machine as directed.

For hand rolled pasta, divide the dough into 4 pieces of equal weight, seal them in plastic and allow them to rest 1 hour at room temperature. Then roll out the dough as thin as possible as directed. (See hand rolled pasta dough.) Hand rolled spinach dough will not roll out quite as thin as other pasta doughs. Each sheet of dough will measure about 14 inches in diameter. Allowing the sheets to dry 30 minutes on each side first, because of their moistness, cut the sheets of pasta into 1/4 inch wide noodles as directed. (See hand cut noodles.)

Hang the machine or hand cut noodles up to dry until they are brittle, then break them into 4 inch long pieces. These noodles can be made well in advance of serving. In which case store them in an unsealed paper bag in a dry place. However, they do not keep quite as well as other dried noodles so use them up in about 1 week.

about 15 ounces dried spinach noodles

A reminder: The eggs called for in this recipe are extra large as are all the other eggs called for in the recipes in this book.

PAELLA

Offer purée of fava bean soup. Then, following this colorful paella, serve a crisp tossed salad mix II with crusty bread and a mild white cheese such as Farmer's cheese. The dessert must, of course, be chilled oranges.

1 cup long grain brown rice - 7 ounces
celery - 2 large ribs - (1 cup cut)
1 1/2 pounds baby artichokes - about 24 - (4 cups trimmed) - or 18 ounces frozen
1 pound 4 ounces green bell peppers - 4 medium small - (2 2/3 cups cut)
1 can pitted black olives - 6 ounces - (1/4 cup broken)
1 jar capers - 3 l/2 ounces - (l/3 cup) - (see note)
1 pound tomatoes - 4 small - (about 2 cups cut)
l/2 teaspoon saffron threads
2 Tablespoons boiling water
1 teaspoon celery salt

1 cup olive oil - divided
2 teaspoons salt - divided
l/2 teaspoon freshly cracked black pepper
2 Tablespoons honey - divided
4 Tablespoons fresh lemon juice

Steam the rice as directed. (See steamed long or short grain brown rice.) Allow the rice to become cold and reserve it.

Trim, scrape the strings from and thinly slice the celery crosswise.

Prepare the baby artichokes as directed. (See preparation of baby artichokes.) Or prepare the frozen artichokes as directed. (See preparation of frozen artichokes.) Then place the frozen artichokes in a colander and allow them to thaw and drain completely.

Core , trim away any white membrane from, and cut the peppers into 3/4 inch squares.

Drain, rinse and drain the olives and break them into pieces.

Drain, rinse and drain the capers.

Peel and seed the tomatoes as directed. (See peeled tomatoes and see seeded tomatoes) . Cut each tomato half into 6 wedges.

Crush the saffron into a tea cup, pour the boiling water over it and allow it to steep.

Now, drain the baby artichokes and blot them, or the thawed artichokes dry on paper towels.

Sauté the celery, sprinkled with the celery salt , in l/2 cup of the oil in a large frying pan (see utensils) over medium heat, 3 minutes. Add the artichokes, peppers, olives, capers, 1 teaspoon of the salt , the black pepper and 1 tablespoon of the honey. Stir the ingredients, then cook the vegetables, covered, for 12 minutes, stirring them once or twice . Using a slotted spoon, remove the vegetable mixture from the pan and reserve it .

Add the remaining l/2 cup of oil to the pan. When it is hot add the cold rice, 1 teaspoon of the salt, the saffron and steeping water,1 tablespoon of the honey and the lemon juice. Using a wooden spatula, gently stir the rice, until It is heated through, all the pan juices have been absorbed and the rice is a beautiful even yellow color throughout .

Now, carefully fold the reserved vegetable mixture and the tomatoes into the rice , stirring only enough to evenly distribute the vegetables. Cover the pan and continue to cook the paella for about 5 minutes longer, until the vegetables are well heated and the tomatoes have wilted. Bring the pan right to the table and serve the paella immediately.

6 servings

Note: Buy the large size capers, if available.

 UMBELLIFERAE PURÉE

The carrot family is presented in a molded purée. Have cream of asparagus for the soup course. Cauliflower florets would be a good choice to serve along with the purée. Next, serve a tossed salad of watercress and some warm rolls. Poached pears complete the dinner.

1/2 teaspoon caraway seeds
I I/2 pounds carrots - 8 large - (4 cups sliced)
about II ounces parsnips - 3 medium large - (2 cups sliced)
1 pound celeriac - I large - (3 cups sliced)
3/4 cup cooked farina - (cooked as directed on the package but without
using salt)
8 Tablespoons butter
2 teaspoons honey
I I/2 teaspoons salt
I/2 celery salt
I/4 teaspoon white pepper
parsley sprigs - a generous number

Toast the caraway seeds in a dry pan over medium heat stirring them for about 3 minutes until they take color and become fragrant. Remove them from the pan immediately and crush them fine in a mortar or use a spice grinder.   Reserve them.

Trim, peel and slice the carrots and parsnips, keeping them separate.

Trim, peel, quarter lengthwise then slice the celeriac.

In a large steamer steam the carrots over already simmering water 10 minutes. Add the parsnips and celeriac and steam the vegetables 25 minutes longer or until they are very soft.

Meanwhile make sure that the farina is well cooked and that all the water has been absorbed. (If the yield is more than 3/4 cup don't use the excess, it would unbalance the recipe.)

Purée the steamed vegetables and cooked farina together through a food mill set over a bowl.

Melt the butter in a large frying pan (see utensils) over medium low heat. Stir in the honey, salt, celery salt, pepper and reserved crushed caraway seed. Add the purée mixture and stir and turn it, using a spatula, for about 10 minutes to dry it out a bit.

Pack the purée into 4 heavily buttered, I cup ovenproof bowls. The top of the purée should be smooth flat and flush with the top of the bowl. (If there is an excess of purée, keep it warm and when the umbelliferae purée has been unmolded decorate the top of each mound with a dollop of the excess.) Bake the purée in a preheated 350 degree oven 25 minutes.

Remove the bowls from the oven and allow them to stand 15 minutes at room temperature. Run a thin knife around the inside edge of each bowl. Cover each bowl with a warm inverted dinner plate and holding the bowl and plate together, turn the two over. Give the back of the bowl a few taps with a wooden spoon to loosen the purée then carefully remove the bowl. Surround each serving with a wreath of parsley sprigs and serve the umbelliferae purée immediately.

4 servings

BLACK BEAN CHIMICHANGAS
with longhorn sauce

These black bean chimichangas have a spicy filling complimented by a mild cheese sauce. The chimichangas will look most attractive if they are served on oval dinner plates. Serve a home style tomato soup then follow the chimichangas with a salad course of avocados on the half shell. Tart pomegranates make a refreshing dessert .

iceberg lettuce - I average head
chimichangas filling - (recipe follows)
Longhorn sauce - (recipe follows)
2 cups plus peanut oil - (see note)
12 flour tortillas - at room temperature - (recipe follows)
cherry tomatoes - 24

Shred the lettuce fine and keep it refrigerated, sealed in plastic until serving.

Reheat the chimichangas filling and keep it warm as directed.

Meanwhile make the longhorn sauce and keep it warm as directed.

Heat the 2 cups of the peanut oil in a 10 inch cast iron frying pan over medium high heat. Place I/4 cup of the warm chimichangas filling in the center of each of 2 tortillas. Fold over 2 sides of each to cover the filling then fold over the ends to form square packages. Just before the oil smokes, slide the 2 packages, folded side down, into the pan and fry the chimichangas about I minute on each side until they are crisp and golden brown. Drain them for a second on paper towels and place the packages, side by side on a warm dinner plate. Ladle a small amount of the cheese sauce over them, surround them with the chilled shredded lettuce and decorate the plate with 4 cherry tomatoes. Serve the black bean chimichangas immediately along with a bowl of the warm Longhorn sauce. They will not wait, so everyone must wait their turn.

Prepare and serve the remaining chimichangas as directed above.

6 servings

Note: Add a little more oil to the pan if necessary as you fry the chimichangas to keep the oil level half way up the packages, but not higher.

chimichangas filling

I generous cup dried black turtle beans - 8 ounces
I bay leaf
1/2 cup long grain brown rice - 3 1/2 ounces
I can peeled tomatoes - 14 1/2 ounces - (about 2 cups)
2 packed teaspoons brown sugar
celery - I large rib - (1/2 cup diced)
green bell pepper - 1/2 medium - (1/2 cup diced)
I teaspoon salt - divided
6 Tablespoons peanut oil
I teaspoon celery salt
I Tablespoon plus I teaspoon ground cumin
2 teaspoons cayenne
I 1/2 teaspoons dried oregano

Soak the beans and cook them with the bay leaf as directed. (See boiled dried, shelled beans.) Do not over cook. Drain them discarding the bay leaf.

Steam the rice as directed. (See steamed long or short grain brown rice.)

Drain the tomatoes into a colander set over a bowl. Remove the stem buttons and cut the tomatoes small, leaving them in the colander to drain further. Dissolve the brown sugar in the drained tomato liquid in the bowl.

Trim, scrape the strings from and dice the celery small.

Core , cut away any white membrane from and dice the green pepper small.

Sauté the celery and green pepper, sprinkled with l/2 teaspoon of the salt in the oil in a large frying pan (see utensils) over medium heat 3 minutes . Using a slotted spoon, remove the vegetables from the pan and reserve them.

Add the beans and the rice to the oil in the pan. Sprinkle them with l/2 teaspoon of the salt , the celery salt , cumin and cayenne , stirring them with a wooden fork. Add the reserved vegetables , the tomatoes and the drained tomato liquid to the pan. Raise the heat to medium high and stir the mixture about 15 minutes until the liquid is absorbed.

(Up to this point the filling can be prepared in advance , cooled to room temperature then covered. If it is refrigerated, bring it to room temperature before continuing with the recipe.)

At serving time, add the oregano, crushing it and reheat the filling, uncovered over very low heat stirring it frequently.

filling for 12 chimichangas

flour tortillas

2 cups unbleached all purpose flour
l teaspoon baking powder
l teaspoon salt
l Tablespoon butter
l/2 to 3/4 cup cold water

Sift the flour, baking powder and salt together into a mixing bowl. Cut in the butter and work the flour through the butter with your finger tips until the mixture is granular. Using a fork stir in only as much of the water as is needed to form dough. Turn the dough out onto a work surface and knead it for 5 minutes. Shape the dough into a cylinder exactly 12 inches long. Using a ruler as a guide, cut the cylinder into l inch pieces. Seal the 12 pieces in plastic and allow them to rest 45 minutes.

On a lightly floured work surface, using a lightly floured rolling pin, roll out I piece of dough at a time into a thin disc, 10 inches in diameter. You can trim the edges of the disc to make it perfectly round but it isn't necessary. Cook the tortilla on a hot, dry griddle over medium heat only, 30 seconds on each side. Transfer the tortilla to a dinner plate and immediately cover it with 2 layers of a clean dish towel. Repeat with the remaining pieces of dough, stacking the tortillas on top of each other under the towel as they are made. The tortillas can be used right away or they can be allowed to cool completely, under the towel, then sealed in plastic and refrigerated up to 24 hours then brought to room temperature before they are used.

12 tortillas

Note: These flour tortillas are of course not completely cooked. They are cooked only enough to make them firm enough to handle . They will finish cooking when the chimichangas are fried. These homemade flour tortillas are much nicer than the store bought kind. They are supple , easy to handle, and they fry up light.

longhorn sauce

12 ounces Longhorn cheese - (3 cups grated)
6 Tablespoons butter
6 Tablespoons flour ,
I/4 teaspoon white pepper
I/2 teaspoon plus optional salt
3 cups milk - at room temperature

Coarsely grate the cheese and reserve it.
Melt the butter in a heavy saucepan over low heat. Using a rubber spatula, blend in the flour, pepper and the 1/2 teaspoon of salt, stirring constantly for 5 minutes. Slowly stir in the milk while raising the heat to medium until the mixture simmers and thickens. Remove the pan from the heat, and I/2 cup at a time, stir the reserved cheese into the sauce until it is melted and the sauce is smooth. You may want to add a little more salt now if the cheese is very mild. Cover the pan with paper towel and lid to keep the Longhorn sauce warm until serving.

about 4 I/2 cups

STROGANOFF

Yogurt rather than sour cream gives this stroganoff its special tang. Serve clear borscht first then have baked Savoy cabbage wedges with the stroganoff. Celery hearts vinaigrette is the salad course served with pumpernickel bread. Fresh plums will be the dessert this evening.

about 1 pound tofu - (4 cups diced) - (recipe follows)
about 1 cup plus 3 Tablespoons soy sauce - divided
1 cup dried black or shiitake mushrooms - (about 1 ounce)
3 quarts plus water
celery - 4 large ribs - (2 cups sliced)
8 ounces fresh mushrooms - large - (about 2 1/2 cups sliced)
4 ounces sweet Gherkin pickles - (1/2 cup sliced)
3 Tablespoons light molasses
3 Tablespoons dry sherry
1 cup yogurt - at room temperature
4 Tablespoons peanut oil
1 Tablespoon plus 1/2 teaspoon salt - divided
1 teaspoon celery salt
4 Tablespoons plus 2 teaspoons butter - divided
1/4 teaspoon freshly cracked black pepper
2 Tablespoons flour
12 ounces medium wide dried egg noodles

Prepare the tofu in advance as directed. Store bought tofu is perfectly acceptable but when you make it yourself you're always sure that it's fresh. Cut the drained tofu into 3/4 inch dice. Place the diced tofu in a bowl just large enough to hold it. Pour the 1 cup of soy sauce over the tofu or enough to keep it submerged. Allow it to marinate for 24 hours, covered and refrigerated, very gently stirring it around several times. Now, drain the tofu well.

In a small saucepan, bring the dried mushrooms in enough water to cover them (they float) to simmer over medium high heat, reduce the heat to low and simmer the mushrooms covered, 45 minutes. Drain them. (Save the strained liquid for a bouillon soup. See bouillon soups.) Trim off and discard the stems. (Save them for that bouillon soup.) Squeeze the mushroom caps to rid them of excess moisture and cut them into 3/16 inch thick slices.

Trim, scrape the strings from, and cut the celery, crosswise, into 1/4 inch thick slices.

Wipe the fresh mushrooms with a damp cloth and trim the butt ends of the stems. Cut the stems, crosswise, into 1/4 inch thick slices. Cut the caps, lengthwise, into 1/4 inch thick slices.

Drain the gherkins, cut them, crosswise into 1/8 inch thick slices and soak them in warm water 5 or 10 minutes to rid them of any excess sweetness. Drain them well.

In a cup, combine the 3 tablespoons of soy sauce, the molasses and sherry.

In a small bowl, stir the yogurt to make it smooth, then set the bowl in a larger bowl partially filled with warm water.

Prepare and set out all the foregoing ingredients in order, just as you would for an oriental stir fry dish.

Sauté the drained tofu in the oil in a large frying pan (see utensils) over medium high heat for about 7 minutes, turning it with a metal spatula until the dice are golden on all sides. Transfer the tofu to paper towels and reserve it.

(At this point set the 3 quarts of water with the 1 tablespoon of salt to boil in a large kettle over high heat.)

Add the celery, sprinkled with the celery salt, to what remains of the oil in the frying pan and sauté it 3 minutes over medium heat. Now, add 2 tablespoons of the butter, the soaked dried mushrooms and the fresh mushrooms to the pan, sprinkle with the 1/2 teaspoon of salt and the pepper and continue to sauté for about 8 minutes longer while increasing the heat to high until all the moisture has evaporated. Reduce the heat to low, sprinkle the flour over the vegetables and, using a wooden spatula, stir and turn them for 3 minutes. Remove the pan from the heat.

Now, drop the noodles all at once into the boiling water, stirring them with a wooden spoon. Cook the noodles, covered with lid ajar, about 6 minutes, or a little less than directed on the package, from the moment they are in the water, regardless of when the water returns to boil, until they are tender-firm "al dente," adjusting the heat to keep the water slowly boiling and stirring occasionally.

Meanwhile, return the pan to low heat, add the reserved tofu, pickles and the sherry mixture and, still using the wooden spatula, gently stir the stroganoff mixture 4 or 5 minutes until the tofu is heated through. Remove the pan from the heat and fold in the yogurt.

When the noodles are ready, drain them well and in the still warm kettle, toss them with the remaining 2 tablespoons plus 2 teaspoons of butter, cut in pieces. Spread the buttered noodles out in a ring on a large warm (blue) serving platter and fill in the center of the ring with the stroganoff mixture. Serve the stroganoff immediately while it's hot.

4 servings

tofu

1 heaping cup dried shelled soy beans - 8 ounces - (see note)
12 3/4 cups water - divided
nigari - 1 1/2 teaspoons crushed - (see note)

Cull the beans and soak them in enough water to cover them by 2 inches, 12 hours or overnight, no longer. Drain and rinse them. The yield will be about 3 3/4 cups soaked beans.

Purée no more than 1 cup of the soaked soy beans, with an equal amount of the water, at a time in the blender for 1 minute. Or process the same amount of beans and water in the processor for 20 seconds.

Line a colander, set over a very large soup kettle, with a double layer of wet, wrung out cheese cloth. Pour the puréed beans into the cheese cloth. Purée the remaining beans as directed, pouring the purée into the cheese cloth.

Reserve 1 cup of the water, then pour the remaining water all over the soy pulp. Tie the corners of the cheese cloth together so that no pulp can escape and place a saucer with a heavy weight upon it on the cheese cloth wrapped pulp. Allow the pulp to drain for about 15 minutes. Remove the colander from the kettle. (Discard the pulp on your garden.)

Place a heat diffuser under the kettle and bring the soy milk slowly to simmer, over medium heat, while stirring occasionally with a long-handled wooden spoon. When the milk simmers, stir it constantly for 5 minutes; be careful as the milk will boil up considerably.

Meanwhile, in a small saucepan, bring the reserved 1 cup of water to boil and dissolve the nigari in it.

Remove the kettle of soy milk from the heat. Slowly pour 1/3 of the nigari water into it, gently stirring the milk 3 or 4 times. Cover the kettle and allow the milk to stand 3 minutes. Now you should be able to see the tofu beginning to form. Sprinkle another 1/3 of the nigari water over the milk and gently stir only the very top of the milk. Cover the kettle and allow it to stand 3 minutes again. By now there should be nice fluffy tofu curds floating in clear yellow whey. If so, the tofu is ready to be drained. If not and the whey is still milky looking, sprinkle the rest of the nigari water over it and gently slide the wooden spoon down into the sides of the kettle to release any milk trapped at the bottom. Cover the kettle and let it stand another 3 minutes.

In either case, line a colander, set in the sink or over a basin, with a double layer of wet, wrung out cheese cloth. Now the tofu curds must be treated very gently. Carefully ladle, don't pour, the curds and whey into the cheese cloth. Then fold the cheese cloth over the tofu and set a saucer with a heavy weight upon it on the cheese cloth wrapped tofu. Allow the tofu to drain and compress for from 15 to 60 minutes, depending on how firm you want it to be. (I prefer 60 minutes.) Place the cheese cloth wrapped tofu in a bowl of cold water and unwrap it under water. Take the tofu out of the water; it is now ready to use.

The tofu may be kept refrigerated, submerged in a covered container of cold water, for up to 1 week, changing the water 3 or 4 times.

about 1 pound

Note: For 8 ounces of soy beans to yield 1 pound of tofu, the beans must be fairly fresh, that is less than 6 months old. If you know ahead of time that your soy beans are old, increase the amount of beans to 10 or 12 ounces but do not increase the water or nigari.

Nigari is a salt derived from sea water and is available at natural food stores.

ASPARAGUS HOLLANDAISE

Processor hollandaise sauce, made in ten minutes, is the wonder of the age. Indeed! Its great advantage is that a double recipe can be made at one time. It is slightly thinner than handmade hollandaise. I prefer handmade hollandaise. If you use a double boiler to make it in, as is often recommended, you may never learn to make handmade hollandaise. Be fearless and make it over direct heat. You will become well acquainted with your stove and sensitive to the sauce you are creating. Use a thin saucepan since it cools quickly when lifted and lift it frequently. I also prefer to use a rubber spatula as its broad blade controls the sauce well. Now, let's get on with the menu. Serve a mushroom bisque for the first course. Then accompany the asparagus hollandaise with baked helianthus tuberosa (jerusalem artichokes). Follow with a tossed salad mix I and some warm dinner rolls. Finish with ripe cherries.

3 pounds asparagus
2 cups handmade or processor hollandaise sauce - (recipes follow)
parsley - 4 sprigs

Prepare the asparagus and tie it in little bundles as directed. (See steamed asparagus.) But don't steam it until after you have made the hollandaise sauce.

Make the hollandaise sauce of your choice and keep it warm or reheat it as directed.

Steam the asparagus as directed. Remove the hot asparagus form the pan, using a pair of tongs. Lay the bundles on 4 warm dinner plates, cutting and removing the ribbons and dividing the asparagus equally. Spoon 1/2 cup of the warm hollandaise sauce across the center of each serving. Tuck a sprig of parsley on the side of each plate, and serve the asparagus hollandaise immediately.

4 servings

handmade hollandaise sauce

3 egg yolks - at room temperature - (see cooked eggs note)
1/2 teaspoon salt
pinch white pepper
1 Tablespoon fresh lemon juice - divided
12 Tablespoon unsalted butter - very cold
1 Tablespoon plus optional hot water

In a bowl, using a wire whisk, beat the yolks until they are light and set them aside.

Dissolve the salt and pepper in 1 teaspoon of the lemon juice in a small saucepan over low heat. Add 1/2 teaspoon of the butter. When it has melted, remove the pan from the heat and, using a rubber spatula, stir in the egg yolks. Return the pan to the low heat, stirring constantly until the yolks have absorbed the butter. Lift or remove the pan from the heat, add another 1/2 teaspoon of butter, return the pan to the heat, stirring constantly until the piece of butter has melted and been absorbed. Continue in this manner, lifting the pan, not allowing it to become too hot, and adding the butter until 4 tablespoons of butter have been used. Add 1 teaspoon of the lemon juice, then increase the additions of butter to 1 teaspoon at a time, adding each teaspoon in 2 thin slices. When 8 tablespoons of butter have been used, add the 1 remaining teaspoon of lemon juice, and increase the additions of butter to 2 teaspoons at a time, adding them in 2 thin slices each. When all the butter has been absorbed, the sauce will be quite thick. Thin it out with the 1 tablespoon of hot water or more as you desire. Hollandaise sauce is served warm, not hot.

1 cup

Note: For emergency procedures have a little pan of simmering water on the stove while you are making the sauce. If it looks at all granular, the sauce is breaking. If the heat is too high, the eggs will scramble. If the butter is added too quickly for the eggs to absorb, the sauce will either not thicken or will separate. In any case, remove the sauce pan from the heat immediately, add 1 teaspoon of simmering water to the sauce, beat it vigorously and continue making the sauce. This remedy can be repeated several times but the sauce will be thinner. If all else fails, the sauce can be started over again using 1 egg yolk and slowly adding the broken sauce to it.

To keep warm or reheat: Remove the pan from the heat, cover it with a paper towel and lid and set it in a basin of lukewarm, not hot, water. When hollandaise stands for even a short amount of time, the lemon flavor becomes more pronounced, so you may want to omit the last teaspoon of lemon juice if the sauce is to be kept warm or reheated. Hollandaise is reheated just as it was made over low heat, stirring constantly and lifting the pan frequently.

To make 2 cups of handmade hollandaise, make 2 sauces rather than trying to double the recipe and subject the eggs to heat for too long a period of time. Keep the first sauce warm while making the second sauce. Then stir the first into the second. Enough said!

processor hollandaise sauce

1 1/2 cups unsalted butter
6 egg yolks - at room temperature - (see cooked eggs note)
1 teaspoon salt
1/8 teaspoon white pepper
2 Tablespoons fresh lemon juice

Melt the butter in a saucepan over low heat. Then transfer the melted butter to a warm pitcher that pours neatly.

Place the yolks, salt, pepper and 2 teaspoons of the lemon juice into the processor. With the motor running, slowly pour 1/2 cup of the butter, in a very, very thin stream, in through the feed tube; this should take about 3 minutes. Add 2 teaspoons of the lemon juice then pour in another 1/2 cup of the butter in a thin stream; this should take about 2 minutes. Add 2 more teaspoons of the lemon juice and pour in the remaining butter in a slightly thicker stream; this should take about 1 minute.

Transfer the hollandaise to a saucepan, and warm it over very low heat for 4 minutes, while stirring constantly with a rubber spatula and lifting the pan frequently. The sauce will thicken slightly as it warms. Hollandaise sauce is served warm not hot.

2 cups

Note: To keep warm or reheat the processor hollandaise, read the handmade hollandaise recipe. (See handmade hollandaise sauce.)

CARROT SOUFFLÉ

A white, straight sided dish is the traditional soufflé dish, but an attractive oven-proof mixing bowl works well too. Let's start with sorrel soup. Next we'll have braised asparagus along with the soufflé and follow with a salad of Boston lettuce and some crusty rolls. Then we'll complete the meal with fresh pears.

8 ounces carrots - about 4 medium - (1 1/2 packed cups grated plus 2
Tablespoons sliced)
parsley leaves - (2 Tablespoons chopped)
1/2 teaspoon salt
4 Tablespoons butter - divided
1/4 cup water
1 cup milk - at room temperature
3 Tablespoons flour
1/8 teaspoon white pepper
2 teaspoons brown sugar
1 teaspoon celery salt

1/4 teaspoon ground coriander
dash mace
4 egg yolks - at room temperature
1 teaspoon dried marjoram
5 egg whites - at room temperature
1/4 teaspoon cream of tartar

Trim and peel the carrots. Starting at the tips of the carrots, cut off enough tiny, very thin slices to equal the 2 tablespoons and reserve them. Coarsely grate the remaining carrots.

Chop the parsley small and reserve it.

Heat the grated carrots, sprinkled with the salt, in 2 tablespoons of the butter in a medium size saucepan over medium heat 3 minutes. Add the water, reduce the heat to low and cook the carrots, covered, about 10 minutes until they are very soft. Uncover the pan, turn up the heat to medium high and stir the carrots for about 2 minutes to evaporate excess moisture. Then, in the blender or processor, purée the carrots with the milk. Reserve the purée.

Melt the remaining 2 tablespoons of butter in a heavy saucepan over low heat. Using a rubber spatula, blend in the flour and pepper stirring constantly until butter is absorbed. Slowly stir in the reserved purée, sugar, celery salt, coriander and mace, while increasing the heat to medium until the sauce simmers and thickens. Remove the pan from the heat and allow it to cool a few moments.

Meanwhile, in a large mixing bowl, using a wire whisk, beat the egg yolks until they are light. Then, very slowly beat in the carrot sauce. Then, whisk in the reserved parsley and the marjoram without crushing it.

Now, in a second large mixing bowl, using the electric mixer, beat the egg whites until they are frothy, add the cream of tartar and continue to beat the whites, at high speed now, until they are glossy and hold stiff but not dry peaks when the beaters are lifted.

Using a wooden spoon, stir 2 rounded tablespoons of the beaten egg whites into the carrot sauce. Then carefully slide the rest of the whites onto the top of the sauce. Using the wooden spoon or a rubber spatula, gently fold the beaten egg whites into the carrot sauce, inserting the spoon into the center of the whites bringing it down underneath, and then using an up and over rolling motion so as not to deflate the whites while intermittently rotating the bowl itself. Do not over do the mixing, a lot of fluffy white curds should still be visible.

Carefully slide half of the soufflé mixture into a buttered 6 cup soufflé dish. Sprinkle on the reserved carrot slices, then slide the rest of the soufflé mixture over them. Using a teaspoon, make a shallow track around the top of the soufflé mixture about 1 1/2 inches from the sides of the dish.

This will cause the soufflé to rise with an attractive break like a top hat. Bake the soufflé in a preheated 325 degree oven 45 minutes. Do not open the oven door during baking time. Serve the puffed and golden carrot soufflé immediately. It will not wait.

4 servings

 # FRIED RICE WITH SNOW PEAS

Have all the ingredients for the fried rice ready before dinner. When guests arrive, enjoy cream of sweet potato soup, then cook the fired rice. To serve the fried rice, if you like, bring the wok directly to the table and set it on a heat proof pie plate. Offer a salad of napa and some sesame crackers. Fresh pineapple will make the perfect desert.

1 1/3 cups long grain brown rice - about 9 1/2 ounces
celery - 2 large ribs - (1 cup diced)
6 ounces rutabaga - 1 piece - (1 cup diced)
1/2 pound unshelled peas - small - (1/2 cup shelled)
6 ounces red bell pepper - 1 medium - (1 cup diced)
about 9 ounces snow peas - young - (3 cups whole)
8 eggs - at room temperature - (see cooked eggs note)
6 Tablespoons peanut oil - divided
1/4 teaspoon liquid smoke
1 teaspoon celery salt - divided
1 1/2 teaspoon salt - divided
1/3 teaspoon freshly cracked black pepper
1 Tablespoon plus 1 teaspoon Oriental sesame oil
Japanese soy sauce

Steam the rice as directed. (See steamed long or short grain brown rice.) Let the rice cool to room temperature then refrigerate it, sealed in plastic, several hours.

Trim, scrape the strings from, and dice the celery the size of a small pea.

Peel and dice the rutabaga the size of a small pea.

Shell the small peas.

Core, cut away any white membrane from and dice the bell pepper the size of a small pea.

Remove the stems from and pull any strings from the snow peas.

Break the eggs into a bowl, but do not stir them. Set them aside. Pour 2 tablespoons of the oil into a 10 inch frying pan, for the eggs, and set it aside.

Place an 8 inch frying pan on or near the stove. Heat 4 tablespoons of the oil with the liquid smoke in a wok over high heat. Before the oil starts to smoke, add the celery, rutabaga and small peas, sprinkle with 1/2 teaspoon of the celery salt and stir fry 4 minutes, using a wok spatula or a long handled spoon. (At this point start heating the oil in the 10 inch frying pan over medium low heat.) Add the bell peppers and snow peas to the wok, sprinkle with the remaining 1/2 teaspoon of celery salt and stir fry 4 minutes longer. Reduce the heat under the wok to medium. Add the rice, sprinkle with 1 teaspoon of the salt and the black pepper and stir fry about 4 minutes longer until the rice is hot. Remove the wok pan from the heat and set it on the 8 inch frying pan.

Pour the sesame oil into a cup and set it near the stove. Now pour the eggs into the heated 10 inch frying pan and gently stir them around with a metal spatula so that the yolks break but remain separate from the whites as much as possible, for color effect, for 1 1/2 minutes. Sprinkle them with 1/2 teaspoon of the salt and the sesame oil and continue to stir for about 30 seconds longer, breaking up any curds that look too large to integrate well with the rice. Turn the eggs into the wok and gently stir them through the fried rice. Serve the fried rice with snow peas immediately along with more than one bottle of soy sauce on the table.

4 generous servings

STOCK VEGETABLE CHARLOTTE
with tomato cream sauce

The stock vegetable charlotte is an amazing little dish. Amazing because it provides six generous servings. Another great feature is that it makes a wonderful party dish since it is prepared in advance and served reheated. Serve a light herb broth, then accompany the charlotte with braised Savoy cabbage. Celeriac remoulade will be a good salad choice and poached pears a pleasant dessert.

8 slices firm, close grain, white bread
8 Tablespoons soft butter - divided
2 cups puréed stock vegetables (see puréed stock vegetables)
2 teaspoons honey
1 teaspoon salt
1 teaspoon celery salt
1/4 teaspoon black pepper
2/3 cup bread crumbs - (see bread crumbs)
Parmesan cheese - (1/3 cup freshly grated)
Romano cheese - (1/3 cup freshly grated)
5 eggs - at room temperature
tomato cream sauce (recipe follows)

Trim the crusts from the bread. Cut out a small circle of bread about 1 1/2 inches in diameter. Place it in the center of the bottom of a round, flat bottomed, 5 cup, oven proof mold. (See note.) Cut out triangular shapes of bread and neatly and tightly fit them around the circle, trimming off the tips and rounding off the outer edges of the triangles to do so. Cut out slightly tapered fingers of bread about 1 inch wide and stand them, narrow end down, tightly together around the sides of the mold and trim them so that they just meet the top edge of the mold. Remove the bread from the mold and, using 4 tablespoons of the butter, lavishly butter one side of each piece of bread. Neatly and tightly replace the pieces of bread in the mold, buttered side against the mold. Set the mold aside.

Melt the remaining 4 tablespoons of butter in a heavy saucepan over low heat. Add the puréed stock vegetables, honey, salt, celery salt and pepper and stir until the purée is warm and the ingredients are well blended. Remove the pan from the heat and stir in the bread crumbs and the cheeses. In a bowl, beat the eggs only until they are well blended then stir them into the purée mixture.

Pour the purée mixture into the bread lined pan, filling it right up to the top of the bread. If more than 1/8 inch of bread stands above the filling, trim it with a sharp knife.

Loosely lay a piece of buttered foil over the mold and bake the charlotte in a preheated 475 degree oven for 1 hour, with a cookie sheet set on the bottom shelf of the oven to diffuse the heat. Remove the mold from the oven, remove the foil (the charlotte will have puffed a bit) and allow the charlotte to cool completely, to room temperature. Cover the mold again, tight now, with foil and refrigerate it overnight. Allowing it to stand several hours gives the charlotte a firmer, more desirable texture. Before reheating the next day, allow 4 or 5 hours to bring the charlotte to room temperature. One hour before serving time, remove the tight foil and reheat the charlotte, loosely covered with foil again, in a preheated 325 degree oven for 45 minutes.

The tomato cream sauce can be prepared and kept warm during the time the charlotte is being reheated, as directed.

Remove the mold from the oven, remove the foil and allow the charlotte to stand 15 minutes. Cover the mold with an inverted, small, round, warm serving platter. Holding the platter and mold together, turn them over and lift the mold off the charlotte. Present the stock vegetable charlotte along with a bowl of the warm tomato cream sauce. At the table, slice the charlotte like a cake and let each diner ladle some of the sauce over his own serving.

6 servings

Note: The mold used here is an aluminum saucepan, 6 3/4 inches in diameter across the top, 5 1/4 inches in diameter across the bottom and 3 1/2 inches deep. Aluminum is desirable since the bread does not pick up an off taste from it, as can happen with other metals, due to the fact that it remains in the pan for as long as 24 hours.

tomato cream sauce

2 Tablespoons butter
3/4 cup tomato paste - 6 ounces
1 cup water
1/2 cup light cream
1/2 teaspoon salt
dash cayenne

Combine all the ingredients in a small, heavy saucepan over medium heat. When the sauce simmers, reduce the heat to low and simmer the sauce, very gently, covered with a piece of trimmed paper towel and lid, 35 minutes. Reduce the heat to very low to keep the sauce warm until serving.

about 2 cups

PARSNIPS À L'ORANGE

This old-time favorite has a great deal of eye appeal. Serve cream of asparagus soup then have buttered spinach with the parsnips. A vinaigrette salad of string beans served with bread and cheese will make a nice salad course. Blackberries over ice cream complete the picture.

1/2 cup shelled walnut halves
1 navel orange
1/4 cup orange juice
4 Tablespoons honey
pinch white pepper
pinch ground cloves
2 pounds parsnips - 10 medium - (6 cups sliced)
1/2 teaspoon salt
8 Tablespoons unsalted butter

Set aside 4 of the larger walnut halves. Using a sharp knife, chop the rest small. Toast the chopped nuts along with the 4 halves in a dry pan over medium heat, stirring for about 3 minutes until they are pale golden. Immediately transfer the nuts to a coarse strainer and shake the strainer to allow any little flakes of walnut skin to fall away. Reserve the walnuts, setting the 4 halves aside separately.

Cut the orange in half lengthwise. Cut 8 thin slices out of the center of each half, discarding the end pieces. Reserve the 16 orange slices.

In a small saucepan over very low heat, warm the orange juice, honey, pepper and cloves until the honey has melted. Keep the mixture warm over the low heat.

Meanwhile, trim, peel and cut the parsnips crosswise into 1/4 inch thick slices.

Sauté the parsnips, sprinkled with the salt, in the butter in a large frying pan (see utensils) over medium heat stirring them with a wooden spatula for 2 minutes. Add the orange juice mixture, cover the pan immediately and cook the parsnips 3 minutes. Increase the heat to high, uncover the pan and cook the parsnips 3 minutes more, stirring them with the wooden spatula. Add the reserved chopped nuts and cook about 2 minutes longer until the moisture has evaporated and the parsnips start to become golden.

Dividing them equally, mound the parsnips in the center of 4 warm dinner plates. Place 4 of the reserved orange slices around each serving of parsnips, tucking the slices under the parsnips so that the straight edges of the slices are hidden. Place 1 reserved walnut half on the top of each mound of parsnips and serve the parsnips à l'orange immediately.

4 servings

 SPANAKOPITTA

Greek spinach pie - a brownie pan is the perfect shape for it - not too deep. Avgolemono would be an ethnically appropriate soup to serve. Accompany this very delicious spanakopitta with some sautéed whole mushrooms. Follow with a salad of fennel in virgin olive oil and some coarse bread. Serve ripe apricots for the finale.

2 pounds untrimmed spinach - (16 tightly packed cups trimmed)
celery - 2 large ribs - (1 cup diced)
dill leaves - (1 packed cup)
Feta cheese - (1 1/4 cups crumbled)
1 teaspoon celery salt
4 Tablespoons olive oil
1/2 teaspoon salt
1/2 teaspoon freshly cracked black pepper
1 Tablespoon plus 1 teaspoon honey
2 Tablespoons fresh lemon juice
2 eggs - at room temperature
1/4 teaspoon freshly grated nutmeg
1/4 cup bread crumbs - (see bread crumbs)
6 Tablespoons butter
10 phyllo leaves - (see note)

Prepare and blanch the spinach as directed. (See blanched spinach.) Immediately turn the drained spinach into a basin of cold water for 1 minute. Then turn it into a colander to drain again. Taking a handful of the spinach at a time, squeeze it hard to remove moisture and coarsely chop it.
(The spinach can be prepared up to 24 hours in advance, sealed in plastic and refrigerated, then brought to room temperature before continuing with the recipe.)

Trim, scrape the strings from, and dice the celery small.

Strip the dill leaves from their branches and coarsely chop them.

Crumble the Feta cheese into small (not fine) even pieces.

In a large frying pan (see utensils) over medium heat, sauté the celery, sprinkled with the celery salt, in the oil for 3 minutes. Add the spinach, salt, pepper and honey. Cover the pan, reduce the heat to low, and warm the spinach for 5 minutes. Uncover the pan and start stirring and turning the spinach with a spatula for about 20 minutes while gradually increasing the heat to medium high until all moisture has evaporated. Reduce the heat to low and add the lemon juice and the dill leaves, stirring well with a fork for about 3 minutes to incorporate the dill into the spinach. Remove the pan from the heat to cool a bit.

In a mixing bowl, using a wire whisk, beat the eggs until they are light, then stir the nutmeg, spinach mixture, cheese and bread crumbs into them in that order.

Melt the butter in a small saucepan over low heat.

Unwrap the phyllo leaves and keep them covered with a towel (they dry out quickly) until they are all used. Lay 1 phyllo leaf in a buttered 7 by 11 by 1 3/8 inch deep, 5 3/4 cup baking pan. It will overhang the edges of the pan. Using a feather pastry brush, brush the phyllo leaf with some of the melted butter. Cover it with another leaf, butter it and repeat the process until 5 leaves have been used. Spoon the spinach into the lined pan and cover it with the remaining 5 leaves, brushing each leaf with melted butter. Trim the over-hanging leaves with a pair of scissors so that there is no more then 1 1/2 inches of overhang all around, then neatly tuck the overhang down into the sides of the pan. Brush the top of the spanakopitta with butter and pierce it through several times with a small skewer to allow steam to escape. Bake it in a preheated 350 degree oven for 45 minutes. Then allow the spanakopitta to stand at room temperature 20 minutes before serving.

6 servings

Note: Phyllo leaves are available in specialty stores. They are very, very thin sheets of fine pastry dough. If you buy them frozen, allow them to thaw in the refrigerator and be sure they are completely thawed before using them.

❧ CAULIFLOWER AND KASHA ❧
BAKED WITH CHEESE

Start this favorite dinner with home style tomato soup. The cauliflower and kasha baked with cheese, incidentally, is a very easy recipe to double for a greater number of guests. And sautéed green bell peppers make an especially good accompaniment. Serve tossed salad mix I after the main course, then poached apricots.

1 cup buckwheat groats - 6 1/2 ounces
3 Tablespoons butter
1 1/4 teaspoons salt - divided
1/4 teaspoon celery salt
1/4 teaspoon black pepper
about 1 pound cauliflower - about 2/3 small head - (4 cups florets)
8 ounces sharp Cheddar cheese - (2 cups grated)
1 cup milk - at room temperature
1 teaspoon English mustard powder
1/8 teaspoon white pepper
1 Tablespoon cold water
3 eggs - at room temperature

Steam the buckwheat as directed. (See steamed buckwheat.) Gently stir the butter, cut in pieces, 1/4 teaspoon of the salt, the celery salt and black pepper into the hot buckwheat.

Break the cauliflower up into even, not too small, florets and trim their stems. Steam the cauliflower until it is not quite cooked. (See steamed cauliflower florets.) Immediately turn the florets into a basin of cold water for 3 minutes. Drain them well and pat them dry with paper towels.

Coarsely grate the cheese and reserve it.

Bring the milk to simmer in a saucepan over medium heat. Immediately remove the pan from the heat and stir the grated cheese into it. In a cup, dissolve 1 teaspoon of the salt, the mustard powder and white pepper in the cold water, then stir the mixture into the cheese sauce. Allow the sauce to cool a bit. In a mixing bowl, using a wire whisk, lightly beat the eggs, then slowly stir the cheese sauce into them.

Now, spread the buckwheat in a buttered, flat, 8 1/4 inch in diameter by 1 3/4 inch deep 5 3/4 cup baking dish. Set the florets, stem side down into the buckwheat, close together so that they cover the dish. Carefully pour the cheese sauce over the florets, using the handle of a spoon to help it run down in between the florets if it looks as if it will overflow.

Bake the dish in a preheated 325 degree oven 45 minutes. Allow the cauliflower and kasha baked with cheese to stand 5 minutes at room temperature before serving

4 servings

Note: When cauliflower is broken up into large florets, their volume of cups per pound increases.

PETIT POIS À LA DUCHESSE

Petit pois à la duchesse is the ultimate presentation for garden fresh peas. Precede them with cream of carrot soup, accompany them with sautéed mushrooms and follow them with a tossed romaine salad and some French bread. Then serve fresh raspberries for a perfectly composed dinner.

2 pounds unshelled peas - (2 cups shelled)
shallot - (1 teaspoon minced)
parsley leaves - (4 teaspoons chopped)
2 1/2 pounds baking potatoes - 6 medium large
2 1/2 cups stock broth - (see stock broth)
1 bay leaf
1 1/2 cups plus 2 Tablespoons unsalted butter - divided
1 teaspoon salt
1 egg - at room temperature
3 egg yolks - at room temperature

Shell the peas.
Peel and mince the shallot.
Chop the parsley fine.
Butter a cookie sheet. With the aid of a ruler, trace 4 well separated circles, each 3 1/2 inches in diameter, in the butter with your finger. Set the sheet aside.
Peel and quarter the potatoes. Bring the potatoes to boil in the stock broth, with the bay leaf, in a large saucepan over high heat. Reduce

the heat to medium low and simmer the potatoes, covered, about 25 minutes or until they are very soft.

Meanwhile, clarify 1 cup, plus 6 tablespoons of the butter as directed. (See clarified butter.) Then in the small saucepan, wilt the minced shallot in the clarified over low heat. Do not allow the shallot to brown. Keep the butter warm.

Drain the cooked potatoes. (Reserve their cooking broth for a bouillon soup. See bouillon soups.) Pass the potatoes through a food mill set over a warm bowl. Add 4 tablespoons of the butter, cut in pieces, and the salt. Using the electric mixer, whip the potatoes, adding the egg and the yolks, one at a time until the potatoes are light and smooth.

Fit a pastry bag with a 1/2 inch fluting tip. Fold half the bag back over itself to form a collar. Fold the tip up to seal it off. Fill the bag with the whipped potatoes, pull up the collar and fill it again. Carefully, pipe the potatoes onto the circles on the baking sheet by gently twisting the bag. (Making separate rosettes close together is the most attractive method.) Make the potato rings 3 rows high. Put the potato rings in a preheated 400 degree oven, 15 minutes, until the edges and tips of the potatoes are golden. If the potatoes must wait a couple of minutes for the peas to be ready, leave them in the oven, and just turn off the heat and open the oven door slightly.

While the potato rings are in the oven, steam the peas as directed. (See steamed peas.) Then using a metal spatula, transfer the potato rings to 4 warm dinner plates and spoon the hot peas into them. If some of the peas spill over, so much the more attractive.

Pour the clarified butter into a small, warm serving bowl, stir in the parsley, and serve it along with the petit pois à la duchesse immediately. The diners spoon the warm butter sauce over their own servings.

4 servings

Note: There may be an excess of whipped potatoes left in the bag, but better too much than too little. Incidentally, the potato rings must be made with hot freshly whipped potatoes. Cold and reheated are not satisfactory.

SPRING FANTASY

A fantasy because chantrelle mushrooms don't appear in the woods in the spring. But if you dry chantrelles in the early fall, you can make your dreams come true. Chantrelles, fiddleheads, and helianthus tuberosa are a natural combination. First, serve cream of parsnip soup then present the spring fantasy on its bed of wild rice. A salad of dandelion greens will be appropriate with biscuits and Cheddar cheese. Offer fresh strawberries for desert.

about 10 ounces chantrelle mushrooms - (3 cups cut) - (see note)
1 cup wild rice - 8 ounces
1 pound fiddlehead ferns - (5 cups) - (see note)
1 1/2 pounds helianthus tuberosa (Jerusalem artichokes) - (4 cups sliced)
2 teaspoons salt
12 Tablespoons butter

Prepare, dry months in advance, then reconstitute the mushrooms as directed.

Prepare and steam the rice as directed. (See steamed wild rice.) Keep the rice warm over hot water.

Take the fiddleheads, a handful at a time, and hold them under a strong stream of running water to remove their paper skins. Blot them dry on paper towels.

Scrub the helianthus tubers with a stiff little brush under running water then dry them well. Trim the tubers and, without bothering to peel them, cut them crosswise, into 1/8 inch thick slices.

Sauté the mushrooms, fiddleheads and tubers, sprinkled with the salt, in the butter, in a large frying pan (see utensils) over medium for about 10 minutes, stirring them occasionally until they are all just tender.

Spread 3/4 cup of the wild rice on each of 4 warm dinner plates. Heap the equally divided vegetables on the center of the rice and serve the spring fantasy immediately.

4 servings

Note: Using a soft little brush, brush the tiny particles of debris from the forest floor off of the mushrooms. Trim, wipe with a damp cloth if necessary, and cut the larger mushrooms lengthwise into 3 or 4 pieces, leaving the smaller mushrooms whole. To dry the mushrooms, thread a fine needle with nylon thread and knot the end of it. Thread the pieces of large mushroom and whole small mushrooms onto the thread like beads on a necklace. Hang them up in an airy room for about 1 week, depending on the weather, until they are completely dry. Store the dried mushrooms in a sealed jar. To reconstitute the mushrooms, simmer them in enough water to cover them (they float) for 45 minutes. Drain them. (Save strained soaking liquid for a bouillon soup. See bouillon soups.) Squeeze the mushrooms to rid them of excess moisture. A word of caution: Never pick wild mushrooms unless you are knowledgeable in their identification and know exactly what you are picking.

Fiddleheads are the tightly furled fronds of a type of fern which look just like the heads of fiddles. They are picked when their little round fiddleheads have just poked above the ground. Look for them in the markets in the early spring.

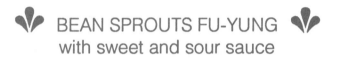

BEAN SPROUTS FU-YUNG
with sweet and sour sauce

Cream of kohlrabi soup starts off this special dinner for two. Sautéed snow peas will be the perfect accompaniment for the bean sprouts fu-yung, if you can handle two frying pans at once. Choose a tossed napa salad served with sesame crackers next. Finish with chilled tangerines.

2 ounces mung bean sprouts - (1 cup) - (recipe follows)
1/2 teaspoon plus salt - divided
1/4 cup peeled almonds - (see almonds)
celery leaves - small tender - (1/4 cup chopped)
sweet and sour sauce - (recipe follows)
4 Tablespoons peanut oil - divided
1 Tablespoon cornstarch - divided
1/8 teaspoon white pepper - divided
1 Tablespoon plus 1 teaspoon cold water - divided
6 egg whites - at room temperature - (3 in each of 2 cups) - (see cooked
eggs note)

Grow the sprouts in advance as directed. Pick any remaining mung bean skins from the sprouts. In a saucepan over high heat, bring to boil 2 cups of water with a pinch of salt. Add the sprouts and blanch them, uncovered, for exactly one minute from the moment they are in the water, regardless of when the water returns to boil. Drain and immediately turn the sprouts into a basin of cold water for one minute. Drain them thoroughly, blot them dry on paper towels, and place them in a bowl.

Chop the almonds small with a heavy knife. Toast them in a dry pan over medium heat for 3 minutes, stirring until they are golden. Immediately transfer them to the bowl with the sprouts.

Chop the celery leaves very small and mix them with the sprouts and nuts.

At this point, make the sweet and sour sauce and keep it warm as directed.

Heat 2 tablespoons of the oil in a 10 inch frying pan over medium heat. Meanwhile, in a mixing bowl, dissolve 1 1/2 teaspoons of the cornstarch and a pinch of the white pepper in 2 teaspoons of the cold water. Using a wire whisk, beat in 3 of the egg whites until they are frothy. Pour the egg mixture into the hot frying pan and allow it to set 15 seconds. Spread half of the bean sprout mixture over the eggs and sprinkle with 1/4 teaspoon of the salt. Using a metal spatula, immediately start pushing the edges of the omelet to the center until it forms a little cake about 5 inches in diameter and 1 1/2 inches thick. Turn the omelet over and cook it until it is a pale golden color on both sides. The omelet should be firm throughout but tender. The entire cooking process will take about 3 minutes; it requires a little technique that is easily acquired. Slip the omelet onto a warm oven proof dinner plate and keep it warm in a preheated 200 degree oven while you make the second omelet.

Drench the omelets with the warm sweet and sour sauce and serve the egg fu yung immediately.

4 servings

mung bean sprouts

1/4 cup dried mung beans
water

Soak the beans in enough warm water to cover them by 2 inches, overnight or for at least 8 hours. Drain them and spread the beans out in the bottom of an 8 cup china or glass bowl, hopefully with its own lid. Cover the beans with 3 layers of paper towels that are wet but not dripping with warm water. The beans must not be allowed to dry out but they must not be standing in water. Cover the bowl with its lid or a plate and put it in a warm place. The beans will sprout best at about 75 degrees. A glass bowl must be in a dark place as well. Allow the beans to stand for from 4 to 8 hours. Remove the towels, fill the bowl with warm water and slip off the skins which will have become loosened and float to the top. Drain the beans well, cover them again with warm wet paper towels and replace the lid. Continue to rinse and drain the beans at least 3 times a day (4 would be better if you have the time) always keeping them covered with paper towels and lid. The sprouts will be ready to eat in 3 or 4 days depending on the temperature; in the winter time they may take 5 days. Well developed mung bean sprouts should be about 1 1/2 to 3 inches long, fat and succulent. Wrap the drained sprouts in paper towels and seal them in a plastic bag. They keep well, refrigerated, 3 or 4 days.

about 6 cups

Note: Extra mung bean sprouts can be used in stir fry dishes and salads, etc.

sweet and sour sauce

3 Tablespoons corn starch
scant 1/4 teaspoon salt
4 1/2 Tablespoons soy sauce
1 1/2 Tablespoons dry sherry
1 Tablespoon California white wine vinegar
1 1/2 teaspoons honey
1 1/2 teaspoons light molasses
2 teaspoons unsalted butter

In a small saucepan, dissolve the cornstarch and salt in the water. Add the soy sauce, sherry, vinegar, honey and molasses. Bring the mixture to simmer over medium heat while stirring constantly with a rubber spatula. When the mixture simmers, reduce the heat slightly and continue to simmer and stir for 2 minutes then stir in the butter. Reduce the heat to very low; cover the pan with a trimmed piece of paper towels and lid and keep the sweet and sour sauce warm until serving.

about 2 cups

SECTION II

SPEZZATINO DI ZUCCHINI

HARICOTS JAUNES AU GRATIN

SOLONACEAE EN CAZUELA

CORN ON THE COB

YELLOW SQUASH PANCAKES with compound herb butter

KOHLRABI MOUSSE

SHISH-KABAB

STUFFED RED BELL PEPPERS

BENNINGTON POT PIES

TEMPURA

HOPPIN' JOHN WITH COLLARDS AND FRIED EGGS

STUFFED SCALLOPED SQUASH

DEEP DISH TOMATOES

HARICTOS VERTS COMBEAU

COUSCOUS THE STEW

JOLIES GATEAUX

STUFFED YELLOW SQUASH

CREOLE CASSEROLE

CHILES RELLEÑOS with salsa rojo

ASSIETTE JARDINIÈRE

STUFFED EGGPLANT

ZUCCHINI GRATINÉ

HARVARD BEETS WITH GREENS

STOCK VEGETABLES AND COUSCOUS WITH CHEESE

PEPERONI AL FORNO

CORN FRITTERS

RATATOUILLE

SWISS CHARD CRÊPES

INDIAN DINNER

STUFFED TOMATOES

SUMMER SQUASH CASSEROLE

EGGPLANT PARMIGIANA

SALSA VERDE TACOS

❧ SPEZZATINO DI ZUCCHINI ❧

This wonderful old recipe makes use of the zucchini juices in a very flavorful tomato sauce. Stracciatella would be an appropriate soup to serve and broccoli a good accompaniment for the zucchini. Sweet Italian frying pepper salad, crusty bread and smoked Mozzarella are a good choice for the salad course. Chilled purple grapes will complete the meal.

3 pounds zucchini squash - 8 medium, 7 to 8 inches long - (about 12 cups cut)
4 Tablespoons olive oil - divided
1 Tablespoon plus 2 1/2 teaspoons salt - divided
1 cup plus 2 Tablespoons tomato paste - 9 ounces
2 cups reserved drained zucchini liquid
1 teaspoon honey
1/4 teaspoon freshly cracked black pepper
1 teaspoon dried basil
3 quarts water
Parmesan cheese - (3 Tablespoons plus freshly grated) - divided
Romano cheese - (1 Tablespoon plus freshly grated) - divided
12 ounces dried orzo pasta
2 Tablespoons plus 2 teaspoons butter - at room temperature

Trim and thinly slice the zucchini crosswise.
Heat 1 tablespoon of the oil in a large frying pan (see utensils) over low heat. Place all the zucchini in the pan, sprinkling it with 2 teaspoons of the salt, layer by layer, as you do so. Cover the pan and allow the squash to warm for 10 minutes, turning it over 2 or 3 times during that period with a large spatula. Place a colander set over a bowl near the stove. Increase the heat to medium and continue to cook the squash, covered, 20 minutes longer, turning it over occasionally and as the zucchini releases its juices, carefully lift the pan, pour the juice through the colander and reserve it. Then, increase the heat to high and continue to cook the zucchini, uncovered now, turning it frequently until all moisture has evaporated. Transfer the zucchini to the colander.
Heat the remaining oil in a heavy, medium size saucepan over low heat. Add the tomato paste, measure out the 2 cups of reserved, drained liquid and slowly stir it into the paste. Add the honey and pepper and increase the heat to medium high. When the sauce simmers, reduce the heat to low and simmer the sauce, uncovered, 55 minutes, stirring occasionally. Add the basil, crushing it and simmer the sauce 5 minutes longer.

(At this point start heating the 3 quarts of water with 1 tablespoon of the salt in a large kettle over high heat for the orzo pasta.) Now carefully fold the reserved zucchini into the sauce and warm it over the low heat until it is heated through. Sprinkle in the 3 tablespoons of Parmesan and 1 tablespoon of Romano. Turn off the heat, cover the pan with paper towels and lid and keep the mixture warm.

When the water boils, drop the orzo in all at once, stirring it with a wooden spoon. Cook the pasta, covered with lid ajar, about 6 minutes or a little less than directed on the package, from the moment it is in the water, regardless of when the water returns to boil, until it is tender but firm, "al dente", adjusting the heat to keep the water slowly boiling and stirring occasionally. Drain the orzo well in a colander, then in the still warm kettle, toss the pasta with the butter, cut in pieces and 1/2 teaspoon of the salt.

Transfer the zucchini mixture, equally divided, to each of 4 very warm dinner plates, heaping it up, then wreath the zucchini with the equally divided orzo. Serve the spezzatino di zucchini immediately along with a bowl of the grated cheeses, mixed in a 3 Parmesan to 1 Romano ratio.

4 servings

Note: You will definitely need a 12 inch frying pan for this amount of squash.

HARICOTS JAUNES AU GRATIN

Start this summertime dinner with jellied consommé Madrilène. Steamed red skinned potatoes, wrapped in a white dinner napkin are served with the haricots jaunes au gratin. Watercress and French bread with unsalted butter is the salad course. Enjoy fresh blackberries for dessert.

2 pounds yellow string beans - (see note)
4 ounces Gruyère cheese - (1 cup grated)
1/2 cup bread crumbs - (see bread crumbs)
7 Tablespoons butter - divided
6 Tablespoons flour

1/8 teaspoon white pepper
2 cups stock broth - (see stock broth)
1/2 teaspoon honey
1 teaspoon salt
1/4 teaspoon ground rosemary - (see ground rosemary)
Parmesan cheese - (6 Tablespoons freshly grated)
Romano cheese - (2 Tablespoons freshly grated)

Trim off only the stem ends of the string beans. Steam them, about 1 minute short of the directed time, until they are tender but still quite firm. (See steamed string beans.) Immediately turn the steamed beans into a basin of cold water for three minutes. Drain them well in a colander then blot them dry on paper towels.

Coarsely grate the Gruyère and reserve it.

Toast the bread crumbs in 1 tablespoon of the butter in a frying pan over medium heat for 3 minutes, stirring constantly, until they are golden. Immediately tranfer them to a bowl and reserve them.

Melt 6 tablespoons of the butter in a heavy, medium size saucepan over medium heat. Using a rubber spatula, blend in the flour and pepper, stirring constantly for 5 minutes. Slowly stir in the broth, then add the honey and salt. When the sauce thickens and starts to bubble, remove the pan from the heat, and add the rosemary and Gruyère, still stirring until the cheese melts.

Lay the string beans, crosswise, in a buttered, 9 by 6 by 1 3/4 inch deep, 6 cup baking dish. Pour the sauce over them, while poking the handle of a spoon down among the string beans, to allow the sauce to run through them.

Toss the Parmesan and Romano with the reserved bread crumbs. Then spread the mixture, thick and even, over the string beans and sauce.

Bake the haricot jaune au gratin in a prehaeated 350 degree oven 25 minutes until the string beans are heated through and the bread crumbs are lightly browned. If the bread crumbs brown too quick, lightly cover the dish with foil.

4 servings

Note: When preparing this dish I only use freshly picked string beans from my own garden and take great care not to overcook them. Store bought beans are a different matter; be sure they are properly steamed before baking.

❦ SOLONACEAE EN CAZUELA ❦

Solonaceae en cazuela with its Mexican overtones tastes and looks best baked and served in an earthenware casserole dish, hopefully with matching lid. Cucumber soup is the first course, then serve coquillages along with the solanaceae en cazuela. Serve a simple black bean vinaigrette for the salad and chilled grapefruit sections for dessert. incidentally, solonaceae is the potato family.

1 pound green tomatoes - 2 medium - (2 cups diced)
1 pound red tomatoes - 2 medium - (2 cups diced)
12 ounces green bell peppers - 2 medium - (2 cuts cut)
12 ounces red bell peppers - 2 medium - (2 cups cut)
12 ounces eggplant - 1 medium small - (2 cups diced)
12 ounces boiling potatoes - 2 medium - (2 cups diced)
4 Tablespoons flour
1 1/4 teaspoons salt
1 teaspoon celery salt
3/4 teaspoon ground cumin
1/4 teaspoon cayenne
6 Tablespoons olive oil
1 Tablespoon honey
1 Tablespoon fresh lemon juice
1 teaspoon dried oregano

Remove the stem buttons and cut the green and red tomatoes into 3/8 inch dice.

Core the green and red bell peppers, trim away any white membrane and cut them into 3/8 inch squares.

Peel the eggplant and cut it into 3/8 inch dice.

Peel the potatoes and cut them into 3/8 inch dice.

Mix all the vegetables together in a large mixing bowl. Mix the flour, salt, celery salt, cumin and cayenne together in a cup, then sprinkle the mixture over the vegetables. Using 2 wooden spoons, toss the vegetables to coat them well with the flour mixture.

Transfer the vegetables to an oiled 12 cup casserole type baking dish or bowl and dribble the oil and honey over them. Cover the dish with a lid or foil and bake it in a preheated 350 degree oven for 45 minutes. Stir in the lemon juice and the oregano, crushing it and bake, still covered, 15 minutes longer. Remove the dish from the oven, uncover, and allow the solonaceae en cazuela to stand 10 minutes before serving.

4 servings.

 CORN ON THE COB

Grow it yourself if you love corn on the cob. To be sure that it is really fresh, go out to the garden just before dinner and pick it. Husk it right there and hide the husks under the mulch. If you're lucky enough to have sorrel growing in that garden you can have sorrel soup as well. And do you have some warm sun ripened tomatoes so that you can have a salad of sliced tomatoes? Let's hope you remembered to plant watermelon.

corn - 12 ears
butter
salt

Husk, trim and boil the corn as directed. (See boiled corn.) On a large serving platter, immediately wrap the drained ears in a clean linen towel and serve the corn on the cob right away. Have plenty of butter and more than one shaker of salt on the table.

4 servings

 YELLOW SQUASH PANCAKES
with compound herb butter

When you are preparing the compound herb butter to spread on the pancakes you might want to make up an extra amount as it is delicious on the accompaniment of green Romano string beans as well. Precede this main course with cream of red bell pepper soup and follow it with fresh coleslaw and some rye bread. Serve chilled cherries for dessert.

compound herb butter - (recipe follows)
6 eggs - at room temperature
1 cup matzoh meal
1 cup water
2 teaspoons honey

1 1/2 teaspoons celery salt
1/4 teaspoon freshly cracked black pepper
1 pound 10 ounces yellow straightneck squash - about 3 medium - (5 cups grated)
1 teaspoon salt
8 Tablespoons unsalted butter - divided

Prepare the compound herb butter as directed and keep it cold.

In a mixing bowl, using a wire whisk, lightly beat the eggs. Stir in the matzoh meal, water, honey, celery salt, and pepper and allow the batter to stand at least 20 minutes.

Meanwhile, trim, quarter lengthwise and scrape only the larger seeds out of the squash. Coarsely grate the squash. Then sauté it, sprinkled with the salt in 4 tablespoons of the butter in a frying pan (see utensils) over medium high heat for about 10 minutes, while turning it with a spatula, until all the juices have evaporated and the squash is tender. Transfer the squash to a bowl to cool a bit then stir it into the matzoh batter.

Melt 1 teaspoon of the butter per pancake in each of 2 frying pans (see utensils) over medium heat. Drop 3 tablespoons of the batter per pancake into the pans and spread it around with the back of the spoon. Each pancake should measure about 5 inches in diameter. Fry the pancakes 5 minutes on each side until the edges are golden brown. Be patient, don't hurry them. Transfer the pancakes, as they are cooked, to a warm heat proof serving platter, (they may overlap each other), and keep them warm in a 200 degree oven until they are all cooked. The yield should be 12 pancakes. Then serve the yellow squash pancakes immediately along with the compound herb butter.

4 servings

Note: I must confess that I use my 15 by 12 inch electric skillet, set at 300 degrees, to cook these pancakes because it is able to accommodate 6 pancakes at a time.

compound herb butter

summer savory leaves - (4 tablespoons minced) - (see note)
1 cup unsalted butter - at room temperature
1/2 teaspoon salt
pinch white pepper

Mince the summer savory leaves very fine. Then in a bowl, cream them with the soft butter, salt and pepper until the mixture is very smooth. Pack the mixture into 4 little ramekins or cups, cover them with foil, and allow them to stand 1 hour at room temperature. Then refrigerate the compound herb butter, keeping it covered, until it is firm.

4 servings

Note: Very likely, you will have to grow the summer savory yourself in order to have fresh leaves, as it is not often seen in the market. However, the plant is prolific and has many uses. Dried savory can not be substituted in this recipe.

KOHLRABI MOUSSE

Tomato essence begins this lovely summer dinner. The kohlrabi mousse is a very elegant dish and deserves to be unmolded onto a silver serving platter. Accompany it with corn, freshly cut from the cob and then serve a salad of zucchini vinaigrette, some bread and a little roundel of herbed cheese. Fresh plums will be the finale.

about 6 pound kohlrabi leaves - (about 4 pounds minus leaves) - 12 bulbs, 2 to 2 1/2 inches in diamter - (6 heaping cups sliced)
4 Tablespoons unsalted butter
1 cup heavy cream - at room temperature
1/2 teaspoon honey
2 teaspoons salt - divided
1/4 teaspoon white pepper
4 eggs - at room temperature
1 pound untrimmed kohlrabi leaves - (4 tightly packed cups trimmed)
2 quarts water
4 Tablespoons butter - (salted)
1/4 teaspoon freshly cracked black pepper
2 teaspoons fresh lemon juice

Reserving the leaves, trim, peel and quarter the kohlrabi bulbs. Steam them over already simmering water about 20 minutes or until they are very soft. Pass the kohlrabi through a food mill set over a bowl, then measure the purée. If it measures more than 2 cups, transfer it to a colander lined with a double layer of wet, wrung out cheese cloth set over a bowl. Place a saucer on the purée and press it gently to drain it. (Save any liqud for a bouillon soup. See bouillon soups.)

Melt the unsalted butter in a small saucepan over low heat. Remove it from the heat and allow it to cool a bit. Transfer the purée to the food processor, add the melted butter, cream, honey, 1 teaspoon of the salt and the white pepper and process 30 seconds. Add the eggs, one at a time and process 5 seconds after each addition. Alternatively place the purée in a mixing bowl and add the other ingredients in the order given, stirrring well after adding each egg. The finished mousse will simply have a coarser texture. Do not eliminate the food mill altogether in favor of the processor. The food mill removes fibers from the kohlrabi. For a really light and smooth mousse, use both the food mill and the processor.

In either case spoon the mousse mixture into a well buttered 1 quart tube pan. Tap the pan down, firmly, on the work surface, once or twice to eliminate air bubbles. Set the tube pan on a trivet (or use 2 chop sticks) in a large baking pan. Pour enough hot water into the baking pan to reach 3/4 of the way up the sides of the tube pan. Lightly cover the tube pan with buttered foil and place the waterbath arrangement in a preheated 325 degree oven and bake the mousse 90 minutes.

Meanwhile sort the kohlrabi leaves, setting aside 1 pound of only the smaller more tender leaves and discarding the rest. (Save them for that bouillon soup.) Cut away the stem and thick rib from each leaf, then rinse and drain them. Bring the 2 quarts of water with 1/2 teaspoon of the salt to boil in a large saucepan over high heat. Blanch the leaves, uncovered, for 10 minutes from the moment they are in the water, regardless of when the water returns to boil. Adjust the heat to keep the water slowly boiling and press the leaves down into the water with a long handled wooden spoon. Drain the kohlrabi leaves into a colander and immediately turn them into a basin of cold water for 1 minute. Then turn the leaves into the colander again, pleace a saucer with a moderate weight upon it on them and allow them to drain 10 minutes. Now, taking the leaves a small handful at a time, cut them into slices about 1/4 inch thick, then toss them in the colander, using a wooden fork to separate them. Reserve them.

When the kohlrabi mousse is done, a toothpick inserted in the center of the custard should come out clean. Remove the foil and lift the tube pan out of the waterbath. Allow it to stand 10 minutes. The mousse will have puffed but it will settle.

Meanwhile, melt the salted butter in a large saucepan over medium low heat. Add the kohlrabi leaves, sprinkle with 1/2 teaspoon of the salt and the black pepper and toss them in the butter for about 3 minutes until they are heated through. Remove the pan from the heat and sprinkle the leaves with the lemon juice.

Now, run the point of a sharp knife around the inside edges of the tube pan. Cover the pan with an inverted, round, flat warm serving platter. Holding the platter and tube pan together, turn them over, tap the back of the pan with a wooden spoon then lift it off the mousse. Heap the kohlrabi leaves into the center of the molded ring and serve the kohlrabi mousse immediately.

4 serving

 SHISH-KABAB

Serve jellied consommé Madrilène to commence this lovely rather middle eastern dinner. Oval dinner plates are both practical and attractive to serve the shish-kabab on. For total effect, leave the vegetables on the skewers, provide each guest with a pot holder (clean) and allow them to remove the skewers themselves. Next, serve a fennel salad accompanied by pita bread and finish with fresh apricots.

2 cups wheat berries - 14 ounces
1 1/4 cups plus water
about 1 pound boiling potatoes - 16 little, new, 1 to 1 1/4 inches in diameter
- (3 heaping cups whole)
1 1/2 pounds red bell peppers - 4 medium, 6 ounces each
about 6 ounces mushrooms - 16 medium, 1 1/2 inches in diameter caps -
(2 cups whole)
about 12 ounces zucchini squash - 2 slender, medium, about 7 to 8 inches
long - (3 heaping cups cut)
12 ounces eggplant - 1 slender, medium small - (2 1/2 heaping cups)
2 cups red wine vinegar
1 1/2 cups olive oil - divided
2 Tablespoons honey

1 teaspoon liquid smoke
1 inch piece cinnamon stick
1/2 teaspoon whole allspice
1/4 teaspoon black peppercorns
5 whole cloves
1 bay leaf
1 Tablespoon plus 1 teaspoon plus salt - divided
2 cups yogurt
1/2 cup pinenuts - 2 ounces

Soak, boil and drain the wheat berries as directed. (See boiled wheat berries.) Reserve them.

Bring enough water to cover the potatoes by 1 1/2 inches to boil in a saucepan over high heat. Add the potatoes and blanch them, uncovered, 10 minutes from the moment they are in the water regardless of when the water returns to boil, adjusting the heat to keep the water slowly boiling. Drain them, turn them into a basin of cold water, slip off their skins and leave them in the water.

Quarter the bell peppers lengthwise, core them and cut away any white membrane.

Wipe the mushrooms with a damp cloth, trim the butt ends of the stems and leave them whole.

Trim the zucchini and cut it crosswise, into 1/2 inch thick slices. Reserve 16 slices.

Select tender young eggplant and trim but don't peel it. Cut it crosswise into 1/2 inch thick slices. Cut each slice into pie shaped thirds. Reserve 16 pieces. (Save any excess zucchini or eggplant for a bouillon soup. See bouillon soups.)

Bring the vinegar, 1 cup of the oil, the 1 1/4 cups of water, the honey, liquid smoke, cinnamon, allspice, peppercorns, cloves, bay leaf and 1 teaspoon of the salt to simmer in a large saucepan over medium high heat. Add the red peppers and the mushrooms and simmer them, uncovered, for 5 minutes from the moment they are in the liquid regardless of when the liquid returns to simmer, adjusting the heat to keep the liquid simmering. Remove the pan from the heat. This will soften the red peppers and mushrooms just enough to keep them from splitting when they are threaded onto the skewers.

Now, drain the potatoes and place them, with the zucchini and the eggplant, in a large bowl, then pour the marinade liquid, with the red peppers and mushrooms, over them. Set a plate with a heavy weight upon it on the vegetables, pressing it down, to keep the vegetables submerged and marinate them 6 hours or all day.

Before serving, drain the vegetables, reserving the marinade liquid, and thread them onto 8 skewers. A potato goes on first, then a red pepper, folded over so that it's double, then a zucchini, horizontally, so that it looks like the face of a clock, then a mushroom, pierced up through the center of the stem, then an eggplant, pierced through the point of the pie shape and out through the skin so that it looks like a fan. Repeat the sequence of vegetables once again.

Set 2 cake racks on a large jellyroll pan. Lay the skewers on the cake racks. Lightly salt the vegetables and brush them with a pastry brush dipped in the reserved marinade. Broil the vegetables, 6 inches from the heat source under a moderately hot broiler, for 10 minutes. Turn the skewers over, lightly salt and brush the vegetables again with the marinade and broil them 10 minutes longer. The vegetables should be just nicely browned around the edges.

Meanwhile, using a wire whisk, lightly beat the yogurt in a serving bowl until it is liquid and set aside.

Using a heavy knife, coarsely chop the pinenuts and toast them in a large dry frying pan (see utensils) over medium heat, for about 3 minutes, stirring, until they become fragrant and start to brown. Remove the pan from the heat, add 1/2 cup of the oil and the reserved wheat berries, sprinkled with 1 tablespoon of the salt. Return the pan to low heat and stir the wheat berries until they are well heated.

When the shish-kabab are ready, divide the wheat berries, equally, among each of 4 warm dinner plates, spreading them out. Then, lay 2 skewers on top of the grain on each plate and serve the shish-kabab immediately, along with the bowl of yogurt which is to be used as a sauce.

4 servings

Note: The broiler should be hot but not too hot, otherwise the vegetables will become charred before they are cooked.

 STUFFED RED BELL PEPPERS

These stuffed red bell peppers are almost heaven, served with buttered lima beans. Have cream of Burssels sprouts soup first, then, after the main course serve a tossed salad mix II and some homemade bread. Chilled canteloupe will complete this meal.

celery - 1 large rib - (1/2 cup diced)
2 pounds red bell peppers - 4 large, 8 ounces each
about 4 ounces green bell pepper - 1 small (1/2 cup diced)
corn - 1 ear - (1/2 cup kernels) - or about 3 ounces frozen
1 1/4 teaspoons plus salt - divided
10 eggs - at room temperature - (see cooked eggs note)
5 Tablespoons light cream - at room temperature
1/4 teaspoon celery salt
6 Tablespoons butter - divided
pinch cayenne
1/4 teaspoon freshly cracked black pepper

Trim, scrape the strings from and dice the celery.

Select well shaped red bell peppers with flat "bottoms" that will sit up properly by themselves. Cut a "lid" out of the stem end of each pepper by carefully cutting a circle down into the pepper in such a way as to retain as much of the "height" of the pepper as possible. Pull the "lid" out, then clean out the pepper, carefully cutting away any white membrane. Reserve the red pepper cups. Remove the flesh from around the "lids" and dice it.

Core, removing any white membrane and dice the green bell pepper. Measure the diced red and green peppers, separately. If either measures more than 1/2 cup, do not use the excess, it would unbalance the recipe. (Save any excess for a bouillon soup. See bouillon soups.)

Prepare and boil the corn as directed, but boil it only 7 minutes. (See boiled corn.) Immediately, turn the drained corn into a basin of cold water for 5 minutes. Drain again and carefully cut the kernels from the cob, separating them and crumbling them into a bowl. If you are using frozen corn, blanch the still frozen corn in enough boiling water to cover it by 1 1/2 inches, in a saucepan, covered with lid slightly ajar, over high heat for 1 minute from the moment the corn is in the water, regardless of when the water returns to boil, stirring the corn with a wooden spoon. Drain it and immediately turn it into a basin of cold water for 3 minutes. Drain and blot it dry on paper towels.

Lightly sprinkle the insides of the red pepper cups with salt, set them on a buttered baking sheet and bake them in a preheated 350 degree oven, 25 minutes.

Meanwhile, break the eggs into a mixing bowl. Add the cream, and using a fork, stir the eggs only enough to just break the yolks. Set the eggs aside.

Sauté the celery, sprinkled with celery salt, in 3 tablespoons of the butter in a large frying pan (see utensils) over medium heat, 2 minutes. Add the diced red and green peppers, sprinkle with 3/4 teaspon of the salt, the cayenne and black pepper and sauté 5 minutes more. Add the corn, sprinkle with 1/2 teaspon of the salt and cook 1 minute longer. Reduce the heat to low and add 3 more tablespoons of the butter to the pan. When the butter has melted, pour the eggs over the vegetables and allow them to set for 1 minute. Then, using a metal spatula, carefully sitr the eggs through the vegetables, taking care not to chop the eggs, until the eggs are evenly cooked but still tender and moist. The eggs will take about 10 minutes to cook.

By now the red pepper cups should be just about done, tender but firm when pierced with a wooden toothpick. Remove the baking sheet from the oven and spoon the hot scrambled egg mixture into the peppers, heaping it up. Transfer the stuffed red bell peppers to 4 warm dinner plates and serve them immediately.

4 servings

BENNINGTON POT PIES

Select deep rather than wide bowls for these pot pies so that the biscuits cover the bowls properly; four inches in diameter is ideal. First, serve sopa de cacahuete then follow the pot pies with a tossed escarole salad. Offer fresh apricots to finish.

celery - 4 large ribs - (2 cups sliced)
about 9 ounces string beans - (2 cups cut)
corn - 4 ears - (2 cups cut) - (see note)
8 ounces zucchini squash - 2 small, 6 inches long - (2 cups cut)
1 pound tomatoes - 2 medium - (2 cups cut)
1 cup plus 3 Tablespoons all purpose flour - divided
1 1/4 teaspoon salt - divided
1 teaspoon sugar
1/2 teaspoon freshly cracked black pepper
fresh thyme leaves - (1 Tablespoon plus 1 teaspoon) - (see note)
10 Tablespoons butter - cold - divided
1 1/2 teaspoons baking powder
1/4 teaspoon baking soda
6 Tablespoons buttermilk

Trim, scrape the strings from and cut the celery, crosswise, into 1/4 inch thick slices.

Trim the stems from and cut the string beans, crosswise, into 3/4 inch long pieces.

Husk the corn and with a sharp knife cut the kernels from the cob. Separate and crumble the kernels into a bowl.

Trim the stems from the zucchini and quarter them lengthwise. Cut the quarters, crosswise into 1/2 inch long pieces.

Peel and seed the tomatoes as directed. (See peeled tomatoes and see seeded tomatoes.) Then cut the tomatoes into 1/2 inch dice.

Mix all the vegetables together in a large mixing bowl, sprinkle the 3 tablespoons of flour over them, and using 2 wooden spoons, toss the vegetables to coat them well with the flour. Then tightly pack the evenly divided vegetables into each of 4 buttered, 2 cup, oven proof bowls, mounding them. Sprinkle each bowl with 1/4 teaspoon of the salt, 1/4 teaspoon of the sugar, 1/8 teaspoon of the pepper and 1 teaspoon of the thyme leaves. Now cover each bowl of vegetables with 2 tablespoons of thinly sliced butter. Tightly cover each bowl with foil, set them on a baking sheet for convenience and bake them in a preheated 375 degree oven 45 minutes.

Meanwhile, prepare a buttermilk biscuit batter. Sift the 1 cup of flour, 1/4 teaspoon of the salt, the baking powder and baking soda into a bowl. Cut in 2 tablespoons of the butter and work the flour through it with your finger tips until the mixture is granular. Then just lightly stir in the buttermilk. Divide the batter into 4 equal parts and with lightly floured hands on a lightly floured surface, shape them into 4 large biscuits 1/2 inch smaller in diameter than the diameter of the bowls.

After the bowls have been in the oven the 45 minutes, remove them from the oven and turn the oven up to 450 degrees. Remove the foil from the bowls and carefully give the vegetables a stir. Don't be concerned if the vegetables appear undercooked at this point. Lay 1 biscuit on top of the vegetables in each bowl, leaving at least 1/4 inch of breathing space all around the edge. When the oven has reached temperature, return the bowls to the oven and bake them 15 minutes longer. Remove the bowls from the oven and allow the Bennington pot pies to stand at least 15 minutes before serving.

4 servings

Note: Bennington pot pies is a summertime dish so use only fresh corn and fresh thyme please!

 TEMPURA

Someday I'd like to get one of those small, deep fryers that you can set right on the dinner table and do tempura in a ceremonious manner before the eyes of my guests, the way it should be done. Have the exotic cream of sweet potato soup for the first course. Then, after the tempura serve a salad of tossed napa and some sesame crackers. Present fresh pineapple for dessert.

assorted vegetables - (about 8 cups whole and cut)
1 1/3 cups long grain white rice - about 9 1/2 ounces
dipping sauce - (recipe follows)
4 cups corn oil
1 Tablespoon Oriental sesame oil
1 egg
1 cup stock broth - ice cold - (see stock broth)
1/2 cup flour
1/2 cup cornstarch
1 teaspoon salt

Prepare the vegetables. Wipe and leave small mushrooms whole. Trim stems and strings from young string beans and snow peas and leave them whole. Peel and cut root vegetables into 1/4 inch thick slices, giving each type a distinctive shape. Break cauliflower and broccoli florets up small. (See preparation of baby artichokes.) Drain and blot dry on paper towels. Trim and cut eggplant, asparagus and use parsley sprigs too, etc, etc, etc.

(All the vegetables can be prepared in advance and sealed in paper or plastic, keeping each type of vegetable separate. If they are refrigerated, bring them to room temperature before continuing with the recipe.)

Steam the rice as directed. (See steamed long or short grain white rice.) Keep the rice warm or reheat it over gently simmering water.

Meanwhile make the dipping sauce as directed.

(Allowing about 15 minutes for the corn oil and sesame oil to heat to temperature together, heat the oils in a deep saucepan, with a cooking thermometer clipped to the inside of it, over medium high heat to 375 degrees. Or use an electric deep fryer set at 375 degrees.)

Arrange the vegetables, keeping each type separate, on a large tray.

In a small mixing bowl, using a fork, beat the egg and stir the stock broth into it. Sift the flour, cornstarch and salt together and add them, all at once, to the egg mixture. Stir the mixture just enough to dissolve large lumps of flour. The batter must be rough and thin and used immediately while it's cold.

Divide the dipping sauce into 4 small cups and set the cups in the center of each of 4 warm dinner plates. Then spread 1 cup of warm rice out around the cup on each plate—just before the vegetables are placed on it.

Using a pair of tongs, dip 1 piece of vegetable at a time into the batter, then hold it up for a second to allow excess batter to drip off, now lower it into the hot oil. In 3 to 4 minutes the little fritter will be a delicate golden color and the vegetable will be cooked. Using a skimmer or slotted spoon, lift it out of the oil, allow it to drain a second and place it on the bed of rice around the dipping sauce. Do not crowd the fryer, frying about 5 assorted pieces of vegetables at once should be the limit. As you work, skim little excess drips of batter off of the oil, discarding them on a paper towel.

Serve each serving of tempura, immediately, as it is completed. The number of pieces of vegetables in each serving will depend on appetite. As in other deep fried dinners everyone waits their turn. Alternatively, fry pieces of one type of vegetable at a time. Serve them on a platter and let everyone serve themselves, so no one waits. Be sure to save an assortment of vegetables for the chef who as always waits till last. The tempura is eaten with either fingers or chopsticks, dipping it into the dipping sauce.

4 servings

dipping sauce

about 8 ounces daikon - 1 piece - (1 cup grated) - (see note)
ginger root - (1/2 teaspoon grated)
1 cup stock broth - (see stock broth)
4 Tablespoons Japanese soy sauce
2 Tablespoons distilled white vinegar
2 Tablespoons honey

Trim and chop the daikon.
Peel and grate the ginger on a medium fine grater.
Combine all the ingredients in the blender and purée. Or process the ingredients 5 seconds in the processor. Transfer the dipping sauce to

a bowl and stir down the foam. Alternatively simply grate the daikon on the same medium fine grater as the ginger, then combine the ingredients in a bowl.

about 2 1/2 cups

Note: Daikon is a very large, long white Japanese radish.

HOPPIN' JOHN
WITH COLLARDS AND FRIED EGGS

Cream of red bell pepper soup makes a good prelude to this soul satisfying dish. Follow the hoppin' john with a salad of pressed cucumbers and some homemade biscuits. Then enjoy fresh peaches.

1 cup long grain brown rice - 7 ounces
1 cup dried blackeyed peas - about 7 1/2 ounces (see note)
1 bay leaf
1 pound untrimmed collard greens - (4 tightly packed cups trimmed)
2 quarts water
2 1/2 teaspoons salt - divided
8 Tablespoons peanut oil - divided
10 Tablespoons butter -divided
1 Tablespoon plus 1 teaspoon honey -divided
1/2 teaspoon liquid smoke
2 teaspoons celery salt - divided
1/4 teaspoon freshly cracked black pepper
1 teaspoon liquid hot red pepper
4 eggs - (see cooked eggs note)
cider vinegar

Cook the rice as directed. (See steamed long or short grain brown rice.)

Cook the blackeyed peas with the bay leaf as directed. (See boiled dried shelled beans.) Drain the peas discarding the bay leaf.

Measure the steamed rice and drained boiled peas. If either measures more than 3 cups, do not use the excess, it would unbalance the recipe. (Save any excess rice or peas for a bouillon soup. See bouillon soups.)

Remove the stems and any thick center rib from the collard leaves, rinse and drain them. Bring the 2 quarts of water with 1/2 teaspoon of the salt to boil in a large saucepan, over high heat. Blanch the leaves, uncovered, for 10 minutes from the moment they are in the water, regardless of when the water returns to boil. Push them down into the water with a longhandled wooden spoon and adjust the heat to keep the water slowly boiling. Drain the collards into a colander and immediately turn them into a basin of cold water for 1 minute. Then turn the leaves into the colander again, place a saucer with a moderate weight upon it on them and allow them to drain 10 minutes. Taking the collards, a handful at a time squeeze them, chop them and toss them in the colander, using a wooden fork to separte them. Set them aside.

In a large saucepan over low heat, warm 4 tablespoons of the oil, 4 tablespoons of the butter, 1 teaspoon of the salt, 2 teaspoons of the honey, the liquid smoke, 1 teaspoon of the celery salt and the black pepper. Gently stir in rice and peas and warm the hoppin' john mixture, covered, 5 minutes or until it is heated through. Now, to facilitate matters, spread the equally divided hoppin' john out on 4 warm dinner plates and keep them warm in a 200 degree oven.

In a large saucepan, over medium low heat, warm 4 tablespoons of the oil, 4 tablespoons of the butter, 1 teaspoon of the salt, 2 teaspoons of the honey, 1 teaspoon of the celery salt and the liquid hot red pepper. Add the reserved collard greens, tossing them with the wooden fork about 3 minutes or until they are heated through.

At the same time fry the eggs in a large frying pan over medium heat in 2 tablespoons of the butter for 2 minutes. Cover the pan and cook them 1 minute longer until the tops are just set.

Remove the plates from the oven and spread the collards in the center of the hoppin' john, then lay a fried egg on the center of the collard greens. Serve the hoppin' john with collards and fried eggs immediately. Have a cruet of cider vinegar on the table, a sprinkling of it enhances all the flavors.

4 servings

Note: When available, fresh blackeyed peas can be substituted for the dried, in this dish. In which case, allow 3 pounds of unshelled blackeyed peas which will yield about 3 cups of shelled peas. Cook the shelled, fresh peas, with the bay leaf, in enough simmering water to cover them until they are just tender.

❦ STUFFED SCALLOPED SQUASH ❦

This dish has a great deal of eye appeal. If you must buy your squash as opposed to growing it, be sure that it is small, young and fresh. Home style tomato soup will be the first course for this summertime dinner. After the stuffed scalloped squash, serve tossed salad mix I along with some warm bread. Follow with chilled cherries.

corn - 3 ears - (1 1/2 cups kernels) - or about 9 ounces frozen
1 1/2 pounds unshelled peas - (1 1/2 cups shelled) - or about 7 1/2 ounces
frozen
9 ounces carrots - 3 large - (1 1/2 cups diced)
2 pounds scalloped squash - 4 small, 8 ounces each, 4 inches in diameter
8 ounces or more Brie cheese - cold
3/4 teaspoon salt
pinch white pepper
2 Tablespoons plus 2 teaspoons butter
parsley - 4 springs

Prepare and boil the corn as directed, but boil it only 5 minutes. (See boiled corn.) Immediately, turn the drained corn into a basin of cold water for 5 minutes. Drain again and carefully cut the kernels from the cob, separating them and crumbling them into a bowl. (Do not use small scrapings.) If you are using frozen corn, simply allow it to thaw and drain completely in a colander, then blot it dry on paper towels.

Shell and steam the peas as directed, but steam them only 8 minutes. (See steamed peas.) Immediately turn them into a basin of cold water for 3 minutes, then drain them well. If you are using frozen peas, blanch the still frozen peas in enough boiling water to cover them by 1 1/2 inches in a saucepan, uncovered, over high heat for 3 minutes from the moment they are in the water, regardless of when the water returns to boil, stirring the peas with a wooden spoon. Make sure they are undercooked. Drain and immediately turn them into a basin of cold water for 3 minutes. Drain again. In either case, blot the peas on paper towels.

Trim, peel and cut the carrots into 3/8 inch dice. Steam them, over already simmering water, 6 minutes. Immediately turn the carrots into a basin of cold water for 3 minutes; drain them and blot them dry on paper towels.

Using a small knife, cut a 1 1/2 inch in diameter cylinder down into the core of the squash around the stem and pull it out. Then scrape out any remaining seeds with a teaspoon.

Trim the rind from the cheese and divide it into 4 equal pieces. Keep the cheese cold. It's best to have extra cheese on hand in case the squash cavities are a little larger than expected.

Set the squash upside down in a buttered baking dish, lightly cover them with foil and bake them in a preheated 375 degree oven for 25 minutes. Remove the dish from the oven, remove the foil and turn the squash right side up. Stuff the cavities with the cheese. Return the dish to the oven and bake the squash, uncovered, 10 minutes longer, until the cheese is well melted. (Watch it! Don't allow the dish to stay in the oven too long or the cheese will run all over.)

Meanwhile, reheat the corn, peas and carrots, sprinkled with the salt and pepper, in the butter, in a medium size saucepan, covered, over medium low heat for about 5 minutes, until they are well heated. Spread the vegetable mixture out on a warm, 10 inch pie plate or similar flat serving dish.

As soon as the squash are done, set them on the mixed vegetables and decorate the top of each squash with a sprig of parsley. Serve the stuffed scalloped squash immediately.

4 servings

 DEEP DISH TOMATOES

A soufflé dish, especially if it's glass, will do nicely for this dish. To serve, scoop the potatoes onto the dinner plates, then spoon the tomatoes over the potatoes. Choose cream of string bean soup to commence. Then buttered Brussels sprouts will go well with the deep dish tomatoes. Next, a crisp tossed salad of chicory and some whole wheat bread would be nice. Offer peaches to complete this dinner.

3 pounds tomatoes - 6 medium
2 teaspoons salt - divided
1 teaspoon sugar
1/4 teaspoon freshly cracked black pepper
3/4 teaspoon dried thyme
9 ounces cucumber - 1 slender, average, about 8 inches long
4 Tablespoons butter - at room temperature - divided

3 pounds baking potatoes - 4 extra large
water
1/2 cup milk - at room temperature

Peel and seed the tomatoes as directed. (See peeled tomatoes and see seeded tomatoes.) Slice them and lay the tomatoes in a buttered, deep, 6 cup baking dish or bowl. In a cup, mix 1 teaspoon of the salt, the sugar, pepper and the thyme, crushing it, and sprinkle half the mixture over the tomatoes. Peel and slice the cucumber thin and spread it over the tomatoes. Cover the cucumber with the rest of the tomatoes and sprinkle the remaining herb mixture over the tomatoes. Dot the tomatoes with 2 tablespoons of the butter, cut in pieces, and bake the dish, uncovered, in a preheated 375 degree oven for 1 hour.

Meanwhile, peel and quarter the potatoes. Bring the potatoes to boil in enough water to cover them by 1 1/2 inches in a saucepan, covered with lid slightly ajar, over high heat. Reduce the heat enough to keep the water slowly boiling and cook the potatoes about 25 minutes or until they are quite soft. Plan the timing so that the potatoes have just finished boiling when the tomatoes are ready to come out of the oven.

Now, turn off the oven, open the door and wait for the tomato liquids to stop boiling before removing the dish from the oven. Remove the dish from the oven and turn the broiler on.

Next, bring the milk to simmer in a small saucepan over medium heat. Drain the potatoes and transfer them to a warm mxing bowl. Using the electric mixer, whip them with 2 tablespoons of the butter, cut in pieces, 1 teaspoon of the salt and only enough of the hot milk to make the potatoes light and fluffy. Then drop heaping tablespoonsful of the potatoes over the tomatoes and run the dish under the preheated broiler, 2 inches from the heat source, for 2 minutes or until the tips of the whipped potatoes are golden brown. Serve the deep dish tomatoes immediately.

4 servings

HARICOTS VERTS COMBEAU

Use only the freshest string beans here. It is essential that the parsley be Italian and make sure that the cashews are fresh too. The success of the haricots verts combeau rests on the quality of these three ingredients. Have a cold curried buttermilk soup, then, following the main course, serve a tossed escarole salad and some crisp dinner rolls. Fresh apricots are a natural choice for dessert.

2 pounds green string beans - (about 7 cups cut)
celery - 4 large ribs - (2 cups cut)
12 ounces red bell peppers - 2 medium - (2 cups cut)
1 pound mushrooms - medium - (5 cups sliced)
Italian parsley leaves - (1/2 cup chopped)
1 cup roasted cashews - 6 ounces - (see cashews)
1 Tablespoon plus 1 teaspoon cornstarch
3 Tablespoons cold water
1 Tablespoon fresh lemon juice
2 teaspoons salt - divided
8 Tablespoons butter
1/2 teaspoon freshly cracked black pepper
1 Tablespoons plus 1 teaspoon honey

Select fresh young string beans and trim off their stems. Cut them, diagonally, into 1 to 1 1/2 inch long pieces. Steam them over already simmering water about 2 or 3 minutes or until they are half cooked. Immediately turn them into a basin of cold water for 3 minutes. Drain them well and blot them dry on paper towels.

Trim, scrape the strings from and cut the celery, diagonally, into 1/4 inch thick slices.

Quarter the bell peppers lengthwise, core them and cut away any white membrane. Cut the quarters crosswise into 1/4 inch wide strips.

Wipe the mushrooms with a damp cloth. Trim the butt ends of the stems and slice each mushroom into thirds, lengthwise.

Coarsely chop the parsley leaves.

Using a heavy knife, coarsely chop the cashews.

In a small cup, dissolve the cornstarch, in the cold water, add the lemon juice and reserve it.

Sauté the celery and bell peppers, sprinkled with 1 teaspoon of the salt in the butter, in a large frying pan (see utensils) over medium heat for 2 minutes. Add the string beans, mushrooms, the remaining 1 teaspoon of salt, the black pepper and the honey. Combine the ingredients well, cover the pan but do not turn down the heat, and cook the mixture 8 minutes. Uncover the pan, add the cashews, turn up the heat to medium high and cook for 2 minutes to reduce the pan liquids a bit. Turn the heat down to medium again, add the parsley, give the reserved cornstarch mixture a stir, pour it into the pan and using a rubber spatula, stir the string bean mixture constantly for about 2 minutes until the pan liquids become thickened and glossy. Serve the haricots verts combeau, immediately, right from the pan.

4 servings

 COUSCOUS THE STEW

Technically, couscous is a grain. In North Africa the grain is steamed over a stew in a two part vessel called a couscoussière. The lower part of the vessel being a pot in which the stew cooks and the upper part a steamer for the grain. The stew is then served over the grain. The combined dish is usually simply called couscous. This slightly updated version requires no special utensil. A chilled consommé Madrilène will make a good first course for this colorful dinner. Then serve a crisp salad of tossed chicory with some pita bread after the spicy couscous. Oranges will be the refreshing dessert.

2 cups commercially precooked couscous - 14 ounces
1/2 cup peeled almonds - about 3 ounces - (see almonds)
3/4 cup dried chick peas - about 6 1/2 ounces
3/4 cup dried fava beans - about 4 ounces
2 bay leaves
3 cups reserved cooking liquid
about 9 ounces carrots - 3 large - (2 cups cut)
about 10 ounces celeriac - 1 medium small - (2 cups cut)
about 10 ounces white turnips - 2 medium large - (2 cups cut)
about 10 ounces sweet potato - 1 medium - (2 cups cut)
about 13 ounces cucumber - 1 large, 10 inches long - (2 cups cut)
about 12 ounces tomatoes - 3 small - (2 cups cut)
8 ounces untrimmed spinach - (4 packed cups trimmed)
1 Tablespoon plus 1/2 teaspoon salt - divided
1 teaspoon celery salt
1 teaspoon sweet Hungarian paprika
1 teaspoon ground coriander
1 teaspoon ground cumin
1 teaspoon ground turmeric

1 1/2 teaspoons cayenne - divided
1/2 teaspoon ground ginger
1/2 teaspoon ground cloves
1/2 teaspoon freshly grated nutmeg
4 Tablespoons butter
1/2 cup golden raisins - about 3 ounces
1 Tablespoon fresh lemon juice
2 teaspoons honey
6 Tablespoons olive oil

Steam, refrigerate and knead the precooked couscous as directed, adjusting the amount of water and salt. (See steamed couscous the grain.) Keep it refrigerated.

Cut the almonds lengthwise into little sticks and toast them in a dry pan over medium heat, stirring about 3 minutes until they are golden. Remove them from the pan immediately and reserve them.

Soak the chick peas and fava beans, separately, then cook them separately, each with a bay leaf as directed. (See boiled dried shelled beans.) Make sure they are well cooked. Drain the chick peas and fava beans saving only the chick pea cooking liquid and if necessary, add to it enough fresh water so that the total amount of liquid measures 3 cups. Reserve the liquid, the bay leaves and the cooked chick peas and fava beans.

Meanwhile, keeping the carrots separate, trim, peel and cut into large, 1 inch dice, the carrots, celeriac, turnips and sweet potato.

Peel and quarter the cucumber lengthwise. Discard the seeds and cut the quarters crosswise into 1 inch pieces.

Peel the tomatoes as directed. (See peeled tomatoes.) Remove the stem buttons. Quarter the tomatoes lengthwise then cut the quarters in half crosswise.

Wash, drain and trim the spinach as directed. (See washed and trimmed spinach.)

In a teacup combine 1 teaspoon of the salt, the celery salt, paprika, coriander, cumin, turmeric, 1 teaspoon of the cayenne, the ginger, cloves and nutmeg.

At this point start reheating the steamed couscous with the reserved almonds in the butter in a large saucepan, uncovered, over very low heat, stirring it occasionally.

In a large, covered soup kettle, bring the 3 cups of reserved cooking liquid with the bay leaves, chick peas and fava beans plus the combined spices, the raisins, lemon juice and honey to boil over medium high heat.

Meanwhile, sauté the carrots, sprinkled with 1/2 teaspoon of the salt, in 1 1/2 tablespoons of the oil in a large frying pan (see utensils) over medium heat for 5 minutes. Transfer them, with their cooking oil, to the kettle and lower the heat under the kettle just enough to keep the liquid slowly boiling.

Sauté the celeriac, turnips and potato together, sprinkled with 1 1/2 teaspoons of the salt in 3 tablespoons of the oil for 5 minutes. Transfer them, with their cooking oil, to the kettle and cook the stew 10 minutes, keeping the liquid slowly boiling.

Now, sauté the cucumbers, sprinkled with 1/2 teaspoon of the salt, in 1 1/2 tablespoons of the oil for 3 minutes. Transfer them, with their cooking oil, to the kettle, add the tomatoes and continue to slowly boil the stew 5 minutes longer.

Then, using a wooden spoon, gently stir the spinach leaves, a few at a time, in with the vegetables. When all the spinach is in the kettle, cook the stew, uncovered, 5 minutes more. Serve the stew while the spinach leaves are still bright green.

Working quickly, heap the equally divided, warm grain in the center of each of 4 well warmed dinner plates. Using a slotted spoon, arrange the vegetables all around the heaps of grain.

Pour the remaining stew liquids into each of 2 small, warm pitchers, each about 1 cup in size. Stir 1/2 teaspoon of the cayenne into the liquid in one of the pitchers.

Serve the couscous immediately. The diners pour some of the stew liquids over their grain from whichever pitcher they prefer.

4 servings

Note: If celeriac is unavailable, celery can be substituted.

 JOLIES GATEAUX

These pretty vegetable cakes are a very appealing dish to children of all ages. I use four little enameled saucepans to make them in; I prefer their slightly wide and shallow shape. The dimensions of the little pans are 4 1/2 inches in diameter at the top, 3 1/2 inches in diameter at the bottom and 2 inches deep. You may want to change the proportions of the ingredients in the recipe slightly to accommodate whatever shape molds or for that matter baking dishes you are using. Mushroom bisque will begin this festive dinner. Offer a wild rice pilaf with the jolies gateaux if you like. Watercress salad with some French bread and Camembert will comprise the salad course. Then finish with fresh rasperries.

2 pounds baking potatoes - 4 medium large
1 teaspoon plus salt - divided
1/4 teaspoon white pepper
1 teaspoon dried marjoram
8 ounces yellow straightneck squash - 1 medium, about 8 inches long
4 ounces carrots - 2 slender medium
1 1/2 pounds unshelled peas (1 1/2 cups shelled) - or about 7 1/2 ounces
frozen
8 ounces green string beans - about 40
8 ounces yellow string beans - about 40
8 ounces Brussels sprouts - about 20 small
about 11 ounces cherry tomatoes - 20
12 Tablespoons unsalted butter
parsley - 4 leaves - (not sprigs)

Boil the potatoes (yes boil the baking potatoes), without peeling them, as directed. (See boiled potatoes.) Peel them and pass them through a food mill set over a bowl. Stir the 1 teaspoon of salt, the pepper and the marjoram, crushing it, into the potatoes.

Trim and thinly slice the squash crosswise. Steam it over already simmering water 5 minutes. Immediately, turn it into a basin of cold water for 2 minutes, drain it and blot it dry on paper towels.

Trim, peel and thinly slice the carrots crosswise. Steam them over already simmering water 5 minutes. Immediately, turn them into a basin of cold water for 2 minutes, drain them and blot them dry on paper towels.

Shell the fresh peas; or allow the frozen peas to thaw and drain completely in a colander, then blot them dry on paper towels. In either case the peas need no precooking.

Cut the green and yellow string beans, crosswise into pieces 1/4 inch shorter than the sides of your molds. You will probably get 2 pieces out of most of the string beans. Steam the green and yellow string beans, separately, over already simmering water 6 or 7 minutes or until they are about three quarters cooked. Immediately, turn them into a basin of cold water for 3 minutes, drain them and blot them dry on paper towels.

Trim the Brussels sprouts and steam them over already simmering water, about 14 minutes or until they are just barely tender when pierced with a wooden toothpick. Immediately, turn them into a basin of cold water for 5 minutes, drain them and blot them dry on paper towels.

Peel the cherry tomatoes just the same as directed for larger tomatoes; but don't bother to remove their tiny stem buttons. (See peeled tomatoes.)

(All the vegetable preparations can be done well in advance. Cover them tight or seal them, separately, in plastic. If you refrigerate them be sure to bring them to room temperature before continuing with the recipe.)

Before assembling the gateaux, butter 4, round, flat bottomed 1 2/3 cup molds, well, and refrigerate them 15 minutes. Very thickly, butter them again and refrigerate them again, 20 minutes. At the same time melt the 12 tablespoons of butter in a small saucepan.

To assemble, lay a parsley leaf in the center of the bottom of each mold. Center a slice of squash on top of it and then arrange the carrot slices around the squash so that they touch the squash and each other, but leave a 1/4 inch space around the edge of the bottom of the mold. Be a little selective with the slices of squash and carrots to make the pattern come out right. Lay the peas close together to form a ring around the carrots and against the bottom of the sides of the mold.

Now, lay alternate green and yellow string beans up against the sides of the mold, standing them on the peas as it were, packing them close together and pressing them into the butter to make sure they stand upright.

Lightly sprinkle the vegetables with salt. Then carefully cover the sides and bottom of the mold of vegetables with 3/4 of the potatoes, working with a spatula and probably your fingers. Don't press them so hard that you disturb the pattern of vegetables.

Next, fill the hollow of potatoes with a mixture of Brussels sprouts, tomatoes and peas, all lightly salted, until the mold is almost full. Cover these vegetables with the remaining potatoes, leaving the ends of the string beans uncovered. Don't mound the potatoes.

Now, slowly and evenly, pour the melted butter over the last layer of potatoes, piercing the potatoes a couple of times with a thin skewer to allow the butter to penetrate down into the mold. Lay the remaining squash slices in a tight overlapping circle over the potatoes and lightly sprinkle them with salt.

Lightly cover each mold, with a piece of buttered foil and bake the gateaux, in a preheated 350 degree oven, 45 minutes. Remove the molds from the oven, remove the foil and allow them to stand 10 minutes. One at a time, cover each mold with a warm, inverted dinner plate. Holding the plate and mold together, turn them over, tap the mold with a wooden spoon, then lift it off the gateau et voila! Serve the jolies gateaux immediately.

4 servings

❦ STUFFED YELLOW SQUASH ❦

Yellow crookneck squash make more attractive stuffed squash than do the straightnecked variety because of their gracefully curved necks and large seed cavities. Sopa di tortilla is the soup course. Braised kohlrabi accompanies the stuffed squash while tortillas go nicely along with tossed salad mix II. Chilled green grapes make a refreshing dessert.

6 ounces green bell pepper - 1 medium - (1 cup diced)
about 2 pounds yellow crookneck squash - 2 very large, about 10 inches
long, about 1 pound each
corn - 4 ears - (2 cups kernels) - (see note)
2 Tablespoons yellow mustard seeds
8 ounces Monterey Jack cheese - (2 cups grated)
1 teaspoon salt - divided
2 Tablespoons corn oil
2 Tablespoons butter
1 teaspoon celery salt
1 teaspoon ground cumin
1/4 teaspoon cayenne
1 teaspoon honey
1 teaspoon dried oregano
2/3 cups whole wheat bread crumbs - (see bread crumbs)
2 eggs - at room temperature

Core, trim any white membrane from and dice the bell pepper.

Cut the squash in half, lengthwise, scoop out and discard the seeds. Using a thin edged spoon, carefully scoop out the flesh, leaving a squash shell about 1/4 inch thick, then chop the flesh. Set the 4 squash shells aside.

Husk the corn and with a sharp knife cut the kernels from the cob. Separate and crumble the kernels into a bowl.

Toast the mustard seeds in a dry pan over medium heat for about 3 minutes stirring, until they all pop. Immediately remove the seeds from the pan and reserve them.

Coarsely grate the cheese and reserve it.

Sauté the diced peppers, sprinkled with 1/2 teaspoon of the salt, in the oil, in a large frying pan (see utensils) over medium high heat, 5 minutes. Using a slotted spoon, remove the peppers from the pan and reserve them.

Reduce the heat to low. Add the butter, chopped squash flesh and corn, sprinkle with 1/2 teaspoon of the salt, the celery salt, cumin, cayenne and the honey to the pan and cook the vegetables, covered, for 10 minutes.

Uncover the pan, add the oregano, crushing it, the reserved mustard seeds and the fried peppers. Turn the heat up to medium high again and cook the vegetables, stirring, for 3 minutes longer, until all the juices have evaporated. turn the mixture into a large bowl to cool for about 10 minutes. Then stir the reserved grated cheese and the bread crumbs into the vegetables. Now using a wire whisk, lightly beat the eggs in a small bowl then thoroughly stir them into the stuffing mixture.

Using the large spoon, stuff the squash shells with the stuffing mixture. Set them on a buttered baking pan and bake them in a preheated 375 degree oven, for 35 minutes. Transfer the stuffed yellow squash to a warm serving platter and serve.

4 servings

Note: The corn must be fresh, no substitutes.

 CREOLE CASSEROLE

Cream of string bean soup begins this dinner with a slight southern drawl. Serve braised turnips with the Creole casserole. A salad of tossed dandelion greens with biscuits follows. Finish with blackberries over ice cream.

1 can peeled tomatoes - 28 ounces - (3 1/2 cups)
1 can peeled tomatoes - 16 ounces - (2 cups)
8 Tablespoons butter - divided
2 Tablespoons tomato paste
1 bay leaf
2 Tablespoons light molasses
1 Tablespoon plus 2 teaspoons light brown sugar
1 Tablespoon soy sauce
1 teaspoon cider vinegar
1 teaspoon liquid hot red pepper
3 drops liquid smoke
1/2 teaspoon celery salt
1/8 teaspoon ground cinnamon

pinch ground cloves
1 can whole yellow hominy - 15 ounces - (about 1 1/3 cups drained)
celery - 2 large ribs - (1 cup cut)
6 ounces green bell pepper - 1 medium - (1 cup cut)
about 8 ounces okra - about 40, 1 1/2 to 3 inch pods - (2 cups cut)
1 1/2 cups water
1 1/2 teaspoons salt - divided
1/2 teaspoon ground turmeric
1/2 cup yellow hominy grits
2 eggs - at room temperature

Turn the tomatoes into a colander, set over a bowl. Holding each tomato over the colander, remove the stem button and carefully quarter it lengthwise then cut each quarter in half crosswise. Return the tomatoes to the colander and allow them to drain for about 10 minutes. Measure out 2 1/2 cups of the drained liquid and reserve it. Let the tomatoes continue to drain until they are called for. (Save any remaining drained liquid for a bouillon soup. See bouillon soups.) The drained tomatoes should measure about 2 1/2 cups.

Melt 2 tablespoons of the butter in a deep (because of spattering) heavy, medium size saucepan over low heat. Add the tomato paste and slowly stir the 2 1/2 cups of reserved liquid into it. Add the bay leaf, molasses, sugar, soy sauce, vinegar, liquid pepper, liquid smoke, celery salt, cinnamon, and cloves. Raise the heat to high and boil the sauce, uncovered, about 30 minutes, stirring frequently and lowering the heat toward the end of the cooking period, as necessary, until the sauce is reduced to 1 cup. Remove the pan from the heat.

Drain, rinse and drain the whole hominy. It should measure about 1 1/3 cups drained. Reserve it.

Trim, scrape the strings from and cut the celery into 1 inch square pieces.

Core, carefully trim away any white membrane from and cut the green peppers into 1 inch square pieces.

Wipe with a damp cloth, if necessary, trim the stems from and cut the okra crosswise into 1/2 inch lengths. Reserve the prepared vegetables.

Bring the water with 1 teaspoon of the salt and the turmeric to boil in a heavy medium size saucepan over high heat. Slowly sprinkle in the grits, stirring with a longhandled wooden spoon. Reduce the heat to low. Simmer and stir the grits for 5 minutes. Remove the pan from the heat and stir in 4 tablespoons of the butter, cut in pieces, and the drained whole hominy. Set the mixture aside to cool a bit.

Meanwhile sauté the celery, bell peppers and okra, sprinkled with 1/2 teaspoon of the salt, in 2 tablespoons of butter in a medium size frying pan (see utensils) over medium heat for 5 minutes. Reduce the heat to low and stir in the drained tomatoes and the sauce and keep the mixture warm.

Now, add the eggs, one at a time to the hominy mixture, beating well with a wooden spoon after each addition.

Spread the okra mixture out in the bottom of a buttered 8 by 8 by 2 inch deep, 8 cup baking dish. Then carefully spoon the hominy mixture over it covering the okra mixture completely and bake the casserole in a preheated 325 degree oven 1 hour. Check after the dish has been in the oven about 40 minutes to see if it's browning too quickly. If so, lightly cover it with foil. Allow the Creole casserole to stand 10 minutes before serving.

4 to 6 servings

Note: You might want to spread a piece of foil, with edges turned up, on the floor of the oven—under the element if it's electric—for possible runover.

CHILES RELLEÑOS
with salsa rojo

These are not the usual batter dipped or breaded chiles relleños. These are simply served plain, with a sauce. The first time I had this delicious type of chiles relleños was in a tiny Mexican restaurant. The Mexican chef not only cooked but waited on tables himself, with obvious pleasure. He loved his work and his customers. I had to suppress a desire to hug him. Serve sopa de cacahuete, then accompany the chiles relleños with a white or brown rice pilaf. Follow with a tossed salad mix II and some warm tortillas and butter. Chilled wedges of honeydew melon will make a happy ending.

frijoles refritos - (recipe follows)
salsa rojo - (recipe follows)
1 1/2 pounds sweet Italian frying peppers - 8 large, 2 1/2 to 3 inches in
          diameter at the top and 5 to 6 inches long, about 3 ounces each
1 pound Munster cheese - (4 cups grated)

The refritos can be prepared in advance and reheated. The salsa rojo and chiles relleños should be prepared in conjunction with one another, starting the salsa first.

Slice off the stem ends of the peppers, core them and carefully remove any white membrane using a small sharp knife. Tap the peppers a few times to dislodge any hidden, clinging seeds. Steam the peppers, 10 minutes over already boiling water. Immediately turn them into a basin of cold water for 3 minutes. Drain them throughly, cut side down, in a colander.

Be sure to select a good quality cheese, it does make a difference. Coarsely grate the cheese.

Stuff the drained peppers, amply, with the grated cheese, forcing it down into the slender part of the pepper with your finger.

To assemble the chiles relleños, divide the hot refritos among 4 ovenproof dinner plates, spreading them out. Lay 2 stuffed peppers side by side in opposite directions on each bed of refritos. They will look like plump little cornucopias. Place the plates in a preheated 325 degree oven for 5 minutes or until the cheese just starts to melt. Do not allow the cheese to become runny. Remove the plates from the oven and spoon a generous band of the hot salsa rojo across the peppers. Serve the chiles relleños immediately along with a warm bowl of the remaining sauce.

4 servings

Note: Sweet Italian frying peppers make an excellent choice for chiles relleños. They do not have to be peeled and there is no guessing about whether they will be mild or not. They are always mild. The hot quality in the dish is provided by the salsa rojo.

salsa rojo

celery - 2 large ribs - (1 cup diced)
3 ounces sweet Italian frying peppers - 1 large - (1/2 cup diced)
parsley leaves - (2 Tablespoons chopped)
1 teaspoon salt
2 Tablespoons olive oil
1 can ground tomatoes - 28 ounces - (3 1/2 cups)
1/4 cup water
1 Tablespoon honey

1 teaspoon ground coriander
1 teaspoon cayenne
1 Tablespoon fresh lime juice
1/2 teaspoon dried basil

Trim, scrape the strings from and dice the celery quite small.
Core the frying pepper, trim away any white membrane and dice it quite small.
Chop the parsley.
Sauté the celery, sprinkled with the salt, in the oil in a heavy saucepan over medium heat 15 minutes, until it starts to shrink. Add the diced pepper and sauté 2 minutes longer.
Add the tomatoes, water, honey, coriander and cayenne. When the sauce comes to simmer, reduce the heat to low and keep the sauce barely simmering, uncovered, for 25 minutes. (Meanwhile, prepare, steam and stuff the chiles relleños. If the sauce must wait for the chiles to be ready, turn off the heat under the sauce and then reheat it when ready, rather than overcook it.) When the chiles relleños go into the oven, add the lime juice, the basil, crushing it, and the parsley to the sauce. Simmer it 5 minutes longer and use it immediately.

4 cups

frijoles refritos

2 1/4 cups dried pink beans - 1 pound
2 bay leaves
reserved cooking liquid
6 Tablespoons olive oil
6 Tablespoons butter
1 teaspoon salt
1/2 teaspoon celery salt
1/4 teaspoon black pepper
1 teaspoon honey
dash cayenne

Soak the beans and cook them with the bay leaves as directed. (See boiled dried shelled beans.) Drain them reserving the cooking liquid and the bay leaves. If the drained cooking liquid measures more than 1 1/2 cups, boil it down over high heat.

Heat the oil and butter in a large frying pan (see utensils) over low heat. Add about 1/4 of the cooked beans to the pan, mashing them with a potato masher and stir in about 3/4 cup of the reserved cooking liquid. (Save the remaining liquid to use if the beans are to be reheated later.) Add the remaining whole beans, the reserved bay leaves and all the rest of the ingredients to the pan. Cook the frijoles refritos, uncovered, stirring occasionally with a metal spatula for about 30 minutes, until they have thickened to the consistency you desire.

4 cups

 ASSIETTE JARDINIÈRE

A vegetable plate is a work of art, a balance of textures, colors and flavors. Cream of celeriac will be the soup course. A tossed endive salad and crisp rolls with perhaps some ripe Bourseau cheese is the salad course served after the assiette jardinière. Strawberries over strawberry ice cream make an elegant finale.

1 1/2 pounds untrimmed spinach - (12 packed cups trimmed)
about 1 3/4 pounds carrots - about 9 large - (4 1/2 cups cut)
about 1 1/2 pounds beets (minus leaves) - 16 small, 1 1/4 to 1 1/2 inches
        in diameter - or 2 cans best quality baby beets, 16 ounces each
corn - 5 ears - (2 1/2 cups kernels) - or about 15 ounces frozen
2 pounds cauliflower - 1 medium small - (about 6 cups florets)
1 pound string beans - (see note)
1 3/4 cups plus 1 teaspoon unsalted butter - divided
about 1 pound mushrooms - 20 medium to large - (about 5 cups whole)
wedge lemon
salt
        Prepare and blanch the spinach as directed. (See blanched spinach.) Immediately turn the drained spinach into a basin of cold water for 1 minute. Then turn it into a colander, place a saucer with a moderate weight upon it on the spinach and allow it to drain for 1 hour, turning it over 2 or 3 times during that period.
        Trim, peel and cut the carrots, crosswise, into 1 inch pieces. Steam them, over already simmering water about 25 minutes or until they are very

soft. Purée the cooked carrots through a food mill set over a bowl. Line a colander with a double layer of wet, wrungout cheese cloth, turn the purée into it, tie the corners of the cheese cloth together and hang the bag up over a bowl to drain for 1 hour. (Save the liquid for a bouillon soup. See bouillon soups.)

Steam, trim and peel the beets as directed. (See steamed beets.) If you are using canned beets, simply drain them. In either case, blot them with paper towels.

Prepare and boil the corn as directed, but boil it only 7 minutes. (See boiled corn.) Immediately, turn the drained corn into a basin of cold water for 5 minutes. Drain again and carefully cut the kernels from the cob, separating them and crumbling them into a bowl. If you are using frozen corn, blanch the still frozen corn in enough boiling water to cover it by 1 1/2 inches, in a saucepan, covered with lid slightly ajar, over high heat, for 1 minute from the moment it is in the water, regardless of when the water returns to boil, stirring the corn with a wooden spoon. Drain it and immediately turn it into a basin of cold water for 3 minutes. Drain again and blot it dry on paper towels.

Prepare but steam the cauliflower 1 minute less than what you would determine to be its full cooking time, as directed. (See steamed cauliflower florets.) Immediately, turn the florets into a basin of cold water for 3 minutes. Then drain them well and blot them dry on paper towels.

Select fresh young string beans. Prepare but steam them 1 minute less than what you would determine to be their full cooking time, as directed. (See steamed string beans.) Immediately, turn the string beans into a basin of cold water for 3 minutes. Then drain them and blot them dry on paper towels.

(These vegetable preparations can be done up to 24 hours in advance. Seal them, separately, in plastic and refrigerate them, but be sure to bring them to room temperature before continuing with the recipe.)

At this point, clarify 1 1/2 cups of the butter as directed. (See clarified butter.)

Now, trim the mushroom stems flush with the caps. (Reserve the stems for the bouillon soup.) Wipe the caps clean with a damp cloth. Using a small sharp knife, flute the caps by starting at the center of the top of each cap and gently pressing the mushroom cap into the blade of the knife to make a long shallow slanted groove down to the edge of the cap while turning the cap, slightly, to achieve a spiral effect. The knife blade will automatically pull up a small strip of skin which is discarded. Keep turning the cap toward you while working away from you, covering the cap with closely parallel grooves. (It's easy once you get the hang of it, like riding a bicycle.) As each mushroom cap is fluted, rub it with the wedge of lemon. Sauté the fluted mushroom caps, lightly sprinkled with salt in 3 tablespoons of the butter, in a large frying pan (see utensils) over medium high heat, for about 10 minutes, turning the caps over occasionally, while raising the heat to high, until all the moisture has evaporated and the mushrooms start to become golden and beautiful. Drain them on paper towels. (The mushrooms can be prepared and sautéed 1 or 2 hours ahead of serving and simply wrapped in the paper towels and kept at room temperature.)

About 30 minutes before serving time, artfully arrange mounds of the spinach, puréed carrots, little beets, corn kernels, cauliflower florets and string beans on each of 4 oven proof dinner plates. (Keep the beets away from the cauliflower or it will get stained.) Hide 1/2 teaspoon of the butter in each mound of spinach and carrots. Lightly sprinkle all the vegetables with salt then arrange 5 mushroom caps at random over the vegetables on each plate.

Lightly but completely, cover each plate with a piece of foil which has been perforated with 5 or 6 small holes. Secure the foil around the edges of the plates and warm the vegetables in a preheated 350 degree oven for just 20 minutes, until they are heated through. Uncover the plates and serve the assiette jardiniere immediately, along with a pitcher of the clarified butter set over a candle warmer and let the diners drench their own vegetables with butter.

4 servings

Note: Preparing this dish, with string beans that are out of season, can be disappointing. Rather than take a chance or do without, I have learned to use a good quality of frozen, whole, small string beans. Blanch the still frozen string beans in enough boiling water to cover them by 1 1/2 inches, in a saucepan, uncovered, over high heat, for 3 minutes from the moment they are in the water, regardless of when the water returns to boil, gently stirring the beans with a wooden spoon. Drain them and immediately turn them into a basin of cold water for 3 minutes. Drain again and blot them dry on paper towels. Then wrap the string beans in more clean, dry paper towels and allow them to stand for 30 minutes so that the towels can absorb any remaining moisture.

STUFFED EGGPLANT

This is perhaps the ultimate stuffed eggplant dish. Watercress soup would make a lovely first course. Serve braised baby artichokes with the eggplant, then have a salad of fennel in virgin olive oil and a basket of warm bread with some Wisconsin Cheddar. Raspberries over ice cream would be the perfect dessert here.

3/4 cup wild rice - 6 ounces
1 1/2 pounds eggplant - 2 medium small - 12 ounces each
2 1/2 teaspoons salt - divided
celery - 2 large ribs - (1 cup diced)
12 ounces green bell peppers - 2 medium - (2 cups diced)
1 pound tomatoes - 4 small - (2 cups diced)
1 cup roasted shelled pecan halves - about 3 1/2 ounces - (see pecans)
parsley leaves - (1/2 cup chopped)
1/3 teaspoon ground rosemary - (see ground rosemary)
1/3 teaspoon ground (rubbed) sage
1/3 teaspoon ground thyme
4 Tablespoons corn oil
8 Tablespoons butter
2 teaspoons honey
1 teaspoon celery salt
1/2 teaspoon freshly cracked black pepper
1 teaspoon dried marjoram
2 eggs

Soak and steam the rice as directed. (See steamed wild rice.) Reserve it.

Do not remove the stems if they're in good shape, but cut the eggplants and their stems in half, lengthwise. Using a teaspoon, carefully scoop out the flesh from the eggplant haves, leaving 1/4 inch thick shells. Reserve the shells. Chop the flesh small, and in a colander, toss it with 1 teaspoon of the salt. Place a saucer with a moderate weight upon it on the chopped eggplant and allow it to drain 1 hour, turning the eggplant over once or twice during that period.

Trim, scrape the strings from and dice the celery.

Core, carefully trim away any white membrane from and dice the bell peppers.

Peel and seed the tomaotes as directed. (See peeled tomatoes and see seeded tomatoes.) Dice the flesh.

Using a heavy knife, coarsely chop the pecans.

Chop the parsley leaves.

Mix the ground rosemary, sage and thyme together in a small cup.

Sauté the celery and bell peppers together, sprinkled with 1/2 teaspoon of the salt, in the oil in a large frying pan (see utensils) over medium heat for 3 minutes. Add the chopped, drained eggplant and the tomatoes, sprinkle with 1/2 teaspoon of the salt and sauté 5 minutes longer.

Reduce the heat to low and add the butter, cut in pieces and the honey. Using a wooden spatula or spoon, gently stir in the reserved wild rice and sprinkle with 1/2 teaspoon of the salt, the ground herb mixture, the celery salt, black pepper and the marjoram, crushing it. Slowly cook the mixture about 3 minutes longer, remove the pan from the heat and allow it to cool a bit.

In a large mixing bowl, using a wire whisk, beat the eggs until they are light. Gently stir in the wild rice mixture, the toasted chopped nuts and the parsley. Set the reserved eggplant shells on each of 4 oven proof dinner plates. Carefully pack the shells with the wild rice mixture, mounding it. Bake the stuffed eggplant in a preheated 350 degree oven for 25 minutes and serve.

4 servings

 ZUCCHINI GRATINÉ

Tomato essence begins this delightful summer dinner. Serve corn off the cob with the zucchini gratiné. Then accompany a kohlrabi vinaigrette with Italian bread. Follow with chilled cherries.

4 Tablespoons bread crumbs - (see bread crumbs)
celery - (1/4 cup diced)
6 ounces sweet Italian frying peppers - 3 medium - (1 cup sliced)
2 pounds zucchini squash - 4 medium large - (6 cups grated)
4 ounces Gruyere cheese - (1 cup grated)
Parmesan cheese - (6 Tablespoons freshly grated)
Romano cheese - (2 Tablespoons freshly grated)
1/2 teaspoon celery salt
4 Tablespoons plus olive oil - divided
1/2 teaspoon plus salt - divided
1/4 teaspoon freshly cracked black pepper
1 teaspoon honey
1/2 cup heavy cream - at room temperature
1/2 teaspoon dried basil
1/2 teaspoon dried oregano
4 eggs - at room temperature

Toast the bread crumbs in a dry pan over medium heat, for about 3 minutes, stirring them constantly, until they start to become golden. Remove the crumbs from the pan immediately and reserve them.

Trim, scrape the strings from and dice the celery small.

Quarter lengthwise and core the frying peppers, carefully trimming away any white membrane. Then thinly slice the quarters crosswise.

Trim and cut one paper thin slice, crosswise, out of the widest part of each zucchini and reserve the slices. Coarsely grate the remaining zucchini.

Coarsely grate the Gruyère and mix it with the Parmesan and Romano.

Sauté the celery and frying peppers, sprinkled with the celery salt, in the 4 tablespoons of oil in a large frying pan over medium heat 3 minutes. Add the grated zucchini, sprinkle with the 1/2 teaspoon of salt and the pepper and stir and turn the vegetables frequently for about 15 minutes, while gradually turning up the heat to high, until all the juices have evaporated. Remove the pan from the heat. Stir in the honey, cream and the basil and oregano, crushing them and allow the mixture to cool a bit.

Using a wire whisk, lightly beat the eggs in a large bowl. Then stir the vegetables and the cheeses into them. Spoon the mixture into each of 4 buttered 1 cup gratin dishes, dividing it equally and spreading it out smooth. Now, evenly sprinkle the reserved bread crumbs over the dishes. Smear a drop of oil and sprinkle a little salt on each of the 4 reserved zucchini slices then gently press 1 slice into the center of each gratin dish.

Bake the dishes in a preheated 325 degree oven for 35 minutes. Allow the zucchini gratiné to stand 10 minutes, then set each gratin dish on a dinner plate to serve.

4 servings

 # HARVARD BEETS WITH GREENS

There's not much room for improvement on that perennial favorite, Harvard beets. However, here they are presented on a bed of their own greens. The tartness of the greens is a perfect counterpoint for the mild sweetness of the beets and combine to make an interesting sweet and sour dish. A cream of cauliflower soup comes first. Then serve buttered yellow string beans with the beets. Iceburg wedges and some large crackers will comprise the salad course, poached pineapple slices the dessert.

2 to 2 1/2 pounds beets (minus greens) - 20 small, 1 1/4 to 1 1/2 inches in diameter
about 2 pounds beet greens - greens from 20 young beets will weigh just about 2 pounds - (16 cups cut)
8 quarts water
1 Tablespoon plus 1 teaspoon salt - divided
1 Tablespoon plus 1 teaspoon cornstarch
1/4 cup cold water
6 Tablespoons cider vinegar
6 Tablespoons honey
3/8 teaspoon black pepper - divided
6 Tablespoons unsalted butter - divided

Select fresh young beets. Cut the greens from the beets, if they are still attached, reserving them, and steam, trim and peel the beets as directed, but leave the roots or "tails" of the beets intact, trimming the long ones only enough so that all the "tails" are about the same length. (See steamed beets.) Drop the beets into a basin of cold water for 5 minutes, drain them, blot them dry with paper towels and reserve them.

Cut the greens and their stems crosswise into 1/4 inch slices. Rinse and drain them in a large colander. Bring the 8 quarts of water with 2 teaspoons of the salt to boil in a large kettle set over high heat. Blanch the greens in the boiling water, uncovered, for 3 minutes from the moment they are in the water, regardless of when the water returns to boil. Push the greens down into the water with a longhandled, wooden spoon and adjust the heat to keep the water slowly boiling. Drain the beet greens into a colander and immediately turn them into a basin of cold water for 1 minute. Then turn the greens into the colander again, place a saucer with a moderate weight upon it on them and allow the greens to drain 30 minutes, turning them over 2 or 3 times during that period.

In a saucepan, large enough to accommodate all the beets, dissolve the cornstarch in the 1/4 cup of cold water. Add the vinegar, honey, 1 teaspoon of the salt, and 1/8 teaspoon of the pepper. Bring the mixture to simmer, over medium heat, while stirring constantly with a rubber spatula. When the mixture simmers, reduce the heat slightly, and continue to simmer and stir for 2 minutes. Add 2 tablespoons of the butter, cut in pieces. When it has melted, add the beets, gently stirring to coat them with the sauce. Reduce the heat to very low, cover the pan with a trimmed piece of paper towel and lid and warm the beets for about 20 minutes or until they are heated through.

Meanwhile, toss the beet greens a bit in the colander, using a wooden fork to separate them. Melt 4 tablespoons of the butter in a large frying pan (see utensils) over low heat. Add the greens, sprinkled with

1 teaspoon of the salt and 1/4 teaspoon of the pepper, and warm them, uncovered, for about 3 minutes, still tossing with the wooden fork, until they are well heated.

Now, spread the equally divided beet greens out, on each of 4 warm dinner plates. Using two spoons, arrange 5 beets, "tail" ends up, close together on the center of the greens on each plate. Then evenly spoon the remaining sauce over the beets and serve the Harvard beets with greens immediately.

4 servings

 ## STOCK VEGETABLES AND COUSCOUS
WITH CHEESE

Serve cream of tomato soup to start off this homey meal. Following the stock vegetables and couscous with cheese, a salad of coleslaw accompanied by some homemade biscuits would be nice. Serve chilled oranges for dessert.

1 1/3 cups commercially precooked couscous - about 9 1/2 ounces
8 ounces or more cheese - (about 2 cups grated) - (see note)
2 1/2 teaspoons salt - divided
1/2 teaspoons freshly cracked black pepper - divided
12 Tablespoons butter - divided
5 to 6 cups drained stock broth vegetables - bay leaf removed - (see stock broth)

Steam, chill and knead the couscous as directed. (See steamed couscous the grain.)

Meanwhile, coarsely grate the cheese and reserve it.

Warm the cold couscous, sprinkled with 1 teaspoon of the salt and 1/4 teaspoon of the pepper, in 4 tablespoons of the butter in a large frying pan (see utensils), over low heat until the couscous is heated through. Keep it warm over the low heat.

Now, warm the drained stock broth vegetables, sprinkled with 1 1/2 teaspoons of the salt and 1/4 teaspoon of the pepper, in 8 tablespoons of the butter in another large frying pan (see utensils) over medium heat, for about 5 minutes until they are heated through, gently stirring them with a wooden spatula because these vegetables are very tired.

Equally divide the couscous among 4 buttered gratin dishes or other individual size, oven proof dishes, spreading it out. Spread the warm vegetables, equally divided, over the couscous. Then sprinkle 1/2 cup or more of the grated cheese over the vegetables on each dish and run the dishes under the broiler, 3 inches from the heat source for about 5 minutes until the cheese is melted and bubbly. Serve the stock vegetables and couscous with cheese immediately.

4 servings

Note: This is a good dish for using up odd amounts of leftover cheese. Use any kind you like; just be sure it's tasty and abundant as it will be the principal flavoring in the dish.

PEPERONI AL FORNO

Al forno means in the oven. Serve sorrel soup before this very small but rich entrée. Buttered broccoli is the accompaniment to the peperoni al forno. For the salad, serve cannellini vinigrette along with some coarse bread sticks. Poached figs complete the meal.

3 pounds red bell peppers - 6 large
2/3 cup bread crumbs - (see bread crumbs)
Parmesan cheese - (4 Tablespoons freshly grated)
Romano cheese - (1 Tablespoon plus 1 teaspoon freshly grated)
1 teaspoon dried oregano
1 teaspoon dried basil
1/2 teaspoon salt
1/8 teaspoon freshly cracked black pepper
4 Tablespoons olive oil

Prepare and peel the bell peppers as directed. (See peeled red bell peppers.)

Toast the bread crumbs in a dry frying pan over medium heat, stirring them constantly, 3 or 4 minutes until they are golden. Immediately transfer them to a mxing bowl. When they have cooled mix the Parmesan, Romano, the oregano and basil, crushing them, and the salt and black pepper into the crumbs.

Lightly oil a 3 or 4 cup flat bottomed baking dish or pan. Sprinkle the bottom and sides of the dish with a little of the bread crumb mixture.

Dredge about 1/3 of the red peppers in the bread crumbs and spread them in the bottom of the dish. Sprinkle 2 tablespoons of the bread crumb mixture over them and then dribble 4 teaspoons of the oil over the bread crumbs. Repeat the layers twice more.

Bake the peppers in a preheated 375 degree overn 20 to 25 minutes until the peppers are heated through and the top of the bread crumbs is golden brown. Allow the peperoni al forno to stand 5 minutes before serving.

4 servings

CORN FRITTERS

Cold curried buttermilk soup is an easy first course for this summer-time dinner. Buttered Swiss chard is the accompaniment to these delicious corn fritters. (Otherwise known as corn critters.) Sliced tomatoes is the salad and fresh blackberries the dessert.

corn - 4 ears - (2 cups kernels) - (see note)
4 cups peanut oil
2 Tablespoons butter
1/2 cup flour
1/2 teaspoon baking powder
3/4 teaspoon plus salt - divided
1/8 teaspoon white pepper
2 eggs - at room temperature

Select freshly picked large ears of sweet corn. Husk it and with a thin sharp knife, cut a line down the center of each row of kernels. Cut the kernels from the cob, separating them, and crumble them into a mixing bowl. Remove any remaining threads of corn silk.

(Allowing about 15 minutes for the oil to heat to temperature, heat the oil in a deep saucepan, with a cooking thermometer clipped to the inside of it, over medium high heat to 375 degrees. Or use an electric deep fryer set at 375 degrees.)

Meanwhile, melt the butter in a small saucepan over low heat. Remove the pan from the heat and allow it to cool a bit.

Sift the flour, baking powder, the 3/4 teaspoon of salt and the pepper over the corn. Combine the ingredients well then stir in the cooled butter.

In a separate bowl, using a wire whisk, beat the eggs until they are light, then stir them into the corn mixture.

When the oil has reached temperature drop the corn mixture, by the tablespoonful, into the hot oil, using a teaspoon to push the mixture off of the tablespoon. Careful! Don't allow the oil to splash and don't crowd the fritters. The fritters should take about 3 minutes to become golden. Using a pair of tongs, turn them over once during the frying time. Using the frying basket or a skimmer, lift the fritters from the oil and drain them on paper towels. Keep them warm, spread out in a single layer on a heat proof serving platter, in a 200 degree oven, until all the fritters are done. The yield should be 20 fritters. Very lightly, salt the corn firtters and serve them.

4 servings

Note: The corn must be fresh, no substitutes.

# RATATOUILLE

Ratatouille, as it is prepared in the Alpes Maritimes province of France, includes potatoes as it does here. Have a cold avocado soup first. If you like, accompany the ratatouille with a rice pilaf. Serve a tossed chicory salad next with some French or Italian bread. Then chilled grapefruit sections will be refreshing.

3 pounds tomatoes - 6 medium - (6 cups chopped)
2 cloves garlic
1 pound boiling potatoes - about 26 tiny, little, new, up to 1 inch in diameter
        - (3 cups whole) - or larger potatoes cut into pieces
about 1 pound green bell peppers - 2 1/2 medium - (2 1/2 cups cut)
12 ounces zucchini squash - 3 small, 6 inches long - (3 cups cut)

2 pounds eggplant - 2 medium - (6 heaping cups diced)
8 Tablespoons olive oil - divided
3 Tablespoons tomato paste
1 Tablespoon plus 1 teaspoon honey
2 teaspoon salt - divided
1 teaspoon celery salt
1/3 teaspoon freshly cracked black pepper
1 bay leaf
1 teaspoon dried basil
1 teaspoon dried marjoram

Peel and seed the tomaotes as directed. (See peeled tomatoes and see seeded tomatoes.)

Peel the garlic.

Peel the potatoes. Yes! Peel the little new potatoes; the white potatoes will look so much more attractive. If you are using larger potatoes, round off the cut edges. In any event, drop the peeled potatoes into a bowl of cold water to cover.

Core, carefully trim away any white membrane from and cut the bell peppers into 3/4 inch pieces.

Trim and quarter the zucchini, lengthwise. Then cut the quarters, crosswise into 3/4 inch pieces.

Trim, peel and cut the eggplant into 3/4 inch dice.

Bring the tomatoes (they'll be juicy) with the garlic and 3 table-spoons of the oil, the tomato paste, honey, 1 teaspoon of the salt, the celery salt, black pepper and bay leaf to boil in a very large, heavy saucepan, uncovered over medium high heat. Drain the potatoes, blot them dry with paper towels and add them to the saucepan. Reduce the heat to medium low and gently simmer the mixture, still uncovered, 40 minutes, stirring occasionally.

Meanwhile, sauté the peppers, sprinkled with 1/4 teaspoon of the salt, in 1 tablespoon of the oil in a large frying pan (see utensils) over medium heat, for 3 minutes. Remove them from the pan and reserve them.

Sauté and reserve the zucchini in like manner.

Sauté the eggplant, sprinkled with 1/2 teaspoon of the salt, in 3 tablespoons of the oil for 3 minutes.

Now add all the sautéed vegetables and their cooking oils to the large saucepan and continue to cook the mixture over medium low heat, covered now, for 20 minutes, stirring occasionally. (The vegetables must not be overcooked as they are to be reheated.)

Transfer the ratatouille to a bowl and allow it to cool, uncovered, to room temperature. Then refrigerate it, covered, 24 hours.

Allow the ratatouille to come to room temperature. About 1 1/2 hours before serving, reheat it in the heavy saucepan, covered, over medium low heat, 25 minutes. Add the basil and marjoram, crushing them and heat 5 minutes longer. Then transfer the ratatouille, evenly divided, to each of 4 individaul size bowls and allow it to stand 1 hour before serving. The flavor peak of ratatouille is just tepid.

4 servings

 SWISS CHARD CRÊPES

This is my mother's recipe. It deserves a lovely saffron consommé royale for the soup course. Serve roast tomatoes with the Swiss chard crêpes and follow with a salad of marinated mushrooms served with French bread. Chilled cantaloupe is the dessert.

12 crêpes - (recipe follows)
2 pounds Swiss chard - (12 packed cups cut)
8 ounces Swiss Ementhal cheese (Swiss cheese) - (2 cups grated)
4 Tablespoons butter - divided
2 Tablespoons flour
1 cup light cream
1 teaspoon plus salt
1/4 teaspoon freshly cracked black pepper

Prepare and the cook the crêpes as directed.
Prepare and blanch the Swiss chard as directed. (See blanched Swiss chard.) Immediately turn the drained Swiss chard into a basin of cold water for 1 minute. Then turn it into a colander, place a saucer with a moderate weight upon it on the Swiss chard and allow it to drain for 30 minutes turning it over 2 or 3 times during that period.
Coarsely grate the cheese and reserve it.
Melt 2 tablespoons of the butter in a large, heavy saucepan over low heat. Using a rubber spatula, blend in the flour, stirring constantly for 3 minutes. Slowly stir in the cream, while gradually raising the heat to medium until the mixture simmers. Add the 1 teaspoon of salt, the pepper and Swiss chard, a handful at a time, stirring it around, to coat it well with the sauce. When all the Swiss chard is in the pan, allow it to continue to heat,

uncovered, for about 8 minutes, stirring occasionally, until the mixture is well heated. Remove the pan from the heat and stir in the reserved cheese, 1/2 cup at a time. The mixture will be thick and stringy.

Lightly sprinkle the least attractive side of 1 crêpe with a little salt. Spoon 2 heaping tablespoons of the warm Swiss chard mixture down the center of it and roll it up. Repeat with the remaining crêpes, arranging 3 stuffed crepes in a slight diagonal on each of 4 oven proof dinner plates. Dot the stuffed crêpes with 2 tablespoons of the butter, equally divided and cut in pieces, then warm them 15 minutes in a preheated 325 degree oven until they are heated through. Serve the Swiss chard crêpes immediately.

4 servings

crêpes

6 1/2 Tablespoons unsalted butter - divided
2 eggs
1/2 cup light cream
1 cup flour
1/4 teaspoon salt
1/2 cup plus sparkling water

Melt 2 tablespoons of the butter in a small pan over low heat. Remove the pan from the heat and allow it to cool a bit. In the blender or processor combine the cooled butter, eggs, cream, flour and salt until the batter is smooth. Alternatively, beat the eggs and cream together in a small bowl using the electric mixer. Sift in the flour and salt and continue to beat until the batter is smooth then beat in the cooled butter. (In either case refrigerate the batter, covered, at least 3 hours or overnight, then bring it to room temperature before continuing with the recipe.)

Clarify 4 1/2 tablespoons of the butter as directed. (See clarified butter.) Keep the butter warm.

(In a soup ladle, using plain water, measure what 3 tablespoons of liquid look like, so that you will be able to estimate and ladle out 3 tablespoons of batter without measuring it every time. Three tablespoons of batter makes a 6 to 7 inch in diameter crêpe.)

Just before making the crêpes, stir the 1/2 cup of sparkling water into the batter. Using a pastry brush, smear the inside of a crêpe pan,

6 1/2 inches in diamter across the bottom, with a little of the warm clarified butter. Set the pan over medium high heat until water sprinkled on it bounces off. Remove the pan from the heat and wait a couple of seconds. (If the pan is too hot the batter will not spread evenly.) Ladle the batter into the center of the pan while quickly but carefully rotating the pan to spread the batter out thin. Return the pan to the heat and cook the crêpe 1 minute. Run a spatula around the edge of the crêpe while it's cooking and shake the pan to be sure it doesn't stick. Flip the crêpe over and cook it 30 minutes longer on the other side. It should have delicate, golden brown spots on it. Slide the crêpe onto a plate and cover it with a towel. Brush the pan again with a little clarified butter and repeat the process with the remaining batter. I generally thin the batter with a little more sparkling water as I go along, adding perhaps as much as 1 teaspoon at a time after about the third, sixth and nineth crêpes have been made, but this varies. The crêpes can be stacked on top of each other under the towel as they are cooked.

(If you are not going to use them immediately, allow the crêpes to cool completely, then seal them in plastic. They can be refrigerated up to 24 hours, but bring them to room temperature before continuing with the recipe.)

12 crêpes

Note: Crêpes require a small amount of technique. The 6 1/2 inch interior bottom diameter of the pan helps to control the size and shape of the crêpe though a larger pan could be used.

INDIAN DINNER

Here is a group of six dishes to be presented all at once, four of which must be served warm. The bean and rice dishes can be kept warm over candle warmers. An Indian dinner translates very easily into a buffet style dinner. Much of it can be prepared in advance and serving it is simple. Everyone helps themselves to some of each dish. Offer pomegrantes to complete the meal. This Indian dinner will serve six to eight people.

suki bhaji

celery - 4 large ribs - (2 cups cut)
12 ounces red bell peppers - 2 medium - (2 cups cut)
12 ounces green bell peppers - 2 medium - (2 cups cut)
8 ounces mushrooms - small - (3 cups whole)
1 pound eggplant - 1 medium - (3 cups diced)
jalapeño peppers - 2
ginger root - (1 teaspoon freshly grated)
1 teaspoon ground turmeric
1 teaspoon ground cumin
2 teaspoons ground coriander
1/4 teaspoon ground cloves
1/4 teaspoon ground cinnamon
1/4 teaspoon ground cardamom
1 teaspoon celery salt
5 1/2 Tablespoons unsalted butter
1 teaspoon black mustard seeds
2 teaspoons salt - divided
1 Tablespoon honey
4 Tablespoons fresh lemon juice
4 Tablespoons water

Trim, scrape the strings from and cut the celery crosswise into 1/2 inch thick slices.

Cut the red and green bell peppers crosswise into 1/2 inch thick slices. Core them, trimming away any white membrane and cut the rings into 1/2 inch squares.

Wipe the mushrooms with a damp cloth, trim the butt ends of the stems and leave them whole.

Select fresh, shiny skinned eggplant. Remove the stem and cut the eggplant into 1/2 inch dice.

Wearing plastic gloves, remove the stems from and dice the jalapeños very small without removing their cores or seeds.

Peel and grate the ginger on a medium fine grater.

In a cup, combine the turmeric, cumin, coriander, cloves, cinnamon, cardamom and celery salt and reserve them.

Clarify the butter as directed. (See clarified butter.) Transfer it to a large frying pan (see utensils) over medium heat. Add the mustard seeds and warm them, covered with lid ajar, 2 or 3 minutes until they have all popped. Remove the lid, add the jalapeños and ginger and heat them 30 seconds. Add the celery, sprinkle it with all of the reserved spice mixture and sauté 3 minutes. Add the red and green bell peppers and the mushrooms, sprinkle with 1 teaspoon of the salt and sauté 5 minutes, stirring occasionally. Add the eggplant, sprinkle wih 1 teaspoon of the salt and sauté 3 minutes, stirring frequently. Add the honey, lemon juice and water, increase the heat to high and cook the vegetables about 8 minutes longer, still stirring frequently until all the liquid has evaporated and the eggplant is tender, turning down the heat toward the end of the cooking period as necessary.

To serve, transfer the suki bhaji to a large, warm, covered serving dish.

chana with whole spices

2 1/4 cups dried chick peas - 1 pound
2 bay leaves
2 cups reserved cooking liquid
1/2 cup tomato paste - 4 ounces
jalapeño peppers - 4
ginger root - (1 teaspoon freshly grated)
4 pods cardamom seeds
1 teaspoon coriander seeds
1 teaspoon fenugreek seeds
1 teaspoon cumin seeds
1 teaspoon celery seeds
8 Tablespoons peanut oil
1 teaspoon black mustard seeds
1 teaspoon salt
1 teaspoon honey
14 cloves
2 pieces cinnamon bark - each 2 inches long
4 Tablespons fresh lemon juice

Soak the chick peas and cook them with the bay leaves as directed. (See boiled dried shelled beans.) Drain the chick peas, reserving them and 2 cups of their cooking liquid and the bay leaves.

In a bowl, stir the 2 cups of reserved cooking liquid into the tomato paste and reserve the mixture.

Wearing plastic gloves, remove the stems from and dice the jalapeños very small without removing their cores or seeds.

Peel and grate the ginger on a medium fine grater.

Shell the cardamom seeds.

In a dry pan over medium heat toast the cardamom, coriander, fenugreek, cumin and celery seeds, stirring, for 2 or 3 minutes until they become fragrant and start to color. Do not allow them to burn. Remove the seeds from the pan immediately and reserve them.

Heat the oil in a large frying pan (see utensils) over medium heat. Add the mustard seeds and warm them, covered with lid ajar, for 2 or 3 minutes until they have all popped. Remove the lid, add the jalapeños and ginger and allow them to heat 30 seconds. Add the reserved chick peas, tomato paste mixture, reserved bay leaves, toasted seeds, the salt, honey, cloves and cinnamon bark. Increase the heat to medium high, when the liquid simmers reduce the heat to low and simmer the mixture, uncovered, about 50 minutes, stirring occasionally, until the liquid has thickened and becomes a binder rather than a sauce. Add the lemon juice and simmer 10 minutes longer.

To serve, transfer the chana with whole spices to a warm, covered serving dish.

Note: Chana with whole spices can be prepared in advance and reheated.

masoor dal

1 cup dried red lentils - about 8 ounces - (see note)
3 cups water
1 bay leaf
1 teaspoon cayenne
1 teaspoon ground tumeric
1/2 teaspoon ground ginger
1/2 teaspoon ground cumin
1/2 teaspoon ground coriander
1/2 teaspoon ground fenugreek
2 Tablespoons peanut oil
1 Tablespoon honey
1 teaspoon salt
1/2 teaspoon celery salt
1 Tablespoon fresh lemon juice
1 Tablespoon unsalted butter

Carefully cull the tiny lentils. There always seems to be more foreign matter among red lentils than among other dried legumes. A few of the lentils will be dark, they are simply lentils with their skin still on. If you think they are unsightly discard them as they will appear as dark specks in the finished dish. Rinse the lentils in a colander lined with cheese cloth.

Bring the lentils, water, bay leaf, cayenne, turmeric, ginger, cumin, coriander, fenugreek, oil and honey to boil in a heavy medium size saucepan over medium high heat. Reduce the heat to low and simmer them, covered with lid slightly ajar, 50 minutes, stirring occasionally. Add the salt, celery salt, lemon juice and butter. The dal should be the consistency of thick pea soup. If it is too thick, add a little more water, if it is too thin, leave the cover off. In either case simmer the dal 10 minutes longer, stirring more frequently.

To serve, transfer the masoor dal to a warm, covered serving dish.

Note: The masoor dal can be prepared in advance and reheated. Red lentils, which are really an apricot color are very tiny split lentils. They are available at natural food and speciality stores. Yellow split peas can be substituted.

basmati rice with coconut

coconut - (1/2 cup grated)
2 cups white basmati rice - 14 ounces

Prepare and grate the coconut as directed. (See coconut.)

In a fine strainer, rinse and drain the rice in 2 or 3 changes of water. Then cook it as directed but boil it only 8 minutes as it is very delicate and overcooks easily. After draining the rice into the steamer, rinse it again, this time under hot running tap water. Then continue with the recipe and steam it as directed. (See steamed long or short grain white rice.) While the rice is still in the steamer, using 2 forks, ever so gently toss the coconut with the rice.

To serve, transfer the basmati rice with coconut to a warm, covered serving dish.

Note: The basmati rice with coconut can be prepared in advance and reheated in the steamer, covered with a trimmed piece of paper towel and lid.

Basmati is a fine, long grain Indian rice available at natural food and specialty stores.

If fresh coconut is unavailable, stir 1 tablespoon of water into a 1/2 cup of dried, unsweetened shredded coconut and allow it to stand 30 minutes.

apple raisin chutney

2/3 cup raisins - about 3 1/2 ounces
1/2 cup boiling water
ginger root - (1 Tablespoon freshly grated)
8 ounces red delicious apple - 1 large
2 Tablespoons fresh lemon juice
1 Tablespoon honey
1/4 teaspoon salt
1/2 teaspoon cayenne
1/4 teaspoon ground cloves
1/4 teaspoon ground cardamom
1/8 teaspoon ground cinnamon

Place the raisins in a small bowl, pour the boiling water over them and allow them to soak 30 minutes.

Peel and grate the ginger on a medium fine grater.

Core but do not peel the apple. Slice it into the container of the blender or processor, add the raisins with their soaking water, the ginger and all the remaining ingredients. Purée or process the mixture only enough to break down the ingredients but yet retain some texture. Alternatively, drain the raisins, reserving their soaking water and put the raisins and sliced apples through an old fashioned food chopper. Then combine them with the soaking water and all the remaining ingredients.

Refrigerate the chutney, covered, for from 3 to 24 hours. The flavors need time to develop and marry. Remove the chutney from the refrigerator 1 hour before serving time. Stir it and turn it into a small serving dish. Serve the apple raisin chutney at room temperature.

cucumber raita

about 1 pound cucumbers - 2 average, 7 to 8 inches long
1 1/4 teaspoons salt - divided
2 cups yogurt
coriander leaves (cilantro) - (1 Tablespoon minced)
1/4 teaspoon ground cumin
coriander - 1 sprig

Peel the cucumbers, cut them in half lengthwise and scoop out the seeds. Grate the cucumbers on a medium size grater. In a bowl, mix the grated cucumber with 1 teaspoon of the salt and refrigerate it, covered, 3 hours. Turn the cucumbers into a colander, place a saucer with a weight set upon it on the cucumbers and allow them to drain 1 hour, turning them over once or twice during that period. Keep the drained cucumbers refrigerated and covered until serving.

Meanwhile, line a colander with a double layer of wet, wrung out cheese cloth. Turn the yogurt into it and allow it to drain 1 hour. Keep the drained yogurt refrigeraged and covered until serving.

Mince the coriander leaves.

At serving time, in a chilled serving dish, combine the drained cucumbers, 1/4 teaspoon of the salt, the yogurt, minced coriander and the cumin. Decorate with the coriander sprig and serve the cucumber raita well chilled.

 STUFFED TOMATOES

Begin with cream of spinach soup this evening. Next, serve buttered yellow string beans with these beautiful stuffed tomatoes. Green bell peppers vinaigrette with crusty bread and some Feta cheese will make a nice salad choice. Then have fresh plums to round out this dinner.

4 Tablespoons sesame seeds
3/4 cup millet

1 teaspoon turmeric
celery - 1 large rib - (1/2 cup diced)
12 ounces broccoli - 1 large head - (3 cups cut)
3 pounds tomatoes - 4 large, 12 ounces each
1 1/2 teaspoons plus salt - divided
1/2 teaspoon celery salt
1/2 cup corn oil - divided
1 Tablespoon plus 1 teaspoon lemon juice
1 Tablespoon plus 1 teaspoon honey
1/2 teaspoon freshly cracked black pepper

Toast the sesame seeds in a dry pan over medium heat for about 3 minutes, stirring, until they start to become golden. Remove them from the pan immediately and reserve them.

Steam the millet as directed adding the turmeric to the water. (See steamed millet.) Set it aside.

Trim, scrape the strings from and dice the celery small.

Cut very short stemmed florets from the broccoli and break them up small. Trim and using a knife, first pull the fiberous skin from the stalk then peel it using a vegetable peeler. Dice the stalk small.

Cut a "lid" out of the stem end of each tomato and using a teaspoon, carefully scoop out the pulp. Chop the pulp, along with useable flesh from the "lids", small and set it aside in a bowl with all the juices. Sprinkle the insides of the tomato shells with a little salt and turn them upside down on paper towels to drain.

Sauté the celery and broccoli, sprinkled with the celery salt, in 4 tablespoons of the oil in a large frying pan (see utensils) over medium heat 5 minutes. Remove them from the pan with a slotted spoon and reserve them.

Add the tomato pulp, 1/2 teaspoon of the salt, the lemon juice, honey and pepper to the pan. Cook the tomato pulp, uncovered, over medium high heat, for about 10 minutes or until the juices are reduced by about half. Lower the heat to medium and add the reserved sesame seeds, the steamed millet, 4 more tablespoons of the oil and 1 teaspoon of the salt. Using a metal spatula, turn and cook the mixture about 5 minutes or until the millet has absorbed the juices. Carefully stir in the reserved celery and broccoli and cook 1 minute longer until they are heated through.

Stuff the tomato shells generously with the hot millet mixture and set them on a lightly buttered earthenware pie plate. Bake the stuffed tomatoes in a preheated 325 degree oven for just 20 minutes and serve them immediately.

4 servings

Note: If the tomatoes are baked at a higher temperature or for a longer period of time the shells tend to fall apart, so watch it.

 ## SUMMER SQUASH CASSEROLE

Make this summer squash casserole when your squash plants are overproducing. It does require a large, deep baking dish or pan, however. First serve sopa de tortilla, then accompany the casserole with fried okra. Have coleslaw for the salad course along with melted Jack cheese on whole tortillas. Fresh peaches are dessert.

1 1/2 pounds zucchini squash - 2 large, about 9 to 10 inches long
1 1/2 pounds yellow squash - 2 large, about 9 to 10 inches long
1 pound scalloped squash - 1 medium, about 6 inches in diameter
2 Tablespoons plus 1 1/4 teaspoons salt - divided
12 ounces red bell peppers - 2 medium
1/2 teaspoon ground rosemary - (see ground rosemary)
1/2 taspoon ground thyme
3 pounds 6 ounces baking potatoes - 6 large
1/4 teaspoon freshly cracked black pepper - divided
8 Tablespoons butter - cold - divided
parsley - 2 sprigs

Lightly scrape or peel only if necessary, cut into quarters lengthwise and seed where necessary, all the squash. Thinly slice it, crosswise. There should be about 12 heaping cups, altogether. In a large bowl, toss the sliced squash with the 2 tablespoons of salt. Cover the bowl and allow the squash to stand in its own salty juices, refrigerated, 12 hours or overnight. Then turn the squash into a colander, place a saucer with a weight upon it on the squash and allow it to drain 30 minutes, turning it over a couple of times during that period. Now, spread the drained squash out on paper towels, cover it with more towels and lightly press it to dry it. Set the squash aside in a bowl or colander.
Meanwhile, starting at the blossom end of the bell peppers, cut 2 or 3 thin slices, crosswise, from each pepper. They will form interesting little shapes and rings. Wrap them in wax paper and reserve them. Quarter, core and thinly slice the rest of the peppers into strips. They should yield about 2 cups.

Blend the ground rosemary and thyme together in an empty salt shaker. Screw on the cap and set it aside.

Set the 2 largest potatoes aside. Peel 2 of the remaining potatoes, slice them thin, crosswise, blot the slices on paper towels and spread them in the bottom of a buttered, flat, 2 1/2 inch deep, 10 cup baking dish. Sprinkle the potatoes with 1/2 teaspoon of the salt. Spread half the squash over the potatoes, then spread half the bell pepper strips over the squash. Sprinkle 1/8 teaspoon of black pepper and only half of the herb mixture (careful, don't let it come out of the shaker too fast) over the bell peppers. Then cover with 3 tablespoons of the butter, thinly sliced. Repeat the layers.

Peel, slice and blot the 2 largest potatoes. Staring at one corner or side of the dish, spread the slices in an overlapping pattern over the dish, so that they cover the buttered edges of the dish as well for the potatoes shrink slightly while baking. Sprinkle with 1/4 teaspoon of the salt and spread 2 tablespoons of thinly sliced butter over the final layer of potatoes. Bake the dish, lightly covered with foil, in a preheated 350 degree oven for 1 hour. Remove the dish from the oven. Remove the foil and artistically arrange the reserved bell pepper rings and shapes, only on the last few potato slices that were layered on the dish, in such a way that they look like a bouquet of flowers. Return the dish to the oven and bake it, uncovered, 15 minutes longer. The edges of the potatoes and peppers should be browned. If they are not, run the dish under the broiler for a couple of minutes until they are. Now, place the parsley sprigs on the dish so that they form leaves for the red bell pepper bouquet. Allow the summer squash casserole to stand 20 minutes before serving.

6 to 8 servings

EGGPLANT PARMIGIANA

Eggplant Parmigiana is so popular I usually double the recipe, using two baking dishes. It's good hot, warm, cold or reheated. Cream of broccoli is the soup course for this rather Italian dinner. Serve buttered Romano string beans with the eggplant. Then have a tossed chicory salad and crusty Italian bread. Chilled wedges of honeydew melon will make an appropriate finale.

Parmigiana sauce - (recipe follows)
1 pound eggplant - 1 medium

salt
1/3 cup flour
1 egg
1 Tablespoon plus water
1 to 2 Tablespoons olive oil
6 ounces Mozzarella cheese - (1 1/2 cups grated)
pinch dried oregano

Prepare the Parmigiana sauce in advance as directed. It does not need to be kept warm or be reheated but have it at room temperature.

Trim, peel and cut the eggplant crosswise into 16 slices, each about 1/8 inch thick. Lay the slices out on a work surface and lightly and evenly salt them. Let them stand 30 minutes, turn them over, salt them again and allow them to stand 30 minutes longer to drain out excess juices.

Place the flour on a dinner plate. In a shallow fruit or cereal bowl, using a fork, beat the egg with the 1 tablespoon of water until it is light. Heat 2 teaspoons of the oil in a large frying pan (see utensils) over medium high heat. Pat 1 slice of eggplant dry on paper towels, lightly dredge it in the flour, then dip it in the beaten egg, lifting it with a fork, allowing the excess egg to drain off. (If the egg eventually becomes thickened with flour, thin it with a little water.)

Lay the slice in the frying pan, immediately flipping it over then fry it about 1 1/2 minutes on each side, turning it over once more, until both sides are light golden. Remove the slice to paper towels. Get a little production line going, but don't crowd the pan. As you go along, add a little more oil to the pan. The whole frying process should not take any longer than 30 minutes. (The eggplant can be prepared early in the day, up to this point, wrapped in foil, refrigerated, then brought to room temperature before the dish is assembled.)

Coarsely grate the Mozzarella.

Smear a little of the sauce in the bottom of a buttered, 8 by 8 by 2 inch deep, 8 cup baking dish. Lay 4 eggplant slices in the dish. Spoon some sauce over each slice, then sprinkle a generous tablespoon of the grated cheese over the sauce on each slice. Repeat the layers until all the eggplant and sauce are used up, ending with a layer of cheese. Sprinkle the oregano, crushing it, over the final layer of cheese.

Lightly cover the dish with foil, securing it to two sides of the dish, so that it arches slightly and does not touch the contents of the dish. Bake the eggplant in a preheated 350 degree oven, 35 minutes. Remove the dish from the oven, remove the foil and allow the eggplant Parmigiana to stand 15 minutes before serving.

4 servings

Note: Yes! It's amazing, eggplant fried in this manner absorbs very little oil. I always use my big electric skillet when frying eggplant, it accomodates so many slices.

parmigiana sauce

celery - 1 large rib - (1/2 cup diced)
8 ounces mushrooms - small - (3 cups whole)
1 can peeled plum tomatoes - 28 ounces - (3 1/2 cups)
2 ounces carrot - 1 medium - (1/2 cup grated)
1/2 teaspoon celery salt
2 Tablespoons olive oil
1/2 teaspoon salt
6 Tablespoons tomato paste
2 teaspoons honey
1 small bay leaf
1/4 teaspoon freshly cracked black pepper
1/2 teaspoon dried oregano

Trim, scrape the strings from and dice the celery small.

Wipe the mushrooms with a damp cloth, trim the butt ends of the stems and thinly slice them lengthwise.

Turn the plum tomatoes into a colander set over a bowl, remove their stem buttons, quarter them lengthwise and allow them to drain a few minutes.

Trim, peel and coarsely grate the carrot.

Sauté the celery, sprinkled with the celery salt, in the oil in a heavy saucepan over medium heat, stirring frequently for about 8 minutes or until it starts to shrink. Add the mushrooms, sprinkle with the salt, and sauté about 8 minutes longer, increasing the heat to high until all the moisture has evaporated. Reduce the heat to low, add the tomato paste, stir in the drained juice from the tomatoes, then add the tomatoes, squeezing them through your (clean) fingers into the pan. Add the grated carrot, honey, bay leaf and pepper and gently simmer the sauce, uncovered, 55 minutes, stirring occasionally. Add the oregano, crushing it, and simmer 5 minutes longer. The sauce will be very thick and rich.

about 3 1/2 cups

❧ SALSA VERDE TACOS ❧

There are some very good commercially prepared tortillas on the market. Making them yourself is not a burning necessity but it can be a lot of fun. Children love it. Have a taco party in the kitchen. Serve cold avocado soup in clear glass mugs. For the tacos, use paper plates supported by those flat wicker baskets just made for the purpose. Set out a big bowl of pink beans vinaigrette and put a watermelon in the fridge.

12 corn tortillas - (recipe follows)
salsa verde taco filling - (recipe follows)
12 ounces Longhorn chesse - (3 cups grated)
1/2 cup roasted pepitas - 3 ounces - (see sunflower and pumpkin seeds)
1 1/2 pounds tomatoes - 3 medium - (3 cups chopped)
salt
iceburg lettuce - 1 small head chilled
peanut oil

Prepare the tortillas in advance as directed.
Prepare the salsa verde taco filling and keep it warm as directed.
Coarsely grate the cheese and heap it in a serving bowl.
Place the pepitas in a small bowl.
Remove the stem buttons from the tomatoes. Do not bother to peel, but seed the tomatoes as directed. (See seeded tomatoes). Dice them, place them in a serving bowl and allow them to stand 15 minutes. Then tip the bowl slightly to drain them. Now, lightly salt the tomatoes.
Shred the lettuce very fine and heap it in a serving bowl.
Set the taco filling, still in the double boiler over hot water, the cheese, pepitas, tomatoes and lettuce out on a table or countertop where they will be easily accessible.
Heat a griddle over medium high heat. Have a little cup of the peanut oil handy and using a pastry brush, generously brush the griddle with the oil. Fry the tortillas, one at a time, for 10 seconds on each side. Then lay a 1 inch thick, 10 or 12 inch long wooden dowel on the center of the tortilla and flip half the tortilla over it. Fry half the tortilla for 1 1/2 minutes, then flip it over and fry the other half about 1 1/2 minutes, keeping the dowel in the center, until the taco shell is fairly crisp and will hold its shape when the dowel is removed. (The shells can be kept warm in a 200 degree oven for a few minutes if you like.)
Let each diner assemble his own salsa verde taco. Heap 2 tablespoons of filling in the taco shell. Sprinkle some cheese over it, then

the pepitas, tomatoes and lots of lettuce. Devour immediately. And oh yes, have plenty of paper napkins on hand!

4 to 6 servings

Note: There are various methods of frying tortillas to form taco shells. Using a dowel is simple, easy and uses very little oil. Wooden dowels are available at your local hardware store.

salsa verde taco filling

1 pound zucchini squash - 2 medium, about 8 inches long - (3 cups grated)
jalapeño peppers - 8
1 1/2 teaspoons salt - divided
6 Tablespoons butter - divided
1/2 teaspoon celery salt
1 teaspoon cumin
2 teaspoon honey
6 eggs - at room temperature - (see cooked eggs note)
1 teaspoon dried thyme
1 teaspoon dried oregano

Trim and coarsely grate the zucchini.
Wearing plastic gloves, trim the stems from and cut the jalapeños in half lengthwise. Remove seeds and membrane and mince the flesh.
Sauté the zucchini, sprinkled with 1 teaspoon of the salt in 2 tablespoons of the butter in a frying pan (see utensils) over medium low heat, about 5 minutes. Add the minced peppers, celery salt, cumin and honey. Toss and turn the mixture, using a metal spatula, for about 10 minutes longer while gradually raising the heat to medium high, until all the zucchini liquid has evaporated. Remove the pan from the heat and allow it to cool a bit.
In a mixing bowl, using a wire whisk, beat the eggs until they are light. Stir in the zucchini mixture and the oregano and thyme, crushing the herbs. Melt 4 tablespoons of the butter in the top of a double boiler set over medium heat. Pour in the egg mixture, sprinkle it with 1/2 teaspoon of the salt and stir it occasionally, using a wooden spoon or rubber spatula, for about 15 minutes, until the eggs are set. Turn off the heat and cover the pan with a paper towel and lid. The egg mixture will stay tender and warm for about 30 minutes, over the hot water.

corn tortillas

1 1/2 cups masa harina - (see note)
1/2 teaspoon salt
1 Tablespoon plus 1 teaspoon corn oil
3/4 cup plus 1 Tablespoon plus 1 teaspoon warm water

In a mixing bowl, toss all the ingredients together with a fork. Gather the dough into a ball then, on a work surface, shape it into an oblong cylinder exactly 12 inches long. Using a ruler as a guide, cut the cylinder into 1 inch pieces. Roll each piece into a ball, place them back in the bowl and cover the bowl.

Using a tortilla press, line it with a sheet of plastic. Place a ball of dough slightly to the back of the center of the press. Loosely fold the plastic over the dough and slowly close the press but not completely. Open the press and turn the tortilla and plastic 90 degrees and slowly close the press but not completely, again. Repeat this step two more times, closing the press completely the last time. These steps insure a more even distribution of the dough. In the absence of a tortilla press, place 1 ball between 2 sheets of wax paper and, using a rolling pin, roll it out into a disc about 6 inches in diameter.

In any case, carefully peel back the top layer of plastic or wax paper from the tortilla. Flip the tortilla onto the palm of your hand and then ever so carefully peel back the remaining plastic sheet or paper. Now flip the tortilla onto a hot, dry griddle over medium heat. Cook the tortilla 30 seconds, turn it over with a metal spatula and cook it 1 minute longer until it becomes flecked with golden brown spots, pressing it with the spatula if it swells too much. Turn it over again and cook about 30 seconds more. Repeat the process with the remaining balls of dough, wrapping the tortillas as they are cooked, together in a linen towel to keep them from drying out.

The tortillas can be used right away or they can be prepared in advance, allowed to cool to room temperature wrapped in the towel, then transfered to a sealed plastic bag and refrigerated up to 24 hours before they are used.

12 tortillas

Note: The cooking temperature is important. If the heat is too high the tortillas will scorch before they are cooked. If the heat is too low, they will take too long to cook and become brittle before they are done.

Adding oil to the batter is not traditional but it makes a more cohesive dough and makes the tortillas easier to handle. Masa harina is a type of corn flour, not to be confused with corn meal. It is available in many super markets and specialty stores.

SECTION III

CHILAQUILES

SWEET POTATO ROULADE with mustard butter sauce

FENNEL À LA GRECQUE

WISCONSIN CHEDDAR PIE

BRUSSELS SPROUTS SUPREME in chestnut sauce

FINNISH MUSHROOM PUDDING

STUFFED BUTTERNUT SQUASH with cranberry sauce

CABBAGE CASSEROLE

FRITTATA

CROQUETTES

BAKED ZITI WITH SWISS CHARD

CAMPFIRE LENTILS

ARTICHOKES POLONAISE

GLAZED ROOT ROAST

GARDEN STYLE BRUSSELS SPROUTS

FEUILLETÉE OF CREAMED ONIONS

PEASANT POTAGE

SUCCOTASH

PENNSYLVANIA DUTCH EGG NOODLES WITH TURNIPS

CELERY AMANDINE

GRAINS AND GREENS

STUFFED SWEET POTATOES

CARAWAY CABBAGE

LASAGNA

ARTICHOKES DELPHINA

BULGARIAN BEET TART

RAGU OF FAVA BEANS

FRIED GREEN TOMATOES

SCALLOPED CELERIAC

BRASSICA BOUQUET with fontina sauce

YANKEE SPOONBREAD

LIMA BEANS PANACHÉ with horseradish-stoneground

mustard sauce

SAUERKRAUT PIE

CHESTNUT DRESSING with brown sauce

 CHILAQUILES

Sopa de cacahuete starts off this decidedly Mexican dinner. Accompany the chilaquiles with some refried pinto beans and then serve avocados on the half shell along with some tortillas for the salad course. Chilled green grapes will be the dessert.

celery - 2 large ribs - (1 cup diced)
4 pounds green tomatoes - 8 medium - (8 cups diced) - (see note)
jalapeño peppers - 6
parsley leaves - (2 Tablespoons chopped)
1 pound Feta cheese - (2 1/2 cups crumbled)
3/4 teaspoon plus salt - divided
2 Tablespoons plus peanut oil - divided
1/2 teaspoon celery salt
1/2 teaspoon ground cumin
4 Tablespoons fresh lemon juice
2 Tablespoons honey
1 teaspoon dried summer savory
12 corn tortillas
1 cup sour cream
paprika

Trim, scrape the strings from and cut the celery into 1/4 inch dice.

Remove the stem buttons and cut the tomatoes into 3/8 inch dice.

Wearing plastic gloves, trim the stems from, cut the jalapeño peppers in half lengthwise, remove seeds and membrane and mince the flesh.

Mince the parsley and reserve it.

Crumble the Feta cheese into small (not fine) even pieces and reserve it.

Sauté the celery, sprinkled with 1/4 teaspoon of the salt in the 2 tablespoons of oil in a large frying pan (see utensils) over medium heat for 3 minutes. Add the tomatoes, jalapeños, 1/2 teaspoon of the salt, the celery salt, cumin, lime juice and honey. Cook the sauce, uncovered, 25 minutes, stirring occasionally. The sauce should be thick and very lumpy. If it looks too liquid turn up the heat a little to evaporate juices. Add the reserved parsley and the savory crushing it, and cook 5 minutes longer. Remove the pan from the heat.

Meanwhile, place some peanut oil in a cup and using a pastry brush, brush a griddle set over medium high heat with it. Fry the tortillas for about 1 minute on each side, until they are fairly crisp, transfer them to paper towels and lightly salt them.

Spread 2 or 3 tablespoons of the tomato sauce in an oiled 10 inch diameter, 2 inch deep, 10 cup cast iron frying pan or baking dish. Tear 4 of the tortillas into bite size pieces and scatter them in the bottom of the pan. Sprinkle 1/3 of the crumbled cheese over them, then spread 1/3 of the remaining sauce over the cheese. Repeat the layers 2 more times, ending with a layer of sauce.

Tightly cover the pan with foil and bake the chilaquiles in a preheated 375 degree overn 35 minutes. Remove the pan from the oven, remove the foil and allow it to stand 15 minutes. Decorate the top of the chilaquiles with a wreath of sour cream dollops. Dust the top of the sour cream with paprika and serve the chilaquiles right from the pan.

4 to 6 servings

Note: The green tomatoes called for in this recipe are the ordinary garden variety not tomatillos.

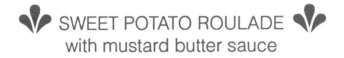

SWEET POTATO ROULADE
with mustard butter sauce

Begin with cream of pea soup. The sweet potato roulade looks very effective presented on a long, narrow cutting board; serve sautéed celery with it. A salad course of tossed iceberg lettuce with some homemade biscuits would be nice followed by fresh blackberries.

1 pound sweet potato - 1 large should do it!
2 pounds untrimmed mustard greens - (8 packed cups trimmed)
4 quarts plus 6 Tablespoons water - divided
1 Tablespoon salt - divided
1/4 cup roasted, peeled peanuts - (see peanuts)
3 eggs - at room temperature
8 Tablespoons butter - divided
4 Tablespoons flour
2 teaspoons honey -divided
6 egg yolks - at room temperature

8 egg whites - at room temperature
1/3 teaspoon cream of tartar
1 Tablespoon fresh lemon juice
1/2 teaspoon freshly cracked black pepper
mustard butter sauce - (recipe follows)

Bake the potato as directed. (See baked sweet potatoes.) Cut it in half and scoop out only enough flesh to measure 1 cup and purée it through a food mill set over a bowl. (Save any excess flesh for a bouillon soup. See bouillon soups.)

Thoroughly wash the greens in a basin or sink full of cold water. Drain them in a colander, removing the stems and any thick center ribs from the leaves. Bring the 4 quarts of water to boil with 1 teaspoon of the salt in a large kettle over high heat. Add the greens and cook them, uncovered, for 15 to 20 minutes, depending upon their maturity, from the moment they are all in the water, regardless of when the water returns to boil. Push the greens down into the water with a longhandled, wooden spoon and adjust the heat to keep the water slowly boiling. Drain the greens into the colander and immediately turn them into a basin of cold water for 1 minute. Then turn them into the colander again, place a saucer with a moderate weight upon it on them and allow them to drain 10 minutes, pressing them several times.

Using a heavy knife, evenly, but not too finely, chop the peanuts.

Hard cook and peel the 3 eggs as directed. (See cooked eggs.)

(Up to this point everything can be prepared as much as 24 hours in advance, separately sealed in plastic and refrigerated then brought to room temperature before continuing with the recipe.)

Purée the hard cooked eggs with the 6 tablespoons of water in the processor. Taking the greens, a handful at a time, squeeze the remaining moisture out of them, place them in the processor with the egg purée and process 5 seconds. Alternatively, put the hard cooked eggs, along with the squeezed greens, through an old fashioned food chopper (see utensils) and then stir in the water. In either case reserve the mixture.

Butter a 17 by 11 inch jelly roll pan. Cover it with a piece of aluminum foil and butter the foil heavily. Set the pan aside.

Melt 4 tablespoons of the butter in a heavy saucepan over low heat. Using a rubber spatula, blend in the flour, stirring constantly until the butter is absorbed. Stir in the puréed potato, 1 teaspoon of the salt and 1 teaspoon of the honey. Remove the pan from the heat and allow it to cool a bit.

Meanwhile, in a large mixing bowl, using a wire whisk, beat the yolks until they are light. Then slowly beat the potato mixture into them.

Now, in a second large mixing bowl, using the electric mixer, beat the whites until they are frothy, add the cream of tartar and continue to beat the whites, at high speed, now, until they are glossy and hold stiff but not dry peaks when the beaters are lifted.

Using a wooden spoon stir 2 tablespoons of the beaten egg whites into the potato mixture. Then carefully slide the rest of the whites onto the top of the mixture. Using the wooden spoon or a rubber spatula, gently fold the beaten egg whites into the potato mixture, inserting the spoon into the center of the whites, bringing it down underneath and then using an up and over rolling motion, so as not to deflate the whites, while intermittently rotating the bowl itself. Don't overdo the mixing, a lot of fluffy white curds should still be visible.

Slide the soufflé mixture into the prepared pan and carefully spread it around with a broad knife or spatula. Evenly sprinkle the chopped peanuts over the soufflé and bake it in a preheated 325 degree oven 25 to 30 minutes until it is golden and firm.

Meanwhile, melt 4 tablespoons of the butter in a saucepan over low heat, add the reserved purée of greens, 1 teaspoon of the salt, 1 teaspoon of the honey, the lemon juice and pepper. Stir well to blend and keep the mixture warm, uncovered, over very low heat.

When the soufflé is ready remove it from the oven, lay a linen towel over it then set the bottom of a large cookie sheet over the towel. Holding the jelly roll pan and the cookie sheet together, turn them over, remove the jelly roll pan then carefully peel away the foil. Working quickly, trim about 1/4 inch off of each short end of the soufflé´ with a sharp knife. Evenly spread the mixture of warm greens over the soufflé, leaving a 1 inch margin uncovered at each short end. Starting at a short end, carefully roll up the roulade, lifting the towel underneath it to assist in the process. Neatly trim about 1/2 inch off of each end of the roulade and carefully roll it onto a warm serving platter or cutting board.

Now, keep the roulade warm in a preheated 200 degree oven for the few minutes it will take to make the mustard butter sauce, since the sauce can not wait. To serve the sweet potato roulade, cut it into 3/4 inch thick slices with a serrated bread knife. Allow 2 slices per serving and ladle a generous amount of the warm mustard butter sauce over the slices as you serve them.

8 servings

mustard butter sauce

2 Tablespoons English mustard powder
2 Tablespoons fresh lemon juice
1 cup butter

In a small cup, dissolve the mustard powder in the lemon juice and reserve it.

Warm 1 tablespoon of butter in a small saucepan over low heat. Just before it is completely melted, add another tablespoon; repeat the process until all the butter has been used. Remove the pan from the heat and stir in the lemon juice. Transfer the sauce to a warm bowl and serve it immediately.

about 1 cup

Note: The result is a slightly thick, melted but not separated butter sauce, so do not try to keep it warm.

 FENNEL À LA GRECQUE

Purée of fava bean will be the soup this evening. Fennel à la grecque is often served cold, as a salad, but it's lovely just slightly warm and served as an entrée, as it is here. The accompaniment of sautéed mushrooms can be served just slightly warm too. A tossed salad of escarole with some pita bread will make a good salad course. Finish with large bunches of purple grapes.

1 1/3 cups long grain brown rice - about 9 1/2 ounces
6 Tablespoons olive oil - divided
1 1/2 teaspoons salt - divided
1 jar pimentos - 4 ounces - (1/2 cup pieces)
1 jar pitted green olives - 2 ounces - (1/2 cup pieces)
1 bay leaf
7 black peppercorns
7 coriander seeds

1/4 teaspoon dried thyme
1/4 teaspoon dried oregano
1/4 teaspoon dried basil
2 cups water
4 Tablespoons fresh lemon juice
1 teaspoon honey
4 pounds fennel with tops - 2 large bulbs
reserved fennel leaves

Steam the rice as directed. (See steamed long or short grain brown rice.) In a warm bowl, toss the rice with 2 tablespoons of the oil and 1/2 teaspoon of the salt. Cover the bowl and keep it warm but not hot over warm water.

Meanwhile, drain, rinse and drain the pimentos and olives. Tear the pimentos and break the olives into pieces and reserve them.

Crushing the bay leaf, tie it, with the peppercorns, coriander seeds, thyme, oregano and basil, in a little cheese cloth bag.

In a large frying pan (see utensils) over high heat, bring the water with 4 tablespoons of the oil, 1 teaspoon of the salt, the lemon juice, honey and the herb bag to simmer, covered. Reduce the heat to medium low and allow the marinade to simmer while you prepare the fennel.

Cut the green tops from and trim the fennel bulbs. Reserve a handful of the leaves. Quarter the bulbs, lengthwise and trim them, discarding any coarse outer ribs. Rinse the quarters. Add the fennel to the pan of simmering marinade and cook it, covered, about 15 minutes from the moment it is in the liquid regardless of when the liquid returns to simmer or until it is just tender when pierced with a wooden toothpick, turning the quarters over once during that period. When the fennel is done, using a pair of tongs, transfer it from the pan to a colander and allow it to drain.

Add the reserved pimento and olive pieces to the marinade liquid in the pan, turn the heat up to high and reduce the liquid, uncovered, to 1 cup. Remove the herb bag and remove the pan from the heat.

Spread the rice on a serving platter and arrange the fennel quarters on it. Spoon the marinade liquid, with the pimentos and olives, over the fennel and rice. Decorate the edges of the platter with the reserved fennel leaves. Serve the fennel à la grecque just slightly warm or at room temperature.

4 servings

WISCONSIN CHEDDAR PIE

Plan your time before beginning to make this really impressive dish for dinner. A cream of lima bean soup and a salad of Brussels sprouts vinaigrette for the same meal can both be prepared a day in advance; and the baking and cooling period for the pie will allow you plenty of time to prepare whipped scalloped squash to serve with the pie. Poached pears will round out the meal.

Cheddar cheese pastry dough - (recipe follows)
6 eggs - at room temperature
1 1/2 pounds boiling potatoes - 8 small
water
2 1/2 teaspoons of salt - divided
1 1/2 pounds tomatoes - 6 small
12 ounces sharp Wisconsin Cheddar cheese - (3 cups grated)
3/4 teaspoon freshly cracked black pepper
flour
3/4 teaspoon ground (rubbed) sage
3/4 teaspoon dried thyme
3 Tablespoons butter - cold
1 egg yolk

Prepare the pastry dough up to 24 hours in advance and refrigerate it as directed.

Hard cook and peel the eggs as directed. (See cooked eggs.) Allow them to cool to room temperature then refrigerate them for 1 hour to help them remain firm while being sliced.

Peel the potatoes and uniformly cut them into 1/16 inch thick slices. Bring enough water to cover the potatoes by 1 1/2 inches, with 1 teaspoon of the salt, to boil in a large saucepan over high heat. Slide the potatoes into the boiling water, all at once, and start counting the cooking time from the moment they are in the water, regardless of when the water returns to boil. Cook the potatoes, covered with lid slightly ajar, just 5 minutes, adjusting the heat to keep the water slowly boiling and stirring them once or twice with a wooden spoon. Drain the potatoes and immediately turn them into a basin of cold water for 3 minutes. Drain them again, well, and blot them dry on paper towels.

Peel and seed the tomatoes as directed. (See peeled tomatoes and see seeded tomatoes.) Cut them crossways into 1/4 inch thick slices and set them aside on a plate and allow them to drain a bit.

Meanwhile, coarsely grate the cheese.

Now, divide the largest piece of pastry dough into 2 equal parts and using a lightly floured rolling pin on a lightly floured work surface, roll out each part into a 15 by 4 1/2 inch rectangle, neatly trimming each end of the rectangles. Fit the rectangles into the sides of a 9 inch in diameter, 3 inch deep, 10 cup springform pan so that the ends of the rectangles overlap each other by 1/2 inch, moistening the ends of the rectangles and pressing them to each other. Firmly press the dough against the sides of the pan, allowing about 1/2 inch of dough to lay all around the edge of the floor of the pan. Let the excess dough at the top of the pan hang over the edges of the pan.

Roll 1 of the other 2 pieces of dough out into a disc, 10 inches in diameter. Neatly trim the edges of the disc and fit it down onto the floor of the pan, 1/2 inch of the dough will stand up all around the edges. Moisten the edges with a little water and press them to the dough on the sides of the pan.

Lay 1/3 of the sliced potatoes in the bottom of the dough lined pan. Sprinkle them with 1/4 teaspoon of the salt and 1/8 teaspoon of the pepper. Slice 2 of the cold, hard cooked eggs very thin and spread them over the potatoes. Blot 1/3 of the sliced tomatoes on paper towels and on a plate, lightly dredge them in flour then spread them over the eggs. Sprinkle them with 1/4 teaspoon of the salt, 1/8 teaspoon of the pepper, 1/4 teaspoon of the sage and 1/4 teaspoon of the thyme, crushing it. Then dot the tomatoes with 1 tablespoon of the butter, cut in small pieces. Spread 1/3 of the grated cheese over all and repeat the layers twice more.

Roll out the remaining piece of dough into a disc, 11 inches in diameter. Lay the disc over the pie and trim both the layers of dough that are hanging over the edges of the pan to 3/4 inch from the rim. Moisten, all around, in between the layers and press them together. Now, moisten the bottom side of the edge of dough and fold it in half, back under itself. Flute the edge of dough with your fingers so that it stands up all around the edges of the pie while pressing it firmly onto the rim of the pan to keep the dough from sliding down into the pan while baking.

Gather up all the scraps of dough into a ball and roll it out. Cut fanciful flower, leaf and vine shapes out of the dough. (I use a small daisy shaped cookie cutter.) Always make decorations larger than necessary since they will shrink while baking. In a cup, using a fork, beat the egg yolk with 1 teaspoon of water. Using a feather pastry brush, lightly paint the entire top and edges of the pie with the beaten egg. Arrange the cut out shapes on top of the pie, a little closer together than it looks as if they should be, then paint them with the beaten egg. Using the tines of a fork, pierce the top of the pie a number of times, in between the decorations.

Bake the pie in a preheated 450 degree oven for 20 minutes. Reduce the heat to 375 degrees and bake 20 minutes longer, lightly covering the pie with foil if it begins to brown too much. Remove the pie from the oven, remove foil if used, and carefully remove the sides of the pan. Return the pie to the oven for 5 minutes. Set the Wisconsin Cheddar pie on a cake rack and allow it to stand at least 30 minutes before serving.

6 generous servings

cheddar cheese pastry dough

4 ounces sharp Wisconsin Cheddar cheese - (1 cup grated)
2 cups minus 2 Tablespoons all purpose flour
2 Tablespoons cornstarch
1 teaspoon English mustard powder
1 teaspoon salt
2/3 cups butter - cold
4 to 5 Tablespoons cold water

Process the cheese about 10 seconds in the processor until it is fine or grate it on a hand grater with small holes.

Sift the dry ingredients together into a mixing bowl. Cut in the butter using a pastry blender then quickly rub the flour through the butter with your fingertips until the mixture is granular. Using a fork thoroughly stir in the cheese. Add the water, a little at a time, still stirring with the fork, using only as much as is necessary until a dough begins to form. Then, with your hands, gather the dough into a ball, handling the dough as little as possible. Divide the dough into 3 parts, 2 equal and one slightly larger. Wrap the pieces of dough, separately, in wax paper then seal them in plastic and allow them to rest, refrigerated, 1 hour.

 BRUSSELS SPROUTS SUPREME
in chestnut sauce

First, present saffron consommé royale before this superb dish of fresh Brussels sprouts in a rich chestnut sauce. Accompany the entrée with braised fennel. Then serve a tossed romaine salad and popovers. Follow with chilled yellow Delicious apples for dessert.

chestnut sauce - (recipe follows)
2 pounds Brussels sprouts - 64 to 80 of equal size - (8 cups whole)
2 Tablespoons unsalted butter - at room temperature
parsley - 4 sprigs

Prepare the chestnut sauce and keep it warm as directed.
Prepare and steam the Brussels sprouts as directed. (See steamed Brussels sprouts.) Working quickly, in a warm pan or bowl, toss the hot Brussels sprouts with the butter, cut into little pieces, until they are well coated.
Pour about 1 cup of the warm chestnut sauce onto each of 4 warm dinner plates. Spoon the Brussels sprouts, equally divided among the 4 plates, on top of the sauce so that they are in but not under the sauce. Tuck a sprig of parsley on the side of each plate and serve the Brussels sprouts supreme in chestnut sauce immediately.

4 servings

chestnut sauce

1 1/4 pounds chestnuts - about 50
3 to 4 cups stock broth - divided - (see stock broth)
1 bay leaf
1 teaspoon salt - divided
reserved cooking liquid
4 Tablespoons unsalted butter
1/2 teaspoon honey
1/8 teaspoon white pepper

Peel the chestnuts as directed. (See peeled chestnuts.)

Simmer the peeled chestnuts in 2 1/2 cups of the stock broth with the bay leaf and 1/2 teaspoon of the salt in a medium size saucepan, covered, over medium low heat 30 minutes or until they are soft. Drain the chestnuts reserving the cooking liquid and discarding the bay leaf. Add enough additional stock broth to the reserved cooking liquid for a total measurement of 2 cups. Purée the chestnuts, along with the 2 cups of liquid in the blender or processor.

Melt the butter in a heavy sauce pan over low heat. Stir in the puréed chestnuts, honey, 1/2 teaspoon of the salt and the pepper. Heat the sauce, below simmering, until it is hot. Cover the pan with a trimmed piece of paper towel and lid and keep the sauce warm over very low heat until serving.

4 cups

FINNISH MUSHROOM PUDDING

When I was a little girl I had a friend whose parents were Finnish. We would ride our bicycles together and stop off at her house, which was on the edge of the woods, for a snack. One day we had a wonderful mushroom pudding that her mother had made. There was much smiling and nodding for her mother did not speak a word of English. Years later when I learned to identify and pick Chanterelle mushrooms, the memory of that wonderful pudding came flooding back to me. It had, of course, been made with Chanterelles. Serve noodle soup first then accompany the pudding with braised rutabaga. A tossed salad of watercress with rye bread is next and the dessert for this very special dinner is fresh blueberries.

2 pounds Chanterelle mushrooms - (10 cups chopped) - (see note)
American type white bread - 6 slices - (3 cups torn)
1 1/2 cups light cream - at room temperature
celery - 2 large ribs - (1 cup chopped)
dill leaves - (1/4 tightly packed cup chopped)
1/2 teaspoon celery salt
6 Tablespoons butter
2 teaspoons salt - divided
7 egg yolks - at room temperature

1 teaspoon honey
1/2 teaspoon white pepper
nutmeg - (1/4 teaspoon freshly grated)
3 egg whites - at room temperature
pinch cream of tartar
2 Tablespoons bread crumbs - (see bread crumbs)

Using a soft little brush, brush the tiny particles of debris from the forest floor off of the mushrooms. Trim, wipe with a damp cloth, if necessary, and coarsely chop the mushrooms. (If you've picked the mushrooms yourself, cleaning them may be time consuming. They can be prepared early in the day and refrigerated in a paper bag until ready to continue with the recipe.)

Tear the bread into pieces without removing the crusts. Place it in a bowl, pour the cream over it and allow it to soak while you prepare the rest of the dish.

Trim, scrape the strings from and dice the celery.

Chop the dill leaves.

Sauté the celery, sprinkled with the celery salt, in the butter in a large frying pan (see utensils) over medium heat, 3 minutes. Add the mushrooms, sprinkle with 1 1/2 teaspoons of the salt and sauté about 10 minutes while gradually increasing the heat to high until all the moisture has evaporated from the mushrooms. Stir in the dill then transfer the mixture to a large mixing bowl and allow it to cool a bit.

Transfer the bread and cream to the container of the processor or blender, add the egg yolks, honey, 1/2 teaspoon of the salt, the pepper and nutmeg and purée the contents. Alternatively, pass the bread with the cream through a food mill, set over a bowl, then beat in the yolks and other ingredients. Now stir the puréed bread mixture into the mushrooms.

In a large mixing bowl, using the electric mixer, beat the egg whites until they are frothy. Add the cream of tartar and continue to beat the whites, at high speed now, until they hold soft peaks when the beaters are lifted. Then carefully slide the beaten whites onto the top of the bread and mushroom mixture. Using a wooden spoon or a rubber spatula, gently fold the beaten whites into the mushroom mixture, inserting the spoon into the center of the whites, bringing it down underneath then using an up and over rolling motion so as not to deflate the whites, while intermittently rotating the bowl itself.

Slide the pudding mixture into a buttered, flat bottomed, 6 cup baking dish or pan and evenly sprinkle it with the bread crumbs. Bake the pudding in a preheated 325 degree oven, 1 hour, until it is firm, puffed and golden. Check it after about 40 minutes in the oven, if it is browning too quickly, lightly cover it with foil. Allow it to stand, 30 minutes, at room temperature before serving. Finnish mushroom pudding is at its flavor peak when served just slightly warm.

6 to 8 servings

Note: Two pounds of Chanterelles sounds extravagant, but if you know where to pick them, they are abundant and they are free. A word of caution: Never pick wild mushrooms unless you are knowledgeable in their identification and know exactly what you are picking.

STUFFED BUTTERNUT SQUASH
with cranberry sauce

Everyone knows how well apple sauce goes with acorn squash, but did you know how well cranberry sauce goes with butternut squash? It does, and the combination has lots of eye appeal. Serve cream of stock vegetable purée soup then accompany the squash with buttered spinach for more glorious color. A salad of kohlrabi vinaigrette is accompanied by cornbread and some Coon cheese. Fresh pears will make the perfect dessert.

cranberry sauce - (recipe follows)
butternut squash - 2 medium, 3 pounds each
1 Tablespoon plus 1 teaspoon butter
salt

Prepare the cranberry sauce and remove it from the refrigerator as directed.
Prepare and bake the squash as directed. (See baked butternut squash.) Set a half squash, cut side up on each of 4 warm dinner plates. Place 1 teaspoon of the butter in each cavity, lightly sprinkle it with salt and fill the cavity with the cranberry sauce, mounding it. Serve the stuffed butternut squash with cranberry sauce along with plenty of extra butter.

4 servings

cranberry sauce

1 pound cranberries - (4 cups)
oranges - 2 or 3 average
2 teaspoons orange zest
1 cup orange juice
2 cups sugar

Cull the cranberries, removing any tiny stems. Rinse and drain them in a colander.

Grate only the thin outer, orange colored part of the orange rind and reserve the zest. Squeeze the orange juice.

Bring the juice with the zest and sugar to boil, in a saucepan large enough to prevent boil overs, over high heat. Add the cranberries all at once and, without stirring, boil them for 5 minutes from the moment they are in the liquid, adjusting the heat to keep the liquid slowly boiling. Remove the pan from the heat, skim off the foam and allow the sauce to cool to room temperature. Refrigerate it, covered, at least 2 hours. Remove the cranberry sauce from the refrigerator 30 minutes before serving and transfer it to a serving dish.

about 3 cups

Note: As with so many things, the flavor of cranberry sauce mellows and develops in 24 hours. So try to prepare it a day in advance if you can.

 CABBAGE CASSEROLE

I use the same large oval baking dish for this cabbage casserole as I use for the summer squash casserole, but any baking dish or pan will do as long as it's deep enough and large enough. Let's start off this rather autumnal dinner with cream of tomato soup. Serve sautéed parsnips with the cabbage casserole. Have a tangy celery hearts vinaigrette for the salad course along with some whole wheat bread. Then set out a bowl of polished apples.

2 1/2 cups dried cranberry beans - 1 pound - (see note)
1 bay leaf
2/3 cup wheat berries - about 5 ounces
water
2 1/2 pounds Savoy cabbage - 1 medium small head - (see note)
2 cups shelled walnut haves - about 8 ounces
8 ounces dill pickles - (1 cup chopped)
2 teaspoons dill seeds
12 ounces extra sharp Vermont Cheddar cheese - (3 cups grated)
5 1/2 Tablespoons butter - divided
4 Tablespoons peanut oil
2 teaspoons salt
2 teaspoons celery salt
1/2 teaspoon freshly grated black pepper
3 Tablespoons honey

Soak the beans and cook them, with the bay leaf, as directed. (See boiled dried shelled beans.) Drain them, discarding the bay leaf.

At the same time, soak, cook and drain the wheat berries as directed. (See boiled wheat berries.)

Fill a large kettle with enough water to cover the head of cabbage and bring it to boil over high heat. Using a small knife cut down deep into the cabbage around the stem to loosen the leaves. With 2 longhandled wooden spoons, lower the cabbage into the boiling water and cook it, covered, 5 minute from the moment it is in the water regardless of when the water returns to boil. Remove the lid and using the 2 wooden spoons, carefully remove each successive leaf as it becomes loosened and set it aside to drain. You may have to remove the cabbage head from the water once and cut down around the stem again in order to loosen the rest of the leaves. When the head becomes too small to handle easily in the water, just take it out to finish removing the small leaves. Reserve the 2 largest best looking leaves then cut the thickest part of the center rib out of all the rest of the leaves. Blot the the leaves dry with paper towels.

Using a heavy knife coarsely chop the walnuts.

Quarter the pickles lengthwise, coarsely chop them then rinse and drain them well.

Toast the dill seeds in a dry, pan over medium heat, stirring constantly for 3 minutes until they become fragrant and take color. Immediately remove them from the pan and crush them, 1/2 teaspoon at a time in a mortar or use a spice grinder.

Coarsely grate the cheese.

In a large frying pan (see utensils) over medium heat, combine 4 tablespoons of the butter, the oil, drained beans, drained wheat berries, chopped nuts and pickles, salt, celery salt, pepper, honey and crushed dill seeds. Turn and stir the ingredients until the seasonings are well distributed and the mixture is heated through.

Spread 1/4 of the cabbage leaves in the bottom of a buttered, flat, 2 1/2 inch deep 10 cup baking dish. Evenly spoon 1/3 of the bean mixture over them then evenly sprinkle 1 cup of the grated cheese over the bean mixture. Repeat the layers twice more. Then, cover the last layer of cheese with the remaining cabbage leaves, using the 2 largest reserved leaves with their center ribs still intact as the final cover, laying them so that the stem ends face each other and neatly tucking the edges of the leaves down into the dish.

Tightly cover the dish with a piece of foil which has been perforated with a number of small holes. Bake the cabbage casserole in a preheated 375 degree oven for 2 hours. Remove the dish from the oven, remove the foil and smear the top of the cabbage leaves with the remaining 1 1/2 tablespoons of butter. Allow the cabbage casserole to stand 15 minutes before serving. To serve, cut down into the casserole with a serrated knife and lift each serving out with a large serving spoon.

8 servings

Note: Dried cranberry beans are available at specialty and natural food stores. Cranberry beans are an old fashioned bean that is also delicious fresh. The pretty cranberry color striped beans are easy to grow. The fresh beans can be substituted for the dried in this cabbage casserole. In which case, allow 4 pounds of unshelled beans which will yield 6 to 7 cups of shelled beans. Cook the shelled, fresh beans, with the bay leaf, in enough simmering water to cover them until they are just tender.

You may want to buy a cabbage which is a little larger than needed since the outer leaves of Savoy cabbage are sometimes tough and must be discarded.

 FRITTATA

Serve a light stracciatella soup before this hearty frittata. A millet pilaf will go nicely with it, if you like. Sliced tomatoes and Italian bread make a good salad course for this meal. Then offer bunches of chilled green grapes.

8 ounces green bell pepper - 1 large - (1 heaping cup sliced)
8 ounces red bell pepper - 1 large - (1 heaping cup sliced)
1 pound mushrooms - medium - (5 cups sliced)
1 1/2 pounds boiling potatoes - 3 medium large - (3 heaping cups sliced)
12 eggs - at room temperature - divided
Italian parsley leaves - (1/2 packed cup chopped)
1 Tablespoon salt - divided
3 Tablespoons olive oil
9 Tablespoons plus butter - at room temperature - divided
1/4 cup milk - at room temperature
1/2 teaspoon ground rosemary - (see ground rosemary)
1 teaspoon celery salt
1/2 teaspoon freshly cracked black pepper
1 teaspoon dried oregano
Parmesan cheese - (1/2 cup freshly grated)

Quarter the green and red bell peppers lengthwise. Core trimming away any white membrane and thinly slice the quarters crosswise.

Wipe the mushrooms with a damp cloth. Trim the butt ends of the stems and thinly slice the mushrooms lengthwise.

Peel and quarter the potatoes lengthwise. Thinly slice the quarters crosswise, dropping them into a bowl of cold water.

(The vegetables can be prepared several hours in advance, up to this point. Wrap the green and red peppers in wax paper, wrap the mushrooms in paper towels and cover the bowl of potatoes. If you refrigerate the vegetables be sure to bring them to room temperature before continuing with the recipe.)

Hard cook and peel 4 of the eggs as directed. (See cooked eggs.) Allow them to cool to room temperature then refrigerate them 1 hour to help them remain firm while being chopped. Coarsely chop and reserve them.

Chop the parsley fine and reserve it.

Generously butter a 10 inch in diameter, 2 inch deep, 10 cup cast iron frying pan, and refrigerate it.

Meanwhile, sauté the green and red bell peppers, together, sprinkled with 1/2 teaspoon of the salt, in the oil, in a large frying pan (see utensils) over medium heat for 10 minutes. Transfer the peppers with their cooking oil to a large bowl and reserve them.

Sauté the mushrooms, sprinkled with 1/2 teaspoon of the salt, in 3 tablespoons of the butter, over medium high heat for about 8 minutes while gradually raising the heat to high until all the moisture has evaporated. Transfer the mushrooms with their cooking butter to the large bowl and reserve them.

Drain the potatoes and blot them dry on paper towels. Sauté them, sprinkled with 1 1/2 teaspoons of the salt, in 4 tablespoons of the butter, over medium heat, for 5 minutes, stirring occasionally. Reduce the heat to low and cook the potatoes, covered, 5 minutes longer. Transfer the potatoes and their cooking butter to the large bowl. Using a wooden spoon, gently, stir all the vegetables together.

Take the cast iron frying pan from the refrigerator and heavily butter it again. Spread a piece of foil, with edges turned up, on the floor of the oven (under the element if it's electric) to catch any possible butter runover.

Now, in a large mixing bowl, using a wire whisk, lightly beat the remaining 8 eggs together with the milk. Using the wooden spoon, stir in 1/2 teaspoon of the salt, the ground rosemary, celery salt, black pepper and the oregano, crushing it, and the cheese. Add the reserved chopped eggs, reserved parsley and the mixed vegetables with all their cooking oil and butter, gently stirring them well to coat them thoroughly with the beaten eggs.

Carefully, pour the mixture into the buttered frying pan, dot with the remaining 2 tablespoons of butter, cut in pieces, and bake it in a preheated 325 degree oven 30 minutes. Lightly cover it with foil and bake it 45 minutes longer. Remove the pan from the oven and allow it to stand 10 minutes. Run a sharp knife down around the inside edges of the pan. Cover it with an inverted, flat, round, warm serving platter about 12 inches in diameter or a pizza pan. Using pot holders, hold the platter and the frying pan together, turn them over, tap the back of the pan with a wooden spoon then lift it off of the frittata. Smear the frittata with a little extra butter to make it shine and allow it to stand 10 minutes longer before serving.

8 servings

 CROQUETTES

Cream of spinach soup is the first course. Serve the croquettes with their beautiful accompaniment of a whole head of cauliflower. Then have a small salad of egg, tomato and lettuce with large crackers. Follow with poached apricots.

2 Tablespoons fennel seeds
1 cup roasted, peeled peanuts - about 4 1/2 ounces - (see peanuts)

2 cups plus 2 Tablespoons plus optional water
4 Tablespoons tomato paste
1/2 teaspoon liquid smoke
2 teaspoons salt - divided
1 cup oat groats - 7 ounces
4 Tablespoons peanut oil
2 Tablespoons light molasses
2 Tablespoons honey
2 Tablespoons soy sauce
2 Tablespoons cider vinegar
2 cups puréed stock vegetables - (see puréed stock vegetables)
nutmeg - (1 teaspoon freshly grated)
1 teaspoon celery salt
1/8 teaspoon cayenne
2 teaspoons dried thyme
3 eggs - divided
1/2 cup flour
3/4 cup bread crumbs - fine - (see bread crumbs)
4 cups peanut oil

Toast the fennel seeds in a dry pan over medium heat, stirring constantly for 3 minutes, until they take color and become fragrant. Remove them from the pan immediately and crush them fine, 1/2 teaspoon at a time, in a mortar or use a spice grinder. Reserve them.

Using a heavy knife or in the blender or for 5 seconds in the processor, chop the peanuts medium small. Reserve them.

Bring the 2 cups of water with the tomato paste, liquid smoke and 1/2 teaspoon of the salt to boil in a large frying pan (see utensils) over high heat. Sprinkle in the oats, reduce the heat to low and cook, covered, 30 minutes or until all the liquid has been absorbed, stirring occasionally. Then, remove the cover, add the 4 tablespoons of oil, the molasses, honey, soy sauce and vinegar and stir the mixture frequently for about 8 minutes, raising the heat to medium then lowering it as necessary until all liquid has been absorbed. Now, add the puréed stock vegetables, and sprinkle with 1 teaspoon of the salt, the reserved fennel, the nutmeg, celery salt and cayenne. Over low heat, stir and turn the mixture, using both a metal and rubber spatula for about 20 minutes until the mixture dries out and becomes pasty. Stir in the reserved peanuts and the thyme, crushing it. Remove the pan from the heat and allow the mixture to cool a bit. Now, thoroughly stir in 1 of the eggs then evenly spread the croquette mixture out on 2 dinner plates and refrigerate it, uncovered, overnight.

Next morning or at least 3 1/2 hours before serving time, in a small bowl, using a fork, beat the 2 remaining eggs with the 2 tablespoons of water and 1/2 teaspoon of the salt. Set out the flour and the bread crumbs, each in a small bowl. Scoop up an ample tablespoon of the croquette mixture, and with floured hands, shape it into a small cylinder about 2 inches long and about 7/8 inch in diameter. Roll the croquettes, one at a time, in the flour, dip them in the egg (if the egg becomes thickened with flour, thin it with a little water) then roll them in the bread crumbs. Lay the croquettes out on 2 dinner plates and refrigerate them for at least 2 hours before frying. (They will be crisper and firmer.) The yield should be 32 to 36 croquettes.

(Allowing about 15 minutes for the 4 cups of oil to heat to temperature, heat the oil in a deep saucepan, with a cooking thermometer clipped to the inside of it, over medium high heat to 375 degrees, or use an electric deep fryer set at 375 degrees).

Fry the croquettes, 6 at a time, for from 3 to 5 minutes or until they are golden brown and crisp. Using a frying basket or a skimmer, lift them from the oil and drain them on paper towels. Keep the croquettes warm on a baking sheet in a 200 degree oven until they are all done. Heap the croquettes on a warm serving platter to serve.

6 to 8 servings

BAKED ZITI WITH SWISS CHARD

Lately I'm enamored of a large, oven proof, rather shallow glass bowl to bake this dish in. Offer consommé jardinière then serve broiled eggplant slices along with the baked ziti with Swiss chard. Follow with a salad of red bell peppers vinaigrette and some crusty Italian bread. Chilled green grapes complete the dinner.

1 1/2 pounds Swiss chard - (9 packed cups cut)
3 cups tomato purée - 24 ounces
4 Tablespoons olive oil
2 teaspoons honey
1 bay leaf
4 1/4 teaspoons salt - divided
1/4 teaspoon celery salt
1/4 teaspoon freshly cracked black pepper
3 4 teaspoon dried basil
3/4 teaspoon dried oregano

1/2 cup milk - at room temperature
1 1/2 cups Ricotta cheese
3 quarts water
12 ounces dried ziti pasta
4 Tablespoons butter - at room temperature
Parmesan cheese - (1 cup freshly grated) - divided

Prepare, slicing it fairly fine, and blanch the Swiss chard as directed. (See blanched Swiss chard.) Immediately, turn the drained Swiss chard into a basin of cold water for 1 minute. Then, turn it into a colander, place a saucer with a moderate weight upon it on the Swiss chard and allow it to drain for 30 minutes turning it over 2 or 3 times during that period.

Meanwhile, in a medium size, heavy saucepan, over medium heat, bring the tomato purée with the oil, honey, bay leaf, 1/4 teaspoon of the salt, the celery salt and pepper to simmer. Reduce the heat to low, cover the pan with a trimmed piece of paper towel and lid and very gently simmer the sauce 25 minutes. Add the basil and oregano, crushing them and simmer 5 minutes longer.

In a small saucepan, bring the milk to simmer over medium heat. Remove the pan from the heat and allow it to cool a couple of minutes. Place the Ricotta in a large mixing bowl and slowly stir the milk into it. Add 1 teaspoon of the salt then thoroughly stir in the drained Swiss chard.

Bring the water to boil with 1 tablespoon of the salt in a large kettle over high heat. Add the ziti all at once, stirring it with a wooden spoon. Cook the pasta, covered with lid ajar, for 5 minutes from the moment it is in the water, regardless of when the water returns to boil. Adjust the heat to keep the water slowly boiling and stir the pasta occasionally. Drain the ziti well in a colander, shaking the colander, return the ziti to the warm kettle and toss it with the butter, cut in pieces, and 1/4 cup of the Parmesan.

Spread 1/3 of the ziti in a buttered, 10 cup oven proof bowl or baking dish. Cover it with 1/3 of the Swiss chard mixture and spoon 1/3 of the sauce over the Swiss chard. Sprinkle 1/4 cup of Parmesan over the sauce. Repeat the layers twice more. Lightly cover the dish with foil and bake it in a preheated 375 degree oven for 40 minutes. Remove the foil and bake 10 minutes longer. Allow the baked ziti with Swiss chard to stand 10 minutes at room temperature before serving.

4 to 6 servings

 CAMPFIRE LENTILS

These are quite literally campfire lentils. I recall having to drive five miles back to the house one time because once we got on the road, headed for a camping trip, I remembered that I had forgotten the bay leaves. Serve a small salad of iceberg wedges and sourdough bread for the salad course. Crisp green apples are dessert.

about 6 ounces small onions - about 8, 1 inch in diameter - (1 1/2 cups)
about 8 ounces boiling potatoes - 8 little new, 1 to 1 1/4 inches in diameter
- (1 1/2 heaping cups)
2 1/4 cups dried lentils - 1 pound
celery leaves - (1/2 cup chopped)
6 cups stock broth - (see stock broth)
2 bay leaves
4 Tablespoons peanut oil
4 Tablespoons butter
1 teaspoon honey
1/2 teaspoon liquid smoke
1 1/2 teaspoons salt
1 1/2 teaspoons celery salt
1/4 teaspoon freshly cracked black pepper
1 teaspoon cider vinegar
1/2 teaspoon ground (rubbed) sage
1/2 teaspoon ground thyme

Peel and prepare the onions as directed. (See peeled onions.)
Scrub the potatoes clean under running water. Do not peel them.
Cull and rinse the lentils.
Chop the celery leaves fine.
In a soup kettle set over high heat, combine the broth, bay leaves, oil, butter, honey, liquid smoke, salt, celery salt and pepper. When the mixture boils, add the onions, potatoes and lentils. When the liquid returns almost to boil, reduce the heat to low and simmer the stew, covered, 45 minutes stirring occasionally.
Add the celery leaves, vinegar, sage and thyme and simmer the campfire lentils 15 minutes longer.

4 servings

❤ ARTICHOKES POLONAISE ❤

Borscht will be the soup course tonight. The artichokes polonaise have maximum eye appeal when served in white dishes. Serve a rye berry pilaf with them. Next have a tossed chicory salad then finish with poached cherries.

2 eggs - at room temperature
6 Tablespoons bread crumbs - (see bread crumbs)
parsley leaves - (1/4 cup minced)
2 pounds 4 ounces baby artichokes - about 36 - (6 cups trimmed) - or 27 ounces frozen
about 1 pound 5 ounces cauliflower - about 1 small head - (4 cups florets)
about 10 ounces mushrooms - small - (4 cups cut)
2 Tablespoons cider vinegar
2 Tablespoons water
2 1/2 teaspoons salt - divided
5 Tablespoons butter - divided
4 Tablespoons olive oil
1/2 teaspoon celery salt
1/4 teaspoon freshly cracked black pepper
1 teaspoon honey
1 teaspoon dried marjoram
parsley - 4 springs

Hard cook and shell the eggs as directed. (See cooked eggs.) Allow the eggs to cool to room temperature then refrigerate them for 1 hour to help them remain firm while being chopped. Cut the eggs in half, separating the yolks from the whites. Crumble the yolks in a small bowl. Chop the whites fine and add them to the bowl of yolks.

Toast the bread crumbs in a dry pan, over medium heat, stirring constantly for 2 or 3 minutes until they are golden. Remove them from the pan immediately and add them to the bowl of eggs.

Mince the parsley leaves, add them to the bowl of eggs and crumbs and reserve the mixture.

Prepare the baby artichokes as directed. (See preparation of baby artichokes.) Or prepare frozen artichokes as directed. (See preparation of frozen artichokes.) Then place the frozen artichokes in a colander and allow them to thaw and drain completely.

Break the cauliflower up into very small florets, cutting them as necessary and trimming the stems. Steam them as directed, until they are just tender. (See steamed cauliflower florets.) Immediately turn the florets into a basin of cold water for 3 minutes. Then drain them well, blot them dry on paper towels and reserve them.

Wipe the mushrooms with a damp cloth, trim the butt ends of the stems and quarter the mushrooms lengthwise.

In a cup, combine the vinegar and the water, and reserve the mixture.

Sauté the mushrooms, sprinkled with 1 teaspoon of the salt in 4 tablespoons of the butter in a large frying pan (see utensils) over medium high heat, for about 8 minutes, while gradually increasing the heat to high until all the moisture has evaporated. Remove the mushrooms from the pan with a slotted spoon and reserve them.

Reduce the heat to medium and add the oil to the pan. Drain the baby artichokes and blot them, or the thawed, drained artichokes dry on paper towels. Sauté the artichokes, sprinkled with 1 teaspoon of the salt, the celery salt and pepper for 1 minute. Remove the pan from the heat, add the reserved vinegar mixture and the honey and cover the pan immediately. Return the pan to the heat and cook the artichokes 5 minutes.

Uncover the pan. Add the reserved cauliflower and mushrooms and the marjoram, crushing it. Using a wooden spatula, turn and mix the vegetables occasionally for about 5 minutes until all the vegetables are heated through and all the moisture has evaporated, turning up the heat if necessary.

Spoon the equally divided vegetables into each of 4 warm 1 cup gratin dishes, or similar small flat dishes, heaping them up.

Now, melt 1 tablespoon of the butter in a small pan over medium heat. Add the egg, crumb parsley mixture and sprinkle with 1/2 teaspoon of the salt. Heat and stir the mixture for about 2 minutes. Then, equally and evenly sprinkle the mixture over the vegetables and decorate the top of each serving with a sprig of parsley and set the dishes on dinner plates. The flavor peak of artichokes polonaise is warm rather than hot.

4 servings

 GLAZED ROOT ROAST

Cream of tomato soup will be served first. Then accompany this simple but unusual dish of glazed root vegetables with a barley pilaf. Yellow string beans vinaigrette served with bread and cheese will be next. Then have blueberries over ice cream.

1 1/2 pounds Swiss chard - (9 packed cups cut)
5 pounds mixed root vegetables of 5 different types - whole or in pieces, each whole or piece weighing about 4 ounces or 1 1/4 pounds per serving -suggested vegetables: carrots, parsnips, potatoes, rutabagas, turnips, beets, sweet potatoes, etc.
lemon juice - optional
1/2 teaspoon plus salt
vegetable glaze - (recipe follows)
4 Tablespoons butter
1/4 teaspoon freshly cracked black pepper

Prepare and blanch the Swiss chard as directed. (See blanched Swiss chard.) Immediately, turn the drained Swiss chard into a basin of cold water for 1 minute. Then turn it into a colander, place a saucer with a weight upon it on the Swiss chard and allow it to drain for 30 minutes, turning it over 2 or 3 times during that period.

Trim and peel the root vegetables. For carrots and parsnips, use only the upper half of extra large vegetables.

(The vegetables can be prepared in advance and most can be sealed in plastic. Parsnips must be covered with cold water in a bowl containing 1 teaspoon of lemon juice per cup of water. Potatoes must be covered with cold water. If the vegetables are refrigerated, be sure to bring them to room temperature before continuing with the recipe.)

Drain any vegetables that have been submerged in water and blot them dry with paper towels. Lightly salt all the root vegetables. Tightly wrap each group of the same type of vegetable in a foil package. Lay the packages on a baking sheet and bake the wrapped vegetables in a preheated 400 degree oven 55 minutes. (Carrots and rutabaga always seem to take a little longer so put them in the oven 10 minutes ahead of the other vegetables.)

Meanwhile make the glaze and reserve it as directed.

At this point, toss the compressed Swiss chard in the colander, using a wooden fork, to separate it.

Test the root vegetables by piercing them with a wooden skewer or toothpick to determine when they are done. When they are ready, remove them from the oven, unwrap them and set them, spaced apart, on the baking sheet, keeping beets on a spread out piece of foil with edges turned up. Using a pastry brush, paint each root vegetable, covering it completely, with the glaze. Then return the baking sheet to the 400 degree oven for about 5 minutes.

Meanwhile, melt the butter in a large saucepan over medium low heat. Add the Swiss chard, sprinkled with the 1/2 teaspoon of salt and the pepper and heat it, uncovered, 4 or 5 minutes, gently tossing it with the wooden fork, until it is just heated through. Then, spread the equally divided Swiss chard out on each of 4 warm dinner plates.

Now, using 2 large spoons, set a mixture of 5 glazed root vegetables on each bed of Swiss chard and serve the glazed root roast, immediately. Have plenty of extra butter on the table.

4 servings

vegetable glaze

2 Tablespoons cornstarch
1/2 cup cold water
4 Tablespoons soy sauce
3 Tablespoons red wine vinegar
4 Tablespoons molasses
2 Tablespoons honey
4 Tablespoons corn oil

In a small saucepan dissolve the cornstarch in the water, soy sauce and vinegar. Add the molasses and honey and bring the mixture to simmer over medium heat, stirring constantly with a rubber spatula. When the mixture simmers, reduce the heat slightly and simmer 2 minutes, still stirring constantly. Remove the pan from the heat and stir in the oil. Cover the pan with paper towel and lid and set it aside; the glaze does not need to be kept warm.

1 1/4 cups

GARDEN STYLE BRUSSELS SPROUTS

It's easy to find very small potatoes of just the right size, for this dish, when you grow them in hay. Otherwise, farm stands and some supermarkets have them toward the end of summer. Serve cream of lima bean soup first and have an oat pilaf with the garden style Brussels sprouts if you like. Follow with a salad of Boston lettuce then offer chilled cantaloupe for dessert.

2 cups butter
4 Tablespoons fresh lemon juice
2 pounds Brussels sprouts - 64 to 80 sprouts, 1 to 1 1/4 inches in diameter
- (8 cups whole)
2 pounds boiling potatoes - about 32 little new, 1 to 1 1/4 inches in diameter
- (6 heaping cups whole)
about 2 pounds 11 ounces cherry tomatoes - (4 heaping cups whole) - at
room temperature
parsley leaves - (1/4 cup chopped)

Melt the butter in a small saucepan over low heat. When it has all melted, raise the heat to medium and stir it frequently. When the butter starts to bubble stir it constantly for about 5 minutes. When it starts to brown, remove the pan from the heat immediately. The butter should be just a delicate golden brown color. Stir the lemon juice into it, cover the pan with paper towel and lid and keep the butter warm.

Trim the Brussels sprouts. Peel the potatoes, even though they are very small, it is necessary for the beauty of this dish. Drop them into a bowl of cold water to cover. Remove any stems from the tomatoes. Leave all 3 vegetables whole. Chop the parsley fine and reserve it.

Butter the entire inside surface of an enameled 4 quart dutch oven or very large oven proof bowl and set it aside.

Steam the Brussels sprouts over already simmering water 20 to 30 minutes. Start testing them at about 18 minutes by piercing them with a wooden toothpick to determine when they will be just tender.

After the Brussels sprouts have been steaming for 10 minutes, start steaming the drained potatoes over already simmering water for about 15 minutes. Pierce them with a wooden toothpick to determine when they are just tender.

After the potatoes have been steaming 5 minutes, put the tomatoes in the dutch oven, tightly cover it and place it in a preheated 200 degree oven. It should take between 15 and 25 minutes for the tomatoes to become heated through, depending upon how ripe they are. Taste one to determine when they are ready.

Remove the dutch oven from the oven, uncover it and add the Brussels sprouts, potatoes, reserved parsley and 2 tablespoons of the browned butter. Using 2 wooden spoons, gently toss the vegetables together. Serve the garden style Brussels sprouts in the dutch oven, uncovered, immediately, along with the rest of the browned butter in individual size candle heated butter warmers and allow each diner to drench his own serving with the butter.

4 servings

Note: The cooking and heating times of the 3 vegetables will vary slightly and must be synchronized as close as possible. If the Brussels sprouts and potatoes must wait for the tomatoes to be ready, simply remove each steamer from the heat, remove the lid and cover the top of the steamer with a paper towel to keep the vegetable warm over the hot water. However, the tomatoes can not wait at all, otherwise they run the risk of becoming mushy. They must be hot but still firm.

FEUILLETÉE OF CREAMED ONIONS

Feuilletée or pâte feuilletée, the French words for puff pastry, is perhaps the ultimate culinary accomplishment. Serve as delicate tomato essence for the soup course. Accompany the feuilletée of creamed onions with buttered whole baby carrots. Then follow with a tossed endive salad, some French bread and Roquefort cheese. Finish with fresh pears.

puff pastry dough - (recipe follows)
about 1 pound onions - 24 small, about 1 inch in diameter - (about 4 cups)
water
1 1/4 teaspoon salt - divided
1 cup reserved blanching liquid
1 1/2 pounds unshelled peas - (1 1/2 cups shelled) - or about 7 1/2 ounces
frozen
3 Tablespoons butter
3 Tablespoons flour
pinch white pepper
1 cup heavy cream - at room temperature

1/2 teaspoon honey
1 egg yolk
1 teaspoon water

Prepare the sheets of puff pastry and keep them refrigerated as directed.

Peel and prepare the onions as directed. (See peeled onions.) In a saucepan over high heat, bring to boil enough water, with 1/2 teaspoon of the salt, to cover the onions by 1 1/2 inches. Add the onions and blanch them, uncovered, for 8 minutes, from the moment they are in the water, regardless of when the water returns to boil, adjusting the heat to keep the water slowly boiling. Drain the onions, reserving 1 cup of the liquid and immediately turn them into a basin of cold water for 3 minutes. Drain them well.

Shell the fresh peas or allow frozen peas to thaw and drain completely in a colander. In either case they do not need precooking.

At this point, remove the pastry sheets from the refrigerator, without unwrapping them, and allow them to become a little bit supple before they are utilized.

Melt the butter in a large, heavy saucepan over low heat. Using a rubber spatula, blend in the flour and pepper until they absorb the butter. Slowly stir in the cream, the 1 cup of reserved blanching liquid, the honey, and 3/4 teaspoon of the salt while raising the heat to medium until the mixture simmers and thickens. Remove the pan from the heat and carefully fold the onions and peas into the cream sauce. Spoon the equally divided creamed onions into each of 4, 5 to 6 inches in diameter, 2 cup, oven proof bowls. There must be 1 inch of headroom between the top of the creamed onions and the top of the bowl so that the bubbling sauce does not touch the pastry as it bakes.

In a cup, using a fork, beat the egg yolk with the 1 teaspoon of water. Unwrap the pastry sheets making note of which is the "up" side. Using a feather pastry brush, paint the "up" side of the sheets, with the yolk mixture, to within 1/4 inch of the 4 edges. Do not allow any of the yolk to drip over the edges, it would inhibit the pastry from rising. Lightly smear the rims of the bowls with the remaining yolk. Now simply lay the sheets, "down" side down, over each of the four bowls, taking care to center them. (The "up" side shrinks slightly when it is baked causing the feuilletée to reveal its many "leaves" in an attractive manner.) For convenience, set the bowls on a baking sheet large enough to accommodate them so that the pastry sheets do not touch one another.

Immediately, place the baking sheet in a preheated 425 degree oven, for 10 minutes. Reduce the heat to 350 degrees and bake 20 minutes longer. The feuilletée will look like puffed golden brown blankets draped over the bowls.

Place the bowls on small size plates set upon dinner plates and serve the feuilletée of creamed onions. Magnifique!

4 servings

Note: The feuilletée of creamed onions is eaten by breaking through the pastry with a fork and allowing the pastry to drop down into the bowl.

puff pastry dough

2 cups plus 2 Tablespoons minus 3/4 teaspoon all purpose flour
2 Tablespoons plus 3/4 teaspoon cornstarch
1 teaspoon salt
1 1/4 cups unsalted butter - cold - divided
8 to 12 Tablespoons ice cold water.

Sift the flour and cornstarch together into a mixing bowl. Remove and reserve 1/4 cup of the mixture.

Transfer the remaining 2 cups of sifted flour and cornstarch to the processor, add the salt and 4 tablespoons of the butter, cut in pieces, and process 20 seconds until the mixture is granular. Now, with the machine still running, slowly add about 8 tablespoons of the water to the processor, through the feed tube, or as much water as is necessary for the dough to form a ball. Then immediately shut the machine off.

Alternatively, add the salt and 4 tablespoons of the butter, cut in little pieces, to the 2 cups of sifted flour and cornstarch remaining in the bowl. Working quickly, with your fingertips, work the flour through the butter until the mixture is granular. Now, using a fork, slowly stir in about 8 tablespoons of the water or as much as is necessary to form a soft dough.

In either case, turn the dough out onto a lightly floured piece of wax paper and with lightly floured hands, shape the dough into a flat, 8 inch square, handling the dough as little as possible. The dough will be very rough looking. Wrap it in the wax paper then refrigerate it, sealed in plastic, for 1 hour.

Place 1 cup of the butter, cut in teaspoon size pieces, in the processor. Add the 1/4 cup of reserved flour mixture and process just until the butter is coarsely granular. Then turn the butter into a mixing bowl.

Alternatively, place 1 cup of the butter, cut in teaspoon size pieces, in a mixing bowl. Sprinkle the butter with the 1/4 cup of reserved flour mixture and using a pastry blender chop the butter until it is coarsely granular.

In either case, using your fingertips now, rub the flour through the butter until the mixture is smooth. Do not overwork the butter until it becomes greasy, it must be pliable but firm. Turn the butter out onto a piece of lightly floured wax paper, and with lightly floured hands, shape the butter into a flat, 5 inch square, wrap it in the wax paper and refrigerate it, sealed in plastic for only 30 minutes. (In other words place the butter in the refrigerator 30 minutes before the dough is ready to come out. Otherwise it may be too firm to roll out easily with the dough.)

Unwrap and lay the dough on a lightly floured work surface. Unwrap and lay the butter on the center of the dough catty-corner to the position of the dough. Fold the corners of the dough up over the butter firmly pressing the edges of the dough together, then press down on the seams with a rolling pin to seal them. The butter will be sealed in a package of dough that looks like the back of a letter envelope.

Now, ever so gently using a lightly floured rolling pin, start rolling out the dough in one direction, starting from the side closest to you. Do not lean on the rolling pin. Let the weight of the rolling pin do the work, just roll it along with long even strokes. Do not allow the rolling pin to roll over and off the far end of the dough. Lift the dough frequently, lightly dusting the work surface as necessary to keep the dough from sticking. Dust the rolling pin also, as needed. Roll the dough until it has reached a rectangular measurement of 6 by 14 inches, block it in with the sides of your hands or a ruler. Using a feather pastry brush, brush excess flour from the dough as you fold the length of the dough over itself in thirds, like a letter, to make the package of dough measure 6 by about 4 inches. Now, rotate the dough 90 degrees so that the narrow end is toward you and the last fold is on top.

Press the rolling pin across the far end of the dough to assist in sealing down the top fold. Then gently roll out and fold the dough again exactly as directed, always keeping the edges of the top fold as even as possible. On this second "turn" the dough may not want to roll out to the full 6 inch width, don't worry about it. You have now made 2 "turns". Wrap the dough in wax paper and refrigerate it, sealed in plastic, for 1 hour. Then make 2 more "turns", that will be 4 "turns" altogether. Now allow the dough to rest, wrapped in wax paper, sealed in plastic and refrigerated 12 hours or overnight.

The next day, using a sharp, heavy knife, cut the unwrapped package of dough crosswise into 2 equal pieces. Wrap, seal and refrigerate 1 piece while you roll out the other half. With the cut edge of the piece of dough toward you, last fold on top, roll the dough out as previously instructed, to a rectangular measurement of 14 1/2 by 6 1/2 inches. With the point of a sharp knife, trim away a long, 1/4 inch wide, strip of dough from all four sides of the rectangle. Now cut the rectangle in half, crosswise, to form 2, 7 by 6 inch sheets of puff pastry dough. (For future information, keep track of which was the "up" side and which was the "down" side of the dough when it was cut. Indicate the sides on the wax paper wrapping.) Wrap the sheets separately in wax paper, seal them in plastic and store them refrigerated. Repeat the steps with the other half of dough. At this point the sheets can be kept refrigerated 2 or 3 days.

4 small sheets of puff pastry dough

Note: You may vary the size of the finished sheets slightly, according to the size of your bowls. These instructions are for 5 inch bowls. For 6 inch bowls simply increase the measurements of each sheet by 1 inch in both length and width. (In other words increase the measurements of the last roll out to 16 1/2 by 7 1/2 inches.) The quantity of dough will easily accommodate it. The sheets must hang over the edge of the bowls by 1 inch on each side in the direction the dough was last rolled out in and only 1/2 inch on each of the other two sides. The reason is, the dough tends to stretch in its sideways direction when it is baked.

The classic method is to give the dough 6 "turns", but when working with a small amount of dough, which this recipe is, the pastry will puff better if only given 4 "turns". It will not be overworked.

Do not make puff pastry during humid or hot weather. A marble work surface is helpful in keeping the dough cool during roll out, but is not absolutely necessary. Before beginning puff pastry it's a good idea to lower the temperature of the room and turn the refrigerator to a warmer setting. If the butter becomes too firm when the dough is refrigerated between "turns" it can cause problems rolling out. To illustrate the proper temperature, there was a time when I would lay the wrapped dough on the cellar floor to rest between turns. That cellar floor was just the right temperature!

 PEASANT POTAGE

Peasant potage is a family favorite which is attractive enough to serve to company on a cold winter night. Since it is really a stew, no soup or accompaniment is necessary. Just serve a cauliflower vinaigrette with some homemade bread and a big piece of Cheddar cheese for the salad course. Blueberries over ice cream complete the meal.

2 cans peeled tomatoes - 28 ounces each - (7 cups)
3 pounds Hubbard squash - piece of a large - (8 packed cups cut)
1 pound untrimmed spinach - (8 packed cups trimmed)
8 Tablespoons butter
2 teaspoons honey
2 teaspoons salt
1/4 teaspoon freshly cracked black pepper
8 eggs - at room temperature - (see cooked eggs note)

Drain the tomatoes into a colander set over a large saucepan. Cut the stem buttons out of the tomatoes and crush the tomatoes through your (clean) fingers leaving them in the colander to drain further.

Meanwhile, scrape any seeds and membrane out of the piece of squash and cut it into 1 inch squares. Then slice off the skin.

Wash, trim and drain the spinach as directed. (See washed and trimmed spinach.)

Now, remove the colander with the tomatoes still in it from the saucepan and set it aside. Bring the liquid in the saucepan to boil over medium high heat. Add the butter, honey, salt, pepper and squash squares. When the liquid returns to boil reduce the heat to low and simmer the squash, covered, 20 minutes, gently stirring it occasionally with a wooden spoon. Then stir in the crushed tomatoes and when the liquid returns to boil again add all the spinach, cover the pan and cook 10 minutes longer, counting the time from the moment the pan is covered, stirring occasionally.

While the vegetables are cooking, cook the eggs 10 minutes and peel them as directed, allowing enough time to peel them. (See cooked eggs.)

When the peasant potage is ready ladle it, equally divided, into 4 warm bowls, nestle 2 eggs into the center of each bowl and serve.

4 servings

SUCCOTASH

This is a new dress for a very old lady, at least 300 years old. But don't be misled, it is hearty pilgrim fare. Start with cream of cauliflower soup. Then serve a traditional accompaniment of baked hubbard squash with the succotash. A tossed iceberg lettuce salad with some buttermilk biscuits will make a good salad course. Follow with poached pears.

corn - 4 ears - (2 cups kernels) - or about 12 ounces frozen
3 1/2 pounds unshelled lima beans - large - (4 cups shelled) - or about 20 ounces large frozen
1 pound red bell peppers - 2 large
celery - 2 large ribs - (1 cup cut)
1/4 teaspoon celery salt
4 Tablespoons butter
1/2 cup heavy cream - at room temperature
1/2 teaspoon honey
1 teaspoon salt
1/4 teaspoon freshly cracked black pepper
1/2 teaspoon dried thyme
1/4 teaspoon ground (rubbed) sage

Prepare and boil the corn as directed; but boil it only 3 minutes. (See boiled corn.) Immediately, turn the drained corn into a basin of cold water for 5 minutes. Drain again and carefully cut the kernels from the cob, separating them and crumbling them into a bowl. If you are using frozen corn, simply allow it to thaw and drain completely in a colander and blot it dry on paper towels. Reserve the corn.

Shell and steam the lima beans as directed, but steam them only 16 minutes. (See steamed lima beans.) Immediately turn them into a basin of cold water for 3 minutes, then drain them. If you are using frozen limas, blanch the still frozen beans in enough boiling water to cover them by 1 1/2 inches in a saucepan, uncovered, over high heat for 5 minutes from the moment they are in the water, regardless of when the water returns to boil, stirring the beans with a wooden spoon. Make sure they are undercooked. Drain and immediately turn them into a basin of cold water for 3 minutes then drain again. In either case, blot the lima beans on paper towels and reserve them.

Prepare and peel the bell peppers as directed. (See peeled red bell peppers.) Cut the quarters, lengthwise, into thin strips about 1/8 inch wide and reserve them.

Trim, scrape the strings from and dice the celery very small.

Sauté the celery, sprinkled with the celery salt, in the butter in a large frying pan (see utensils) over medium heat for 3 minutes. Remove the pan from the heat, add the cream, honey, salt, black pepper, thyme and sage then return it to the heat. Stir in the reserved corn and lima beans and cook the succotash, covered, 5 minutes, stirring once with the wooden spoon. Uncover the pan, increase the heat to medium high and cook the succotash, 5 minutes longer, gently stirring, until all the cream has been absorbed.

Pack the succotash, spreading it out, into 4 warm, 1 cup gratin dishes or other small, somewhat flat, oven proof dishes. Now, working quickly, lay the strips of red bell pepper over the succotash, about 3/4 inch apart, in a lattice pattern, using about 1/2 bell pepper per dish. Run the dishes under a preheated broiler, 3 inches from the heat source, for 2 minutes. Set the dishes on dinner plates and serve the succotash immediately.

4 servings

PENNSYLVANIA DUTCH EGG NOODLES WITH TURNIPS

Actually, I serve this noodle dish in a large, shallow, rectangular, enameled oven pan, rather than the recommended bowl in the recipe. It makes it easier to toss the noodles and turnips together and somehow noodles look just right in an enameled pan. Cream of pumpkin soup is the first course and green string beans is the accompaniment vegetable. The salad is sweet Italian frying peppers served with some sourdough bread and Farmers cheese. Dessert can be fresh cherries.

egg noodles - (recipe follows)
1 rounded teaspoon dried juniper berries - about 24
1/4 teaspoon black peppercorns
1 cup California white wine vinegar
3 1/2 quarts plus 1 cup water - divided
2 Tablespoons honey
1 bay leaf
2 teaspoons dried thyme - divided

1 Tablespoon plus 2 1/2 teaspoons salt - divided
1/2 cup bread crumbs - (see bread crumbs)
12 Tablespoons butter - divided
2 pounds white turnips - 8 medium - (6 cups cut)

Prepare the egg noodles in advance as directed.

Lightly crush the juniper berries in a mortar. Then toast them along with the peppercorns in a dry saucepan over medium heat, stirring, for 3 minutes. Add the vinegar and the 1 cup of water, the honey, bay leaf, 1 teaspoon of the thyme and 1 teaspoon of the salt. Increase the heat to medium high, when the liquid comes to simmer reduce the heat to low and simmer the mixture, covered, 10 minutes. Remove the pan from the heat and allow the mixture to steep while the rest of the dish is being prepared.

Toast the bread crumbs in 1 tablespoon of the butter in a heavy frying pan over medium heat, stirring constantly, for 3 minutes, until they are golden brown. Transfer the bread crumbs to a small bowl, toss them with 1 teaspoon of the thyme, uncrushed, and reserve them.

For convenience, cut 8 tablespoons of the butter into small pieces and set them out on a dinner plate to soften.

Trim, peel and cut the turnips in half, lengthwise. Lay the halves, cut side down, and cut each half, lengthwise, into 3 pieces of equal size. Thinly slice the pieces, crosswise.

(At this point set the 3 1/2 quarts of water with 1 tablespoon plus 1/2 teaspoon of the salt to boil in a large kettle over high heat.)

Now, sauté the turnips in 3 tablespoons of the butter in a large frying pan (see utensils) over medium heat, 3 minutes. Pour in the vinegar mixture (careful of steam) through a fine strainer discarding the spices. Increase the heat to high and boil the turnips, uncovered, about 12 minutes, stirring occasionally, and turning down the heat towards the end of the cooking period until all the liquid has evaporated. If the turnips must wait for the egg noodles to be ready, turn off the heat and cover the pan to keep them warm. Ideally the egg noodles should start cooking about 5 minutes before the turnips are done.

Drop the egg noodles all at once into the boiling water, stirring them with a wooden spoon. Cook the noodles, covered with lid ajar, 2 to 3 minutes from the moment they are in the water, regardless of when the water returns to boil, until they are tender firm, "al dente", adjusting the heat to keep the water slowly boiling and stirring occasionally. Drain the noodles well in a colander, shaking the colander.

Then turn them into a large, warm serving bowl. Using two wooden spoons or forks toss the noodles with the 8 cut tablespoons of butter and 1 teaspoon of the salt until they are well coated with the butter. Add the turnips and continue to toss until the noodles and turnips are combined.

Sprinkle the reserved bread crumbs over all and serve the Pennsylvania dutch egg noodles with turnips immediately.

4 to 6 servings

Note: The egg noodles must be swimming in butter - don't skimp!

egg noodles

about 2 cups unbleached all purpose flour
1/2 teaspoon salt
2 eggs - at room temperature
3 egg yolks - at room temperature - (see note)

Sift about 1 1/2 cups of the flour and the salt together into a mixing bowl. In another bowl, using a wire whisk, beat the eggs and yolks together until they are light. Then, using a fork, stir them into the flour until a just barely manageable dough forms. Turn the very loose dough out onto a lightly floured surface. With lightly floured hands, start kneading the dough while gradually incorporating only as much of the remaining flour as is necessary to form a smooth dough which no longer sticks to your hands. If the dough is going to be rolled out by machine, a little extra flour can be added to form a firmer dough. (The dough will be sticky at first and you may have to wash, dry and flour your hands once or twice.) Knead the dough more vigorously now folding it over itself and pressing it out repeatedly with the heel of your hand. If the dough is going to be rolled out by machine, only knead it vigorously for 3 minutes to form a cohesive mass, even though the pasta machine will knead the dough later. If the dough is going to be rolled out by hand, knead it vigorously for 10 minutes. The egg noodle dough will weigh about 18 ounces.

For machine (see utensils) rolled pasta, divided the dough into 8 pieces of equal weight, seal them in a plastic, they will not need to rest. Put 2 tablespoons of flour on a 12 inch square of wax paper and place it near the machine. Flatten 1 piece of the dough with your hands, flour it lightly and pass it through the widest setting of the smooth rollers of the machine. Turn the roller setting down 1 notch and run the dough through again. Lightly dust the dough with flour on both sides and continue to run the dough through progressively narrower settings, dusting it every other time and stopping at the setting just before the narrowest.

For hand rolled pasta, divide the dough into 4 pieces of equal weight, seal them in plastic and allow them to rest 1 hour. Then roll out the dough as directed. (See hand rolled pasta dough.) Each sheet of dough will measure about 16 inches in diameter.

Now, cut either the machine or hand rolled sheets of dough into 3/4 inch wide noodles as directed. (See hand cut noodles.)

Hang the noodles up to dry until they are brittle then break them into 2 inch long pieces. (See dried noodles.) These noodles can be made well in advance of serving. In which case, store them in an unsealed paper bag in a dry place. They keep well up to at least 4 weeks.

about 15 ounces dried egg noodles

A reminder: The eggs called for in this recipe are extra large as are all the other eggs called for in the recipes in this book.

CELERY AMANDINE

Begin this dinner with cream of pea soup. Celery amandine looks best served on oval dinner plates, if you have them. It's pretty vegetable accompaniment is baked acorn squash. Then have a tossed romaine salad and some warm rolls. Finish with an elegant fresh pineapple.

1/2 cup sliced unblanched almonds - about 2 1/2 ounces
celery - 1 very large bunch
4 cups stock broth - (see stock)
1 bay leaf
1 3/4 cups reserved cooking liquid
3 Tablespoons cornstarch
1/8 teaspoon white pepper
1/4 cup cold water
1 teaspoon salt
4 Tablespoons butter

Toast the almonds in a dry pan over medium heat, stirring for about 3 minutes until they are golden. Remove them from the pan immediately and reserve them.

Select a handsome bunch of celery and, crosswise, cut off the lower 6 inches. (Save the tops for a bouillon soup. See bouillon soups.) Trim the bottom of the bunch and scrape the strings from the outer ribs. Carefully quarter the bunch lengthwise, leaving the little yellow inner leaves intact. Then spray water down into the wedges to remove any soil.

Bring the broth with the bay leaf to boil in a medium size saucepan over high heat. Add the quartered celery to the broth pushing it down so that the broth covers it. Cook the celery, covered, for 5 minutes from the moment it is in the broth, regardless of when the broth returns to boil, adjusting the heat to keep the liquid slowly boiling. Remove the pan from the heat and drain off the liquid, reserving 1 3/4 cups of it. (Save remaining liquid for that bouillon soup.) Leave the celery in the covered saucepan to keep it warm, off the heat.

In a small saucepan dissolve the cornstarch and pepper in the cold water then stir in the reserved liquid. Bring the mixture to simmer over medium heat while stirring constantly with a rubber spatula. When the mixture simmers, reduce the heat slightly and continue to simmer and stir for 2 minutes. Add the salt, butter, and reserved almonds to the sauce and remove the pan from the heat.

Place the quartered celery on each of 4 warm dinner plates, spoon the amandine sauce, equally divided, over the celery and serve the celery amandine immediately.

4 servings

 GRAINS AND GREENS

Kale, Swiss chard, and parsley are still standing in the garden after a heavy frost. God bless them! Serve home style tomato soup and accompany the grains and greens with yellow summer squash. (You'd better have picked the squash before that frost.) Then serve a robust salad of rutabaga vinaigrette with bread and Liederkranz cheese. Have poached plums for dessert.

1/3 cup wheat berries - about 2 1/2 ounces
1/3 cup rye berries - about 2 1/2 ounces
2/3 cup long grain brown rice - about 5 ounces

3/4 cup roasted sunflower seeds - about 4 1/2 ounces - (see sunflower and pumpkin seeds)
about 10 ounces untrimmed kale - (4 tightly packed cups trimmed)
about 10 ounces Swiss chard - (4 packed cups cut)
celery leaves - (1 packed cup chopped)
parsley leaves - (1 packed cup chopped)
10 Tablespoons butter - divided
1 Tablespoon plus 1 teaspoon honey
1 teaspoon salt
1 teaspoon celery salt
1/2 teaspoon freshly cracked black pepper
2 cups yogurt - at room temperature
2 Tablespoons flour
2 eggs - at room temperature

Soak, boil, and drain the wheat and rye berries, together, as directed. (See boiled wheat berries or see boiled rye berries.) Steam the rice as directed. (See steamed long or short grain brown rice.) Mix the 3 grains together and allow them to cool then mix the sunflower seed in with the grains.

Prepare and blanch the kale as directed. (See blanched kale.) Immediately turn the drained kale into a basin of cold water for 1 minute. Then, turn it into a colander, place a saucer with a moderate weight upon it on the kale and allow it to drain for 30 minutes, turning it over several times and pressing on it during that period. (Water is more reluctant to drain out of kale than spinach or Swiss chard.) Now, cut the compressed kale into slices about 1/4 inch thick.

Prepare and blanch the Swiss chard as directed. (See blanched Swiss chard.) Immediately turn the drained Swiss chard into a basin of cold water for 1 minute. Then, turn it into a colander, place a saucer with a moderate weight upon it on the Swiss chard and allow it to drain for 30 minutes turning it over 2 or 3 times during that period.

(Up to this point the grains, seeds, kale, and Swiss chard can be prepared in advance. Seal the grains and seeds together and the kale and Swiss chard together, in plastic, and refrigerate them up to 24 hours. Bring them to room temperature before continuing with the recipe.)

Chop the celery leaves small.

Coarsely chop the parsley leaves.

Melt 8 tablespoons of the butter in a large frying pan (see utensils) over low heat. Add the grains and seeds, the kale, Swiss chard, celery leaves, parsley leaves, honey, salt, celery salt, and pepper. Using 2 forks, stir and fold the ingredients until the grains are well mixed with the greens and all are well coated with butter. Pack the mixture into a buttered 6 cup soufflé dish or similar oven proof dish and bake it, uncovered, in a preheated 350 degree oven, for 20 minutes.

Meanwhile, using a wire whisk, beat the yogurt in a bowl until it is liquid. Melt 2 tablespoons of the butter in a small heavy saucepan over low heat. Using a rubber spatula, blend in the flour until the butter is absorbed. Add the yogurt all at once and cook it, stirring constantly, in one direction only, for about 8 minutes, while slowly turning up the heat to medium until the yogurt simmers. Reduce the heat slightly and continue to simmer and stir 2 minutes longer. Remove the pan from the heat and allow it to cool a bit.

In a bowl, using the whisk, beat the eggs until they are light, then slowly stir the stabilized yogurt into them.

Remove the grains and greens from the oven and pour the yogurt mixture over them. Return the dish to the oven and bake 30 minutes longer. Remove the dish from the oven and allow the grains and greens to stand 10 minutes before serving.

4 to 6 servings

STUFFED SWEET POTATOES

Creamy mushroom bisque is always a delightful first course. Serve buttered kale along with the stuffed sweet potatoes. A salad of celery hearts vinaigrette will make a good counter point to the sweetness of the potatoes. Have some whole wheat biscuits with the salad and finish with fresh peaches.

3 pounds sweet potatoes - 4 medium large
1 can crushed pineapple - 8 ounces
1/2 cup shelled pecan halves - about 1 3/4 ounces
12 Tablespoons unsalted butter - at room temperature
3/4 packed cup dark brown sugar
1 teaspoon salt
1/2 teaspoon ground ginger

Scrub the potatoes, pierce them with a fork and bake them in a preheated 375 degree oven 1 hour or until they are just tender when pierced with a wooden skewer.

Meanwhile, drain the pineapple in a colander. Place a saucer with a weight upon it on the pineapple and allow it to drain thoroughly. The yield should be about 1 cup drained.

Using a heavy knife, chop the pecans small.

When the potatoes are done, holding each potato with a pot holder, slice off a quarter of it, lengthwise, then carefully scoop out all the hot flesh from both pieces of the potato into a bowl, leaving 1/4 inch of flesh in the larger shell and discarding the smaller piece of skin. Using an old fashioned potato masher, (it gives the right texture) mash the potato flesh with the butter, cut in pieces, sugar, salt, and ginger. Then, using a fork, stir in the drained pineapple and chopped nuts.

Pack the potato mixture into the potato shells, heaping it up. Use a metal spatula to assist in handling the stuffed potatoes as their skin is more delicate than that of white potatoes. Set the potatoes on a baking sheet and return them to a preheated 400 degree oven for 15 minutes. Transfer the stuffed sweet potatoes to a warm serving platter and serve.

4 servings

CARAWAY CABBAGE

Commence with noodle soup; then accompany the caraway cabbage with baked beets. A salad of pressed cucumbers would be apropos with more rye bread if you like. Poached apricots are dessert.

2 teaspoons caraway seeds
4 pounds Savoy cabbage - 1 large head - (20 tightly packed cups cut) - (see note)
5 or 6 oval slices Jewish rye bread with caraway seeds -depending on size
8 Tablespoons butter - divided
2 teaspoons salt
1/4 teaspoon freshly cracked black pepper
1 teaspoon honey
2 Tablespoons hot water
1 1/2 cups sour cream - at room temperature

Toast the caraway seeds in a dry pan over medium heat, stirring constantly for 3 minutes until they become golden, fragrant and start to pop. Remove them from the pan immediately and crush them, 1/2 teaspoon at a time, in a mortar or use a spice grinder. Reserve them.

Quarter and core the cabbage; cut the quarters crosswise into 1/2 inch thick slices. Pull the leaf layers apart. (It will seem like a tremendous amount.) Set the cabbage aside.

Cut the slices of bread in half and toast half of the slices in 2 tablespoons of the butter in a large frying pan over medium heat. Toast the slices on both sides, while pressing them with a metal spatula, until they are golden brown. Repeat with the remaining slices and 2 more tablespoons of the butter. Arrange the toasted slices around the edge of a 10 inch pie plate or similarly shaped serving dish.

Melt 4 tablespoons of the butter in a very large saucepan or kettle over medium low heat. Add the crushed caraway seeds and the cabbage and sprinkle with the salt and pepper. Dissolve the honey in the 2 tablespoons of hot water and add the mixture to the pan. Cook the cabbage, covered, 15 minutes while stirring and turning it occasionally and gradually increasing the heat to high.

At this point place the pie plate in a preheated 150 degree oven to warm the bread.

Now, uncover the pan and cook the cabbage 10 minutes longer, on high heat, while stirring and turning almost constantly. Remove the pan from the heat, if there is any moisture left in the bottom, drain it out. Then thoroughly stir the sour cream into the cabbage. Remove the plate from the oven and heap the cabbage into the center of the circle of toast and serve immediately. To serve the caraway cabbage place 2 or 3 pieces of toast on each dinner plate and spoon the cabbage over it..

4 to 6 servings

Note: You may want to buy a cabbage which is a little larger than needed since the outer leaves of Savoy cabbage are sometimes tough and must be discarded.

 LASAGNA

A light herb broth is served before this delicious lasagna which is followed by a tossed chicory salad and perhaps some bread if appetites still allow. Chilled green grapes will complete the dinner.

lasagna noodles - (recipe follows)
lasagna sauce - (recipe follows)
3 ounces untrimmed spinach - (1 1/2 packed cups trimmed)
1 Tablespoon plus 2 teaspoons olive oil - divided
about 12 ounces zucchini squash - 3 small, 6 inches long - (about 2 cups
cut)
1 Tablespoons salt - divided
6 ounces sweet Italian frying peppers - 3 medium
2 eggs - at room temperature
1 1/2 cups Ricotta cheese - at room temperature
Parmesan cheese - (7 Tablespoons plus 1 teaspoon freshly grated) -
divided
Romano cheese - (2 Tablespoons plus 2 teaspoons freshly grated) -
divided
8 ounces Mozzarella cheese - (2 cups shredded)
2 quarts water
bowl of cold water

Prepare the lasagna noodles in advance as directed.

Prepare the lasagna sauce in advance as directed. It does not need to be kept warm or be reheated but have it at room temperature.

Select large spinach leaves. Remove the stems, rinse them in cold water and spin them absolutely dry. Sauté the spinach in 1 teaspoon of the oil in a frying pan (see utensils) over medium high heat for about 2 minutes. Quickly stir the leaves around, with a wooden spatula until they become just barely wilted. Remove the spinach to paper towels and very carefully spread the leaves out.

Trim the zucchini. Cut it in half lengthwise. Lay the halves cut side down and cut them into thirds crosswise. Cut the thirds into thin slices lengthwise. Sauté the zucchini slices, sprinkled with 1/4 teaspoon of the salt in 2 teaspoons of the oil in the frying pan over medium high heat, stirring constantly, for about 5 minutes or until they begin to become translucent. Do not allow the zucchini to become overcooked. Spread it out on paper towels.

Core the frying peppers, trimming away any white membrane. Cut the peppers lengthwise into long strips, about 3/4 inch wide. Sauté the peppers, sprinkled with 1/4 teaspoon of the salt in 2 teaspoons of the oil in the frying pan over medium high heat, 5 minutes or until they are wilted. Spread them out on paper towels.

(The vegetables can be prepared early in the day, up to this point, lightly covered with paper towels and left at room temperature.)

About 2 hours before serving time, using a wire whisk,beat the eggs in a mixing bowl until they are light. Then stir in the Ricotta (if whey has separated from the Ricotta, pour it off and discard it), 6 tablespoons of the Parmesan, 2 tablespoons of the Romano and 1/2 teaspoon of the salt.

Coarsely shred the Mozzarella.

Smear a little of the lasagna sauce in the bottom of a buttered 7 1/2 by 12 by 2 inch deep, 8 cup baking dish. Bring the 2 quarts of water to boil with 2 teaspoons of the salt in a large saucepan over high heat. Blanch 4 of the lasagna noodles for 1 or 2 minutes, depending on how fresh or how dry they are, until they are supple, from the moment they are in the water, regardless of when the water returns to boil. Carefully lift them out with a slotted spoon and immediately drop them into the bowl of cold water. Drain them well and pat them good and dry on paper towels. Lay the noodles in the baking dish, allowing them to overlap and trimming off any ends that are too long with a sharp knife. Spread about 1 cup of the sauce over the noodles then sprinkle 1/3 of the Mozzarella over the sauce. Lay 4 more noodles over the Mozzarella and spread 1/2 of the Ricotta mixture over the noodles. Evenly distribute half the spinach, zucchini and peppers over the Ricotta, spreading out the spinach leaves. Cover the vegetables with another layer of noodles, spoon about 1 cup of the sauce over them, sprinkle 1/3 cup of the Mozzarella over the sauce and cover with 4 more noodles. Repeat the layers starting with the Ricotta mixture. Smear the top of the noodles with the remaining sauce and sprinkle the remaining 1 tablespoon plus 1 teaspoon of Parmesan and 2 teaspoons of Romano over the sauce.

Lightly cover the lasagna with foil, securing it to the ends of the dish, so that it arches slightly and does not touch the contents of the dish. Bake the lasagna in a preheated 375 degree oven, 35 minutes. Remove the foil and bake 15 minutes longer. Allow the lasagna to stand 15 minutes before serving.

8 servings

Note: You may want to place a small baking sheet on the oven shelf below the one that the lasagna is on to diffuse the heat and keep the bottom layer of noodles from possibly browning.

lasagna noodles

pasta dough - (see pasta dough)

Roll out the dough as directed. (See machine rolled pasta dough.) On a flat work surface, using a sharp knife, cut each sheet of dough, crosswise, into 6, 6 by 3 inch rectangular noodles.

Alternatively, roll out the dough as directed. (See hand rolled pasta dough.) Roll each sheet of dough out as thin as possible into an 18 by 12 inch rectangle. Cut the sheet in half lengthwise then cut it crosswise into 12, 6 by 3 inch rectangular noodles.

In either case the total number of noodles should be 24. The noodles can now be allowed to dry on a towel, 15 minutes on each side, then used right away. Or they can be hung to dry and stored as directed. (See dried noodles.) If they are hung to dry on the pasta drying rack, hang them across 2 rungs at a time or hang them on a thick broom handle. This will keep the wide noodles from sticking to themselves which they are prone to do.

Note: If the noodles are not quite as large as the 6 by 3 inch measurement, don't worry about it, they swell from 1/2 to 1 1/2 inches when cooked especially the machine rolled noodles. Also, remember that the bottom of the baking dish will be smaller than the top so smaller noodles can be used on the bottom.

lasagna sauce

1 can peeled tomatoes - 28 ounces - (3 1/2 cups)
2 Tablespoons olive oil
3/4 cup tomato paste - 6 ounces
2 teaspoons honey
1/2 teaspoon salt
1/2 teaspoon celery salt
1/4 teaspoon freshly cracked black pepper
1/2 teaspoon dried oregano
1/2 teaspoon dried basil
1/2 teaspoon dried thyme

Drain the peeled tomatoes in a colander set over a bowl.

Heat the oil in a heavy saucepan over low heat. Add the tomato paste and stir the drained liquid from the peeled tomatoes into it. Remove the stem buttons from the tomatoes, carefully quarter them then crush them through your (clean) fingers into the sauce. Add the honey, salt, celery salt, and pepper and gently simmer the sauce, covered, 55 minutes, stirring occasionally. Add the oregano, basil, and thyme, crushing them and simmer the sauce 5 minutes longer. Remove the pan from the heat. The sauce will be very thiçk.

3 1/2 cups

ARTICHOKES DELPHINA

Make this a romantic little dinner for just the two of you. Serve a cream of carrot soup first. Follow the main course with a tossed endive salad then finish with poached pears.

2 large slices homemade type white bread
2 pounds artichokes - 2 large
1 cup sauce delphina - (recipe follows)
2 eggs - very fresh - at room temperature - (see cooked eggs note)

Hopefully you will have nice slices of bread, 1 inch thick and about 4 1/2 inches square. Remove the crusts and trim the slices to make them round. Reserve the bread.

Using a serrated knife, trim off the stems flush with the bottom leaves of the artichokes. Lay the artichokes on their sides on a cutting board and cut off the top third of each artichoke. Using a pair of scissors, trim off the tips of the remaining leaves. Then cook and drain the artichokes as directed. (See boiled whole artichokes.) Using a small spoon, carefully remove their thistle centers or "chokes," taking care not to damage the bottoms of the artichokes. If they must wait, set the artichokes upside down in the empty, warm kettle in which they were cooked, covered with the lid to keep warm.

While the artichokes are cooking, make the sauce delphina and keep it warm as directed.

About 12 minutes before the artichokes are ready, warm the slices of bread in a preheated 350 degree oven until they are lightly toasted on the outside but still soft on the inside.

About 5 minutes before the artichokes are ready, poach, drain and trim the eggs as directed. (See poached eggs.)

Now, working quickly, place a slice of toast on each of 2 warm salad size plates. Set the artichokes, right side up, on each slice of toast and slip a poached egg into the cavity of each artichoke. Spoon the sauce over the eggs, filling the cavities to their brims. Set the salad plates on dinner plates and serve the artichokes delphina immediately.

2 servings

Note: Synchronization is the key to this recipe, be organized. To eat the artichokes, pull off the leaves with your fingers, one at a time, dip each leaf into the sauce and eat only the thick tender part at the base of each leaf. Provide each diner with a bowl for the discarded leaves. When you get to the poached egg, proceed with a knife and fork.

sauce delphina

dill pickles - (2 teaspoons chopped)
pitted green olives - (2 teaspoons chopped)
capers - (2 teaspoons chopped)
3 egg yolks - at room temperature - (see cooked eggs note)
1/2 scant teaspoon salt
pinch white pepper
1/4 teaspoon English mustard powder
1 Tablespoon plus 1 teaspoon cider vinegar - divided
12 Tablespoons unsalted butter - very cold
2 teaspoons plus optional hot water
1/4 teaspoon dried tarragon

Drain, rinse and drain the pickles, olives and capers. Chop them fine then blot them on paper towels and reserve them.

In a bowl, whisk the yolks until they are light and set them aside.

Dissolve the salt, pepper, and mustard powder in 1 teaspoon of the vinegar in a small saucepan over low heat. Add 1/2 teaspoon of the butter, when it has melted, remove the pan from the heat, and using a rubber spatula, stir in the egg yolks. Return the pan to low heat, stirring constantly until the yolks have absorbed the butter. Lift or remove the pan from the heat, add another 1/2 teaspoon of the butter, return the pan to the heat, stirring constantly until the piece of butter has melted and been absorbed. Continue in this manner, lifting the pan, not allowing it to become too hot and adding the butter until 4 tablespoons of butter have been used. Add 1 teaspoon more of the vinegar then increase the additions of butter to 1 teaspoon at a time, adding each teaspoon in 2 thin slices. When 8 tablespoons of butter have been used, add 1 teaspoon of the vinegar and increase the additions of butter to 2 teaspoons at a time, adding them in 2 thin slices each. When all the butter has been absorbed, the sauce will be quite thick. Thin it out with the 1 remaining teaspoon of vinegar and the 2 teaspoons of hot water or more as you desire. Now stir in the reserved pickles, olives, and capers then add the tarragon, crushing it. Sauce delphina is served warm not hot.

1 cup

Note: To keep the sauce warm or for emergency procedures read the handmade hollandaise recipe. (See handmade hollandaise sauce.)

BULGARIAN BEET TART

This is a very pretty not red but pink and violet tart with a touch of green. The first course is matzoh balls in garlic broth. The beet tart is accompanied by fresh peas then followed by a tossed spinach salad and some dark bread. Poached plums is the dessert course.

1 pound beets, minus leaves - 2 large, 2 1/2 inches in diameter
water
2 1/2 pounds red cabbage - 1 medium small
1 teaspoon dill seeds
1 cup yogurt - at room temperature
8 ounces Cream cheese - at room temperature

4 eggs - at room temperature
1 1/2 teaspoons salt
1 1/2 teaspoons sugar
1/4 teaspoon white pepper
1 teaspoon distilled white vinegar
4 Tablespoons butter
dill or parsley - 1 sprig

Bake, trim, and peel the beets as directed. (See baked beets.) Coarsely grate the baked beets and reserve them.

Meanwhile fill a large kettle with enough water to cover the head of cabbage and bring it to boil over high heat. Trim a slice, about 1 inch thick, off of the bottom of the head of cabbage and discard it. Also discard any coarse outer leaves. (Save them for a bouillon soup. See bouillon soups.) Using a small knife, cut down deep into the cabbage around the stem to loosen the leaves. With 2 longhandled wooden spoons, lower the cabbage into the boiling water and cook it, covered, 5 minutes from the moment it is in the water regardless of when the water returns to boil. Uncover the kettle. Using the 2 wooden spoons, carefully remove each successive leaf as it becomes loosened and set it aside to drain, until 7 or 8 leaves have been removed. (Save what remains of the head of cabbage for that bouillon soup.) Blot the leaves dry with paper towels and cut most of the thick center rib out of each leaf. Arrange 6 or 7 of the leaves in a buttered 10 inch in diameter 6 cup pie plate so that they overlap each other and about 1/3 of each leaf hangs over the edge of the plate. Cover the bottom of the plate with 1 large leaf and set the plate aside.

Toast the dill seeds in a dry pan over medium heat, for about 3 minutes, stirring constantly, until they become golden and fragrant. Remove them from the pan immediately, crush them, 1/2 teaspoon at a time, in a mortar or use a spice grinder and reserve them.

In a mixing bowl, using a wooden spoon, work the yogurt, a little at a time, through the Cream cheese until they are smoothly blended. Then thoroughly stir in the eggs, 1 at a time.

Warm the reserved beets, sprinkled with the salt, sugar, pepper, the reserved crushed dill seeds and the vinegar in the butter in a medium size saucepan over low heat. Stir them gently with a rubber spatula for about 5 minutes until they are heated through and well coated with the butter. Remove the pan from the heat, allow it to stand a minute then turn the beets and all their butter into the cheese and yogurt mixture and combine them well with the rubber spatula.

Carefully pour the beet mixture into the cabbage leaf shell, evenly spreading it around. Neatly fold the overhanging cabbage leaves over the edges of the beet mixture to frame it. Lay the sprig of dill or parsley in the center of the tart.

Lightly but completely, cover the tart with a piece of foil which has been perforated with 10 or 12 small holes. Do not allow the foil to touch the tart but secure it around the edges of the plate. Bake the tart in a preheated 325 degree oven for 1 hour and 15 minutes. Remove the plate from the oven and set it on a cake rack. Remove the foil and allow the Bulgarian beet tart to stand 20 minutes before serving.

6 servings

Note: If a little liquid has drained from the cabbage leaves while cooking, blot it up with paper towels before serving.

RAGU OF FAVA BEANS

A small salad of fennel in virgin olive oil would be a good choice for the salad course after this robust stew. Then offer chilled cantaloupe.

2 1/4 cups dried fava beans - 1 pound
2 bay leaves
reserved cooking liquid
2 Tablespoons flour
celery - 4 large ribs - (2 cups cut)
about 11 ounces rutabaga - piece - (2 cups cut)
8 ounces mushrooms - medium - (2 1/2 cups cut)
12 ounces green bell peppers - 2 medium - (2 cups cut)
1 pound tomatoes - 2 medium - (2 cups cut)
2 cups dry red wine
7 Tablespoons olive oil - divided
1 Tablespoon honey
 3 1/2 teaspoons salt - divided
1 1/2 teaspoons celery salt
1/4 teaspoon freshly cracked black pepper
1/8 teaspoon cayenne
5 Tablespoons butter - divided
1 quart water
4 ounces dried rotelle pasta - (see note)
1 1/2 teaspoons dried oregano
1 pound pecorino Romano cheese

Soak the beans and cook them with the bay leaves as directed. (See boiled dried shelled beans.) Drain and reserve the beans, the bay leaves and the cooking liquid. If there are more than 2 cups of the liquid, boil it down, if there are less, add fresh water. Purée 2 cups of the reserved beans with the flour and the 2 cups of liquid in the blender or processor or pass the beans through a food mill set over a bowl and then combine them with the flour and water. Reserve the purée.

Meanwhile, trim, scrape, the strings from and cut the celery crosswise into 1/2 inch pieces.

Trim, peel, and cut the rutabaga into 1/2 inch dice.

Wipe the mushrooms with a damp cloth, trim the butt ends of the stems and quarter the mushrooms lengthwise.

Core the bell peppers, trimming away any white membrane and cut them into 1/2 inch squares.

Peel and seed the tomatoes as directed. (See peeled tomatoes and see seeded tomatoes.) Remove the stem buttons and cut the halves into sixths, lengthwise.

Place the reserved bean purée in a large, attractive, heavy soup kettle set over medium heat. Stir in the wine, 4 tablespoons of the olive oil, the honey, 1 1/2 teaspoons of the salt, the celery salt, black pepper, cayenne, the remaining reserved whole beans and the reserved bay leaves. Cover the kettle and reduce the heat enough to keep the liquid just gently simmering.

Sauté the celery, sprinkled with 1/4 teaspoon of the salt in 1 tablespoon of the oil in a frying pan (see utensils) over medium heat 5 minutes. Add the celery and its cooking oil to the bean mixture, adjusting the heat if necessary to keep the liquid simmering, still keeping the kettle covered. Sauté and add the rutabaga in like manner. Sauté and add the mushrooms in like manner, but use 1 tablespoons of the butter instead of oil. (At this point, start heating the 1 quart of water with 1 teaspoon of the salt in a large saucepan over high heat for the pasta.) Sauté in oil and add the bell peppers in like manner to the preceding vegetables. The vegetables must be sautéed and added to the kettle in the order given. When all the sautéed vegetables are in the kettle, cook the ragu 5 minutes then add the tomatoes and cook 5 minutes more. Add the oregano, crushing it and cook 10 minutes longer.

At the same time as the tomatoes are added to the ragu, drop the rotelle into the boiling water all at once. Give it a stir with a wooden spoon and cook the pasta, covered with lid ajar for 15 minutes, or a little less than directed on the package, from the moment it is in the water, regardless of when the water returns to boil or until it is tender but firm, "al dente," adjusting the heat to keep the water slowly boiling and stirring occasionally. Drain the pasta and in the still warm saucepan, toss it with 4 tablespoons of the butter, cut in pieces.

Carefully stir the buttered rotelle into the ragu using a wooden spoon and serve it immediately. Bring the kettle directly to the table and ladle out the ragu of fava beans with rotelle into warm bowls. Pass the chunk of Romano around with a small hand grater and let everyone grate some cheese over their own serving. Freshly grated!

6 servings

Note: Sometimes identified by other names, rotelle is the pasta that looks like tightly twisted corkscrews.

 FRIED GREEN TOMATOES

These are so good, you'll pick all your tomatoes before they ripen. The fried tomatoes can not be kept warm in the oven so have everyone assemble and wait their turn. Start with cream of stock vegetable purée soup. Then baked sweet potatoes make the perfect vegetable accompaniment. Iceberg wedges is the salad course and fresh pears the dessert.

3 pounds green tomatoes - 12 small, 2 to 2 1/2 inches in diameter
2 cups plus optional water
1 Tablespoon English mustard powder
4 Tablespoons tomato paste
2 Tablespoons plus peanut oil - divided
4 Tablespoons cider vinegar
4 Tablespoons soy sauce
4 Tablespoons honey
2 teaspoons plus salt - divided
1 teaspoon celery salt
2 dashes cayenne
drained marinade liquid
5 Tablespoons cornstarch
about 1 cup flour

Prepare and start marinating the tomatoes early in the day. Cut the stem button out of each tomato and cut it in half lengthwise. Trim off a small slice on the round side of each tomato half and discard it. Then cut each half, lengthwise, into 2 slices, each about 1/2 inch thick. Pack the tomato slices into a bowl.

In a saucepan, slowly stir the 2 cups of water into the mustard powder and tomato paste until the mixture is smooth. Add the 2 tablespoons of oil, the vinegar, soy sauce, honey, the 2 teaspoons of salt, the celery salt and cayenne. Bring the mixture to simmer over medium heat then simmer it, uncovered, for 5 minutes. Pour the hot marinade over the tomatoes in the bowl and set a saucer with a weight upon it on them to keep them submerged, and allow them to marinate at least 6 hours.

Just before serving time, drain the tomatoes in a large strainer set over a bowl. Measure out the drained marinade liquid and add enough water to it if necessary to bring the total measurement to 3 cups. Dissolve the cornstarch in the liquid and bring it to simmer in a heavy saucepan over medium heat while stirring constantly, with a rubber spatula. When the liquid simmers, reduce the heat slightly and simmer 2 minutes longer, still stirring constantly. The sauce will be very thick and is meant to be so. Keep the sauce warm, covered with a trimmed piece of paper towel and lid, over very low heat until serving.

Heat 1/4 inch of the oil in a heavy, 10 inch frying pan over medium high heat. There will be 8 tomato slices per serving so work in batches of 8. Meanwhile, lightly salt both sides of each slice, dredge it in a bowl of the flour and set it on a plate. (Do not dredge more than 8 slices ahead of time, they get soggy.) Fry the floured tomato slices for 2 to 2 1/2 minutes on each side until they are golden brown. Do not overcook them. They retain their heat for a long time and consequently continue to cook after they are removed from the pan. We want them to remain crisp. Drain the fried slices for a moment on paper towels. Transfer them to a warm dinner plate and serve the fried green tomatoes, immediately, along with a small, warm bowl of the equally divided marinade sauce.

6 servings

 SCALLOPED CELERIAC

The menu tonight is consommé jardinière, scalloped celeriac accompanied by buttered kale, yellow string beans vinaigrette with French bread and chilled purple grapes.

1 cup milk - at room temperature
2 teaspoons honey
8 ounces Provolone cheese - (2 cups grated) - (see note)
parsley - (3 Tablespoons chopped)
tomatoes - 2 medium, 6 ounces each
2 pounds celeriac - 2 large
2/3 cup flour
1 teaspoon salt - divided
1/4 teaspoon freshly cracked black pepper - divided
3 Tablespoons butter - divided

Bring the milk and honey to simmer in a small saucepan over medium heat. Remove the pan from the heat and reserve it.

Coarsely grate the cheese.

Chop the parsley fine.

Peel the tomatoes as directed. (See peeled tomatoes.) Remove the stem buttons and cut the tomatoes, crosswise, into 1/4 inch thick slices. About 7 slices will be needed. Discard end slices. (Save them for a bouillon soup. See bouillon soups.) Spread the slices out on a plate to drain a bit.

Scrub, trim, and peel the celeriac. Cut the bulbs in half, lengthwise. Thinly slice only 1/3 of the total amount of celeriac at a time crosswise. Lightly dredge each slice in a bowl of the flour and spread the slices in a buttered, flat, round, 8 1/4 inch in diameter by 1 3/4 inch deep, 5 3/4 cup baking dish. Sprinkle them with 1/3 each of the salt and pepper and dot with 1 tablespoon of the butter cut in pieces. Then spread 1/3 of the cheese over all and sprinkle 1/3 of the parsley over the cheese. Repeat the layers twice again, omitting the last layer of cheese and parsley.

Pour the reserved milk over the dish, lightly cover it with foil and bake it in a preheated 350 degree oven 55 minutes. Remove the dish from the oven and turn on the broiler. Remove the foil and spread the remaining cheese over the celeriac. Place 1 tomato slice on the center of the dish and place the remainder of the slices around it. Sprinkle the remaining parsley over all and run the dish under the broiler, 3 inches from the heat source, for 5 minutes, until the edges of the tomatoes start to brown. Remove the dish from the broiler and allow the scalloped celeriac to stand 10 minutes before serving.

4 to 6 servings

Note: Be sure that you have a well aged cheese that will melt nicely. Try to use the best Italian Provolone you can find for this dish. If you are using domestic Provolone you may want to increase the salt slightly.

BRASSICA BOUQUET
with fontina sauce

A bouquet to be sure! Members of the cabbage family make up this impressive presentation. The soup will be matzoh balls in garlic broth. An oat pilaf will go nicely with the brassica bouquet. Then serve a lima bean vinaigrette salad followed by crisp yellow delicious apples.

2 pounds cauliflower - 1 medium small head
2 1/2 pounds red cabbage - 1 medium small head - (12 1/2 tightly packed cups cut)
1 pound rutabaga - 1 small
1 pound broccoli - 2 average heads
8 ounces Brussels sprouts - 16 to 20 of equal size - (2 cups whole)
Fontina sauce - (recipe follows)

Prepare and steam the whole cauliflower as directed but steam it 1 minute less than what you would determine to be its full cooking time, testing it with a wooden tooth pick. (See steamed whole cauliflower.) Immediately turn the cauliflower into a basin of cold water for 5 minutes. Then drain it well and blot it dry on paper towels as best you can.

Prepare and blanch the cabbage exactly as directed. (See blanched red cabbage.) Immediately turn the drained cabbage into a basin of cold water for 3 minutes. Drain again and spread the cabbage out on paper towels and blot it dry with more towels.

Trim, peel, and cut the rutabaga in half lengthwise. Lay the halves cut side down and cut them, crosswise, into slices 1/2 inch thick. Then cut the slices into long fingers 1/2 inch wide. Cut one end of the rutabaga fingers square then cut the other end into a point like a picket fence. Steam the rutabaga over already simmering water for about 10 minutes or 1 minute less than what you would determine to be its full cooking time, testing it with a wooden tooth pick. Immediately, turn the rutabaga into a basin of cold water for 3 minutes. Drain and blot it dry on paper towels.

Cut the broccoli florets, with 1 inch of stem, off of the stalks. (Reserve the stalks for another purpose.) Separate and cut the larger clusters into smaller florets and steam them as directed; but steam them 1 minute less than what you would determine to be their full cooking time, testing them with a wooden tooth pick. (See steamed broccoli.) Immediately turn the florets into a basin of cold water for 3 minutes. Drain them well and blot them dry on paper towels.

Prepare and steam the Brussels sprouts as directed but steam them 1 minute less than what you would determine to be their full cooking time, testing them with a wooden tooth pick. (See steamed Brussels sprouts.) Immediately, turn them into a basin of cold water for 5 minutes. Drain and blot them dry on paper towels.

(All the vegetable preparations can be done well in advance. Seal them, separately, in plastic. If you refrigerate them, be sure to bring them to room temperature before continuing with the recipe.)

About 1 hours before serving time, make the Fontina sauce and keep it warm as directed.

Now, tightly wrap the cauliflower in foil and warm it in a preheated 350 degree oven, for 15 minutes, ahead of the other vegetables, as in this case it will take longer to reheat.

Meanwhile, evenly spread the red cabbage ribbons out, covering a buttered 12 inch in diameter, round, shallow baking pan or pizza pan. Then arrange the rutabaga fingers in a fanned out circle on the cabbage so that the pointed ends point to the edges of the pan and the square ends touch shoulders forming a tight circle. Next, remove the cauliflower from the oven, unwrap it and set it on the center of the rutabaga circle. Now, with the aid of a teaspoon handle, insert the little broccoli florets into the cauliflower head, gently pressing them in between the cauliflower florets. Finally, set 1 Brussels sprout in each space between the rutabaga fingers, placing it against the base of the cauliflower head. (If you put 1 or 2 extra Brussels sprouts on the pan, you can use them for a test to determine when the vegetables are hot.)

Lightly, but completely, cover the bouquet with a large piece of foil which has been perforated with 10 or 12 small holes. Secure the foil around the edges of the pan and warm the vegetables in a preheated 350 degree oven for 25 to 30 minutes until they are heated through. Uncover the vegetables and serve the brassica bouquet, immediately, along with a bowl of warm the Fontina sauce. Let each of the diners spoon the sauce over their own serving.

6 servings

Note: You'll want a large knife with which to carve the cauliflower.

fontina sauce

1 pound Fontina cheese - (4 cups grated)
1 1/2 cups dry white wine
1 cup water - cold
4 Tablespoons butter
4 Tablespoons flour
1/8 teaspoon white pepper

Coarsely grate the cheese and reserve it.

In a small saucepan, over high heat, boil the 1 1/2 cups of wine, uncovered, down to 1 cup. Remove the pan from the heat and add the water to the wine.

Melt the butter in a heavy saucepan over low heat. Using a rubber spatula, blend in the flour and pepper, stirring constantly for 3 minutes. Slowly stir in the wine mixture while raising the heat to medium until the mixture simmers and thickens.

Reduce the heat to very low and place a heat diffuser under the pan. Cover the pan with a trimmed piece of paper towel and lid and keep the sauce warm until serving. Just before serving, remove the pan from the heat and add the cheese, 1/2 cup at a time, stirring until the cheese has melted and the sauce is smooth.

about 4 cups

YANKEE SPOONBREAD

Cream of red bell pepper soup makes a colorful first course. Serve zucchini fans with this easy entrée which can serve at least eight people. Tossed salad mix I is the salad and fresh blueberries the dessert.

corn - 3 ears - (1 1/2 cups kernels) - or about 9 ounces frozen
1 pound extra sharp Vermont Cheddar cheese - (4 cups grated) - (see note)
1 1/2 cups plus 1 Tablespoon plus 1 teaspoon stoneground yellow corn meal - divided

2/3 cup cold water - divided
1 1/4 teaspoons salt - divided
4 Tablespoons butter
3 Tablespoons honey
1 cup buttermilk - at room temperature
2 teaspoons baking powder
1 teaspoon baking soda
1 teaspoon celery salt
1 teaspoon English mustard powder
1/4 teaspoon cayenne
1/2 teaspoon dried thyme
4 eggs - at room temperature

Prepare and boil the corn as directed, but boil it only 3 minutes. (See boiled corn.) Immediately, turn the drained corn into a basin of cold water for 5 minutes. Drain again and carefully cut the kernels from the cob, separating and crumbling them into a bowl. If you are using frozen corn, simply allow it to thaw and drain completely in a colander and blot it dry on paper towels. Reserve the corn.

Coarsely grate the cheese and reserve it.

In a measuring cup, stir 1/3 cup of the corn meal into 1/3 cup of the cold water. In a heavy, medium size saucepan, over medium high heat, bring the remaining 1/3 cup of the water with 1/4 teaspoon of the salt to boil. Slowly, pour the corn meal slurry into the boiling water, while stirring, constantly, with a long handled wood spoon. When the mixture returns to boil, reduce the heat to low and cook the corn meal, 5 minutes, stirring frequently, smoothing out any lumps. Remove the pan from the heat and stir in the butter, cut in pieces, until it has melted. Then stir in the honey and buttermilk.

Sift the remaining 1 1/4 cups of the corn meal, the baking powder, baking soda, 1 teaspoon of the salt, the celery salt, mustard powder, cayenne and the thyme, crushing it, into a mixing bowl. Return any coarse corn meal which wouldn't go through the sieve to the mixture in the bowl. Then slowly stir in the buttermilk mixture, in 3 parts. Using a wire whisk, thoroughly beat in the eggs, 1 at a time. Now, stir in the reserved corn kernels and cheese.

Spoon the mixture into a well buttered 10 inch in diameter, 2 inch deep, 10 cup cast iron frying pan and bake it in a preheated 350 degree oven, 50 minutes. If the spoonbread browns too quickly during the last 10 minutes of the baking period, lightly cover it with foil. Remove the pan from the oven; remove the foil if you used it, and allow it to stand 15 minutes. Bring the pan right to the table and serve the Yankee spoonbread cut in wedges.

8 servings

Note: Be sure your cheese is good and sharp. I buy a small, wax covered, 3 pound wheel of extra sharp Vermont Cheddar whenever I think of it and hide it in a cool place for 6 months. Then I know I've got extra sharp cheese.

LIMA BEANS PANACHÉ
with horseradish-stoneground mustard sauce

I like to present this dish on some pretty pottery plates which I otherwise keep on display. Serve borscht to begin. Then have red cabbage wedges with the lima beans panaché. Pressed cucumbers will make a light salad and poached plums will complete the dinner.

2 1/2 cups dried lima beans - large - 1 pound
1 bay leaf
1/2 cup reserved cooking liquid
1 pound 14 ounces unshelled lima beans - baby - (2 cups shelled) or about
                                              10 ounces frozen
celery - 2 large ribs - (1 cup cut)
about 13 ounces carrots - 6 medium - (2 cups sliced)
parsley leaves - (4 Tablespoons chopped)
horseradish - stoneground mustard sauce - (recipe follows)
6 Tablespoons butter - divided
4 Tablespoons peanut oil
2 teaspoons salt - divided
1 teaspoon celery salt
1/4 teaspoon freshly cracked black pepper
1 Tablespoon honey
2 drops liquid smoke
4 eggs - at room temperature
2 Tablespoons warm water - in a cup.

Cook the dried lima beans, with the bay leaf, as directed. (See boiled dried shelled beans.) Do not over cook them. Drain them, reserving the beans and the 1/2 cup of their cooking liquid and discarding the bay leaf.
Meanwhile, shell the fresh lima beans.

Trim, scrape the strings from and cut the celery crosswise into 1/8 inch thick slices.

Trim, peel, and cut the carrots crosswise into 1/8 inch thick slices. Chop the parsley small.

At this point, prepare the horseradish - stoneground mustard sauce and keep it warm as directed.

In a very large saucepan, set over very low heat, combine the drained cooked dried lima beans, the 1/2 cup of reserved cooking liquid, 4 tablespoons of the butter, the peanut oil, 1 1/2 teaspoons of the salt, the celery salt, pepper, honey and liquid smoke. Cover the pan and keep the mixture warm.

Meanwhile steam the shelled fresh lima beans over already simmering water, about 20 minutes or until they are just tender. Then turn them into the saucepan of dried lima beans.

At the same time hard cook and peel the eggs as directed. (See cooked eggs.) Place the peeled eggs in a bowl of hot water to keep them warm.

If you are using frozen lima beans, about 12 minutes after the eggs have started cooking, blanch the still frozen lima beans in enough boiling water to cover them by 1 1/2 inches in a large saucepan, uncovered, over high heat for just 8 minutes from the moment they are in the water, regardless of when the water returns to boil, stirring with a wooden spoon. Drain and turn them into the saucepan of dried lima beans.

Now, sauté the celery and carrots together, sprinkled with 1/2 teaspoon of the salt in 2 tablespoons of the butter in a frying pan (see utensils) over medium heat, 3 minutes. Remove the pan from the heat, add the 2 tablespoons of warm water, quickly cover the pan, return it to the heat and cook the vegetables, 5 minutes. Uncover the pan and cook them 2 minutes longer until the water has evaporated. Add the vegetables and their cooking butter along with the chopped parsley into the saucepan of lima beans and gently stir the mixture using a wooden spoon.

Spread the lima bean mixture out on each of 4 warm dinner plates. Spoon the mustard sauce, equally divided onto the center of the bean mixture on each plate, reserving a little for decoration. Drain, dry and cut each of the hardcooked eggs in half lengthwise. Place 2 halves on the sauce on each plate, cut sides up and wide ends touching. Dribble the remaining sauce over the eggs where they touch and serve the lima beans panaché immediately.

4 servings

Note: A really simple country dish that requires organized timing. To save time and energy the eggs can be hardcooked in the simmering water in the bottom of the double boiler over which the mustard sauce is being kept warm.

horseradish - stoneground mustard sauce

2 Tablespoons butter
3 ounces Cream cheese - at room temperature
1 cup prepared horseradish - stoneground mustard - (a fresh jar)
1/2 cup warm water

Melt the butter and cheese in the top of a double boiler over gently simmering water. Slowly stir in the mustard until the mixture is reasonably smooth. Then slowly stir in the warm water.
Cover the sauce with a trimmed piece of paper towel and lid and keep it warm over barely simmering water until ready to serve.

about 2 cups

SAUERKRAUT PIE

There are certain people who have to be restrained from over-indulging in sauerkraut pie. Have cream of pumpkin soup then serve buttered green string beans with the pie. A salad of beets vinaigrette and pumpernickel bread go nicely with this meal. Then have some polished red apples.

prebaked 7 inch bottom diameter by 1 1/2 inch deep pie shell (recipe
follows)
2 pounds fresh sauerkraut - (4 drained, lightly packed cups) - or 2 cans,
27 ounces each
1 quart plus water - divided
8 Tablespoons butter - at room temperature - divided
3 Tablespoons cider vinegar
1 Tablespoon honey
2 Tablespoons prepared grey mustard
1/8 teaspoon cayenne
1/2 cup prepared mayonnaise
6 ounces Swiss emmenthal cheese (Swiss cheese) - (1 1/2 cups grated)
2 pounds baking potatoes - 4 medium large

about 1 cup reserved cooking liquid
1 1/2 teaspoons salt
2 Tablespoons bread crumbs - fine - (see bread crumbs)

Prepare and bake the pie shell in advance as directed.

Immerse the drained fresh sauerkraut in cold water and drain it again. Bring the 1 quart of water to boil in a saucepan over high heat. Add the drained sauerkraut and cook it, covered, 30 to 40 minutes from the moment it is in the water, regardless of when the water returns to boil, reducing the heat to keep the water gently simmering until the sauerkraut is almost tender. Drain it thoroughly. Or immerse the drained, canned sauerkraut in cold water and drain it again very well.

In either case, melt 4 tablespoons of the butter in a frying pan (see utensils) over medium low heat. Add the vinegar, honey, and drained sauerkraut. Cook the sauerkraut, uncovered, stirring it frequently with a wooden fork for about 20 minutes until all the moisture has evaporated. Remove the pan from the heat and allow it to cool a bit. In a cup, blend the mustard and cayenne into the mayonnaise then stir the mixture into the cooled sauerkraut.

Coarsely grate the cheese and reserve it.

Peel and quarter the potatoes. Bring the potatoes to boil in enough water to cover them by 1 1/2 inches in a saucepan, covered with lid slightly ajar, over high heat. Reduce the heat enough to keep the water slowly boiling and cook the potatoes about 25 minutes or until they are quite soft. Drain the potatoes, reserving about 1 cup of the cooking liquid, and transfer them to a warm mixing bowl. Using the electric mixer, whip the potatoes with 4 tablespoons of the butter, cut in pieces, the salt and only enough of the reserved cooking liquid to make the potatoes light and very smooth.

Spoon the sauerkraut into the pie shell, evenly smoothing it down. Evenly sprinkle the reserved cheese over the sauerkraut. Cover the cheese with the potatoes taking care not to get any on the rim of the shell. Spread the potatoes with the broad blade of a knife so that they will be smooth and slightly domed. Evenly sprinkle the bread crumbs over the potatoes. If the crumbs fall on the rim of the shell, whisk them off with a pastry brush.

Bake the pie in a preheated 350 degree oven for 35 minutes. Set it on a cake rack and allow the sauerkraut pie to stand 15 minutes before serving.

8 servings

Note: Quantities of canned saurkraut can, after it is drained and packed, vary considerably, sometimes as much as a cup! To be on the safe side have a greater quantity on hand than would appear necessary. However, do not use any extra quantity as it would unbalance the recipe.

prebaked pie shell

plain pastry dough - (see plain pastry dough)

Prepare, rest and roll out the dough into a disc, 13 inches in diameter, as directed. Fold the disc in half and then again in half. Place the point of the folded dough in the center of a 7 inch bottom diameter by 1 1/2 inch deep pie plate. (See utensils.) Then unfold the dough, encouraging it to relax down into the plate. There should be 1 inch of dough hanging down all around the outside of the pie plate; trim the edges even. Dip your finger in some water and dampen 1/2 inch all around the underside of the overhanging dough. Now, fold the overhanging dough up under itself onto the rim of the plate. Then artfully crimp the dough by pressing your thumb against your crooked index finger to form an attractive scalloped edging.

Carefully fit aluminum foil down into the shell, without disturbing the edging. Fill the foil lined shell with about 4 1/2 cups of dried shelled beans which you reserve solely for this purpose. Then lightly cover the whole with more foil so that the scalloped edging is completely covered.

Bake the shell in a preheated 400 degree oven for 15 minutes. Remove the plate from the oven and remove the light foil covering. Using a large spoon, remove the beans then carefully remove the remaining foil. The pie shell can be baked several hours in advance of being filled. In which case, carefully slip the shell out of the pie plate onto a cake rack. When it is completely cool, seal it in plastic and leave it at room temperature. However, return the shell to its pie plate before it is filled and the sauerkraut pie is baked.

prebaked pie shell
7 inch bottom diameter by 1 1/2 inch deep

CHESTNUT DRESSING
with brown sauce

The elegant saffron consommé royale is the first course for this special autumn dinner. Serve braised green cabbage along with the chestnut dressing. Fennel in virgin olive oil with crackers and Stilton cheese is the salad course. Offer fresh pears to finish.

12 slices firm, close grain white bread - (8 cups torn)
1 pound chestnuts - (2 cups broken)
3 cups stock broth - (see stock broth)
celery - 4 large ribs - (2 cups diced)
11 ounces carrots - 4 medium large - (2 cups shredded)
parsley leaves - (1/2 cup chopped)
1/2 teaspoon ground rosemary - (see ground rosemary)
1/2 teaspoon ground (rubbed) sage
3/4 teaspoon ground ginger
1/2 teaspoon freshly cracked black pepper
1 1/2 teaspoon dried thyme
1 1/2 teaspoon dried marjoram
1 teaspoon celery salt
12 Tablespoons butter
1/2 cup currants
2 Tablespoons honey
1 teaspoons salt
brown sauce - (recipe follows)
2 eggs

Do not bother to trim the crusts from the bread but tear it into pieces the size of a dried bean. Spread the torn bread out, in one layer, on each of 2, 17 by 11 inch jelly roll pans. Allowing the bread to stand, uncovered, 2 or 3 hours will shorten oven time. In any case, dry the bread out in a preheated 200 degree oven for about 25 minutes, stirring it around once or twice. Watch it, do not let the bread to become toasted. Immediately transfer the bread to a paper bag and reserve it.

(The bread can be prepared up to 1 week in advance and stored in a dry place.)

Shell and peel the chestnuts as directed. (See chestnuts.) Bring the stock broth to simmer in a medium size saucepan over medium heat. Add the peeled chestnuts, reduce the heat to medium low and gently simmer the chestnuts, covered, about 20 minutes until they are just tender. Drain the chestnuts. (Reserve the cooking broth for the brown sauce. See brown sauce.) Break the chestnuts into pieces and reserve them.

Trim, scrape the strings from and dice the celery fairly small.

Trim, peel, and coarsely shred the carrots.

Chop the parsley small.

In a cup, mix the rosemary, sage, ginger, pepper and the thyme and marjoram, crushing them, together.

Sauté the celery, sprinkled with the celery salt in all the butter in a large frying pan (see utensils) over medium heat 3 minutes. Add the reserved chestnuts, the carrots, currants, honey, salt and mixed herbs and spices and cook the ingredients 5 minutes. Transfer the mixture to a large mixing bowl and stir the reserved dried bread pieces and the chopped parsley into it. Combine the ingredients well so that the bread absorbs the butter. Let the mixture cool completely then tightly cover the bowl and refrigerate the dressing 24 hours in order to allow the flavors to blend. Bring the dressing to room temperature before continuing with the recipe.

Prepare the brown sauce and keep it warm as directed.

In a small bowl beat the eggs until they are light then stir them into the dressing. Pack the dressing into 4, buttered, 1 1/2 cup, oval gratin dishes and tightly cover them with foil. Bake the dressing in a preheated 325 degree oven for 35 minutes. Uncover the dishes and serve the chestnut dressing along with a bowl of the warm brown sauce.

4 servings

brown sauce

7 Tablespoons butter
7 Tablespoons flour
1 Tablespoon tomato paste
3 cups reserved cooking broth - cold - (see chestnut dressing with brown
sauce)
1 teaspoon plus optional water
2 Tablespoons light molasses
3 Tablespoons soy sauce
1/2 teaspoon plus optional honey
1/2 teaspoon celery salt
1/8 teaspoon freshly cracked black pepper
1/8 teaspoon ground thyme

Melt the butter in a heavy medium size saucepan over medium heat and allow it to brown slightly. Immediately remove the pan from the heat and when the foaming subsides return the pan to low heat. Blend in the flour using a rubber spatula and stir the roux for 5 minutes. Add the tomato paste and slowly stir in the reserved broth adding a little water if the broth doesn't quite measure the 3 cups. Add the molasses, soy sauce, the 1/2 teaspoon of honey, the celery salt and pepper while gradually increasing the heat to medium. When the sauce simmers reduce the heat to low again, cover the pan with a trimmed piece of paper towel and lid and slowly cook the sauce for 25 minutes. Now in a cup make a paste out of the thyme and the 1 teaspoon of water and add it to the sauce. Taste. If necessary add a little more honey. Cook the sauce 5 minutes longer. Keep it warm, still covered with paper towel and lid over very low heat.

about 3 1/2 cups

SECTION IV

STUFFED HEAD OF RED CABBAGE

CROUSTADES OF WHITE ROOT VEGETABLES

STOCK VEGETABLE OMELETS

BROCCOLI BEATRICE with roquefort sauce

STUFFED IDAHOES

CELERY AND MILLET BAKED WITH SMOKED CHEESE

THREE DAY RUTABAGA

SPRING ROLLS

BOSTON BAKED BEANS (for the new age)

GOULASH with spätzle

STUFFED ACORN SQUASH with apple sauce

STEAMED VEGETABLES WITH NOODLES and a fukien sauce

RED BEAN HASH WITH POACHED EGGS and ketchup

NEW ENGLAND BOILED DINNER

SUPER CHIPS

CABBAGE ROLLS

ENCHILADAS DE LEGUMBRES with bean sauce

BROILED EGGPLANT MEDALLIONS with mushroom sauce

GERMAN STYLE RED CABBAGE

SAVORY TURNOVERS

SCALLOPED WHITE TURNIPS

STUFFED GREEN BELL PEPPERS with paprika sauce

PETITE MARMITE

POLENTA

RUTABAGA IN A POT

STUFFED MUSHROOMS

CHILE CASA MIA

COLCANNON

WHOLE ARTICHOKES WITH GARLIC BUTTER

CABBAGE STRUDEL

STUFFED HEAD OF RED CABBAGE

Stuffed head of red cabbage is fun to serve. It's a bit of magic and it looks especially effective surrounded by its accompaniment vegetable of buttered carrots. Serve cucumber soup first then following the main course serve marinated mushrooms and whole wheat bread with some Cheddar cheese. Crisp yellow apples are dessert and don't forget the mixed nuts!

1 1/3 cups dried lentils - about 10 ounces
1 bay leaf
1/2 cup reserved cooking liquid
water
4 pounds red cabbage - 1 large head
celery - 2 large ribs - (1 cup diced)
1 1/2 teaspoons salt
4 Tablespoons peanut oil
1 1/2 teaspoons English mustard powder
1 1/2 teaspoons celery salt
1/4 teaspoon cayenne
1 1/2 Tablespoons cider vinegar
2 Tablespoons tomato paste
2 Tablespoons soy sauce
2 Tablespoons honey

Cook the lentils with the bay leaf as directed. (See boiled dried shelled beans.) Drain them reserving 1/2 cup of their cooking liquid and discarding the bay leaf. If the drained lentils measure more than 4 cups, do not use the excess, it would unbalance the recipe. (Save any excess lentils for a bouillon soup. See bouillon soups.) Reserve the lentils.

Meanwhile, fill a large kettle with enough water to cover the head of cabbage and bring it to boil over high heat. Trim a slice, about 1 inch thick, off of the bottom of the head of cabbage and discard it. Using a small knife, cut down deep into the cabbage all around the stem to loosen the leaves. Using 2 long handled wooden spoons, lower the cabbage into the boiling water and cook it, covered, 5 minutes, from the moment it is in the water regardless of when the water returns to boil. Uncover the kettle. Using the 2 wooden spoons, carefully remove each successive leaf as it becomes loosened and set it aside to drain until 10 leaves have been removed. Lift what remains of the cabbage head out of the water, quarter, core and chop it fine. Cut a small triangle out of the thick base of each of the drained leaves and discard it. Blot the leaves dry with paper towels and reserve them.

Trim, scrape the strings from and dice the celery small.

Sauté the chopped cabbage and diced celery, sprinkled with the salt, in the oil in a large frying pan (see utensils) over medium heat, 5 minutes. Cover the pan, reduce the heat to low and cook 10 minutes. Meanwhile, in a small bowl dissolve the mustard powder, celery salt, and cayenne in the vinegar. Stir in the tomato paste, soy sauce and the 1/2 cup of reserved cooking liquid. Uncover the pan and add the liquid mixture, the reserved lentils and the honey. Increase the heat to medium high and cook the lentil mixture, stirring and turning it with a metal spatula, for about 10 minutes until it becomes somewhat dry, soft and pasty. Remove the pan from the heat.

Lay 2 long sheets of aluminum foil, crisscross, in a round bottomed 2 quart oven proof bowl, letting the long ends of the sheets hang over the sides of the bowl.

Now, we are going to reform the head of cabbage in the bowl. Place the 4 largest leaves, overlapping each other, stem end up, in the bowl. Using the back of a soup spoon, evenly spread not quite 1/3 of the lentil mixture around the inside of the leaves. Arrange 3 more cabbage leaves inside the now formed head and spread not quite another 1/3 of the lentil mixture around inside of them. Then arrange 2 leaves inside of that and fill them with not quite another 1/3 of the lentils, folding the base of the 2 leaves over it. Now, spread 1/2 of the remaining lentil mixture over the base of the 2 leaves. Fold down the base of the next 3 leaves and spread the remainder of the lentils over them. Fold over the base of the 4 large leaves and cover them with the last remaining leaf. Draw the foil up tight around the cabbage head, leaving a small opening at the top for steam to escape.

Bake the cabbage head in a preheated 375 degree oven for 1 hour and 45 minutes. Remove the bowl from the oven, open up the steam hole a little more and lay an inverted cake rack over the bowl. Holding them together, turn the bowl and rack over, set them over a pan and allow the cabbage to drain 10 minutes. Turn the bowl and rack over again, remove the rack, open up the foil completely now and fold it back over the sides of the bowl. Place a warm, round, inverted, serving platter over the bowl and holding them together, turn them over. Remove the bowl and carefully remove the foil. Let the beautiful, round, firm, cabbage head stand for 5 minutes. If any more moisture drains away from it, blot it up with a paper towel. To serve the stuffed head of red cabbage, cut it into wedges with a serrated knife, like a cake.

8 servings

Note: Be sure that the bowl you reshape the head of cabbage in has a round bottom.

CROUSTADES
🌿 OF WHITE ROOT VEGETABLES 🌿

Croustades is a French word for crusts. Do make an effort to obtain good quality, crusty, hard rolls. Herb broth will make a light first course and tossed iceberg lettuce a refreshing third course. Poached peaches are the simple dessert.

A combination of any of the following vegetables: celeriac, parsnips, potatoes, white turnips, white sugar beets, salsify, helianlhus tuberose, white radishes, etc., in whatever proportions are desirable or available - (8 cups)

lemon juice - optional
boiling water
salt
4 hard rolls
4 eggs - at room temperature
8 Tablespoons butter
7 Tablespoons flour
1/4 teaspoon white pepper
3 cups light cream - at room temperature
1 cup dry white wine
2 teaspoons salt
1 1/2 teaspoons celery salt
1 1/2 teaspoons honey
1 teaspoon ground (rubbed) sage
1 teaspoon ground thyme
1/2 teaspoon ground rosemary - (see ground rosemary)
1 Tablespoon cold water

Trim, peel and cut the vegetables into 3/8 inch dice. As each vegetable is diced, keeping each type of vegetable separate, drop it into a bowl containing enough cold water to cover it. For celeriac, parsnips, and salsify add 1 teaspoon of lemon juice per cup of water to help keep the vegetables from discoloring. Then drain the vegetables, one at a time, and blanch them, individually, in 2 cups of boiling water with 1/4 teaspoon of salt per cup of diced vegetable, in a saucepan, set over high heat. Start counting the cooking time from the moment the vegetable is in the water, regardless of when the water returns to boil. Cover the saucepan, with lid ajar, and adjust the heat to keep the water slowly boiling. The diced vegetables will take anywhere from 1 1/2 to 2 1/2 minutes to be done. Celeriac will take about 1 1/2 minutes, parsnips 2 minutes, potatoes and turnips 2 1/2 minutes, etc. The vegetables must be just barely tender firm, as they are going to be reheated later. The only way to be sure when the vegetable is ready is to taste a piece of it. The moment the vegetable is ready, drain it and turn it into a basin of cold water for 2 minutes. Then drain the vegetable well and blot it dry on paper towels. Mix all the vegetables together in a bowl.

(The vegetables can be prepared up to 24 hours in advance and stored, refrigerated, altogether in a sealed plastic bag then brought to room temperature before continuing with the recipe.)

Set the hard rolls on a cookie sheet in a preheated 250 degree oven, for 10 minutes. Remove them from the oven. Now, neatly cut "lids" out of the tops of the rolls, not too large nor too small, as you would a pumpkin. Then pick the warm soft inside out of the rolls and "lids" with your finger tips and discard it. It is easiest to do this while the rolls are hot, but don't burn your fingers. Set the shells and "lids" aside, keeping the proper shells and "lids" together.

(The rolls can be prepared several hours in advance and stored in an unsealed paper bag.)

Hard cook and peel the eggs as directed. (See cooked eggs.) Allow them to cool to room temperature then refrigerate them for 1 hour to help them remain firm while being chopped. Chop them about the same size as the diced vegetables and reserve them.

Melt the butter in a large saucepan over low heat. Using a rubber spatula, blend in the flour and pepper, stirring constantly, for 5 minutes. Slowly stir in the cream, wine, 2 teaspoons of salt, the celery salt, and honey, while gradually raising the heat to medium high, until the sauce comes to a lively simmer. Add all the vegetables. When the sauce returns to simmer, reduce the heat to low, place a heat diffuser under the pan and heat the vegetables, covered with a trimmed piece of paper towel and lid 10 minutes. In a teacup make a paste out of the sage, thyme, rosemary and the 1 tablespoon of cold water. Then stir the paste into the sauce and continue to heat the vegetables, covered, 5 minutes longer.

Meanwhile, replace the hard roll shells and "lids" on the cookie sheet, cut sides up, and return them to a 250 degree oven, for 5 minutes.

To serve, cover each of 4 warm dinner plates with a ladleful of the vegetable and sauce mixture. Set a warm shell on top of each and fill the shells full to overflowing with the remainder of the vegetable and sauce mixture. Then sprinkle the evenly divided chopped eggs over each. Set the proper "lid" on top of each shell and serve the croustades of white root vegetables immediately.

4 servings

Note: White sugar beets make a delicious ingredient in this dish. Most people are unfamiliar with them as a table vegetable. However, if you use them, the salt and honey may need adjusting.

❧ STOCK VEGETABLE OMELETS ❧

This method of omelet making never fails to produce a beautiful, well shaped, tender omelet. It takes 2 or 3 minutes longer to make than the classic French method but the entire process is under your calm control every second and it never fails. (French omelets without tears!) Cream of celeriac is the soup, then have coleslaw and baking powder biscuits with some Cheddar cheese following the omelets. Complete this homey repast with frozen bananas.

3/4 to 1 cup warm stock vegetable omelet filling - (recipe follows)
1 teaspoon corn oil
3 eggs - at room temperature - (see cooked eggs note)
1 Tablespoon warm water
1 Tablespoon butter - at room temperature - divided
salt and pepper

Prepare the omelet filling and keep it warm as directed.

Warm the oil in an omelet pan (see utensils) which has an inside bottom measurement of 7 inches in diameter, over medium heat, about 5 minutes, depending upon the heaviness of the pan, until the pan is well heated. The heat setting may vary slightly according to your stove.

Meanwhile, using a wire whisk, beat the eggs and water together, in a mixing bowl, just until they are light.

When the pan is ready, add 2 teaspoons of the butter. The butter should sizzle and foam but not so much that it burns. If it starts to darken too quickly, lift the pan immediately and reduce the heat slightly. Allow the butter to become a delicate, light shade of brown to give color to the omelet. (The eggs themselves, however, must not brown.) When the butter stops foaming, pour in the eggs and wait about 30 seconds until they begin to set. Then, using a metal spatula and working quickly, lift the edges of the omelet while tilting the pan to allow the top, still liquid portion of the eggs to flow down into the pan. This process should take 30 to 45 additional seconds. Now, cover the pan with a tight fitting lid, remove the pan from the heat and allow it to stand from 2 to 3 minutes, depending upon how well done you like your omelet, to permit the eggs to finish cooking.

For easy access, set the saucepan of warm stock vegetable omelet filling next to a warm dinner plate. Remove the lid from the omelet pan and slide half of the omelet out onto the center of the plate. Using a large spoon, spoon 3/4 to 1 cup of the filling onto it then deftly flip the other half of the omelet over the filling, using the edge of the pan. Quickly smear the top of the omelet with the remaining 1 teaspoon of soft butter and serve the stock vegetable omelet immediately along with salt and pepper on the table.

1 omelet - 1 serving

Note: Repeat the recipe and continue making up to 6 omelets until everyone is served. If you like, it's a simple matter to produce omelets in quick succession, by using 2 pans.

stock vegetable omelet filling

2 Tablespoons butter
3/4 cup tomato paste - 6 ounces
1 cup water
1 Tablespoon cider vinegar
2 teaspoons honey
1/2 teaspoon salt
1/2 teaspoon celery salt
1/2 teaspoon paprika
1/4 teaspoon ground allspice
1/8 teaspoon cayenne
1/2 teaspoon dried oregano
1/2 teaspoon dried basil
1/2 teaspoon dried thyme
5 to 6 cups drained stock broth vegetables - bay leaf removed - (see stock broth)

Combine the first 10 ingredients in a large heavy saucepan over low heat and allow them to very gently simmer, uncovered, 30 minutes. Add the 3 herbs, crushing them. Gently fold the stock vegetables into the sauce and warm them, covered, over the low heat 15 minutes.
Keep the filling warm, covered with a trimmed piece of paper towel and lid over very low heat.

5 to 6 cup filling

Note: 5 to 6 cups is enough filling for six 3 egg omelets.

 BROCCOLI BEATRICE
with roquefort sauce

Serve noodle soup first. Then accompany this very simple but rich entrée with baked butternut squash. Tossed romaine is a good salad choice. Serve poached cherries to finish.

2 pounds of broccoli - 4 average heads
Roquefort sauce - (recipe follows)
salt

Trim and cut the broccoli as directed but do not steam it just yet. (See steamed broccoli.)

Prepare the Roquefort sauce and keep it warm as directed.

Now, steam the broccoli as directed. Then arrange the hot broccoli on each of 4 warm dinner plates so that the heads of the florets face in two opposite directions and the extra stem pieces are neatly arranged with the stems of the florets. Lightly sprinkle the broccoli with salt and spoon the equally divided, warm sauce over the stems so that the florets remain visible at each end. Serve the broccoli Beatrice with Roquefort sauce immediately.

4 servings

roquefort sauce

4 ounces Roquefort cheese - (1 cup crumbled)
1 Tablespoon butter
1 cup small curd Cottage cheese
1 cup sour cream - at room temperature
1/4 teaspoon salt

Crumble the Roquefort cheese, and in the top of a double boiler over simmering water, combine it with the butter and Cottage cheese, stirring. When the cheeses have melted the mixture should still be slightly lumpy. Remove the double boiler from the heat, and when the water in the lower half stops simmering, stir the sour cream and salt into the cheese mixture. Cover the top of the pan with a paper towel and lid and keep the Roquefort sauce warm over the hot water until serving.

about 3 cups

STUFFED IDAHOES

Some years ago my French grandmother came to visit us and fell in love with Idaho potatoes. She took some back to France and planted them. However, in French soil they only grew to be moderate size potatoes and she was sorely disappointed. The soup selection is cream of tomato then buttered spinach will go well with these very special stuffed potatoes. Serve celery hearts vinaigrette with some bread and cheese for the salad course then follow with poached peaches.

3 pounds Idaho potatoes - 4 extra large, 12 ounces each
1 1/2 pounds white turnips - 4 large
celery - 2 large ribs - (1 cup diced)
1 teaspoon celery salt - divided
1 Tablespoon plus 1 teaspoon peanut oil - divided
6 ounces green bell pepper - 1 medium - (1 cup diced)
3/4 cup butter
1 teaspoon salt
1/4 teaspoon freshly cracked black pepper

Scrub the potatoes under running water and dry them well. Pierce each potato a couple of times with the tines of a fork and bake them in a preheated 425 degree oven, 1 hour.

Trim, peel, and tightly wrap the turnips, individually, in foil. Bake them in a preheated 425 degree oven about 40 minutes until they are very tender. Purée them through a food mill set over a bowl then turn them into a colander lined with a double layer of wet wrung out cheese cloth, set over a bowl. Place a saucer with a moderate weight upon it on the turnips and allow them to drain while you prepare the rest of the dish. (Save the drained liquid for a bouillon soup. See bouillon soups.)

Trim, scrape the strings from and dice the celery small. Sauté it, sprinkled with 1/2 teaspoon of the celery salt, in 2 teaspoons of the oil in a frying pan (see utensils), over medium heat about 5 minutes or until it starts to shrink and become golden. Transfer the celery to paper towels and reserve it.

Core, trim away any white membrane from the bell pepper and dice it small. Sauté it, sprinkled with 1/2 teaspoon of the celery salt, in 2 teaspoons of the oil in the frying pan over medium heat, 5 minutes, or until it starts to brown. Transfer the pepper to paper towels and reserve it.

Melt the butter in a small saucepan over low heat and keep it warm.

Pierce the potatoes with a wooden skewer to determine when they are done. Holding each potato with a pot holder, slice off a quarter of it, lengthwise, then carefully scoop out all the hot flesh from both pieces of the potato into the food mill set over a bowl, leaving 1/4 inch of flesh in the larger shell and discarding the smaller piece of skin. Purée the potatoes into the bowl then thoroughly stir the drained turnip, melted butter, salt and pepper into them. Fold in the reserved celery and bell pepper.

Now, stuff the potato shells with the potato mixture, heaping it high. Set the stuffed potatoes on a baking sheet and place them under a preheated broiler, 6 inches from the heat source for about 10 minutes until the tips of the potato mixture brown and the potatoes are heated through. Transfer the stuffed Idahoes to a warm serving platter and use two large spoons with which to serve them,

4 servings

CELERY AND MILLET BAKED WITH SMOKED CHEESE

Before preparing this easy dish make sure that you have a well aged smoked cheese which will melt nicely. Serve cream of carrot soup to begin. Then accompany the celery with sweet Italian frying peppers. Red cabbage vinaigrette with whole wheat bread is the salad course and chilled oranges the dessert.

7/8 cup millet - about 6 1/2 ounces
celery - 1 average bunch - (about 6 cups cut)
12 ounces smoked Cheddar cheese - (3 cups grated) - divided
1 jar pimento stuffed green olives - 5 ounces - (1 cup sliced)

1 teaspoon celery salt
8 Tablespoons butter - divided
3 Tablespoons hot water - in a cup
1 teaspoon honey
1/2 teaspoon salt
1/2 teaspoon freshly cracked black pepper

Steam the millet as directed. (See steamed millet.) Let it get cold and reserve it.

Select a handsome bunch of celery with plenty of fresh green leaves on it. Spray water down into the bunch of celery to dislodge any dirt. Turn it upside down in a colander to drain then wrap it in a clean dish towel and dry it well. Lay the bunch of celery on a cutting board. Using a large serrated knife and starting at the top of the bunch, cut the celery, crosswise, into slices no thicker than 1/4 inch.

Coarsely grate the cheese and reserve it.

Drain, rinse, and drain the olives. Cut them thin, crosswise, and reserve them, setting 16 slices aside for decoration.

Sauté the celery, sprinkled with the celery salt, in 4 tablespoons of the butter in a large frying pan (see utensils), over medium heat for 3 minutes. Reduce the heat to low, remove the pan from the heat, add the hot water and cover the pan immediately. Return it to the low heat for 4 minutes. Increase the heat to high, uncover the pan and cook the celery about 2 minutes longer, stirring it until all the moisture has evaporated. Reduce the heat to low again, add 4 more tablespoons of the butter, the honey, reserved millet, salt and pepper. Stir the mixture well with a wooden fork until the millet absorbs the butter. Then transfer the mixture to a mixing bowl and allow it to cool a bit. Now, stir in 2 cups of the reserved cheese and the reserved olives.

Pack the mixture into each of 4 buttered, 1 1/2 cup gratin dishes or oven proof bowls. Sprinkle 1/4 cup of the remaining cheese over each dish and decorate each with 4 of the remaining olive slices. Bake the dishes 30 minutes in a preheated 325 degree oven. Then set the gratin dishes on dinner plates and serve the celery and millet baked with smoked cheese.

4 servings

 THREE DAY RUTABAGA

The flavor of the rutabaga needs three days to fully develop and tastes divine, just divine. Start with matzoh balls in garlic broth then accompany the rutabaga with buttered Swiss chard. Next a pressed cucumber salad is served with rye bread and Jarlesberg cheese. Mixed fruit over ice cream will round out the meal.

4 pounds rutabaga - 2 medium small
8 Tablespoons unsalted butter
1 teaspoon plus salt - divided
1/4 teaspoon freshly cracked black pepper
4 Tablespoons heavy cream
2 red Delicious apples, - fresh and firm
2 Tablespoons butter - (salted)
4 teaspoons granulated sugar - divided
parsley - 8 sprigs

Trim, peel, and quarter the rutabaga, lengthwise. Wrap the quarters, separately, in a double layer of aluminum foil. Place the wrapped pieces on a baking sheet and bake them in a preheated 400 degree oven for 1 hour or until they are very soft when pierced with a wooden toothpick. Unwrap the pieces and purée the rutabaga through a food mill set over a bowl.

Line a colander with a double layer of wet wrung out cheese cloth. Place the purée in it, tie the corners of the cheese cloth together and hang the bag up over a bowl to allow the rutabaga to drain for 1 hour. The yield should be 4 cups of drained purée. (Save the liquid for a bouillon soup. See bouillon soup.)

Melt the 8 tablespoons of butter in a heavy, medium size saucepan over low heat. Thoroughly stir the purée, the 1 teaspoon of salt and the pepper into the butter. Remove the pan from the heat, allow the rutabaga to cool to room temperature then refrigerate it, covered, overnight.

About 24 hours later warm the rutabaga, uncovered, over low heat for about 15 minutes, stirring occasionally, until it is heated through. Allow it to cool to room temperature and refrigerate it again, covered, overnight.

Before serving, warm the rutabaga again, uncovered, over low heat, this time stirring in the cream, for about 20 minutes until it is hot. Divide the purée equally among 4 warm, 1 cup gratin or similar dishes smoothing it out. Place the dishes in a preheated 250 degree oven to keep warm while you prepare the apples.

Using a vegetable peeler, peel the apples and cut a thin slice off the top and bottom of each apple and discard them. Then cut each apple, crosswise into 4 slices each about 1/2 inch thick. Using a sharp pointed knife, cut the core out of each slice in a neat little circle. Sauté the 8 slices together, sprinkled with 2 teaspoons of the sugar and a dash of the salt, in the 2 tablespoons of butter in a large frying pan (see utensils), over medium high heat for about 1 minute. Using a metal spatula, turn the slices over, sprinkle them again with 2 teaspoons of the sugar and a dash of the salt and sauté them about 2 minutes. Turn them over again and sauté them 1 minute longer. The slices must be just tinged a crisp golden brown, but do not allow the butter or sugar to scorch or the apples to overcook.

Arrange 2 slices, one slightly overlapping the other, on each dish of purée and tuck a sprig of parsley into the hole in each slice. Set the gratin dishes on dinner plates and serve the three day rutabaga immediately.

4 servings

 SPRING ROLLS

As everyone must know by now the true name of egg rolls is spring rolls. They are always served on Chinese new year as well as at other times. Cream of kohlrabi is a good soup for this Oriental dinner. Have one or two bottles of soy sauce on the table as well as the plum and mustard sauces. Follow with a white turnip vinaigrette and some rice wafers. Complete this festive dinner with fresh tangerines.

plum sauce - (recipe follows)
12 spring roll wrappers - (recipe follows)
spring roll filling - (recipe follows)
5 cups peanut oil
1 Tablespoon flour
2 Tablespoons cold water
mustard sauce - (recipe follows)

The plum sauce can be prepared far in advance as directed.
The spring roll wrappers can be prepared 2 or 3 days in advance as directed.

The spring roll filling should be prepared just before assembly.

(Allowing about 15 minutes for the oil to heat to temperature, heat the oil in a deep saucepan, with a cooking thermometer clipped to the inside of it, over medium heat to 350 degrees. Or use an electric deep fryer set at 350 degrees.)

In a small cup, make a thin paste out of the flour and water.

Keeping the remaining wrappers sealed in plastic, lay 1 wrapper out, catty-corner, in front of you and slice off about 1 inch of the corner nearest you, to form a blunt corner. (Dry the scraps and save them for a bouillon soup. See bouillon soups.) Dip your finger in the flour and water paste and smear the edges of the 3 pointed corners and the 2 full length sides of the wrapper with it. Now, place 2 heaping tablespoons of the filling just below the center of the wrapper arranging it in an oblong shape about 5 inches long, parallel with the blunt corner. Pull the blunt corner up over the filling and carefully fold in the 2 side corners adding a little more paste where necessary to keep the ends of the spring roll tightly sealed. Then just finish rolling it up, pressing the fourth corner flap to the body of the spring roll. The completed spring roll should be about 5 inches long.

Make another spring roll, and when the oil has reached temperature, deep fry the 2 spring rolls together, for about 3 minutes, pushing them down into the oil and turning them over with a skimmer or slotted spoon, until they are just a pleasing golden color. Lift them from the oil, using the skimmer, and drain them on paper towels.

Assemble, fry and drain the remaining spring rolls, 2 at a time until they are all done. Allow the spring rolls to cool completely then wrap them in paper towels and refrigerate them, sealed in plastic several hours or overnight.

Just before serving prepare the mustard sauce as directed.

At serving time, reheat the oil to 365 degrees and deep fry the cold spring rolls, 3 at a time now, for 5 minutes until they are a beautiful crisp golden brown. If they should brown too quickly, lower the heat as they will require the full 5 minutes to become heated through. Drain them on paper towels and serve the spring rolls immediately along with small dishes of the plum sauce and mustard sauce.

Three spring rolls constitute one serving. To serve them crisp and hot, either place three rolls on a warm dinner plate and serve just one guest, letting the others wait their turns, or place the three spring rolls on a small platter and let each guest serve himself to one spring roll while the next batch is being fried. Cook is served last.

The diners serve themselves to the sauces and place a little of each on their dinner plates. To eat them, cut the spring rolls crosswise with serrated knives provided for the purpose and dab the filling with a little plum sauce and mustard sauce. You can use chop sticks or a fork to hold the spring rolls if you like but fingers are entirely acceptable. In which case you might want to provide finger bowls scented with almond extract at the end of the course.

4 servings

Note: Happy New Year!

plum sauce

2/3 cup pitted dried prunes - 4 ounces
1/4 cup dried apricot halves - 1 1/2 ounces
boiling water
1 cup reserved soaking water
2 Tablespoons soy sauce
1 Tablespoon distilled white vinegar
2 Tablespoons light molasses
2 Tablespoons honey
2 Tablespoons brown sugar
1/4 teaspoon salt
1/2 teaspoon Chinese five spices

Place the prunes and apricots in a bowl and add enough boiling water to cover them by 1 inch. Allow them to stand 1 hour or until they are very soft. Drain them, reserving 1 cup of the soaking water. Purée the soaked prunes, apricots, the reserved soaking water and all the remaining ingredients in the blender. (Purée not liquefy.) Serve the plum sauce at room temperature, in small dishes.

about 1 1/2 cups plum sauce

Note: Plum sauce may be stored, refrigerated, in a covered glass jar. Chinese five spices is a mixture of spices, commercially packaged and available in specialty stores, natural food stores and some supermarkets.

spring roll wrappers

1 cup minus 1 Tablespoon all purpose flour
1 Tablespoon cornstarch
1/4 teaspoon salt
4 Tablespoons plus 1 1/2 to 2 teaspoons cold water

      Combine the flour, cornstarch, salt and the 4 tablespoons plus 1 1/2 teaspoons water in the processor and process them 15 seconds. Stop the machine, scrape down the bowl and pinch the granular mixture together between your fingers. If it does not cling together to form dough, add 1/2 teaspoon more water. In either case, process 15 seconds longer, turn the still granular mixture out onto a very lightly floured work surface, gather the dough together and knead it 1 minute. The dough will weigh 8 ounces. Divide the dough into 4 pieces of equal weight and seal them in plastic. They do not need to rest.

      Alternatively, sift the flour, cornstarch and salt together into a mixing bowl. Sprinkle them with the 4 tablespoons plus 1 1/2 teaspoon of water and stir the ingredients with a fork. Now, using your hand knead the very crumbly mixture about 5 minutes or until a very rough dough begins to form. At this point, decide whether to add the 1/2 teaspoon more water. Turn the dough out onto a very lightly floured work surface and knead it, as best you can, for 3 minutes to form a cohesive mass even though the pasta machine will knead the dough later. Divide and seal the dough as directed above.

      Roll out either the processor or hand made dough as directed but use cornstarch rather than flour to dust it with. (See machine rolled pasta dough.) The dough may be very ragged during the first 1 or 2 passes through the rollers but it quickly smooths out and behaves. The finished sheet should measure 18 by 6 inches, like pasta dough. If, because this dough is firmer, the sheet should not be quite long enough, run it through the machine 1 more time. As soon as each sheet of dough is rolled out, lay it on a flat work surface and cut it into 3, 6 inch squares. Lightly dust the squares with cornstarch, stack them on top of each other and seal them in plastic immediately. The wrappers can be made 2 or 3 days in advance of assembling the spring rolls and stored refrigerated.

12 spring roll wrappers

      Note: We want this dough to be nice and firm so resist adding the extra 1/2 teaspoon of water if you can. Do not let the dry roughness of the dough discourage you, especially if you are kneading the dough by hand. The processor is the preferred method here but it is not absolutely necessary. However, it is necessary to use the pasta machine to roll out this very firm dough.

Good quality spring roll wrappers are available in many super markets. However, once you have made your own you will probably prefer them. These wrappers fry up light and crisp.

spring roll filling

1 pound mushrooms - medium - (5 cups sliced)
12 ounces green bell peppers - 2 medium - (2 cups sliced)
celery - 4 large ribs - (2 cups sliced)
8 ounces water chestnuts - about 16 - (1 cup cut)
1 pound napa (Chinese celery cabbage) - 1 small head - (4 cups sliced)
ginger root - (1 Tablespoon freshly grated)
2 Tablespoons peanut oil
1 1/2 teaspoon salt - divided
4 ounces mung bean sprouts - (2 cups)
1/4 cup reserved drained vegetable juice
2 teaspoons cornstarch
1/4 teaspoon superfine sugar
2 Tablespoons soy sauce

Wipe the mushrooms with a damp cloth and trim the butt ends of the stems. Thinly slice the stems crosswise and the caps lengthwise.

Quarter the bell peppers lengthwise and core them, cutting away any white membrane. Thinly slice the quarters crosswise.

Trim, scrape the strings from and thinly slice the celery crosswise.

Trim, peel and cut the water chestnuts into little matchsticks.

Cut the napa in half lengthwise. Lay it cut side down and very thinly slice it crosswise.

Peel and grate the ginger root on a medium fine grater.

Heat the oil in a wok or large frying pan (see utensils), over high heat. Just before the oil starts to smoke add the ginger and heat it 15 seconds. Then add the mushrooms, sprinkle with 1/2 teaspoon of the salt and stir fry about 8 minutes or until all their moisture has evaporated. Now add the bell peppers, celery and water chestnuts and stir fry 2 minutes more, add the napa, sprinkle with 1 teaspoon of the salt and stir fry 4 minutes. Then add the sprouts and stir fry 2 minutes longer. Immediately turn the vegetables into a colander set over a bowl. Place a saucer with a moderate weight upon it on them and allow the vegetables to drain 1 hour, turning them over several times during that period. Transfer the vegetables to a mixing bowl. Measure out 1/4 cup of the drained vegetable juices and reserve it. (Save any extra juices for a bouillon soup. See bouillon soup.)

In a small saucepan, dissolve the cornstarch and sugar in the 1/4 cup of reserved juice and the soy sauce. Bring the mixture to simmer over medium heat stirring constantly with a rubber spatula. When the mixture simmers, reduce the heat slightly and continue to simmer, 2 minutes still stirring constantly. Pour the sauce over the vegetables and using two forks toss them to distribute the sauce evenly and coat the vegetables well.

filling for 12 spring rolls 5 inches long

chinese mustard sauce

1 part Chinese mustard powder - (see note)
2 or 3 parts cold water

In a small dish make a paste of 2 or 3 tablespoons of the mustard powder and some water gradually adding more water to make a slurry. Chinese mustard sauce is very powerful, not much will be required, do not make too much. Allow the mustard sauce to stand about 15 minutes before serving.

Note: Chinese mustard powder is available in the Oriental section of super markets and in specialty or natural food stores. If Chinese mustard powder is unavailable use English mustard powder and make the sauce in the proportions of 1 part mustard powder, 2 parts water and 1 part distilled white vinegar.

BOSTON BAKED BEANS
(for the new age)

Start off with cream of parsnip soup on this cold winter evening. Then have baked cabbage wedges with these delicious baked beans. Carrot and currant salad with steamed brown bread and Cream cheese are good choices for the next course. Follow with yellow Delicious apples.

2 1/4 cups dried marrow beans or yellow eyed beans - 1 pound - (see note)
1/3 cup wheat berries
3 cups stock broth - (see stock broth) - divided
2 Tablespoons tomato paste
1/3 cup light molasses
1 Tablespoon honey
1/2 teaspoon liquid smoke
3 Tablespoons butter
3 Tablespoons peanut oil - divided
1/4 teaspoon black pepper
1 1/4 teaspoon salt - divided
1 teaspoon celery salt
2 teaspoons English mustard powder
1 teaspoon cider vinegar
boiling water - optional
celery - 2 large ribs - (1 cup diced)

Cull the beans and soak them, in water to cover by 2 inches, overnight. (Do not precook the beans.)

Start soaking the wheat berries about 1 hour before the beans go into the oven. Soak, cook and drain the wheat berries as directed. (See boiled wheat berries.) If the cooked wheat berries measure more than 1 cup, don't use the excess it would unbalance the recipe. (Use any excess in a bouillon soup. See bouillon soups.)

Drain the beans and place them in a deep 6 cup baking dish, preferably an earthenware bean pot with a close fitting lid. In a saucepan, over high heat, bring 2 cups of the stock broth, with the tomato paste, molasses, honey, liquid smoke, butter, 2 tablespoons of the oil and the pepper to boil. Immediately pour the boiling mixture over the beans. Tightly cover the dish with the lid or aluminum foil and bake the beans in a preheated 250 degree oven 3 hours, without stirring them. Check them from time to time to be sure that the liquid is always at least even with the surface of the beans. If necessary heat the remaining 1 cup of stock broth to boiling in a saucepan and add some of it to the beans.

At the end of the 3 hour baking period, using a wooden spoon, carefully stir the drained, boiled wheat berries, 1 teaspoon of the salt and the celery salt into the beans and cook them, covered, 1 hour longer.

Now, in a cup dissolve the mustard in the vinegar and add the paste to the beans, plus any remaining hot stock broth. If the beans still require more liquid simply add a little boiling water and bake the beans, uncovered now, 30 minutes.

Meanwhile trim, scrape the strings from and dice the celery small. When the beans have baked, uncovered, for the 30 minute baking period, sauté the celery, sprinkled with 1/4 teaspoon of the salt in 1 tablespoon of the oil in a frying pan over medium heat for 3 minutes. Then gently stir the celery and its cooking oil into the beans and bake the beans, still uncovered 30 minutes more. Remove the beans from the oven and allow them to stand, covered now, 30 minutes before serving.

6 to 8 servings

Note: I like the flavor of marrow beans for this dish, but they are not often seen in the market. I grew them one year but they were not productive. However, yellow eyed beans are tasty and the Mainiacs (people in Maine), who grow a lot of them prefer them for baked beans. In either case they do not need to be precooked as old recipes indicate. Today, it is not so much a question of being sure the beans are cooked as it is a question of being careful not to overcook them.

GOULASH
with spätzle

Goulash looks very much at home in a blue agateware soup kettle with a wire handle. Spätzle are delightful little free-form dumplings. This simple dish can easily feed eight people so follow it with a double recipe of tossed salad mix I plus some dark bread and a mild Cheddar. Blackberries over ice cream is a multipliable dessert.

celery - 4 large ribs - (2 cups sliced)
8 ounces carrots - 4 medium - (1 1/2 cups sliced)

1 1/2 pounds cabbage - 3/4 small head - (7 1/2 tightly packed cups cut)
12 ounces green bell peppers - 2 medium - (2 cups cut)
1 Tablespoon caraway seeds
8 Tablespoons butter - divided
4 Tablespoons flour
6 1/2 cups water - divided
3/4 cup tomato paste - 6 ounces
1 can peeled tomatoes - 28 ounces - (3 1/2 cups)
1 can peeled tomatoes - 16 ounces - (2 cups)
4 Tablespoon sweet Hungarian paprika
2 teaspoons hot Hungarian paprika
2 Tablespoons plus 1 teaspoon honey
1 teaspoon celery salt
1 Tablespoon salt - divided
2 teaspoons dried marjoram

Trim, scrape the strings from and cut the celery, crosswise into 3/8 inch thick slices.

Trim, peel and cut the carrots, crosswise, into 3/8 inch thick slices.

Quarter the cabbage lengthwise, trimming away the core. Cut the wedges into 1 inch dice, then carefully pull the leaves apart.

Cut the bell peppers crosswise into 1 inch thick slices. Core them, trimming away any white membrane and cut the rings into 1 inch squares.

Toast the caraway seeds in a dry pan over medium heat for about 3 minutes, stirring constantly, until they deepen in color, become fragrant and start to pop. Remove the seeds from the pan immediately and crush them, 1/2 teaspoon at a time in a mortar or use a spice grinder.

Melt 2 tablespoons of the butter in a large soup kettle over low heat. Using a rubber spatula, blend in the flour until the butter is absorbed. Gradually stir in 2 cups of the water until the mixture is perfectly smooth. Then stir in the tomato paste. Drain the tomato juices into the kettle, cut the stem buttons out of the tomatoes, quarter them lengthwise and add them to the kettle. In a cup, make a paste out of the sweet and hot paprika and 1/2 cup of the water then add it to the kettle. Add the crushed caraway, the honey, celery salt and the remaining 4 cups of water. Increase the heat to medium high, when the liquid simmers, reduce the heat to low and simmer the mixture, covered, 30 minutes.

Now, sauté the celery and carrots together, sprinkled with 1 teaspoon of the salt, in 2 tablespoons of the butter in a large frying pan (see utensils), over medium heat for 5 minutes. Add the celery, carrots and all their butter to the kettle. Sauté the cabbage in exactly the same manner and add it to the kettle, then the bell peppers in like manner. When all the vegetables are in the kettle, continue to simmer the goulash, covered, 25 minutes. Add the marjoram, crushing it, and simmer 5 minutes longer.

Meanwhile, about 15 minutes before the goulash is ready, prepare the spätzle as directed. When the goulash is done, turn the drained spatzle into it and serve the goulash with spätzle immediately.

8 servings

spätzle

3 to 4 Tablespoons plus water
1 teaspoon salt - divided
1 cup flour
2 eggs

Half fill a deep saucepan with water, add 1/2 teaspoon of the salt and bring it to simmer over medium heat.

Meanwhile, sift the flour and 1/2 teaspoon of the salt into a mixing bowl. In a measuring cup, using a fork, lightly beat the eggs with the 3 to 4 tablespoons of water or enough water so that the total volume measures 2/3 cup. Using a rubber spatula, stir the egg mixture into the flour until it is a fairly smooth, very thick, sticky batter.

Now, pass the batter through a spätzle maker (see utensils), set over the simmering water. Alternatively, place a coarse, flat grater (the one you would coarsely grate cheese on) smooth side up, over the simmering water. Scoop up 1 heaping tablespoon of the batter at a time and using a wooden spatula, press it through the grater with a scraping motion. (This closely simulates the action of a spätzle maker.) In either case, adjust the heat to keep the water gently simmering. When all the spätzle are in the water continue to simmer them, covered, for about 5 minutes until they are tender. Drain the spätzle in a colander.

about 2 cups

 STUFFED ACORN SQUASH
with apple sauce

Begin this homey dinner with cream of pea soup. Accompany the squash with braised red cabbage and serve buttermilk biscuits with a salad of green bell peppers vinaigrette. Blueberries over ice cream will be dessert.

apple sauce - (recipe follows)
acorn squash - 2 medium, 1 1/2 pounds each
1 Tablespoons plus 1 teaspoon of butter
salt
ground cinnamon

Prepare the apple sauce as directed and have it at room temperature.

Remove any stems and cut a little slice off of the pointed end of each squash to make it flat. Cut the squash in half crosswise and scoop out seeds and membrane. Lay the halves, cut side down on a buttered jellyroll pan and bake the squash about 40 minutes in a preheated 375 degree oven. Pierce the squash with a wooden toothpick to determine when it is just tender. Use a metal spatula to remove the squash from the pan.

Set half a squash, cut side up, on each of 4 warm dinner plates. Place 1 teaspoon of butter in each cavity, lightly sprinkle it with salt and fill the cavity with the apple sauce, then dust the apple sauce with cinnamon. Serve the stuffed acorn squash with apple sauce along with plenty of extra butter.

4 servings

apple sauce

about 1 1/2 pounds Cortland apples - 4 medium
2 Tablespoons water
about 1 1/2 pounds Macintosh apples - 4 medium
about 6 Tablespoons sugar
1/4 teaspoon ground cinnamon
1/8 teaspoon ground cloves.

Cut the Cortlands, lengthwise, into eighths. Core but do not peel them. Cook them, with the water, in a large, heavy saucepan, covered, over low heat, 15 minutes. Meanwhile cut and core the Macintoshes. When the Cortlands have cooked the 15 minutes, add the Macintoshes to the pan and continue to cook the apples 30 minutes longer, keeping the liquid gently simmering and stirring occasionally.

When the apples are very soft, pass them through a food mill set over a bowl. Discard skins that won't go through.

Return the purée to the saucepan, over low heat, add the sugar to your taste, the cinnamon and cloves and simmer the sauce, uncovered, 5 minutes longer. Remove the pan from the heat and allow the apple sauce to cool to room temperature.

about 6 cups

STEAMED VEGETABLES WITH NOODLES
and a fukien sauce

Hot spices are used in the cooking of the Fukien Province of China. Egg drop will be the appropriate soup to serve. Follow the main course with a tossed salad of napa and some sesame crackers. Then have poached pineapple slices and almond cookies.

8 ounces untrimmed spinach - (4 packed cups trimmed)
celery - 4 large ribs - (2 cups sliced)
6 ounces carrots - 3 slender medium - (1 heaping cup sliced)
1 pound broccoli - 2 average heads - (4 cups florets and cut)
8 ounces mushrooms - small - (3 cups whole)
Fukien sauce - (recipe follows)
3 quarts water
1 Tablespoon plus 1 teaspoon salt - divided
6 Tablespoons corn oil - divided
12 ounces fine dried egg noodles

Prepare and blanch the spinach as directed but leave the leaves whole. (See blanched spinach.) Immediately turn the drained spinach into a basin of cold water for 1 minute. Then turn it into a colander, place a saucer with a moderate weight upon it on the spinach and allow it to drain for 1 hour, turning it over 2 or 3 times during that period. Now, carefully separate the leaves and spread them out on a plate.

Trim, scrape the strings from and cut the celery, on a steep diagonal, into 3/8 inch thick slices. Steam the celery over already simmering water 7 minutes, turn it into a basin of cold water for 3 minutes then drain it well in a colander.

Trim, peel and cut the carrots, on a steep diagonal, into 3/8 inch thick slices. Steam the carrots over already simmering water 10 minutes, turn them into a basin of cold water for 3 minutes then drain them well in a colander.

Cut the florets off of the broccoli stalks with about 1 inch stems. Trim and, using a knife, pull the fibrous skin from the stalks then peel them with a vegetable peeler. Cut the stalks crosswise into 3/8 inch thick slices. Steam the broccoli over already simmering water 5 minutes, turn it into a basin of cold water for 3 minutes then drain it well in a colander.

Trim the butt ends of the stems and wipe the mushrooms with a damp cloth. If any mushrooms are too large, cut them in half. Steam the mushrooms over already simmering water for 3 minutes then wrap them in paper towels.

(All the vegetables can be prepared up to 24 hours in advance. Cover the spinach with plastic wrap, seal the celery, carrots and broccoli in plastic and keep the mushrooms wrapped in paper. If they are refrigerated bring them to room temperature before continuing with the recipe.)

Make the Fukien sauce now and keep it warm as directed.

(At this point set the water with 1 tablespoon of the salt to boil in a large kettle over high heat.)

Heat the celery, carrots, broccoli and mushrooms, sprinkled with 1 teaspoon of the salt, in 3 tablespoons of oil in a large frying pan (see utensils), over medium low heat, stirring gently for 4 minutes. Add the spinach leaves, a few at a time, still stirring and heat the vegetables 3 minutes longer or until they are all thoroughly heated through.

At the same time as the spinach is added to the pan, drop the noodles, all at once into the boiling water, stirring them with a wooden spoon. Cook the noodles, covered with a lid ajar, about 3 minutes, or a little less than directed on the package, from the moment they are in the water, regardless of when the water returns to boil, until they are tender firm, "al dente", adjusting the heat to keep the water slowly boiling and stirring occasionally. Drain the noodles well and, in the still warm kettle, toss them with 3 tablespoons of the oil.

Equally divide the noodles among 4 warm dinner plates, spreading them out in a ring. Spoon the equally divided hot vegetables into each ring of noodles. Serve the steamed vegetables with noodles along with a bowl of the warm Fukien sauce set over a candle warmer on the table and let everyone help themselves to the sauce.

4 servings

fukien sauce

2 Tablespoons corn oil
6 Tablespoons tahini (sesame paste)
4 Tablespoons tomato paste
6 Tablespoons light molasses
6 Tablespoons soy sauce
6 Tablespoons dry sherry
2 teaspoons honey
1/2 cup plus optional water
1/2 teaspoon celery salt
1 teaspoon salt
1 teaspoon or more cayenne

In a small heavy saucepan, over medium heat, blend the corn oil into the tahini and tomato paste until the mixture is smooth. Gradually stir in the remaining ingredients then simmer the sauce gently, 10 minutes, stirring frequently,. The sauce is by nature very thick. If you would like to thin it, simply add a little more water. Cover the pan with a trimmed piece of paper towel and lid and keep the Fukien sauce warm over very low heat, stirring occasionally.

about 2 1/2 cups

Note: I find that each time I make this sauce I add more cayenne.

RED BEAN HASH WITH POACHED EGGS
and ketchup

New York State Cheddar soup precedes this hearty bean dish. Serve coleslaw following the red bean hash, along with some bread if you think anyone has room for it. Chilled green apples will be refreshing.

ketchup - (recipe follows)
2 cups dried red beans - about 14 1/2 ounces
1 bay leaf
12 ounces boiling potatoes - 2 medium - (2 cups diced)
celery - 4 large ribs - (2 cups diced)
12 ounces green bell peppers - 2 medium - (2 cups diced)
6 Tablespoons peanut oil
1/4 teaspoon liquid smoke
1 1/2 teaspoon salt - divided
3 Tablespoons cider vinegar
6 Tablespoons butter
1 teaspoon celery salt
1/2 teaspoon freshly cracked black pepper
1/2 teaspoon dried thyme
4 eggs - at room temperature - (see cooked eggs note)

Prepare the ketchup at least 24 hours in advance as directed. Bring it to room temperature before serving.

Soak the beans and cook them with the bay leaf as directed. (See boiled dried shelled beans.) They must be very well cooked, allow them to cook a little longer if necessary. Drain them discarding the bay leaf. If the drained beans measure more than 4 cups, do not use the excess, it would unbalance the recipe. (Save any excess for a bouillon soup. See bouillon soups.)

Peel and cut the potatoes into 1/4 inch dice. Soak them in a bowl of cold water to cover for 1 hour. Drain and blot them dry on paper towels.

Meanwhile trim, scrape the strings from and cut the celery into 1/4 inch dice.

Core, trim the white membrane from and cut the green peppers into 1/4 inch dice.

Warm the oil and liquid smoke in a large frying pan (see utensils), over medium high heat. Add the drained beans sprinkled with 1 teaspoon of the salt and the vinegar. Fry the beans, 10 to 15 minutes, crushing about 1/3 of them with the back of fork then turning them over, spreading them out and pressing them down 3 or 4 times with a metal spatula until they are lightly browned. Remove the beans from the pan and reserve them.

Now in the same pan over medium heat sauté the potatoes, sprinkled with 1/2 teaspoon of the salt, in the butter 5 minutes. Add the celery and green peppers, sprinkle with the celery salt, black pepper and the thyme, crushing it and sauté the vegetables 5 minutes longer.

Reduce the heat to low and carefully stir in the reserved beans. Make 4 depressions in the hash with the back of a large spoon. Break 1 egg into each of the depressions. Cover the pan and poach the eggs about 20 minutes until they are set.

Uncover the pan and bring it right to the table. Use the metal spatula to serve the red bean hash with poached eggs. Have a bowl of the ketchup on the table, along with a little ladle with which to serve it.

4 servings

ketchup

3 1/2 cups tomato purée - 28 ounces
3 Tablespoons cider vinegar
3 Tablespoons light brown sugar
1 bay leaf
1 teaspoon salt
1 teaspoon paprika
1/2 teaspoon celery salt
1/4 teaspoon ground cinnamon
1/4 teaspoon ground allspice
1/8 teaspoon cayenne
pinch ground cloves

Combine all the ingredients in a heavy saucepan over low heat. Cook the ketchup, uncovered, barely simmering, stirring occasionally, for 1 hour. Allow it to cool to room temperature. Store the ketchup refrigerated in a sealed glass jar. It keeps well up to 1 week.

about 3 cups

Note: Make the ketchup at least 24 hours in advance of serving to allow time for the flavors to marry.

❧ NEW ENGLAND BOILED DINNER ❧

Served along with a thick, pungent, old fashioned horseradish sauce, New England boiled dinner is a triumph of puritanical simplicity. Present it on an antique platter if possible. Cream of pumpkin soup would be apropos for the soup course and tossed iceberg lettuce a good salad selection, served with anadama bread and Vermont Cheddar. Poached cherries could be served for dessert.

2 pounds cabbage - 1 small compact head
1 pound rutabaga - 1 small or 1 piece
1 pound carrots - 8 medium
celery - 4 large ribs
8 ounces onions - 12 small, about 1 inch diameters
about 2 pounds boiling potatoes - 10 small, about 2 inch diameters
8 ounces parsnips - 2 large
cold water
lemon juice
4 ounces horseradish - 1 piece - (3/4 cup chopped) - (see horseradish)
1 bay leaf
2 teaspoons salt - divided
4 cups boiling stock broth - (see stock broth)
3 cups reserved cooking liquid - divided
7 Tablespoons butter
7 Tablespoons flour
1 teaspoon honey
1 Tablespoon distilled vinegar

Trim and cut the cabbage lengthwise into eighths. Do not core the wedges, it holds them together.

Trim, peel and cut the rutabaga, crosswise, into 1/2 inch thick slices. Cut the slices into pie shaped pieces.

Trim and peel the carrots. Leave them whole.

Trim, scrape the strings from and cut the celery ribs crosswise into 1 inch pieces.

(The vegetables can be prepared in advance up to this point, sealed in plastic, refrigerated then brought to room temperature before continuing with the recipe.)

Peel and prepare the onions as directed. (See peeled onions.)

Peel the potatoes and leave them whole dropping them into a bowl of cold water to cover.

Trim, peel and cut the parsnips crosswise into 1/2 inch thick slices. Drop them into a bowl of cold water to cover and add 1 teaspoon of lemon juice per cup of water.

Trim, peel and chop the horseradish small.

Place the rutabaga, carrots, celery, onions and the drained potatoes in a large enameled dutch oven. Set the cabbage wedges on top of the other vegetables. Tuck in the bay leaf and sprinkle the vegetables with 1 teaspoon of the salt. Set the dutch oven over high heat and pour in the boiling stock broth. Cover with lid slightly ajar and start counting the cooking time immediately. Cook the vegetables 15 minutes. As the broth returns to a full boil, reduce the heat to medium to keep the liquid slowly boiling.

Drain and add the parsnips to the dutch oven and continue to cook the vegetables 10 minutes longer. (Do not overcook the vegetables, they must remain firm at this point.) When the vegetables have cooked 25 minutes altogether, carefully drain the cooking liquid into a bowl and reserve it. Leave the vegetables in the covered dutch oven and set the dutch oven aside.

In a blender, grate the chopped horseradish with 1 cup of the reserved liquid (careful of your eyes) and reserve it.

Melt the butter in a heavy, medium size saucepan over low heat. Using a rubber spatula, blend in the flour, stirring the roux constantly for 5 minutes without permitting it to brown. Slowly stir 2 cups of the remaining reserved cooking liquid plus the horseradish mixture into the roux, while gradually increasing the heat to medium high until the sauce simmers. Add the honey, vinegar and 1 teaspoon of the salt and simmer 1 minute longer. Transfer the sauce to a warm serving bowl.

Arrange the cabbage wedges around the edge of a large, warm serving platter then arrange the rest of the vegetables in the center of them. Serve the New England boiled dinner immediately and let everyone help themselves to the horseradish sauce.

4 servings

Note: When the vegetables are drained they should be barely tender. The recipe is timed to allow them to go on cooking in the hot dutch oven after it has been removed from the heat. When they are placed on the platter, the vegetables will be just tender and steaming hot.

SUPER CHIPS

Start with cream of stock vegetable purée soup. Then a heaping mound of sauerkraut is served with these super chips which really are super. Have string beans vinaigrette for the salad with some dark rye bread then offer shiny red apples.

allow 9 ounces or more baking potato per serving - 1 large - (about 14 to 16 slices)
4 cups peanut oil
salt

Early in the day, peel the potatoes and carefully cut them, lengthwise, into 1/8 inch thick, even slices. In an ample bowl, soak the potato slices in enough very cold water to cover, for 1/2 hour. Drain and rinse them then cover them again with cold water and allow them to soak 1 hour longer. Drain and blot the slices dry on paper towels.

(Allowing about 15 minutes for the oil to heat to temperature, heat the oil in a deep saucepan, with a cooking thermometer clipped to the inside of it, over medium high heat to 370 degrees or use an electric deep fryer set at 370 degrees).

Fry 14 to 16 potato slices at a time, 5 minutes, stirring them occasionally with a skimmer or slotted spoon, until they are a pale golden color. Using a frying basket, skimmer or spoon, drain the potatoes, and spread them out on paper towels to cool. Repeat the process with the remaining slices. When all the potatoes have cooled, cover them with paper towels until serving time.

At serving time reheat the oil to 390 degrees. Fry the potatoes again, 14 to 16 slices at a time. Stirring them gently for about 3 or 4 minutes or until they are the golden brown color you want them to be. Transfer the potatoes to paper towels to drain for a couple of seconds. Then heap each serving in an individual size, paper napkin lined, basket and serve the super chips immediately, they will not wait. Let each one salt their own serving and don't stand on ceremony, eat them while they're hot!

CABBAGE ROLLS

Cabbage rolls take time to prepare and require 24 hours to become full flavored. However, they ask only to be reheated in their wine sauce before serving. While they are heating you'll have plenty of time to enjoy a cream of celeriac soup and to sauté some cucumbers to go along with the cabbage rolls. String beans vinaigrette, some pita bread and Feta cheese will make a good salad course, followed by poached figs.

1 can peeled plum tomatoes - 14 1/2 ounces - (about 2 cups)
water
2 1/4 pounds cabbage - 1 medium small head
8 ounces mushrooms - medium - (2 1/2 cups sliced)
parsley leaves - (1 cup chopped)
1/2 cup roasted, peeled hazelnuts - about 2 1/2 ounces - (see hazelnuts)
1 1/2 teaspoons salt - divided
4 Tablespoons butter - divided
1 Tablespoon sweet Hungarian paprika
3/4 teaspoon celery salt
1/4 teaspoon cayenne
1/4 teaspoon ground cinnamon
1/8 teaspoon ground cloves
2 teaspoons honey -divided
1 egg - at room temperature
1/2 cup plus 2 Tablespoons buckwheat groats - about 3 1/2 ounces
1/2 cup dry red wine
1/2 cup tomato paste - 4 ounces

Turn the tomatoes into a colander set over a bowl. Then, holding each tomato over the colander, remove the stem button and carefully cut it into little pieces. Drop the pieces into the colander and allow them to drain while you prepare the rest of the vegetables.

Fill a large kettle with enough water to cover the head of cabbage and bring it to boil over high heat. Trim a slice about 1 inch thick, off of the bottom of the head of cabbage and discard it. Using a small knife, cut down deep into the cabbage around the stem to loosen the leaves. With 2 longhandled, wooden spoons lower the cabbage into the boiling water and cook it, covered, 5 minutes from the moment it is in the water regardless of when the water returns to boil. Uncover the kettle. Using the 2 wooden spoons, carefully remove each successive leaf as it becomes loosened and set it aside to drain until 12 to 14 leaves have been removed. It is wise to have a couple of extra leaves in case of tears. Remove the remaining cabbage head from the water, quarter, lengthwise, core and shred it fine crosswise.

Wipe the mushrooms with a damp cloth, trim the butt ends of the stems and thinly slice the mushrooms lengthwise.

Chop the parsley leaves fine and reserve them.

Using a heavy knife or in the blender or processor chop the hazelnuts small and reserve them.

Cook the shredded cabbage, sprinkled with 1/2 teaspoon of the salt, in 1 tablespoon of the butter in a large frying pan (see utensils), covered, over medium low heat, 15 minutes, stirring occasionally. Uncover the pan and stir the cabbage, constantly now, while gradually increasing the heat to medium high until the cabbage is cooked and all the moisture has evaporated. Remove the cabbage from the pan and reserve it.

Sauté the mushrooms, sprinkled with 1/2 teaspoon of the salt in 1 tablespoon of the butter in the frying pan over medium high heat about 8 minutes gradually increasing the heat to high until all the moisture has evaporated. Remove the mushrooms from the pan and reserve them.

Measure out 1 cup of the drained tomato liquid. Place the paprika, celery salt, cayenne, cinnamon and cloves in a small saucepan. Slowly stir the tomato liquid into them until the mixture is smooth. Add 1 1/2 teaspoons of the honey, set the pan, uncovered, over medium high heat and slowly boil the mixture about 5 minutes or until it is reduced to 3/4 cups. Continue to keep the liquid slowly boiling.

At the same time, using a fork, lightly beat the egg, in a bowl. Discard 1 1/2 tablespoons of it, this will be half the egg. (Save the discarded half egg for a bouillon soup. See bouillon soups.) Stir the buckwheat into the egg in the bowl then transfer the mixture to a large, dry (clean) frying pan (see utensils), over medium heat. Using a spatula stir the buckwheat constantly for 3 minutes until each grain becomes separate and dry. Do not allow the mixture to scorch. Remove the pan from the heat, pour in the boiling tomato liquid, cover the pan and return it to low heat. Now, cook the buckwheat 10 minutes. Uncover the pan. Add 1 tablespoon of the butter, the reserved, shredded cabbage, the mushrooms and the tomato pulp. Cook the ingredients about 5 minutes, mixing them well and turning up the heat slightly, if necessary until the mixture is fairly dry. Remove the pan from the heat, stir in the chopped parsley and nuts and allow the mixture to cool a bit.

Cut a little triangle out of the base of each leaf to remove the thickest part of the rib. Blot each leaf dry with paper towels. Place 2 heaping tablespoons of the buckwheat mixture on the center of one leaf. Roll the leaf up from the bottom folding in the sides as you go and finally folding over the top of the leaf. Stuff 12 cabbage leaves, packing them into a buttered 10 by 6 by 1 3/4 inch deep, 6 cup baking dish as they are completed. They should just fill the dish in 1 layer. Tightly cover the dish with a piece of foil which has been perforated with a number of small holes. Bake the cabbage rolls in a preheated 350 degree oven 45 minutes. Remove the dish from the oven, remove the foil, and allow it to stand 30 minutes.

Lay a cutting board over the dish and tilt it to drain any liquid into a measuring cup. Measure out 1/2 cup of the liquid. If there is not enough, add water to it. If no liquid drains out of the dish then use all water. In any case, combine it with the wine. In a small, heavy saucepan, stir the wine mixture into the tomato paste. Add 1/2 teaspoon of the salt, 1 tablespoon of the butter and 1/2 teaspoon of the honey and simmer the sauce, covered, over low heat, 1 hour. Pour the sauce over the cabbage rolls allowing it to run down into the dish by carefully separating the rolls slightly with the handle of a spoon. When the dish has cooled completely, tightly cover it with foil and refrigerate it 24 hours.

Before serving, bring the dish to room temperature, this will take about 4 hours. Bake the cabbage rolls, now, lightly covered with foil, in a preheated 350 degree oven, 45 minutes. Uncover the dish and allow the cabbage rolls to stand 10 minutes before serving.

4 servings

ENCHILADAS DE LEGUMBRES
with bean sauce

Enchiladas de legumbres are always a favorite. Have home style tomato soup first then serve avocados on the half shell following the enchiladas. Then chilled grapefruit sections will be refreshing.

bean sauce - (recipe follows)
about 4 ounces rutabaga - piece of medium large
1 teaspoon plus salt
1 Tablespoons plus 1 teaspoon plus peanut oil
6 Tablespoons hot water - in a cup - divided
celery - 3 large ribs
2 or 3 ounces string beans - 12 long
8 ounces green bell pepper - 1 large

1 1/3 cups long grain white rice - about 9 1/2 ounces
1 teaspoon turmeric
8 ounces Monterey Jack cheese - (2 cups grated)
12 ounces tomatoes - 2 medium small
iceberg lettuce - 1/2 head
12 corn tortillas
1 1/2 cups reserved thick bean sauce - (see bean sauce)
4 Tablespoons butter

Prepare the bean sauce 24 hours in advance. Reheat, thin and keep it warm as directed.

Select a rutabaga with a 6 inch diameter. Peel and cut 24 large matchsticks, 6 inches long and about 3/16 inch square, out of the widest part of it. Sauté the rutabaga sticks, lightly sprinkled with salt, in 1 teaspoon of the oil in a frying pan (see utensils), over medium heat, two minutes. Reduce the heat to low, remove the pan from the heat, add 2 tablespoons of the hot water, cover the pan immediately, return it to the heat and braise the rutabaga, 5 minutes, until it is tender but still quite firm. Transfer the rutabaga to paper towels.

Trim, scrape the strings from and cut the celery into 24, 6 inch long, about 3/16 inch square matchsticks. Cook the celery in the same manner as the rutabaga, but braise it only 3 minutes.

Trim the stems from the string beans and cut them in half lengthwise. Cook the string beans in the same manner as the preceding vegetables but braise them 8 minutes.

Core, trim away any white membrane from and cut the bell pepper, lengthwise into long, about 3/16 inch wide strips. Cook the pepper strips in the same manner as the other vegetables but do not add water to the pan however cook them, covered, 8 minutes.

(All these vegetables can be prepared, cooked in advance and sealed in plastic. If they are refrigerated, bring them to room temperature before continuing with the recipe.)

Cook the rice as directed, adding the turmeric to the initial cooking water. (See steamed long or short grain white rice.) Keep the rice warm, in the steamer, over hot water.

Coarsely grate the cheese and reserve it.

Remove the stem button and cut each tomato in half, lengthwise. Lay the halves cut side down and cut 6 crescent shaped slices, lengthwise, out of each half. Reserve the slices.

Shed the lettuce very fine, seal it in plastic and refrigerate it until serving time.

This is the point at which to reheat the sauce.

To assemble the enchiladas, put some peanut oil in a cup and using a pastry brush, brush a griddle set over medium high heat with it. Fry each tortilla 10 seconds on each side to make it pliable. Transfer it to paper towels and lay 2 strips each of rutabaga, celery, string beans and bell pepper down the center of the tortilla. Spread 1 heaping tablespoon of the reserved thick, bean sauce over the vegetables. Sprinkle about 1 table-spoon of the cheese over the bean sauce and lay 2 tomato slices on the cheese. Roll up the enchilada, secure it with a wooden toothpick and place it on a lightly buttered oven proof dinner plate. There will be 3 enchiladas on each of 4 dinner plates. Loosely, but well, cover the plates with foil and warm the enchiladas in a preheated 350 degree oven for 20 minutes.

This is the point at which to thin the remaining sauce and keep it warm.

Meanwhile, in a warm bowl, toss the 1 teaspoon of salt and the butter, cut in pieces, with the warm rice. When the enchiladas are ready, remove the foil and tooth picks, and working quickly, spoon the rice around the enchiladas on each plate. Then sprinkle a small amount of the shredded lettuce over each plate and serve the enchiladas de legumbres along with a bowl of the warm bean sauce and a bowl of the chilled lettuce and let everyone help themselves to the sauce and the lettuce.

4 servings

bean sauce

2 1/4 cups dried pink beans - 1 pound (see note)
reserved cooking liquid
1 cup peanut oil
1 1/2 teaspoons plus optional salt
1 1/2 teaspoons celery salt
1 teaspoon ground cumin
3 Tablespoons plus optional cayenne - (that's right!)
2 Tablespoons plus optional honey
4 Tablespoons fresh lemon juice
1 teaspoon plus optional dried oregano

Soak and cook the beans as directed. (See boiled dried shelled beans.) Drain them, reserving their cooking liquid.

Heat the oil in a large frying pan over low heat. Add the drained beans, the 1 1/2 teaspoons of salt, the celery salt, cumin, the 3 tablespoons of cayenne, the 2 tablespoons of honey and the lemon juice. Using a large fork, crush all the beans, while slowly adding enough of the reserved cooking liquid to make a thick, lumpy, pasty sauce. Permit the beans to very gently cook for about 30 minutes, adding more liquid as is necessary.

(Up to this point prepare the sauce 24 hours in advance, cool it to room temperature, cover it and store it refrigerated. Like most bean dishes the flavor of the sauce has a chance to develop when prepared in advance and reheated.)

Reheat the sauce over low heat before assembling the enchiladas. Add the 1 teaspoon of oregano now, crushing it and cook 5 minutes more. Then remove the 1 1/2 cups of thick sauce that will go into the enchiladas and reserve it.

While the enchiladas are in the oven, thin the remainder of the sauce with any remaining cooking liquid or use water, to a pourable consistency. You may want to add a dash more salt, a dab of honey, a dusting of crushed oregano and yes, more cayenne to make a really firery sauce. Cover the pan with a trimmed piece of paper towel and lid and keep the bean sauce warm over very low heat until serving.

about 4 cups

Note: If pink beans, which are sometimes called by the pretty name of "rositas", are not available, substitute pinto beans.

BROILED EGGPLANT MEDALLIONS
with mushroom sauce

Cream of cauliflower soup precedes this delightful entrée. Serve baked potatoes with the eggplant then, with asparagus vinaigrette, offer bread and Camembert. Serve the ever popular strawberries over strawberry ice cream for dessert.

mushroom sauce - (recipe follows)
1 1/2 pounds eggplant - 1 large
salt
2 Tablespoons plus 2 teaspoons butter

Make the mushroom sauce and keep it warm, as directed.

Trim, peel, and cut the eggplant in half lengthwise. Now, ever so carefully and precisely, cut each half lengthwise, into 2, 3/4 inch thick slices of even thickness throughout, so that you have 4 large, full slices. (Save the rounded end slices for a bouillon soup. See bouillon soups.)

Lay the slices on a buttered aluminum baking sheet (other metals discolor eggplant); lightly salt them and dot each slice with 1 teaspoon of butter. Broil the eggplant, in a preheated broiler, 6 inches from the heat source, for 5 minutes. Remove the sheet from the broiler and turn the slices over with a metal spatula. Sprinkle them again with salt and dot them with the remaining butter. Return the sheet to the broiler for 5 minutes. Do not over cook the eggplant as it retains its heat and goes on cooking after it has been removed from the broiler.

Using the metal spatula, transfer the slices to each of 4 warm dinner plates. Spoon 1/4 cup of the warm mushroom sauce over each slice and serve the broiled eggplant medallions immediately along with a warm bowl of the remaining sauce.

4 servings

mushroom sauce

about 5 ounces mushrooms - small - (2 cups sliced)
1/2 teaspoon salt
2 Tablespoons butter
2 Tablespoons cornstarch
2 cups stock broth - cold - (see stock broth)
1 teaspoon light molasses
1/4 teaspoon celery salt
pinch freshly cracked black pepper

Wipe the mushrooms with a damp cloth and trim the butt ends of the stems. Very thinly, slice the mushrooms lengthwise. Sauté them sprinkled with the salt, in the butter in a frying pan over medium high heat about 8 minutes while gradually raising the heat to high until all the moisture has evaporated. Remove the pan from the heat and allow the mushrooms to cool a bit.

In a small saucepan, dissolve the cornstarch in the stock broth. Add the molasses, celery salt and pepper. Bring the mixture to simmer over medium heat while stirring constantly, with a rubber spatula. When the mixture simmers, reduce the heat slightly and continue to simmer and stir for 2 minutes then stir in the mushrooms. Reduce the heat to very low, cover the pan with a trimmed piece of paper towel and lid and keep the mushroom sauce warm until serving.

about 2 cups

GERMAN STYLE RED CABBAGE

I like to use wild apples in this dish when I can. In which case the number of apples must be increased since they are small. Serve cream of lima bean soup. Then have whole boiled, peeled potatoes along with the cabbage. Follow with a salad of pressed cucumbers accompanied by Westphalian pumpernickel and Limburger cheese. Complete the meal with poached apricots.

4 pounds red cabbage - 1 large head - (16 tightly packed cups cut)
8 Tablespoons butter
1/2 cup plus 2 Tablespoons cider vinegar - divided
2 Tablespoons honey
2 Tablespoons brown sugar
2 teaspoons salt
1 teaspoon celery salt
1/2 teaspoon freshly cracked black pepper
1 bay leaf
3 whole cloves
about 1 1/2 pounds tart green apples - 4 - divided

Quarter the cabbage lengthwise. Core and cut the quarters crosswise into 1/4 inch thick slices.

Melt the butter in a large, heavy, enameled kettle over medium low heat. Add the 1/2 cup vinegar, the honey, sugar, salt, celery salt, pepper, bay leaf, and cloves. Then add the cabbage and gently cook it, covered, 1 hour. Stir it occasionally with a wooden spoon. This will be a little difficult at first but will become easier as the cabbage gradually cooks down.

Now, do not peel but quarter, core, and thinly slice 2 of the apples crosswise. Add the sliced apples to the kettle and continue to cook the cabbage, uncovered now, 30 minutes longer while gradually turning up the heat, still stirring occasionally, until most of the moisture has evaporated and the apples have disintegrated. The cabbage must be well cooked but not over done.

Meanwhile, do not peel but cut the 2 remaining apples in half lengthwise. Core them using a melon ball cutter and thinly slice the halves crosswise, discarding the end pieces and dropping the slices into a bowl containing the 2 tablespoons of vinegar and enough water to cover.

When the cabbage is ready to be served, drain the sliced apples and pat them dry on paper towels. Heap the cabbage on a warm (white oval if you have one) serving platter and arrange the apple slices in a wreath, about 3 layers deep, around it with their cut sides tucked down into the cabbage. Serve the German style red cabbage immediately.

about 8 servings

 SAVORY TURNOVERS

Cream of Brussels sprouts will be the soup course this evening. Then these glossy, golden yellow turnovers are eaten from the hand. Their accompaniment of stewed tomatoes is served in small bowls set upon dinner plates. Tossed salad mix I is the salad course and bananas the dessert.

1/4 cup barley
1/2 cup lentils - about 4 ounces
1 bay leaf
1 3/4 teaspoons salt - divided
1 cup roasted, peeled hazelnuts - about 5 ounces - (see hazelnuts)
celery - 4 large ribs - (2 cups diced)
ginger root - (2 teaspoons freshly grated)
2 Tablespoons fresh lemon juice
12 ounces tart green apples - 2 medium - (2 cups grated)
4 Tablespoons peanut oil
4 Tablespoons butter
1 teaspoon celery salt
1/4 cup dried currants
4 teaspoons honey
1 Tablespoon ground cumin

1 Tablespoon ground coriander
1 teaspoon cayenne
2 teaspoons dried oregano
1 egg
Cream cheese pastry dough - (recipe follows)
1 egg yolk
1 teaspoon water

Cook the barley as directed. (See steamed barley.)

Cull, rinse and cook the lentils with the bay leaf and 1/4 teaspoon of the salt as directed. (See boiled dried shelled beans.) Take care not to over cook them. Drain them.

Measure the steamed barley and boiled, drained lentils, separately. If the barley measures more than 3/4 cup and the lentils measure more than 1 1/2 cups, do not use the excess it would unbalance the recipe. (Save any excess for a bouillon soup. See bouillon soups.)

Using a heavy knife, coarsely chop the hazel nuts.

Trim, scrape the strings from and dice the celery.

Peel and grate the ginger on a medium fine grater.

Place the lemon juice in a mixing bowl. Peel, core, and grate the apples on a coarse grater into the bowl. Toss the apples with the lemon juice.

Heat the ginger in the oil and butter in a large frying pan (see utensils), over medium heat for about 30 seconds. Add the celery, sprinkle with the celery salt and sauté it 3 minutes. Using a wooden fork, stir in the barley, lentils, hazelnuts and currants, sprinkling with 1 1/2 teaspoons of the salt. Add the honey, cumin, coriander, and cayenne. Cook the mixture, stirring frequently for 5 minutes. The mixture should be fairly dry. Remove the pan from the heat, stir in the apples and lemon juice and the oregano, crushing it. Allow the mixture to cool a bit.

In a large mixing bowl, using a fork, beat the egg until it is light then stir the mixture into it. Allow the mixture to cool to room temperature then refrigerate it, covered, 12 hours or overnight.

At this point the Cream cheese pastry dough can be prepared as directed either the night before or the following morning.

About 1 hour and 45 minutes before serving, transfer half of the filling mixture to another bowl and return the other half to the refrigerator. Remove 6 of the balls of dough from the refrigerator, keeping them wrapped. On a lightly floured work surface roll out one ball at a time, into a disc 6 inches in diameter. Place 2 great heaping tablespoons (1/4 cup) of the filling mixture just below the center of the disc. Dip your finger in water and moisten the edge of the lower half of the disc then fold the upper half of the dough over the filling to meet the edge of the lower half. Seal the edges of the turnover with the tines of a fork and trim the edges with a sharp knife so that they are neat and even. Place the turnover on an ungreased cookie sheet. (Each turnover takes 4 to 5 minutes to make.) Make the remaining turnovers.

In a cup, using a fork, beat the egg yolk and the 1 teaspoon of water together. Using a feather pastry brush, brush the beaten yolk over the tops of the turnovers then go over them a second time. Now decoratively pierce each turnover 3 times with the tines of a fork. Rock the fork back and forth a little to make sure the holes are well open as the egg yolk glaze tends to seal them while baking. Bake the turnovers in a preheated 375 degree oven for 25 minutes. Check them after they have been in the oven about 15 minutes. If they are browning too quickly, lightly cover them with foil.

Using a metal spatula, transfer the turnovers to a cake rack and allow them to cool 25 minutes. Heap the savory turnovers on a platter or in a napkin lined basket and serve.

6 to 12 servings

cream cheese pastry dough

2 cups minus 2 Tablespoons all purpose flour
2 Tablespoons cornstarch
1 teaspoon salt
1/2 teaspoon ground turmeric
1/2 cup unsalted butter - cold
6 ounces Cream cheese - cold
2 to 3 Tablespoons cold water

Sift the flour, cornstarch, salt, and turmeric into a mixing bowl. Cut in the butter and cheese, using a pastry blender. Then quickly rub the flour through the butter and cheese with your fingertips until the mixture is granular. Add the water, a little at a time, stirring it in with a fork, using only as much as is necessary until dough begins to form. Then, with your hands, shape the dough into a cylinder, 12 inches long, handling the dough as little as possible. Using a ruler as a guide, divide the cylinder into 12 pieces and roll the pieces into balls. Wrap the balls, 6 together, first in wax paper, then seal the 12 balls of dough in each of 2 plastic bags and allow them to rest, refrigerated, 1 hour or overnight.

❧ SCALLOPED WHITE TURNIPS ❧

Potato dumplings in paprika broth is the warming soup this evening. Serve buttered peas with the scalloped turnips and have whole wheat bread with a tossed spinach salad. Poached plums will be dessert.

6 eggs - at room temperature
1 pound white turnips - 4 medium - (4 cups sliced)
3 Tablespoons butter
3 Tablespoons flour
1/8 teaspoon white pepper
2 cups plus 2 Tablespoons milk - at room temperature
1/2 teaspoon honey
1 1/2 teaspoon salt - divided
1/4 teaspoon celery salt
1 teaspoon dried summer savory

Hard cook and peel the eggs as directed. (See cooked eggs.) Allow the peeled eggs to cool to room temperature then refrigerate them, 1 hour, to help them remain firm while being sliced. Cut the cold eggs crosswise into 1/4 inch thick slices, and reserve them.

Trim, peel, and cut the turnips in half lengthwise. Thinly slice the halves crosswise.

Melt the butter in a medium size saucepan over low heat. Using a rubber spatula, blend in the flour and pepper until they absorb the butter. Slowly stir in the milk, the honey, 1/2 teaspoon of the salt and the celery salt. Gradually increase the heat to medium high until the sauce simmers and thickens. Add the summer savory, crushing it, and simmer the sauce, stirring, 2 minutes. Remove the pan from the heat.

Spread a small amount of the sauce in the bottom of a buttered, round, 8 inch diameter by 2 inch deep, 5 cup baking dish. Lay half of the sliced turnips over the sauce and, reserving the large better looking slices for the top layer, spread half of the sliced eggs over the turnips. Evenly sprinkle the eggs with 1/2 teaspoon of the salt and spoon half of the remaining sauce over the eggs. Repeat the layers once more.

Bake the turnips in a preheated 375 degree oven, 1 hour. If the dish is browning too much after about 45 minutes in the oven, lightly cover it with foil. However, the top of the dish should be a lovely golden color. Allow the scalloped white turnips to stand 10 minutes before serving.

4 servings

STUFFED GREEN BELL PEPPERS
with paprika sauce

Offer cream of stock vegetable purée soup. Then braised celeriac accompanies these very hearty stuffed peppers. A crisp tossed escarole salad follows and poached cherries will complete this dinner.

1 cup dried pea beans - about 7 1/2 ounces
2/3 cup rye berries - about 5 ounces
celery - 2 large ribs - (1 cup diced)
about 13 ounces savoy cabbage - part of a small - (4 packed cups shredded)
1 1/2 pounds green bell peppers - 4 medium, 6 ounces each
about 1 1/2 ounces horseradish - 1 piece - (1/4 cup chopped) - (see horseradish)
paprika sauce - (recipe follows)
1 cup reserved sauce - (see paprika sauce)
1 Tablespoons sweet Hungarian paprika
2 teaspoons honey
1 1/2 teaspoons salt - divided
1/4 teaspoon cayenne
1 teaspoon celery seed
1 teaspoon celery salt
4 Tablespoon peanut oil
4 Tablespoons butter
1/4 teaspoon liquid smoke
1/2 cup roasted sunflower seeds - about 3 ounces - (see sunflower and pumpkin seeds)

Soak and cook the beans as directed, taking care not to over cook them. (See boiled dried shelled beans.) Drain them.

Soak and cook the rye berries as directed. (See boiled rye berries.) Drain them.

Measure the drained beans and rye berries separately. If either measures more than 2 cups do not use the excess it would unbalance the recipe. (Save any excess for a bouillon soup. See bouillon soups.) Now, using the back of a fork, thoroughly crush 1 cup of the beans on a dinner plate. Reserve the whole and crushed beans and the rye berries.

Trim, scrape the strings from and dice the celery.

Quarter lengthwise, core, and shred the cabbage fine crosswise. Then coarsely chop it.

Select well shaped bell peppers with "flat bottoms" that sit up properly by themselves. Cut a "lid" out of the stem end of each pepper by carefully cutting a circle down into the pepper to retain as much of the "height" of the pepper as possible. Pull the "lid" out then clean out the pepper, carefully trimming away any white membrane. Reserve the pepper cups. Remove the flesh from around the "lids" and dice it.

Trim, peel and chop the horseradish small.

At this point, prepare the paprika sauce as directed, reserving the 1 cup and setting the rest aside. It does not need to be kept warm.

Place the chopped horseradish, the 1 cup of reserved sauce, the paprika, honey, 1/2 teaspoon of the salt and the cayenne in the blender or processor, purée the mixture (careful of your eyes) and reserve it. Alternatively simply grate the piece of horseradish fine, by hand, then combine it with the other ingredients.

Stirring constantly, toast the celery seeds in a dry pan over medium heat for 2 or 3 minutes until they become fragrant. Remove them from the pan and reserve them.

Sauté the diced celery sprinkled with the celery salt, in the oil and butter with the liquid smoke in a large frying pan (see utensils), over medium heat for 3 minutes. Add the shredded cabbage and diced peppers sprinkle with 1 teaspoon of the salt and sauté 2 minutes longer, stirring the vegetables. Reduce the heat to low and cook the vegetables, covered, 10 minutes, stirring once. Increase the heat to medium high and cook uncovered, 3 minutes longer, stirring, until all the moisture has evaporated.

Reduce the heat to low again and add the reserved celery seeds. Then, sprinkle the sunflower seeds and rye berries, a few at a time, into the vegetables stirring the mixture with a wooden fork. Now, stir in the mashed beans and the reserved horseradish mixture. Gently stir in the whole beans, combining the mixture well and remove the pan from the heat.

Carefully pack the stuffing mixture into the reserved pepper cups, pressing it down with the back of a spoon, and generously heaping it up.

Select a saucepan with about a 10 cup capacity or a pan just large enough to hold the 4 peppers close together so that they remain upright while cooking. Pour the remaining paprika sauce into the saucepan and then set the stuffed peppers down into it. Two large spoons are helpful in handling the peppers.

Set the saucepan on a heat diffuser over medium low heat or just enough heat to keep the sauce simmering and steam the peppers, covered, about 50 minutes or until their flesh is tender when pierced with a toothpick. Do not over cook them.

To serve, lift the peppers out of the pan using the two large spoons and set them on each of 4 warm dinner plates. Stir the sauce and generously spoon it around and over each of the peppers.

4 servings

Note: If the peppers do not quite fill the space in the pan, tuck a long slender olive jar half filled with water and covered with a lid down inbetween them before they start to cook to help keep them upright.

paprika sauce

2 Tablespoons butter
2 Tablespoons flour
1 1/2 cups tomato paste - 12 ounces
2 cups water
2 teaspoons honey
1 teaspoon salt
1/2 teaspoon celery salt
1/4 teaspoon cayenne
1 Tablespoon sweet Hungarian paprika
1/4 cup sour cream - at room temperature
6 Tablespoons warm water
2 teaspoons dried tarragon

Melt the butter in a medium size, heavy saucepan over low heat. Using a rubber spatula, blend in the flour until the butter is absorbed. Add the tomato paste and slowly stir in the 2 cups of water until the mixture is smooth.

At this point remove 1 cup of the sauce and reserve it for the stuffed peppers.

Now add the honey, salt, celery salt, and cayenne to the sauce in the pan. In a cup, stir the paprika into the sour cream, then stir in the 6 tablespoons of warm water until the mixture is smooth. Stir the sour cream mixture and the tarragon, crushing it into the sauce in the pan and remove it from the heat.

about 3 1/4 cups

 PETITE MARMITE

I've been making this stew for years. In the beginning I had a French earthenware pot, taller than it was wide, called une petite marmite. Anything cooked in the petite marmite was delicious. It was magic. Alas! It is no more. But I continue to make the stew in a dutch oven and still call it une petite marmite. A romaine salad, bread, cheese and a bowl of yellow apples will round out the meal.

12 ounces Brussels sprouts - (3 cups)
1 pound carrots - 8 medium - (2 cups cut)
about 10 ounces mushrooms - small - (4 cups whole)
celery - 6 large ribs - (3 cups cut)
12 ounces green bell peppers - 2 medium - (2 cups cut)
3/4 cup flour
1 pound 12 ounces unshelled lima beans - large - (2 cups shelled) - or about
10 ounces frozen
1 pound boiling potatoes - about 16 little new, 1 to 1 1/4 inches in diameter
- (3 heaping cups whole)
4 cups water
2 bay leaves
2 teaspoons salt - divided
9 Tablespoons butter - divided
3 cups reserved cooking liquid
1 Tablespoon tomato paste
3 Tablespoons soy sauce
3 Tablespoons light molasses
1 Tablespoons honey
1 teaspoon celery salt
1/2 teaspoon freshly cracked black pepper
1 teaspoon dried thyme

Trim the Brussels sprouts if necessary.
Trim, peel, and cut the carrots crosswise into 1 inch pieces.
Wipe the mushrooms with a damp cloth and trim the butt ends of the stems. Leave them whole.
Trim, scrape the strings from, and cut the celery crosswise into 1 inch pieces.
Cut the bell pepper crosswise into 3/4 inch thick slices. Core them, carefully trimming away any white membrane and cut the rings into 3/4 inch squares.

(Up to this point the vegetables can, and should for the sake of the cook be prepared up to 24 hours in advance. Seal the Brussels sprouts, carrots and celery in plastic, the mushrooms in a paper bag and the bell peppers in wax paper. Refrigerate, but bring them to room temperature before continuing with the recipe.)

In a dry, heavy frying pan over medium low heat, brown the flour, stirring it constantly with a spatula for about 15 minutes or until it is a medium beige color. Remove it from the pan immediately. (Browned flour loses its thickening qualities and for this reason we must use twice as much as would otherwise be necessary.) The flour can be prepared in advance.

Shell fresh lima beans or place frozen in a colander and allow them to thaw and drain completely.

Peel the potatoes.

Bring the 4 cups of water to boil with the bay leaves and 1 teaspoon of the salt in a large, enameled dutch oven over high heat. Add the Brussels sprouts and potatoes counting the cooking time from the moment they are in the water, regardless of when the water returns to boil. Cook the vegetables, covered, 5 minutes, adjusting the heat to keep the water slowly boiling.

Add the carrots and fresh lima beans (see below for frozen), adjusting the heat again if necessary to keep the water slowly boiling.

As soon as the carrots and beans are in the water (split timing here), in a large frying pan (see utensils), over medium high heat, individually and in the following order, sauté the mushrooms, celery, and bell peppers, each sprinkled with 1/3 teaspoon of the salt, each in 1 tablespoon of the butter for 3 minutes. Then add each vegetable, in turn, to the dutch oven. If you are using frozen lima beans add them to the dutch oven now. When all the vegetables are in the dutch oven, cook them 5 minutes longer.

(At this point, total cooking time in the dutch oven should be 20 minutes.) Now, immediately and very carefully, drain all the liquid from the dutch oven into a bowl. Set the dutch oven aside, covered. Measure out 3 cups of the drained liquid and reserve it.

In a heavy, medium size saucepan over low heat, melt 6 tablespoons of the butter. Then increase the heat to medium high until the butter foams up for a minute or two and slightly browns. Remove the pan from the heat. Reduce the heat to low. When the foam subsides, return the pan to the low heat and using a rubber spatula, blend in the browned flour then the tomato paste. Slowly stir in the 3 cups of reserved liquid, the soy sauce, molasses, honey, celery salt and black pepper, while gradually increasing the heat to medium high until the sauce simmers. Simmer the sauce 2 minutes. (It should take no more than 12 minutes to make the sauce.) Add the thyme, crushing it and pour the sauce over the vegetables in the dutch oven, gently stirring them with a wooden spoon.

Return the dutch oven to low heat and cook the stew, covered, for 5 minutes. Serve the petite marmite immediately bringing the dutch oven right to the table and ladling the stew into warm bowls.

4 generous servings

Note: There is an art to making a stew, timing is essential. It takes organization and planning. All the vegetables must be cooked to an equal degree of tenderness, slightly more done than stir fried vegetables would be.

 POLENTA

As long as you plan ahead, this is a very easy way to feed 8 people. Serve stracciatella for the soup course. Follow the polenta with a make ahead broccoli vinaigrette salad and some Italian bread sticks, the coarse, crusty kind. Finish with poached figs and ammeretti cookies.

polenta the grain - (recipe follows)
3 cans ground tomatoes - 16 ounces each - (6 cups)
4 Tablespoons olive oil - divided
2 teaspoons honey
1 teaspoon plus dried oregano - divided
celery - 2 large ribs - (1 cup sliced)
6 ounces green bell pepper - 1 medium - (1 cup sliced)
about 5 ounces mushrooms - small - (2 cups sliced)
5 ounces pitted black olives - (1 cup sliced)
Parmesan cheese - (6 Tablespoons freshly grated)
Romano cheese - (2 Tablespoons freshly grated)
1 pound Mozzarella cheese - (4 cups grated)
2 Tablespoons plus 2 teaspoons butter
1/2 teaspoon salt
pinch freshly cracked black pepper

Prepare polenta the grain in advance as directed and keep it cold.
Bring the ground tomatoes, 2 tablespoons of the oil and the honey to simmer in a large, heavy saucepan over medium heat. Reduce the heat to low and gently simmer the sauce, uncovered, 25 minutes. Add 1 teaspoon of the oregano, crushing it, simmer 5 minutes longer then keep the sauce warm, uncovered over very low heat.

Trim, scrape the strings from and very thinly slice the celery crosswise.

Quarter the bell pepper lengthwise, core it and trim away any white membrane. Very thinly slice the quarters crosswise.

Wipe the mushrooms with a damp cloth, trim the butt ends of the stems and very thinly slice the mushrooms lengthwise.

Drain, rinse, drain and thinly slice the olives crosswise.

Mix the Parmesan and Romano together in a cup.

Coarsely grate the Mozzarella.

Now, remove the cold polenta loaf from the dish and slice it crosswise into 16 slices, each 1/2 inch thick. Lay 2 slices in each of 8 buttered gratin or shallow oven proof dishes. Dot each serving of polenta with 1 teaspoon of the butter. Place the dishes (they will need two shelves) in a preheated 350 degree oven for 15 minutes.

Meanwhile, 5 minutes before the polenta is ready, sauté the celery, bell pepper, mushrooms, and olives, sprinkled with the salt and black pepper in 2 tablespoons of the oil in a frying pan (see utensils), over medium high heat for 5 minutes.

Remove the dishes from the oven and spoon the equally divided warm sauce over the polenta. Sprinkle 1 tablespoons of the Parmesan mixture over the sauce in each dish. Spread the equally divided sautéed vegetables over the Parmesan then cover the vegetables with the equally divided Mozzarella. Sprinkle a pinch of oregano, crushing it, over each serving and return the dishes to the oven for 5 minutes or until the cheese has melted. Remove the dishes from the oven and allow the polenta to stand 5 minutes. Set the gratin dishes on dinner plates to serve.

8 servings

polenta the grain

2 cups cold water
2 cups stone ground yellow corn meal
2 cups water
2 teaspoons salt
1 Tablespoons plus 1 teaspoon honey

In a mixing bowl, stir the cold water into the corn meal. Bring the other 2 cups of water, with the salt and honey to boil in a large saucepan over high heat. Using a long handled wooden spoon, stir the corn meal slurry into the boiling water then stir constantly until the mixture returns to boil. Remove the pan from the heat and immediately pour the mixture into a 9 by 5 by 2 1/2 inch deep, 4 cup baking dish then tightly cover the dish with foil. Place the dish on a trivet (a 2 inch high tin can with both ends cut out works fine) in a very large kettle containing 1 inch of water. Cover the kettle with a lid and set it over high heat. When the water boils, reduce the heat to low and steam the corn meal for 3 hours. (If or when necessary, add already boiling water to the kettle to keep the water level constant.)

Remove the dish from the kettle and remove the foil. Cover the polenta with a folded paper towel and replace the foil. Allow the polenta to cool to room temperature, replacing the paper towel 2 or 3 times as it absorbs the moisture of condensation as the polenta cools. (We are keeping it covered to prevent a skin from forming.) Now, refrigerate the polenta, covered with a dry towel and foil, overnight or for up to a week

Note: If you have ever spent an hour stirring corn meal in the traditional manner to make polenta, you will appreciate this effortless way of steaming it. All you have to do is be home.

RUTABAGA IN A POT

The pot or saucepan used here should be the type with a handle on either side. But a large, ovenproof bowl will also do nicely, so long as it has a flat bottom. This delicious dish was really meant for a wood stove. It needs long baking in order for the juices to be absorbed and the flavors to marry. While you're waiting for the rutabaga to be ready serve some New York State Cheddar soup. Sautéed celery will be the accompaniment vegetable and a tossed spinach salad will follow. Enjoy poached cherries for dessert.

2 1/4 cups dried yellow split peas - 1 pound
1 bay leaf
1 Tablespoon plus 2 teaspoons salt - divided
2/3 cup millet - about 5 1/2 ounces
2 pounds rutabaga - 1 medium small about 4 1/2 inches in diameter
2 Tablespoons plus sweet Hungarian paprika - divided

2 teaspoons dried thyme
1/2 teaspoon black pepper
cayenne
8 Tablespoons unsalted butter - very cold
4 teaspoons superfine sugar
4 cups tomato juice
1 cup sour cream - at room temperature

Cull, rinse and cook the beans with the bay leaf and 1 teaspoon of the salt as directed. (See boiled dried shelled beans.) Take care not to overcook them, they must be tender but not disintegrating. Drain them well in a colander for about 5 minutes, shaking the colander a couple of times and discarding the bay leaf.

Steam the millet as directed. (See steamed millet.) In a large bowl, combine the millet with the drained peas, tossing them together with a wooden fork.

Meanwhile, trim, peel and quarter the rutabaga lengthwise. Very thinly slice the quarters crosswise, keeping the slices from each quarter separate on 4 plates.

Set out 4 teacups. Place 1/2 teaspoon of the salt, 1 1/2 teaspoons of the paprika, 1/2 teaspoon of the thyme, crushing it, 1/8 teaspoon of the black pepper and a dash of cayenne in each cup. (This will save confusion later on.)

Cover the edges of a buttered, deep, about 8 inches in diameter, 10 cup saucepan with a strip of aluminum foil reaching 1 inch down into the pan, as a spatter guard.

Spread 1/4 of the pea and millet mixture in the bottom of the pan. Sprinkle it with 1/2 teaspoon of the salt and dot it with 1 tablespoon of the butter, cut in pieces. Cover the butter with 1/4 of the rutabaga slices, evenly spread out. Dissolve 1 teaspoon of the sugar in 1 cup of the tomato juice and pour it over the rutabaga. Evenly sprinkle the spice mixture from 1 of the teacups over the tomato juice then dot it with 1 tablespoon of the butter, cut in pieces. Repeat the layers 3 more times.

Bake the rutabaga, lightly covered with foil in a preheated 375 degree oven for 1 hour. Remove the foil cover and bake 45 minutes longer. Slip a thin knife down in around the edges of the pan to allow the butter which has bubbled to the top to run down again. Bake 10 to 20 minutes longer, covering with foil again if it has browned enough, or until a wooden skewer pierced down into the center of the rutabaga meets no resistance. Remove the foil covering if you used it and spread the sour cream over the rutabaga to within 1 inch of the edge of the pan. Liberally sprinkle it with paprika and return the pan to the oven for 5 minutes longer. Remove the pan from oven, remove the foil spatter guard and allow the rutabaga in a pot to stand 10 minutes before serving.

6 servings

❧ STUFFED MUSHROOMS ❧

I'd love to have one of those Middle Eastern tin lined copper trays that looks as if it's been polished by the sands of the desert to serve these stuffed mushrooms on. Purée of fava bean will be an appropriate soup for this dinner. Serve braised fennel with the mushrooms then have artichokes vinaigrette, pita bread and Feta cheese for the salad course. Bunches of purple grapes are the dessert course.

2 pounds untrimmed spinach - (16 packed cups trimmed)
1 cup plus 2 Tablespoons bulghar - about 7 1/2 ounces
1 1/2 cups stock broth - (see stock broth)
boiling water
4 Tablespoons raisins
capers - (4 Tablespoons chopped)
about 15 to 20 pitted black olives - (4 Tablespoons chopped)
2 Tablespoons pine nuts
about 2 1/4 pounds mushrooms - 12 very large, about 3 inch in diameter
caps
2 1/4 teaspoons plus salt - divided
12 Tablespoons butter - divided
2 eggs
2 Tablespoons fresh lemon juice
1 Tablespoon honey
4 Tablespoons curry powder - (that's right!)
2 teaspoons cinnamon
3/8 teaspoon cayenne
1 1/2 teaspoons celery salt - divided
6 Tablespoons bread crumbs - (see bread crumbs)
1 ounce dried fidelini or vermicelli pasta - (1/4 cup broken)
2 cups water
1/4 teaspoon freshly cracked black pepper

Prepare and blanch the spinach as directed. (See blanched spinach.) Immediately, turn the drained spinach into a basin of cold water for 1 minute. Then turn it into a colander to drain again. Taking a handful of the spinach at a time squeeze it as dry as possible. Then mince the spinach in the processor or with a chopper, mincer, heavy knife, etc., and reserve it.

Steam the bulghar as directed, but use the stock broth rather than water. (See steamed bulghar.) Reserve it.

In a bowl pour boiling water over the raisins and allow them to soak

5 or 10 minutes until they are soft. Drain, squeeze and chop them fine. Place them in a small bowl.

Drain, rinse and drain the capers. Coarsely chop them and add them to the bowl of raisins.

Drain, rinse and drain the olives. Chop them small, add them to the small bowl and reserve the mixture.

Using a heavy knife, coarsely chop the pine nuts and toast them in a dry pan over medium heat, stirring constantly, for about 3 minutes until they are golden. Immediately, remove them from the pan and reserve them.

(Up to this point, everything can be prepared in advance, sealed separately in plastic and refrigerated, but brought to room temperature before continuing with the recipe.)

Wipe the mushrooms with a damp cloth, remove the stems and reserve the caps. Trim the butt ends of the stems and chop them fine.

Sauté the chopped stems, sprinkled with 1/4 teaspoon of the salt, in 6 tablespoons of the butter in a frying pan over medium high heat for about 3 minutes. Reduce the heat to low, add the reserved raisin mixture and cook about 2 minutes longer until the mixture is fairly dry. Remove the pan from the heat and allow it to cool a bit.

In a mixing bowl, using a wire whisk, beat the eggs until they are light. Stir in the reserved spinach, the cooled sautéed mixture, the reserved nuts, the lemon juice, honey, curry powder, cinnamon, cayenne, 1 teaspoon of the celery salt, the bread crumbs and 1 teaspoon of the salt.

Lightly salt the inside of each mushroom cap and spoon the spinach mixture into the caps, mounding it. Set the stuffed mushrooms on a lightly buttered baking sheet and bake them just 20 minutes in a preheated 350 degree oven.

Meanwhile, break the fidelini into small pieces about 1/2 inches long. Bring the 2 cups of water to boil in a saucepan over high heat. Add the pasta all at once, stirring it with a wooden spoon. Cook the pasta, covered with lid ajar, about 4 minutes or a little less than directed on the package, from the moment it is in the water, regardless of when the water returns to boil, until it is "al denté". Drain it well and in the saucepan, over low heat, toss it with 6 tablespoons of the butter, cut in pieces, the reserved bulghar, 1 teaspoon of the salt, 1/2 teaspoon of the celery salt and the black pepper until the bulghar is heated through.

Spread the pilaf mixture out on a warm, round, 10 inch in diameter, serving platter, set the mushrooms on it and serve the stuffed mushrooms immediately.

4 servings

Note: Interestingly, the spinach balances the curry and this is not an overwhelmingly curry flavored dish.

CHILE CASA MIA

Heap this fiery chile in pottery bowls to serve and provide wooden spoons with which to eat it. Offer a basket of warm tortillas to go with tossed salad mix I, then have chilled grapefruit sections.

fried gluten bits - (recipe follows)
2 1/4 cups dried red kidney beans - 1 pound
2 bay leaves
2 cans peeled plum tomatoes - 28 ounces each - (7 cups)
celery - 2 large ribs - (1 cup diced)
about 1 pound green chile peppers (Anaheim or California) - 6, about
                 1 3/4 inches in diameter at top and 5 inches long
4 Tablespoons masa harina - (see note)
1 Tablespoon paprika
2 1/2 teaspoons ground cumin
2 teaspoons cayenne
2 teaspoons celery salt
1/2 cup beer - flat
4 Tablespoons light molasses
4 Tablespoons soy sauce
2 teaspoons honey
1/2 teaspoon liquid smoke
8 Tablespoons peanut oil
1 teaspoon salt
4 Tablespoons butter
1/2 teaspoon dried thyme
1 teaspoon dried oregano

Prepare the fried gluten bits in advance as directed and have them at room temperature.

Soak the beans and cook them, with the bay leaves, as directed, making sure that they are well cooked. (See boiled, dried, shelled beans.) Drain them reserving the bay leaves. Purée 1 1/2 cups of the cooked beans through a food mill set over a bowl and then stir any skins that would not go through the mill into the purée. Reserve the purée and the remaining whole beans.

Meanwhile, turn the tomatoes into a large colander set over a bowl. Then, holding each tomato over the colander, remove the stem button and carefully cut it into 1/2 inch pieces. Drop the pieces into the colander and allow them to drain while you prepare the rest of the vegetables.

Trim, scrape the strings from, dice the celery and reserve it.

Prepare and peel the chile peppers as directed. (See peeled red bell peppers.) Handle the chile peppers carefully, their skin is tougher but their flesh is more delicate than red bell peppers. Cut the flesh into 1/2 inch squares and reserve them.

Combine the masa harina, paprika, cumin, cayenne, and celery salt in a large, heavy kettle set over low heat. Slowly add the drained tomato liquid while stirring constantly to make a smooth slurry. Next, add the beer, molasses, soy sauce, honey and liquid smoke. Cover the kettle, increase the heat to medium and stir occasionally until the liquid simmers. Then add all the fried gluten bits. (At first there will seem to be far too much but as the gluten softens it shrinks, becomes chewy and becomes incorporated into the dish.) Adjust the heat to keep the liquid gently simmering and cook, covered, 15 minutes, stirring occasionally and basting the gluten with the liquid.

Add the reserved bay leaves and stir in the puréed beans, the whole beans, the drained tomatoes and the peanut oil. Cover the kettle with lid ajar only enough to allow the kettle to breathe and cook the mixture 25 minutes while stirring frequently and adjusting the heat to keep the liquid just barely simmering.

Now, in a small frying pan, (see utensils), over medium heat, sauté the reserved celery, sprinkled with the salt in the butter for 5 minutes. Transfer the celery and all their cooking butter to the kettle and cook the chile 15 minutes longer still stirring frequently.

Add the reserved chile peppers, the thyme and the oregano crushing them and cook 10 minutes longer. To serve, ladle the chile casa mia into warm, individual bowls.

4 to 6 servings

Note: Masa harina is a corn flour available at specialty stores, natural food stores and some supermarkets.

fried gluten bits

1 cup 100% wheat gluten flour - (see note)
6 to 8 Tablespoons luke warm water
3 cups peanut oil

Place the flour in a mixing bowl and, using a fork, stir in only as much of the warm water as is necessary for a dough to form. The dough should be quite dry. Transfer the dough to a work surface and knead it 3 or 4 minutes. The dough will be very, very rough and tough. When 100% wheat gluten flour absorbs water it is immediately transformed into a rubbery mass, with no effort. The yield should be 1 cup of stringy, rubbery gluten. It can be used right away or it can be refrigerated, sealed in plastic, for at least 24 hours then brought to room temperature before continuing with the recipe.

Allowing about 15 minutes for the oil to heat to temperature, heat the oil in a deep saucepan, with a cooking thermometer clipped to the inside of it, over medium heat to 375 degrees, or use an electric deep fryer set at 375 degrees. Meanwhile, cut or pull little pieces off of the mass of gluten. Do not make them too large, they expand as they cook. Set the pieces out on a cutting board or a couple of dinner plates so that the pieces do not touch each other.

Drop enough of the gluten bits into the hot oil (be very careful of splashing) to cover the surface of the oil. Fry the gluten bits 5 minutes, stirring occasionally with a skimmer or slotted spoon until they are a medium golden color. Do not allow them to become too dark. Lift the fried bits out of the oil with the skimmer or spoon and transfer them to paper towels. Repeat the process, in 3 or 4 more batches, until all the gluten has been fried. The bits will be very puffed and crisp.

The fried gluten bits are now ready to go right into the chili or they can, when cool, be wrapped in paper towels, sealed in plastic and refrigerated 24 hours. Then brought to room temperature before they are used.

Note: One hundred percent wheat gluten flour is available in natural food stores. If 100% wheat gluten flour is unavailable, gluten can be made with any kind of wheat flour but it is a considerably longer process. In which case, place 4 cups of flour in a large mixing bowl and, using a fork, stir in only as much of about 1 1/3 cups of luke warm water as is necessary for a dough to form. The dough should be quite dry and very rough. Transfer the dough to a work surface and knead it vigorously for exactly 20 minutes, lightly flouring your hands and the work surface as necessary.

Place the ball of dough in a bowl, cover it with cold water and allow it to stand 1 hour.

Now, start kneading the dough while it is still in the water. The water will become white with starch. Pour the water out through a fine strainer to catch any little particles of gluten and replace the water with more cool water. Keep kneading the dough under fresh water, changing the water frequently until the water finally remains almost clear. The water kneading process will take about 25 minutes. At the end, squeeze the mass of gluten in your hands to get remaining water out of it. The yield should be about 1 cup of stringy, rubbery gluten.

Gluten bits made from ordinary wheat flour will fry up exactly like those made from 100% wheat gluten flour. Either type of gluten has little taste of its own but readily absorbs the flavors of that with which it is cooked.

 COLCANNON

A celestial dish to serve on Saint Patrick's Day! Have cream of pumpkin soup first. Accompany the colcannon with buttered boiled onions. A vinaigrette salad of beets served with some Irish soda bread would be fine. Crisp green apples will be in keeping with the day.

1 pound untrimmed kale - (6 tightly packed cups trimmed)
2 1/2 pounds baking potatoes - 4 large to extra large
water
2 eggs - at room temperature
12 Tablespoons butter
1 cup reserved cooking liquid
1 teaspoon salt
1 teaspoon celery salt
1/2 teaspoon freshly cracked black pepper

Prepare and blanch the kale as directed, but blanch it 20 minutes. (See blanched kale.) Immediately, turn the drained kale into a basin of cold water for 1 minute. Then turn it into a colander, place a saucer with a moderate weight upon it on the kale and allow it to drain 30 minutes, turning it over and pressing on it several times during that period. Then taking the kale a handful at a time, squeeze remaining moisture out of it, chop it fine and reserve it.

Peel and quarter the potatoes. Bring the potatoes to boil in enough water to cover them by 1 1/2 inches, in a saucepan covered with lid slightly ajar, over high heat. Reduce the heat enough to keep the water slowly boiling and cook the potatoes about 25 minutes or until they are quite soft.

In the meantime, hard cook and peel the eggs as directed. (See cooked eggs.) If they must wait, keep the peeled eggs warm in a bowl of warm water.

Melt the butter in a saucepan over very low heat and keep it warm.

When the potatoes are ready, drain them, reserving the 1 cup of cooking liquid. Pass the potatoes through a food mill into a warm bowl. Using a wooden spoon, slowly stir in the reserved cooking liquid, the salt, celery salt and pepper until the potatoes are smooth and light. Stir in the reserved kale until the mixture is completely blended. Heap the mixture in a buttered oven proof serving dish the size of a 9 inch in diameter pie plate. Using the back of a large spoon, make a round depression, about 4 1/2 inches in diameter, in the center of the colcannon and set the dish in a preheated 325 degree oven to warm for about 10 minutes.

Now, drain and dry the eggs on paper towels and quarter them lengthwise. Remove the dish from the oven and place the egg quarters, prominently and evenly spaced, around the top of the depression in the colcannon. Pour the warm, melted butter into the depression and serve the colcannon immediately.

4 servings

Note: One must be dexterous to serve colcannon!

 WHOLE ARTICHOKES WITH GARLIC BUTTER

Select the largest most beautiful artichokes ever seen for this simplest of main dishes. Don't try to serve an accompaniment vegetable with it, there just isn't time for it, the artichokes keep you too busy. The interesting soup will be potato dumplings in paprika broth. A salad of celeriac remoulade with some French bread and Camembert follow the artichokes. Mixed fruit over ice cream makes an elegant dessert.

4 pounds artichokes - 4 large, 1 pound each
2 cups unsalted butter
garlic - 1 clove
1 Tablespoon plus 1 teaspoon fresh lemon juice

Trim, boil and drain the artichokes as directed. (See boiled whole artichokes.)

Meanwhile, peel the garlic and clarify the butter as directed, putting the garlic clove in with the butter during the clarifying process and then removing it. (See clarified butter.) Add the lemon juice to the clarified butter and divide it equally among 4 warm tea cups.

Set the drained artichokes and the tea cups on each of 4 warm dinner plates and serve the whole artichokes with garlic butter immediately.

4 servings

Note: To eat the artichokes, pull off the leaves with your fingers, one at a time, dip each leaf in the butter and eat only the thick tender part at the base of each leaf. Provide each diner with a bowl for the discarded leaves. When you get to the choke, scrape it away and discard it. Using a knife and fork, cut up the bottom of the artichoke (sometimes called the heart) and dip it in the butter.

 CABBAGE STRUDEL

I'm sometimes asked which of my recipes is my own totally original creation. Food has been around for a long time and there's very little in cooking that could be called totally original. However, I have never seen this method of stretching strudel dough, using oil, anywhere else. The idea might be original with me. It makes a very thin, light, crisp pastry using ordinary flour, quickly and with little effort. Serve cream of stock vegetable purée soup then accompany the cabbage strudel with buttered lima beans. Carrot and currant salad with dark bread will be the salad course and a big bowl of red apples the dessert.

strudel filling - (recipe follows)
4 Tablespoons butter - divided
strudel dough - (recipe follows)
1/2 cup bread crumbs - fine - (see bread crumbs)
2 ounces Limburger cheese - cold

Prepare and cool the filling as directed.

Melt the butter in a small saucepan over low heat. Place a cookie sheet on the bottom shelf of the oven to diffuse the heat as the strudel dough is very delicate.

Be sure to have everything in readiness before the dough is stretched. Prepare and stretch the strudel dough as directed.

Using a pastry feather, brush the entire surface of the rectangular sheet of dough with 3 tablespoons of the melted butter then evenly sprinkle it with the bread crumbs. Lay half of the cabbage mixture in a 3 inch wide strip down a 16 inch side of the sheet of dough, 1 inch in from the side and leaving about 1/4 inch of dough showing at either end of the cabbage strip. Cut the cheese into thin slices and evenly lay it on the cabbage then cover it with the remaining cabbage. Fold the 1 inch edge of the dough over the cabbage and continue rolling the dough over itself, using your hands, until the strudel is formed. This comparatively small sheet of strudel dough is easily handled and peels right up off of the oiled surface.

Lift the strudel onto a buttered 11 by 17 inch jelly roll pan and brush the top of it with the remaining butter. Pierce the strudel several times with a thin skewer and bake it in a preheated 350 degree oven for about 55 minutes until it is golden and crisp. Transfer the strudel to a cutting board and allow it to stand 10 minutes. Bring the cutting board right to the table and use a serrated knife to cut the cabbage strudel.

4 to 6 servings

strudel filling

celery - 2 large ribs - (1 cup sliced)
3 pounds cabbage - 1 medium head - (12 tightly packed cups sliced)
1/2 teaspoon celery salt
6 Tablespoons butter
1 teaspoon salt
1/2 teaspoon freshly cracked black pepper
1/2 teaspoon sugar

Trim, scrape the strings from and very thinly slice the celery crosswise.

Quarter the cabbage lengthwise. Core it and very thinly slice it crosswise.

Sauté the celery, sprinkled with the celery salt, in the butter in a large frying pan (see utensils), over medium heat for 3 minutes. Reduce the heat to low. Add the cabbage, sprinkle it with the salt, pepper and sugar and very slowly cook it, covered, for 30 minutes. As the cabbage begins to wilt, turn it occasionally with a metal spatula, so that it will cook evenly. Now, uncover the pan, raise the heat to high and stir the cabbage almost constantly for about 30 minutes, using both the metal spatula and a fork. The cabbage must brown evenly. As the juices begin to evaporate, turn down the heat a little to keep the cabbage from scorching. At about the end of the cooking period, the cabbage should be fairly dry and nicely browned. Transfer it to a bowl to cool completely.

strudel dough

1 1/2 cups all purpose flour
1 1/2 Tablespoons plus corn oil - divided
1/4 teaspoon salt
6 Tablespoons plus tepid water - divided
1 1/2 teaspoons cider vinegar

Sift the flour into a mixing bowl. Using a fork, stir in the 1 1/2 tablespoons of corn oil. In a cup, dissolve the salt in the 6 tablespoons of water then add the vinegar to it. Slowly pour the water mixture into the flour while stirring with the fork. Then, start working the mixture with your hand, adding only as much additional water, by the teaspoonful, as is necessary until dough begins to form. Transfer the dough to a very, very lightly floured work surface and vigorously knead the dough for 10 minutes.

Now, form the dough into a slightly oblong shape. Take hold of one end of it and slam the rest of it against the edge of the work surface (counter or table) 100 times, reversing sides and ends. This will activate the gluten. Shape the dough into a ball, seal it in plastic and allow it to rest 1 hour at room temperature.,

Pinch a piece of the dough. If the pinch stands up, remains firm and does not snap back, the dough is ready to be stretched. If it snaps back, let it rest a while longer.

Lightly oil a rolling pin and a work surface which has at least 3, preferably 4 open sides around which you can walk. (If you are using a wooden table you might want to cover it first with a plastic table cloth, securing it around th edges under the table with thumb tacks. However the oil will not hurt the wood.)

First, using the rolling pin, roll out the dough as thin as possible on the oiled surface. Now, carefully start stretching the dough by slipping your hands under it and gently pulling it toward you with the back of your hands.

Keep moving slowly around the work surface while stretching the dough. The dough will cling to the oiled surface and this aids greatly in the stretching process. If a hole develops, quickly pinch it with a drop of water and then avoid that spot. When the dough has reached a size that can have a 16 by 26 inch rectangle cut out of it by trimming off the slightly thicker edges, stop, or make it even thinner if you dare. Remember, strudel dough should be thin enough to read a newspaper through. Now, using a sharp knife, trim away the slightly thicker edges from around the 16 by 26 inch rectangle. It should not take any longer than 10 minutes to roll out, stretch and trim the strudel dough.

ACCOMPANIMENT VEGETABLES

In the menu suggestions that appear at the beginning of each main dish recipe, the accompaniment vegetable is only included in dinners that have the previously discussed entrée as the main dish. The accompaniment vegetable is meant to enhance the qualities of the entrée as well as round out the course. You will find the preparation, cooking and presentation of the accompaniment vegetables have been intentionally kept simple in order not to detract from but rather to compliment the entrée. There are several considerations in the selection of the accompaniment vegetable . They are seasonal availability, taste, color, type, texture, tradition and cooking method. The seasonal availability should coincide, the taste and color must flatter, the type and texture must compliment plus it is well to respect tradition. In addition the cooking method should be diverse from that of the entrée. Such perfect harmony is not always attainable but we can aim in that direction.

Seasonal availability: Seasonal availability are words that hardly seem to matter anymore. Even asparagus are seen in the markets in December. However, though a vegetable may be physically present all year round it has a seasonal flavor peak that must be taken into consideration whether planning an entrée or selecting an accompaniment vegetable . The importance of seasonal availability really comes into focus when you are working with vegetables from your own garden.

Taste: The taste of the accompaniment vegetable must compliment the taste of the entrée with which it is served. This can be subtle but a very clear example of it would be the sweetness of baked sweet potatoes played against the tartness of fried green tomatoes.

Color: The color of the accompaniment vegetable must also compliment the entrée. Let's not have red tomatoes with stuffed red bell peppers. Rather, make it green zucchini.

Type: Select an accompaniment vegetable whose type and family differ from those of the entrée. That is to say if the main dish were composed of root vegetables the accompaniment should be a vegetable of a lighter nature such as spinach. And keep family in mind. A dinner with an entrée of broccoli and an accompaniment of turnips would not be very interesting. But an accompaniment of butternut squash would—shall we say flatter the broccoli?

Texture: Texture is not only the natural quality of a given vegetable but the way in which it is cut or prepared. The preparation and presentation of the accompaniment vegetable is an art. Handle the vegetables as if they were flowers. Many vegetables have wonderful shapes which must be carefully preserved. While others require slicing, dicing, cutting into little matchsticks in the French julienne fashion or slicing on a steep diagonal in the Oriental manner, shredding or puréeing to enhance their best aspects and give them added distinction and a style of their own. What must be considered here is the texture of the accompaniment vegetable in relation to the main dish. For instance if the entrée is a solid mass such as a stuffed head of red cabbage an accompaniment of a mass of small things like sliced carrots would compliment it. Conversely if the main dish is a lot of little things such as croquettes it is complimented by an accompaniment such as a head of cauliflower which is a mass.

Tradition: If the principal presentation has an ethnic theme it will influence the selection of the accompaniment vegetable in yet another way. After all we are not going to serve baked potatoes with egg fu-yung are we? There are other patterns of tradition too of things that just go well together like sauerkraut and potatoes or corn and tomatoes. However do not overlook innovation. If we don't experiment how will we make progress?

Cooking Method: A dinner has more character when the accompaniment vegetable has been cooked by a different method than the entrée. Hopefully the preparation, cooking and presentation of the accompaniment will dovetail nicely into those of the main dish. Generally the accompaniment vegetable can be prepared in advance and cooked at the last minute to coincide with the presentation of the entrée. Read the recipe for the entrée over carefully and decide at what point the accompaniment must start cooking in order to be ready to serve at the same moment with it. Vegetables which have been prepared in advance may be stored, covered, refrigerated but must be brought to room temperature before cooking—for these recipes.

Once the accompaniment vegetable is cooked it must be turned into a warm serving dish and served immediately. If you have no other means to warm the serving dish just fill it with hot water about five minutes before emptying it, drying it, and placing the vegetable in it. Covered serving dishes are elegant pieces to own and are almost a necessity for starchy vegetables such as boiled potatoes, lima beans, and peas which always seem to cool too quickly. Like the entrée the accompaniment must be presented in an appropriate and attractive dish which enhances its appearance. Color is important; for instance carrots look well in a blue dish, beets in a white one. If you do not have the proper serving dish, place the vegetables in a seven inch glass pie plate and set the pie plate on a dinner plate. The effect is of a matching serving piece to the dinner plates. And incidentally if you must use little side dishes because there is not enough room on the dinner plates for the accompaniment vegetable , make certain that the little dishes are just as warm as the dinner plates.

After all these considerations in the selection of an accompaniment vegetable, seasonal availability, taste, color, type, texture, ethnic tradition and cooking method, there is one more consideration which came into play in designing the menu suggestions for this book and it is this. I have tried to use every commonly available vegetable at least once. Do not allow your menus to fall into the rut of playing favorites. Some very good and I might add economical vegetables are overlooked simply because they are out of style and too many favorites become a bore. Variety is the spice of life. When selecting vegetables try to keep that in mind.

The amounts of sliced, diced, grated, etc. vegetables have been carefully measured in this section as well as throughout the book. However these measurements do not meet any particular recognized standard of measurement.

Weights and measures of vegetables can vary considerably depending on moisture content. Consequently, wherever possible, each vegetable is always listed with its weight, size and cut measurement to aid in greater accuracy both in shopping and cooking.

artichokes

asparagus

lima beans

string beans

beets

broccoli

brussels sprouts

cabbage

red cabbage

savoy cabbage

carrots

cauliflower

celeriac

celery

corn

cucumbers

eggplant

fennel

helianthus tuberosa

kale

kohlrabi

mushrooms

onions

okra

parsnips

peas

snow peas

green bell peppers

red bell peppers

sweet italian frying peppers

potatoes

sweet potatoes

rutabaga

spinach

summer squash

swiss chard

tomatoes

white turnips

artichokes

Would that I could grow these thistles in my garden; artichokes are the elegant flower buds of a member of the thistle family. The very small buds are usually called baby artichokes when fresh and artichoke hearts when frozen. Artichoke bottoms are also frequently called hearts.

Large artichoke are available all year but most abundant in the springtime and the baby artichokes are much more widely available now than they once were. Fortunately the baby artichokes also freeze well.

boiled whole artichokes

water
2 teaspoons cider vinegar per quart water
1/2 teaspoon salt per quart water
7 black peppercorns
1 bay leaf
artichokes — medium to large

In a saucepan (see utensils) just large enough to hold them, set over high heat, bring to boil enough water to cover the artichokes by 1 1/2 inches, with the vinegar, salt, peppercorns, and bay leaf.

Meanwhile, using a stainless steal serrated knife, trim off the stems flush with the bottom leaves of the artichokes. Add the artichokes to the boiling water, laying a plate on top of them if necessary to keep them submerged. Cook them, covered with lid ajar, for from 30 to 40 minutes, depending on their size, from the moment they are in the water, regardless of when the water returns to boil, adjusting the heat to keep the water slowly boiling. Pierce the bottom of each artichoke with a wooden toothpick or skewer to determine when it is just tender. Drain them upside down for a couple of minutes.

preparation of baby artichokes

1 cup water per 2 cups baby artichokes
2 Tablespoons fresh lemon juice per cup water
baby artichokes

In a bowl, combine the required amount of water with the necessary lemon juice.

Using a stainless steel serrated knife, trim off the stems flush with the bottom leaves of the artichokes. Lay the artichokes on their sides on a cutting board and cut off the top third of each artichoke. Remove tough outer leaves (more than you think necessary) and quarter the artichokes lengthwise. There will be no "chokes". Immediately drop the trimmed artichokes into the acidulated water; they discolor very quickly.

boiled baby artichokes

baby artichokes
water
1/2 teaspoon salt per quart water

Prepare the artichokes as directed. (See preparation of baby artichokes.)

In a saucepan, (see utensils) over high heat, bring to boil enough water to cover the artichokes by 1 1/2 inches, with the necessary amount of salt. Drain the artichokes, add them to the boiling water and cook them, covered with lid ajar, for about 10 minutes from the moment they are in the water, regardless of when the water returns to boil, adjusting the heat to keep the water slowly boiling. Pierce the bottom of the artichokes with a wooden toothpick to determine when they are just tender. Drain them.

preparation of frozen artichokes

frozen artichoke hearts

In a colander run enough warm water over the artichoke hearts to separate, but not thaw them. Now while they are still frozen, using a stainless steel serrated knife, trim them. (Frozen artichoke hearts are never quite properly trimmed.) See that all the hearts have been quartered, that longer leaves are trimmed of tips that might be tough and that bottoms are neatly pared.

Note: Disregard any instructions or measurements on the package.

blanched frozen artichokes

frozen artichoke hearts
water
1/2 teaspoon salt per quart water

Prepare the artichokes as directed. (See preparation of frozen artichokes.)

In a saucepan, (see utensils) over high heat, bring to boil enough water to cover the artichokes by 1 1/2 inches, with the necessary amount of salt. Drop the still frozen artichokes into the boiling water and blanch them, covered with lid, ajar, for 5 minutes from the moment they are in the water, regardless of when the water returns to boil, adjusting the heat to keep the water slowly boiling. Drain them.

braised baby artichokes

1 1/2 pounds baby artichokes - about 24 - (4 cups trimmed) or

18 ounces frozen

2 Tablespoons cider vinegar
2 Tablespoons water
1 teaspoon salt
1/4 teaspoon freshly cracked black pepper
6 Tablespoons olive oil

Prepare the baby artichokes as directed. (See preparation of baby artichokes.) Or prepare the frozen artichokes as directed. (See preparation of frozen artichokes.) Then place the frozen artichokes in a colander, and allow them to thaw and drain completely.

In a cup, combine the vinegar and the water and reserve the mixture.

Drain the baby artichokes, blot them or the thawed artichokes, on paper towels. Sauté the artichokes, sprinkled with the salt and pepper, in the oil in a large frying pan (see utensils) over medium heat for 1 minute. Remove the pan from the heat, add the reserved vinegar mixture, cover the pan immediately and return it to the heat for 5 minutes. Uncover the pan, increase the heat to high, and cook the artichokes about 5 minutes longer, turning them with a metal spatula until all the moisture has evaporated and the artichokes are golden and a little crisp in the same way that you would want fried potatoes to be.

Turn the braised artichokes into a serving dish and allow them to stand 10 minutes. Their flavor peak is warm rather than hot.

4 servings

asparagus

When I planted my first garden, naively, I sowed a package of asparagus seeds. It takes a minimum of three years for the plants to develop to eating size, five years really. However, it was an easier and less expensive way to plant asparagus than setting out roots would have been. In retrospect, it wasn't such a bad idea. Asparagus will naturalize themselves almost anywhere, but they prefer a light loose soil. Drop a few seeds in an out of the way place and see what happens. Store bought asparagus are usually peeled to some degree before cooking but fresh young asparagus from your garden may not have to be peeled at all.

steamed asparagus

Select spears of equal thickness. Rinse the spears in a basin of cold water and drain them. Snap off the butt end of each spear at the point where it breaks most easily. Lay the asparagus out with tips evenly lined up and trim off the lower end of any spears that are excessively long. Using a vegetable peeler, lightly peel the asparagus below the head. Tie the asparagus into bundles of 5 thick or 6 or 7 more slender spears with dressmaker tape or ribbon that will not cut into the asparagus. Tie each bundle twice, once near the top and once near the bottom.

Bring 1 inch of water to boil in the lower part of a double boiler set over high heat and stand the bundles up in it. Cover the asparagus with the inverted upper part of the double boiler. Reduce the heat to medium low and steam the asparagus 8 to 10 minutes or until they are just tender when pierced with a wooden skewer or toothpick.

Note: If you are only steaming 1 or 2 bundles, set a glass jar, half filled with water, in the pan before steaming the asparagus so that there will be no room for the bundles to fall over.

buttered steamed asparagus

2 pounds asparagus
butter
salt and pepper

Prepare and steam the asparagus as directed. (See steamed asparagus.) Using a pair of tongs, remove the hot asparagus from the pan. Lay the bundles on a warm serving platter with the tips all pointing in the same direction. Then cut and remove the ribbons. Serve the asparagus immediately along with plenty of butter, salt and pepper on the table.

4 servings

Note: Tongs are handy for serving the asparagus

braised asparagus

about 2 pounds asparagus - (4 cups trimmed and cut)
1/2 teaspoon salt
4 Tablespoons butter
4 Tablespoons hot water - in a cup

Select asparagus spears of equal thickness. Rinse the spears in a basin of cold water then drain them. Snap off the butt end of each spear at the point where it breaks most easily. Using a vegetable peeler, lightly peel the asparagus below the head. Cut the spears, diagonally, into 1 to 1 1/2 inch long pieces.

Sauté the asparagus, sprinkled with the salt, in the butter, in a large frying pan (see utensils) over medium heat, 2 minutes. Remove the pan from the heat, add the hot water, cover the pan immediately and return it to the heat for 3 minutes. Increase the heat to high, uncover the pan and cook the asparagus about 1 minute longer until all the moisture has evaporated and the pieces are just tender when pierced with a wooden toothpick. Serve the braised asparagus immediately.

4 servings

lima beans

Lima beans are delicious either as freshly shelled beans or as dried shelled beans. They are grown in both a large variety and a small variety, referred to a "baby limas."

steamed lima beans

unshelled lima beans

Shell the lima beans and steam either the large or small variety over already simmering water for from 20 to 25 minutes depending on their size. If your steamer is not very large (the little folding type) do not steam more than 2 cups at a time or they will not steam evenly.

buttered steamed lima beans

1 pound 12 ounces large or 1 pound 14 ounces baby unshelled lima beans
- (2 cups shelled)
1 Tablespoon plus 1 teaspoon butter - at room temperature
salt and pepper to taste

Shell and steam the lima beans as directed. (See steamed lima beans.) In a warm serving dish, toss the hot beans with the butter, cut in pieces, the salt and pepper and serve them, covered, immediately.

4 servings

string beans

String beans are also called snap beans. Unless you have eaten them freshly picked from the garden, you have never really tasted string beans. Green or yellow, narrow or wide and flat, string beans are grown as bush plants or climb poles as vines. Yellow string beans are generally called wax beans, abut some old timers call them butter beans.

steamed string beans

green or yellow, slender or wide and flat string beans

Rinse if necessary, drain and trim off only the stems of the string beans. Steam them over already simmering water for an average of 10 minutes for store bought beans. Freshly picked home grown string beans take as little as 5 minutes to steam. The wide flat pod varieties are especially tender so pay close attention! Taste the string beans to determine when they are just tender.

buttered steamed string beans

1 pound green or yellow, slender or wide and flat string beans
2 Tablespoons butter - at room temperature
salt and pepper to taste

Prepare and steam the string beans as directed. (See steamed string beans.) In a warm serving dish, toss the hot string beans with the butter, cut in pieces, the salt and pepper and serve immediately.

4 servings

beets

Leaving part of the leaf stems, the skin and the root of the beet intact while it is cooking helps it to retain its lovely ruby color.

steamed beets

beets - small, 1 1/4 to 1 1/2 inches in diameter

Scrub the beets well under running water. Trim off all but 1 inch of their leaf stems and leave the roots intact. Steam them over already simmering water for about 50 minutes or until they are just tender when pierced with a wooden toothpick. Hold the beets under running warm water to trim off the stems and roots and slip off the skins.

boiled beets

beets
water

Scrub beets of any size well, under running water. Trim off all but 1 inch of their leaf stems and leave their roots intact. In an adequate size saucepan over high heat bring to boil enough water to cover the beets by 1 1/2 inches. Add the beets and cook them, covered, for from 30 to 60 minutes depending on their size, from the moment they are in the water, regardless of when the water returns to boil, adjusting the heat to keep the water slowly boiling. Pierce the beets with a wooden skewer or toothpick to determine when they are just tender. Drain them and hold the beets under warm running water to trim off the stems and roots and slip off the skins.

baked beets

beets

Scrub the beets well under running water. Trim off all but 1 inch of their leaf stems and leave their roots intact. Tightly wrap the beets, individually, in aluminum foil and bake them in a preheated 400 degree oven for from 40 to 60 minutes depending on their size. Check the beets to determine when they are just tender by unwrapping them slightly and piercing them with a wooden skewer or toothpick. When they are done, unwrap them and hold the beets under running warm water to trim off the stems and roots and slip off the skins.

buttered baked beets

1 1/4 pounds beets - 2 medium, 2 inches in diameter
salt and pepper to taste
2 Tablespoons plus 2 teaspoons unsalted butter

Prepare, bake, trim, and peel the beets as directed. (See baked beets.) Cut the baked beets, crosswise, into slices about 3/16 inch thick. Reheat the sliced beets, dusted with salt and pepper in the butter in a covered saucepan over low heat for about 3 minutes until they are heated through. Serve the beets immediately.

4 servings

broccoli

The flavors of the broccoli florets and stalks are distinctively different. They can be served together or separately. The florets can be served as a vegetable accompaniment while the stalks can be saved for a vinaigrette salad or vice versa. Harvest or buy broccoli while the heads are still tightly compact.

steamed broccoli

broccoli

Cut the broccoli florets from the stalk with enough stem so that the florets, including their stems, measure about 4 inches long. Cut or break the larger florets down to the size of the smaller ones, where necessary so that the florets are all of a uniform size, as much as possible. Their stems will be tapered. Trim and peel the remainder of the large stalk, first pulling off the fibrous skin with a knife and then using a vegetable peeler. Then cut the stalk lengthwise into quarters or eighths depending on its thickness. The pieces should be 3 to 4 inches long.

Steam the broccoli florets and stalk pieces over already simmering water for from 10 to as much as 20 minutes. Start testing the broccoli at 8 minutes by piercing the stems with a wooden toothpick to determine when it will be just tender.

buttered steamed broccoli

1 1/2 pounds broccoli - 3 average heads, 1 bunch - (6 cups florets and cut)
2 Tablespoons plus 2 teaspoons butter - at room temperature
salt and pepper to taste

Prepare and steam the broccoli as directed. (See steamed broccoli.) In a warm serving dish, toss the hot broccoli with the butter, cut in pieces, the salt and pepper and serve immediately.

4 servings

brussels sprouts

For a real treat, grow them yourself. Brussels sprout plants take a long time to develop. Start them 2 weeks earlier than you think you should, you won't regret it.

steamed brussels sprouts

Brussels sprouts

Make an effort to obtain Brussels sprouts of equal size. Trim them only if necessary and steam the sprouts over already simmering water for from 15 to 30 minutes, depending on their size. Start testing the Brussels sprouts at about 13 minutes by piercing them with a wooden toothpick to determine when they will be just tender.

buttered steamed brussels sprouts

1 pound Brussels sprouts - 32 to 40 of equal size - (4 cups whole)
2 Tablespoons plus 2 teaspoons butter - at room temperature
1 teaspoon salt

Prepare and steam the Brussels sprouts as directed. (See steamed Brussels sprouts.) In a warm serving dish toss the hot Brussels sprouts with the butter, cut in pieces, and the salt and serve immediately.

4 servings

cabbage

The common cabbage reaches far back into history. It is an extremely versatile as well as abundant vegetable. Universally popular green cabbage has three distinctive head shapes, conical, round and flattened. Pale green cabbage is the one we make coleslaw out of and is also called white cabbage.

baked cabbage wedges

2 pounds cabbage - 1 small head
4 Tablespoons butter - cold
salt

Cut the cabbage lengthwise into 6 wedges. The rounded side of each wedge should measure 3 to 4 inches at its widest point. Trim the wedges as necessary but do not core them. Tuck about 2 teaspoons of the butter, cut into thin slivers, between the leaves of each wedge and lightly salt the wedges. Tightly wrap each wedge in foil, set them on a baking sheet for convenience, resting on their rounded side, and bake them in a preheated 375 degree oven 30 minutes. Unwrap the cabbage wedges, place them on a warm platter and serve immediately.

6 servings

braised cabbage

2 pounds cabbage - 1 small head - (10 tightly packed cups cut)
1 teaspoon salt
2 Tablespoons plus 2 teaspoons butter
2 Tablespoons hot water - in a cup

Quarter the cabbage lengthwise, core it and cut the quarters into 1 inch dice, separating the interlocking leaves. Cut any thick pieces smaller.

Sauté the cabbage, sprinkled with the salt, in the butter, in a large frying pan (see utensils) over medium heat 2 minutes, stirring and turning it over to coat it well with the butter. Reduce the heat to low, remove the pan from the heat, add the hot water, cover the pan immediately and return it to the low heat for 10 minutes, turning the cabbage over 2 or 3 times. Increase the heat to medium high, uncover the pan and cook the cabbage 3 minutes longer, turning it until all the moisture has evaporated. Serve the braised cabbage immediately.

4 servings

sauerkraut

3 pounds fresh sauerkraut - (6 drained, lightly packed cups) -
or 3 cans 27 ounces each - (see note)

6 cups water
6 Tablespoons butter
2 teaspoons honey
1/4 teaspoon cracked black pepper

      Immerse the drained fresh sauerkraut in cold water and drain it again. Bring the 6 cups of water to boil in a large saucepan over high heat. Add the drained sauerkraut and cook it, covered, 30 or 40 minutes from the moment it is in the water, regardless of when the water returns to boil, reducing heat to keep the water gently simmering until the sauerkraut is almost tender. Drain it thoroughly. Or immerse the drained, canned sauerkraut in cold water and drain it again very well.

      In either case melt the butter in a medium size saucepan over low heat. Add the honey, pepper and drained sauerkraut, gently stirring it, with a wooden fork to coat it well with the butter mixture. Warm the sauerkraut, covered, 20 minutes until it is heated through. Serve the sauerkraut immediately.

4 to 6 servings

Note: Quantities of canned saurkraut can, after it is drained and packed, vary considerably, sometimes as much as a cup! To be on the safe side have a greater quantity on hand than would appear necessary. However, do not use any extra quantity as it would unbalance the recipe.

red cabbage

      The handsome big red cabbage is really more purple than red. Of slightly heavier texture than green cabbage, the flavor of red cabbage has an affinity for vinegar which in turn helps it to retain its beautiful color.

baked red cabbage wedges

2 pounds red cabbage - 1 small head
4 Tablespoons butter - cold
salt

Prepare, bake and serve the red cabbage wedges as directed but bake them an extra 5 minutes. (See baked cabbage wedges.)

6 servings

blanched red cabbage

red cabbage
1 quart boiling water per 2 tightly packed cups cut red cabbage
1 teaspoon distilled white vinegar per quart water
1/4 teaspoon salt per quart water

Quarter the red cabbage lengthwise, core it and cut the quarters, crosswise, into 1/2 inch thick slices. Carefully separate the interlocking leaves. In a large kettle set over high heat, blanch the cabbage, in boiling water with vinegar and salt, uncovered, for 3 minutes from the moment it is all in the water, regardless of when the water returns to boil. Push the cabbage down into the water with a long handled wooden spoon and adjust the heat to keep the water slowly boiling. Drain the cabbage into a colander.

braised red cabbage

2 pounds red cabbage - 1 small head - (10 tightly packed cups cut)
2 Tablespoons cider vinegar
1 teaspoon salt
4 Tablespoons butter

Quarter the cabbage lengthwise, core it and cut the quarters into 1 inch dice, separating the interlocking leaves. Cut any thick pieces smaller, warm the vinegar in a small saucepan over low heat.
Sauté the red cabbage, sprinkled with the salt, in the butter, in a large frying pan (see utensils) over medium heat 2 minutes, stirring and

turning it over to coat it well with the butter. Reduce the heat to low, remove the pan from the heat, add the warm vinegar, cover the pan immediately and return it to the low heat for 15 minutes, turning the cabbage over occasionally. Increase the heat to medium high, uncover the pan and cook the cabbage 3 minutes longer, turning it, until all the moisture has evaporated. Serve the braised red cabbage immediately.

4 serving

savoy cabbage

Savoy cabbages are a deeper shade of green than other cabbages. Their distinctive flavor seems to favor the Brussels sprout side of the family. Crinkly leafed Savoy cabbage plants are so graceful that it's worth growing them just for their beauty alone.

baked savoy cabbage wedges

2 pounds Savoy cabbage - 1 small head
4 Tablespoons butter - cold
salt

Prepare, bake and serve the Savoy cabbage wedges exactly as directed. (See baked cabbage wedges.)

6 servings

braised savoy cabbage

2 pounds Savoy cabbage - 1 small head - (10 tightly packed cups cut)
1/2 teaspoon salt
1/4 teaspoon freshly cracked black pepper
4 Tablespoons butter
2 Tablespoons hot water - in a cup

Prepare and cook the Savoy cabbage exactly as directed for braised cabbage but add the pepper with the salt and cook the cabbage, covered, 15 minutes rather than the recommended 10 minutes. (See braised cabbage.)

4 servings

Note: For accurate measurement, you may want to buy a cabbage which is a little larger than needed since the outer leaves of Savoy cabbage are sometimes tough and must be discarded.

carrots

There can be quite a range of sweetness in carrots, depending upon the soil in which they are grown. Raw carrots are the perfect diet snack. In which case cut them, crosswise, into carrot coins about 1/4 inch thick and keep them on hand in the refrigerator. Pop one into your mouth when you feel hunger pangs.

steamed carrots

carrots - large or very small

Trim, peel and cut large carrots diagonally into 3/4 inch thick slices. Using your sharp little paring knife, trim the cut edges of the carrot slices so that they will be rounded and look like little pieces of soap. Or select very small carrots about 3 to 4 inches long and not more than 3/4 inch in diameter at the top. Trim the small carrots and just scrub them with a stiff brush rather than peel them. Steam either the large cut or whole very small carrots over already simmering water about 15 minutes until they are just tender when pierced with a wooden toothpick.

buttered steamed carrots

1 pound 4 ounces carrots - 6 or 7 large or 1 pound - 24 very small
4 Tablespoons unsalted butter - at room temperature
3/4 teaspoon salt
1/4 teaspoon freshly cracked black pepper

Prepare and steam the large or very small carrots as directed. (See steamed carrots.) In a warm serving dish, toss the hot carrots with butter, cut in pieces, the salt and pepper and serve immediately.

4 servings

braised carrots

1 pound 4 ounces carrots - 10 medium - (3 cups sliced)
1 1/2 teaspoons honey
3 Tablespoons hot water
3/4 teaspoon salt
1/4 scant teaspoon freshly cracked black pepper
4 Tablespoons unsalted butter

Trim, peel and cut carrots, crosswise, into 1/8 inch thick slices. In a cup dissolve the honey in the hot water and reserve the mixture.

Sauté the carrots, sprinkled with the salt and pepper in the butter in a frying pan (see utensils) over medium heat 2 minutes. Reduce the heat to low, remove the pan from the heat, add the reserved hot water mixture, cover the pan immediately and return it to the low heat for 4 minutes, shaking the pan once or twice. Increase the heat to high, uncover the pan and cook the carrots 1 minute longer until all the moisture has evaporated. Serve the braised carrots immediately.

4 servings

Note: Pay close attention, braised carrots can overcook easily!

cauliflower

Cauliflower is the flower of the vegetable garden and the queen of the table. Some gardeners tie the leaves of the plant up over the white flower head while it is developing to keep it all the whiter.

steamed cauliflower florets

cauliflower

Trim the cauliflower and separate the head into florets. Cut or break down larger florets to the size of the smaller ones, where necessary so that the florets are, as much as possible, all of a uniform size. Neatly trim the little stems.

Steam the florets over already simmering water for from 10 to 20 minutes, 15 minutes being the average. Start testing the cauliflower at 8 minutes, by piercing the stems with a wooden toothpick to determine when it will be just tender.

buttered steamed cauliflower florets

about 2 pounds 11 ounces cauliflower - 1 medium large head -
(8 cups florets)
2 Tablespoons plus 2 teaspoons butter - at room temperature
salt to taste

Prepare and steam the cauliflower as directed. (See steamed cauliflower florets.) In a warm serving dish, toss the hot cauliflower florets with the butter, cut in pieces, and the salt and serve immediately.

4 servings

steamed cauliflower head

cauliflower

Remove the leaves and leaving enough of the stem to hold the head together, trim the stem flush with the head of the cauliflower. Steam the cauliflower, stem side down over already simmering water for from 10 to 25 minutes. Start testing the cauliflower at 8 minutes by piercing the stem with a wooden skewer to determine when it will be just tender.

buttered steamed cauliflower head

2 pounds cauliflower - 1 medium small head
butter
salt

Prepare and steam the cauliflower as directed. (See steamed cauliflower head.) Transfer the hot cauliflower head to a warm serving platter. Carve it with a knife at the table and let everyone butter and salt their own serving.

4 servings

celeriac

Celeriac is a celery plant bred for the root rather than the ribs. Its flavor is dramatic and intense and were it more abundantly available it could make an interesting addition to many dishes.

braised celeriac

1 pound celeriac - 1 large or 2 small - (3 cups cut)
1 Tablespoon fresh lemon juice
1/2 teaspoon salt
1/2 teaspoon celery salt
1/4 teaspoon freshly cracked black pepper
2 Tablespoons plus 2 teaspoons butter
4 Tablespoons hot water - in a cup

Scrub the celeriac under running water. Trim, peel and cut it into eighths lengthwise. Cut the eighths, crosswise, into 3/16 inches thick slices, dropping them into a bowl containing the lemon juice and enough cold water to cover them.

(The celeriac can be prepared several hours in advance up to this point. Cover the bowl and refrigerate it, but bring the celeriac to room temperature before continuing with the recipe.)

Drain and blot the celeriac slices dry on paper towels.

Sauté the celeriac, sprinkled with the salt, celery salt and pepper in the butter in a frying pan (see utensils) over medium heat 2 minutes. Reduce the heat to low, remove the pan from the heat, add the hot water, cover the pan immediately and return it to the low heat for 3 minutes.

Increase the heat to high, uncover the pan and cook the celeriac, 1 minute longer, stirring it gently with a wooden spatula until all the moisture has evaporated. Serve the braised celeriac immediately.

4 servings

celery

Celery, so often eaten raw, is a delicious cooked vegetable too and a wonderful flavoring agent.

braised celery

celery - 10 large ribs - (5 cups cut)
1/2 teaspoon salt
1/4 teaspoon freshly cracked black pepper
2 Tablespoons plus 2 teaspoons peanut oil
3 Tablespoons hot water - in a cup

Trim, scrape the strings from and cut the celery, diagonally, into 1/2 inch thick slices.

Sauté the celery, sprinkled with the salt and pepper in the oil in a frying pan (see utensils) over medium heat 3 minutes. Reduce the heat to low, remove the pan from the heat, add the hot water, cover the pan immediately and return it to the low heat for 4 minutes. Increase the heat to high, uncover the pan and cook the celery, 2 minutes longer, stirring until all the moisture has evaporated. Serve the braised celery immediately.

4 servings

corn

There's only one foolproof way I know of to keep raccoons from stealing your corn. String a low voltage electric fence around the garden or corn patch, about 3 inches off the ground. Like the electric fencing used to keep horses and cows in check, it's not enough voltage to harm them, just enough to scare them. Keep the weeds under the fence pulled or clipped so that they don't touch the wire and ground it out. Then sit back and enjoy the fruits of your labor.

boiled corn

water
corn ears

Bring enough water to cover the ears by 1 1/2 inches to boil in an adequate size saucepan or kettle over high heat.

Meanwhile, husk the corn, removing the silk and trimming the stems and the tips of the ears.

Lower the corn into the boiling water and boil it, covered with lid ajar, 8 minutes from the moment all the corn is in the water, regardless of when the water returns to boil, adjusting the heat to keep the water slowly boiling. Drain it.

Note: You may want to drain the corn by lifting it from the water with a large pair of tongs; since a large kettle of corn could be very heavy.

corn off the cob

corn - 4 ears - (2 cups kernels)
4 Tablespoons butter
4 Tablespoons hot water - in a cup
1/2 teaspoon salt

Husk the corn, remove the silk and carefully cut the kernels from the cobs, separating them and crumbling them into a bowl.

(Try not to cut the kernels off the cobs any longer ahead of cooking time than is absolutely necessary. If they must wait, keep the kernels, covered, in a cool, not cold, place for no longer than 1 hour.)

Melt the butter in a frying pan (see utensils) over medium heat. Add the kernels and water and cook the corn, covered, 8 minutes, shaking the pan occasionally. Uncovered the pan, all water will have been absorbed. Sprinkle the corn with the salt, stir it around for 30 seconds and serve it immediately.

4 servings

Note: Corn off the cob should be as freshly picked as corn on the cob. It's a delightful surprise for anyone who has never tried it this way. If the pan is a little hot and some of the kernels brown a bit, it simply adds a tasty new dimension to the corn.

cucumbers

Cucumbers are members of the ubiquitous squash family. Like celery, and even more so, cucumbers are so often eaten raw (or pickled) that few people realize what an interesting flavor they have when cooked.

sautéed cucumbers

2 pounds 4 ounces cucumbers - 4 average, 7 to 8 inches long -
(4 heaping cups sliced)
2 Tablespoons cider vinegar
1 teaspoon superfine sugar
1/2 teaspoon salt
1/4 teaspoon freshly cracked black pepper
2 Tablespoons butter

Peel and cut the cucumbers in half lengthwise. Using a teaspoon, scoop out the seeds and cut the halves crosswise into 1/4 inch thick slices. Warm the vinegar with the sugar in a small saucepan over low heat.

Sauté the cucumbers, sprinkled with the salt and pepper in the butter in a frying pan (see utensils) over medium high heat, 2 minutes. Add the warm vinegar mixture and cook the cucumbers, stirring frequently to assist in even cooking, for 8 minutes, while gradually increasing the heat to high, until all the moisture has evaporated and the cucumbers are just tender. Serve the sautéed cucumbers immediately.

4 servings

eggplant

The ancient eggplant lends itself to a great variety of dishes, almost as many as its cousins the potato and the tomato.

buttered broiled eggplant

2 pounds eggplant - 2 medium
salt and pepper
6 or 7 Tablespoons butter

Fresh, shiny eggplant need not be peeled. Remove the stems and cut the eggplant, crosswise, into uniformly thick 3/4 inch slices, discarding the end slices.

Spread the slices out on a buttered aluminum baking sheet or use aluminum foil. (Other metals discolor eggplant.) Lightly sprinkle the slices with salt and pepper and lay a very thin slice of butter on each. Broil the eggplant in a preheated broiler, 6 inches from the heat source for 5 minutes. Remove the sheet from the broiler, using a metal spatula, turn the slices over, sprinkle them again with salt and pepper and lay a thin slice of butter on each. Return the sheet to the broiler for 5 minutes. Do not overcook the eggplant as it retains its heat and goes on cooking after it has been removed from the broiler. Slide the buttered eggplant onto a warm serving platter to serve.

4 servings

Note: If you like your eggplant well charred, broil it closer to the heat source. I like to sprinkle white wine vinegar on my serving!

fennel

Occasionally when buying fennel, someone in the market will say to me, "What do you do with that?" I hope that people will become more familiar with the interesting flavor of fennel, both raw and cooked.

braised fennel

3 pounds fennel with tops - 2 medium bulbs
1 teaspoon salt
4 Tablespoons butter
4 Tablespoons hot water - in a cup

Cut the green tops from, trim, and quarter the fennel bulbs lengthwise, reserving a handful of the leaves. Spray water down into the quarters to remove any soil then slice the quarters, lengthwise, into thin wedges.

Sauté the fennel wedges, sprinkled with the salt, in the butter, in a large frying pan (see utensils) over medium heat 5 minutes, while turning the wedges over with a spatula. Reduce the heat to low, remove the pan from the heat, add the hot water, cover the pan immediately and return it to the low heat for 10 minutes. Increase the heat to high, uncover the pan, add the reserved leaves and cook the fennel 2 minutes longer while turning it with the spatula until all the moisture has evaporated. Serve the braised fennel immediately.

4 servings

helianthus tuberosa

Helianthus tuberosa is a tuberous member of the sunflower family which is native to the north American continent. Commonly called Jerusalem artichokes, the word Jerusalem is supposed to be a corruption of the Italian word for sunflower. How the word artichoke became associated with them is a mystery. They are also sometimes called sunchokes. To end the confusion, I find that I must use their Latin name. Better yet, let's find out what the north American Indians called them and use that name.

buttered baked helianthus tuberosa

1 1/2 pounds helianthus tuberosa - 12 large
butter - divided
salt and pepper

Scrub the tubers under running water and dry them well. Pierce each with the tines of a fork to allow them to release moisture while baking. Thoroughly rub the tubers with some of the butter, lightly salt them all over and place them, well spaced, on a buttered baking dish. Bake the tubers in a preheated 400 degree oven for 40 to 45 minutes, depending on their size. (Slightly larger tubers can be put in the oven 5 minutes ahead of the others.) Turn the tubers over once or twice during the baking period so that they will be golden brown on all sides. Pierce them with a wooden toothpick to determine when they are done.

Serve the helianthus tuberosa immediately with plenty of additional butter, salt and pepper on the table.

4 servings

Note: Be sure to select firm tubers since helianthus tuberosa soften comparatively quickly.

kale

Kale is the last vegetable to succumb to winter. It can be seen poking up through the snow still green and still edible.

trimmed and washed kale

kale

Trim away the stem and thick center rib from each leaf. Wash the trimmed kale in a basin or sink full of cold water then drain it in a large colander.

blanched kale

kale
1 quart boiling water per 2 tightly packed cups trimmed kale
1/4 teaspoon salt per quart water

   Trim and wash the kale as directed. (See trimmed and washed kale.) In a large kettle set over high heat, blanch the kale in boiling salted water, uncovered, for 10 minutes from the moment it is all in the water, regardless of when the water returns to boil. Push the kale down into the water with a long-handled wooden spoon and adjust the heat to keep the water slowly boiling. Drain the kale into a colander.

buttered kale

1 1/2 pounds untrimmed kale - (9 tightly packed cups trimmed)
4 Tablespoons plus butter - divided
1/2 teaspoon salt
1/4 teaspoon freshly cracked black pepper
   Prepare and blanch the kale as directed. (See blanched kale.) Immediately turn the drained kale into a basin of cold water for 1 minute. Then turn it into a colander, place a saucer with a moderate weight upon it on the kale and allow it to drain for 30 minutes, turning it over several times during that period and pressing on it. Now, cut the compressed kale into slices about 1/4 inch thick.
   (Up to this point the kale can be prepared in advance, sealed in plastic and refrigerated as long as 24 hours, then brought to room temperature before continuing with the recipe.)
   Just before serving time, toss the kale in a colander with a wooden fork to separate it then carefully pull the compressed kale apart with your fingers. (It will heat better and look better.)
   At serving time, melt the 4 tablespoons of butter in a sauce pan over medium low heat. Add the kale, sprinkle with the salt and pepper and heat it, uncovered, about 4 minutes, tossing it gently with the wooden fork, until it is just heated through. Serve the buttered kale immediately with extra butter on the table.

4 servings

   Note: Do not warm for too long or it will discolor.

kohlrabi

I tasted kohlrabi for the first time when I grew it myself. Now, I wouldn't plant a garden without it. Its delicate flavor lies somewhere between that of cauliflower and potato. For full flavor, it must be freshly picked. Its smokey tasting leaves makes delicious greens.

braised kohlrabi

about 2 1/2 pounds kohlrabi, minus leaves -
(about 3 3/4 pounds with leaves) - 8 bulbs, 2 to 2 1/2 inches
in diameter - (4 heaping cups sliced)
1 teaspoon salt
1/4 teaspoon freshly cracked black pepper
2 Tablespoons plus 2 teaspoons butter
4 Tablespoons hot water - in a cup

Trim, peel and cut the kohlrabi bulbs in half lengthwise. Cut the halves, crosswise into half moon shaped slices, 1/8 inch thick.

Sauté the kohlrabi, sprinkled with the salt and pepper, in the butter in a frying pan (see utensils) over medium heat 3 minutes. Reduce the heat to low, remove the pan from the heat, add the hot water, cover the pan immediately and return it to the low heat for 8 minutes. Increase the heat to medium high, uncover the pan and cook the kohlrabi 1 minute longer, until all the moisture has evaporated. Serve the braised kohlrabi immediately

4 servings

mushrooms

Mushrooms are available all year round. (Thank goodness!) Transfer them to a roomy brown paper bag as soon as you get them home and store them refrigerated. Mushrooms will keep better in paper than tightly wrapped in plastic.

sautéed mushrooms

1 1/4 pounds mushrooms - medium, 1 1/2 inch in diameter caps -
(6 generous cups sliced)
1/2 teaspoon salt
1/4 teaspoon freshly cracked black pepper
3 Tablespoons butter

Trim the butt end of the mushroom stems and wipe the mushrooms with a damp cloth. Cut the stems off flush with the caps, then cut the stems, crosswise, into 1/4 inch thick slices.

Sauté the mushroom caps and sliced stems, sprinkled with the salt and pepper in the butter in a large frying pan (see utensils) over medium high heat, for about 8 minutes, while gradually increasing the heat to high until all the moisture has evaporated and the mushrooms just start to become golden. Serve the sautéed mushrooms immediately.

4 servings

okra

Be sure your okra pods have been picked young. A southern favorite, their mucilaginous quality thickens soups and stews.

fried okra

1 pound okra - about 80 small pods 1 1/2 to 2 1/2 inches long
4 Tablespoons peanut oil
4 Tablespoons butter
salt

Trim off the okra stems taking care not to cut into the pods. Wipe the pods with a damp cloth as you would mushrooms. (Do not rinse the okra as that encourages it to become gooey.)

Heat the oil and butter in a large frying pan (see utensils) over medium low heat. Add the okra, lightly sprinkle with salt and cook it, uncovered, for about 20 minutes, turning the pods individually with a small pair of wooden tongs or collectively with a spatula until they become brown and crisp on all sides. Serve the fried okra immediately.

4 servings

Note: This is an East Indian style of frying okra. The okra must be carefully tended, turning all the pods so that they brown evenly.

onions

"Consider the lilies of the fields how they grow—." Onions, scallions and their close relatives leeks, garlic, shallots and chives with their pretty little globular shaped lavender flowers all belong to the lily family.

peeled onions

small onions
boiling water

In a bowl, pour enough boiling water over the onions to cover them and allow them to stand 5 minutes. Drain them and cover them with cold water. Taking the onions out of the water, one at a time, trim and carefully peel them. If the onions are going to be cooking whole, run a wooden toothpick twice through the diameter of each onion at cross-angles. This will keep the center of the onion from popping out during cooking.

boiled onions

small onions
water
1/2 teaspoon salt per quart water

    Peel and prepare the onions as directed. (See peeled onions.) In an adequate size saucepan over high heat, bring to boil enough salted water to cover the onions by 1 1/2 inches. Add the onions and cook them, uncovered, 20 to 25 minutes from the moment they are in the water, regardless of when the water returns to boil, adjusting the heat to keep the water slowly boiling, until they are just tender when pierced with a wooden toothpick. Drain them.

buttered boiled onions

about 1 pound onions - 24 small, about 1 inch in diameter - (4 cups)
1 Tablespoons plus 1 teaspoon butter - at room temperature
salt and pepper to taste

    Prepare and boil the onions as directed. (See boiled onions.) In a warm serving dish, toss the hot onions with the butter, cut in pieces, the salt and pepper and serve them immediately.

4 servings

parsnips

    If you are growing parsnips yourself, leave some in the ground, covered with hay, all winter. The cold will turn the starch to sugar and when you dig them in the early spring you will find that they will have gained in both sweetness and flavor.

braised parsnips

1 pound parsnips - 5 or 6 medium - (3 cups cut)
1 Tablespoon fresh lemon juice
1 Tablespoon plus 1 teaspoon brown sugar
2 Tablespoons hot water
3/4 teaspoon white pepper
2 Tablespoons plus 2 teaspoons unsalted butter

Trim, peel and cut the parsnips crosswise into 1 1/2 inch long pieces. Quarter the pieces lengthwise then cut each quarter lengthwise into wedge shaped strips about 1/4 inch wide on the rounded side. Trim the core out of each strip and discard it. As they are trimmed, drop the parsnip strips into a bowl containing the lemon juice and enough cold water to cover them.

(The parsnips can be prepared several hours in advance up to this point. Cover the bowl and refrigerate it but bring the parsnips to room temperature before continuing the recipe.)

Drain and blot the parsnips strips dry on paper towels. In a cup, dissolve the sugar in hot water and reserve the mixture.

Sauté the parsnips, sprinkled with the salt and pepper in the butter in a frying pan (see utensils) over medium heat 2 minutes. Reduce the heat to low, remove the pan from the heat, add the reserved hot water mixture, cover the pan immediately and return it to the low heat for 2 minutes. Increase the heat to high, uncover the pan and cook the parsnips 1 minute longer stirring them gently with a wooden spatula until all the moisture has evaporated. Serve the braised parsnips immediately, they will not wait.

4 servings

Note: Pay close attention, braised parsnips can overcook easily!

peas

Peas are the first seeds to go into the ground in the spring, the first plants to break ground in their race to the top of the fence and the first summer vegetable of the season on the table. If you must buy yours, be sure that they have not been allowed to overdevelop.

steamed peas

unshelled peas

Shell the peas and steam them over already simmering water for about 10 minutes depending on their size. If your steamer is not very large (the little folding type) do not steam more than 2 cups at a time or they will not cook evenly.

buttered steamed peas

2 pounds unshelled peas (2 cups shelled)
1 Tablespoon plus 1 teaspoon butter - at room temperature
Salt and pepper to taste
Shell and steam the peas as directed. (See steamed peas.) In a warm serving dish toss the hot peas with the butter, cut in pieces, the salt and pepper and serve them, covered, immediately.

4 servings

snow peas

Edible podded snow peas are also sometimes called sugar peas. they develop so quickly on the vine that it's hard to keep up with them. Snow peas are best eaten when the pods are 1 1/2 to 2 inches long and the tiny peas are just barely visible.

braised snow peas

12 ounces snow peas - 1 1/2 to 2 inches long - (4 packed cups)
1/2 teaspoon salt

2 Tablespoons plus 2 teaspoons peanut oil
2 Tablespoons hot water - in a cup

Remove the stems and pull the little strings from each edge of the snow pea pods.

(Up to this point the snow peas can be prepared in advance, sealed in plastic and refrigerated as long as 24 hours, then brought to room temperature before continuing with the recipe.)

Sauté the snow peas, sprinkled with the salt, in the oil, in a large frying pan (see utensils) over medium high heat 1 minute, turning them over with a wooden spatula to coat them well with the oil. Remove the pan from the heat, add the hot water, cover the pan immediately and return it to the heat for 3 minutes, shaking the pan occasionally. Increase the heat to high, uncover the pan, and cook the snow peas 1 minute longer until all the moisture has evaporated. Serve the braised snow peas immediately.

4 servings

Note: Do not permit the snow peas to overcook, they must retain a certain crispness.

green bell peppers

It is obvious by their large cavity and blocky shape that Mother Nature designed green bell peppers specifically to be stuffed.

braised green bell peppers

1 1/2 pounds green bell peppers - 4 medium - (4 cups cut)
3/4 teaspoon salt
1/4 teaspoon celery salt
1/4 teaspoon freshly cracked black pepper
2 Tablespoons olive oil

Cut the bell peppers lengthwise into 3/4 inch thick slices. Core the slices, trimming away any white membrane. Then cut the rings into 3/4 inch squares.

Sauté the bell peppers, sprinkled with the salt, celery salt and black pepper in the oil, in a large frying pan (see utensils) over medium heat 2 minutes, turning them over to coat them well with the oil. Reduce the heat to low and cook the peppers, covered, for 8 minutes, stirring them once and shaking the pan a few times to keep them from sticking. Increase the heat to high, uncover the pan and cook the peppers about 2 minutes longer, turning them, until the edges just start to brown. Serve the braised green bell peppers immediately

4 servings

red bell peppers

Red bell peppers are, of course, fully ripe green bell peppers.

braised red bell peppers

1 1/2 pounds red bell peppers - 4 medium - (4 cups cut)
1 teaspoon salt
1/2 teaspoon freshly cracked black pepper
2 Tablespoons plus 2 teaspoons olive oil

Quarter the bell peppers lengthwise. Core them, trimming away any white membrane. Then cut the quarters lengthwise into strips 1/4 inch wide.

Sauté the bell peppers, sprinkled with the salt and black pepper in the oil, in a large frying pan (see utensils) over medium heat, 2 minutes, turning them over to coat them well with the oil. Reduce the heat to low and cook the peppers, covered, for 5 minutes, stirring them once and shaking the pan a few times to keep them from sticking. Increase the heat to high, uncover the pan and cook the peppers about 2 minutes longer, turning them. Serve the braised red bell peppers immediately.

4 servings

Note: Braised red bell peppers look best in a white serving dish.

peeled red bell peppers

red bell peppers

Large fully ripe peppers of the first quality peel the easiest. Quarter the peppers lengthwise then core them, trimming away any white membrane. Lay the quartered peppers, cut side down, on an ungreased cookie sheet. Flatten them, despite the fact that they will split and tear a bit, they will blister more evenly and the skins will peel off more easily.

Roast the peppers, 3 inches from the heat source, under a preheated broiler for 10 to 15 minutes until they become well blistered and charred. Using a metal spatula, immediately transfer the peppers to a paper bag. Close the bag tight and leave the peppers in it for 15 minutes. Now the peppers are ready to peel, slip the skins off with your fingers, they should come off easily.

sweet italian frying peppers

The sweet Italian frying pepper is a medium size, tapered, yellowish green pepper. It resembles the California anaheim or green chili in size but its flesh, when cooked, is always sweet and mild.

braised sweet italian frying peppers

1 1/2 pounds sweet Italian frying peppers - 12 medium, 2 to 2 1/2 inches in diameter at the top and 4 to 5 inches long
2 Tablespoons plus 2 teaspoons olive oil
1 teaspoon salt

If you select frying peppers which are all the same shade of green, they will all cook in the same amount of time. Cut the peppers in half lengthwise then core them, trimming away any white membrane.

Heat the oil in a large frying pan (see utensils) over very low heat for about 5 minutes. Then lay the pepper halves in the pan, cut side down, in a single layer if possible. Cover the pan and cook the peppers 15 minutes. Uncover the pan, turn the peppers over so that they are cut side up and sprinkle them with the salt. Continue to cook the peppers, uncovered now, 10 minutes longer while gently flattening them with a spatula. At this point, most of the pepper halves will be cooked, transfer them to a serving dish. Continue to cook any remaining peppers, transferring them to the dish when done. If after 5 minutes 1 or 2 peppers yet remain, simply turn off the heat, cover the pan and allow them to finish cooking in the warm pan another few minutes. The braised sweet Italian frying peppers are best served just warm rather than hot.

4 servings

Note: This is another dish in which my 11 1/2 by 14 1/2 inch electric griddle is put to good use.

potatoes

Potatoes are the most versatile and perhaps the most popular of all vegetables. There are two principal types of potato, the mealy type for baking and deep frying and the waxy type for boiling and pan frying. Not surprisingly, home grown potatoes are more flavorful than store bought and it's so easy to grow them. Simply spread a 3 or 4 inch layer of hay on the ground, distribute the seed potatoes on it, then cover them with about 8 inches more hay. Check them during the summer to make sure they stay well covered. That's all there is to it, no digging at all, and what an easy, clean, bountiful harvest.

steamed potatoes

boiling potatoes - little new, 1 to 1 1/4 inches in diameter or small

Scrub the potatoes clean under running water. Steam them either peeled or unpeeled, as directed by the need or recipe, over already simmering water. Peeled potatoes take 5 minutes less to steam than unpeeled potatoes. Little, new potatoes will take about 15 or 20 minutes and small potatoes will take about 25 or 30 minutes. Pierce the potatoes with a wooden toothpick to determine when they are just tender.

buttered steamed potatoes

about 1 pound 4 ounces boiling potatoes - 20 little new, 1 to 1 1/4 inches in diameter - (4 heaping cups whole)
butter
salt and pepper

Do not peel but scrub and steam the potatoes as directed. (See steamed potatoes.) Serve the hot potatoes wrapped in a clean white linen napkin on a serving platter. Have plenty of butter, salt and pepper on the table.

4 servings

Note: The red skinned variety of potatoes look especially effective wrapped in the white linen napkin.

boiled potatoes

boiling potatoes - (see note)
water
1/2 teaspoon salt per quart water

Scrub the potatoes clean under running water. The potatoes can be boiled either peeled or unpeeled as the need or recipe indicate. Peeled potatoes will take a little less time to cook than unpeeled potatoes. In an adequate size saucepan over high heat, bring to boil enough salted water to cover the potatoes by 1 1/2 inches. Add the potatoes and cook them, covered with lid slightly ajar, counting the time form the moment they are in the water, regardless of when the water returns to boil, adjusting the heat to keep the water slowly boiling, until they are just tender when pierced with a wooden skewer or toothpick. Drain the potatoes. Return them to the empty pan, set over low heat, and "dry them out," covered, for 2 to 3 minutes while shaking the pan constantly.

Note: Whole, unpeeled small, 3 ounce potatoes will take 30 to 35 minutes, medium, 6 ounce potatoes, 40 to 45 minutes and large, 9 ounce potatoes, 50 to 55 minutes to cook.

buttered boiled potatoes

1 1/2 pounds boiling potatoes - 8 small or 6 medium or 1 pound 11 ounces
boiling potatoes - 3 large
butter
salt and pepper

Prepare and boil the potatoes as directed. (See boiled potatoes.) The small potatoes are served in their skins, the medium potatoes are peeled after they are boiled. (Hold them in a pot holder to peel them rather than disfigure them by piercing them with a fork to hold them.) The large potatoes are peeled and quartered before they are boiled. In which case, adjust the time accordingly. Simply serve the small, medium or large hot boiled potatoes in a warm, covered serving dish along with plenty of butter, salt and pepper on the table.

4 servings

baked potatoes

baking potatoes

Be sure to select mature baking potatoes, they bake mealy and fluffy the way baked potatoes should be. Scrub the potatoes under running water and dry them well. Pierce them each a couple of times with the tines of a fork to allow them to release moisture while baking. Bake the potatoes in a preheated 425 degree oven for 1 hour. Pierce them with a wooden skewer to determine when they are done.

buttered baked potatoes

3 pounds baking potatoes - 4 extra large, 12 ounces each
butter - divided
salt and pepper

Prepare and bake the potatoes as directed. (See baked potatoes.) When they are done, using a knife, make a lengthwise slash, about 3 inches long in the skin of each potato. Press the sides of the potatoes slightly to push the flesh up out of the skin a bit. Insert a large chunk of the butter in each potato and serve them immediately along with plenty of additional butter and salt and pepper on the table.

4 servings

fried potatoes

2 pounds boiling potatoes - 4 medium large - (5 cups diced)
1 1/2 teaspoon salt
1/8 teaspoon freshly cracked black pepper
4 Tablespoons corn oil
4 Tablespoons butter

Peel and cut the potatoes into 3/8 inch dice, dropping them into a bowl of cold water to cover. When they are all in the water allow them to stand 5 minutes then drain, rinse and drain them. Cover them again with cold water and allow the potatoes to stand 1 hour. Drain them well again and blot them dry on paper towels using more towels.

Sauté the diced potatoes, sprinkled with the salt and pepper, in the oil and butter, uncovered, in a large frying pan (see utensils) over medium high heat. Using a spatula stir the potatoes almost constantly for about 15 minutes until they are lightly browned. Serve the fried potatoes immediately.

4 servings

sweet potatoes

Can you tell the difference between a sweet potatoes and a yam. I've had it explained to me a number of times but I fail to grasp the full particulars. A yam is darker in color than a sweet potato—but not always! One is longer, the other more slender, but which? At any rate, in cooking, they are interchangeable. As far as I'm concerned there's nothing quite as delectable as a baked sweet potato with lots of butter on it. Or do I mean yam?

baked sweet potatoes

sweet potatoes

Scrub the sweet potatoes under running water and dry them well. Pierce them each a couple of times with the tines of a fork to allow them to release moisture while baking. Bake the sweet potatoes in a preheated 375 degree oven for 45 minutes to 1 hour, depending upon their size. Pierce them with a wooden skewer to determine when they are done.

buttered baked sweet potatoes

3 pounds sweet potatoes - 4 medium large
butter - divided
salt and pepper

Prepare the sweet potatoes as directed. (See baked sweet potatoes.) When they are done, using a knife, make a lengthwise slash, about 3 inches long in the skin of each potato. Press the sides of the potatoes slightly to push the flesh up out of the skin a bit. Insert a large chunk of butter in each sweet potato and serve them immediately along with plenty of additional butter and salt and pepper on the table.

4 servings

rutabaga

Rutabaga gives an excellent return on your investment. Just put the tiny seed into the ground and in about 90 days you have something approaching the size of a basket ball.

braised rutabaga

1 pound rutabaga - 1 small - (4 moderate handfuls cut)
1/2 teaspoon salt
1/4 teaspoon freshly cracked black pepper
2 Tablespoons plus 2 teaspoons butter
3 Tablespoons hot water - in a cup

Trim, peel, and cut the rutabaga in half lengthwise. Lay the halves cut side down and cut them, crosswise, into 1/2 inch thick slices. Then cut the slices into long fingers 1/2 inch wide.

Sauté the rutabaga, sprinkled with the salt and pepper, in the butter in a large frying pan (see utensils) over medium heat 3 minutes, turning the rutabaga to coat it well with the butter. (You may have to use 2 spatulas.) Reduce the heat to low, remove the pan from the heat, add the hot water, cover the pan immediately and return it to the low heat for 8 minutes, giving the pan a good shake once or twice. Increase the heat to high, uncover the pan and cook the rutabaga 1 minute longer until all the moisture has evaporated. Serve the braised rutabaga immediately.

4 servings

Note: In this case hands give a more accurate measurement than cups.

spinach

There is an art to growing spinach. Despite the fact that it is always in abundant supply in the market, it is finicky about growing conditions and must have cool weather. I haven't had all that much luck with it. Someone told me to plant the rows running north and south. I'll have to try that next time.

washed and trimmed spinach

spinach

Thoroughly wash the spinach, in a basin or sink full of cold water. Remove the spinach from the water. Drain and clean the basin or sink. Repeat the process 2 or 3 times depending on how sandy the spinach is. Then drain the spinach in a large colander. Tear the stems from the leaves and tear the leaves into bit size pieces.

blanched spinach

spinach
1 quart boiling water per 2 packed cups trimmed spinach
1/4 teaspoons salt per quart water

Wash and trim the spinach as directed. (See washed and trimmed spinach.) In a large kettle set over high heat, blanch the spinach in boiling, salted water, uncovered, for 3 minutes from the moment it is all in the water, regardless of when the water returns to boil. Push the spinach down into the water with a long-handled, wooden spoon and adjust the heat to keep the water slowly boiling. Drain the spinach into a colander.

buttered spinach

2 pounds untrimmed spinach - (16 packed cups trimmed)
4 Tablespoons plus butter - divided
1/2 teaspoon salt
1/4 teaspoon freshly cracked black pepper

Prepare and blanch the spinach as directed. (See blanched spinach.) Immediately turn the drained spinach into a basin of cold water for 1 minute. Then turn it into a colander, place a saucer with a moderate weight upon it on the spinach and allow it to drain for 1 hour, turning it over 2 or 3 times during that period.

(Up to this point the spinach can be prepared in advance, sealed in plastic and refrigerated as long as 24 hours, then brought to room temperature before continuing with the recipe.)

Just before serving time, pull the compressed spinach apart with your fingers dropping it into a colander. (Slightly time consuming but it makes the best looking spinach ever seen on a plate.)

At serving time, melt the 4 tablespoons of butter in a saucepan over medium low heat. Add the spinach, sprinkle it with the salt and pepper and heat it, uncovered, 4 or 5 minutes, tossing it gently with a wooden fork until it is just heated through. Serve the buttered spinach, immediately, with extra butter on the table.

4 servings

scalloped squash

Scalloped squash are also sometimes called pattypan or cymling. They have a lovely delicate flavor and are best picked when no more than 4 inches in diameter. Their creamy white color and pretty scalloped edging make them so attractive and distinctive looking that it seems a shame to cut them up.

whipped scalloped squash

3 pounds scalloped squash - 6 small, about 4 inches in diameter -

(9 cups sliced)

3/4 teaspoon salt
pinch white pepper
4 Tablespoons butter
1 teaspoon honey

Remove the stems and cut the squash in half lengthwise but do not bother to remove the seeds or membrane. Then slice the halves very thin.

In a large, heavy saucepan, over medium low heat, cook the squash, sprinkled with the salt and pepper in the butter and honey, covered, for 25 minutes, stirring occasionally. Uncover the pan and increase the heat to high. Stir and mash the squash frequently with a spatula for about 20 minutes, being careful not to allow it to scorch and lowering the heat a little as necessary, until almost all the moisture has evaporated and the squash is thick. Serve the whipped scalloped squash immediately.

4 servings

yellow squash

The name "summer squash" is sometimes singularly applied to yellow squash. However, that name also often encompasses both the zucchini and scalloped squash tribes and rightly so for all are summer squash. Yellow squash is available in both a straight neck and crook neck variety.

sautéed yellow squash

2 1/4 pounds straight neck yellow squash - about 6 small, 6 inches long -
(6 cups cut)
1/2 teaspoon salt
3 Tablespoons plus 2 teaspoons butter - at room temperature - divided
1/8 teaspoon freshly cracked black pepper

Trim the squash and cut it crosswise into pieces 1 1/2 inches long. Quarter the pieces, trimming away any seeds and membrane, and cut them into little wedge shaped matchsticks about 3/16 inch wide on the rounded side.

Sauté the squash, sprinkled with the salt in 2 tablespoons plus 2 teaspoons of the butter in a large frying pan over medium high heat for 3 minutes while turning it over with a spatula. Increase the heat to high and sauté 2 minutes longer until the moisture has evaporated and the squash is tender but still firm.

In a warm serving dish, toss the squash with 1 tablespoon of the butter, cut in pieces and the pepper and serve the sautéed yellow squash immediately.

4 servings

zucchini squash

Zucchini are the delicious green squash with the Italian name. There is a striped variety called cocozelle. Zucchini are best picked when they are about 6 inches long, but are famous for quickly becoming overgrown.

sautéed zucchini squash

1 pound zucchini squash - 4 small, about 6 inches long

2 Tablespoons olive oil
salt
1/4 teaspoon freshly cracked black pepper - divided
1/2 teaspoon superfine sugar - divided
1/2 teaspoon vinegar - divided
1/2 teaspoon dried basil

Trim the squash and cut it lengthwise, into 6 or 7 slices, to within about 1/4 inch of the stem end so that all the slices remain attached.

Heat the oil in a large frying pan (see utensils) over medium high heat. Lay the zucchini in the pan and using a spatula, gently spread them out like little fans. Lightly sprinkle them with salt, half the pepper, half the sugar and half the vinegar. Cook the zucchini for 7 minutes, then carefully grasping the stem ends, with a pair of tongs, flip them over and spread them out again. Sprinkle again lightly with salt and the remaining pepper, sugar and vinegar and the basil, crushing it and cook the zucchini 7 minutes longer. The edges of each slices should be golden and crisp. Carefully transfer the zucchini to a warm serving platter, fanning them out, and serve the sautéed zucchini immediately.

4 servings

acorn squash

Dark green acorn squash are the smallest of the winter squash and so easy to grow. Serve them cut crosswise to show off their distinctive ribbed shape.

buttered baked acorn squash

3 pounds acorn squash - 3 small, 1 pound each
salt and pepper
butter

Remove the stem then cut off and discard a thin slice from both the stem and blossom end of each squash. Cut the remainder of the squash, crosswise, into slices about 5/8 inch thick. Scrape the seeds and membrane out of the center of each slice. Then neatly cut a hole in the center of the solid end slices so that all the slices will be uniform. The yield should be about 6 slices per squash.

Lay the slices in a well buttered jellyroll pan. Lightly sprinkle them with the salt and pepper and dot each slice with butter. Bake the squash in a preheated 375 degree oven for 20 minutes. Using a metal spatula, turn the slices over, and again, sprinkle them lightly with salt and pepper and dot them with butter. Bake the squash 15 minutes longer or until it is just tender when pierced with a wooden toothpick. Arrange the slices in an overlapping pattern on a warm serving platter and serve the acorn squash immediately.

4 servings

butternut squash

They used to call butternut squash, banjo squash. Which makes sense because in its more natural state it does resemble a banjo. Today the butternut squash has been bred to make it so stocky that it almost looks square. However, it contains a large portion of thick sweet flesh.

baked butternut squash

butternut squash

Cut the squash in half lengthwise, scrape out the seeds and membrane and lay the squash, cut side down on a buttered jellyroll pan. Bake the squash in a preheated 375 degree oven for 45 minutes. Pierce it with a wooden skewer to determine when it is just tender. Use a metal spatula to remove the squash from the pan.

buttered baked butternut squash
(That's a mouthful!)

4 pounds butternut squash - 2 small, 2 pound each
butter
salt and pepper

Prepare and bake the squash as directed. (See baked butternut squash.) Serve the butternut squash, cut side up, along with plenty of butter, salt and pepper on the table. Incidentally, the skin of baked butternut squash can be eaten just like the skin of a baked potato.

4 servings

Note: For an accompaniment vegetable, it's sometimes fun to serve a very large gourd shaped baked butternut squash with a long curved neck, if you can find one. Present it, cut in half lengthwise, on a large platter to display its dramatic shape. Allow 1 pound per serving and cut the squash into pieces at the table to serve it.

hubbard squash

Hubbard squash always look like prehistoric monsters, especially the nubby so-called blue variety. There are blue, green, and gold varieties of Hubbard Squash. They can weigh as much as 20 pounds, but require a long growing season, 4 months of hot weather to develop their sweet dry flesh.

baked hubbard squash

Hubbard squash

Select a well developed squash that weights at least 13 pounds and is heavy for its size. A well developed Hubbard squash will have flesh that is at least 1 to 1 1/2 inches thick. Cutting them up can present a problem. A frozen food saw is the ideal implement for the job. Cut the squash in half, scrape out the seeds and membrane then cut the squash into pieces of the desired size. Bake the squash pieces, cut side down, on a buttered jellyroll pan in a preheated 400 degree oven for from 60 to 90 minutes. The thicker pieces near the stem end will take the longer cooking time. Pierce the squash with a wooden skewer to determine when it is just tender. Use a metal spatula to remove the squash from the pan.

buttered baked hubbard squash

6 pounds Hubbard squash - 4 pieces, 1 1/2 pounds each
butter
salt and pepper

Prepare and bake the squash as directed. (See baked Hubbard squash.) Serve the Hubbard squash, cut side up, along with plenty of butter, salt and pepper on the table.

swiss chard

If you don't have luck growing spinach, try Swiss chard. It's infallible. It grows right through summer heat and keeps going 'til snowfall. Why don't commercial growers make more use of it? Unlike most other greens, the stems of the Swiss chard plant are as desirable as its dark green leaves.

cut and washed swiss chard

Swiss chard

First, slit only the leaves of the Swiss chard in half lengthwise. Then cut the leaves and the stems, crosswise, into 1/4 inch thick slices. Wash the cut Swiss chard in a basin or sink full of cold water then drain it in a large colander. (Cutting the Swiss chard before it is washed will make it much easier to handle. It may lose some vitamins but it sure saves the cook.)

blanched swiss chard

Swiss chard
1 quart boiling water per 2 packed cups cut Swiss chard
1/4 teaspoon salt per quart water

Cut and wash the Swiss chard as directed. (See cut and washed Swiss chard.) In a large kettle set over high heat, blanch the Swiss chard in boiling, salted water, uncovered, for 5 minutes from the moment it is all in the water, regardless of when the water returns to boil. Push the Swiss chard down into the water with a long-handled wooden spoon and adjust the heat to keep the water slowly boiling. Drain the Swiss chard into a colander.

buttered swiss chard

1 1/2 pounds Swiss chard - (9 packed cups cut)
4 Tablespoons plus butter - divided
1/2 teaspoon salt
1/4 teaspoon freshly cracked black pepper

Prepare and blanch the Swiss chard as directed. (See blanched Swiss chard.) Immediately turn the drained Swiss chard into a basin of cold water for 1 minute. Then, turn it into a colander, place a saucer with a moderate weight upon it on the Swiss chard and allow it to drain for 30 minutes turning it over 2 or 3 times during that period.

(Up to this point, the Swiss chard can be prepared in advance, sealed in plastic, and refrigerated as long as 24 hours, then brought to room temperature before continuing with the recipe.)

Just before serving time, toss the compressed Swiss chard in a colander, using a wooden fork to separate it.

At serving time melt the 4 tablespoons of butter in a saucepan over medium low heat. Add the Swiss chard, sprinkle it with the salt and pepper and warm it, uncovered, 4 or 5 minutes, gently tossing it with the wooden fork until it is just heated through. Serve the buttered Swiss chard, immediately, with extra butter on the table.

4 servings

tomatoes

I could easily rhapsodize for five or six pages about the pleasures of the tomato. Though it is available in the market all year, still it remains the most seasonal of vegetables. Nothing can quite replace the flavor of a fresh summer tomato. Interestingly, however, it is the most universally accepted of all canned vegetables. From paste to juice, we just can't do without it.

peeled tomatoes

tomatoes

Place several tomatoes in a large strainer or similar utensil. Plunge the strainer into an adequate size kettle of boiling water for about 20 seconds. Over ripe tomatoes will take slightly less. Lift the strainer out of the boiling water and immediately plunge it into an adequate size basin of cold water for 1 minute. Drain the tomatoes, remove the stem buttons with a small sharp knife and peel them.

If you are just peeling 1 or 2 tomatoes, a small saucepan and a slotted spoon will be adequate utensils.

seeded tomatoes

tomatoes

Cut unpeeled or peeled tomatoes in half crosswise and using the handle of a teaspoon, scoop the seeds out of their little cavities. (Drop the seeds into a fine strainer, set over a bowl. Save the flavorful juices that will drain way from the seeds for a bouillon soup. See bouillon soups.)

roast tomatoes

1 pound tomatoes -4 small, 2 1/2 to 3 inches in diameter
olive oil
salt and pepper

Select ripe but firm tomatoes and have them at room temperature. Peel the tomato and remove the stem buttons as directed. (See peeled tomatoes.) Smear each tomato with a little olive oil and dust them with salt and pepper. Set the tomatoes, stem side down, on a lightly buttered pie plate or oven proof serving dish. Bake the tomatoes in a preheated 325 degree oven for 20 minutes. Serve the roast tomatoes immediately.

4 servings

stewed tomatoes

2 quarts home canned tomatoes - (see home canned tomatoes)
2 tablespoons olive oil
1 teaspoon honey
salt to taste - optional (see note)
1/8 teaspoon freshly cracked black pepper
1/4 teaspoon dried thyme

Turn the tomatoes into a colander set over a bowl and allow them to drain 30 minutes. Transfer the drained juices to a large saucepan set over high heat. Add the oil, honey, optional salt and the pepper. When the liquid boils, reduce the heat to medium and slowly boil it, uncovered, until the juice is reduced by half, stirring occasionally. Now, reduce the heat to low, add the drained tomatoes plus anymore juice that drained out of them and the thyme, crushing it, to the pan. Warm the tomatoes, covered, for about 10 minutes, giving them a gentle stir once or twice, until they are heated through. To serve, divide the tomatoes among 4 warm 1 1/2 cup bowls.

4 servings

Note: You will have already salted the tomatoes to some degree when you canned them.

home canned tomatoes

tomatoes - medium to small
salt

Use either narrow or wide mouthed 1 quart canning jars that have 2 piece metal caps with rubber compound around the edge of the disc part of the cap or that have separate rubber rings. In either case, be sure to use brand new discs and new rubber rings too, if you are using that kind of cap. Check to make sure that there are no cracks or chips around the mouths of the jars and wash them thoroughly. Leave the jars in clean hot water until they are ready to be filled.

For a canner all you need is a big, old fashioned, inexpensive, water bath kettle equipped with a jar rack. Fill the kettle half full of water and set it over medium heat so that the water will be hot but not boiling when the jars are lowered into it.

Allow about 2 pounds of tomatoes per quart jar, equalling 4 or 5 medium to small tomatoes plus 1 medium or 2 small tomatoes to be used for juice. Be sure to select ripe, firm, unblemished tomatoes. Peel them as directed. (See peeled tomatoes.) Set aside the tomatoes to be used for juice and coarsely chop them. Then liquify them 2 or 3 at a time, briefly in the blender or processor and reserve the juice in a large pitcher. Skim off any foam. Cut the rest of the tomatoes in half lengthwise and tightly pack them into the drained jars, without crushing them. Add 1/2 teaspoon of salt to each jar then pour in enough of the reserved juice to come to within 1/2 inch of the top of the jar. Run a rubber spatula down against the inside of the jars to release air bubbles. Wipe the rim and threads of the jars with a clean damp cloth, lay the rubber rings on the rims of the jars if you are using them and, in either case, screw the 2 piece caps on tight.

Set the jars in the rack and lower it into the water bath. If necessary, pour enough additional hot water into the water bath so that the jars are covered by 1 1/2 inches of water. Cover the kettle, increase the heat to high and when the water boils, start counting the time. Then adjust the heat to keep the water slowly boiling and boil the jars 45 minutes if you live at an altitude of up to 1,000 feet above sea level. For higher altitudes, add 2 minutes boiling time for each additional 1,000 feet above sea level. In other words if you live at 1,000 feet, boil the jars 47 minutes and so on. (See jar or water bath manufacturer's instructions.) Carefully remove the jars from the water and allow them to cool for 12 hours, away from drafts. The metal lids will make popping noises as they cool which means they are sealing themselves. After a jar has cooled, if you can still press the center of the lid down with your finger, it has not sealed, (hardly ever happens) in which case refrigerate the jar and use it soon. Store the jars of home canned tomatoes in a cool dark place.

Note: A recipe for the simple process of canning tomatoes hardly needs to be written out again, the world abounds with them. However, few people take the time to can anymore and they're missing out on a flavor that commercially canned tomatoes just don't have. You'll find that canning tomatoes is a very satisfying accomplishment. So much the more if you have grown the tomatoes yourself.

white turnips

The flavor of white turnips is ambiguous. It can be either mild or strong. Don't overlook using tender young turnip tops for greens.

braised white turnips

1 pound white turnips - 4 medium - (4 loosely packed cups cut)
3 Tablespoons light cream
1 teaspoon superfine sugar
1 teaspoon salt
1/4 scant teaspoon freshly cracked black pepper
1 Tablespoon plus 1 teaspoon butter

Trim, peel, and cut the turnips crosswise into 3/16 inch thick slices. Cut the slices into matchsticks 3/16 inch wide. (There will seem to be too great a volume for 4 servings but turnips cook down.) Warm the cream and sugar in a small saucepan over low heat.

Sauté the turnips, sprinkled with salt and pepper, in the butter, in a large frying pan (see utensils) over medium heat 2 minutes. Reduce the heat to low, remove the pan from the heat, add the warm , sweetened cream, cover the pan immediately and return it to the low heat for 2 1/2 minutes, shaking the pan once or twice. Increase the heat to high, uncover the pan and cook the turnips 1 minute longer until all the moisture has evaporated. Serve the braised white turnips immediately.

4 servings

Note: Pay close attention, turnips overcook easily.

GRAINS PASTA
DRIED SHELLED BEANS

There are nine grains in common use today. Rice, wheat, rye, buckwheat, millet, oats, barley, wild rice and corn. Included here are the basic methods for cooking the grains plus a very simple pilaf recipe for each grain with the exception of corn. For corn, there is a tasty little dish with southwestern overtones, that uses corn meal to be served in place of a pilaf. The corn dish and each pilaf has been mentioned at least once in the menu suggestions. But any of these dishes can be used in almost any dinner, at your discretion. They make light meals more substantial and entrées go farther. Also included are all the basic pasta making recipes as well as a buttered noodle recipe. The last of which is the quickest and easiest meal stretcher of them all when extra guests arrive. Grains are wonderful staples to have on hand, all of them.

This section also contains directions for soaking and boiling dried shelled beans plus a recipe for refried beans. Refried beans can be served in exactly the same way as pilafs and noodles - as meal stretchers.

barley

buckwheat

corn

millet

oats

rice

wild rice

rye

wheat

pasta

dried shelled beans

barley

Hopefully, if you buy barley in the natural food store it will only have been lightly hulled and retain some color and some nutrients. Most commercial barley has been ground repeatedly to remove all the hull and unfortunately most of the nutrients and is called "pearled" barley.

steamed barley

3 cups water
1/2 teaspoon salt
1 1/3 cups barley - about 9 1/2 ounces

Bring the water with the salt to boil in a saucepan over high heat. Sprinkle in the barley. When the water returns to boil reduce the heat to low and simmer the barley, covered, 15 minutes. Drain the barley into a steamer.

Bring 1 inch of water to simmer in a saucepan over medium heat. Set the barley in the steamer over it and steam the barley, covered with a trimmed piece of paper towel and lid, 15 minutes.

4 cups

barley pilaf

1/4 cup cashews
parsley leaves - (2 Tablespoons chopped)
4 cups steamed barley - cold - (see steamed barley)
1 teaspoon salt
1 teaspoon celery salt
1/4 teaspoon freshly cracked black pepper
2 Tablespoons olive oil
2 Tablespoons butter

Using a heavy knife, chop the cashews small and in a dry pan over medium heat, toast them, stirring 3 minutes until they are golden. Remove them from the pan immediately and reserve them.

Chop the parsley fine and reserve it.

Warm the barley, sprinkled with the salt, celery salt and pepper in the oil and butter in a large frying pan (see utensils), uncovered, over low heat until it is heated through. Add the reserved nuts and parsley, heat 2 minutes longer and serve the barley pilaf immediately.

4 to 6 servings

buckwheat

Did you know that buckwheat belongs to the rhubarb family? It's distinctive flavor is a great favorite in Eastern Europe.

steamed buckwheat

1 egg
1 1/4 cups buckwheat groats (whole grain buckwheat) - about 8 ounces
1/2 teaspoon salt
1 1/2 cups boiling water

In a bowl, using a fork, beat the egg until it is light, then stir the buckwheat into it. Transfer the mixture to a large dry frying pan (see utensils), over medium heat. Using a metal spatula, stir the buckwheat constantly for 3 minutes or until each grain becomes dry and separate. Do not allow the mixture to scorch. Reduce the heat to low and remove the pan from the heat. Add the salt to the boiling water, pour the boiling water into the pan (careful of steam) and cover the pan immediately. Return the pan to the low heat and cook the buckwheat 10 minutes. Remove the pan from the heat and allow it to stand, covered, 10 minutes. Uncover the pan and gently stir the buckwheat with a fork.

4 cups

Note: Buckwheat is graded into 3 sizes, fine, medium and coarse. For the recipes in this book the medium size is preferred. Buckwheat is available both unroasted and lightly roasted. Roasting intensifies the flavor. Roasted buckwheat is a medium russet color. Of the two, roasted buckwheat is the more commonly available, or at least more popular, and the word roasted is generally dropped. It is understood that the recipes in this book call for the roasted variety. If you find yourself with white, which is a plain tan color, unroasted buckwheat and want to roast it, spread the grain out in one uncrowded layer on a jellyroll or pizza pan and roast the buckwheat in a preheated 275 degree oven 20 minutes, stirring it around every 5 minutes until the color of the grain has deepened. Do not let it get too dark. Remove the roasted buckwheat from the pan immediately.

Incidently, buckwheat is frequently listed under the name Kasha.

buckwheat pilaf

1/4 cup roasted, peeled hazelnuts - (see hazelnuts)
parsley leaves - (2 Tablespoons chopped)
4 cups steamed buckwheat - cold - (see steamed buckwheat)
1/2 teaspoon salt
1/2 teaspoon celery salt
1/4 teaspoon freshly cracked black pepper
4 Tablespoons olive oil

Using a heavy knife, chop the hazelnuts small and reserve them. Chop the parsley fine and reserve it.

Warm the buckwheat, sprinkled with the salt, celery salt and pepper in the oil in a large frying pan (see utensils), uncovered, over low heat until it is heated through. Add the reserved nuts and parsley, heat 2 minutes longer and serve the buckwheat pilaf immediately.

4 to 6 servings

corn the grain

Corn is the only grain we also eat as a vegetable. In its dried form, corn does not lend itself well to a pilaf in the way that other grains do but more than makes up for it by its great versatility.

coquillages

1/4 cup roasted pepitas - (see sunflower and pumpkin seeds)
3 cups cold water - divided
1 Tablespoons plus 1 teaspoon honey
1 teaspoon salt
1 teaspoon celery salt
1 teaspoon ground cumin
1/2 teaspoon ground turmeric
1/4 teaspoon cayenne
1 cup stoneground yellow corn meal - about 5 1/2 ounces
4 Tablespoons butter

Using a heavy knife, coarsely chop the pepitas and reserve them.
Bring 2 cups of the water with the honey, salt, celery salt, cumin, turmeric and cayenne to boil in a medium size, heavy saucepan over high heat. In a spouted, 2 cup measuring cup, stir 1 cup of the water into the corn meal. Then slowly stir the slurry into the boiling water. When the corn meal mixture returns to boil, reduce the heat to medium low and place a heat diffuser under the pan. Cook the corn meal, uncovered, while it slowly "erupts", for 30 minutes, stirring it frequently with a long handled wooden spoon, smoothing it out.
Remove the pan from the heat and stir in the butter and the reserved pepitas.
Spoon the mixture into 4 scallop shells, roundly smoothing it and allow the corn meal to cool completely and become firm.
(Up to this point the coquillages can be prepared 2 or 3 days in advance, wrapped in paper towels, sealed in plastic and refrigerated. In which case, unwrap them and bring them to room temperature before continuing with the recipe.)

At serving time, place the shells on a baking sheet, for convenience, and broil them, 6 inches from the heat source under a preheated broiler for about 10 minutes until they become golden brown and slightly charred around the edges. Using 2 large spoons, transfer the shells to a serving platter and serve the coquillages immediately.

4 servings

Note: Scallop shells can be found at kitchenware stores --- or on the beach!

millet

This nutritious but unassuming little grain is delicious mixed with toasted sesame seeds.

steamed millet

1 cup minus 2 Tablespoons millet - 7 ounces
1/2 teaspoon salt
1 3/4 cups boiling water

In a large, dry frying pan (see utensils), over medium heat, toast the millet, stirring constantly, for 5 minutes until it starts to color, become fragrant and pop.

Reduce the heat to low and remove the pan from the heat. Add the salt to the boiling water, then pour the boiling water into the pan. (Careful of steam.) Return the pan to the low heat and cook the millet, tightly covered, 25 minutes. Remove the pan from the heat and allow the millet to stand, still tightly covered, 10 minutes. Uncover the pan. The millet will be dry and fluffy.

4 cups

millet pilaf

2 Tablespoons sesame seeds
parsley leaves - (2 Tablespoons chopped)
4 cups steamed millet - cold - (see steamed millet)
1 teaspoon celery salt
1/4 teaspoon freshly cracked black pepper
6 Tablespoons butter

Toast the sesame seeds in a dry pan over medium heat, stirring for 3 minutes until they take color and become fragrant. Remove them from the pan immediately and reserve them.

Chop the parsley fine and reserve it.

Warm the millet, sprinkled with the celery salt and the pepper, in the butter in a large frying pan (see utensils), uncovered, over low heat until it is heated through. Add the reserved sesame seeds and parsley, heat 2 minutes longer and serve the millet pilaf immediately.

4 to 6 servings

oats

Familiar as a breakfast cereal and famous for sticking to your ribs, oats make a wonderfully chewy pilaf.

steamed oats

3 cups water
1/2 teaspoon salt
1 1/3 cups oat groats (whole grain oats) - about 9 1/2 ounces.

Bring the water with the salt to boil in a saucepan over high heat. Sprinkle in the oats. When the water returns to boil reduce the heat to low and simmer the oats, covered, 15 minutes. Drain the oats into a steamer.

Bring 1 inch of water to simmer in a saucepan over medium heat. Set the oats in the steamer over it and steam the oats, covered with a trimmed piece of paper towel and lid, 15 minutes.

4 cups

oat pilaf

1/4 cup hulled sunflower seeds
parsley leaves - (2 Tablespoons chopped)
4 cups steamed oats - cold - (see steamed oats)
3/4 teaspoon salt
3/4 teaspoon celery salt
1/4 teaspoon freshly cracked black pepper
5 Tablespoons butter

Toast the sunflower seeds in a dry pan over medium heat, stirring, about 3 minutes until they take color and become fragrant. Remove them from the pan immediately and reserve them.

Chop the parsley fine and reserve it.

Warm the oats, sprinkled with the salt, celery salt and pepper in the butter in a large frying pan (see utensils), uncovered, over low heat until they are heated through. Add the reserved sunflower seeds and parsley, heat 2 minutes longer and serve the oat pilaf immediately.

4 to 6 servings

rice

Brown rice has been hulled and remains firm and flavorful when cooked. White rice has been both hulled and polished and is more delicate. The grains of either brown or white, long grain rice, when cooked, remain distinct and separate. Short grain brown or white rice, is slightly more mucilaginous, when cooked.

steamed long or short grain brown rice

3 cups water
1/2 teaspoon salt
1 1/3 cups long or short grain brown rice - about 9 1/2 ounces

Bring the water with the salt to boil in a saucepan over high heat. Sprinkle in the rice. When the water returns to boil reduce the heat to low and simmer the rice, covered, 20 minutes. Drain the rice into a steamer.
Bring 1 inch of water to simmer in a saucepan over medium heat. Set the rice in the steamer over it and steam the long or short grain brown rice, covered with a trimmed piece of paper towel and lid 15 minutes.

4 cups

steamed long or short grain white rice

(See steamed long or short grain brown rice.) Follow the recipe but boil the white rice just 10 minutes and steam it only 8 to 10 minutes or until the grains are separate and fluffy.

brown or white rice pilaf

1/4 cup peeled almonds - (see almonds)
parsley leaves - (2 Tablespoons chopped)
4 cups steamed long grain brown or white rice - cold - (see steamed long
or short grain brown rice or see steamed long or short grain
white rice)
1 teaspoon salt
1/2 teaspoon celery salt
1/4 teaspoon freshly cracked black pepper
4 Tablespoons butter

Using a heavy knife, chop the almonds small and in a dry pan over medium heat, toast them, stirring, 3 minutes until they are golden. Remove them from the pan immediately and reserve them.
Chop the parsley fine and reserve it.
Warm the rice, sprinkled with the salt, celery salt and pepper, in the butter in a large frying pan (see utensils), uncovered, over low heat until it is heated through. Add the reserved nuts and parsley, heat 2 minutes longer and serve the brown or white rice pilaf immediately.

4 to 6 servings

Note: Long grain rice is preferred for pilafs but short grain rice can also be used.

wild rice

Wild rice, that delicious native American, is not a rice at all, but is more closely related to grass.

steamed wild rice

1 cup wild rice - 8 ounces
3 cups water
1/2 teaspoon salt

Soak the wild rice in cold water to cover 3 hours. Drain and rinse it.

Bring the 3 cups of water with the salt to boil in a saucepan over high heat. Sprinkle in the rice. When the water returns to boil reduce the heat to low and simmer the rice, covered, 20 minutes. Drain the rice into a steamer and rinse it under hot running water.

Bring 1 inch of water to simmer in a saucepan over medium heat. Set the rice in the steamer over it and steam the wild rice, covered with a trimmed piece of paper towel and lid, 15 minutes.

4 cups

wild rice pilaf

1/4 cup shelled pecan halves
parsley leaves - (2 Tablespoons chopped)
4 cups steamed wild rice - cold (see steamed wild rice)
1/2 teaspoons salt
1/2 teaspoon celery salt
1/4 teaspoon freshly cracked black pepper
3 Tablespoons butter

Using a heavy knife, chop the pecans small and in a dry pan over medium heat, toast them, stirring, 3 minutes until they are golden. Remove them from the pan immediately and in a coarse strainer, shake them to allow little flakes of skin to fall away. Reserve the pecans.

Chop the parsley fine and reserve it.

Warm the wild rice, sprinkled with the salt, celery salt and pepper in the butter in a large frying pan (see utensils), uncovered, over low heat until it is heated through. Add the reserved nuts and parsley, heat 2 minutes longer and serve the wild rice pilaf immediately.

4 to 6 servings

Grains 433

rye

Rye is a hardy grain which will grow where other grains will not. It is combined so often with caraway seed that people mistake the flavor of the seed for the grain.

boiled rye berries

1 1/3 cups rye berries (whole grain rye) about 9 1/2 ounces
4 cups water
1/2 teaspoon salt

In a colander rinse the rye berries well, under running water.

In a medium size saucepan, soak the rye berries in the 4 cups of water 3 hours add the salt and bring the rye berries to boil in their soaking water, in the saucepan set over high heat. Reduce the heat to low and simmer the rye berries, covered, about 1 hour until they are chewy and some of the berries have popped open. Drain them.

4 cups

rye berry pilaf

1/4 cup shelled walnut halves
parsley leaves - (2 Tablespoons chopped)
4 cups boiled rye berries - cold - (see boiled rye berries)
1 teaspoon salt
1/2 teaspoon celery salt
1/4 teaspoon freshly cracked black pepper
2 Tablespoons peanut oil
2 Tablespoons butter

Using a heavy knife, chop the walnuts small and in a dry pan over medium heat, toast them, stirring, 3 minutes until they are golden. Remove them from the pan immediately and in a coarse strainer, shake them to allow little flakes of skin to fall away. Reserve the walnuts.

Chop the parsley fine and reserve it.

Warm the rye berries, sprinkled with the salt, celery salt and pepper in the oil and butter in a large frying pan (see utensils), uncovered, over low heat until they are heated through. Add the reserved nuts and parsley, heat 2 minutes longer and serve the rye berry pilaf immediately.

4 to 6 servings

wheat

Wheat, which gives us pilafs of wheat berries, bulghar and couscous, is also the papa of the pasta family.

boiled wheat berries

1 1/3 cup wheat berries (whole grain wheat) - about 9 /12 ounces
4 cups water
1/2 teaspoon salt

In a colander, rinse the wheat berries well under running water.

In a medium size saucepan soak the wheat berries in the 4 cups of water 3 hours add the salt and bring the wheat berries to boil in their soaking water in the saucepan set over high heat. Reduce the heat to low and simmer the wheat berries, covered, about 1 hour until they are chewy and some of the berries have popped open. Drain them.

4 cups

wheat berry pilaf

3 Tablespoons pinenuts
parsley leaves - (2 Tablespoons chopped)
4 cups boiled wheat berries - cold - (see boiled wheat berries)
1/2 teaspoon salt
1/2 teaspoon celery salt
1/4 freshly cracked black pepper
4 Tablespoons olive oil

Using a heavy knife, coarsely chop the pinenuts and in a dry pan over medium heat, toast them, stirring 3 minutes until they are golden. Remove them from the pan immediately and reserve them.

Chop the parsley fine and reserve it.

Warm the wheat berries, sprinkled with the salt, celery salt and pepper in the oil in a large frying pan (see utensils), uncovered, over low heat until they are heated through. Add the reserved nuts and parsley, heat 2 minutes longer and serve the wheat berry pilaf immediately.

4 to 6 servings

steamed bulghar

1 1/2 cups water
1/2 teaspoon salt
1 cup plus 2 Tablespoons bulghar (commercially precooked cracked
wheat) - about 8 ounces

Bring the water with the salt to boil in a medium size saucepan over high heat. Slowly, so that the water never stops boiling, sprinkle in the bulghar while stirring. Remove the pan from the heat, cover it with a paper towel and lid and allow the bulghar to stand 1 hour. All the water will be absorbed. Gently stir the bulghar with a fork.

4 cupS

bulghar pilaf

(1/4 teaspoon liquid smoke)
1/4 cup roasted peeled peanuts - (see peanuts)
parsley leaves - (2 Tablespoons chopped)
4 cups steamed bulghar - cold - (see steamed bulghar)
1/2 teaspoon salt
1 teaspoon celery salt
1/4 teaspoon freshly cracked black pepper
1 1/2 Tablespoons peanut oil
1 1/2 Tablespoons butter

(The liquid smoke is added to the water in the steamed bulghar recipe. See steamed bulghar.)

Using a heavy knife, chop the peanuts small and reserve them.

Chop the parsley fine and reserve it.

Warm the bulghar sprinkled with the salt, celery salt, and pepper in the oil and butter in a large frying pan (see utensils), uncovered, over low heat until it is heated through. Add the reserved nuts and parsley, heat 2 minutes longer and serve the bulghar pilaf immediately.

4 to 6 servings

steamed couscous the grain

1 1/3 cups water
1/2 teaspoon salt
1 1/3 cups commercially precooked couscous (a cracked wheat very much
like semolina) - about 9 1/2 ounces - (see note)

Bring the water with the salt to boil in a medium size sauce pan. Remove the pan from the heat, sprinkle in the couscous, cover the pan with a paper towel and lid and allow the couscous to cool completely. The water will be absorbed. Transfer the couscous to a sealed plastic bag and refrigerate it for at least 1 hour. Now knead the couscous with your finger tips, through the plastic bag until all the grains are separate.

4 cups

Note: If commercially precooked couscous is not available you may have to use old fashioned couscous which is not precooked. To prepare old fashioned couscous, spread it out in 1 layer on a jelly roll pan and sprinkle it with 4 tablespoons of water per cup of grain. Then transfer the couscous to a steamer and steam it, uncovered, over already simmering water, 20 minutes. Again, spread the couscous out on the pan, breaking up any lumps with a fork and sprinkle it this time with 6 tablespoons of water per the original cup of grain. Return it to the steamer and steam the couscous, again uncovered, about 20 minutes longer or until it is tender.

couscous pilaf

1/2 cup peeled, toasted pistachios - about 2 1/4 ounces (see pistachios)
parsley leaves - (2 Tablespoons chopped)
4 cups steamed couscous - cold - (see steamed couscous the grain)
1 teaspoon salt
1/2 teaspoon celery salt
1/4 teaspoon freshly cracked black pepper
2 Tablespoons olive oil
2 Tablespoons butter

Using a heavy knife, coarsely chop the pistachios and reserve them.
Chop the parsley fine and reserve it.
Warm the couscous, sprinkled with the salt, celery salt and pepper, in the oil and butter in a large frying pan (see utensils), uncovered, over low heat until it is heated through. Add reserved pistachios and parsley, heat 2 minutes longer and serve the couscous pilaf immediately.

4 servings

pasta

What would we do without it?

pasta dough

1 cup minus 2 Tablespoons unbleached all purpose flour
1/4 teaspoon salt
1 egg - at room temperature
1 to 2 teaspoons tepid water

Sift the flour and salt together into a mixing bowl. In a small bowl, using a fork, beat the egg until it is light, then stir it into the flour. Now stir in only as much of the water as is necessary to form dough. If the dough is going to be rolled out by the pasta machine, use a lesser amount of water for a firmer dough, allowing the dough to be slightly drier than you think it should be. If the dough is going to be rolled out by hand, use the greater amount of water for a more pliable dough. Gather up the dough and place it on a lightly floured work surface. With lightly floured hands, knead the dough vigorously, folding it over itself and pressing it out repeatedly with the heel of your hand.

If the dough is going to be rolled out by machine, knead it for 3 minutes to form a cohesive mass, even though the pasta machine will knead the dough later. Divide it into 4 pieces of equal weight and seal them in plastic. They do not need to rest. If the dough is going to be rolled out by hand, knead it 10 minutes, divide it into 2 pieces of equal weight and allow it to rest, sealed in plastic, for 1 hour at room temperature.

about 7 to 7 1/2 ounces pasta dough

A reminder: The egg called for in the recipe is extra large as are all other eggs called for in the recipes in this book.

machine rolled pasta dough

2 Tablespoons flour
pasta dough, hand kneaded 3 minutes and not allowed to rest - (see
pasta dough)

Before beginning, put the 2 tablespoons of flour on a 12 inch square piece of wax paper and place it near the pasta machine. (See utensils.)

Flatten 1 piece of the dough with your hands and pass it through the widest setting of the smooth rollers of the machine. Fold the piece of dough in half, lightly dust both sides of it with flour and pass it through the widest setting again. Continue to fold and pass the dough through the widest setting, 8 more times, dusting it only on every other turn or as is necessary. The piece of dough will be an odd shape. The foregoing are kneading steps.

Now, fold the longest ends of the piece of dough over themselves, more or less like a business letter, to form a 5 1/2 inch long piece of dough. Turn the roller setting down 1 notch and run the "letter" through the rollers "sideways" so that the piece of dough is almost as wide as the rollers. The trailing end of the sheet of dough is usually ragged. Squarely fold it over itself and feed that end through first next time. Always feed the dough through slowly, guiding it with your hand to keep it centered. Continue to run the sheet of dough through progressively narrower settings, very lightly dusting it with flour on both sides after passing it through the midpoint setting, only if necessary, until the narrowest setting has been reached. The sheet of dough should be 18 inches long and 6 inches wide. Repeat with the remaining pieces of dough.

hand rolled pasta dough

pasta dough, hand kneaded 10 minutes and allowed to rest 1 hour -
(see pasta dough)

On a lightly floured work surface, using a lightly floured rolling pin, roll out 1 piece of the dough at a time. Keep rotating the sheet of dough as you work to keep the thickness even, while gently lifting it and lightly flouring the work surface and rolling pin if and as necessary. Rolling out 1 piece of dough as thin as possible should take about 8 minutes, beyond 10 minutes the dough will start to dry. The sheet of dough will be a disc about 15 inches in diameter. Repeat with the remaining piece of dough.

Note: Hand rolled pasta dough, when properly cooked has a nice firm toothsome quality. It may take 3 or 4 minutes longer to cook than machine rolled pasta dough, depending upon how thin you rolled out the dough.

machine cut noodles

sheets of machine rolled pasta dough - (see machine rolled pasta dough)

Spread the sheets of pasta out on clean towels on a table or drape them over the backs of chairs. Allow the sheets to dry 15 minutes. Turn them over and allow them to dry 15 minutes longer. Do not let the edges of the sheets of pasta become brittle. The pasta should dry only long enough so that it will not stick to itself. If the 18 inch long sheets of pasta seem too long and awkward, cut them in half crosswise before feeding them through the noodle cutter; the noodles will be shorter and easier to handle.

To make the noodles, feed each sheet of dough through either the 1/16 inch narrow or the 1/4 inch wide noodle cutting rollers of the pasta machine, (see utensils), slowly guiding the dough through.

If the noodles are to be cooked immediately, toss them out onto a towel and allow them to dry 15 minutes. If they are to be dried, dry them as directed. (See dried noodles.)

hand cut noodles

sheets of pasta dough - either machine rolled or hand rolled -(see
machine rolled pasta dough or see hand rolled pasta dough)

Spread the sheets of pasta out on clean towels on a table or drape them over the backs of chairs. Allow the sheets to dry 15 minutes. Turn them over and allow them to dry 15 minutes longer. Do not let the edges of the sheets of pasta become brittle. The pasta should dry only long enough so that it will not stick to itself.

To make the noodles, fold each sheet of dough in half and again half and then again until it is only about 1 1/2 inches wide, folding machine rolled sheets the short way. Now, on a cutting board, using a sharp knife, cut the dough, crosswise, into whatever width slices you want, from 1/16 inch to as much as 1 inch if you like. Unfold the noodles.

If the noodles are to be cooked immediately, toss the unfolded noodles out onto a towel and allow them to dry 15 minutes. If they are to be dried, dry them as directed. (See dried noodles.)

dried noodles

machine or hand cut noodles - (see machine cut or see hand cut noodles)

Hang the noodles up to dry on a pasta drying rack, a clothes drying rack or a broom handle resting between the backs of two chairs. Allow the noodles to dry several hours or overnight until they are perfectly brittle. There will be variations in drying time depending on the thickness of the pasta and the weather. The noodles may now either by left whole or broken into the desired lengths. Store the dried noodles in an unsealed paper bag in a dry place. They will keep well up to at least 4 weeks.

Fourteen or 15 ounces of pasta dough will lose from 1 to 3 ounces in weight when rolled and dried. In other words 15 ounces of pasta dough may produce as little as 12 ounces of noodles.

Note: Dried pasta will take a little longer to cook than fresh pasta, depending upon how long it had been dry. Dried pasta is the best convenience food yet invented!

buttered noodles

1 teaspoon poppy seeds
3 quarts water
1 Tablespoons plus 1/2 teaspoon salt - divided
about 15 ounces fresh or about 12 ounces dried noodles - (see machine cut
          noodles or see hand cut noodles or see dried noodles)
6 Tablespoons butter - at room temperature
pinch freshly cracked black pepper

Toast the poppy seeds in a dry pan over medium heat for about 3 minutes, stirring, until they become fragrant. Remove them from the pan immediately and reserve them.

Bring the water with the 1 tablespoon of salt to boil in a large kettle over high heat. Add the noodles all at once, stirring them with a wooden spoon. Cook the noodles, covered with lid ajar, about 2 or 3 minutes or 4 or 5 minutes, depending upon how fresh or dry they are, from the moment they are in the water, regardless of when the water returns to boil, until they are tender firm "al dente", adjusting the heat to keep the water slowly boiling and stirring occasionally. Drain the noodles well and, in a large, warm serving dish, toss them with the butter, cut in pieces, the 1/2 teaspoon of salt, the pepper and the reserved poppy seeds. Serve the buttered noodles immediately.

4 servings

Note: "Al dente!" It sounds like someone's name but it means that the pasta is tender-firm when you bite it.

dried shelled beans

There's nothing like a pot of beans quietly simmering on the back of the stove to establish a homey atmosphere. Dried shelled beans, believe it or not, like other vegetables are best fresh. They are meant to be stored only over the winter, not forever. The individual varieties of beans each retain their own distinctive flavor identity and are tastier too if they are cooked when they are not more than six months old. Buy only the very best dried shelled beans that are available to you. Their quality and flavor can vary with the soil and climate in which they are grown.

There are so many more varieties of dried beans easily available than most people have any idea of. In this cookbook alone twenty two different varieties are called for. If you can't find what you want in the super market, frequent natural food stores, speciality shops and ethnic markets.

boiled dried shelled beans

Most dried shelled beans measure 2 1/4 cups per pound with a few measuring more, such as blackeyed peas, limas and cranberry beans measuring 2 1/2 cups per pound and fava beans measuring 3 cups per pound.

Almost all dried shelled beans need to be soaked before cooking. Cull the beans and in a bowl with enough water to cover by 2 inches, soak them 12 hours or overnight, no longer. Drain and rinse them. There is also the quick soaking method of bringing the beans to boil in their soaking water, then turning off the heat and allowing the beans to soak 1 hour in the hot water. Then drain and rinse them and continue with the recipe. However if you are uncertain about the age of the beans you are using, the longer soaking method is the safer method. A few dried beans such as splitpeas, lentils, blackeyed peas and lima beans do not generally need any soaking at all.

The rule of thumb is 3 cups of cooking water per cup of dried shelled beans. Do not use salt in the cooking water, it tends to toughen the beans and prolong the cooking period. Salt is added to the beans after they are cooked, with the exception of lentils which fall apart so quickly that you may want to add salt to the water to help them retain their shape. Cook all beans in a large kettle, covered with lid ajar only enough to allow the kettle to breathe. Set the kettle over high heat until the water boils. Then reduce the heat to low and keep the water slowly simmering, stirring the beans a few times to help them cook evenly. However, be careful of the delicate lentils, blackeyed peas, limas and fava beans or you will break them, stir them only at the beginning of the cooking period. Cooking time can vary considerably, depending on the age and variety of bean. Most dried shelled beans will take between 40 to 90 minutes to cook with those which do not require any soaking taking the lesser amount of time. Be alert and do not permit them to overcook. Chick peas and fava beans usually require about 90 minutes. If you must add more water during the cooking period to the longer cooking beans, to keep them covered, make sure it is boiling water. Beans that have been quick soaked often seem to require extra water. Then there are those times when you bought some beans that your grocer was hoping to keep for his retirement. In that case, if the beans have cooked 30 minutes beyond their recommended cooking time and they are not done yet, just turn off the heat and allow them to soak for 1 hour. Then turn on the heat again, they always cook quickly after that.

The yield per cup of dried shelled beans is between 2 to 2 1/2 cups of cooked, drained beans with lentils, blackeyed peas and cranberry beans usually yielding 3 cups. But here again it depends upon the age and variety of bean. In any case, always cook enough dried shelled beans for the recipe. Don't be caught short. Plan ahead!

Note: The drained cooking water from dried beans is often tasty, chick peas in particular, and always nutritious. (If not otherwise put to use, add it to a bouillon soup. See bouillon soups.)

refried beans

1 pound dried shelled beans - any kind - (2 1/4 to 2 1/2 cups)
2 bay leaves
reserved bean cooking liquid
celery - 1 large rib - (1/2 cup diced)
1 teaspoon salt - divided
6 Tablespoons peanut oil
6 Tablespoons butter
1 teaspoon honey
1/2 teaspoon cider vinegar
1/2 teaspoon celery salt
1/4 teaspoon black pepper
1/8 teaspoon liquid smoke
pinch cayenne

Soak the beans and cook them with the bay leaves as directed. (See boiled dried shelled beans.) Drain the beans reserving both the bay leaves and the cooking liquid. If the drained bean liquid measures more than 1 1/2 cups, boil it down over high heat.

Trim, scrape the strings from and dice the celery small. Sauté it, sprinkled with 1/4 teaspoon of the salt in the oil and butter in a large frying pan (see utensils), over medium heat 5 minutes. Remove the celery from the pan with a slotted spoon and reserve it.

Reduce the heat to low. Add half the cooked beans to the pan and using a potato masher, mash them. Stir in 1 cup of the reserved bean cooking liquid. (Save the remaining 1/2 cup to use in case you should want to reheat the beans later.) Add the remaining whole beans to the pan, the reserved bay leaves and celery and all the remaining ingredients. Cook the refried beans, uncovered, stirring occasionally with a metal spatula for about 30 minutes until they have thickened to the consistency you desire.

about 6 servings

Note: As with most bean dishes refried beans are even tastier reheated the next day.

SALADS

Salad must be enjoyed in a course all to itself with the accompaniment of some bread and perhaps some cheese, whether it be a simple tossed salad served in the second or third course or a principal salad served as the main course.

The selection of second or third course salads is fairly easy. A tossed green salad is usually the universal favorite. But if the entrée or principal soup already contain greens such as spinach or cabbage then a vinaigrette salad or one of the small salads might be more appropriate. In which case some of the menu design standards must be considered, season, taste, type, texture, color and a nod to ethnic tradition.

Speaking of ethnic tradition, I've come to include a tossed salad in dinners which have an Oriental entrée, though tossed salads, as we know them, are not traditional in the Orient. However the salad is a tossed napa or Chinese cabbage salad which somehow makes it very acceptable. Serve it with sesame crackers or rice wafers. Another good salad selection for an Oriental dinner would be white turnips vinaigrette. Tradition can be yielding!

tossed salads

There is nothing quite as refreshing as a tossed green salad. It can be either a combination of mixed salad greens or just a single salad green simply dressed. The quality of the oil and vinegar used will make all the difference to the success of a tossed salad.

In the French tradition the tossed salads listed here have no vegetables mixed in with them with one exception. I have included thinly sliced mushrooms in the spinach salad for what seems to have become an American tradition.

The greens must be fresh and crisp, washed in cold water, torn into bite sized pieces, spun dry in a spinner or swung dry in a salad basket. When I was a child, swinging the salad basket was a special privilege. You really had to step out the door to do it. With our French mother in the kitchen, I do not think we ever sat down to a dinner that did not include a tossed green salad. It is for me the staff of life.

Also in the French fashion, when a tossed salad follows the entrée, I always serve the salad before the dinner plates have been cleared away and the salad is eaten from the hopefully empty dinner plates. Otherwise, salad plates are provided.

No discussion of tossed salad would be complete without mentioning three or four other salad greens which are not listed in these recipes because of their limited availability. Anyone of them would make a wonderful addition to the mixed tossed salads. The first is roquette, also called rocket, rugula or arugula which is very easy to grow and I would not dream of going through the summer without its peppery, smoky flavor in my garden. The second is the perennial lemon flavored sorrel which is discussed in the note at the end of the sorrel soup recipe. The third is the mild, also easy to grow, corn salad, which is also called lambs lettuce or mâché. And fourth is the colorful, tart radicchio which looks like a small head of red cabbage.

tossed salad mix I with oil and vinegar dressing

tossed salad mix II with oil and lemon dressing

romaine salad with mimosa dressing

escarole salad with roquefort dressing

boston lettuce salad with cream dressing

chicory salad with parmesan dressing

spinach salad with soy dressing

iceberg lettuce salad with tomato dressing

endive salad with red wine vinegar dressing

watercress salad with grey mustard dressing

dandelion salad with honey-mustard dressing

napa salad with sesame dressing

tossed salad mix I
with oil and vinegar dressing

iceberg lettuce, escarole and spinach - (8 loosely packed cups torn)
1/4 teaspoon salt
1/4 teaspoon celery salt
1 Tablespoon cider vinegar
3 Tablespoons olive oil
1/4 teaspoon freshly cracked black pepper

Tear the iceberg and escarole into bite size pieces. Submerge them in cold water, drain them well and spin them dry. Trim the spinach and tear it into bite size pieces. Submerge the spinach in 2 or 3 changes of cold water until it is clean, drain it well and spin it dry. Place all the greens in a salad bowl.

In a cup, dissolve the salt and celery salt in the vinegar. Using a fork, beat in the oil and the pepper then pour the dressing over the greens. Lightly but well, toss it and serve the tossed salad mix I immediately.

4 servings

tossed salad mix II
with oil and lemon dressing

romaine, Boston lettuce and chicory - (8 loosely packed cups torn)
1/8 teaspoon salt
1/4 teaspoon celery salt
1/4 teaspoon superfine sugar
1 Tablespoon fresh lemon juice
4 Tablespoons olive oil
1/4 teaspoon freshly cracked black pepper

Using a stainless steel knife, split the ribs of the larger romaine leaves in half lengthwise then tear all the greens into bite size pieces. Submerge them in cold water, drain them well and spin them dry. Place them in a salad bowl.

In a cup, dissolve the salt, celery salt and sugar in the lemon juice. Using a fork, beat in the oil and the pepper then pour the dressing over the greens. Lightly but well, toss it and serve the tossed salad mix II immediately.

4 servings

romaine salad
with mimosa dressing

2 eggs - at room temperature
romaine - (8 loosely packed cups torn)
1/2 teaspoon salt - divided
1/4 teaspoon celery salt
1/2 teaspoon superfine sugar
1 Tablespoon plus 1 teaspoon cider vinegar
4 Tablespoons olive oil
1/4 teaspoon freshly cracked black pepper
1/2 teaspoon dried tarragon

Hard cook and peel the eggs as directed. (See cooked eggs.) Cut them in half separating the yolks and whites, discarding the whites. (Save them for a lunch time salad.) Crumble the yolks, spreading them out on a piece of brown paper and sprinkle them with 1/4 teaspoon of the salt. Allow the yolks to dry for about 2 hours, stirring them around a couple of times during the period so that they dry out evenly. When dried in this way the color of the yolks intensify and they remain firm and do not disintegrate in the dressing.

Using a stainless steel knife, split the ribs of the larger romaine leaves in half lengthwise then tear all the leaves into bite size pieces. Submerge the greens in cold water, drain them well and spin them dry. Place them in a salad bowl.

In a cup, dissolve 1/4 teaspoon of the salt, the celery salt and sugar in the vinegar. Using a fork beat in the oil and the pepper then add the tarragon, crushing it. Pour the dressing over the greens then sprinkle the dried egg yolks over them. Lightly but well, toss it and serve the romaine salad immediately.

4 servings

escarole salad
with roquefort dressing

escarole - (8 loosely packed cups torn)
1 ounce Roquefort cheese - (1/4 cup crumbled)
1/2 teaspoon salt
1/4 superfine sugar
1/4 teaspoon white pepper
1 Tablespoon distilled white vinegar
1 Tablespoon fresh lemon juice
4 Tablespoons corn oil

Cut off the bottom of the core of a head of escarole to release the leaves then tear them into bite size pieces. Submerge the greens in cold water, drain them well and spin them dry. Place them in a salad bowl.
Crumble the cheese.
In a cup dissolve the salt, sugar and pepper in the vinegar and lemon juice. Using a fork, beat in the oil then add the crumbled cheese. Pour the dressing over the greens and lightly but well, toss the salad. Serve the escarole salad immediately.

4 servings

boston lettuce salad
with cream dressing

Boston lettuce - (8 loosely packed torn)
parsley leaves - (2 Tablespoons chopped)
1/2 teaspoon salt
1/4 teaspoon celery salt
1/2 teaspoon superfine sugar
1/8 teaspoon white pepper
2 teaspoons California white wine vinegar
2 teaspoons water
2 Tablespoons corn oil
1 Tablespoon plus 1 teaspoon heavy cream

Tear the lettuce into bite size pieces. Submerge the greens in cold water, drain them well and spin them dry. Place them in a salad bowl.

Chop the parsley small and sprinkle it over the lettuce.

In a cup dissolve the salt, celery salt, sugar and pepper in the vinegar and water. Using a fork beat in the oil and the cream then pour the dressing over the greens. Lightly but well, toss it and serve the Boston lettuce salad immediately.

4 servings

chicory salad
with parmesan dressing

chicory - (8 loosely packed cups torn)
1/4 teaspoon salt
1/4 teaspoon celery salt
1 Tablespoon plus 1 teaspoon cider vinegar
2 teaspoons cold water
4 Tablespoons olive oil
1/4 teaspoon freshly cracked black pepper
3 Tablespoons freshly grated Parmesan cheese - (see note)

Cut off the bottom of the core of a head of chicory to release the leaves then tear them into bite size pieces. Submerge the greens in cold water, drain them well and spin them dry. Place them in a salad bowl.

In a cup dissolve the salt and celery salt in the vinegar and water. Using a fork, beat in the oil and the pepper then pour the dressing over the greens. Lightly but well toss the salad then sprinkle the cheese over it, toss it again and serve the chicory salad immediately.

4 servings

Note: Use the very best Parmesan available to you. Grate the cheese only just before preparing the dressing. Make sure the greens are well coated with the dressing before adding the cheese or the cheese will absorb the dressing and prevent it from coating the greens.

spinach salad
with soy dressing

12 ounces untrimmed spinach - (8 loosely packed cups trimmed)
about 4 ounces mushrooms - medium (1 1/2 cups sliced)
1/4 teaspoon salt
1/4 teaspoon celery salt
1 Tablespoon soy sauce
1 Tablespoon cider vinegar
3 Tablespoons olive oil
1/4 teaspoon freshly cracked black pepper

Trim the spinach and tear it into bite size pieces. Submerge the greens in 2 or 3 changes of cold water, until they are clean, drain them well and spin them dry. Place them in a salad bowl.

Trim the butt ends of the stems and wipe the mushrooms with a damp cloth. Slice the mushrooms thin lengthwise and toss them with the spinach.

In a cup, dissolve the salt and celery salt in the soy sauce and vinegar. Using a fork, beat in the oil and the pepper then pour the dressing over the greens. Lightly but well, toss it and serve the spinach salad immediately.

4 servings

iceberg lettuce salad
with tomato dressing

1/2 teaspoon dried thyme
1/2 teaspoon dried basil
1 teaspoon boiling water
1 Tablespoon fresh lime juice
3 dashes liquid hot red pepper
1/2 teaspoon salt
1 teaspoon English mustard powder
1/2 teaspoon sweet Hungarian paprika
1 packed Tablespoon plus 1/2 teaspoon dark brown sugar

2 Tablespoons tomato purée (not paste)
3 Tablespoons corn oil
iceberg lettuce - (8 loosely packed cups torn)

Place the thyme and basil in a cup, crushing them. Pour the boiling water over the herbs and allow them to steep 10 minutes. Then stir in the lime juice, liquid pepper, salt, mustard, paprika and sugar. Next, using a fork, beat in the purée and oil. Let the dressing stand at room temperature 15 minutes to allow the flavor to develop.

Meanwhile, tear the lettuce into bite size pieces. Submerge the greens in cold water, drain them well and spin them dry. Place them on each of 4 small salad plates. Spoon the dressing over each of the salads, do not toss them, but serve the iceberg lettuce salad immediately.

4 servings

Note: Iceberg lettuce salad is, of course, a tossed salad but it makes a more attractive presentation served on a salad plate with its dressing just decorating it and not yet tossed

endive salad
with red wine vinegar dressing

endive - 4 heads, 3 ounces each
1/4 teaspoon salt
1/4 teaspoon celery salt
1/4 teaspoon superfine sugar
3 Tablespoons plus 1 teaspoon red wine vinegar
5 Tablespoons olive oil
1/4 teaspoon freshly cracked black pepper

Select compact endive heads which do not show any green at the tip. Using a stainless steel knife, trim the bottom of the core and cut each head lengthwise into eighths. Place the prepared endives in a rectangular dish of adequate size.

In a cup, dissolve the salt, celery salt and sugar in the vinegar. Using a fork, beat in the oil and pepper then pour the dressing over the endive. Lightly and carefully but well, toss it and serve the endive salad immediately.

4 servings

Note: Endive is one of the great loves of my life. Please don't ever serve it cut crosswise or mixed into any other salad.

watercress salad
with grey mustard dressing

about 2 bunches watercress - (8 loosely packed cups leaves and tips)
1 Tablespoon plus 1 teaspoon cider vinegar
2 teaspoons prepared grey mustard
1/4 teaspoon salt
1/4 teaspoon celery salt
1/4 teaspoon superfine sugar
4 Tablespoons olive oil
1/4 teaspoon freshly cracked black pepper

Pull the leaves and just the tiny branch tips from the watercress stems. Watercress does not generally need to be washed, however, to be sure it is dry; spin it if you have to. Place the leaves and tips in a salad bowl.

In a cup stir the vinegar into the mustard until the mixture is smooth. Then dissolve the salt, celery salt and sugar in the mixture. Using a fork, beat in the oil and the pepper then pour the dressing over the greens. Lightly but well, toss it and serve the watercress salad immediately.

4 servings

dandelion salad
with honey-mustard dressing

dandelion greens (8 loosely packed cups cut) - (see note)
1 teaspoon honey
2 teaspoons prepared yellow mustard
1 Tablespoon plus 1 teaspoon cider vinegar
1/4 teaspoon salt
1/4 teaspoon celery salt
4 Tablespoons olive oil
1/4 teaspoon freshly cracked black pepper

Trim any roots from the dandelions and using a stainless steel knife cut each leaf, crosswise, into 2 or 3 pieces. Submerge the greens in cold water, drain them well and spin them dry. Place them in a salad bowl.

In a cup, stir the honey into the mustard then gradually stir in the vinegar until the mixture is smooth. Then dissolve the salt and celery salt in the mixture. Using a fork beat in the oil and the pepper then pour the dressing over the greens. Lightly but well toss it and serve the dandelion salad immediately.

4 servings

Note: Dandelion greens are available, sold in bunches, in some markets. I more often pick mine and find that a fistful of leaves generally equals 1 cup of cut greens. Be sure to pick dandelion greens early in the season before the flowers start to appear. Look for clumps that are not growing in grass, grass is difficult to sort out. If there is grass among your greens sort it out before the greens are washed, (voice of experience) it will be easier.

napa salad
with sesame dressing

2 teaspoons sesame seeds
napa (celery cabbage) - (8 loosely packed cups cut)
1/2 teaspoon salt
1 Tablespoon plus 1 teaspoon California white wine vinegar
1 teaspoon Oriental sesame oil
4 Tablespoons corn oil
1/4 teaspoon freshly cracked black pepper

Toast the sesame seeds in a dry pan over medium heat, stirring, for about 3 minutes until they become golden and fragrant. Remove them from the pan immediately and reserve them.

Using a stainless steel knife, split the napa leaves in half, lengthwise, then cut them crosswise into 1/2 inch slices. Submerge the napa in cold water, drain it well and spin it dry only if necessary. Place the napa in a salad bowl.

In a cup dissolve the salt in the vinegar. Using a fork beat in the sesame and corn oils and the pepper. Pour the dressing over the napa then sprinkle the reserved sesame seeds over it. Lightly but well, toss it and serve the napa salad immediately.

4 servings

small salads

Small salads are just that, not tossed salads, too small to be principal salads yet more diverse in style than the vinaigrettes. These small, second or third course salads are presented already on small size salad plates.

avocados on the half shell

sliced tomatoes

pressed cucumbers

carrot and current salad

coleslaw

marinated mushrooms

iceberg wedges

celeriac remoulade

fennel in virgin olive oil

egg tomato and lettuce salad

sweet italian frying pepper salad

potatoes in dill mayonnaise

avocados on the half shell

Boston lettuce - 4 to 8 leaves
1 1/2 pounds avocados - 2 medium, 12 ounces each
4 Tablespoons plus virgin olive oil
1 Tablespoon plus 1 teaspoon plus California white wine vinegar
salt and freshly cracked black pepper to taste

Rinse the lettuce leaves in cold water, spin them dry and arrange them, equally divided, in each of 4 small (berry) dishes. Cut the avocados in half lengthwise and discard the pits. (Plant them.) Set an avocado half on the lettuce in each dish. Place 1 tablespoon of the oil, 1 teaspoon of the vinegar and a dash of salt and pepper in the cavity of each avocado half. Set the small dishes upon larger plates and serve the avocados on the half shell immediately along with cruets of extra oil and vinegar plus salt and pepper on the table.

4 servings

sliced tomatoes

2 pounds firm ripe tomatoes - 4 medium
basil leaves - (1 Tablespoon minced)
3 Tablespoons olive oil
1 Tablespoon cider vinegar
1/2 teaspoon salt
1/4 teaspoon freshly cracked black pepper

Peel the tomatoes as directed. (See peeled tomatoes) Remove the stem buttons and cut the tomatoes crosswise into slices about 3/16 inch thick. Place the slices in a colander and allow them to drain 20 minutes.
Mince and reserve the basil.
Arrange the sliced tomatoes, equally divided, in an overlapping pattern, on each of 4 small salad plates. In a cup, combine the remaining ingredients then dribble 1 tablespoon of the dressing over each serving. Sprinkle the equally divided basil over the tomatoes and set the small plates upon larger plates to serve the sliced tomatoes.

4 servings

pressed cucumbers

4 1/2 pounds cucumbers - 8 average, 7 to 8 inches long - (8 heaping cups
sliced)
2 1/4 teaspoons salt
3 Tablespoons olive oil
9 Tablespoons cider vinegar
1/3 teaspoon celery salt
1/3 teaspoon freshly cracked black pepper
1 teaspoon superfine sugar

Trim the tip off either end of, peel and thinly slice the cucumbers crosswise. In a large mixing bowl, toss them with the salt and allow them to stand 1 hour at room temperature. Then refrigerate them, covered, 12 hours or overnight. Turn the cucumbers into a colander, place a saucer with a weight upon it on them and allow them to drain 30 minutes, turning them over several times during that period.

In a mixing bowl, toss the drained cucumbers with the remaining ingredients and refrigerate them again, covered, for 1 hour.

About 20 minutes before serving time, remove the bowl from the refrigerator. Just before serving, transfer the equally divided cucumbers to each of 4 small (berry) dishes. Set the small dishes upon larger plates to serve the pressed cucumbers.

4 servings

carrot and currant salad

about 1 pound carrots - 3 large - (4 cups shredded)
dried currants - (1/4 cup)
3 Tablespoons corn oil
3 Tablespoons cider vinegar
1 teaspoon salt
1/4 teaspoon freshly cracked black pepper
about 1 1/2 teaspoons superfine sugar (see note)
3/4 teaspoon dried marjoram - crushed

Trim, peel, and shred the carrots on a medium fine grater. In a mixing bowl, using 2 forks, toss the carrots with the remaining ingredients and refrigerate them, covered, for 1 hour.

About 20 minutes before serving time remove the bowl from the refrigerator and toss the carrots again. Just before serving transfer the equally divided carrots to each of 4 small salad plates. Set the small plates upon larger plates to serve the carrot and currant salad.

4 servings

Note: The amount of sugar will depend upon how sweet the carrots are.

coleslaw

2 pounds cabbage - 1 small head - (8 tightly packed cups shredded)
3 Tablespoons corn oil
6 Tablespoons cider vinegar
1 1/2 teaspoons salt
1/8 teaspoon cayenne
1 1/2 Tablespoons superfine sugar
1/4 teaspoon celery seeds

Quarter lengthwise, discarding any tough outer leaves and core the cabbage. Slice the quarters crosswise as fine as possible.

In a mixing bowl very thoroughly toss the shredded cabbage with the remaining ingredients. Allow the coleslaw to stand 1 hour at room temperature tossing it several times during that period. Then refrigerate it, covered, 1 hour.

About 20 minutes before serving time remove the bowl from the refrigerator. Just before serving, transfer the equally divided coleslaw to 4 small salad plates. Set the small plates upon larger plates to serve the coleslaw.

4 generous servings

marinated mushrooms

1 pound mushrooms - small - (5 1/2 cups trimmed)
6 Tablespoons olive oil
2 Tablespoons cider vinegar
1/4 teaspoon freshly cracked black pepper
1/2 teaspoon dried marjoram
1/2 teaspoon salt
1/4 teaspoon celery salt

Trim off the mushroom stems flush with the caps and discard them. (Save the stems for a bouillon soup. See bouillon soups.) Wipe the caps with a damp cloth and in a mixing bowl, combine them with the oil, vinegar, pepper and the marjoram, crushing it. Allow the mushrooms to marinate for 1 hour at room temperature, tossing them occasionally during that period.

Just before serving, add the salt and celery salt and transfer the equally divided mushrooms to each of 4 small (berry) dishes. Set the small dishes upon larger plates to serve the marinated mushrooms.

4 servings

iceberg wedges

1 cup mixer mayonnaise - (see mixer mayonnaise)
2 eggs - at room temperature
1/4 teaspoon salt
2 Tablespoons cold water
1 teaspoon California white wine vinegar
iceberg lettuce - 4 wedges - (each about 1/6 of a large head) - chilled

Prepare the mayonnaise in advance and keep it refrigerated as directed.

Hard cook and peel the eggs as directed. (See cooked eggs.) Allow the peeled eggs to cool to room temperature then refrigerate them, at least 1 hour, to help them remain firm while being chopped.

Now, cut the chilled eggs in half lengthwise. Separating the yolks from the whites, crumble the yolks and chop the whites fine. In a small mixing bowl dissolve the salt in the water and vinegar, stir in the mayonnaise until the mixture is smooth then stir in the crumbled yolks and chopped whites.

Arrange the iceberg wedges on each of 4 small, chilled salad plates and spoon the equally divided dressing over each wedge. Set the small plates upon larger plates to serve the iceberg wedges.

4 servings

celeriac rémoulade

1/4 teaspoon salt
1/4 teaspoon celery salt
1/2 teaspoon superfine sugar
4 Tablespoons cider vinegar
2 Tablespoons prepared grey mustard
8 Tablespoons olive oil
1/4 teaspoon freshly cracked black pepper
2 Tablespoons capers - small
dill pickles - 2 small, 3 inches long by 3/4 inches wide - (1/2 cup sliced)
about 1 pound celeriac - 2 medium small - (3 heaping cups sliced)

In a mixing bowl, dissolve the salt, celery salt and sugar in the vinegar. Stir in the mustard until the mixture is smooth. Beat in the oil and pepper. Drain, rinse and drain the capers. Very thinly slice the pickles crosswise, rinse and drain the slices well. Add the capers and pickles to the dressing.

Scrub the celeriac under running water. Trim, peel and cut them lengthwise into eighths. Very thinly slice the eighths crosswise, dropping the slices into the dressing. Allow the salad to stand 1 hour at room temperature, tossing it several times during that period. Then refrigerate it covered for 23 hours.

About 20 minutes before serving time, remove the bowl from the refrigerator. Just before serving, transfer the equally divided celeriac to each of 4 small salad plates. Set the small plates upon larger plates to serve the celeriac rémoulade.

4 servings

Note: This method of slicing the celeriac rather than the conventional julienne shows the interesting pattern of the grain of the vegetable.

fennel in virgin olive oil

1 1/2 pounds fennel with top - 1 medium bulb - (4 cups sliced)
6 Tablespoons virgin olive oil
1/2 teaspoon salt

Cut the green top from, trim, and cut the fennel bulb in half lengthwise, reserving a heaping tablespoon of the leaves. Slice the halves very thin crosswise. If the fennel has to be rinsed to remove any soil, drain it well and blot it dry on paper towels. Coarsely chop the reserved leaves.

In a mixing bowl, toss the sliced fennel and chopped leaves with the remaining ingredients. Transfer the equally divided fennel to each of 4 small salad plates. Set the small plates upon larger plates and serve the fennel in virgin olive oil right away.

4 servings

egg tomato and lettuce salad

4 eggs - at room temperature
1 cup mixer mayonnaise - (see mixer mayonnaise)
iceberg lettuce - 4 to 8 leaves
1 1/2 pounds tomatoes - 4 medium small - 6 ounces each

Hard cook and peel the eggs as directed. (See cooked eggs.) Allow the peeled eggs to cool to room temperature then refrigerate them, at least 1 hour, to help them remain firm while being cut.

Prepare the mayonnaise in advance and refrigerate it as directed.

Just before serving, arrange 1 or 2 lettuce leaves on each of 4 small salad plates. Remove the stem buttons from the tomatoes and quarter them lengthwise.. Quarter the eggs lengthwise. Arrange the equally divided tomato and egg quarters alternately in a circle on the lettuce on each plate then heap 4 tablespoons of the mayonnaise in the center of each circle. Set the small plates upon larger plates to serve the egg, tomato and lettuce salad.

4 servings

sweet italian frying pepper salad

This is exactly the same recipe as braised sweet Italian frying peppers. (See braised sweet Italian frying peppers.) What makes them a salad is that they are allowed to cool to room temperature. Place the equally divided peppers on each of 4 small salad plates. Set the small plates upon larger plates to serve the sweet Italian frying pepper salad.

4 servings

potatoes in dill mayonnaise

3 pounds boiling potatoes - 6 medium large - (9 cups sliced)
1 teaspoon dill seeds
1 1/2 cups mixer mayonnaise - (see mixer mayonnaise)
2 teaspoons salt
1/2 teaspoon superfine sugar
cider vinegar
peanut oil - (see note)
1/4 teaspoon freshly cracked black pepper
1 teaspoon dried dill weed
water

Peel and quarter the potatoes lengthwise. Cut the quarters crosswise into 1/8 inch uniformly thick slices, dropping them into a large bowl of enough cold water to cover them and allow them to stand 1 hour.

Meanwhile, toast the dill seeds in a dry pan over medium heat for about 3 minutes, stirring until they become golden and fragrant. Remove them from the pan immediately, crush them fine, 1/2 teaspoon at a time in a mortar or use a spice grinder. Reserve them.

Prepare the mixer mayonnaise as directed with the following exceptions. Dissolve the 2 teaspoons of salt, in addition to the salt already called for in the mayonnaise recipe plus the 1/2 teaspoon of sugar in the amount of vinegar called for, substituting cider vinegar for the white wine vinegar and peanut oil for the olive oil called for. When the mayonnaise is completed, stir in the reserved crushed dill seed, the black pepper, and dill weed.

Drain the potatoes. In a large saucepan over high heat, bring to boil enough water to cover the potatoes by 1 1/2 inches. Turn the drained potatoes into the boiling water and cook them, covered with lid slightly ajar, for about 6 minutes from the moment they are in the water, regardless of when the water returns to boil. Adjust the heat to keep the water slowly boiling and stir them once or twice with a wooden spoon until the potatoes are tender but firm. Taste them to determine when they are done. Drain the potatoes and immediately turn them into a basin of cold water for 3 minutes. Drain them again, spread them out on paper towels and blot them dry with more towels.

In a mixing bowl, using a rubber spatula, gently combine the potatoes well with the dill mayonnaise. Transfer the equally divided potatoes to each of 4 small salad plates. Set the small plates upon larger plates and serve the potatoes in dill mayonnaise at room temperature.

8 servings

Note: For a richer flavor, use strained peanut oil that has been used for deep frying. (See utensils.)

vinaigrette salads

In this instance, vinaigrette salads consist of cooked vegetables which have been marinated in oil and vinegar, usually with herbs. The vinaigrette salads can be an economy in wintertime when the price of your favorite salad green has gone sky high. Out smart the situation, by serving a cooked vegetable vinaigrette salad. The vinaigrettes can be a help in the summertime too when your garden is over producing and there is an abundance of a certain vegetable that you must do something with right away. The vinaigrette salads are great to have on hand for an instant lunch with bread and cheese. They must marinate twenty four hours and generally keep well up to forty eight hours in which case they seem like a found salad if not a down right surprise.

Included here are recipes for sixteen vegetables which take especially well to the vinaigrette dressing plus the ubiquitous dried bean vinaigrettes of many varieties.

You will notice in the vinaigrette salad recipes that the vegetables are usually placed in a jar to marinate. Because of the shape of the jar, the dressing will cover the vegetables more completely than it would in a dish. It also becomes an easy matter to toss the vegetables in their dressing by simply rotating the jar and consequently they marinate more evenly. Become a jar collector. Before you throw an empty jar away look at it and think "cauliflower", "asparagus."

These second or third course vinaigrette salads look great served on small, white, oval plates, bistro style.

To avoid repetition, the following are general marinating and serving instructions which apply to most of the vinaigrette salads.

general marinating and serving instructions

Cover the jar with wax paper and screw the lid on tight. Lay the jar on its side and rotate it frequently for 1 hour at room temperature. Then refrigerate the jar, on its side, 23 hours, rotating it occasionally.

About 30 minutes before serving time, remove the jar from the refrigerator. Just before serving, transfer the equally divided vegetables, with their dressing, to each of four small salad plates. Set them upon larger plates and serve the vinaigrette salad chilled but not cold.

baby artichokes vinaigrette

asparagus vinaigrette

dried shelled beans vinaigrette

lima beans vinaigrette

string beans vinaigrette

beets vinaigrette

broccoli vinaigrette

brussels sprouts vinaigrette

red cabbage vinaigrette

cauliflower vinaigrette

celery hearts vinaigrette

kohlrabi vinaigrette

green bell peppers vinaigrette

red bell peppers vinaigrette

rutabaga vinaigrette

white turnips vinaigrette

zucchini vinaigrette

baby artichokes vinaigrette

1 1/2 pounds baby artichokes - about 24 - (4 cups trimmed) or
18 ounces frozen
8 Tablespoons olive oil
2 Tablespoons plus 2 teaspoons California white wine vinegar
1 Tablespoon plus 1 teaspoon fresh lemon juice
1/2 teaspoon salt
1/2 teaspoon celery salt
1/2 teaspoon freshly cracked black pepper
1/2 teaspoon cayenne
1/2 teaspoon dried marjoram

Prepare and boil the artichokes as directed. (See boiled baby artichokes.) Or prepare and blanch frozen artichokes as directed. (See blanched frozen artichokes.) In either case, immediately turn the drained artichokes into a basin of cold water for 3 minutes. Drain them well in a colander and blot them dry with paper towels.

In a large jar combine the artichokes with all the remaining ingredients crushing the marjoram.

To marinate and serve, see general instructions at the beginning of this section.

4 servings

asparagus vinaigrette

2 pounds asparagus
4 Tablespoons olive oil
2 Tablespoons cider vinegar
1/2 teaspoon salt
1/4 teaspoon freshly cracked black pepper
1/8 teaspoon superfine sugar
1/4 teaspoon dreid tarragon

Prepare and steam the asparagus, until they are just tender, as directed. (See steamed asparagus.) Using a pair of tongs, immediately transfer the bundles of asparagus to a basin of cold water for 3 minutes. Cut and remove their ribbons while they are in the water. Drain the asparagus well and blot them dry on paper towels.

Lay the asparagus, parallel, in a long, large jar, with their tips all pointing toward the mouth of the jar, and add all the remaining ingredients, crushing the tarragon.

To marinate and serve, see general instructions at the beginning of this section.

4 servings

Note: In the absence of a long enough jar, a loaf dish can be substituted. Rotate the asparagus with a wooden spoon and cover the dish with foil.

dried shelled beans vinaigrette

3 cups cooked, drained, dried shelled beans - any kind cooked with 1 bay leaf - (see boiled dried shelled beans)
1 reserved bay leaf
celery - (3 Tablespoons diced very small)
3 Tablespoons olive oil
6 Tablespoons cider vinegar
1/2 teaspoon salt
1/4 teaspoon celery salt
1/4 teaspoon freshly cracked black pepper
3/4 teaspoon superfine sugar
pinch cayenne
1/2 teaspoon equally mixed dried thyme, basil and oregano
3 Tablespoons roasted sunflower seeds - (see sunflower and squash seeds)

In a large jar, combine the cooked beans with their reserved bay leaf and all the remaining ingredients, crushing the herbs, except the sunflower seeds.

To marinate and serve, see general instructions at the beginning of this section, removing the bay leaf and tossing the sunflower seeds with the beans just before dividing the salad.

4 servings

lima beans vinaigrette

1 pounds 12 ounces unshelled lima beans - large - (2 cups shelled) or
10 ounces frozen
4 Tablespoons olive oil
2 Tablespoons cider vinegar
1/4 teaspoon salt
1/4 teaspoon celery salt
1/4 teaspoon freshly cracked black pepper
1/4 teaspoon dried thyme

Shell and steam the lima beans, until they are just tender, as directed. (See steamed lima beans.) Immediately turn them into a basin of cold water for 3 minutes, then drain them. If you are using frozen limas, blanch the still frozen beans in enough boiling water to cover them by 11/2 inches in a large saucepan, uncovered, over high heat for about 8 minutes from the moment they are in the water, regardless of when the water returns to boil, stirring the beans with a wooden spoon, until they are just tender. Drain and immediately turn them into a basin of cold water for 3 minutes then drain again. In either case blot the lima beans dry on paper towels.

In a large jar, combine the beans with all the remaining ingredients, crushing the thyme.

To marinate and serve, see general instructions at the beginning of this section.

4 servings

string beans vinaigrette

1 pound green or yellow slender or wide and flat string beans
4 Tablespoons olive oil
2 Tablespoons cider vinegar
1/4 teaspoon salt
1/4 teaspoon celery salt
1/4 teaspoon freshly cracked black pepper
1/4 teaspoon ground rosemary - (see ground rosemary)

Prepare and steam the string beans, until they are just tender, as directed. (See steamed string beans.) Immediately turn the beans into a basin of cold water for 3 minutes. Drain them and blot them dry on paper towels.

In a large jar, combine the string beans with all the remaining ingredients.

To marinate and serve, see general instructions at the beginning of this section.

4 servings

beets vinaigrette

1 1/4 pounds beets - 10 small or 4 medium
4 Tablespoons olive oil
2 Tablespoons cider vinegar
1/4 teaspoon salt
1/4 teaspoon celery salt
1/4 teaspoon freshly cracked black pepper
1/4 teaspoon superfine sugar
1/2 teaspoon dried dill weed

Scrub, boil, trim and peel the beets as directed. (See boiled beets.) Immediately drop the peeled beets into a basin of cold water for 5 minutes. Drain and cut them crosswise into 3/16 inch thick slices. Blot the slices dry on paper towels.

In a large jar combine the sliced beets with all the remaining ingredients, crushing the dill weed.

To marinate and serve, see general instructions at the beginning of this section.

4 servings

broccoli vinaigrette

1 1/2 pounds broccoli - 3 average heads - 1 bunch - (6 cups florets and cut)
6 Tablespoons olive oil
3 Tablespoons cider vinegar
3/4 teaspoon salt
1/4 teaspoon freshly cracked black pepper
1/3 teaspoon superfine sugar
1/2 teaspoon dried oregano

Cut the broccoli florets from the stalks with enough stem so that the florets, including their stems, measure 2 inches long. Separate the larger clusters of florets into smaller clusters, cutting them apart where necessary, so that the florets are all of a uniform size. Trim and peel the remainder of the large broccoli stalks, first pulling off the fibrous skin with a knife and then using a vegetable peeler. Cut the stalks crosswise into 1/4 inch thick slices. Steam the broccoli over already simmering water for from 10 to as much as 20 minutes. Start testing it at 8 minutes by piercing it with a wooden toothpick to determine when it will be just tender. Immediately turn the broccoli into a basin of cold water for 3 minutes. Drain it well in a colander and blot it dry on paper towels.

In a large jar, combine the broccoli with all the remaining ingredients, crushing the oregano.

To marinate and serve, see general instructions at the beginning of this section.

4 servings

brussels sprouts vinaigrette

1 pound Brussels sprouts - 32 to 40 of equal size - (4 cups cut)
6 Tablespoons olive oil
2 Tablespoons fresh lemon juice
1 teaspoon salt
1/4 teaspoon freshly cracked black pepper
1/2 teaspoon superfine sugar

Trim the Brussels sprouts and cut them in half lengthwise. Steam the spouts over already boiling water 13 to 15 minutes or until they are just tender when pierced with a wooden toothpick. Immediately turn the sprouts into a basin of cold water for 3 minutes. Drain them well in a colander and blot them dry on paper towels.

In a large jar, combine the Brussels sprouts with all the remaining ingredients.

To marinate and serve, see general instructions at the beginning of this section.

4 servings

red cabbage vinaigrette

2 pounds red cabbage - 1 small head - (10 tightly packed cups, cut)
4 Tablespoons corn oil
4 Tablespoons California white wine vinegar
1 1/2 teaspoons salt
1/4 teaspoon freshly cracked black pepper
1 Tablespoon brown sugar
1/8 teaspoon ground cloves

Prepare and blanch the cabbage as directed. (See blanched red cabbage.) Immediately turn the drained cabbage into a basin of cold water for 1 minute. Drain it well in a colander then spread the cabbage out on paper towels and blot it dry with more towels.

Combine all the remaining ingredients in a mixing bowl. Add the cabbage, toss it well with the dressing and allow it to marinate 1 hour at room temperature, tossing it several times. Cover the bowl tight and refrigerate it 1 hour.

About 20 minutes before serving time, remove the bowl from the refrigerator, uncover it, and toss the cabbage again, once or twice. Just before serving, transfer the equally divided cabbage, with its dressing, to each of 4 small salad plates. Set them upon larger plates and serve the red cabbage vinaigrette chilled but not cold.

4 servings

Note: For convenience, the red cabbage can be marinated over night like other vinaigrette salads but it is not necessary.

cauliflower vinaigrette

about 2 pounds 11 ounces cauliflower - 1 medium large head -

(8 cups florets)

8 Tablespoons olive oil
4 Tablespoons cider vinegar
1 teaspoon salt
1/4 teaspoon freshly cracked black pepper
1/4 teaspoon superfine sugar
1/2 teaspoon dried thyme

Prepare and steam the cauliflower florets, until they are just tender, as directed. (See steamed cauliflower florets.) Immediately turn the florets into a basin of cold water, for 3 minutes. Drain them well in a colander and blot them dry with paper towels.

In a large jar, combine the cauliflower florets with all the remaining ingredients, crushing the thyme.

To marinate and serve, see general instructions at the beginning of this section.

4 servings

Note: Cauliflower florets by nature of their bulky structure, require more dressing than other vinaigrette salads. If you cannot find a jar large enough to accommodate the cauliflower, use a mixing bowl. Toss the florets with a wooden spoon and cover the bowl with foil.

celery hearts vinaigrette

about 2 1/2 pounds celery - 1 average bunch
6 Tablespoons olive oil
4 1/2 Tablespoons cider vinegar
3/4 teaspoon salt
3/4 teaspoon celery salt
2 teaspoons superfine sugar
1/4 teaspoon liquid hot red pepper - or to taste

Crosswise, cut off the lower 6 inches of the bunch of celery. (Save the upper part for a bouillon soup. See bouillon soups.) Trim the bottom of the bunch and using a vegetable peeler scrape the strings from the outer ribs. Carefully cut the bunch into eighths lengthwise. Leave the little yellow inner leaves intact. Then spray water down into the wedges to remove any soil. Steam the celery over already boiling water for about 10 minutes or until it is just tender when pierced with a wooden toothpick. Immediately turn the celery into a basin of cold water for 3 minutes. Drain it well in a colander and blot it dry on paper towels.

Lay the celery wedges, parallel, in a long, large jar and add all the remaining ingredients.

To marinate and serve, see general instructions at the beginning of this section.

4 servings

Note: In the absence of a long enough jar, a loaf dish can be substituted. Rotate the celery with a wooden spoon and cover the dish with foil.

kohlrabi vinaigrette

about 2 1/2 pounds kohlrabi, minus leaves - (about 3 3/4 pound with leaves)
8 bulbs, 2 to 2 1/2 inches in diameter - (4 heaping cups sliced)
4 Tablespoons olive oil
2 Tablespoons cider vinegar
1 teaspoon salt
1/4 teaspoon superfine sugar
1/2 teaspoon dried summer savory

Trim, peel and cut the kohlrabi bulbs in half lengthwise. Cut the halves, crosswise, into half moon shaped slices, 1/8 inch thick. Steam the kohlrabi over already simmering water for about 7 minutes or until it is just tender when pierced with a wooden toothpick. Immediately turn the kohlrabi into a basin of cold water for 2 minutes. Drain it and blot it dry on paper towels.

In a large jar, combine the kohlrabi with all the remaining ingredients, crushing the savory.

To marinate and serve, see general instructions at the beginning of this section.

4 servings

green bell peppers vinaigrette

1 1/2 pounds green bell peppers - 4 medium - (4 cups cut)
4 Tablespoons olive oil
2 Tablespoons cider vinegar
1/2 teaspoon salt
1/4 teaspoon freshly cracked black pepper
1/2 teaspoon superfine sugar
1/4 teaspoon dried marjoram

Cut the bell peppers crosswise into 3/4 inch thick slices. Core the slices, trimming away any white membrane. Cut the rings into 3/4 inch squares. Steam the bell pepper squares about 5 minutes over already simmering water or until they are just tender. Immediately turn the peppers into a basin of cold water for 1 minute. Drain them and blot them dry on paper towels.

In a large jar, combine the bell peppers with all the remaining ingredients, crushing the marjoram.

To marinate and serve, see general instructions at the beginning of this section.

4 servings

red bell peppers vinaigrette

2 pounds red bell peppers - 4 large
4 Tablespoons olive oil
1 Tablespoon plus 1 teaspoon cider vinegar
1/2 teaspoon salt
1/4 teaspoon freshly cracked black pepper
1/4 teaspoon dried basil

Select deep red, fully ripe bell peppers. Prepare and peel them as directed. (See peeled red bell peppers.)

In a large jar, combine the bell peppers with all the remaining ingredients, crushing the basil.

To marinate and serve, see general instructions at the beginning of this section.

4 servings

rutabaga vinaigrette

1 pound rutabaga - 1 small - (3 cups cut)
1/2 teaspoon dill seeds
6 Tablespoons corn oil
3 Tablespoons cider vinegar
1/2 teaspoon salt
1/2 teaspoon celery salt
1/3 teaspoon freshly cracked black pepper
1/4 teaspoon superfine sugar

Trim, peel and cut the rutabaga crosswise into 3/4 inch thick slices. Then cut the slices into long pieces about 1 1/2 inches wide. Now, cut the pieces, crosswise, into slices about 1/8 inch thick. Steam the rutabaga over already simmering water about 7 minutes or until it is just tender when pierced with a wooden toothpick. Immediately turn the rutabaga into a basin of cold water for 2 minutes. Drain it and blot it dry on paper towels.

Toast the dill seeds in a dry pan over medium heat, stirring for 3 minutes until they start to pop and become golden. Remove them from the pan immediately and crush them in a mortar or spice grinder.

In a large jar, combine the rutabaga with the crushed dill seed and all the remaining ingredients.

To marinate and serve, see general instructions at the beginning of this section.

4 servings

white turnips vinaigrette

1 pound white turnips - 4 medium - (4 loosely packed cups cut)
boiling water
1 1/2 teaspoons English mustard powder
2 teaspoons brown sugar
1/2 teaspoon salt
1/4 teaspoon celery salt
1/8 teaspoon white pepper
6 Tablespoons California white wine vinegar
2 Tablespoons corn oil

Trim, peel and cut the turnips, crosswise, into 3/16 inch thick slices. Cut the slices into matchsticks 3/16 inch wide. Blanch the turnips in enough boiling water to cover them by 1 1/2 inches in a large saucepan, uncovered, over high heat for 2 1/2 minutes from the moment they are in the water, regardless of when water returns to boil. Drain them and immediately turn them into a basin of cold water for 2 minutes. Drain the turnips and blot them dry on paper towels.

In a cup dissolve the mustard, sugar, salt, celery salt and pepper in the vinegar. Using a fork beat in the oil until the mixture is smooth. In a large jar, combine the turnips with the dressing.

To marinate and serve, see general instructions at the beginning of this section.

4 servings

zucchini vinaigrette

1 1/2 pounds zucchini squash - 6 small, 6 inches long - (6 cups sliced)
1/2 teaspoon plus salt - divided
6 Tablespoons olive oil - divided
2 Tablespoons cider vinegar
1/4 teaspoon freshly cracked black pepper
1/4 teaspoon superfine sugar
1/4 teaspoon dried oregano

Trim and cut the zucchini, crosswise, into 1/4 inch uniformly, thick slices. Sauté only 2 cups of the slices at a time, (it is important not to crowd the pan) lightly sprinkled with salt, in 1 tablespoon of the oil, in a large frying pan (see utensils) over high heat for 3 minutes, turning them with a metal spatula until they start to blister and become golden. Undercook rather than overcook the zucchini, it must be just tender but still very firm. Transfer the sautéed sliced to paper towels.

In a large jar, combine the zucchini with 3 tablespoons of the oil, the 1/2 teaspoon of salt and all the remaining ingredients, crushing the oregano.

To marinate and serve, see general instructions at the beginning of this section.

4 servings

PRINCIPAL SALADS

A large salad as the main course in a summer dinner or a winter dinner too for that matter, preceded by a light soup, accompanied by some bread and often some cheese and followed by fresh fruit is a delightful meal. Like a soup supper and the dîner dessert it is a comparatively simple meal and a very good one for company since the major part of most principal salads can be prepared in advance.

A principal salad can have a diverse number of ingredients and can be comprised of both raw and cooked vegetables, grains, legumes, nuts, seeds, eggs, cheese, bread and fruit as well as salad greens. Their shapes include the curried rice dome, tomato aspic, stuffed avocados and the impressive glacée of marinated vegetables as well as large salad bowls.

Within the realm of principal salads are the composed salads, those which are already arranged on individual salad plates. They allow an opportunity to vent artistic skills and make beautiful arrangements.

Also within the realm of the principal salad are the antipasto, hors d' oeuvre and smörgåsbord salads. They are groupings of small salads, vinaigrettes, pickles, olives, cheeses and breads among other things, each presented separately in little dishes.

SECTION I

WHOLE ARTICHOKES WITH OIL AND VINEGAR

CAPONATA

STUFFED LETTUCE LEAVES

GREEN GARDEN SALAD

SALADE RUSSE

CURRIED RICE DOME

PRIMAVERA SALAD

ANTIPASTO

WHOLE ARTICHOKE
 WITH OIL AND VINEGAR

French onion soup is the perfect foil for cold artichokes. I like to buy medium size artichokes for this dish and allow 2 or 3 per serving—if the price is right. They look very luxurious, heaped on a platter in the center of the table and guests can help themselves to what they want. Serve French bread and Gruyère cheese with the artichokes. Then offer raspberries over ice cream for dessert.

artichokes - 2 or 3 medium, about 10 ounces each
1/4 teaspoon salt
1/4 teaspoon celery salt
1 Tablespoon cider vinegar
3 Tablespoons olive oil
1/4 teaspoon freshly cracked black pepper

Prepare, boil and drain the artichokes as directed then allow them to cool to room temperature. (See boiled whole artichokes.)

In a teacup dissolve the salt and celery salt in the vinegar. Using a fork, beat in the oil and pepper. Set the cup on a large salad plate and place it at a place setting on the dinner table. Multiply this recipe as desired.

Heap the artichokes on a serving platter to serve the whole artichokes with oil and vinegar.

1 serving

Note: Are you wondering how to eat the artichokes? (See whole artichokes with garlic butter.) Provide each diner with a bowl for the discarded leaves.

 CAPONATA

Serve a lovely cold avocado soup first. Then have some hearty Italian bread sticks and some Gorgonzola cheese with the caponata. Follow with poached figs.

1/2 teaspoon fennel seeds
1 jar capers - 2 ounces - (1/3 cup)
1 can pitted black olives - 3 ounces - (1/2 cup broken)
1 can pitted green olives - 3 ounces - (1/2 cup broken)
3/4 cup water
1 can tomato paste - 6 ounces
9 Tablespoons olive oil - divided
2 Tablespoons plus 2 teaspoons red wine vinegar - divided
1 Tablespoon plus 1 teaspoon honey
1 teaspoon plus salt - divided
1/2 teaspoon celery salt
1/2 teaspoon plus freshly cracked black pepper - divided
pinch cayenne
2 teaspoon dried basil
2 teaspoon fresh lemon juice
celery - 6 large ribs (3 cups cut)
2 pounds eggplant - 2 medium (6 heaping cups diced)
escarole leaves - (4 loosely packed cups torn)

Toast the fennel seeds in a dry pan over medium heat, stirring for about 3 minutes until they become golden and fragrant. Remove them from the pan immediately, crush them in a mortar or spice grinder and reserve them.

Drain, rinse and drain the capers and black and green olives. Break the olives into pieces. Reserve the capers and olives.

In a heavy, medium size saucepan over low heat, stir the water into the tomato paste then add 8 tablespoons of the oil, 2 tablespoons of the vinegar, the honey, the 1 teaspoon of salt, the celery salt, the 1/2 teaspoon of black pepper, the cayenne, reserved fennel and the reserved capers and olives. Slowly cook the sauce, covered, over the low heat for 55 minutes. Then add the basil, crushing it, and cook 5 minutes longer. Turn the sauce into a large mixing bowl and stir in the lemon juice. The sauce will be very thick and oily.

Meanwhile, trim, scrape the strings from and cut the celery into pieces about 1 inch square. Steam it over already simmering water for 11 or 12 minutes or until it is just tender. Immediately turn the celery into a basin of cold water for 2 minutes, drain it well, blot it dry on paper towels and using a rubber spatula, fold it into the tomato sauce.

Trim the eggplant, and unless it is very fresh, peel it. Cut it into 3/4 inch dice. (Unless you have a large size steamer, steam the eggplant in 3 batches so that it will be evenly cooked.) Steam the eggplant over already simmering water for 6 to 7 minutes; pierce 1 or 2 pieces with a wooden toothpick to determine when it is just tender. Immediately turn the eggplant into a basin of cold water for 3 minutes, drain it well and blot it dry on paper towels. Fold the eggplant into the tomato sauce, combining the mixture well. Allow the caponata to stand, covered, 1 hour at room temperature, gently turning and folding it over itself once or twice during that period then refrigerate it, covered 23 hours.

Remove the bowl from the refrigerator 2 hours before serving time and allow the caponata to come to room temperature. Rinse the escarole in cold water, tear it into bite size pieces and spin it dry. Just before serving time, in a cup dissolve 1/8 teaspoon of salt in 2 teaspoons of the vinegar then using a fork beat in 1 tablespoon of the oil and a pinch of black pepper. On a serving platter, toss the escarole with the dressing and arrange the leaves in a wreath around the edges of the platter then heap the caponata in the center of the wreath of escarole and serve.

4 servings

Note: Pay close attention to steaming the celery and eggplant, they must be tender but firm. Their texture is very important to the success of the caponata.

 STUFFED LETTUCE LEAVES

Cream of tomato soup is the first course for this dinner which is otherwise eaten out of hand. I usually serve the stuffing mixture in a crock, taller than it is wide and let guests serve themselves with a longhandled wooden spoon. Have pita bread on the table, as some people like to slip their stuffed lettuce leaf inside a pita pocket. A bunch of bananas will be dessert for this informal dinner.

7 Tablespoons millet - about 3 1/4 ounces
4 eggs - at room temperature
12 ounces green bell peppers - 2 medium - (2 cups diced)
8 ounces red radishes, minus leaves - about 20 - (2 cups diced)
celery - 4 large ribs - (2 cups diced)
2 1/2 teaspoons salt - divided
1 jar pitted green olives - 3 1/2 ounces - (2/3 cup chopped)
about 3 1/2 ounces hickory smoked Cheddar cheese - (2/3 cup diced)
2/3 cup roasted peeled peanuts - about 3 1/2 ounces - (see peanuts)

iceberg lettuce - 2 heads
1/2 teaspoon freshly cracked black pepper
1/2 teaspoon sugar
1/4 teaspoon cayenne
1 cup prepared mayonnaise

Steam the millet as directed. (See steamed millet.) If the steamed millet measures more than 2 cups, do not use the excess, it would unbalance the recipe. (Save any excess for a bouillon soup. See bouillon soups.) Allow the millet to cool to room temperature then refrigerate it covered, for at least 2 hours.

Hard cook and peel the eggs as directed. (See cooked eggs.) Allow them to cool to room temperature then refrigerate them for 1 hour to help them remain firm while being chopped.

Core the green bell peppers, trimming away any white membrane and dice them very small. Trim and dice the radishes very small. Trim, scrape the strings from and dice the celery very small. In a bowl, toss the 3 diced vegetables together with 1 teaspoon of the salt and refrigerate them, covered, at least 1 hour.

Drain, rinse and drain the olives. Using a mincer, chop them small and blot them dry on paper towels. Dice the cheese very small. Using a heavy knife, coarsely chop the peanuts. In a large mixing bowl, mix the olives, cheese and peanuts together and refrigerate them, covered, at least 30 minutes.

(Up to this point everything can be prepared as much as 24 hours in advance and refrigerated as directed.)

About 45 minutes before serving, using a small sharp knife, core the heads of lettuce and run cold tap water into the hole. The leaves will separate themselves without tearing. Using only the medium size leaves, blot them well with paper towels and refrigerate them in a sealed plastic bag until ready to serve.

Turn the diced vegetables into a colander set over a bowl. Place a saucer with a weight set upon it on the vegetables and return them, in the colander over the bowl, to the refrigerator and allow them to drain for 20 minutes. Then blot the drained vegetables dry on paper towels.

Meanwhile, cut the hard cooked eggs in half, separating the yolks from the whites. Crumble the yolks and chop the whites very small.

Now, tossing the mixture well, combine the millet, crumbled and chopped eggs, diced vegetables, 1 1/2 teaspoon of the salt, the black pepper, sugar and cayenne with the olives, cheese and peanuts in the large mixing bowl. Then fold in the mayonnaise and transfer the stuffing mixture to an attractive serving bowl.

Arrange the chilled lettuce leaves on a large serving tray and present it along with the bowl of stuffing. Each diner places a couple of tablespoons of the stuffing mixture in a lettuce leaf, rolls it up and eats the stuffed lettuce leaf out of hand.

about 8 servings

 GREEN GARDEN SALAD

Precede this sumptuous salad with a cream of carrot soup. Offer warm dinner rolls with the salad and follow with chilled tangerines.

baby artichokes vinaigrette - (see baby artichokes vinaigrette)
asparagus vinaigrette - (see asparagus vinaigrette)
string beans vinaigrette - (see string bean vinaigrette,
                using slender, green, string beans) - (see note)
broccoli vinaigrette - (see broccoli vinaigrette)
green bell peppers vinaigrette - (see green bell peppers vinaigrette,
                substituting 1/4 teaspoon dried basil for marjoram called for
                in recipe)
1 1/2 cups mixer mayonnaise - (see mixer mayonnaise)

Prepare and marinate the five vinaigrette salads as directed but instead of placing them on little salad dishes drain each of them very well, separately, in a colander. Alternatively, just place each vegetable on a plate and tilt the plate to drain off the dressing. (Save the dressings for a lunchtime salad.) Then blot the vegetables on paper towels.

Meanwhile, prepare the mixer mayonnaise as directed, transfer it to a serving dish and refrigerate it, covered, until serving.

Arrange the vegetables, equally divided, on each of 4 large salad plates, artichokes heaped in the center, asparagus (trim butt ends a little if too long) and string beans opposite each other on either side and broccoli and bell peppers opposite each other on the remaining two sides. All very neatly done please.

Refrigerate the plates for 20 minutes before serving to chill them. Then serve the green garden salad along with the dish of mayonnaise and let everyone help themselves to the mayonnaise as they desire.

4 servings

Note: If prime string beans are not available at the same time as asparagus, see the note at the end of the assiette jardiniére recipe. (See assiette jardiniére.)

SALADE RUSSE

Salade Russe is usually served already mixed with its mayonnaise but it's far more attractive served this way, with the mayonnaise kept separate so that the jewel-like beauty of the vegetables is revealed. Serve mushrooms bisque for the first course then have a very nice loaf of French bread with the salad. Fresh plums will round out the meal.

1 1/2 cups mixer mayonnaise - (see mixer mayonnaise)
about 10 ounces beets - 2 medium - (2 cups diced)
12 ounces boiling potatoes - 2 medium - (2 cups diced)
water
12 ounces carrots - 4 large - (2 cups diced)
1 1/2 pounds unshelled peas - (1 1/2 cups shelled) or about
                              7 1/2 ounces frozen - (see note)
corn - 3 ears - (1 1/2 cups kernels) or about 9 ounces frozen - (see note)
6 Tablespoons olive oil - divided
3 Tablespoons cider vinegar - divided
2 3/4 teaspoons salt - divided
1/2 teaspoon plus freshly cracked black pepper - divided

Prepare the mayonnaise and keep it refrigerated as directed.
Scrub, boil, trim and peel the beets as directed. (See boiled beets.) Immediately drop the peeled beets into a basin of cold water for 5 minutes. Then drain them and cut them into 3/8 inch dice. Blot the diced beets dry on paper towels and place them in a small mixing bowl.
After each of the remaining vegetables has been cooked (and drained) immediately turn it into a basin of cold water for at least 3 minutes. Drain it, blot it dry on paper towels then combine all the vegetables except the beets in a large mixing bowl.
Peel the potatoes and cut them into 3/8 inch dice. In a medium size saucepan over high heat, bring to boil enough water to cover the potatoes by 1 1/2 inches. Add the potatoes to the boiling water and cook them, covered with lid slightly ajar, for about 6 to 7 minutes from the moment they

are in the water regardless of when the water returns to boil. Adjust the heat to keep the water slowly boiling and stir them once or twice with a wooden spoon until the potatoes are just tender. Taste them to determine when they are done. Do not allow them to overcook. Drain them.

Trim, peel and cut the carrots into 3/8 inch dice. Steam them over already simmering water for about 6 or 7 minutes until they are just tender.

Shell and steam the peas as directed. (See steamed peas.) If you are using frozen peas, blanch the still frozen peas in enough boiling water to cover them by 1 1/2 inches in a saucepan, uncovered, over high heat for 3 minutes from the moment they are in the water regardless of when the water returns to boil, stirring the peas with a wooden spoon. Do not allow them to overcook. Drain them.

Husk the corn and boil it as directed, (see boiled corn) but leave the corn in the basin of cold water 5 minutes then drain and blot it. Carefully cut the kernels from the cob. Do not use scrapings from the cob. Separate and crumble the kernels into the large bowl. If you are using frozen corn, blanch the still frozen corn in enough boiling water to cover it by 1 1/2 inches, in a saucepan over high heat, covered with lid ajar, for 3 minutes from the moment it is in the water, regardless of when the water returns to boil, stirring the corn with a wooden spoon. Drain it.

Now, in the small mixing bowl, toss the beets with 1 tablespoon of the oil, 1 teaspoon of the vinegar, 1/4 teaspoon of the salt and a dash of pepper. Then in the large mixing bowl toss all the other vegetables with 5 tablespoons of the oil, 2 tablespoons plus 2 teaspoons of the vinegar, 2 1/2 teaspoons of the salt and the 1/2 teaspoon of pepper. Allow the 2 bowls to stand 1 hour at room temperature, gently and frequently tossing the contents of each. Then refrigerate the bowls, covered, 23 hours, tossing occasionally.

Before serving, turn the contents of each mixing bowl, separately, into a colander set over a bowl and allow the vegetables to drain 30 minutes. (Save the dressing for a lunch time salad.) Then toss all the drained vegetables together in a chilled glass serving bowl. Using a teaspoon, spoon the mayonnaise all around the edges of the bowl, like a wreath and serve the salade Russe immediately.

4 servings

Note: If you must use frozen peas or corn, select those which are not too small so that their size will be in keeping with the diced vegetables.

 CURRIED RICE DOME

This salad looks just like the dome of Saint Peter's Basilica! Serve cucumber soup first. Then have some large crackers along with the salad and finish with chilled oranges.

2 cups long grain brown rice - 14 ounces
1 teaspoon turmeric
6 Tablespoons olive oil
6 Tablespoons cider vinegar
2 teaspoons curry powder
1 1/2 teaspoons salt
1/2 teaspoon superfine sugar
1/4 teaspoon cayenne
12 ounces baby artichokes - about 12 - (2 cups trimmed) - or
9 ounces frozen
1 pound asparagus
8 ounces mushrooms - medium - (2 1/2 cups)

Steam the rice as directed putting the turmeric in the initial cooking water. (See steamed long or short grain brown rice.) Turn the steamed rice into a large mixing bowl, and using a wooden spoon, gently but thoroughly, toss the rice with the oil, vinegar, curry powder, salt, sugar and cayenne.

Prepare and blanch the artichokes as directed, but rather than quarter them, leave them in halves. (See blanched baby artichokes.) Or prepare and blanch the frozen artichokes as directed leaving them in halves. (See blanched frozen artichokes.) In either case immediately turn the drained artichokes into a basin of cold water for 5 minutes. Drain them well and blot them dry on paper towels. Reserve 6 of the best looking artichoke halves and chop the rest small.

Prepare and steam the asparagus as directed. (See steamed asparagus.) Immediately turn the steamed asparagus into a basin of cold water for 5 minutes. Drain them, untie the strings and blot them dry on paper towels. Reserve 6 of the best looking spears, cut the heads off of the rest of the spears and slice the remainder of the spears crosswise into 1/4 inch thick slices.

Wipe the mushrooms with a damp cloth and trim the butt ends of the stems. Select 3 mushrooms, cut them in half lengthwise and reserve them. Chop the remaining mushrooms small.

Wrap the reserved artichoke halves, the whole asparagus and the mushroom halves in wax paper and refrigerate them.

Add the chopped artichokes, the asparagus tips and slices and the chopped mushrooms to the bowl of rice. Using the wooden spoon, and again very gently but thoroughly, mix the vegetables with the rice. Cover the bowl and allow the mixture to stand 1 hour at room temperature. Then refrigerate it covered, at least 1 hour.

Remove the wrapped vegetables and the rice mixture from the refrigerator 30 minutes before serving. About 10 minutes before serving, mound the rice mixture up on a round serving plate, using your (clean) hands, to form a firm dome. Then lay the whole asparagus spears over the dome so that their butt ends rest on the plate and their tips meet at the top of the dome, like the spokes of a wheel. Now, carefully press the artichoke halves, cut side out, flush into the dome between the asparagus around the bottom of the dome. Finally, press the mushroom halves, cut side out, into the dome above the artichokes. Serve the curried rice dome immediately.

4 to 6 servings

PRIMAVERA SALAD

Watercress soup will make a perfect first course this evening. The primavera salad is so complete in itself that it really requires no bread or cheese. However, if you feel the need, serve pita bread and perhaps some Feta cheese. Chilled cherries are the natural dessert selection.

A combination of any of the following young garden vegetables:
asparagus, string beans, broccoli florets, carrots, cucumbers, cauliflower florets, fennel, helianthus tuberosa, kohlrabi, peas, snowpeas, peppers, zucchini, etc., in whatever proportions are desirable or available. - (8 cups cuts)
8 Tablespoons olive oil
2 Tablespoons plus 2 teaspoons cider vinegar
1 teaspoon salt
1/2 teaspoon celery salt
1/2 teaspoon freshly cracked black pepper
1/4 teaspoon superfine sugar
2 pita bread loaves - 7 inches in diameter
butter - at room temperature
parsley leaves - (4 Tablespoons)

Rinse and drain when necessary, trim and cut the vegetables so that they are all of an approximately similar size. In a large serving bowl, toss the vegetables with the oil, vinegar, salt, celery salt, pepper and sugar. Cover the bowl and allow the vegetables to marinate 2 hours at room temperature, turning them frequently. Then refrigerate them for 1 hour, turning them occasionally.

Meanwhile, carefully split the pita loaves in half to form 4 discs. Spread the discs with butter and cut them into many small pie shaped pieces only about 3/8 inch wide at the rounded side. Place the little pieces of bread on a baking sheet and dry them out in a 225 degree oven for about 40 minutes. Immediately transfer the bread to an unsealed paper bag and reserve it.

Remove the vegetables from the refrigerator about 30 minutes before serving. To serve, toss the parsley leaves and the reserved bread with the vegetables and serve the primavera salad.

4 servings

Note: If you do not have quite enough vegetables to measure 8 cups use sliced celery as a filler.

# ANTIPASTO

An antipasto dinner is ideal for a party on the deck, porch or patio. Most of the dishes in this casual meal can be prepared in advance. All the dishes can be doubled or tripled as the case may be. More cheeses, breads, pickles and salad dishes can be added to the list but remember to keep the theme Italian.

stuffed eggs - (recipe follows)
cannellini vinaigrette - (see dried shelled beans vinaigrette)
baby artichokes vinaigrette - (see baby artichokes vinaigrette)
kohlrabi vinaigrette - (see kohlrabi vinaigrette) - (cauliflower can substitute)
red bell peppers vinaigrette - (see red bell peppers vinaigrette)
Gorgonzola cheese
Fontina cheese
smoked Provolone cheese
Italian bread sticks

butter
fennel
jar pepperoncini - hot green Italian peppers
jar Italian oil cured black olives
jar Italian mixed garden pickles
honeydew melon

Place a stack of salad plates on the table as well as paper napkins, flatware, plenty of serving pieces and more than one pair of salt and pepper. The stuffed eggs is the featured dish. The cannellini vinaigrette, baby artichokes vinaigrette, kohlrabi vinaigrette and red bell peppers vinaigrette are presented in serving dishes and on platters. The cheeses can be arranged on a cheese basket or tray. Put the bread sticks in big jars. See that the fresh fennel is trimmed, quartered, separated, chilled and crisp. Serve the pepperoncini and olives, etc., in little dishes. Have the well chilled honeydew cut into wedges and set on individual dessert plates.

4 servings

stuffed eggs

6 eggs - at room temperature
1 can asparagus pieces - 14 1/2 ounces
1 1/2 Tablespoons cider vinegar
1 Tablespoons plus 1 teaspoon prepared yellow mustard - divided
1/2 teaspoon salt
1/8 teaspoon white pepper
1/2 cup plus about 2 1/2 Tablespoons prepared mayonnaise - divided
1 teaspoon ground turmeric
paprika
parsley - 2 sprigs

Hard cook and peel the eggs as directed. (See cooked eggs.) Allow them to cool to room temperature then refrigerate them for 1 hour to help them remain firm while being cut.
Drain, rinse and drain the asparagus, sorting out and discarding any tough pieces. Place the asparagus in a colander, set a saucer with a weight upon it on them and allow them to drain 30 minutes, turning them over 2 or 3 times during that period. Then, taking the asparagus in 2 or 3

batches, squeeze them in your (clean) hands to press out the last drop of moisture. Using a knife, mince the asparagus fine. Place the minced asparagus in a small bowl and stir the vinegar, the 1 tablespoon of mustard, the salt and pepper into it to form a paste.

Cut the eggs in half lengthwise and pop the yolks out into a dinner plate. Using a fork, mash the yolks well blending the asparagus paste into them. Now, add about 2 1/2 tablespoons of the mayonnaise to the mixture, 1 teaspoon at a time. Do not use too much, keep the mixture fairly dry.

Discard 4 of the egg white halves. (Save them for a lunch time salad.) Very generously stuff the 8 remaining halves with the asparagus mixture. Round and smooth the mixture leaving a visible lip all around the edge of the egg white.

Now in a small bowl, stir the 1 teaspoon of mustard and the turmeric into the 1/2 cup of mayonnaise. Glaze the stuffed eggs with the yellow mayonnaise, covering the stuffing and just meeting the edge of the lip. Sprinkle the top of each egg with a dash of paprika.

Place a white paper plate (to keep the eggs from sliding) on a dinner plate and arrange the eggs in a circle on it. Refrigerate the eggs 1 hour. Then decorate the center of the plate with the sprigs of parsley and serve the stuffed eggs chilled.

4 servings

SECTION II

SALADE NIÇOISE

LEGUMINOSAE SALAD

STUFFED TOMATO SALAD

POTATO SALAD

GLACEE OF MARINATED VEGETABLES

TABBOULEH

HORS D'OEUVRE

GREEK SALAD

 SALADE NIÇOISE

This lovely salad really looks best arranged on white oval plates. Serve cold avocado soup. Then offer bread sticks to go along with the salade Niçoise. Ripe cherries will be the perfect dessert.

12 ounces boiling potatoes - 6 rather small - (2 heaping cups sliced)
water
9 ounces string beans - (2 cups cut)
13 Tablespoons olive oil - divided
6 Tablespoons plus 2 teaspoons cider vinegar - divided
1 teaspoon salt - divided
1 teaspoon celery salt - divided
1 teaspoon freshly cracked black pepper - divided
1/4 teaspoon superfine sugar - divided
4 eggs - at room temperature
unpitted canned black olives - 28 small - chilled
capers - 4 Tablespoons small - chilled
4 ounces smoked Mozzarella cheese - (1 cup cut) - chilled
cherry tomatoes - 20 - chilled
Boston lettuce - 20 medium size leaves
1/2 teaspoon dried basil
1/2 teaspoon dried oregano

Peel and quarter the potatoes lengthwise. Cut the quarters crosswise into 1/16 inch uniformly thick slices, dropping them into a bowl of enough cold water to cover them and allow them to stand 1 hour then drain them.

In a medium size saucepan over high heat, bring to boil enough water to cover the potatoes by 1 1/2 inches. Turn the drained potatoes into the boiling water and cook them, covered with lid slightly ajar, for about 5 minutes from the moment they are in the water, regardless of when the water returns to boil. Adjust the heat to keep the water slowly boiling and stir them once or twice with a wooden spoon, until the potatoes are tender but firm. Taste them to determine when they are done. Drain the potatoes and immediately turn them into a basin of cold water for 3 minutes. Drain them again, spread them out on paper towels and blot them dry with more towels.

In a jar, combine the potatoes with 3 tablespoons of the oil, 3 tablespoons of the vinegar, 1/4 teaspoon each of the salt, celery salt and pepper and 1/8 teaspoon of the sugar. Cover the jar with waxed paper and screw the lid on tight. Lay the jar on its side and rotate it frequently for 1 hour at room temperature. Then refrigerate the jar, on its side 23 hours, rotating it occasionally.

Trim and cut the string beans crosswise into pieces 1 inch long. Steam them over already simmering water for an average of 10 minutes for store-bought string beans. Freshly picked home grown string beans may take as little as 5 minutes. Taste them to determine when they are just tender. Immediately turn them into a basin of cold water for 3 minutes, drain them then blot them dry on paper towels.

In a jar, combine the string beans with 2 tablespoons of the oil, 1 tablespoons of the vinegar, 1/4 teaspoon each of the salt, celery salt and pepper and 1/8 teaspoon of the sugar. Then marinate them as directed for the potatoes.

Hard cook and peel the eggs as directed. (See cooked eggs.) Allow them to cool to room temperature then refrigerate them 1 hour to help them remain firm while being cut.

About 30 minutes before serving, remove the potatoes, string beans and eggs from the refrigerator. Cut the eggs in half lengthwise, then cut the halves into quarters lengthwise. Drain, rinse and drain the olives and capers. Blot them dry on paper towels. Cut the cheese into little match sticks 1 inch long. Quarter the cherry tomatoes lengthwise. Rinse the lettuce leaves in cold water and spin them dry.

Arrange 5 lettuce leaves around the edge of 4 large salad plates. Then, equally dividing them among the 4 plates, arrange the cheese, tomatoes, olives, the potatoes and string beans with their dressing, and the eggs, in that order, in diagonal strips side by side in the center of the lettuce leaves and then sprinkle 1 tablespoon of capers over each plate. In a cup, dissolve 1/2 teaspoon each of the salt and celery salt in 2 tablespoons plus 2 teaspoons of the vinegar. Using a fork, beat in 8 tablespoons of the oil, 1/2 teaspoon of the pepper and the basil and oregano, crushing them. Sprinkle the equally divided dressing over each plate and serve the salade Niçoise.

4 servings

Note: It's worth the effort to scout around in speciality stores to find the true, tiny black Niçoise olives packed in oil — in which case drain but do not rinse the olives.

 LEGUMINOSAE SALAD

Sopa de tortilla would be a good selection for the first course. Leguminosae is a Latin name for the bean family. This five bean salad has a warm Mexican accent so accompany it with tortillas. Chilled cantaloupe will make a refreshing finale.

1 heaping cup dried black turtle beans - 8 ounces
1 heaping cup dried kidney beans - 8 ounces
1 1/2 cups large dried lima beans - 8 ounces
sweet gherkin pickles - (1/2 cup sliced)
1 jar pitted green olives - 2 1/2 ounces - (1/2 cup sliced)
3 canned jalapeño peppers
4 Tablespoons superfine sugar
1 cup cider vinegar
1/2 cup olive oil
2 teaspoons salt
2 teaspoons celery salt
2 teaspoons ground cumin
2 teaspoons dried oregano
about 8 ounces green string beans - (1 3/4 cups cut)
about 8 ounces yellow string beans - (1 3/4 cups cut)
iceberg lettuce - 1/2 head - chilled

Soak and cook the three dried beans, separately, as directed. (See boiled dried shelled beans.) Drain them.

Drain, rinse and drain the pickles and olives. Slice them thin crosswise..

Wearing plastic gloves, drain, rinse and drain the jalapeños. Cut them in half lengthwise, remove the seeds and membrane and mince the flesh.

In a large mixing bowl, dissolve the sugar in the vinegar, then using a fork, beat in the oil, salt, celery salt, cumin and the oregano crushing it. Add the pickles, olives, jalapeños and the cooked dried beans, tossing them with wooden spoons to coat them well with the dressing. Allow the mixture to stand 1 hour at room temperature, tossing it occasionally. Then refrigerate it, covered, 23 hours, tossing it twice during that period. Avoid tossing the mixture too often, it may break the beans.

Now, trim and cut the green and yellow string beans into pieces 1 to 1 1/2 inches long. Steam them separately, until they are just tender, as directed. (See steamed string beans.) Immediately turn them into a basin of cold water for 3 minutes then drain and blot them dry on paper towels. Fold the string beans into the dried bean mixture and refrigerate the salad, covered, 24 hours longer, carefully tossing it twice.

About 30 minutes before serving remove the salad from the refrigerator. Just before serving turn it into a serving bowl. Then shred the chilled iceberg lettuce fine and lay it in a wreath around the edge of the beans. Serve the leguminosae salad right away.

4 to 6 servings

 STUFFED TOMATO SALAD

The shape of the soup plate helps to maintain the shape of the very large tomato. This recipe can easily be multiplied a number of times. Enjoy sorrel soup first then serve some whole wheat rolls with the salad and follow with fresh peaches.

2/3 cup small curd Cottage cheese
radishes - (1/4 cup diced)
green bell pepper - (2 Tablespoons diced)
celery - (2 Tablespoons diced)
carrot - (1 Tablespoon diced)
1/3 teaspoon plus salt
parsley leaves - (1 Tablespoon chopped)
oak leaf lettuce - 7 or 8 leaves
1 teaspoon cider vinegar
1 Tablespoon olive oil
dash freshly cracked black pepper
about 14 ounces tomato - 1 very large
2 Tablespoons prepared mayonnaise
dash cayenne

See that the Cottage cheese and all the vegetables are well chilled before beginning preparation of the salad.

Hang the Cottage cheese up in a wet, wrung out cheese cloth bag to drain while the vegetables are being prepared.

Trim the radishes. Core the green pepper, trimming away any white membrane. Trim and scrape the strings from the celery. Trim and peel the carrot. Dice these vegetables very small and in a bowl toss them together with the 1/3 teaspoon of the salt. Chop the parsley fine.

Rinse the lettuce leaves in cold water and spin them dry. In a chilled soup plate, dissolve a pinch of salt in the vinegar. Using a fork, beat in the oil and pepper then toss the lettuce with the dressing. Arrange the leaves so that the tips point out like the spokes of a wheel.

Cut the stem button out of the tomato and cut it into eighth's, or twelfth's if it's very large, lengthwise. Do not cut the wedges too thin. Set the wedges in a circle on the lettuce leaves, sharp points up, to loosely reform the tomato, as it were. Lightly sprinkle the tomato with salt.

Now, thoroughly stir the drained Cottage cheese, chopped parsley, mayonnaise and cayenne, into the diced vegetables. Then heap the Cottage cheese mixture into the center of the tomato wedges and serve the stuffed tomato salad immediately.

1 serving

 # POTATO SALAD

An old world recipe this, the potatoes are cooked after they are sliced and for better penetration the dressing is thickened after it has already flavored the salad. Enjoy home style tomato soup then have some light crackers with the potato salad which looks attractive served on an oval platter. Fresh blueberries will be a good dessert choice.

3 pounds boiling potatoes - about 50 little new, 1 1/4 inches in
                                        diameter - (9 heaping cups sliced)
water
celery - half of 2 large ribs - (1/2 cup sliced)
1 teaspoon superfine sugar
6 1/2 Tablespoons cider vinegar - divided
7 1/2 Tablespoons olive oil - divided
1 1/2 teaspoon salt
1/4 teaspoon freshly cracked black pepper
1 rounded teaspoon cornstarch
parsley leaves - (1 Tablespoon chopped)
chicory - (4 loosely packed cups torn)
1/8 teaspoon salt
1/8 teaspoon freshly cracked black pepper
1/8 teaspoon celery salt

Peel the potatoes and cut them into slices no more than 1/16 inch thick. It is of the utmost importance that the slices be of a uniform thickness. As they are sliced, drop the potatoes into a bowl of cold water and allow them to stand 1 hour then drain them.

In a large saucepan over high heat, bring to boil enough water to cover the potatoes by 1 1/2 inches. Turn the drained potatoes into the boiling water and cook them, covered with lid slightly ajar, for about 5 minutes from the moment they are in the water regardless of when the water returns to boil. Adjust the heat to keep the water slowly boiling and stir the potatoes once or twice with a wooden spoon, until they are tender but firm. Taste them to determine when they are done. Drain the potatoes and immediately turn them into a basin of cold water for 3 minutes. Drain them again, spread them out on paper towels and blot them dry with more towels.

Trim, scrape the strings from and thinly slice only the upper, narrower part of the celery ribs, crosswise. The slices will look like little horse shoes.

In a cup dissolve the sugar in 6 tablespoons of the vinegar. In a large mixing bowl, combine the sliced potatoes, celery, 6 tablespoons of the oil, the vinegar mixture, the 1 1/2 teaspoons of salt and the 1/4 teaspoon of pepper. Gently toss the ingredients using wooden spoons and allow the potatoes to stand 1 hour at room temperature, tossing occasionally. Then refrigerate them, covered, 22 hours, tossing them once or twice.

Now, turn the potatoes into a large strainer set over a saucepan and allow them to drain well for 20 minutes. Return the potatoes to the mixing bowl. Dissolve the cornstarch in the dressing in the saucepan. Bring the mixture to simmer over medium heat, stirring constantly with a rubber spatula. Then reduce the heat slightly and continue to simmer and stir for 2 minutes. Now, pour the hot dressing over the potatoes and using the wooden spoons, gently toss them. Cover the bowl and return it to the refrigerator for 1 hour.

Meanwhile chop the parsley and reserve it.

Thirty minutes before serving time remove the potatoes from the refrigerator. Rinse the chicory in cold water, tear it into bit size pieces and spin it dry. Just before serving, in a cup dissolve 1/8 teaspoon each of the salt and celery salt in 1 1/2 teaspoons of the vinegar. Using a fork, beat in 1 1/2 tablespoons of the oil and 1/8 teaspoon of the pepper. On a chilled serving platter, toss the chicory with the dressing and arrange the leaves in a wreath around the edges of the platter. Lightly mix the reserved parsley with the potatoes then heap the potatoes on the platter in the center of the wreath of chicory and serve the potato salad.

4 servings

GLACÉE OF MARINATED VEGETABLES

This is one of the most glamorous of all salads. Offer your guests cream of spinach soup first then have French bread and ripe Goat cheese with the glacée of marinated vegetables. Finish with fresh pears.

6 ounces red bell pepper - 1 medium - (1 cup cut)
6 ounces carrots - 2 large - (about 1 cup cut)
1 pound cauliflower - about half small head - (2 cups florets)
6 ounces yellow straight or crookneck squash - 1 small, 6 inches long -
(1 cup cut)
12 ounces baby artichokes - about 12 - (2 cups trimmed) or 9 ounces frozen
1 pound unshelled peas - (1 cup shelled) or 5 ounces frozen
1 1/2 teaspoons salt - divided
3 pinches freshly cracked black pepper - divided
8 Tablespoons olive oil - divided
8 Tablespoons California white wine vinegar - divided
glace - (recipe follows)
parsley - about 20 tiny leaves

Core the bell pepper, trimming any white membrane and cut it into little 3/4 inch triangles, then peel the triangles as directed. (See peeled red bell peppers.)

After each remaining vegetable has been cooked, turn it into a basin of cold water for 3 minutes. Then drain it well and blot it dry on paper towels.

Select long slender carrots. Trim, peel and cut the carrots crosswise into 1/4 inch thick slices. Steam the carrots over already simmering water. Start testing them after 10 minutes by piercing them with a wooden toothpick to determine when they are just tender.

Break the cauliflower up into small florets of a uniform size and trim the butt ends of their little stems. Steam the florets over already simmering water. Start testing them after 5 minutes by piercing them with a wooden toothpick to determine when they are just tender.

Trim the squash and cut it crosswise into 1 1/2 inch long pieces. Cut the pieces lengthwise into little wedge shaped sticks about 1/4 inch wide. Trim away the seeds and steam the little sticks over already simmering water just 5 minutes.

Prepare and boil the artichokes as directed, (see boiled baby artichokes) or prepare and blanch frozen artichokes as directed. (See blanched frozen artichokes.)

Shell the peas and steam them over already simmering water for about 10 minutes, depending on their size, until they are just tender. Or blanch the still frozen peas in enough boiling water to cover them by 1 1/2 inches in a medium size saucepan, uncovered, over high heat 1 minute less than the recommended cooking time on the package, from the moment they are in the water, regardless of when the water returns to boil, stirring the peas with a wooden spoon. Do not overcook them. Drain them.

Place the red bell pepper and carrots in a jar (or a bowl). Place the cauliflower and squash in another jar and the artichokes and peas in a third. Sprinkle 1/2 teaspoon of the salt and a pinch of the black pepper into each jar. Pour 4 tablespoons of the oil and 4 tablespoons of the vinegar into the cauliflower jar and 2 tablespoons of the oil and 2 tablespoons of the vinegar into each of the other two jars. Cover the jars with wax paper and screw the lids on tight. Lay the jars on their sides and rotate them frequently for 1 hour at room temperature. (Or toss vegetables in bowls frequently and keep the bowls covered.) Then refrigerate the jars, on their sides, 23 hours, rotating them occasionally.

Several hours before serving, turn all the vegetables into a colander, set over a bowl and allow them to drain for 1 hour, red peppers on the bottom. (Save the drained marinade for a lunch time salad.) Then blot the vegetables dry on paper towels and artfully arrange them in 4 shallow, 1 cup gratin dishes or other small 1 inch deep dishes. Evenly divide each type of vegetable among the 4 dishes, mounding the arrangements slightly. Then refrigerate the dishes for 30 minutes.

At this point prepare the glace and keep it warm as directed.

Now, remove the dishes from the refrigerator and tuck the tiny parsley leaves in among the vegetables, evenly distributing them. Then carefully pour the warm glace mixture over the vegetables until the liquid reaches to within 1/4 inch of the rim of the dishes. Return the dishes to the refrigerator for 5 minutes or until the gelatin is lightly set. Then, taking 2 dishes from the refrigerator at a time and using a feather pastry brush, carefully paint a thin coat of glace over the vegetables then return the dishes to the refrigerator again for about 2 minutes while the next 2 dishes are being painted. Continue in this manner, gradually building up thin coats of glace over the vegetables until about 7 coats have been applied to each dish.

Now, refrigerate the dishes for at least 3 hours before serving. To serve the glacée of marinated vegetables, set each dish on a folded dinner napkin placed upon an individual salad plate.

4 servings

glace

3 cups clarified stock broth - cold - (see clarified stock broth)
1/2 cup cold water
1 teaspoon California white wine vinegar
1/2 teaspoon honey
1/2 teaspoon salt
3 Tablespoons agar-agar granules - (see note)

Combine all the ingredients in a medium size saucepan and bring them to boil over high heat while stirring constantly. Reduce the heat to medium high and slowly boil the mixture 10 minutes, still stirring constantly. Reduce the heat to very low to keep the mixture warm, uncovered.

3 cups

Note: Agar-agar is a gelatin derived from seaweed and is available at natural food stores.

TABBOULEH

No matter how you spell it tabbouleh is a unique salad. We used to frequent a quaint Syrian restaurant which served a wonderful tabbouleh so thick with parsley that the grain was hardly visible. Be sure to use Italian parsley and, of course, fresh mint. Purée of fava bean soup will make an appropriate first course. You might like to serve some Feta cheese and pita bread along with the salad. Fresh apricots will make an excellent dessert selection.

celery - 1 1/2 ribs - (about 3/4 cup diced)
1 pound tomatoes - 2 medium - (2 cups diced)
Italian parsley leaves - (3 packed cups)
mint leaves - (3 packed cups)
1 1/2 cups bulghur - 10 1/2 ounces
9 Tablespoons olive oil
9 Tablespoons fresh lemon juice
2 1/4 teaspoons salt

1 1/2 teaspoons sugar
3/4 teaspoon freshly cracked black pepper
3/4 teaspoon celery salt
6 Tablespoons pine nuts
romaine leaves - about 1 head

Trim, scrape the strings from and dice the celery small.

Remove the stem buttons and seed the tomatoes as directed. (See seeded tomatoes.) Dice them small.

If the parsley or mint need to be rinsed, spin them and blot them dry on paper towels. Chop them fine with a mincer or in the processor, etc.

In a bowl, combine all the ingredients except the pine nuts and romaine. Refrigerate them, covered, no less than 24 hours, tossing them 2 or 3 times.

Using a heavy knife, chop the pine nuts and toast them in a dry pan over medium heat, stirring about 3 minutes until they are golden. Remove them from the pan immediately and toss them with the tabbouleh.

Separate the romaine leaves. If they need to be rinsed, spin them dry. Arrange the more tender leaves around the edge of each of 4 large chilled salad plates. Heap the tabbouleh in the center of the leaves and serve. The tabbouleh is eaten by scooping it up with the romaine leaves and eating it along with the leaves.

4 servings

Note: That's right, the bulgur does not need to be steamed.

 HORS D'OEUVRE

The following are suggestions for a buffet style dinner with a French theme. Most of the dishes in this casual meal can be prepared well in advance. All the dishes can be doubled or tripled as the case may be. More cheeses, breads, pickles and salad dishes can be added to the list but remember to keep the theme French.

oeufs en gelée - (recipe follows)
lentils vinaigrette - (see dried shelled beans vinaigrette)
sliced tomatoes - (see sliced tomatoes)

marinated mushrooms - (see marinated mushrooms)
celeriac remoulade - (see celeriac remoulade)
Roquefort cheese
Gruyère cheese
French bread
radishes
unsalted butter
jar cornishon - (tiny French pickles)
jar olives niçoise - (packed in oil)
jar tiny white asparagus
pears

Place a stack of salad plates on the buffet as well as paper napkins, flatware, plenty of serving pieces and more than one pair of salt and pepper. The oeufs en gelée is the featured dish. The lentils vinaigrette, sliced tomatoes, marinated mushrooms and celeriac remoulade are presented in serving dishes and on platters. The cheese can be arranged on a cheese basket or tray. Place the bread on a bread board along with a bread knife. See that the radishes are fresh and chilled. They are eaten with a dab of butter. Serve the pickles and olives, etc., in little dishes. The pears are eaten out of hand.

4 servings

oeufs en gelée
(eggs in aspic)

4 eggs - at room temperature - (see cooked eggs note)
watercress leaves - (1/4 packed cup chopped) plus 4 small leaves and 8
sprigs
2 cups clarified stock broth - cold - (see clarified stock broth)
1/2 cup cold water
2 Tablespoons agar-agar granules - (see note)
1 teaspoon fresh lemon juice
1/2 teaspoon honey
1/4 teaspoon salt

Cook the eggs for 8 minutes and peel them as directed. (See cooked eggs.) Allow the eggs to cool to room temperature, then refrigerate them for 2 hours.

Chop the watercress leaves fine and reserve them.

Combine the broth, water, agar-agar, lemon juice, honey and salt in a medium size saucepan and bring them to boil over high heat, while stirring constantly. Reduce the heat to medium high and slowly boil the mixture, 10 minutes, still stirring constantly. Reduce the heat to very low to keep the mixture warm, uncovered.

Ladle 1 tablespoon of the broth mixture into each of 4 chilled, little metal eggs in aspic molds or glass custard cups and refrigerate them 2 or 3 minutes or until the gelatin is lightly set.

Dip the 4 small watercress leaves into the broth mixture and, with the aid of a wooden toothpick, spread one over the center of the gelatin in the bottom of each mold then refrigerate the molds again for 2 or 3 minutes. The leaves must be set enough so that they do not move when the eggs are laid over them.

Now, lay 1 cold egg in each mold and ladle enough of the broth mixture into the molds to only barely cover the eggs. Refrigerate the molds again for 3 minutes.

Stir the reserved chopped watercress leaves into the remainder of the broth mixture. Then ladle the rest of the broth mixture into the molds, filling them to the brim and refrigerate the molds for at least 1 hour. (However, do not prepare the oeufs en gelée too far in advance for after a while the aspic begins to color the eggs.)

To serve, run the point of a thin knife around the inside edge of each mold. Then very carefully slip the knife down in between the aspic and the mold, only enough to break the suction. (The molds do not need to be dipped in hot water.) Cover each mold with an inverted, chilled, small plate. Holding them together, turn the two over, then carefully remove the mold. Garnish each plate with 2 sprigs of watercress.

4 servings

Note: Agar-agar is a gelatin derived from seaweed and is available at natural food stores.

This recipe can easily be doubled, but in that case do not double the amount of water.

 GREEK SALAD

Avgolemono is the soup, naturally! Serve crusty bread with the salad then finish with chilled purple grapes.

12 ounces tomatoes - 1 1/2 medium
3 ounces green bell pepper - 1/2 medium
cucumber - 1/2 slender average
celery - 1/2 rib
2 ounces Feta cheese - divided
basil - (1 Tablespoon chopped)
5 Calamata olives - greek olives
2 Tablespoons olive oil
3 Tablespoons red wine vinegar
1/2 teaspoon salt
1/4 teaspoon freshly cracked black pepper

See that stem buttons have been removed and that the tomatoes have been cut in half crosswise. Using only 3 halves, cut each half into 8 wedges.

See that the green pepper has been cut in half lengthwise. Core the half, carefully removing any white membrane. Cut the half pepper in half crosswise then cut the 2 pieces lengthwise into strips, 1/4 inch thick.

See that the cucumber has been cut in half crosswise. Peel the half, quarter it lengthwise and cut the quarters crosswise into 1/4 inch thick slices.

Using only the white, lower half of the celery rib, scrape the strings from it and cut it crosswise into 1/4 inch thick slices.

Dice small or crumble the cheese.

Chop the basil fine and reserve it.

In a bowl, toss the prepared vegetables, 1/2 of the cheese and all the olives with the oil, vinegar, salt and pepper. Arrange the salad on an individual salad plate. Then combine the remaining cheese with the reserved basil, sprinkle the mixture over the Greek salad and serve.

1 serving

Note: Greek salad must be prepared and served in individual portions. If a number of servings are all mixed together and then served, the cheese falls to the bottom and no one seems to get an equal portion of anything.

SECTION III

WALDORF SALAD

GADO GADO

STUFFED AVOCADO SALAD

ITALIAN SALAD

SMÖRGÅSBORD

LENTIL AND RICE SALAD

CRUDITÉ WITH THREE DIPS

 WALDORF SALAD

Here's a new twist on a standard favorite. Cheddar cheese is a logical as well as delicious addition to Waldorf salad. Have a cream of celeriac soup then serve whole wheat bread with the salad. Dessert will be bunches of green grapes.

1 1/2 cups roasted walnut halves - about 6 ounces - (see walnuts)
6 ounces extra sharp Cheddar cheese - (1 1/2 cups diced)
celery - 4 large ribs - (2 cups diced)
6 Tablespoons prepared mayonnaise
1 1/2 pounds Macintosh apples - 4 large - (4 heaping cups diced)
1/2 teaspoon salt

Using a heavy knife, coarsely chop the walnuts.
Make a point of obtaining well aged cheese for this salad. Dice it small or crumble it to conform with the size of the chopped walnuts.
Select well developed, succulent celery. Trim, scrape the strings from and dice the ribs small.
Place the mayonnaise in a large mixing bowl.
Select apples with rosy cheeks and core but do not peel them. Dice the apples somewhat small and as you do so, drop them into the mayonnaise, using a rubber spatula combine them well to keep the apples from discoloring. Then, still using the spatula, fold in the walnuts, cheese and celery. Cover the bowl and refrigerate it at least 1 hour.
Thirty minutes before serving remove the bowl from the refrigerator. To serve, the Waldorf salad, sprinkle it with the salt and turn it into an attractive serving bowl.

4 to 8 servings

 GADO GADO

Gado Gado is a salad from southeast Asia where it is often decorated with edible flowers. Nasturtium blossoms make a lovely addition if you have them. The salad which is served at room temperature with a warm dressing or sauce is truly a feast. Serve cream of kohlrabi soup first, then accompany the salad with rice wafers, if you like. Fresh pineapple completes this pretty picture.

2 pounds cabbage - 1 small head - (8 tightly packed cups shredded)
water
1 1/2 teaspoons plus salt
about 14 ounces boiling potatoes - 12 little new, 1 to 1 1/4 inches in diameter
8 ounces carrots - 4 medium - (1 1/3 cups cut)
about 9 ounces string beans - (2 cups cut)
2 ounces mung bean sprouts - (1 cup)
4 eggs - at room temperature
celery - upper green branches - (1/2 cup diced)
1/4 cup roasted, salted, unpeeled Spanish peanuts
8 ounces tofu - (2 cups diced)
2/3 cup cornstarch
1/2 cup peanut oil
boiling water
peanut sauce - (recipe follows)
8 ounces cucumber - 1 slender average, 7 to 8 inches long - (1 cup sliced)

Quarter the cabbage lengthwise, core and shred it fine crosswise. In a large kettle over high heat, bring to boil 4 quarts of water with 1 teaspoon of the salt. Add the cabbage and blanch it, uncovered, for 3 minutes from the moment it is all in the water, regardless of when the water returns to boil. Push the cabbage down into the water with a longhandled wooden spoon and adjust the heat to keep the water slowly boiling. Drain and immediately turn the cabbage into a basin of cold water for 1 minute. Drain the cabbage very thoroughly, spin it and blot it dry on paper towels.

Scrub the potatoes clean under running water. In an adequate size saucepan over high heat, bring to boil enough water to cover the potatoes by 1 1/2 inches, with 1/2 teaspoon of the salt. Add the potatoes and cook them, covered with lid slightly ajar, for about 20 minutes from the moment they are in the water, regardless of when the water returns to boil, adjusting the heat to keep the water slowly boiling, until they are just tender when pierced with a wooden toothpick. Drain the potatoes and immediately turn them into a basin of cold water for 5 minutes. Drain and peel them.

Trim, peel and cut the carrots, diagonally, into 1/4 thick slices. Steam them over already simmering water for about 3 minutes, until they are just tender. Immediately turn them into a basin of cold water for 2 minutes. Drain them and blot them dry on paper towels.

Trim and cut the string beans crosswise into pieces 1 inch long. Steam them over already simmering water for an average of 10 minutes for store bought string beans. Freshly picked home grown string beans may take as little as 5 minutes. Taste them to determine when they are just tender. Immediately turn them into a basin of cold water for 3 minutes, drain them and blot them dry on paper towels.

Pick any remaining mung bean skins from the bean sprouts. In a saucepan over high heat, bring to boil 2 cups of water with a pinch of salt. Add the sprouts and blanch them, uncovered, for exactly 1 minute from the moment they are in the water, regardless of when the water returns to boil. Drain and immediately turn the sprouts into a basin of cold water for 1 minute. Drain them thoroughly and blot them dry on paper towels.

(All the foregoing vegetables can be prepared up to 24 hours in advance, sealed, separately, in plastic and refrigerated then brought to room temperature before the salad is assembled.)

Hard cook and peel the eggs as directed. (See cooked eggs.) Allow them to cool to room temperature then refrigerate them for 1 hour to help them remain firm while being sliced.

Trim any leaves from the celery and dice it very small.

Slip the skins off of the peanuts and coarsely chop them with a heavy knife.

(Like the cooked vegetables, the eggs, celery and peanuts may be prepared well in advance, etc.)

Two or three hours before serving time, cut the tofu into 1/2 inch dice, blot it on paper towels and lightly sprinkle it with the salt. Dredge 1 cup of the diced tofu in 1/3 cup of the cornstarch, shaking off excess. Heat the 1/2 cup of oil in an 8 inch frying pay (the oil should measure about 1/4 inch deep) over medium high heat. Before the oil starts to smoke, add the dredged tofu. Fry it for about 5 minutes, carefully and constantly stirring it with a wooden spatula until the cubes become golden on all sides. Do not allow them to scorch. Drain the fried tofu on paper towels. Repeat the process with the remaining tofu. Now transfer all the fried tofu to a bowl, pour boiling water over it to cover and allow the tofu to stand 2 minutes. (This improves texture.) Drain the tofu well and set the cubes out on a platter, without touching each other, to dry until serving, turning them over once.

Prepare the peanut sauce and keep it warm or reheat it as directed.

Just before assembling the salad, prepare the cucumber. If the cucumber is unwaxed, do not peel it. Otherwise, peel it. In either case, score the cucumber lengthwise all around, with the tines of a fork and thickly slice it crosswise.

To assemble the salad, spread the cabbage out on a very large serving platter or tray, about 16 by 20 inches. Place the whole potatoes, evenly spaced, around the edge of the cabbage. Arrange the carrots all around and on top of the edge of the cabbage inside the ring of potatoes. Lay the string beans in a ring on the cabbage inside the ring of carrots. Arrange the cucumber slices all around the inside edge of the string beans. Slice the eggs crosswise and lay them, evenly spaced, on top of the cucumbers. Spread out the tofu inside the ring of cucumbers and eggs. Sprinkle the diced celery and chopped peanuts over all the vegetables. Then sprinkle the bean sprouts over all.

Present the gado gado along with a bowl of the warm peanut sauce set over a candle warmer on the dinner table. Allow the diners to serve themselves and spoon the peanut sauce over their servings.

4 to 6 servings

peanut sauce

coconut - (3 cups freshly grated) - (see coconut)
reserved coconut water
1 cup roasted, salted, unskinned Spanish peanuts - about 6 ounces
2 Tablespoons peanut oil
3 Tablespoons fresh lemon juice
1 Tablespoon plus 1 teaspoon tamari
1 teaspoon honey
1/2 teaspoon salt
1 teaspoon curry powder
2 teaspoons cayenne

Prepare and grate the coconut as directed reserving the drained coconut water. Place the grated coconut in the blender or processor.

Strain the reserved coconut water through a fine strainer into a measuring cup. If necessary, add enough tap water to the coconut water for a total measurement of 2 cups. Bring the coconut water to simmer in a saucepan over medium heat. Then pour it over the coconut and allow it to stand a few minutes to cool a bit. Now, purée the mixture. Pour the puréed coconut into a colander, lined with a double layer of wet wrung out cheese cloth set over a bowl. Twist the corners of the cheese cloth together to form a bag. Gently squeeze the bag until all the liquid has been pressed out of it into the bowl. The yield will be 2 cups of coconut milk.

Place the unskinned peanuts in the (clean) blender or processor with all the remaining ingredients and purée the mixture. Transfer the peanut purée to a medium size, heavy saucepan. Rinse out the container of the blender or processor with the coconut milk and then stir the coconut milk into the peanut purée. Now, set the saucepan over medium heat and bring the sauce to simmer, uncovered, while stirring constantly. Simmer the sauce until it thickens. If it thickens too much, add a little water. The sauce can be kept warm, uncovered, over low heat.

(The peanut sauce can be prepared in advance, in which case allow it to cool completely before covering it. If it is refrigerated bring it to room temperature before it is reheated. Reheat the sauce, uncovered, over low heat, stirring constantly.)

To serve the peanut sauce, transfer it to a warm heat-proof serving bowl.

about 3 cups

Note: If fresh coconut is unavailable use 1 1/2 cups dried, unsweetened coconut and 2 cups of (cows) milk rather than water. In which case, allow with the dried coconut to soak in the hot milk for 1 hour before the mixture is puréed. Another alternative is to use canned coconut milk. It comes in 12 ounce cans, is very thick and can be thinned with water to produce the required 2 cups.

 STUFFED AVOCADO SALAD

Unctuous cream of red bell pepper soup is served preceding this very special stuffed avocado salad. Offer some light bread with the salad, or maybe bread sticks. Then present a platter of chilled grapefruit sections.

3/4 cup mixer mayonnaise - (see mixer mayonnaise)
1 pound tomatoes - 2 medium - (2 cups diced)
celery - 1/2 large rib - (1/4 cup diced)
about 1 1/2 ounces green bell pepper - (1/4 cup diced)
canned hearts of palm - 4 hearts
1/3 cup roasted cashews - (see cashews)
parsley leaves - (1/4 cup chopped) - divided
2 Tablespoons plus 2 teaspoons fresh lemon juice
2 pounds avocados - 2 large, 1 pound each

2 teaspoons salt
1/2 teaspoon freshly cracked black pepper
Boston lettuce - about 12 large leaves

Prepare the mayonnaise and keep it refrigerated, as directed, until ready to serve.

Do not bother to peel, but remove the stem buttons then seed the tomatoes as directed. (See seeded tomatoes.) Coarsely chop the tomatoes and place them in a colander to drain for 20 minutes.

Trim, scrape the strings from and dice the celery small.

Core, cut away any white membrane and dice the green pepper small.

Drain, rinse and drain the hearts of palm. Cut them crosswise into 1/4 inch thick slices and blot the slices dry on paper towels.

In a bowl combine the drained tomatoes, the diced celery and bell pepper and the hearts of palm, refrigerate them, covered, and reserve them.

Using a heavy knife, coarsely chop the cashews.

Chop the parsley leaves small.

Place the lemon juice in a mixing bowl. Cut the avocados in half lengthwise discarding the pits. (Plant them.) Using a small spoon, scoop out the flesh by the half teaspoon full and drop it into the lemon juice, reserving the avocado shells. Add the reserved, mixed vegetables, the chopped cashews and the chopped parsley to the avocado flesh, reserving about 1/2 teaspoon of the parsley. Sprinkle the mixture with the salt and pepper and using a wooden spoon gently combine it well.

Rinse the lettuce leaves in cold water and spin them dry. Arrange the equally divided leaves in each of 4 small (berry) dishes and set the reserved avocado shells on them. Drop 2 tablespoons of mayonnaise into each shell then carefully and generously heap the avocado salad mixture over the mayonnaise. Top each stuffed avocado with 1 tablespoon of mayonnaise then sprinkle a pinch of the reserved chopped parsley over each dollop of mayonnaise. Set each dish on an individual salad plate and serve the stuffed avocado salad right away.

4 servings

 ITALIAN SALAD

Begin with stracciatella for the soup course. Next, have some nice crusty Italian bread and some String cheese with the salad. Are you familiar with String cheese? Chilled honeydew melon is the finale.

1 pound cauliflower - about 1 small head - (3 cups florets)
1 pound broccoli - 2 average head - (4 cups florets and cut)
about 13 1/2 ounces yellow string beans - (3 cups cut) - (see note)
12 ounces zucchini squash - 3 small, 6 inches long - (3 cups cuts)
1 pound 2 ounces red bell pepper - 3 medium - (3 cups cut)
3/4 cup olive oil
3/4 cup red wine vinegar
1 Tablespoons superfine sugar
1 Tablespoons salt
1/2 teaspoon freshly cracked black pepper
1 teaspoon dried basil - crushed
1 teaspoon dried oregano - crushed

As soon as each vegetable has been steamed immediately turn it into a basin of cold water, cauliflower, broccoli and string beans for 3 minutes and zucchini and bell peppers for 1 minute. Drain them well and blot them dry on paper towels.

Prepare and steam the cauliflower as directed. (See steamed cauliflower florets.)

Cut the florets off of the broccoli on short stems. Separate large clusters of florets into smaller clusters so that the florets are all of a uniform size. Cut the remaining slender branches into pieces about 1 inch long. Then trim and peel the remainder of the large stalks, first pulling off the fibrous skin with a knife and then using a vegetable peeler. Cut the large stalks crosswise into 1/4 inch thick slices and steam the broccoli over already simmering water for from 10 to as much as 20 minutes. Start testing it at 8 minutes by piercing it with a wooden toothpick to determine when it will be just tender.

Prepare and steam the string beans as directed, cutting them into pieces about 1 inch long. (See steamed string beans.)

Trim the zucchini, quarter it lengthwise, trim away any large seeds and cut the quarters into pieces 3/4 inch long. Steam the zucchini about 5 minutes over already simmering water or until it is just tender.

Cut the bell peppers crosswise into 3/4 inch thick slices. Core the slices, trimming away any white membrane. Cut the rings in 3/4 inch squares. Steam the bell pepper squares about 5 minutes over already simmering water or until they are just tender.

In a large mixing bowl combine all the vegetables with all the remaining ingredients. Allow them to stand 1 hour at room temperature, frequently and gently tossing them using a wooden spoon. Then refrigerate the bowl, covered, and allow the vegetables to marinate, 23 hours, tossing them occasionally. About 30 minutes before serving transfer the vegetables and their dressing to a glass serving bowl and serve the Italian salad

about 8 servings

Note: If prime yellow string beans are not available see the note at the end of the assiette jardiniére recipe. (See assiette jardiniére.)

SMÖRGÅSBORD

Arrange this Scandinavian smörgåsbord on a table or a sideboard. Most of the dishes in this casual meal can be prepared well in advance. All the dishes can be doubled or tripled as the case may be. More cheeses, breads, pickles and salad dishes can be added to the list but remember to keep the theme Scandinavian.

Scandinavian eggs - (recipe follows)
kidney beans vinaigrette - (see dried shelled beans vinaigrette)
pressed cucumbers - (see pressed cucumbers)
potatoes in mayonnaise - (see potatoes in mayonnaise)
coleslaw - (see coleslaw)
Danish Blue cheese
Tilsit or Cream Havarit cheese
Jarlsberg cheese
assorted Scandinavian cracker breads
butter
carrot coins
big dill pickles
jar sliced pickled beets
jar dilly beans
red apples

Place a stack of salad plates on the table or sideboard as well as paper napkins, flatware, plenty of serving pieces and more than one pair of salt and pepper. The Scandinavian eggs is the featured dish. The kidney beans vinaigrette, pressed cucumbers, potatoes in mayonnaise and coleslaw are presented in serving dishes and on platters. The cheeses can be arranged on a cheese basket or tray. Place the assorted breads in a large flat basket. See that the peeled and thickly sliced carrots are fresh and chilled. Serve the dill pickles and pickle beets etc., in little dishes. The apples are eaten out of hand.

4 servings

scandinavian eggs

about 3/4 cup mixer mayonnaise - (see mixer mayonnaise)
4 thick slices white bread
4 very fresh eggs - at room temperature - (see cooked eggs note)
tomatoes - about 2 large - (4 slices)
salt
parsley leaves - (2 teaspoons minced)

Prepare the mayonnaise and keep it refrigerated as directed.
Cut round pieces out of the bread slices, with the same diameters as the tomato slices you will be using. If, at this point, the bread is left to stand, uncovered, 2 or 3 hours it will reduce oven time. In any case, place the bread on a cookie sheet and dry it out in a preheated 200 degree oven for about 40 minutes or until it begins to lightly take color. Immediately transfer the bread to an unsealed paper bag and reserve it.
Poach the eggs and reserve them in a bowl of cold water, refrigerated, as directed. (See poached eggs.)
Choose large, ripe, firm tomatoes which are about 2 1/2 to 3 inches in diameter. Cut 4 slices, each 1/2 inch thick out of the tomatoes. Lightly salt the slices and allow them to drain, 20 minutes, in a colander.
Mince the parsley and reserve it.
Drain the eggs, trimming off any streamers as directed and pat the eggs dry on paper towels. Blot the tomato slices on paper towels and set them on a cookie sheet. Place a poached egg on each tomato slice then mask each egg with the mayonnaise without covering the tomato slice. Sprinkle a little of the reserved minced parsley on the top of each masked egg.

(At this point the eggs can be returned to the refrigerator for about 1 hour if it is necessary to wait.)

At serving time set each egg covered tomato slice on a piece of the reserved dried bread, transfer it to a serving platter and serve the Scandinavian eggs immediately.

4 servings

LENTIL AND RICE SALAD

Cold curried buttermilk soup is the first course this evening. Lentil and rice is such a hearty salad that no bread or cheese is usually served with it, but that's up to you. Oranges will make a light dessert.

2 3/4 cups lentils - about 18 ounces
1 bay leaf
2/3 cup long grain brown rice - about 5 ounces
celery - 2 large ribs - (1 cup chopped)
1/2 cup olive oil
1 cup cider vinegar
2 teaspoons plus salt - divided
1 1/2 teaspoons celery salt
1 1/2 teaspoons superfine sugar
3/4 teaspoons freshly cracked black pepper
1 1/2 teaspoons dried basil
1/2 cup roasted, peeled hazelnuts - about 2 1/2 ounces - (see hazelnuts)
about 1 1/2 pounds tomatoes - 6 small
escarole leaves - (2 cups shredded)

Cull and cook the lentils, with the bay leaf, as directed. (See boiled dried shelled beans.) It is important not to overcook the lentils, for this recipe, so watch them. Thoroughly drain them, reserving the bay leaf. If the cooked lentils measure more than 8 cups, do not use the excess, it would unbalance the recipe. (Save any excess for a bouillon soup. See bouillon soups.)

Steam the rice as directed. (See steamed long or short grain brown rice.) If the steamed rice measures more than 2 cups, do not use the excess. (Save it for the bouillon soup.)

Trim, scrape the strings from and chop the celery fine.

In a large mixing bowl, toss the lentils, rice, celery and the reserved bay leaf with the oil, vinegar, the 2 teaspoons of salt, the celery salt, sugar, pepper and the basil, crushing it. Allow the mixture to stand 1 hour at room temperature, tossing it frequently with a wooden spoon. Then refrigerate it, covered, 23 hours, tossing it occasionally. About 30 minutes before serving time, remove the bowl from the refrigerator.

Remove the stem buttons from the tomatoes and slice them crosswise. Lightly salt the slices and place them in a colander to drain for 20 minutes.

Meanwhile, using a heavy knife, chop the nuts small and reserve them.

Select tender escarole leaves, rinse them in cold water and spin them dry. Cut the leaves in half lengthwise then shred them very, very fine crosswise.

Just before serving toss the reserved chopped nuts and the shredded escarole with the lentil and rice mixture. Then heap the equally divided mixture in each of 6 individual wooden salad bowls. Tuck the equally divided sliced tomatoes in under the salad mixture, around the edges of each bowl, in such a way that half of each tomato slice is sticking up above the edge of the bowl and serve the lentil and rice salad.

6 servings

CRUDITÉS WITH THREE DIPS

Otherwise known as garden city salad, loosely translated, crudité is French for raw. Serve herb broth as the first course to this very casual dinner. Along with the impressive tray of vegetables, serve bread sticks, cut up pita bread, tortilla chips or any little bread shapes which can also be used in the dips. Chilled cantaloupe completes the feast.

assorted vegetables - asparagus, string beans, broccoli, carrots,
cauliflower, celery, cucumber, fennel, mushrooms, snow peas,
bell peppers, zucchini, cherry tomatoes, etc. -
(about 12 cups whole and cut)
hummus bi tahini - (recipe follows)

Blue cheese dip - (recipe follows)
guacamole - (recipe follows)
6 trays of ice cubes

Trim, peel, core, seed, cut, slice or leave the vegetables whole as necessary so that they are all of a size which is easy to use in the dips.

(The vegetables can all be prepared in advance, sealed in plastic with the exception of mushrooms which should be wrapped in paper towels and bell peppers which should be wrapped in wax paper and refrigerated until serving.)

Prepare the three dips as directed, bringing them to room temperature before serving.

Wrap the ice cubes, 1 tray at a time, in a clean terry cloth towel. Lay the towel on a work surface and using a hammer or other heavy object, crack the ice cubes. The cracked ice can be stored in a sealed plastic bag in the freezer.

At serving time set a bowl of each of the three dips on opposite sides of the dinner table for easy access.

Cover a tray or large serving platter with the cracked ice then arrange the cold prepared vegetables, in groups of kind, alternating colors and textures, on the cracked ice. Set the platter of crudités on the center of the table and supply everyone with a salad plate. The diners simply select the vegetables they desire and dunk them into the dip of their choice.

6 servings

hummus bi tahini

1 can chick peas - 16 ounces - (2 cups drained)
1/2 cup reserved drained chick pea liquid
1/2 cup tahini - sesame paste - (stir it up before using)
2 Tablespoons olive oil
2 Tablespoons California white wine vinegar
1 Tablespoons soy sauce
1 Tablespoon plus 1 teaspoon honey
1 teaspoon ground coriander
1/2 teaspoon ground cumin
1/2 teaspoon salt

1/2 teaspoon celery salt
1/4 teaspoon white pepper
1/4 teaspoon ground ginger.

Liquefy the drained chick peas with all of the remaining ingredients in the blender or processor until they are smooth. Alternatively, pass the chick peas through a food mill set over a bowl then, combine them with the remaining ingredients, in which case the mixture will not be as smooth. The hummus bi tahini can be prepared in advance and refrigerated in a sealed container but must be brought to room temperature before serving. To serve the hummus bi tahini divide it between each of 2 small serving bowls.

about 3 cups

blue cheese yogurt dip

8 ounces Blue cheese - (2 cups crumbled)
2 cups yogurt
1 Tablespoon plus 1 teaspoon fresh lemon juice
1/2 teaspoon salt
1/4 teaspoon white pepper

Using a fork, mash the cheese well on a dinner plate. Transfer the cheese to a bowl and slowly stir the yogurt and the remaining ingredients into it. The Blue cheese dip can be prepared in advance and refrigerated, covered, but must be brought to room temperature before serving. To serve the Blue cheese dip, divide it between each of 2 small serving bowls.

about 3 cups

guacamole

about 8 ounces green chile peppers (Anahiem or California) -
        3, about 1 3/4 inches in diameter at top and 5 inches long
celery - half large rib - (1/4 cup minced)

1 1/2 pounds avocados - 3 small
1 Tablespoon olive oil
1 Tablespoon fresh lemon juice
1 teaspoon salt
1/8 teaspoon cayenne

Prepare and peel the chile peppers as directed. (See peeled red bell peppers.) Handle the chile peppers carefully, their skin is tougher but their flesh is more delicate than the red bell peppers. Mince the chile peppers with a knife or mincer and reserve them.

Trim, scrape the strings from, mince the celery and reserve it.

Select avocados with dark, rough skin. Peel them and separate them from their large pits, reserving 2 of the pits. Using the back of a fork, mash the avocados on a large plate, until creamy but still a little lumpy. Transfer the avocado to a bowl and blend in the oil, lemon juice, salt, cayenne and the reserved chile peppers and celery. Then put the 2 reserved pits in the guacamole. The guacamole can be prepared in advance and refrigerated, covered, but must be brought to room temperature before serving. To serve the guacamole place 1 avocado pit in each of 2 small serving bowls and heap the equally divided guacamole over them.

about 2 cups

Note: By a miraculous mystery of nature the pits keep the guacamole from discoloring.

SECTION IV

ORANGE AND AVOCADO SALAD

with mousseline mayonnaise

DELPHINA'S PÂTÉ MAISON

PICKLED BEET AND EGG SALAD with green mayonnaise

CHICK PEA BROCCOLI AND PASTA SALAD

RAW SLAW with soy mayonnaise dressing

TOMATO ASPIC

STUFFED GREEN BELL PEPPER SALAD

❧ ORANGE AND AVOCADO SALAD ❧
with mousseline mayonnaise

Sopa de cacahuete is the first course for this lovely dinner which could, interestingly, bring a touch of summer to a grey winter day. Almost any type of bread or cheese would work well as an accompaniment to the salad. Present fresh pineapple for an appropriate finale.

navel oranges - 4 large
water
mousseline mayonnaise - (recipe follows)
watercress - 2 bunches - (8 loosely packed cups leaves and tips)
1/2 teaspoon plus salt - divided
1 Tablespoon California white wine vinegar
3 Tablespoons olive oil
1/4 teaspoon freshly cracked black pepper
2 pounds avocados - 4 small, 8 ounces each
pomegranate - 1 large

To easily peel the oranges, bring to boil enough water to cover the oranges in a saucepan over high heat. Blanch the oranges 5 seconds, drain them and transfer them to a basin of cold water for 5 minutes. Peel them, carefully removing all white membrane and separating the segments. Refrigerate the orange segments, covered, until ready to serve.

At this point, prepare the mousseline mayonnaise and keep it cold as directed.

Pull the leaves and only the tiny branch tips from the stems of the watercress. In a mixing bowl, dissolve the 1/2 teaspoon of salt in the vinegar. Using a fork, beat in the oil and pepper and toss the watercress with the dressing. Then arrange the watercress, equally divided, in a wreath around the edge of 4 large chilled salad plates.

Remove the orange segments from the refrigerator and count them. Then, cut the avocados, lengthwise, discarding the pits (plant them) into as many slices as there are orange segments. Carefully pull the skins from the avocado slices and then arrange them, alternately, with the orange segments, like the spokes of a wheel on the salad plates, inside the wreaths of watercress. Break open the pomegranate and sprinkle about 2 tablespoons of the seeds over each salad plate then lightly sprinkle the salads with salt. Now, heap the mousseline mayonnaise, equally divided, in the center of each orange and avocado salad and serve them immediately.

4 servings

mousseline mayonnaise

1/2 cup mixer mayonnaise - (see mixer mayonnaise)
1/2 cup heavy cream - cold

   Before beginning, place a small mixing bowl in the refrigerator to keep it cold..
   Prepare the mixer mayonnaise as directed. Then very thoroughly wash the beaters and refrigerate them for a few minutes. Now, in the cold bowl, using the cold beaters, beat the heavy cream at medium speed until it is very thick. Then, using a rubber spatula, carefully fold the whipped cream into the mayonnaise and refrigerate the mousseline mayonnaise, covered, until ready to serve.

about 1 1/2 cups

DELPHINA'S PÂTÉ MAISON

   I always bake the pâté in a little, round, white, odd size, ceramic baking dish because the pâté looks good in it—which is important. If you have nothing else use a standard loaf dish but do look for an attractive pâté dish, there are some around. Serve jellied consommé Madrilène to begin this delightful meal. Following the pâté and salad offer strawberries over ice cream.

1/2 teaspoon ground rosemary - (see ground rosemary)
1/2 teaspoon ground (rubbed) sage
1/2 teaspoon ground thyme
1/4 teaspoon freshly grated nutmeg
1/4 teaspoon ground cloves
pinch ground ginger
1/2 teaspoon celery salt
1/4 teaspoon white pepper
4 eggs - divided
1 can pitted black olives - 3 ounce - (1/2 cup chopped)
1 pound mushrooms - medium - (5 cups whole)

1 teaspoon salt
8 Tablespoons butter
2 cups stock vegetable purée - (see stock vegetable purée)
2 Tablespoons Madeira
2 Tablespoons honey
1/4 cup bread crumbs - (see bread crumbs)
1 bay leaf

In a cup, combine the rosemary, sage, thyme, nutmeg, cloves, ginger, celery salt and white pepper. Reserve the mixture.

Hard cook and peel 2 of the eggs as directed. (See cooked eggs.) Allow them to cool to room temperature then refrigerate them 1 hour to help them remain firm while being chopped. Cut the eggs in half, separating the whites and yolks. Crumble the yolks and chop the whites small.

Drain, rinse and drain the olives. Chop them small.

Wipe the mushrooms with a damp cloth, trim the butt ends of the stems and chop them small.

Sauté the mushrooms, sprinkled with the salt, in the butter in a large frying pan (see utensils) over medium high heat for about 10 minutes or until all moisture has completely evaporated. Reduce the heat to medium low. Add the crumbled yolks, chopped whites, chopped olives, stock vegetable purée Madeira and honey to the pan. Using a metal spatula, stir and turn the mixture over for about 10 minutes to dry out the purée. Blend in the reserved herb and spice mixture and the bread crumbs. Remove the pan from the heat and allow the mixture to cool a bit.

In a mixing bowl, using a wire whisk, beat the 2 remaining eggs until they are light then gradually stir the pâté mixture into them. Now, pack the pâté mixture into an attractive, buttered, 3 1/2 to 4 cup baking dish, such as a 9 by 5 inch loaf dish and lightly press the bay leaf onto the top of the center of the pâté. Using a piece of foil which has been perforated with a number of small holes, tightly cover the dish, but so that the foil does not touch the pâté itself.

Bake the pâté in a preheated 350 degree oven for 1 1/2 hours. Remove the dish from the oven and allow the pâté to cool completely. Remove the foil and cover the dish with a fresh piece of foil (without holes), then refrigerate the pâté at least 24 hours to allow the flavors to ripen. The pâté keeps very well, refrigerated, up to 5 days. Remove the dish from the refrigerator and uncover it at least 1 hour before serving. Serve Delphina's pâté maison just slightly cool along with some very good French bread to spread it on and a tossed salad mix I or II. (See tossed salad mix I or see tossed salad mix II.)

about 3 1/2 cups

Note: The pâté must be neither too fine nor too coarse. Its texture will depend upon how you chop the egg whites, olives and mushrooms.

❧ PICKLED BEET AND EGG SALAD ❧
with green mayonnaise

This is possibly the most beautiful of all salads. The color combination of dark green spinach, ruby red beets, white and yellow eggs and the pale green mayonnaise is very dramatic. Vichyssoise would be a good soup choice. Next, serve Westphalian pumpernickel bread and unsalted butter with the salad. Finish with chilled yellow delicious apples.

8 pickled beets - (recipe follows)
8 pickled eggs - (recipe follows)
1 cup green mayonnaise - (recipe follows)
1 pound untrimmed spinach - (8 packed cups trimmed)
1/4 teaspoon salt
1/4 teaspoon celery salt
1 Tablespoon cider vinegar
3 Tablespoons olive oil
1/4 teaspoon freshly cracked black pepper

Prepare the pickled beets and eggs as directed.
Prepare the green mayonnaise and keep it cold as directed.
Wash and trim the spinach as directed then spin it dry. (See washed and trimmed spinach.) In a bowl, dissolve the salt and celery salt in the vinegar. Using a fork, beat in the oil and pepper and toss the spinach with the dressing. Then spread the equally divided spinach out on each of 4 large salad plates. Drain the beets and cut them in half crosswise so that their pretty pattern of rings is evident. Lay 4 halves, on the spinach on each plate, cut side up, in the shape of a cross, leaving a space at the center of it. Now, cut the drained eggs in half lengthwise and lay them in a cross in between the beets. Heap 6 tablespoons of the mayonnaise in the center of each salad to serve the pickled beet and egg salad with green mayonnaise.

4 servings

PICKLED BEETS AND EGGS

2 1/2 pounds beets - 8 medium
3 cups cider vinegar
1 cup water
1 cup sugar
2 bay leaves
1 teaspoon salt
1 inch piece cinnamon bark
1 teaspoon black peppercorns
1 teaspoon whole cloves
1 teaspoon whole allspice
8 eggs - at room temperature

Boil, trim and peel the beets as directed, leaving them whole. (See boiled beets.) Immediately drop the peeled beets into a basin of cold water for 5 minutes. Drain them.

Bring all the remaining ingredients, except the eggs, to simmer in a saucepan over high heat. Reduce the heat to low and gently simmer the mixture, uncovered, 15 minutes. Place the beets in a very large, hot, sterilized jar and pour the hot liquid and spices over them. When cool, cover the jar and allow the beets to marinate 48 hours at room temperature.

About 18 hours before the pickled beet and egg salad with green mayonnaise is to be served, in other words just before you go to bed the night before, hard cook and peel the eggs as directed. (See cooked eggs.) Drop the eggs into the marinade with the beets, making sure the eggs are completely covered with the liquid so that they color evenly.

In 18 hours the eggs will absorb just enough of the beet coloring to make a pretty edging on the egg whites when they are cut open. Do not allow them to marinate longer. If the timing does not coincide with the preparation of the salad, simply remove the eggs from the marinade and refrigerate them, covered, until about 30 minutes before serving.

green mayonnaise

2 ounces untrimmed spinach - (1 packed cup trimmed)
1 1/2 cups mixer mayonnaise - (see mixer mayonnaise)
1 egg yolk - at room temperature
1 Tablespoon cider vinegar

Prepare and blanch the spinach as directed. (See blanched spinach.) Squeeze the spinach dry in your (clean) hand. Place the ball of spinach in the blender or processor with 1/2 cup of the oil from the mixer mayonnaise recipe and liquefy the spinach. Transfer the liquified spinach to a little pitcher or measuring cup which has a spout. Rinse out the blender or processor with the remaining oil from the mixer mayonnaise recipe then pour the oil into the pitcher. Alternatively, pass the squeezed spinach through a food mill set over a bowl then stir the oil into it. The mayonnaise will not be as smooth.

Prepare the mixer mayonnaise as directed, using 3 yolks instead of the 2 called for, the spinach oil, cider vinegar instead of the white wine vinegar called for and omitting the water at the end of the recipe. Refrigerate the green mayonnaise, covered, until serving.

about 1 3/4 cups

CHICK PEA BROCCOLI AND PASTA SALAD

I like to serve this salad in a big white ironstone bowl that used to be a wash basin. Start with home style tomato soup. Then, following the chick pea, broccoli and pasta salad, serve poached pineapple slices.

1 3/4 cups dried chick peas - about 14 ounces
2 teaspoons superfine sugar
8 Tablespoons cider vinegar
4 Tablespoons prepared yellow mustard
1 Tablespoon plus 1 teaspoon salt - divided
1 teaspoon celery salt
1/2 teaspoon freshly cracked black pepper
8 Tablespoons olive oil
1 1/2 pounds broccoli - 3 average heads, 1 bunch - (6 cups cut)
1 can pitted black olives - 6 ounces - (1 cup cut)
2 quarts water
8 ounces dried small elbow macaroni
1 teaspoon dried oregano

Soak and cook the chick peas as directed. (See boiled dried shelled beans.) Be sure they are well cooked. Drain them. If the cooked chick peas measure more than 4 cups do not use the excess, it would unbalance the recipe. (Save any excess for a bouillon soup. See bouillon soups.) Spread the drained chick peas out on a tray, which is lined with paper towels to dry off a bit. Slip off as many loose skins as you can and discard them.

In a cup, dissolve the sugar in the vinegar, then in a mixing bowl, stir the vinegar into the mustard. Add 1 teaspoon of the salt, the celery salt, pepper, oil and chick peas. Combine the ingredients well and allow the chick peas to stand 1 hour at room temperature, tossing frequently. Then refrigerate them, covered, 23 hours, tossing occasionally.

About 1 1/2 hours before serving time, trim the florets off of the broccoli, giving them stems about 1/4 inch long. Separate large clusters of florets into smaller clusters so that the florets are all of a uniform size. Cut the remaining slender branches into pieces 3/8 inch long. Then trim the remainder of the large stalks, first pulling off the fibrous skin with a knife and then using a vegetable peeler. Dice the stalks to match the size of the chick peas. Steam the broccoli over already simmering water for from 10 to as much as 20 minutes. Start testing it at 8 minutes by piercing it with a wooden toothpick to determine when it will be just tender. Immediately turn the broccoli into a basin of cold water for 3 minutes, drain it and blot it dry on paper towels. Refrigerate the broccoli in a covered bowl for at least 1 hour.

Drain, rinse and drain the olives. Cut them crosswise into slices 1/4 inch thick, usually 3 slices per olive. Refrigerate the olives, covered, at least 30 minutes.

Just before serving time bring the water to boil, with 2 teaspoons of the salt, in a large saucepan over high heat. Drop the macaroni into the boiling water all at once, give it a stir with a wooden spoon and cook the pasta, covered with lid ajar for 12 minutes, or a little less than directed on the package, from the moment it is in the water, regardless of when the water returns to boil or until it is tender but firm, "al dente", adjusting the heat to keep the water slowly boiling and stirring occasionally. Turn the macaroni into a colander and drain it well, shaking the colander. Allow it to cool 4 or 5 minutes.

Meanwhile, transfer the chick peas and all their dressing to a large salad bowl. In its separate bowl, toss the broccoli and 1 teaspoon of the salt and the oregano, crushing it. Then toss the broccoli, the sliced olives and the macaroni with the cold chick peas and serve the chick pea, broccoli and pasta salad immediately.

4 to 6 servings

Note: Please do not mix the ingredients together ahead of time or allow the pasta to become stone cold. The warm pasta and the cold chick peas balance each other and the salad will be a pleasantly cool one.

RAW SLAW
with soy mayonnaise dressing

This is a great salad to have in mid-winter when you're craving raw vegetables. The salad is showed off to its advantage if it is arranged in a shallow pasta bowl. Serve matzoh balls in garlic broth first. Accompany the salad with a coarse dark bread then complete the meal with crisp green apples.

soy mayonnaise dressing - (recipe follows)
2 ounces carrot - 1 medium
celery - part of 8 ribs - (2 cups sliced)
4 ounces green bell pepper - 1 small - (3/4 cup sliced)
4 ounces red radishes, minus leaves - about 10 (1 cup sliced)
about 2 pounds red cabbage - 1 small head - (5 or 6 outer leaves plus 4
cups shredded)

Prepare the dressing and keep it refrigerated as directed.

Trim and peel the carrot. Then still using the vegetable peeler, with a light touch, continue to peel long thin strips from the carrot, dropping them into a bowl of ice water. Let the carrot strips remain in the ice water while the rest of the vegetables are being prepared.

Trim and scrape the strings from the celery. Using only the lower, whiter half of each rib cut the celery, diagonally, into long thin slices.

Quarter the green pepper lengthwise, core it and trim away any white membrane. Cut the quarters, lengthwise into long thin strips.

Trim and slice the radishes thin crosswise.

Reserve 5 or 6 of the large outer cabbage leaves. Quarter and core the remaining head and shred the quarters crosswise.

Drain the carrot strips and blot them dry on paper towels. Toss all the prepared vegetables together and refrigerate them, along with the reserved cabbage leaves, sealed in plastic, for about 1 hour. Fifteen minutes before serving arrange the cabbage leaves in a large bowl and place the tossed vegetables in the center of them. Serve the raw slaw along with a bowl of soy mayonnaise dressing and let everyone spoon the dressing over their own serving.

4 servings

soy mayonnaise dressing

1 teaspoon superfine sugar
1 Tablespoons plus 2 teaspoons soy sauce
1 Tablespoons plus 2 teaspoons cider vinegar
2 teaspoons water
1 1/4 cups prepared mayonnaise

In a cup dissolve the sugar in the soy sauce, vinegar and water. Place the mayonnaise in a small serving bowl and stir the liquid mixture into it. Refrigerate the soy mayonnaise dressing, covered, until serving.

about 1 1/2 cups

 TOMATO ASPIC

Serve vichyssoise, either hot or cold to start. Fancy little dinner rolls and perhaps some cheese would go nicely with the tomato aspic. Offer poached peaches to finish.

3 cups tomato juice - cold
1 1/2 cups stock broth - cold - (see stock broth)
4 Tablespoons agar-agar granules - (see note)
2 teaspoons fresh lemon juice
1/2 teaspoon salt
1/2 teaspoon sugar
pinch cayenne

celery - (3 Tablespoons diced)
green bell pepper - (3 Tablespoons diced)
boiling water
1 1/2 cups mixer mayonnaise - (see mixer mayonnaise)
1 pint cherry tomatoes - chilled - (2 heaping cups whole)
parsley - several sprigs

In a medium size saucepan, combine the tomato juice, stock broth, agar-agar, lemon juice, salt, sugar and cayenne and bring the mixture to boil over high heat, while stirring constantly. Reduce the heat to medium high and slowly boil the mixture 10 minutes, still stirring constantly. Then pour the mixture into a 4 cup plain ring mold and allow the aspic to stand 1 hour at room temperature to cool and partially solidify.

Meanwhile, see that the strings have been scraped from the celery and dice it very small. Blanch it in a little boiling water for 2 minutes, drain it, turn it into a basin of cold water for 1 minute and drain it. See that any white membrane has been cut away from the cored bell pepper and dice it very small. Blanch it in a little boiling water for 1 minute, drain it, turn it into a basin of cold water for 1 minute and drain. Blot the celery and bell pepper dry on paper towels, evenly sprinkle them over the partially solidified aspic then, using a wooden spoon, gently fold them into it. Allow the aspic to cool 1 more hour at room temperature then refrigerate it for 3 hours.

Meanwhile prepare the mayonnaise as directed. Transfer it to a small serving bowl and keep it refrigerated, covered, until serving.

At serving time run the point of a thin knife around the inside edges of the ring mold. Then very carefully slip the knife down in between the aspic and the mold, in several places, only enough to break the suction. (The mold does not need to be dipped in hot water.) Cover the mold with an inverted, round, flat, chilled serving platter. Holding the platter and mold together, turn them over, tap the back of the ring mold with a wooden spoon then lift it off of the aspic. Fill the center of the ring of aspic with the cherry tomatoes, stems removed, then decorate both the cherry tomatoes and the edges of the platter with the parsley sprigs. Serve the tomato aspic along with the bowl of mayonnaise and let everyone serve themselves to the mayonnaise.

4 servings

Note: Agar-agar is a gelatin derived from seaweed and is available at natural food stores.

STUFFED GREEN BELL PEPPER SALAD

Potato dumplings in paprika broth will be the first course. A favorite with those who love egg salad, this recipe can easily be multiplied. Serve whole wheat crackers with the salad. Blackberries over ice cream round out this salad dinner which can be served at any time of year.

celery - 1 large rib
1 ounce carrot -1 small
radishes - 3
6 ounces green bell pepper - 1 medium
3 eggs - at room temperature
3 Tablespoons prepared mayonnaise
1 teaspoon prepared gray mustard
1/8 teaspoon salt
1/4 teaspoon freshly cracked black pepper
about 1 ounce alfalfa sprouts - (1 cup) - chilled
parsley - 3 sprigs

Trim, scrape the strings from and cut 3 pieces, each 2 inches long, crosswise from the celery rib. Now, make many, close parallel cuts lengthwise in either end of each piece almost to the center of the piece, like the teeth of a comb. Drop the celery pieces into a bowl of ice water. Finely dice enough of what remains of the celery rib to measure 2 tablespoons and reserve it.

Trim, peel and cut the carrot in half lengthwise. Using a vegetable peeler, peel 3 wide, thin slices from the inside of the carrot. Roll the slices up, secure them with a toothpick and drop them into the bowl of ice water with the celery pieces.

Trim the tops and roots from the radishes. Make 4 thin, leaf shaped slices around each radish, starting at the root end and extending 3/4 of the way up the radish without cutting them off. Drop the radishes into the bowl of ice water and refrigerate the bowl.

Select a well shaped bell pepper with a "flat bottom" that sits up properly by itself. Slice a "lid" off of the stem end of the pepper and core it, carefully trimming away any white membrane. Wrap the pepper cup in wax paper, refrigerate and reserve it. Finally dice enough of the sliced off "lid" to measure 2 tablespoons and reserve it.

Hard cook and peel the eggs as directed. (See cooked eggs.) Allow them to cool to room temperature then refrigerate them for 1 hour to help them remain firm while being chopped. Then cut the eggs in half separating the yolks from the whites. Chop the whites small and crumble the yolks into a bowl. Stir the mayonnaise, mustard, salt and black pepper into the yolks then fold in the chopped whites and reserve diced celery and bell pepper. Refrigerate the egg salad until it is thoroughly chilled.

(Up to this point all the preparations can be done several hours in advance.)

Assemble the salad just before serving. With the aid of a fork, to separate the alfalfa sprouts, spread the sprouts out on a large chilled salad plate. Stuff the reserved bell pepper cup with the egg salad, mounding it up and set the pepper on the center of the sprouts. Drain the bowl of ice water, remove the toothpicks from the carrot curls and blot the vegetables on paper towels. The celery will have spread like fans, the carrots will remain curled and the radishes will have opened to look like tiny roses. Artfully arrange the vegetables around the stuffed pepper. Garnish the plate with the parsley sprigs and serve the stuffed green bell pepper salad.

1 serving

BREAD AND CHEESE

Unfortunately bread is a subject too vast to be contained within the confines of this book, as would be a discussion of table cheese.

However, bread, like the other components of a perfect meal, must be appropriate. Occasionally I have suggested, but there are so many types from which to choose and circumstance vary so, that I must let you make the final decision yourself. Home baked bread is wonderful and it's quality would be dependable. Even if you do not have time to make yeast breads there are many quick breads that can easily be made such as Irish soda bread, corn bread, buttermilk biscuits, popovers, and fried breads, such as tortillas and chipatees. But barring that, seek out the best quality you can find. Look for a good bakery, very often it's the natural food store that supplies the best bread in town.

In dinners where soup, salad or dessert are the main dish bread can assume a slightly more important role. A thick loaf of peasant bread can be sliced on a bread board right at the table. Or warm some French style bread to make it crustier and serve it in a long narrow basket. Or serve Italian bread sticks, Westphalian pumpernickel or buttery warm dinner rolls wrapped in a napkin. Big round flat discs of Scandinavian rye bread, the kind with the hole in the middle, are always a show stopper. Or how about a basket of mixed crackers of varying sizes. I often offer both salted and sweet butter with bread. Bread and butter plates are sometimes provided but not usually with a tossed salad that follows an entrée and is eaten from the dinner plate. Their use is flexible, it's a question of convenience. If you are using a white table cloth you could just lay the bread right on the table in the old fashioned way. Then use the little pan and brush called a "crumber" designed for the purpose of sweeping up the crumbs before dessert is served.

Cheese is frequently offered along with the bread in the salad course but only when it has not been predominantly incorporated into some other part of the dinner and never in an Oriental dinner, of course. A wedge of cheese served at room temperature, under a glass dome is a visual as well as alimentary pleasure. Cheese can round out some of the lighter menus very nicely and from Brie to Cheddar the choice is vast. I especially like the soft cheeses with the diner dessert menus. While the hard Cheddars always seem to go well with the soup suppers. The dinners where salad is the principal dish require perhaps the most careful selection of a cheese accompaniment—and so on.

Once again, as with all food, be absolutely certain of the quality of the bread and cheese you serve.

DESSERTS

Desserts, like soups and salads can be divided into two categories. They are either the light course after a full meal or they are treated like a main dish, the feature of the dinner, as in the dîner dessert menus. In any case, dessert is always a final course before coffee and tea.

LIGHT DESSERTS

Very often a beautiful dessert, which after all may have taken as much effort and time to prepare as an entrée, will receive little attention simply because the diners are sate. The foregoing meal was delicious and generous and everyone is satisfied. A simple offering of fresh fruit and nuts or poached fruit and cookies or frozen fruit over ice cream would have been a better choice and in that case the diners would be more inclined to feel free to pass up dessert without fear of offending the host or hostess. No one would regret anything especially the cook who prepares the beautiful desserts. Following are some light and almost effortless fruit dessert suggestions.

FRESH FRUIT

Fresh fruit, in its natural simplicity, at the peak of ripeness, lush and full flavored, served for dessert makes dessert the easiest course to select. The prime consideration is seasonal availability. Then give taste, color and tradition some thought. Fresh fruit requires little effort and is always beautiful, served slightly chilled and attractively presented. The golden rule to follow when serving fresh fruit is to always be absolutely certain of the quality of the fruit before serving it.

Strawberries, raspberries, blackberries and blueberries are served in little fruit dishes along with a pitcher of rich cream and a bowl of superfine, granulated sugar.

Cherries, peaches, plums and apricots look natural heaped in a basket.

The vast melon family cut in wedges or slices, should always be served on chilled plates.

Grapes, in varying shades of purple and green are perhaps the most elegant of fruits and look classic draped over a pedestal dish. Do you have grape shears for snipping off a small bunch of grapes?

For apples and pears I use an antique fruit service consisting of twelve small, delicately proportioned knives and forks in a gold colored metal. They are just meant for cutting up fruit; each diner carves his own. Try serving apples and pears with small knives and forks sometime, it is old world and guests find it amusing.

Grapefruit, oranges, mandarins or tangerines belong to the citrus family. To peel grapefruit immerse it in boiling water for 5 seconds, drain it and immerse it in a basin of cold water for 5 minutes. The grapefruit will now be easy to peel. Carefully remove all the white membrane. To serve the grapefruit, separate the segments and arrange them in two concentric circles on a serving plate. To serve oranges, without peeling them, cut the oranges in half crosswise then cut each half into eighths and heap the pieces in a bowl. They are eaten right off the skin. Mandarin oranges or tangerines as they are called are served whole.

Bananas are the prefect dessert after a meal, such as tacos or stuffed lettuce leaves that you have been eating with your hands. They are the one fruit which is usually served at room temperature. Serve them still in the bunch and let everyone select their own, peel it and eat it. (Like monkeys!) Or if you want to be more dignified, carefully cut the bananas in half lengthwise, peel them, wrap each half in foil and put them in the freezer for a couple of hours. To serve them unwrap the still frozen bananas and lay two halves, "back to back" on a chilled glass dessert plate. Eat them with a spoon or fork. It's the civilized way, really!

Pineapple is so beautiful it's a shame to cut it. However, slice off the top, keeping all the leaves in tact, and set it aside. Now, you can use the pineapple coring device which both cores the pineapple and cuts away the rind, then cut the pineapple into cubes. If you do not have such a device, cut the pineapple crosswise into 1 inch thick slices. Trim the piney rind from the slices and cut them into wedges about 1 inch wide at the rounded side then trim away the hard core from the pointed end of the wedges. In any case set the pineapple top on the center of a round serving platter and arrange the pineapple cubes around it. Stick a tooth pick in each cube for easy handling.

Serve pomegranates heaped in a bowl along with plenty of paper napkins. The little seeds are juicy.

And then there are the more exotic fruits, fresh figs, mangoes, papayas ad infinitum. Substitute them in the menu suggestions at your discretion. A bowl of nuts, either a single variety or a mixed bowl, is always served with the fresh fruit. Be sure to have a nut cracker for each diner. The nuts accompany not only the fruit but the lingering dinner conversation.

POACHED FRUIT

If you had a peach tree in your yard which bore delicious fruit, you would be tempted to can some of it wouldn't you? The following winter you would be proud to serve fruit that you canned yourself. If you do not have a yard or a tree, you can buy fresh fruit in season at a local farm stand, take it home, can it, and feel as if you do have a yard and a tree—and be just as proud. Quality canned fruit will greatly supplement the very limited range of fully ripe fresh fruit available in winter time. If a certain fruit that you like will not grow in your area, it's fun to make an overnight trip and drive to an area where the fruit does grow and bring back baskets of it for canning. We like to make a camping trip out of it and it's an event that we look forward to.

What I am trying to say is that I would like to encourage you to discover the satisfaction of canning fruit yourself but that there is not enough room here to give you the instructions. However, you can get instructions from any good canning book—like the one that comes with the jars. Canning fruit is really a very simple process. Unfortunately, the word "canned" has fallen into such disrepute that I almost hesitate to use it. But canned fruit could also be called poached fruit so let us call it that and when poached fruit is called for in the menu suggestions you will know that I really mean some special fruit which you canned yourself last summer. Serve homemade cookies with the chilled fruit, if you can. It's a nice touch. Find a recipe for Swedish butter cookies in the miscellaneous section of this book.

Also, there are some very nice commercially prepared canned fruits available, some put up in glass jars. Search out those which meet your standards and keep them on hand in case of emergency. By the same token, some good quality cookies are being commercially packaged these days, they aren't hard to find. Be sure not to overlook that old favorite chocolate covered graham crackers.

FROZEN FRUIT

Freezing, as well as canning fresh fruit while it is flavorful and abundant is not only a good idea, it is economical too. All the berries freeze especially well. Again, due to the lack of space, I shall have to ask you to find freezing instructions in a book dedicated to the subject. Thawed frozen berries served over ice cream is a favorite with everyone. Keep the ice cream flavors uncomplicated but don't forget to serve those wonderful strawberries you picked at the berry farm last spring over strawberry ice cream on Valentines Day.

PRINCIPAL DESSERTS

Now that we have agreed that a light fruit dessert after a full meal is a wise choice, what about the beautiful and sometimes rich desserts we all love? Featuring our important dessert as the main dish is a solution to the situation. The dinner is designed around the dessert. A light soup, a tossed salad and appetites are saved for the pièce de résistance, the principal dessert. It makes sense doesn't it? The dessert dinner or dîner dessert to give it a distinctive name then becomes a special, slightly festive occasion. It is a dinner to look forward to, perhaps served only on Sundays or some other day. Or maybe a certain favorite dessert is served only on a particular occasion. It can say "Happy Birthday" in a special way.

SECTION I

DEEP DISH RHUBARB PIES

STRAWBERRY MOUSSE

RASPBERRY CREAM PUFFS

BLACKBERRY SHERBET in meringue shells

BLUEBERRY PIE

 DEEP DISH RHUBARB PIES

Vichysoisse, hot or cold, would make a good first course for this springtime, dîner dessert. Then a tossed salad of dandelion greens would be very appropriate, served with homemade biscuits. These delicious old fashioned looking rhubarb pies use only honey and bananas as sweetening agents.

plain pastry dough - (see plain pastry dough)
2 pounds 4 ounces rhubarb - 12 to 14 ribs - (6 cups cut)
ripe bananas - 2 large
8 Tablespoons honey
10 Tablespoons plus 1 teaspoon cold water - divided
1/8 teaspoon salt
2 Tablespoons cornstarch
1 egg yolk - at room temperature

Prepare the pastry dough as directed, dividing it into 4 flattened balls of equal size before refrigerating it.

Select nice ruby red rhubarb ribs of uniform size. Trim the ribs, lay them, flat side down, on a cutting board and using a serrated knife, cut them crosswise into 3/4 inch long pieces. Pack the cut rhubarb into each of 4, 1 1/2 cup, oven proof bowls.

Peel the bananas and together with the honey, 6 tablespoons of the water and the salt, in the blender, in two batches, or in the processor, make a slurry out of them. The slurry should be slightly lumpy. Alternatively, using a fork, mash the bananas on a dinner plate, transfer them to a bowl and stir in the other ingredients. In any case, in a cup, dissolve the cornstarch in 4 tablespoons of the water then stir the mixture into the slurry. Spoon the equally divided banana slurry over the rhubarb in the 4 bowls.

Roll out 1 of the balls of dough into a disc 1 inch in diameter larger than the diameter of the bowls. Using the point of a sharp knife, cut the dough into long strips, 1/2 inch wide.

In a cup, using a fork, beat the yolk with the 1 teaspoon of water. Using a pastry feather, brush the rim and 1/2 inch down around the outside of 1 of the bowls, with some of the yolk. Now, cover the bowl with the strips of dough in a slightly oblique, interwoven lattice pattern. Press the overhanging dough against the outside of the bowl and trim the strips of dough, evenly, to within 1/2 inch of the rim of the bowl. Then carefully paint the lattice pattern with some of the yolk. Repeat the process with the remaining balls of dough and bowls of rhubarb.

For convenience, set the bowls on a baking sheet and bake them in a preheated 400 degree oven for 40 minutes, covering the bowls with foil after about 20 minutes if the pastry is browning too quickly. Remove the bowls from the oven and allow the deep dish rhubarb pies to cool to room temperature before serving.

4 servings

STRAWBERRY MOUSSE

Be sure to use fresh, ripe strawberries in season, there's just no substitute for their flavor. French onion soup is the first course. Next, serve asparagus vinaigrette with some French bread and have a piece of Gruyère on the table if you like. You may want to serve some little cookies such as Swedish butter cookies with the strawberry mousse.

1/2 cup heavy cream
strawberries - 1 pint - (2 heaping cups)
1 cup superfine sugar - divided
2 egg whites - at room temperature - (see cooked eggs note)
1/8 teaspoon cream of tartar

Refrigerate the cream and a large size mixing bowl for at least 1 hour before whipping the cream. Refrigerate electric mixer beaters also.

Meanwhile, cull the strawberries, reserving 4 to 6 berries for decoration. Hull the remaining berries and in the processor or blender, purée them with 1/3 cup of the sugar. Transfer the purée to a bowl and refrigerate it, covered.

In the cold bowl, using the cold beaters, at medium speed, whip the cream until it starts to thicken. Then reduce the speed to low and continue to whip the cream while slowly adding 1/3 cup of the sugar until the cream is very thick. Now, gently stir the cold strawberry purée into the whipped cream and refrigerate the mixture, covered.

Thoroughly wash and dry the beaters and in a medium size bowl beat the egg whites until they are frothy. Add the cream of tartar and continue to beat the whites, at high speed, now, while slowly adding the remaining 1/3 cup of sugar, 1 teaspoon at a time, until the whites hold glossy peaks when the beaters are lifted.

Remove the strawberry mixture from the refrigerator, uncover it and slide the beaten egg whites onto the top of it. Then, using a wood spoon or rubber spatula gently fold the whites into the strawberry mixture, inserting the spoon into the center of the whites, bringing it down underneath and then using an up and over rolling motion so as not to deflate the whites, while intermittently rotating the bowl itself.

Spoon the mousse into each of 4 to 6 (depending on appetites) chilled, large, long stemmed glasses and decorate each serving with a reserved, whole, unhulled strawberry. Set the glasses upon doily covered saucers, place the saucers upon larger plates and serve the strawberry mousse immediately.

4 to 6 servings

RASPBERRY CREAM PUFFS

Cream puffs are fun and people like to see them being made so have the raspberry sauce and the pastry cream ready in advance. Invite your guests into the kitchen to watch the cream puff preparation. While the puffs are baking, enjoy sorrel soup followed by a salad of celeriac vinaigrette with a light bread and a mild cheese. Afterward, assemble and serve the raspberry cream puffs to your delighted guests.

raspberry sauce - (recipe follows)
pastry custard - (recipe follows)
6 cream puff shells - (recipe follows)

Prepare the raspberry sauce in advance as directed. Then remove it from the refrigerator about 40 minutes before serving time so that it will be just cool but not chilled when served.

Prepare the pastry custard in advance as directed. Be sure that it is at room temperature before assembling the cream puffs.

Prepare the cream puff shells as directed. When they have cooled to room temperature, fill them with the equally divided pastry custard and replace their little cut out bottoms. Set the cream puffs, right side up, on dessert plates set upon larger plates. Spoon about 3 tablespoons of the sauce over each puff and serve the raspberry cream puffs immediately.

6 servings

raspberry sauce

raspberries - 1 pint - (2 heaping cups)
1/4 cup water
6 Tablespoons superfine sugar

Cull the raspberries, setting aside 1/2 cup of the firmest, best looking berries. Liquefy the rest of the berries with the water in the processor or blender. Then, stirring it with a spoon, strain the liquid through a fine sieve into a bowl.

Add the sugar to the liquid and allow it to stand 1 hour at room temperature, stirring occasionally, until all the sugar is thoroughly dissolved. Then, add the reserved berries and refrigerate the raspberry sauce, for at least 1 hour before serving.

about 1 1/4 cups

Note: Divine nectar!

pastry custard
(crème patissière)

1 1/2 cups milk - at room temperature
1 teaspoon vanilla extract
1/2 teaspoon almond extract
2 Tablespoons plus 2 teaspoon cornstarch
2 Tablespoons cold water
4 eggs yolks - at room temperature
10 Tablespoons sugar

Bring the milk to simmer in a small, heavy saucepan over medium heat. Add the vanilla and almond extract.

Meanwhile, in a cup, dissolve the cornstarch in the water. In a mixing bowl, using a wire whisk, beat the egg yolks until they are light then whisk the cornstarch mixture and the sugar into them. Now, very slowly pour half of the simmering milk into the yolk mixture while stirring vigorously with the whisk. Then, using a rubber spatula, stir the yolk mixture into the remaining milk in the pan over the medium heat. Raise the heat slightly to bring the custard to a slow boil then reduce it again slightly and slowly boil the custard for 2 minutes while stirring it thoroughly and constantly. Scrape the bottom and sides of the pan, do not allow the custard to scorch. Remove the pan from the heat and continue to stir the custard 1 minute longer. Cover the pan with a paper towel and lid and allow the custard to cool to room temperature.

about 2 cups

cream puff shells

1/2 cup all purpose flour
4 Tablespoons butter
1/2 cup plus 1 teaspoon water
1 teaspoon sugar
dash salt
2 eggs - at room temperature
1 egg yolk

Sift the flour into a mixing bowl.

Melt the butter in a medium size, heavy saucepan over low heat. Add the 1/2 cup of water, the sugar and salt. Raise the heat to medium high and when the water comes to boil remove the pan from the heat. Add the sifted flour all at once and using a wooden spoon, stir the batter vigorously until it is well blended. Return the pan to the medium high heat and continue to stir the batter for 2 minutes vigorously flattening it out and turning it over to "dry" it on all sides. Immediately transfer the batter to the mixing bowl and, using a rubber spatula, beat in the eggs, 1 at a time, until each is well incorporated and the batter is smooth.

Drop the equally divided batter on a lightly buttered baking sheet, 1 heaping tablespoon at a time, into 6 mounds, spaced 3 inches apart, rounding off the mounds and leaving no "tails". In a cup, using a fork, beat the yolk with the 1 teaspoon of water. Using a pastry feather, brush just the top of each mound with the yolk. Do not allow the yolk to drip down, it may inhibit the pastry from puffing. Place the baking sheet in the middle of a preheated 400 degree oven and bake 15 minutes. Then slip another baking sheet onto the bottom shelf of the oven to keep the bottom of the puffs from scorching. The pastry will have already puffed at this point and may be lightly covered with foil if you think it is necessary to keep it from browning too much. Continue to bake the puffs 15 minutes longer.

Then remove the sheet from the oven, and using a potholder, turn each puff upside down and with the point of a sharp knife cut a circle into each around the area where they rested on the baking sheet. Now, return the upside down puffs to the turned off oven, with door ajar, for 10 minutes, to allow steam to escape and their interiors to dry. Then remove the puffs from the oven and lift the little cut out from each puff. Using a small spoon, very carefully scrape any remaining moist dough out of the puffs. Keeping each puff with its own cut out together, set the puffs on a cake rack and allow them to cool to room temperature

6 cream puff shells

BLACKBERRY SHERBET
in meringue shells

Wear old clothes if you're picking wild blackberries because the thorns will tear them to pieces. This dessert is worth it though, a lovely color combination of green pistachios on lavender sherbet. Serve watercress soup then have a salad of yellow string beans vinaigrette with French bread. Finally, present this delicate and delicious dessert.

meringue shells - (recipe follows)
blackberry sherbet - (recipe follows)
1 Tablespoon shelled pistachios

Make the meringue shells in advance as directed.

Make the blackberry sherbet as directed. Use it while it is firm, but not hard.

Peel the pistachios as directed. If they have already been roasted, just dry them out as directed. If they have not been roasted, roast them as directed. (See pistachios.) In either case, using a heavy knife, coarsely chop the pistachios.

At serving time set the 6 meringue shells on individual dessert plates. Scoop the sherbet into the meringue shells, heaping it and rounding it. Sprinkle 1/2 teaspoon of chopped pistachios over each serving and, of course, serve the blackberry sherbet in meringue shells immediately.

6 servings

meringue shells

3 eggs whites - at room temperature - (see cooked eggs note)
dash salt
1/8 rounded teaspoon cream of tartar
2/3 cup superfine sugar
1/2 teaspoon vanilla extract

Cover a cookie sheet with parchment or brown paper and set it aside.

Place the egg whites in a mixing bowl then set the bowl inside of a larger bowl which is half filled with hot water. Using a hand held electric mixer, beat the whites until they are frothy. Add the salt and cream of tartar and continue to beat the whites, at high speed now, until they hold soft peaks when the beaters are lifted. Now continue beating while slowly adding the sugar, 1 teaspoon at a time, until all the sugar is added and the whites hold stiff glossy peaks when the beaters are lifted. Add the vanilla. The entire beating operation should take no more than 15 minutes.

Using a large spoon, drop 6 large, well separated dollops, each about 3 inches in diameter, of the equally divided meringue on the paper covered cookie sheet. Using the back of a soup spoon, dipped in cold water, make a depression in the center of each dollop to fashion a free form cup. Place the meringues in a preheated 150 to 200 degree oven for from 1 1/2 to 2 hours. The object is to dry out the meringues without permitting them to color. (See note.)

When cooled, the 6 lovely white meringue shells can be stored in a sealed plastic bag for an indefinite period of time. Make them on a dry winter day and they will be like a gift on that hot summer day when you make blackberry sherbet. Never place meringue shells in the refrigerator as they would absorb moisture.

6 meringue shells

Note: The temperature setting and length of time will depend upon your oven. (All ovens are not calibrated the same, my children.) In the oven I now have the lowest temperature setting is 175 degrees and I must leave the oven door slightly ajar during the 2 hours of drying out time. Then I turn off the heat, close the oven door and allow the meringue shells to remain in the oven until the oven has cooled. These steps may not be necessary with your oven, but it's nice to have a few tricks up your sleeve.

blackberry sherbet

blackberries - 1 pint - (2 heaping cups)
1/2 cup plus optional water
1 cup sugar
1 teaspoon lemon juice
2 cups milk - at room temperature

Cull and hull the blackberries. In a large, heavy saucepan over medium high heat, combine the berries with the 1/2 cup of water and the sugar, mashing the berries with a potato masher. When the mixture comes to boil, reduce the heat to medium and continue to slowly boil it, uncovered, for 10 minutes. Pass the mixture through a food mill set over a bowl to eliminate seeds. Then strain it through a fine strainer into a bowl, stirring the pulp and pressing it with the back of a spoon. Measure the liquid in the bowl. If it does not measure 2 cups, pour more water over the pulp still in the strainer. If the total liquid measurement is more than 2 cups, boil it down. Discard the pulp.

Now, in the bowl, combine the 2 cups of blackberry syrup with the lemon juice and the milk. (If the milk appears to curdle, don't worry about it, it will straighten out later.) Allow the mixture to cool to room temperature. Then either pour it into 2 freezer trays (freezes quicker) or leave it in the bowl. In either case, put it in the freezer for 2 or 3 hours until it is hard. Then take the sherbet out of the freezer and break it up into chunks not larger than 1 inch. In the food processor, process the chunks of sherbet, in 2 batches, for about 20 seconds each, until it is smooth. Return the sherbet to the trays or the bowl and freeze it for 1 or 2 hours until it is firm but not hard.

Alternatively, use the electric mixer and beat the sherbet in the bowl while it is still in the slush stage, repeating the procedure 2 or 3 times. Or you can even beat the sherbet right in the freezer trays with a fork, but, of course, the processor will give smoother results than either of these methods.

If you have an ice cream maker, freeze according to the manufacturer's directions.

about 3 cups

 BLUEBERRY PIE

I use a pretty flower shaped cookie cutter to make the cut out in the crust of this clever blueberry pie. Offer tomato essence first, then serve a salad of Boston lettuce, from your garden hopefully, before presenting the pie.

2 pints blueberries - (5 heaping cups)
5 Tablespoons plus 1 teaspoon cold water - divided
1 cup sugar
4 Tablespoons cornstarch
1 teaspoon fresh lemon juice
1 1/2 Tablespoons unsalted butter
plain pastry dough - double recipe - (see plain pastry dough)
1 egg yolk

Cull the blueberries. In a large, heavy saucepan over medium low heat, combine the berries with 1 tablespoon of the water and the sugar. Heat the berries, covered, about 15 minutes, until their juices start to run and simmer. Uncover the pan and continue to simmer the berries 20 minutes longer, stirring occasionally with a wooden spatula. Remove the pan from the heat. In a cup, dissolve the cornstarch in 4 tablespoons of the water. When the berries have stopped simmering completely (important) pour the cornstarch mixture over them while gently and constantly stirring the berries with the spatula. Return the pan to medium low heat and continue to constantly stir the berries until the juices come to simmer. Then simmer and stir the berries 2 minutes. Remove the pan from the heat and stir in the lemon juice and butter. Transfer the berry mixture to a bowl and allow it to cool to room temperature. Cover the bowl with a paper towel and lid and refrigerate it overnight. The berries must be very cold before the pie is filled.

The following morning prepare the double recipe of plain pastry dough as directed, dividing the dough into 2 flattened balls and wrapping them separately before refrigerating them.

Roll out 1 of the balls of dough as directed into a disc at least 13 inches in diameter. Fold the disc of dough in half and then again in half. Place the point of the folded dough in the center of a 7 inch bottom diameter by 1 1/2 inch deep pie plate. (See utensils). Then unfold the dough, encouraging it to relax down into the plate. There should be about 1 inch of dough hanging down all around the outside of the plate.

Roll out the second ball of dough into a disc at least 12 inches in diameter. Using a small cookie cutter or a small drinking glass, cut a hole in the center of the dish then cover the dough with a clean towel.

In a cup, using a fork, beat the yolk with the 1 teaspoon of water. Using a pastry feather, paint the entire surface of the dough inside the pie plate with the yolk. Reserve the remainder of the yolk in the cup. Dip your finger in some water and dampen the dough on the rim of the plate, all around. Remove the berries from the refrigerator and spoon the cold berries into the dough lined pie plate. Stick a toothpick in the very center of the berries. Now, uncover and carefully lift the second disc of dough, placing it on the pie and centering the cut out on the toothpick. Remove the toothpick. Evenly trim away all but 1 inch of the overhanging dough all around the outside of the pie plate. Dip your finger in water again and dampen 1/2 inch all around the underside of the overhanging dough. Now, fold the overhanging dough up under itself onto the rim of the plate. Flute the folded dough all around by pinching it between the tips of the thumb and index finger of one hand onto the tip of the index finger on the other hand. Brush the entire top of the pie with the reserved remaining yolk.

Bake the pie on the bottom shelf of a preheated 450 degree oven for 18 minutes. Cover the pie with foil and bake 7 minutes longer. Remove the foil and set the pie plate on a cake rack and allow the pie to cool at least 6 hours. Serve the blueberry pie at room temperature.

6 to 8 servings

Note: This is a foolproof method for a non-boil over berry pie. The pie should really be baked in the morning to give it plenty of time to cool.

SECTION II

CHOCOLATE CHERRY CLAFOUTI

APRICOT DUMPLINGS

BLUE PLUM COBBLER

PEACH TART

WATERMELON BASKET

❧ CHOCOLATE CHERRY CLAFOUTI ❧

The first time I can remember tasting cherry clafouti was at the home of relatives in the Burgundy region in France. It was unforgettable. Start with sorrel soup. Next, offer a salad of cauliflower vinaigrette and country bread. Then finish with this special clafouti.

1 cup sugar
6 Tablespoons 100% cocoa - (see note)
1/8 teaspoon salt
1 1/4 cups milk - at room temperature
1/2 teaspoon almond extract
1 pound dark, sweet cherries - (2 heaping cups)
3 eggs - at room temperature
2/3 cup flour
1 teaspoon confectioners sugar

Sift the sugar, cocoa and salt together into a saucepan. Stir in the milk and almond extract. Set the pan over medium low heat and stir frequently until the sugar and cocoa have dissolved. Remove the pan from the heat and allow the mixture to cool a bit.

Meanwhile, remove the stems from and split the cherries on one side only, removing their pits with the tip of a sharp little knife. (It's really not hard to do if you don't happen to own a cherry pitter.) Reserve the cherries.

Using the electric mixer or in a mixing bowl, using a wire whisk, beat the eggs until they are light and stir the cocoa mixture into them. Sift the flour over the mixture, then beat the ingredients only until they are smooth. The batter will be very thin.

Butter a flat, round 8 1/4 inch in diameter by 1 3/4 inch deep 5 3/4 cup baking dish. Pour a 1/4 inch thick layer of batter into the bottom of the dish and place it in a preheated 375 degree oven for 3 minutes. Remove the dish from the oven and turn the oven heat down to 350 degrees. Evenly distribute the cherries, cut side down, in the dish, then carefully pour the rest of the batter over the cherries. Bake the clafouti in the 350 degree oven 35 to 40 minutes. (If your oven heats unevenly, turn the dish around after it has been in the oven 20 minutes.) Insert a wooden toothpick into the center of the clafouti, if it comes out clean, it is done. It will be quite puffed. Allow the clafouti to cool for at least 30 minutes. Dust the top with the confectioners sugar sifted through a fine sieve and serve the chocolate cherry clafouti warm.

6 to 8 servings

Note: In other words a cocoa with no sugar in it.

APRICOT DUMPLINGS

This is the kind of dessert that should be served on a platter covered with paper doilies. For the soup and salad courses, precede the apricot dumplings with borscht and a tossed spinach salad served with a light rye bread.

almond paste - (recipe follows)
1 cup minus 1 Tablespoon all purpose flour
1 Tablespoon cornstarch
2 Tablespoons sugar
1/4 teaspoon salt
2 Tablespoons butter - cold
1 egg
1/2 teaspoon almond extract
1 to 2 Tablespoons milk - cold
about 1 pound apricots - 12
boiling water
6 cups water
4 cups corn oil
confectioners sugar

Prepare the almond paste in advance as directed and keep it refrigerated.

Sift the flour, cornstarch, sugar and salt together into a bowl and cut in the butter with a pastry blender. Then quickly rub the flour through the butter with your fingertips until the mixture is granular. Stir in the egg and almond extract with a fork. Add the milk, a little at a time, using only as much as is necessary until dough begins to form. Then, with your hands, shape the dough into a cylinder 12 inches long, handling it as little as possible. Using a ruler as a guide, divide the cylinder into 12 pieces, seal them in plastic and allow them to rest, refrigerated, 1 hour.

Meanwhile, blanch the apricots, 20 seconds, in enough boiling water to cover them. Drain them and immediately turn them into a basin of cold water. Drain them and slip their skins off. (See note.) Cut each apricot in half and remove the pit. Place all the apricot halves in a colander. Bring the 6 cups of water to boil in a large saucepan over high heat. Slide all the apricots into the boiling water at once. Blanch them for 1 minute from the moment they are in the water, regardless of when the water returns to boil. Drain them and immediately turn them into a basin of cold water for 3 minutes. Drain the apricot halves and blot them dry on paper towels.

(Allowing about 15 minutes for the oil to heat to temperature, heat the oil in a deep saucepan, with a cooking thermometer clipped to the inside of it, over medium high heat to 375 degrees, or use an electric deep fryer set at 375 degrees.)

Meanwhile, shape some of the cold almond paste into 12 pieces the size of almond pits. Set them aside.

Keeping the unused pieces of dough sealed in plastic, roll out 1 piece of dough at a time, on a lightly floured surface with a lightly floured rolling pin, into a thin disc. Place an almond paste pit between 2 halves of apricot and set it on the center of the disc of dough. Carefully pull the dough up around the apricot, enclosing it completely in the dough, sealing the dough with your fingertips, using a drop of water if necessary. Make 2 more dumplings. When the oil has reached temperature, deep fry the 3 dumplings together for 5 minutes, pushing them down into the oil and turning them over occasionally with a skimmer or slotted spoon so that they brown evenly. Meanwhile, make 3 more dumplings. Using the skimmer, lift the cooked dumplings from the oil, drain them on paper towels for a second then roll them in a bowl of the confectioners sugar and transfer them to a pretty serving platter. Repeat the process until all the dumplings are made. Apricot dumplings are best served within 30 minutes of being fried. They are eaten with knife and fork.

4 to 6 servings

Note: If you are using store bought apricots, keep in mind that because of their perishability, apricots are shipped before they are fully ripe. This sometimes makes them difficult to peel. In which case, do not blanch them any longer but rather peel them with a sharp little knife.

almond paste

1/2 cup blanched almonds - about 2 1/2 ounces - (see almonds)
1 cup confectioners sugar
1 teaspoon almond extract
2 Tablespoons corn oil

Process the almonds and sugar together in the processor until the nuts are chopped as fine as possible or use the blender. Then, using the flat solid disc, pass the mixture through the food chopper into a bowl. (See utensils.) This will enable the chopped almonds to be transformed into a paste. Alternatively, the nuts can be chopped fine with a heavy knife then combined with the sugar and passed through the chopper. In any case, sprinkle the extract over the mixture. Then, while dribbling the oil over it a little at a time, start working the mixture with your hand until a "dough" forms.

Wash and dry your hands well and flour them with confectioners sugar. Transfer the "dough" to a surface lightly dusted with confectioners sugar and knead the "dough" just as you would flour dough until it is a smooth mass. The almond paste will keep well refrigerated in a sealed glass jar at least 6 months.

about 1/2 pounds almond paste

Note: The food chopper step can be eliminated but the finished product will not be as smooth.

BLUE PLUM COBBLER

Begin with cucumber soup this evening. Then a salad of green string beans vinaigrette and a little goat cheese with some dinner rolls will be nice to serve before this easy dessert. The blue plum cobbler looks especially pretty baked in a glass soufflé dish.

2 pounds blue plums (prune plums) - 26 to 32 - (6 cups sliced)
1 Tablespoon cornstarch
2/3 cup honey
1 teaspoon ground cinnamon
1/4 teaspoon freshly grated nutmeg
1/4 teaspoon plus salt - divided
3 Tablespoons butter - cold - divided
1 cup all purpose flour
1 1/2 teaspoons baking powder
2 Tablespoons sugar
1/2 cup milk - at room temperature
1/2 teaspoon vanilla extract

Pit the plums and thinly slice them, dropping them into a deep 6 cup oven proof bowl.

In a small bowl, vigorously stir the cornstarch into the honey until it is dissolved then pour the honey over the plums. Sprinkle the cinnamon, nutmeg and a dash of salt over the plums and dot them with 1 tablespoon of the butter, cut in little pieces. Tightly cover the dish with foil and bake the plums in a preheated 425 degree oven for 30 minutes.

About 15 minutes before the plums are ready, prepare the biscuit topping. Sift the flour, baking powder. the 1/4 teaspoon of salt and the sugar together into a mixing bowl. Cut in 2 tablespoons of the butter with a pastry blender then quickly rub the flour through it with your fingertips until the mixture is granular. Add the milk and vanilla, all at once, and using a fork, stir only until the flour has absorbed the liquid.

When the plums are ready remove the dish from the oven and uncover it. Drop the biscuit batter by the teaspoonful (for more even distribution than tablespoonfuls would make) evenly over the hot plums. Return the dish to the 425 degree oven and bake if for 25 minutes longer until the biscuit topping is nicely browned. Remove the dish from the oven and allow the blue plum cobbler to stand 20 minutes before serving.

4 to 6 servings

 PEACH TART

Offer consommé Madrilène for the first course then serve a romaine salad with some bread sticks. Finally, for this mid-summer diner dessert, present the beautiful peach tart which you baked in the cool of the morning.

prebaked tart shell 12 by 8 by 1 inch deep - (recipe follows)
about 3 1/2 pounds peaches - 14 medium - (14 cups sliced)
3 Tablespoons plus water
1 Tablespoon lemon juice
1 cup sugar

Prepare, bake and cool the tart shell in advance as directed.

Select your peaches very carefully. They must be all of a uniform size, ripe but firm and unblemished. Blanch the peaches 20 seconds in a saucepan of boiling water. Drain them and immediately immerse them in a basin of cold water. Drain, peel, cut them in half and remove the pits. Slice each half into thirds or into wedges 1 to 1 1/4 inches wide on the rounded side.

Combine the sliced peaches, the 3 tablespoons of water, the lemon juice and sugar in a large, heavy saucepan over medium low heat. As the juices from the peaches start to flow and the sugar dissolves, increase the heat to medium high until the juices come to boil. Then adjust the heat to keep the juices slowly boiling for 1 hour, uncovered, stirring occasionally with a wooden spatula. Then, reduce the heat enough so that the juices only simmer gently. Stir more frequently now and ever so carefully for about 30 minutes or until all the peach slices have become translucent and the juices are thick and syrupy. Pay close attention toward the end of the cooking period, do not allow the mixture to scorch. Remove the pan from the heat.

Place the cooled prebaked tart shell on a cutting board nice enough to be brought to the table. Using 2 spoons, lift the peach slices, 1 at a time, and place them in the shell arranging them, curve on curve, in 6 neat, closely packed rows running parallel with the 8 inch sides of the shell. There will probably be a few slices left over but better safe than sorry. Dip a pastry brush into the remaining syrup in the pan and carefully brush it all over the edges and sides of the tart shell to glaze it. Allow the peach tart to stand 1 hour before serving.

12 servings

prebaked tart shell

3/4 cup shelled pecan halves - about 3 ounces
1 cup plus 1 Tablespoon all purpose flour
1 Tablespoon cornstarch
2 teaspoon salt
1/2 teaspoon ground cinnamon
3/4 cup sugar
12 Tablespoons butter - very cold for processor -

otherwise at room temperature

1 egg
1 teaspoon vanilla extract
3/4 cup bread crumbs - (see bread crumbs)

Process the nuts in the processor, 15 seconds. Alternatively, grind them in the blender or use a heavy knife. In any event they must be chopped fine. Reserve them.

Sift the flour, cornstarch, salt and cinnamon together and reserve them.

In the processor, process the sugar and butter, cut in pieces, together 20 seconds. Alternatively, cream them using the electric mixer until they are light or use a large mixing bowl and a wooden spoon. Add the egg and the vanilla and process 5 seconds, or add them to the electric mixer or mixing bowl and beat well. Add the flour mixture and process 10 seconds, or beat in the flour mixture, in 3 parts, in the mixer or mixing bowl. Then, if you are using the processor, transfer the mixture to a large mixing bowl and use the wooden spoon. In any case, stir the bread crumbs and the reserved ground nuts into the dough.

Using a spatula, roughly spread the dough out in an 8 by 12 by 1 inch deep, false bottom pan. Wrap the pan, first in wax paper, then seal in plastic and refrigerate it 30 minutes. Then take the pan out, uncover it and go over the dough again with the spatula, smoothing it out and pressing it against the sides of the pan to form about 1/4 inch thick sides to the tart shell. Now, with the tip of your finger, press the rim of the tart sides down, all around, to 1/4 inch below the sides of the pan, making an attractive little pattern of indentations. The dough swells as it bakes and the edges must not be too high. Wrap the pan in wax paper, seal in plastic again and refrigerate it at least 3 hours or overnight.

To bake the shell, remove the plastic and wax paper and lay a large piece of aluminum foil over the dough fitting it down into the shell and fill it with about 4 cups of dried beans which you reserve solely for this purpose. Fold the edges of the foil over the edges of the pan to cover the dough completely.

Bake the shell in a preheated 325 degree oven 20 minutes. Remove the pan from the oven and using a large spoon remove the beans then the foil. Return the pan to the oven and bake the shell 20 minutes longer. Now, remove the pan from the oven, set it on a cake rack and allow the shell to cool 1 hour. Then remove the sides of the pan and slip a thin knife between the shell and the pan bottom to loosen it. Carefully slide the tart shell off of the pan bottom onto the cake rack and allow it to cool 2 hours longer. The shell must be completely cooled and very firm like a large cookie which is what it really is.

prebaked tart shell
12 by 8 by 1 inch deep

 WATERMELON BASKET

This melon basket is so festive looking it suggests a gala event. Serve a cold curried buttermilk soup then have sliced tomatoes with crusty bread and some special cheese. Be sure to have chilled fruit dishes on hand for the melon.

watermelon - 1 average
cantaloupes - 2 average
honeydews - 2 average

Roll the watermelon around to let it find its natural resting place. Then with the point of a knife lightly etch the outline of a basket on the upper third of the melon. This will seem high but it will not be later. Make the handle about 2 1/4 inches wide, if it is too wide it will look clumsy. Now, carefully insert a long, thin, sharp knife into the melon along the etched line and remove the pieces. Scoop out the watermelon flesh with a melon ball cutter. Much of the melon will not be usable as it will be riddled with seeds but there will be enough watermelon balls to equal the number taken out of the cantaloupes and honeydews. Set the melon balls aside in a large bowl. When all the melon balls have been removed, scrape out the inside of the melon basket with a large spoon until it is reasonably smooth. It is not necessary to scrape it down to the white layer.

Now, using a tape measure and the point of a knife, lightly mark out a scalloped edging along the edge of the basket. Make the scallops about the size of a fifty cent piece, rounded side up. Space the scallops so that there will be a full rounded scallop against each side of the basket handle. The basket will look best if a scallop is centered at each end of the melon. Using a small sharp knife, carve out the scallops. The edges of the handle are left smooth.

Cut the cantaloupes and honeydews in half and remove their seeds and membrane. Scoop as many melon balls out of them as you can. Mix all the melon balls together in the large bowl and refrigerate them, covered, along with the melon basket, 1 hour.

Just before serving, carefully drain both the melon balls and the basket. (A slight amount of liquid will have collected.) Heap the mixed melon balls in the watermelon basket and serve.

about 8 servings

Note: One picture would be worth a thousand words.

SECTION III

CONCORD GRAPE JELLY ROLL

STUFFED PEARS in custard sauce

APPLE CAKE

PUMPKIN CARAMEL CUSTARD

FLAMING FIG PUDDING with brown sugar hard sauce

 CONCORD GRAPE JELLY ROLL

Definitely a do ahead dessert, this delightful confection is a simple way to feature homemade jelly. Serve stracciatella to begin then a salad of fennel in virgin olive oil with some Gorgonzola and Italian bread. Present the Concord grape jelly roll and finish the dinner with a strong espresso.

Concord grape jelly - (recipe follows)
5 1/2 Tablespoons unsalted butter
1 cup minus 2 Tablespoons all purpose flour
2 Tablespoons cornstarch
1/4 teaspoon salt
5 eggs - at room temperature
2/3 cup superfine sugar
3/4 teaspoon vanilla extract
1 Tablespoon confectioners sugar

The jelly should, of course, have been prepared well in advance.
First, butter an 11 by 17 inch jelly roll pan, fit an 11 by 17 inch piece of wax paper into it and butter the wax paper. Set the prepared pan aside.
Clarify the butter as directed. (See clarified butter.) Remove the pan from the heat and allow it to cool a bit.
Sift the flour, cornstarch and salt together and reserve the mixture.
Place the eggs in a warm mixing bowl and set the bowl inside of a larger bowl which is half filled with hot water. Using a hand held electric mixer, beat the eggs at high speed for 10 minutes while slowly adding the superfine sugar. Beat in the vanilla and remove the bowl from the water. The eggs should have tripled in volume and be thick and creamy. Now, with the mixer running at low speed, add 1 heaping tablespoon of the reserved flour mixture at a time, to the eggs, alternating the flour with small amounts of the clarified butter until all the flour and butter have been added.
Spread the batter in the prepared pan, rotating the pan to spread the batter evenly. Bake the cake in a preheated 375 degree oven for just 12 minutes or until the edges of the cake pull away from the sides of the pan. Remove the pan from the oven and cover the cake with a piece of wax paper then set the bottom of a large cookie sheet over the wax paper. Holding the jelly roll pan and the cookie sheet together, turn them over, remove the jelly roll pan then carefully peel away the first piece of wax paper. The adhering "skin" of the cake will peel away with it, the way it does when the paper is peeled off of the bottom of a cupcake. Trim a long strip, 1/4 inch wide off of the 2 short sides of the cake. Now, starting from a short side roll the cake

up tight in the second piece of wax paper, rolling the paper right in with the cake. Set the rolled up cake, seam side down, on a cake rack to cool for 1 1/2 hours.

(The cake can be made ahead up to this point, slipped into a plastic bag, tightly sealed and refrigerated for at least 3 or 4 days. It keeps very well.)

To fill the cake, unroll it on a work surface and carefully peel off the second piece of wax paper and the "skin" along with it. Now, spread about 3/4 cup of the grape jelly on the "inside" of the cake, taking care not to use too much or it will ooze out of the cake. Then roll the cake up tight and using a serrated knife trim a slice about 1/4 inch thick off of each end of the roll to make it even.

(The cake can at this point be slipped into the plastic bag again, sealed and kept at room temperature a few hours until serving time.)

At serving time sift the powdered sugar, through a fine strainer, all over the top of the cake then set the cake on a serving tray which has been covered with paper doilies. To serve the Concord grape jelly roll cut it crosswise into 3/4 inch thick slices and allow 2 slices for each serving.

about 6 servings

Note: A cake made by this classic method is called a Génoise.

concord grape jelly

3 pounds Concord grapes - (8 cups grapes)
1/2 cup plus optional water - divided
1 block paraffin - 4 ounces
4 cups sugar
3 ounces fruit pectin

Rinse and drain the grapes. Pluck them from their stems and using a fork, lightly crush them, about 1/2 cup at a time, on a dinner plate. Transfer them to a large enameled kettle, add the 1/2 cup of water, bring them to simmer over medium heat and simmer them, covered, 10 minutes, stirring occasionally. Then pour the grapes into a colander lined with a double layer of wet, wrung out cheese cloth, set over a bowl. Tie the corners of the cloth together and hang the bag up over the bowl to drip for 2 hours. Be patient. If you don't care whether the jelly is crystal clear, gently press the bag a few times during the last half hour to get the full amount of juice out of it. If you do care, don't do it.

Meanwhile, sterilize 7 or 8, 3/4 cup glass jars in boiling water for 10 minutes. Leave them in hot water until ready to be used. Melt the paraffin in the top of a double boiler set over low heat.

Now, measure out 3 cups of the grape juice. If there is not quite enough, pour a little water through the grapes. In the large enameled kettle set over high heat, bring the juice to boil with the sugar, while stirring constantly with a long handled wooden spoon. (The kettle must be large and the handle must be long because the liquid boils up quite a bit.) As soon as the liquid comes to a hard boil, pour in all the pectin, all at once, and allow the liquid to boil hard for 1 minute, while stirring constantly. Remove the kettle from the heat and using a metal spoon, skim off the foam and wipe it on paper towels.

Drain the hot jars, one at a time, and ladle the hot liquid into them, leaving at least a 3/4 inch head room. Carefully wipe the inside edges of the jars with a clean cloth, wrung out in hot water, so that the paraffin will seal properly. Now, very carefully pour a 1/8 inch thickness of hot paraffin over the hot jelly. Allow the jelly and paraffin to cool completely. Then reheat the remaining paraffin, over low heat, and pour another 1/8 inch of hot paraffin over the cold paraffin. When the paraffin is cold, cover the jars with caps or dust covers and store them in a cool, dark, dry place.

5 to 6 cups jelly

STUFFED PEARS
in custard sauce

Consommé jardiniére is the first course in this rather esthetic dîner dessert. Next offer a tossed escarole salad accompanied by French bread. The stuffed pears look especially pretty served in colored glass bowls.

3 cups plus optional water
1 1/2 cups sugar
2 Tablespoons fresh lemon juice
2 pounds Bosc pears - 4 large
1/4 cup golden raisins

1/4 cup roasted macadamias - (see macadamias)
crystalized ginger - (1 Tablespoon chopped)
1 teaspoon honey
fresh green leaves - 4 small - (see note)
custard sauce - (recipe follows)

Bring the 3 cups of water, the sugar and lemon juice to simmer in a covered saucepan, just large enough to hold the pears, lying on their sides, over medium heat until the sugar dissolves.

Select ripe but firm pears with their stems still attached. Trim a thin slice from the bottom of each pear so that it sits up properly. Carefully cut or rather scrape the core out of each pear; a vegetable peeler works well for this. Still using the vegetable peeler peel the pears leaving the stems intact.

Place the pears in the simmering poaching liquid. They should be covered with liquid, if they are not, add a little water. Adjust the heat to keep the liquid simmering and poach the pears, covered, for 10 to 15 minutes from the moment they are in the liquid depending upon how ripe they are until they are tender but still slightly firm. Using a slotted spoon, transfer the pears from the liquid to paper towels and allow them to drain and cool.

Meanwhile, using a heavy knife, chop the raisins, nuts and ginger fairly small. In a bowl, mix them well with the honey. Now, using your fingers, gently but firmly stuff the mixture into the cavities in the pears. Paper towels are sometimes helpful in holding the pears.

Insert the stem of a small green leaf into each pear right next to its stem. Set each pear in an individual fruit dish and chill them while the sauce is being prepared.

At this point make the custard sauce as directed.

Spoon the custard sauce around the pear in each dish. Ideally, the pears should be just chilled, not cold, and the sauce tepid, not warm. Serve the stuffed pears in custard sauce immediately.

4 servings

Note: Leaves from a fruit tree would be perfect, but lacking those, tiny leaves from an unsprayed house plant such as English ivy could be substituted very well. The leaves, though they are inedible, add just the right touch of "authentic" decoration to the pears. They are indispensable really.

custard sauce
(stirred custard, crème anglaise)

1 1/2 cups milk - at room temperature
1/4 cup sugar
pinch salt
3 inch piece vanilla bean - (cut in half lengthwise)
4 egg yolks - at room temperature - (see cooked eggs note)

Slowly bring the milk with the sugar, salt and vanilla bean to simmer in a saucepan (not a heavy one) over low to medium heat. Remove the pan from the heat and allow the mixture to steep 30 minutes. Remove the vanilla bean and bring the milk to simmer again over medium heat then remove the pan from the heat.

Meanwhile, stirring them gently, strain the yolks through a fine strainer into a small bowl. Then, very slowly stir half of the hot milk into the yolks. Now, slowly stir the yolk mixture into the milk in the pan while stirring constantly.

Return the pan to medium low heat and using a rubber spatula, stir the sauce constantly, lifting the pan frequently as for a hollandaise sauce, 7 or 8 minutes until the mixture thickens and "coats the spoon" as they say. Do not permit the sauce to simmer.

Remove the pan from the heat and cover it with a paper towel and lid. Allow the custard sauce to cool until it is just tepid.

about 2 cups

 APPLE CAKE

Begin with borscht this evening then have a tossed salad mix II and some bread if you like but be sure to save enough room for this most attractive and delicious of apple cakes.

1 1/2 cups whole wheat pastry flour
1 cup unbleached all purpose flour

2 teaspoons baking powder
2 teaspoons ground cinnamon
nutmeg - (1/2 teaspoon freshly grated)
1/4 teaspoon ground cloves
1/4 teaspoon salt
1/4 cup stone ground yellow corn meal
1 cup shelled walnut halves - about 4 ounces
about 2 1/4 pounds Cortland apples - 6 medium
3/4 packed cup dark brown sugar
1 cup white sugar - divided
12 Tablespoons butter - very cold for processor - otherwise at room
temperature
2 eggs - at room temperature

Sift the two flours, baking powder, cinnamon, nutmeg, cloves, salt and corn meal together into a mixing bowl. Return any coarse corn meal which wouldn't go through the sieve to the mixture in the bowl.

Chop the walnuts small, processing them 5 seconds in the process. Alternatively chop them in the blender or use a heavy knife. In any case stir the chopped nuts into the flour mixture.

Cut 1 apple in half, lengthwise and reserve 1 of the halves. Using a vegetable peeler, peel 2 1/2 apples. Core, quarter and grate them in the processor using the coarse disc etc. The grated apples should measure 2 cups if there is an excess, do not use it. It would unbalance the recipe. Sprinkle the grated apples into the flour mixture, a little at a time, tossing them with a wooden fork, until they are well coated and separate.

In the processor, process the brown sugar and 3/4 cup of the white sugar with the butter, cut in pieces, 20 seconds. Alternatively, cream them together using the electric mixer until they are light or in a large mixing bowl using a wooden spoon. Add the eggs, 1 at a time, to the processor and process 5 seconds after each addition, or add the eggs, 1 at a time, to the electric mixer or the mixing bowl, beating well after each addition. Then, if you are using the processor, transfer the mixture to a large mixing bowl and using the electric mixer or wooden spoon, beat in the flour mixture, 2 or 3 heaping tablespoons at a time. The batter will be very stiff. Turn the batter into a well buttered, 9 inch in diameter, 2 1/2 inch deep springform pan, spreading it out even.

Peel the remaining 3 1/2 apples, cutting the whole apples in half lengthwise. Core the 7 halves with a melon ball cutter and trim out each end of the cores. Lay the halves, cut side down, and thinly slice the apples, crosswise without cutting down too deep so that the slices remain attached at either end. Set the halves on the batter, 1 in the center and 6 around it. Gently but firmly, press the halves well down into the batter and evenly sprinkle the entire top of the cake with the remaining 1/4 cup of white sugar. Bake the cake in a preheated 375 degree oven 1 hour and 25 minutes, covering it with foil after about 60 minutes if it is browning too quick. Remove the cake from the oven and allow it to stand 3 hours. Then run a thin knife around the inside edge of the pan and remove the sides. The apple cake is now ready to serve.

Note: Cortland is the preferred apple for this cake.

PUMPKIN CARAMEL CUSTARD

Like pumpkin soup, pumpkin custard is really made with buttercup squash and what an elegant turnout for a squash. Sopa de tortilla is the soup course. Sweet Italian frying pepper salad with Jack cheese and tortillas are next. Then present the pumpkin caramel custard.

2 pounds buttercup squash - 1 small - (1 1/2 cups puréed)
1/2 cup sugar
3 Tablespoons water
1 cup milk - at room temperature
1 cup heavy cream - at room temperature
3 eggs - at room temperature
3/4 packed cup dark brown sugar
1 Tablespoon light molasses
1 Tablespoon ground cinnamon
1 1/2 teaspoons ground cloves
pinch ground mace
1/2 teaspoon salt

Prepare and bake the squash as directed. (See baked butternut squash.) Scoop the flesh out of the skin and purée it through a food mill set over a bowl. Turn the purée into a colander lined with a double layer of wet, wrung out cheese cloth. Tie the corners of the cheese cloth together and hang the bag up over a bowl. Allow the purée to drain 1 hour, gently pressing the bag occasionally. (Save drained liquid for a bouillon soup. See bouillon soups.) If the drained purée measures more than 1 1/2 cups do not use the excess, it would unbalance the recipe. (Save it for the bouillon soup.) Reserve the purée.

Heat the sugar and water together in a small very clean saucepan over medium low heat for about 10 minutes without stirring but rotating the pan frequently until the sugar has completely dissolved. (A tiny speck of dirt or stirring would encourage crystallization.) When the liquid is clear, increase the heat to high and boil the liquid 3 or 4 minutes while rotating the pan constantly until the liquid is a lovely amber color. Now, one at a time, pour the equally divided caramel into each of 6, 2/3 cup capacity, custard cups, quickly rotating the cup to spread the caramel around the inside. Then invert the cup and set it down on paper towels. The caramel will harden.

Bring the milk to simmer in a saucepan over medium heat. Remove the pan from the heat and stir the cream into it. In a bowl, beat the eggs using a wire whisk, just until they are light, then stir the milk and cream into them.

In a large bowl, combine the reserved purée, brown sugar, molasses, cinnamon, ginger, cloves mace and salt. Then stir the egg mixture into them. Pour the equally divided custard mixture into the 6 caramel lined custard cups.

Set the cups, well spaced, on a trivet (cake rack) in a large baking pan. Pour enough hot water into the baking pan to reach 3/4 of the way up the sides of the custard cups. Place the waterbath arrangement in a preheated 325 degree oven and bake 50 minutes or until a wooden toothpick inserted in the center of the custard comes out clean.

Lift the cups out of the waterbath and allow the custard to cool to room temperature then refrigerate them for 1 hour. At serving time, run the point of a sharp knife around the inside edges of the cups. Cover each cup with an inverted dessert plate. Holding the plate and cup together, turn them over, tap the back of the cup with a wooden spoon then lift it off the custard. The caramel sauce will flow over and around the custard. Serve the pumpkin caramel custard immediately.

6 servings

FLAMING FIG PUDDING
with brown sugar hard sauce

This impressive dessert, which has been prepared well in advance, is the perfect dessert for Christmas Day or New Years Eve. Offer mushroom bisque followed by a tossed endive salad, French bread and some expensive little cheeses that you wouldn't ordinarily buy. Then bring on the flaming spectacle.

1/2 cup roasted, peeled hazelnuts - about 2 1/2 ounces - (see hazelnuts)
boiling water
9 ounces dried figs - about 20 - (1 1/2 packed cups chopped)
1 1/4 cups unbleached all purpose flour
6 ounces dried pitted dates - (1 cup chopped)
1 cup dried currants - about 5 ounces
1 teaspoon baking powder
1 teaspoon salt
2 teaspoons ground cinnamon
1 teaspoon ground ginger
1 teaspoon ground cloves
1 teaspoon freshly grated nutmeg
pinch cayenne
1/2 cup milk
1/4 cup honey
1/4 cup light molasses
1 cup butter - very cold for processor - otherwise at room temperature
1 packed cup dark brown sugar
3 eggs - at room temperature
3/4 cup bread crumbs - (see bread crumbs)
brown sugar hard sauce - (recipe follows)
6 Tablespoons cognac

    Using a heavy knife, chop the hazelnuts small and reserve them.
    In a bowl, pour boiling water over the figs and allow them to soak about 20 minutes or until they have softened. Drain them, remove their little stems and chop them small. As the figs are chopped drop them into a mixing bowl containing the 1 1/4 cups of flour.
    Chop the dates the same size as the figs, dropping them into the bowl of flour.
    Add the currants to the bowl and toss the fruits to coat them well with the flour. Then transfer the fruits and flour to a large coarse strainer set over a bowl and shake the strainer so that all the excess flour falls away from the fruits into the bowl. Reserve the fruits.
    There will be about 3/4 to 1 cup of excess flour in the bowl. Sift it together with the baking powder, salt, cinnamon, ginger, cloves, nutmeg and cayenne and reserve the mixture.
    Warm the milk, honey and molasses in a small saucepan over low heat until the honey and molasses have melted. Remove the pan from the heat and allow the mixture to cool a bit.
    In the processor, process the butter and sugar together 10 seconds. Alternatively, cream them together using the electric mixer until they are light or in a large mixing bowl, using a wooden spoon. Add the eggs,

1 at a time, and process each egg 5 seconds, or beat in the eggs 1 at a time. Add the flour mixture and process 5 seconds, then add the milk mixture and process 5 seconds. Or beat in the flour mixture, 1/2 cup at a time, alternately with the milk mixture, 1/2 cup at a time.

Now, if you are using the processor transfer the batter to a large bowl. In any case, stir the bread crumbs first then the reserved nuts and fruits thoroughly into the batter.

Pack the pudding mixture into a well buttered 6 cup steamed pudding mold, tamping it down with the blade of a table knife to release air pockets. The batter will fill the mold only 3/4 full, it swells while cooking. Cover the mold with its lid and place the mold on a trivet in a large kettle containing 1 inch of simmering water, set over low heat, cover the kettle and steam the pudding 3 hours. Should the kettle need more water during that period, be sure the water is simmering before adding it.

Remove the mold from the kettle and remove its lid. Allow the pudding to stand 10 minutes then cover it with an inverted cake rack and holding the rack and mold together, turn them over and remove the mold. Allow the pudding to cool completely for 3 or 4 hours to room temperature. Then tightly wrap the pudding in aluminum foil and refrigerate it for at least 1 week or up to 2 weeks. (Do not try to store the pudding in the pudding mold, it would affect the taste.)

Before serving the pudding, prepare the hard sauce and refrigerate it as directed.

To serve, bring the wrapped pudding to room temperature then warm it, still wrapped, in a preheated 325 degree oven for 35 minutes. Unwrap the pudding and place it on a flame proof serving plate. It is best served warm rather than hot.

When ready to serve, have your audience ready. Warm the cognac in a small saucepan over low heat. After a couple of minutes, ignite the rising alcohol fumes by holding a lighted, long wooden match over the pan. (See note.) Immediately and very carefully pour the flaming cognac over the pudding and carry the flaming fig pudding to the table with haste as the flames only last about 1 1/2 minutes. Serve along with the dish of cold brown sugar hard sauce.

8 to 12 servings

Note: It's a good idea to wear an oven mitten while igniting the alcohol. Incidentally, if your mold is the type with a hole down the middle, don't pour the flaming cognac down the hole. It will put out the flame.

brown sugar hard sauce

1/2 cup butter - very cold for processor - otherwise at room temperature
1/2 cup dark brown sugar
1/2 cup sugar
1 teaspoon vanilla extract

Process all the ingredients in the processor for 10 seconds until smooth. Alternatively, cream them together using the electric mixer or in a bowl, using a wooden spoon. If using the processor transfer the mixture to a bowl. In any case, refrigerate the mixture, covered, until firm.

At serving time, using a spoon, transfer the mixture to a serving dish and serve the brown sugar hard sauce cold.

about 1 cup

SECTION IV

ORANGE AMBROSIA

PINEAPPLE CHEESE CAKE

LEMON MERINGUE TARTS

BANANA BREAD AND BUTTER PUDDING

GRAPEFRUIT CUPS

ORANGE AMBROSIA

Purée of fava bean soup will be the first course for this dinner in a Middle Eastern mood. Baby artichokes vinaigrette served with pita bread and some Feta cheese make a good salad selection. Orange blossom honey gives the ambrosia a certain exotic flavor and it looks especially beautiful served in a cobalt blue dish.

Navel oranges - 8 large - divided
4 Tablespoons orange blossom honey - no substitute
bananas - 2 large
4 Tablespoons sweetened shredded coconut

Squeeze the juice of 2 of the oranges into a small saucepan, add the honey and set the pan over low heat until the honey has melted. Pour the juice mixture into a mixing bowl.

Peel the bananas and cut them crosswise into 3/16 inch thick slices dropping them into the juice. Gently stir them with a rubber spatula to be sure they are well coated with the citrus juice.

Lay a small cutting board across the mixing bowl. On it, cut the remaining 6 oranges crosswise into 1/4 inch thick slices, discarding the end slices and allowing the juices to run down into the bowl. As each slice is cut lay it on the cutting board and run the point of a sharp knife around the edge of the fruit cutting away the skin and white membrane and leaving a perfectly round slice of orange. Drop the slices into the bowl. Cover the bowl and refrigerate it for 1 hour.

Remove the bowl from the refrigerator 20 minutes before serving. Just before serving, transfer the ambrosia mixture to an attractive 6 cup serving dish and sprinkle it with the shredded coconut. Serve the orange ambrosia chilled but not cold.

4 servings

 PINEAPPLE CHEESE CAKE

Cheese cake is so very easy to make. Start off with matzoh balls in garlic broth. Next, serve beets vinaigrette along with pumpernickel bread. Then present this rich, velvety, cheese cake for the grand finale.

3 zwieback crackers - (3 Tablespoons crushed)
1/2 cup canned pineapple juice
2 cups sugar
4 Tablespoons flour
1/4 teaspoon salt
2 1/2 pounds Cream cheese - 5 packages, 8 ounces each - at room
temperature
1/2 teaspoon vanilla extract
6 eggs - at room temperature
1 jar apricot preserves - 10 ounces
4 or 5 dried pineapple rings

Spin the zwieback crackers around in the processor or blender a few seconds until they become crumbs. Or roll them with a rolling pin. Then sprinkle the cracker crumbs around in a buttered 9 inch in diameter, 3 inch deep, 10 cup springform pan. Rotate the pan so that it becomes well coated with the crumbs and set the pan aside.

Bring the pineapple juice to boil in a small saucepan over medium high heat. Reduce heat slightly and slowly boil the juice for about 10 minutes until it is reduced by half. Remove the pan from the heat and reserve the juice.

Being sure that the bowl of the processor is clean, spin the sugar, flour and salt around together a couple of seconds until they are blended. Alternatively, sift the sugar, flour and salt into a mixing bowl. Add all the Cream cheese at once and process 20 seconds. Or beat it in, 1/2 pound at a time, using the electric mixer or a wooden spoon. Add the reserved pineapple juice and the vanilla extract and process 20 seconds longer. Or beat them in. Add the eggs, 1 at a time, and process 5 seconds after each addition, scraping down the bowl of the stopped processor just before adding the third egg. Or beat the eggs in one at a time until the mixture is smooth.

Pour the cheese mixture into the prepared pan, if bubbles rise to the surface, pop them with point of knife. Bake the cheese cake in a preheated 325 degree oven for 1 hour. Then turn off the heat, open the oven door, just ajar, and allow the cake to slowly cool, in the oven for 1 hour. The cake will have puffed and will drop slightly. Then open the oven door wide and allow the cake to cool completely to room temperature. Now, cover the top of the cake pan with foil and refrigerate the cake about 24 hours.

Remove the cake from the refrigerator at least 2 hours before serving, removing the foil and the sides of the pan, as it is best served chilled but not cold. Meanwhile, empty the jar of apricot preserves into a small, heavy saucepan over medium low heat. When the preserves have melted, pass them through a fine strainer into a small bowl. Using a feather pastry brush, glaze the top of the cheese cake, covering the slightly raised edge of the cake.

Next, cut the pineapple rings into little triangular segments not more than 1/4 inch wide on their outer rounded sides. Arrange the segments with a cut side down, in a small circle on the center of the top of the cake so that only the widest sides of the little triangles are just barely touching each other. Arrange 2 more increasingly large circles around the first circle in such a way that the 3 circles cover the top of the cake and the raised edge forms a natural rim. Now, carefully glaze all the pineapple segments so that the whole top of the cake glistens. The pineapple cheese cake is now ready to serve.

 LEMON MERINGUE TARTS

Tart tarts! Isn't it wonderful, one lemon can make enough dessert for 6 people? Sopa de cacahuete is the soup course this evening. Next, have a tossed salad mix I with some dinner rolls and a mild cheese. Finish with these classic favorites.

prebaked tart shells - (recipe follows)
lemon - 1 large - (1 teaspoon grated zest)
4 Tablespoons fresh lemon juice
4 eggs - at room temperature
1 egg white - at room temperature
1 1/2 cups water - cold
1 1/4 cups sugar
4 Tablespoons cornstarch
1/8 teaspoon plus salt
1 Tablespoon unsalted butter - at room temperature
1/4 scant teaspoon cream of tartar
6 Tablespoons superfine sugar

Prepare and bake the tart shells in advance as directed. Set the cooled shells on a baking sheet.

Grate just the yellow part of the lemon rind on a fine grater, measure and reserve it. Squeeze, strain through a fine strainer and measure the lemon juice and reserve it.

Separate the whole eggs, putting yolks in a small bowl and whites in a large mixing bowl. Add the extra white to the bowl of whites and reserve them. Using a wire whisk, beat the yolks while slowly pouring the water into them.

Sift the 1 1/4 cups of sugar, the cornstarch and the 1/8 teaspoon of salt together into a medium size saucepan. Then slowly stir the egg yolk and water mixture into them until the sugar, cornstarch and salt are dissolved.

Set the saucepan over medium heat, and using a rubber spatula, constantly stir the mixture until it comes to a slow boil. Reduce the heat a bit and continue to stir the slowly boiling mixture for another 2 minutes until it thickens. Remove the pan from the heat, add the butter, reserved zest and slowly pour in the reserved lemon juice while continuing to very gently stir the mixture, for 5 minutes longer to release the heat. Spoon the equally divided lemon mixture into the 6 prebaked tart shells, smoothing it out.

Now, using the electric mixer, beat the egg whites until they are foamy. Add the cream of tartar and a pinch of salt and continue to beat, at high speed now, while slowly adding the superfine sugar, 1 teaspoon at a time, until the whites hold glossy peaks when the beaters are lifted. Spoon the equally divided meringue over the lemon filling, swirling it in an attractive manner, and covering the rims of the pastry shells with it.

Place the baking sheet in a preheated 400 degree oven and bake the tarts 8 minutes or until the meringue peaks are a delicate golden brown. Using a metal spatula, carefully transfer the tarts to a cake rack and allow them to cool at least 3 hours. To serve, set each tart on an individual dessert plate and serve the lemon meringue tarts at room temperature.

6 servings

Note: Choose a low humidity day to make the lemon meringue tarts since the meringue draws moisture from the atmosphere.

prebaked tart shells

1 1/2 cups minus 1 1/2 Tablespoons all purpose flour
1 1/2 Tablespoons cornstarch
2 Tablespoons superfine sugar
1/8 teaspoon salt
6 Tablespoons unsalted butter
2 Tablespoons margarine
3 to 3 1/2 Tablespoons plus 1 teaspoon cold water
1 egg yolk - (save white for meringue)

Using all the above ingredients except the 1 teaspoon of water and the egg yolk, prepare, sifting the sugar with the other dry ingredients and dividing the dough into 6 flattened balls of equal weight, rest and roll out the sweet pastry dough, 1 ball at a time into a disc, 7 inches in diameter, using only the directions for plain pastry dough. (See plain pastry dough.) Fold the disc of dough in half and then again in half. Place the point of the folded dough in the center of a 3 inch bottom diameter by 1 inch deep, false bottom tart pan. (See utensils.) There should be 1 inch of dough hanging down all around the outside of the pan, trim the edges even. Dip your finger in some water and dampen the whole 1 inch of overhanging dough, all around, on the side that is facing you. Then fold the overhanding dough back into the shell, pressing it against the sides of the pan so that the dough pops up about 1/8 inch above the rim of the pan. Wrap the little pan first in wax paper then seal in plastic and allow the shell to rest, refrigerated, at least 30 minutes. Repeat with the remaining balls of dough.

Now, remove the plastic and wax paper and fit aluminum foil down into the shells carefully folding the foil over the edges of the tart shells to cover the dough completely. Fill the foil covered shells with dried shelled beans which you reserve solely for this purpose. The shells will require about 4 1/2 cups of beans.

Set the tart pans on a cake rack for convenience, place the rack in a preheated 450 degree oven and bake the shells 30 minutes. Remove the cake rack with the pans from the oven. Using a spoon, remove the beans, then carefully remove the foil. In a cup, beat the egg yolk with the 1 teaspoon of water. Using a feather pastry brush, paint the entire inside of each shell with the beaten yolk. Return the cake rack with the tart pans on it to the 450 degree oven and bake the shells 5 minutes longer. Take the rack out of the oven, remove the sides of the pans and carefully slide the tart shells off of the little pan bottoms onto the cake rack and allow them to cool. The tart shells can be baked several hours in advance of being filled. In which case, when they are completely cool, seal them in plastic and leave them at room temperature. These small tart shells will not have to be returned to their tart pans before they are filled and the lemon meringue tarts are baked.

6 prebaked tart shells
3 inch bottom diameter by 1 inch deep

 # BANANA BREAD AND BUTTER PUDDING

Noodle soup starts off this cozy diner dessert. Serve a broccoli vinaigrette salad next. Then enjoy this generous banana bread and butter pudding which everyone loves.

1/2 cup roasted, peeled Brazilnuts - about 3 ounces - (see Brazilnuts)
8 French type dinner rolls - 1 or 2 days old - about 12 ounces - (8 cups cubed)
3 1/2 cups light cream - at room temperature
1 cup honey
1 teaspoon vanilla extract
2 teaspoons freshly grated nutmeg
6 Tablespoons unsalted butter
5 eggs - at room temperature
1/2 cup raisins - about 3 ounces
3 ripe firm bananas - (3 cups sliced)

Using a heavy knife, chop the Brazilnuts small and reserve them.
Cut the rolls into 1/2 inch cubes. Spread them out in a large oven pan and dry them out a bit in a preheated 250 degree oven for about 20 minutes, stirring them around 3 or 4 times. Immediately, transfer the bread to a large mixing bowl.
Combine the cream, honey, vanilla and nutmeg in a saucepan over medium heat. When the honey has melted and the mixture comes to simmer remove the pan from the heat and allow it to cool a bit.
Melt the butter in a small saucepan over low heat. Then dribble the melted butter over the bread cubes tossing them well.
In another mixing bowl, using a wire whisk, beat the eggs until they are light. Slowly beat the cooled cream into them then pour the mixture over

the bread cubes and stir in the raisins. Allow the combined ingredients to stand 1 hour or longer to allow time for the bread to absorb the liquid.

Now peel and cut the bananas crosswise into slices about 3/16 inch thick. Fold them into the bread mixture along with the reserved nuts. Using a large spoon, spoon the pudding mixture into a buttered, flat, 2 1/2 inch deep, 10 cup baking dish. Bake the pudding in a preheated 325 degree oven 45 minutes. Lightly cover the dish with foil to keep the pudding from browning too much and bake it 45 minutes longer. Remove the pudding from the oven and allow it to stand at least 10 minutes before serving. The banana bread and butter pudding may be served hot, warm or at room temperature.

8 servings

 GRAPEFRUIT CUPS

First, serve cold avocado soup then a tossed salad mix II with homemade biscuits and some Cream Havarti cheese. The grapefruit cups look especially attractive if they are set on glass sauces which have been refrigerated to make them frosty.

pink grapefruit - 2
4 Tablespoons fresh lime juice
4 Tablespoons superfine sugar - or to taste
Macintosh apple - 1/2
pineapple - 1/2 medium - (1 1/2 cups cut)
kiwifruit - 1
4 ounces purple grapes

Draw an imaginary line, crosswise, around the widest part of 1 grapefruit. Holding the fruit over a mixing bow, to catch the juices, insert the point of a paring knife halfway into the fruit in a zig-zag or a sawtooth pattern all around the imaginary line. Then gently pull the two halves of the grapefruit apart. Now, using the knife, cut out and remove the grapefruit sections, just as you always do. They will be a little more difficult to see than usual. Drop the sections into the bowl. With the assistance of the paring knife, carefully pull the membrane out of the grapefruit shell. Squeeze the membrane over the bowl to get any remaining juices out of it and discard it. Repeat with the second grapefruit and refrigerate the 4 shells, sealed in plastic, until serving time.

Stir the lime juice and sugar into the grapefruit sections in the bowl.

Cut the 1/2 apple, lengthwise, into quarters. Core the quarters but do not peel them. Cut the quarters crosswise into 1/4 inch thick slices and toss them with the grapefruit sections so that the apples are will coated with the citric juices.

Cut 2 or 3 slices, each 1/2 inch thick, crosswise, from the bottom of the pineapple. Cut the slices into little wedges 1/2 inch wide at the rind side. Trim off the thick rind and the pointed tip of the wedge which is the core of the pineapple. Add the pineapple pieces to the bowl.

Quarter the kiwifruit lengthwise. Peel them with a vegetable peeler and cut them crosswise into 1/4 inch thick slices. Add them to the bowl.

Cut the grapes in half lengthwise, pick out the pits and toss the grapes with the other fruit in the mixing bowl. Cover the bowl and refrigerate the fruit at least 1 hour.

Remove the bowl from the refrigerator about 20 minutes before serving. Just before serving time fill the grapefruit shells with the mixed fruit, arranging it artistically so that some of each kind of fruit is visible in each shell. Set the grapefruit cups on each of 4 saucers then set the saucers on salad plates. Serve the grapefruit cups chilled but not cold.

4 servings

COFFEE AND TEA

Coffee and tea are a course as important in themselves as the entrée. Brew the coffee while the dessert is being enjoyed. Be sure to offer both regular and decaffinated coffee. If you serve espresso it's nice to have the small cups that are traditional and serve each with a twist of lemon peel. As well as regular tea, there are so many lovely herb teas on the market today that it's an easy matter to have a number of them on hand. Tea pots are as collectable as soup tureens, not to mention tea cozies.

Coffee and tea are served just at the point when dessert is finished but the dessert plates have not been removed. Guests are still cracking nuts or nibbling cookies and may need them. Coffee and tea provide a graceful ending to dinner and people must not feel hurried. The nicest compliment I've ever received was when I suggested, at the end of dinner, that we adjourn to the living room and one of the guest countered, "Oh no, let's stay here, it's so pleasant!"

BLUE PLATE SPECIAL

A blue plate special is a name some old time restaurants used for the economy speciality of the day. We have some blue plates with a little raised ridge on them that divides each plate into three separate sections, one section slightly larger than the other two. You know the type. Picnic plates are often designed that way. We use them for the blue plate special dinners.

This interpretation of the blue plate special is what to have for dinner when the string beans in your garden are coming ready all at once. Or you just got an excellent buy on cauliflower at the market. Or the first asparagus of spring are in. Or you just plain love baked potatoes in the wintertime. Or whatever your personal preferences are. The only prerequisite is that the vegetable in question be abundant. In other words you make a principal presentation out of the accompaniment vegetable while getting the meal onto one plate.

The vegetable, cooked in its simplest form is heaped into the largest section of the plate. A pilaf and a small salad or vinaigrette salad will be in the two remaining smaller sections. But the portions can be reversed. If you love buckwheat pilaf have a mountain of it with a small serving of a vegetable and a salad of your choice or a large serving of salad and small ones of vegetable and pilaf.

For the soup course, serve one of the bouillon soups or play it by ear. Have you ever tried hot tomato juice? It's very satisfying. In any event, serve the soup in mugs. For dessert have some fresh fruit that can be eaten out of hand or ice cream cones or anything that doesn't require a plate.

The blue plate special must be portable. Have it on tray tables by the fire or in front of the T.V. Or out on the deck or patio. Or balance it on your knees while sitting on the back stoop. It is a simple meal that is special. The plate does not need to be divided and it does not need to be blue, but it's fun if it is. There is no reason why the blue plate special can not be served to guests as long as they are informed in advance about how informal the meal might be. Following are some blue plate special suggestions.

buttered asparagus with a wild rice pilaf and

marinated mushrooms

sweet Italian frying pepper salad with an oat pilaf and

buttered cauliflower florets

buckwheat pilaf with fried red bell peppers and

avocados on the half shell

baked red cabbage wedges with a rye pilaf and

pressed cucumbers

egg tomato and lettuce salad with buttered broccoli and

a wheat berry pilaf

buttered peas with a barley pilaf and

carrot and current salad

buttered noodles with buttered string beans and

coleslaw

braised baby artichokes with a bulghar pilaf and

sliced tomatoes

fennel in virgin olive oil with a rice pilaf and

sautéed mushrooms

MISCELLANEOUS

These are the little recipes upon which some of the larger recipes rest.

stock broth

clarified stock broth

puréed stock vegetables

clarified butter

mixer mayonnaise

bread crumbs

plain pastry dough

swedish butter cookies (cookie gun cookies)

ground rosemary

horseradish

cooked eggs

poached eggs

almonds

brazilnuts

cashews

chestnuts

coconuts

hazelnuts

macadamias

peanuts

pecans

pinenuts

pistachios

walnuts

sunflower and pumpkin seeds

stock broth

1/4 cup dried chick peas
9 cups water
1 bay leaf
3 ounces carrot - 1 large - (1 cup chopped)
about 6 ounces rutabaga - 1 piece - (1 cup chopped)
6 ounces potato - 1 medium - (1 cup chopped)
about 3 ounces mushrooms - medium - (1 cup sliced)
6 ounces green bell pepper - 1 medium - (1 cup chopped)
celery - 2 large ribs - (1 cup chopped)
8 ounces tomato - 1 medium - (1 cup chopped)
2 ounces untrimmed spinach - (1 packed cup trimmed)
celery leaves - (1/2 packed cup)
parsley leaves - (2 Tablespoons)
1 teaspoon honey
1/4 teaspoon freshly cracked black pepper
1 teaspoon salt

Soak the chick peas in water to cover 12 hours or overnight. Drain and rinse them.

Bring the 9 cups of water to boil in a large enameled soup kettle over high heat. Add the chick peas and bay leaf, reduce the heat to low and simmer them, covered, while the vegetables are being prepared. As the vegetables are prepared, place them in a large bowl or colander.

Scrub the carrot well, do not peel but trim and chop it.

Peel the piece of rutabaga and chop it.

Scrub the potato well but do not peel it. Chop it.

Wipe the mushrooms with a damp cloth, trim the butt ends of the stems and slice them.

Core, trim away any white membrane and chop the bell pepper.

Trim the celery and chop it.

Remove the stem button and chop the tomato.

Wash and trim the spinach as directed. (See washed and trimmed spinach.)

Chop the celery leaves.

Add the parsley leaves to the bowl or colander.

Increase the heat under the kettle to high. When the water comes to boil, add all the prepared vegetables, the honey and black pepper. When the water returns to boil, reduce the heat to low and simmer the stock broth, covered, 1 hour. Then turn off the heat, add the salt and allow the broth to stand 1 hour.

Turn the broth and vegetables into a colander set over a large bowl and allow them to drain 15 minutes, turning them over 2 or 3 times. Now, strain just the stock broth through a second colander, lined with a double layer of wet wrung out cheese cloth, set over a large bowl.

8 cups stock broth

Note: The stock broth will be slightly cloudy, which is quite acceptable for many of the recipes that use it. However, some of the consommé and broth soup recipes etc., call for clarified broth. In which case, clarify it. (See clarified stock broth.)

The stock broth keeps, refrigerated in covered glass jars, up to 5 days and indefinitely frozen. Freezing it in 2 cup containers is handy. You will notice that stock broth prepared in the summertime is especially tasty. If you have room enough in your freezer you may want to prepare several batches in the summertime for winter use. The importance and usefulness of good stock broth can not be over estimated. It is the basis for many soups as well as other dishes.

For recipes utilizing the drained stock broth vegetables: (See stock vegetable omelets, stock vegetables and couscous with cheese and puréed stock broth vegetables.)

clarified stock broth

2 eggs whites - at room temperature
8 cups stock broth - at room temperature

In a mixing bowl, using a wire whisk, beat the egg whites until they are foamy. Slowly stir in the broth. Then pour the mixture into a large saucepan set over medium heat. Using a wooden spatula, stir the broth constantly to keep the egg whites from settling to the bottom for about 15 minutes or until the broth just barely starts to simmer. Do not let it. Immediately reduce the heat as low as possible, so that the broth stays below the simmering point. (Use a heat diffuser if necessary to accomplish this.) Also, immediately stop stirring the broth but continue to heat it for 10 minutes. A thick foamy substance will form a covering over the surface of the broth. Using a spoon, carefully push the covering away from the edge of the pan a little to make an opening so you can see the broth. If the temperature is correct the broth will be in motion and tiny particles of substance will slowly be rising to the surface. Now, very carefully, without agitating the foamy substance too much, pour the broth into a colander lined with 4 layers of wet wrung out cheese cloth, set over a bowl. Let the foamy substance go into the colander too and let it drain 10 minutes.

The egg whites will have enveloped all the minute particles of vegetable and floated them to the surface leaving a crystal clear broth.

about 7 1/2 cups clarified stock broth

puréed stock vegetables

To purée the stock broth vegetables, pass them through a food mill set over a bowl. Then turn the puréed vegetables into a colander lined with a double layer of wet, wrung out cheese cloth set over a bowl. Tie the corners of the cheese cloth together and hang the bag up over the bowl to drain for 1 hour. Gently press the bag every now and then. The yield will be about 2 1/2 cups of drained stock broth vegetable purée and about 1/2 cup of cloudy broth. The cloudy broth can be used along with clearer broth in recipes where clearness is not important.

For recipes using the puréed stock vegetables: (See cream of stock vegetable soup, cold curried buttermilk soup, stock vegetable charlotte, stock vegetable croquettes and Delphina's pâté maison.)

clarified butter

unsalted butter

Melt the butter in a small, (so that the liquefied butter will be deep rather than shallow) heavy saucepan. Using a small spoon, skim the foam off of the butter as it rises to the surface and wipe the spoon on a paper towel. Now, using a large spoon, spoon the clear butter out of the pan into a container, leaving the milky solids in the bottom of the pan. (The milk solids can go into a bouillon soup. See bouillon soups.) The clarified butter can be used right away or it can be stored, refrigerated in a sealed jar, indefinitely.

1 cup unsalted butter yields 3/4 cup clarified butter

mixer mayonnaise

1/2 teaspoon salt
1 Tablespoon California white wine vinegar
1/4 cup olive oil
3/4 cup corn oil
2 egg yolks - at room temperature - (see cooked eggs note)
1/2 teaspoon English mustard powder
generous pinch white pepper
2 teaspoons boiling water

In a teacup dissolve the salt in the vinegar. Combine the olive and corn oils in a measuring cup that has a spout and set the measuring cup on a saucer to keep things neat.

Fill a small mixing bowl with hot water. Allow it to stand a few minutes to warm the bowl, then empty and dry it. Place the yolks, mustard, pepper and 1 teaspoon of the salted vinegar in the bowl. Using a hand held or standard electric mixer beat the yolks for a few seconds at medium speed. Then add the oil mixture drop by drop until about 3 tablespoons of oil have been added. Continue to slowly add the oil in a very thin stream now, until 1/3 of the oil has been used, while occasionally turning the bowl. Add 1 teaspoon more of the salted vinegar and another 1/3 of the oil, pouring it in a little faster now, but only as fast as the forming mayonnaise can absorb it. (If the oil is added too quick the mayonnaise will separate. Should that happen, start over again with 1 egg yolk in another bowl, slowly adding the separated mayonnaise to it.) Add the last teaspoon of vinegar and pour in the remaining oil in a thicker stream. Thin the mayonnaise slightly with the boiling water which will also stabilize it and keep it smooth.

This entire procedure should take about 12 minutes. The electric mixer makes an excellent thick mayonnaise as it should be. Store the mayonnaise, tightly covered in the refrigerator.

1 1/2 cups

Note: The flavor of the mayonnaise will depend upon the quality of the olive oil. The proportions of olive and corn oil can be varied according to taste.

bread crumbs

best quality white or whole wheat bread

Without removing the crust, crumble the bread into pieces the size of a dried bean and spread them out in 1 layer on a jelly roll pan. Half of a 1 pound loaf will fill an 11 by 17 inch pan. Allowing the crumbled bread to stand, uncovered 2 or 3 hours will shorten oven time. In any case place the pan in a preheated 250 degree oven for about 15 minutes, stirring the bread around once or twice during the period, closely watching it until it is just a very pale delicate golden color. The sugars in the flour will have caramelized slightly and will make tasty bread crumbs. Remove the bread from the pan immediately.

Transfer no more than 1 cup of the bread at a time to the blender or processor. "Grate" the bread giving the machine 3 on-off turns. Empty the crumbs into a coarse strainer set over a bowl and shake the strainer a bit. Whatever does not go through goes back into the cup, the cup is filled with bread again, the bread is transferred to the machine, "grated" and sifted. Repeat the steps until all the bread crumbs have been made. Whatever does not go through the strainer on the last sifting is discarded.

This method provides even textured crumbs. Allowing all the bread to remain in the machine until all of it is reduced to crumbs will result in powdery crumbs. If at anytime finer crumbs are needed simply add the required amount to the machine until they are the desired consistency.

Store the crumbs in a jar with a loosely closed lid.

1 pound of bread yields 3 1/2 to 4 cups crumbs

Note: Alternatively crumbs can be made by placing the dried bread in a clean pillow case and pounding and rolling it with a rolling pin.

plain pastry dough

1 cup all purpose flour minus 1 Tablespoon
1 Tablespoon cornstarch
1/2 teaspoon salt
4 Tablespoons unsalted butter - cold
1 Tablespoon plus 1 teaspoon margarine - cold
2 to 2 1/2 Tablespoons cold water

Sift the flour, cornstarch and salt together into a mixing bowl; cut in the butter and margarine with a pastry blender. Then quickly rub the flour through the butter and margarine with your fingertips until the mixture is granular. Add the water, a little at a time, stirring it in with a fork and using only as much as is necessary until dough begins to form. Then, using your hands shape the dough into a flattened ball, handling it as little as possible. Wrap the dough first in wax paper then seal in plastic and allow it to rest, refrigerated, 1 hour.

To roll out the dough, place it on a lightly floured work surface. With a lightly floured rolling pin, using long even strokes, roll the dough out into a disc while rotating and lifting it and lightly flouring the work surface and rolling pin as necessary until the disc reaches the diameter and thinness desired.

swedish butter cookies
(cookie gun cookies)

1 cup unsalted butter - very cold for processor - otherwise at room
temperature.

1 cup sugar
2 egg yolks
3/4 teaspoon almond extract
1 3/4 cups all purpose flour
1/4 cup cornstarch
1/4 teaspoon salt

Process the butter and sugar together in the processor 20 seconds. Alternatively, cream them together in the electric mixer until they are light or use a wooden spoon and a mixing bowl. Add the yolks and extract and process 5 seconds or mix or stir them in until the mixture is smooth.

Sift the flour, cornstarch and salt together into a bowl. Then add them, 1 cup at a time, to the processor and process 10 seconds after each addition, allowing the last addition to form a ball of dough. Alternatively, add 1/2 cup of the flour mixture at a time to the mixer or mixing bowl and mix or stir thoroughly after each addition.

On a piece of wax paper, shape 1/4 of the dough into a long cylinder with a diameter slender enough to fit into the cookie gun and wrap the cylinder up in the wax paper, then seal it in plastic. Repeat with the remaining dough. Refrigerate the 4 wrapped cylinders 30 minutes if made in the processor or 45 minutes if made in the mixer or by hand. Then, taking each cylinder out of the refrigerator in succession, allow it to stand for 20 minutes at room temperature just before it is put into the cookie gun. The dough must be just the right temperature. If it is too cold and hard, it will not come out of the gun. If it is too warm and soft the cookies will spread too much while baking.

Load a cylinder of dough into the cookie gun, fitted with the disc pattern of your choice. Press the cookies out, about 1 inch apart, onto a cold, lightly buttered cookie sheet. The cookie sheet must be cold. After each use, rinse it off under cold running water, wipe it dry and lightly butter it again. To expedite matters, work with two cookie sheets, covering one with cookies while the other is in the oven.

Bake the cookies, in a preheated 350 degree oven, 9 to 10 minutes or until their edges are a light golden brown. Using a metal spatula, carefully transfer them to a cake rack to cool. As they become cool enough to handle, transfer the cookies to plates and allow them to "cure" 2 hours at room temperature. Now the cookies are ready to serve or they may be stored in paper bags inside of tightly sealed plastic bags and refrigerated up to 5 days.

about 6 dozen (72) cookies

Note: The cookie gun comes with quite a number of disc patterns. The discs can be changed while the dough is in the gun to produce a mixed batch of cookie patterns. However, some cookie patterns bake slightly quicker than others so you may want to experiment. Be sure to read the manufacturers instructions.

ground rosemary

1/2 teaspoon dried rosemary

Place the rosemary in a mortar and grind it with a pestle. Place the ground rosemary in a small fine strainer set over a tea cup and stir it with a teaspoon until all the ground rosemary falls through and nothing but the chaff remains.

about 1/4 teaspoon ground rosemary

horseradish

Horseradish is that big ugly often dirty looking root seen in the market in the fall—you think what on earth is that? Tangy, piquant, pungent! All those names apply to horseradish. Scrub it clean, dry it well, wrap it in plastic and store it in your refrigerator three or four months over the winter, changing the wrapper every week or two. Just cut off small pieces of the root as they are needed.

cooked eggs

eggs - (see note)
water

These cooking times are for extra large room temperature eggs. The shells of room temperature eggs are less likely to crack when immersed in simmering water than those of cold eggs. Allow refrigerated eggs to stand at least 3 hours at room temperature before cooking. If time is short, immerse refrigerated eggs in luke warm water for 20 minutes. However, in that case, results may be variable and experience will be the teacher.

Bring to a boil enough water to cover the eggs by 1 inch in a saucepan over high heat. Reduce the heat to low and when the water is barely simmering, lower the eggs into it, adjusting the heat to keep the water barely simmering. (That is to say the bottom of the pan is covered with bubbles and a few rise to the surface.) Gently roll the eggs around every 2 or 3 minutes while they are cooking for well centered yolks. Time the eggs from the moment they are in the water and cook them uncovered.

8 minute eggs (mollet): Tender firm whites and slightly runny yolks.
10 minute eggs: Medium firm whites and still brightly colored, slightly translucent yolks.
17 minute eggs (hard cooked): Firm whites and yolks with no grey rim around the yolks.

In all 3 cases remove the eggs from the simmering water immediately and submerge them in cold water. Shell them immediately by gently tapping them all over to crack the shells then peel them.

Note: Fresh eggs do not peel well. If you write the date of purchase on the carton you will know how old they are. Keep eggs refrigerated at least 10 days before cooking 8, 10, or 17 minute eggs.

If there is any question of Salmonella, (a possible health risk in undercooked eggs) being present in the eggs in your area, as a precaution, call your County Extension Service for further information.

poached eggs

eggs - (see note) - (see cooked eggs note)
water
1 teaspoon distilled white vinegar per cup water

These cooking times are for extra large, room temperature eggs. Allow refrigerated eggs to stand at lest 3 hours at room temperature before cooking. If time is short, immerse refrigerated eggs in luke warm water for 20 minutes. However, in that case results may be variable and experience will be the teacher.

Break each egg into an individual tea cup. Bring 2 inches of water plus the correct amount of vinegar to boil in an 8 to 10 inch frying pan, depending upon the number of eggs to be poached, over high heat. Turn off the heat, and the moment the water stops boiling, slide the eggs into the water, one at a time. Using a wooden spoon, gently roll the eggs around to help them retain their shape.

Poach eggs to be served hot, 4 minutes. Using a slotted spoon and working quickly, lift the eggs out of the hot water, one at a time. Rinse them in warm water and allow them to drain in the slotted spoon while trimming off the streamers with a pair of scissors. Serve hot poached eggs immediately.

Poach eggs to be served cold, 6 minutes. Using a slotted spoon lift the eggs out of the hot water and submerge them in a bowl of cold water. Allow them to remain in the cold water, refrigerated if necessary, until just before serving time. At which time, drain the eggs and trim off the streamers.

Note: A fresh egg holds its shape when it is poached better than other eggs do. However, in this modern age of refrigeration the fresh egg is relatively unknown and unidentifiable. The whites of most eggs break down, and form what are called streamers, when they are poached. The solution is to trim off the undesirable streamers.

almonds

To peel: In a bowl pour boiling water over shelled almonds. Allow them to soak 3 minutes. Then peel them, they pop right out of their skins. The unpeeled almonds remain in the water until they are peeled.

To dry: Spread the peeled almonds on a baking sheet and dry them out in a preheated 200 degree oven 15 minutes, stirring them around every 5 minutes. Remove them from the baking sheet immediately.

To roast: 'Roast as for to dry using a 275 degree oven for 20 minutes.

1 cup shelled almonds - about 5 1/2 ounces

brazilnuts

Refrigerating brazilnuts for a few hours before shelling them will make the shells more brittle and easier to crack.

To roast or peel: (See peanuts.) The skins can be obstinate. Do not expect great results, but don't despair, peel off any remaining skin with a vegetable peeler.

1 cup shelled brazilnuts - about 5 ounces

cashews

Cashews always reach the market peeled. Raw cashews are available in natural food stores. If you are using already roasted, salted cashews, shake them in a coarse strainer to rid them of excess salt.

To roast: Roast cashews on a baking sheet in a preheated 250 degree oven 20 minutes, stirring them around every 5 minutes. Remove them from the baking sheet immediately.

1 cup cashews - about 6 ounces

chestnuts

Chestnuts appear in some markets as early as September. Buy them as soon as you see them for use in November and December. They will keep well, stored in a brown paper bag in your refrigerator and be in better condition than those you would otherwise buy at holiday time.

For accurate measurement it's wise to buy 2 or 3 more nuts than your recipe calls for as there are often 2 or 3 spoiled nuts per pound.

To shell and peel: Using a small sharp knife slash a cross, not too deep, on the rounded side of each chestnut. Spread the chestnuts out on any adequately sized baking sheet and place them in a preheated 425 degree oven for 15 minutes. Turn off the oven and remove the chestnuts, 3 at a time, using a potholder. The chestnuts will be very hot so hold them in the potholder or paper towels while you shell and peel them, one at a time with the aid of the sharp little knife. Most of the chestnuts will be whole and perfect when shelled and peeled using this method. They are not however, cooked, but ready to go into any recipe. Chestnuts can be shelled and peeled a day in advance, cooled and refrigerated in a covered bowl until they are ready to be used.

30 to 40 unshelled chestnuts depending upon how plump they are = 1 pound

2 1/2 cups whole shelled and peeled chestnuts = 1 pound

2 cups broken chestnut pieces = 1 pound

coconuts

When you shake a fresh coconut you can hear liquid sloshing around inside. Select a fresh coconut. Using a small (clean) screwdriver and a hammer, puncture the three little eyes at one end of the coconut. Let the coconut water drain out through the holes. (Save it if desired.) Wrap a towel around the coconut, place it on a hard surface (the floor) and whack it with the hammer in several places to crack it. Using the little screwdriver pry the flesh loose from the shell. Then peel the skin off of the flesh with a vegetable peeler.

To grate: Break the flesh into 1 inch pieces and process them for 15 seconds in the food processor. Alternatively grate the pieces on a medium fine grater. Freshly grated coconut will keep up to 1 week refrigerated in a sealed glass jar depending upon how fresh the coconut was when cracked open.

An average coconut weighs about 1 1/2 pounds and yields about 3 cups of grated flesh.

hazelnuts

To roast and peel: (See peanuts.) Hazelnuts are also called filberts.

1 cup shelled hazelnuts - about 5 ounces

macadamias

The macadamia is a very hard nut to crack. For most practical purposes they are sold everywhere shelled, peeled, roasted, lightly salted and canned. Shake canned macadamias in a coarse strainer to rid them of excess salt. However, they are also available from large mail order gift package type nut retailers shelled, peeled, unroasted and unsalted, but in quantities larger than you probably want to buy.

To roast: Roast shelled, peeled macadamias on a baking sheet in a preheated 250 degree oven 20 minutes, stirring them around every 5 minutes. Remove them from the baking sheet immediately.

1 cup fresh or canned macadamias - about 5 ounces

peanuts

Raw peanuts are available in natural food stores. If you are using already roasted, peeled and salted peanuts, shake them in a coarse strainer to rid them of excess salt. Peanuts, of course, are a bean not a nut. But everyone knows that!

To roast and peel: Roast shelled peanuts on a baking sheet in a preheated 275 degree oven 20 minutes, stirring them around every 5 minutes. Remove them from the baking sheet immediately. Taking a small handful of peanuts at a time (careful, they're hot) rub off the brittle skins in a clean dish towel.

1 cup shelled peanuts - about 4 1/2 ounces

pecans

To roast: (See walnuts.)

1 cup shelled pecan halves - about 3 1/2 ounces

pinenuts

Pinenuts are the seeds that come from the pinecones of certain pine trees.

To roast: Roast pinenuts on a baking sheet in a preheated 250 degree oven 12 minutes stirring them around once or twice. Remove them from the baking sheet immediately. Pinenuts are almost always available with their skins removed. However, if not, peel them as for peanuts. (See peanuts.)

1 cup pinenuts - about 4 ounces

pistachios

When pistachios are ripe their little shells open slightly and this facilitates shelling them. Pistachios are often roasted and salted while they are still in the shell and are sold unshelled. The shells are sometimes dyed red. Undyed, unsalted, raw, unshelled pistachios are available in natural food stores. If you are using already roasted, salted pistachios shake the shelled nuts in a coarse strainer to rid them of excess salt or if you are going to peel them soaking will dissolve the salt.

To peel: In a bowl pour boiling water over shelled pistachios and allow them to soak 1 or 2 minutes. Then peel them, they pop right out of their skins. The unpeeled pistachios remain in the water until they are peeled.

To dry: Spread the peeled pistachios on a baking sheet and dry them out in a preheated 200 degree oven 15 minutes stirring them around every 5 minutes. Remove them from the baking sheet immediately.

To roast: Roast as for to dry using a 275 degree oven.

1 cup shelled pistachios - about 4 ounces
(1 cup unshelled pistachios - about 4 1/2 ounces)

walnuts

To roast: Roast shelled walnut halves on a baking sheet in a preheated 275 degree oven 20 minutes, stirring them around every 5 minutes. Remove them from the baking sheet immediately. Walnuts are not ordinarily peeled but if they are to be roasted and chopped they can, after chopping, be shaken in a coarse strainer to allow little flakes of skin to fall away.

1 cup shelled walnut halves - about 4 ounces

sunflower and pumpkin seeds

Raw hulled sunflower and pumpkin seeds are available in natural food stores. Pumpkin seeds swell when toasted and are called pepitas in Mexican cooking.

To roast: Roast hulled sunflower or pumpkin seeds on a baking sheet in a preheated 275 degree oven 15 minutes until they are a pale golden color, stirring them around every 5 minutes. Remove them from the baking sheet immediately.

1 cup hulled sunflower or pumpkin seeds - about 6 ounces

UTENSILS

As I glance around my kitchen at the sizeable collection of cooking utensils, I remember that it was not always so. I started cooking with very few utensils just like most people do. Over the years as my interest in food and cooking grew and grew, so did my "batterie de cuisine." To begin with, only a few key implements for daily living are what is needed. Then, as ability and interest increase, pieces are gradually added for a more expanded culinary repertoire. The following utensils listed here are not all necessary at once. At times, something can be improvised, if you are a little bit ingenious, or something can be substituted and make-do surprisingly well. What is important is that when you do buy, buy quality, first, last and always. It is money well spent. Good utensils last a very long time and some can even be handed down to the next generation. Treasure your cooking utensils the way that you do your good china and treat them well.

FRYING PANS

Aluminum, cast iron and copper spread heat well. Aluminum and iron can discolor food. The solution is stainless steel, clad aluminum and enameled, cast iron. Copper must be lined with tin to be usable. Stainless steel clad copper is another alternative. When a recipe in this cook book calls for a large frying pan, it means 12 inches in diameter across the top. A large frying pan allows plenty of room which is essential for sautéing a large quantity of vegetables. My 12 inch enameled frying pan has curved sides and its own domed lid. I find it indispensable. However, I get plenty of use out of my old 10 and 8 inch plain, cast iron pans. A plain, cast iron griddle is wonderful for tortillas etc., and a 9 inch aluminum "no stick" pan is very handy. A personal favorite is a 12 by 15 inch electric skillet which, though not a necessity, sometimes takes the place of two pans.

OMELET PANS

An omelet pan usually has curved sides which make it easy to work with. However, most frying pans can be used as omelet pans, provided they are the correct size and conduct heat well. If the pan is too small it will make manipulation difficult, if it is too large the omelet will be too thin and in both cases there will be a variation in cooking time.

It is the inside bottom measurement of the pan that counts. An inside bottom measurement of 7 inches in diameter is ideal for a 3 egg omelet. The inside top measurement of a pan is usually 2 inches larger in diameter than the bottom measurement. It is best to reserve and maintain an omelet or frying pan just for omelets so that there will never be any problem with sticking. If possible, after use, simply wipe out the pan with paper towels. If it must be washed and scrubbed, after drying it, set it over medium low heat and spread about 1/2 teaspoon of vegetable oil in the pan, rubbing it around with a paper towel. Then remove the pan from the heat and wipe off any excess oil with paper towels leaving a fine film of oil on the surface. Of course, no stick omelet pans will not need this treatment.

CRÊPE PANS

The crêpe pan has an inside bottom measurement of 6 1/2 inches in diameter, which helps to control the size of the crêpe, and has sloping sides. The crêpe pan is maintained in exactly the same manner as the omelet pan. (See omelet pans.)

WOK

No household is complete without this Oriental cooking pan. Despite the fact that they are sometimes made in other metals and come in a variety of sizes, the most common woks are rolled carbon steel and are about 12 inches in diameter. Woks are equipped with a large domed lid and a ring to place around a gas or electric burner to set the wok upon for stability. When using an electric stove, set the wok over the largest burner. Follow manufacturer's directions to season a brand new wok. Maintain your wok in much the same manner as you would an omelet pan. (See omelet pans.) This will protect the wok from rust. Do not leave food in a carbon steel wok after it has cooled.

DEEP FRYERS

A deep fryer can simply be a saucepan fitted with a basket to lift the cooked fried foods up out of the deep oil. The saucepan should have a cooking thermometer clipped to the inside of it for an accurate oil temperature reading. An electric deep fryer is an asset. The thermometer is built in and all you have to do is set the dial to the desired temperature. The electric deep fryer produces foods of a consistent quality. In either case the oil for deep frying can be reused if, after it has cooled, it is filtered through a paper coffee filter.

SAUCEPANS & KETTLES   In selecting saucepans and kettles follow the same criteria you would when choosing frying pans. With enamel and stainless steel there is no question of food discoloration. How many saucepans and kettles does a well equipped kitchen need? There never seem to be enough. Start with a little 2 cup saucepan and move right up at about 2 cup intervals to 12 cups. Then proceed to 16 cups. This 4 quart kettle can be an enameled, oval Dutch oven shape which is good for stews and makes an attractive appearance when brought to the table. Next, move on to 6, 8, and 10 quarts. For the 6 quart kettle it's good to have the "spaghetti pot," mentioned under steamers. It is fitted with its own large draining basket for corn and pasta as well as the steaming basket. The large 10 quart kettle is handy for sterilizing jars when making jelly and other bulky jobs. And you will also want the big water bath canner with its own jar rack for canning. Before leaving the subject, let's not forget the double boiler for the sauces which require it.

BAKING DISHES   The ovenproof glass baking dish comes in a variety of sizes and shapes, round, oval, square, and rectangular. In clear, amber, or white, it's the great American baking dish. Very practical are those which can go from freezer to oven. Earthenware and enameled metal dishes are attractive and add a look of diversity. The deep, straight sided soufflé dish can also serve other purposes. Don't forget the bean pot is a baking dish too as are individual gratin dishes. Plain and fancy molds for custard type preparations can also be used for gelatins.

QUICHE PANS & PIE PLATES   For this cookbook, the quiches, tarts, and their shells were baked in metal, false bottom pans. If you are using those which have a black finish you may want to decrease the baking time by 5 minutes as pastry browns quicker in a dark pan. The pies and their shells were baked in glass pie plates. If you are using an earthenware plate, increase the baking time by 5 minutes. If you are using a metal plate decrease the time by 5 minutes.

BAKING SHEETS & PANS   Baking sheets are usually aluminum these days and come in sizes up to 14 by 17 inches. They have no sides and are also referred to as cookie sheets. Insulated cookie sheets are desirable to keep baked goods from browning too quick on the bottom. Jelly roll pans come in sizes up to 11 by 17 inches and have shallow sides 3/16 inch deep. They are useful not only for jelly rolls but for baking slightly juicy items or items that must be contained. The good old pizza pan comes in handy too!

STEAMERS   The handy little folding steamer that fits into almost any pot is the one most people own. I also have a 6 cup steamer with a lid which sits on top of its own 6 cup saucepan and it is the one I use most frequently. A large 6 quart kettle called a "spaghetti pot" has a good size steaming basket which is very necessary for steaming large quantities of vegetables. The multi-storied bamboo steaming baskets which sit on top of the wok are also useful. Lacking a large steamer, a colander, covered with a lid and set in a large kettle can substitute.

THE MACHINES   Concerning the food processor and the electric mixer, what the machine will do for you will depend upon the size of the motor and the type and number of attachments that you have to fit the machine. Every year the manufacturers seem to come out with yet another new attachment. They are really all quite wonderful. For using this cookbook, the basic attachments that will be necessary are the steel blade and a grating disk for the processor and the beaters for the electric mixer. The electric blender, though a simpler machine than the last two, is also nice to have in certain instances, for perhaps smaller quantities. It does a good job of liquefying and is a good nut chopper too. The hand held electric mixer, though not so powerful as the big standard machine, is handy and versatile. Though there is usually an alternative to these machines, they sometimes save hours of work and have so integrated themselves that they have become indispensable for certain recipes.

PASTA MAKER
Pasta makers knead, roll out, and cut the pasta dough. My pasta maker is the hand crank type. Different brands of pasta makers have varying numbers of roller settings. If the narrowest setting on your machine does not produce a fine enough pasta to suit you, run the dough through the narrowest setting 2 or 3 times until you get the quality you desire. By the same token, if the narrowest setting makes the pasta too thin, omit using it. The cutting rollers for wide or narrow noodles are sometimes a separate attachment. A ravioli maker is an optional attachment. If you own a glamorous motorized pasta maker, follow the manufacturers instructions.

SPÄTZLE MAKER
There are two types of spätzle makers. One looks like a flat cheese grater with a sliding collar on it. The other resembles a food mill.

PASTA DRYING RACK
You can use a broom handle or the back of a chair if you like but a pasta drying rack is very satisfactory and folds up for easy storage.

FOOD MILL & FOOD CHOPPER
These two old fashioned utensils are still put to good use despite the fact that the processor, blender, and mixer attachments do a quicker job with less effort. The food mill retains a certain desirable texture when foods are puréed through it that the electric machines do not retain. The food mill also separates coarse fiber and seed

from vegetables to a large extent. The food chopper, that's the one that clamps onto the side of a table or work counter, and has a big crank handle is useful for turning nuts into paste as well as chopping food.

GRATERS, CHOPPERS, MINCERS & GRINDERS   There is a plethora of these items available. Most are still manual but there are some nifty little electrified versions. The processor, blender, and electric mixer attachments can do most of these jobs but we're talking about small quantities when you perhaps don't want to use the big machine. The four sided grater is the most common grater, with the flat grater running a close second. The hand held grater is next. It's a good idea to keep an extra pepper mill to use for grinding other spices. Finally, we come to what is perhaps the most ancient of all kitchen utensils, the mortar and pestle. Wood and marble models still in use do an excellent job of grinding and pulverizing spices and other food materials.

MIXING BOWLS   Almost any kind of bowl can be used as a mixing bowl, from the very largest right down to a teacup. So much the better if it is oven proof and can double as a baking dish.

COLANDERS & STRAINERS   A big colander for draining large quantities of vegetables such as spinach is necessary. A large coarse strainer on a stand is also very useful. Do have at least one very good fine strainer about 6 inches in diameter as well as the small, fine "tea" strainer. Remember that colanders and strainers can also be used as steamers.

SALAD BASKETS   Wire salad baskets could be grouped with colanders and strainers. But the plastic salad spinners that dry your lettuce with centrifugal force should be listed under fun!

MARBLE SLAB & ROLLING PIN   A marble slab to roll out pastry on isn't absolutely necessary but it does help to keep pastry dough cool when working with it during warmer weather. I use an 18 inch long European type of rolling pin without handles.

PASTRY BAG & TIPS   A pastry bag with a few plain and fluting tips is a little luxury that is worth the professional looking results it produces.

MEASURING UTENSILS   These include measuring cups and spoons as well as an accurate food scale. A cooking thermometer is also a measuring utensil and so is a timer. Every kitchen should also have a wooden ruler.

SPOONS, SPATULAS, WHISKS & ETCETERA   A variety of spoons, large and small, is useful. Wooden spoons, as well as forks, can be used not only for tossing salads but for stirring delicate things that a metal implement might break. Metal spoons also include a utilitarian soup ladle as well as a slotted spoon and a skimmer. The wonderful rubber spatula must be treated with care, it is not heat proof. Replace it often. A wooden spatula is a must for the tenuous lining of "no stick" pans. The metal spatula is, of course, also called an egg turner. The wire whisk or whip has many beating and stirring jobs. And the pastry blender and potato masher deserve mention.

CUTTING IMPLEMENTS   The little paring knife is the basic tool of the kitchen. A well equipped kitchen has several knives in graduated sizes for slicing, dicing, chopping, and mincing, the largest of which is the chefs' knife with a 10 to 12 inch long blade. Carbon steel knives take a very fine edge but must be sharpened regularly. Carbon steel will discolor certain vegetables such as artichokes. Stainless steel knives hold a more lasting edge than carbon. Serrated knives are used in instances where a sawing action is necessary. This group includes the grapefruit knife, bread knife, and frozen food knife as well as others. It is wise to have more than one vegetable peeler just in case someone wants to help you. Replace vegetable peelers when they get dull. A melon ball cutter can also be used to core fruit. An apple corer is nice to have and a cherry pitter is a luxury. Keep your kitchen scissors sharpened. They can be used for cutting herbs. Last but not least is the zig zag rolling cutter used for ravioli and certain pastry.

TORTILLA PRESS

Unless you are uncommonly skilled at patting out tortillas, you will need a tortilla press.

COOKIE GUN

The cookie gun, like the tortilla press, is a boon to unskilled artisans. Some are even motorized.

ICE CREAM MAKER

The simple ice cream makers of today have come a long way from the old recipe that tells you to throw a piece of carpet over the ice cream maker to keep it cool.

JUICERS

A juicer can be a separate electrical appliance or it can be an optional attachment to one of the machines. It can also be a hand press or a glass dish.

SKEWERS AND TOOTHPICKS

As well as for shish-kabab, metal skewers can also be used to determine when vegetables are cooked. However, I prefer a wooden skewer or toothpick for the job. Metal slides in and out too easy where as wood creates drag and gives a more accurate reading, I feel.

BRUSHES

Set aside a scrub brush that is not used for pots and pans with which to scrub vegetables. It is good to have a soft brush for mushrooms too. Pastry brushes are a must and the old ones can be used for greasing griddles. I like a feather brush for delicate pastry.

FOIL, PLASTIC WRAP, PAPERS, CHEESE CLOTH, AND ETCETERA

How did the kitchen ever function before aluminum foil, plastic wrap, plastic bags and plastic gloves were invented? It functioned with parchment paper, wax paper and brown paper bags and they are still used today despite the modern conveniences. Buy medical quality cheese cloth in a drug store. The type sold in kitchenware stores is better suited to polishing the car. Keep soft string or tape on hand for tying up asparagus and other things. As mentioned elsewhere, coffee filters can be used for filtering oil as well as coffee.

HEAT DIFFUSER   A heat diffuser set over the burner under the pan is invaluable. As they say, it makes a double boiler out of any pan.

PLASTIC SQUEEZE BOTTLES   I like plastic squeeze bottles for measuring out honey. Mine is shaped like a bear and he comes to the table for tea!

A

D

E